AUTOMOTIVE TUNE-UP PROCEDURES

William L. Husselbee

Reston Publishing Company, Inc.
A Prentice-Hall Company
Reston, Virginia

Library of Congress Cataloging in Publication Data

Husselbee, William L.
   Automotive tune-up procedures.

   1. Automobiles--Maintenance and repair.   I. Title.
TL152.H89 1983   629.28722   82-13192
ISBN 0-8359-0295-1

10 9 8 7 6 5 4 3 2 1

Printed in the United States of America

CONTENTS

Chapter 12
Principles of Electricity and Magnetism   271

Chapter 13
Automotive Storage Batteries   305

Chapter 14
Battery Maintenance   323

Chapter 15
Standard Ignition Systems   345

Chapter 16
Standard Ignition System
Service   373

Chapter 17
Electronic Ignition
Systems   413

Chapter 18
Electronic Ignition System
Testing   431

PREFACE

Each year, the automotive repair industry has a need for a large number of new tune-up technicians. These people will perform tune-ups on current- as well as millions of older-model, domestic- and foreign-built motor vehicles on the highways in this country. These new technicians will work alongside other master mechanics in new-car agencies, independent garages, and tune-up specialty shops; and they will have a lifetime rewarding career with excellent compensation.

The word "tune-up" means different things to various people. To some people, a tune-up means simply replacing spark plugs, distributor points, and condenser, and adjusting the carburetor. However, due to state, local, and federal emission-control laws as well as the need for better fuel economy, an engine tune-up now comprises a great deal more. Consequently, a new tune-up mechanic must be able to diagnose and perform given repairs and adjustments to the engine and the fuel, ignition, and emission-control systems.

Obviously, then, the job of a tune-up technician requires a great deal of knowledge and hand skills. *Automotive Tune-up Procedures* meets these requirements by providing not only all the necessary related information on the systems mentioned above, but also the techniques used to diagnose and repair the many components of these systems.

The design of this text is such that it meets the needs of several categories of people. First, the book serves as an excellent reference source for the high-school, trade school, or community college student in a tune-up course. Second, this text serves adequately as a training tool for any automotive mechanic who desires to master the tune-up procedure. Finally, *Automotive Tune-up Procedures* is a valuable source of information for any "do-it-yourself" person: the automotive hobbyist or any consumer who desires to know something about the area of automotive tune-up.

To perform its overall purpose, the book is divided into chapters on theory followed by chapters on how to perform specific procedures and/or repairs. A chapter on theory describes a particular system component and explains the principles of operation. Immediately following a chapter on principles is a "how-to" chapter, which presents up-to-date troubleshooting, service, and repair methods of the components within a specific system. Thus, the book provides the reader with a firm conceptual understanding of the theory behind the many engine systems involved in a tune-up while providing him or her with the testing and repair techniques necessary to become a qualified tune-up mechanic.

Because the tune-up technician must possess a great deal of knowledge and must be able to perform a variety of tests, adjustments, and repairs, the overall scope of *Automotive Tune-up Procedures* is quite large. Included are not only the principles of operation, but also the types of service procedures for the engine, the battery, the fuel system, ignition system, charging system, starting system, and emission-control system.

This book also explains the types of automotive test equipment and how to use these instruments to perform various checks. Specifically, the equipment discussed includes the vacuum gauge, compression and leakage testers, voltmeter, ammeter, ohmmeter, hydrometer, infrared analyzer, propane-enrichment tool, oscilloscope, and dynamometer. Chapter 24, for example, provides information on the infrared analyzer and the propane-enrichment tool and explains how to use this equipment to check and/or adjust and engine's air/fuel ratio.

In Chapters 25 and 26, detailed information on the engine analyzer and dynamometer is presented. Within Chapter 25, the reader will find an explanation not only of the various instruments found on a typical engine analyzer, but will also learn how to interpret oscilloscope patterns. Chapter 26 details a complete tune-up test procedure using the engine analyzer and dynamometer explained in Chapter 25.

Review questions are included at the end of each chapter. The answers to these questions are found in the Appendix. After reading the entire text and completing all chapter review questions, the reader should be able, with very little difficulty, to pass the National Institute for Automotive Service Excellence (NIASE) test for automotive tune-up technicians.

Definition

The term *tune-up* as applied to vehicle service work can mean various things to different people. For example, to the average vehicle owner, a tune-up is something done by a mechanic to the engine to make it operate more efficiently and achieve better fuel economy. To a few mechanics, a tune-up is nothing more than the cleaning, regapping, or replacing of the spark plugs in addition to possibly replacing the points and condenser, adjusting the carburetor in order to achieve the proper idle mixture and speed, and sometimes performing a few other minor service operations.

But to the highly skilled tune-up specialist, a tune-up means a great deal more. To this person, *a tune-up is a service procedure that restores the engine and its accessories to factory specifications and peak performance.* This procedure, of course, is only possible if the engine is in reasonably good mechanical condition that will allow factory-designated output.

Many people also apply the word *tune-up* to other service operations on a vehicle, unrelated to the engine. For instance, it is not uncommon to see advertisements for automatic transmission, front-end, or cooling system tune-ups. A tune-up in these situations also refers to some form of service procedure to restore the particular unit or system as closely as possible to factory specifications.

Extent of Tune-Up Work

A thorough tune-up consists of service procedures that restore the engine, its accessories, and subsystems to factory specifications. However, a tune-up is not a cure for a sick engine. In fact, a large

Chapter 1

ENGINE TUNE-UP

number of vehicles coming into a shop cannot be tuned by the mechanic because a preliminary checking procedure indicates that the engine requires mechanical repair before a tune-up job could be successful. Therefore, attempting to tune-up an engine that has worn or defective bearings, rings, pistons, or valves is very difficult, if not impossible, and is a waste of a technician's time and the customer's money.

A tune-up mechanic then checks engine condition as part of the job but will not rebuild the engine if it is worn out. This specialist on occasion will do some minor engine repair or service procedures such as adjusting valves, replacing valve-cover gaskets, and retorquing cylinder heads.

The remaining emphasis of a .thorough tune-up is checking, servicing, and electrically testing the accessories and subsystems of the engine, the powerplant. This procedure consists of checking, servicing, and testing the battery, starting, generating, and ignition systems and includes necessary repairs, replacements, and adjustments. In addition, a tune-up includes testing, overhauling, and replacing the components of the fuel and emission-control systems. Finally, a tune-up specialist inspects and performs minor service on the cooling and lubrication systems such as inspection and replacement of heater and radiator hoses, fan belts, and thermostat plus the condition and level of the engine's lubricating oil and its system for external leakage.

Tune-Up: A Sequence of Small Operations

A complete tune-up, like any other service operation, is nothing more than a series of simple steps (operations) with each step leading to a desired result. In other words, the skilled mechanic breaks down the complicated task into simple and smaller parts with each part building on the other until the tune-up is complete. Every thoroughly trained specialist knows this fact and follows the necessary steps in each phase of the tune-up.

A complete tune-up consists of three or four individual service operations, depending on the type of equipment that the technician is using. The first task is a visual inspection and repair of the battery, cooling system components, fan belts, exhaust system, oil and fluid levels, air cleaner, vacuum hoses, and evaporation control system canister.

The second operation is a test of the mechanical condition of the engine, accomplished in one of two ways. First, the mechanic removes the spark plugs and performs a compression or leakage test on the engine itself. Either of these checks will indicate the serviceability of the engine's rings, valves, and head gaskets.

Second, the specialist can test engine performance *as part of* phase 3 of the tune-up sequence. In this instance, the mechanic utilizes an electronic engine analyzer (Fig. 1-1) to perform a power check on each of the engine cylinders. The value of this testing method is that it very quickly informs the mechanic if each individual cylinder is producing power and compares each cylinder's output against the rest. This is commonly known as *checking engine balance*, which is extremely important for smooth engine performance, especially at idle.

However, a balance test will not usually reveal what is wrong within a cylinder with low output. To locate the source of power loss, if not due to a fuel or ignition problem, the technician must remove the spark plugs and conduct either a compres-

Fig. 1-1. A typical electronic diagnosis engine tester or engine analyzer.

sion or leakage test. These tests are necessary to determine the mechanical condition of the rings, pistons, valves, and head gaskets.

A modern engine analyzer also tests many other things very accurately. With this machine, the mechanic can quickly determine the operating efficiency of the battery, charging, starting, and ignition systems in addition to overall performance of the carburetor and emission control systems. With the aid of these analyzers, the specialist can determine what replacement parts or services are necessary to restore these units to factory specifications.

The final phase of any thorough tune-up is repairing, replacing, and rechecking malfunctions located with the analyzer. This operation may include replacing such items as the points and condenser, spark plugs and wires, ignition coil, or components of the high-energy ignition (HEI) system. The repair procedures may also call for rebuilding the carburetor and repairing or replacing the alternator or starter. No matter what the repair or replacement, the last step in a tune-up before a road test is always rechecking the repaired or replaced units on the analyzer.

This final check is necessary to ensure that all repaired units are functioning normally.

Major Components of Engine Operation

As noted, many steps are necessary to complete a tune-up that will make an engine operate more efficiently; these steps relate closely to the three components of engine operation: compression, ignition, and carburetion. Adequate *compression* is, for example, necessary to induce and crowd (compress) sufficient fuel into the combustion chamber for satisfactory engine performance. The compression process causes a greater utilization of the fuel for power output because a compressed fuel charge burns more efficiently.

Ignition is the second component necessary for engine operation. Ignition is the firing of the compressed fuel/air charge inside the engine cylinders, and it is the task of the ignition system. This system must not only produce a spark but also time this firing process so that it occurs at a precise moment during the engine's cycle. Furthermore, the system must alter the moment it fires every spark plug to match the speed—revolutions per minute (rpm)—of the engine. In other words, at slower engine speeds it retards the firing point, and at higher rpm it advances the sparking sequence.

The final element necessary for engine operation is *carburetion*. The carburetion process converts liquid fuel to vapor and mixes it with air to form a highly combustible air/fuel mixture. This action takes place in the carburetor, which not only performs this converting process but also varies the quantity of fuel admitted to the cylinders by mechanical linkage attached to the accelerator pedal.

If any one of these components—compression, ignition, or carburetion—does not function properly, it will directly affect engine performance. If the degree of efficiency loss is great enough, the engine will not run at all. Consequently, it is extremely important that the mechanic check these operational components during the various phases of a tune-up.

Consequence of Normal Wear

Satisfactory performance of the modern powerplant requires the maintenance of the engine, its accessories, and subsystems to keep them in a condition equivalent to new. But as soon as a vehicle leaves the dealer's showroom floor and the owner places it into service, the vehicle begins to wear out. As a rule, this process continues for the life of a properly maintained automobile for about 150,000 miles.

Some of the wear on the key components affecting engine performance is very predictable. For instance, friction causes wear on the engine's bearings, cylinder walls, pistons, and rings. In the standard ignition system, spark plugs and breaker points in the distributor deteriorate with use. Furthermore, some of the distributor's mechanical parts such as the distributor shaft, bearings, driving gear, breaker-plate bearings, and internal electrical connections may wear out or become defective. Both the high- and low-tension wiring are also subject to deterioration due to oxidation, heat, oil deposits, and age; their terminals can become loose or corroded. In the fuel system, the fuel

pump may require replacement due to a ruptured diaphragm. Also, the carburetor may malfunction because of deposits in its circuits due to dirty fuel or air filters.

It is therefore the task of the tune-up technician to locate the worn or deteriorated parts affecting engine performance. The technician must then report these problems to the owner and correct them by either the adjustment, repair, or replacement of affected components, except the engine. The end result of the tune-up will be the restoration of these operational components as close to their original condition as possible.

Testing Equipment

In order to locate a worn or defective part quickly and accurately, the tune-up mechanic can utilize seven types of testing equipment: the engine analyzer, combustion or exhaust-gas analyzer, dynamometer, distributor tester, timing light, vacuum gauge, and compression or leakage testers. The *engine analyzer* (Fig. 1-1), as its name implies, diagnoses engine problems simply and quickly. The machine itself, depending on the manufacturer, will consist of an oscilloscope, volt and dwell meters, tachometer, combustion analyzer, or HC (hydrocarbon) and CO (carbon monoxide) meters.

The *oscilloscope* is a diagnostic device that quickly pinpoints troubles within the ignition system. The scope, as most people call it, is a type of voltmeter that uses a televisionlike picture tube to show ignition voltages. In operation, the scope draws a picture of the ignition voltages on the face of the picture tube, and the picture readily shows what is taking place in the ignition system. If there is a problem in the system, the picture shows what it is.

The *voltmeter* measures the potential difference (voltage) between two points in an electrical circuit. In this situation, the meter measures total voltage or voltage drop in the battery, starter, ignition, or alternator circuit.

The *dwell meter* is also a precision electrical instrument. Its primary usage in diagnostic work is that of measuring distributor dwell. *Dwell* is the number of degrees the contact points, inside the distributor, are closed while the engine is running.

The *tachometer* measures engine speed or rpm. The technician uses this instrument when setting engine idle speed to specifications and while checking such other factors as the distributor's advance curve, carburetor balance, and cylinder output or balance.

The *exhaust-gas analyzer* may be part of the engine analyzer or a separate unit. In either case, a modern unit measures the amount of hydrocarbons and carbon monoxide in the engine's exhaust. By doing this, the instrument indicates to the mechanic whether the emission controls on the vehicle are functioning and whether the idle mixture requires adjustment.

A *chassis dynamometer* (Fig. 1–2) tests engine output under various operating conditions. The device itself duplicates any type of road test at any load or speed desired, and, at the same time, instruments on its test panel measure vehicle speed and engine horsepower.

A *distributor tester* (synchroscope) checks a distributor removed from the engine (Fig. 1–3). The machine itself tests distributor dwell and the centrifugal- and vacuum-advance mechanisms. This tester will also detect distributor shaft eccen-

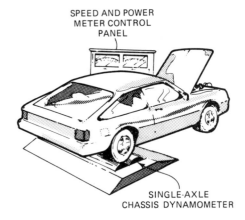

SPEED AND POWER METER CONTROL PANEL

SINGLE-AXLE CHASSIS DYNAMOMETER

Fig. 1–2. A common chassis dynamometer and control panel.

Fig. 1–3. A distributor tester shows the firing pattern and checks the automatic and vacuum advance units.

tricity caused by a worn bearing or a bent shaft.

A *timing light* can be a separate unit or built into an engine analyzer. In either case, the timing light (Fig. 1–4) is nothing more than a stroboscopic light used to check basic ignition timing on most engines. In normal operation, the light flashes every time the number one spark plug fires; the technician uses this light to check the positioning of the timing marks when the engine is running.

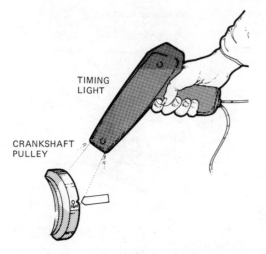

Fig. 1-4. A timing light is necessary in most cases to check ignition timing.

The *vacuum gauge* may also be a separate unit or incorporated into an engine analyzer (Fig. 1-5). The gauge itself measures the amount of intake manifold vacuum in inches or millimeters of mercury (Hg). The vacuum within the intake manifold varies with various operating conditions and with different engine defects. Therefore, the way in which the vacuum gauge readings vary from normal indicate what is wrong inside the engine.

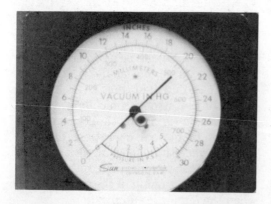

Fig. 1-5. A typical vacuum gauge.

The *cylinder compression tester* (Fig. 1-6) measures the ability of the engine cylinder to build and hold compression pressure. The pressure acts on a dia-

Fig. 1-6. A common compression tester.

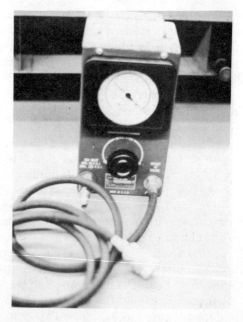

Fig. 1-7. A cylinder leakage tester measures the amount of air loss from a cylinder.

phragm inside the tester itself. This action forces the needle on the face of the tester to move around, indicating the pressure within the cylinder.

A *cylinder leakage tester* (Fig. 1–7) does about the same job as the compression tester but in a slightly different manner. This device applies air pressure to each cylinder with its piston at top dead center (TDC) on the compression stroke with both valves closed. The cylinder leakage tester then measures the amount of pressure loss from the cylinder; this loss normally should be very small.

Qualifications of Prospective Tune-Up Technician

A person desiring to become a tune-up specialist should be analytical and dedicated, in addition to being dexterous. The quality of being analytical will enable the person to learn difficult procedures and operational theories along with being able to diagnose problems or troubleshoot. The mechanic must be able, for example, to read and understand complicated tune-up procedures from various types of service manuals. The technician must also know the operational theories of the engine, ignition, fuel, and emission-control systems and be able to apply these principles in trouble-shooting malfunctions, which frequently occur on these units.

The tune-up specialist should be dedicated to the profession. This person should always do the very best to give the customer the service being paid for. *Work quality is never sacrificed to achieve quantity.* Finally, the technician must keep up with current developments in the tune-up area by learning about the most current, effective methods and equipment available.

The mechanic must possess a great deal of dexterity. A tune-up technician must work a great deal manually with various types of tools and delicate equipment. Also, the mechanisms worked on are intricate and for the most part expensive to replace if broken during tune-up.

Job Opportunities

Because of local, state, and government laws regarding emission levels from motor vehicles and the escalating cost of fuel, engine tune-ups have become an important aspect of overall vehicle maintenance. In the past, many vehicle owners bypassed the normal tune-ups as long as the engine appeared to perform well. But now people are paying more attention to preventive maintenance, especially in the area of tune-ups, because of the necessity of adhering to emission laws or to conserve fuel. The result of this, of course, is the need for more, highly trained and skilled tune-up specialists to perform this increased volume of service work.

A tune-up specialist can work in a dealership, independent garage or service center, or a tune-up shop. A tune-up mechanic employed at a new-car dealership will be only one type of technician working at the agency. The tune-up mechanic's specialty, of course, will be tune-ups; the others will specialize in either brakes and front-end, new-car service, automatic transmission, or engine service. However, all these technicians will usually work only on one type, or family, of vehicles.

A tune-up person at an independent garage or service center also will work with other specialized mechanics, with one difference. In this situation, these specialists will work on almost all types of vehicles. This, in most cases, makes all their jobs more difficult and demanding.

Finally, a person employed in a tune-up specialty shop—these have become increasingly popular—will work with a number of other tune-up people. They all will perform nothing but tune-ups on various types of vehicles; the customer must take a vehicle to an agency or garage for all other types of service work.

Review

This section will assist you in determining how well you remember the material in this chapter. Read each item carefully. If you can't complete the statement, review the section in the chapter that covers the material.

1. Unless the _____ is in reasonably good mechanical condition, a tune-up will not be successful.
   a. brakes
   b. starter
   c. engine
   d. fuel pump

2. A tune-up technician usually will not overhaul or replace the _____ .
   a. engine
   b. carburetor
   c. distributor
   d. fan belts

3. The second step in a tune-up procedure is to check the _____ _____ of the engine.
   a. lubricating system
   b. cooling system
   c. smog system
   d. mechanical condition

4. Most modern engine analyzers can check the _____ _____ of each cylinder.

   a. compression pressure
   b. exhaust pressure
   c. intake vacuum
   d. power output

5. The final phase of any tune-up is repairing, replacing, and _____ those malfunctions located with the analyzer.
   a. rechecking
   b. recalibrating
   c. resizing
   d. reinstalling

6. The final element necessary for engine operation is _____ .
   a. ignition
   b. compression
   c. carburetion
   d. power

7. A carburetor may malfunction due to _____ in its circuits.
   a. water
   b. deposits
   c. air
   d. oil

8. The device that quickly pinpoints problems in the ignition system is the _____ .
   a. voltmeter
   b. exhaust-gas analyzer
   c. tachometer
   d. oscilloscope

9. The machine that tests engine output under various operating conditions is the _____ .
   a. compression tester
   b. leakage tester
   c. dwell meter
   d. dynamometer

10. The device that applies air pressure to each cylinder is the _____ .
    a. compression tester

b. leakage tester
c. dynamometer
d. oscilloscope

11. To be able to work with tools and delicate equipment, the prospective tune-up mechanic must possess _____.

a. loyalty
b. integrity
c. dexterity
d. dedication

12. The average motorist is adhering to normal intervals between engine tune-ups in order to conserve _____ _____.

a. fuel
b. horsepower
c. emissions
d. air

13. A tune-up technician who works on all types of automobiles performing only tune-ups will be employed at either an independent garage or a _____ _____.

a. new-car dealership
b. tune-up shop
c. vehicle factory
d. salvage facility

For the answers, turn to the Appendix.

Before fully understanding and appreciating how an engine operates and develops its power from the burning of fuel, one must understand the basic structure of the engine and know the function of its various parts. With this in mind, let's examine the construction of a conventional piston-type engine, beginning with the block and then moving to the many components that it houses or supports.

Engine Block and Accessories

The engine block forms the main framework, or foundation, of the water-cooled engine (Fig. 2–1). Manufacturers cast the block mainly from gray iron or iron alloyed with other metals such as nickel or chromium. However, some blocks have been made from aluminum. In any case, the block itself has many components cast into it or assembled onto it.

Cast into the block, for example, are the *cylinders*. The cylinders are circular, tubelike openings in the block, which act as guides for the pistons as they move up and down. Engine blocks have four, six, or eight openings, or cylinders. In aluminum blocks, the manufacturer usually installs cast-iron or steel cylinder sleeves (liners) because these metals can withstand the wear caused by the moving pistons better than aluminum can.

Also cast into the block are the *water jackets*. The water jackets are open spaces between the inner and outer surfaces of the block and cylinders through which the *coolant* flows. The coolant, in turn, removes heat from the metal surfaces around such areas as the cylinder walls and valve seats and carries the heat to the

Chapter 2

ENGINE CONSTRUCTION

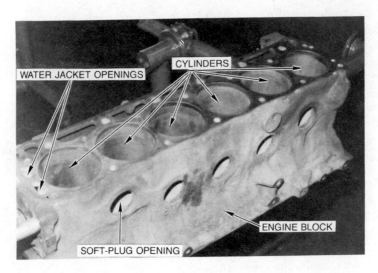

Fig. 2-1. The engine block forms the foundation for the entire engine.

radiator where it releases into the air. Cast-iron blocks usually have a number of holes along the side and in the end leading into the water jackets. These holes provide access into the interior of the block during the casting process, and the manufacturer seals these openings with soft-steel plugs, often called *freeze-out plugs* (Fig. 2-2).

Finally, the block has cast-in bores for both the camshaft and crankshaft (Fig. 2-3). The *camshaft bore* has a machined

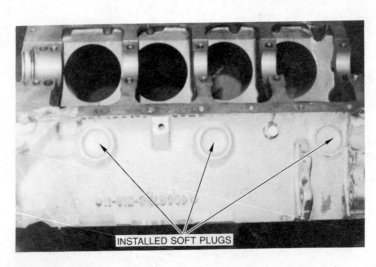

Fig. 2-2. Soft-steel plugs cover the opening in the block used during its manufacture.

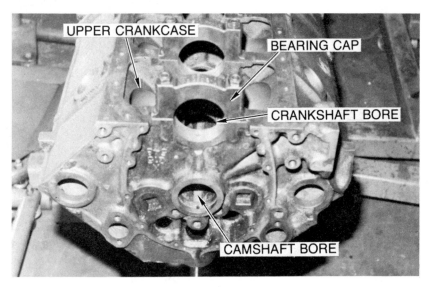

Fig. 2-3. The upper crankcase area of the typical block with its main and cam bearing bores.

finish, which accommodates a bushing that actually supports the revolving shaft in the block. However, only half the crankshaft bore is cast into the block. The manufacturer machines the other half into a *bearing cap*. The block bearing saddles (the half bores) and the caps also have a machine finish, which accommodates the main bearings, which in turn support the crankshaft.

Many parts also attach by fastening devices to the average engine block (Fig. 2-4). These items include the water pump, oil pan, timing gear or chain cover, the flywheel or clutch housing, the ignition distributor, oil and fuel pump, and the cylinder head. The water pump is a component of the cooling system. The crankshaft usually rotates this unit by means of a belt. When revolving, the water pump circulates coolant between the engine water jackets and the radiator.

The oil pan and the lower portion of the block together are known as the *crankcase;* they enclose or encase the crankshaft. The manufacturer usually forms the oil pan of pressed steel. The pan itself is also a reservoir, which usually holds 4 to 9 quarts of lubricating oil, depending on the design of the engine (Fig. 2-5).

When the engine is operating, the oil pump of the lubricating system draws oil from the pan and pumps it to all the moving parts of the engine. After the oil lubricates these parts, it drains off and runs back down into the pan. Consequently, there is a constant circulation of oil between the pan and the moving parts of the engine.

The *timing gear or chain cover,* as its name implies, encloses and protects the timing gears or timing chain and sprockets from foreign materials. This cover (Fig. 2-6), like the oil pan, can be

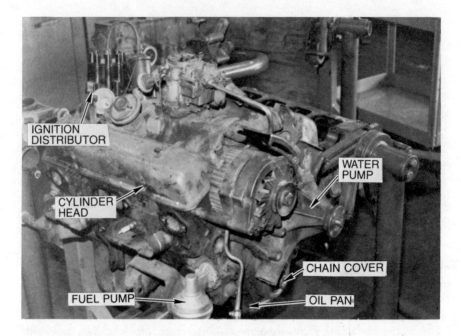

Fig. 2–4. Many components like the water pump, oil pan, timing cover, flywheel cover, ignition distributor, fuel pump, and cylinder head attach to the outside of the block.

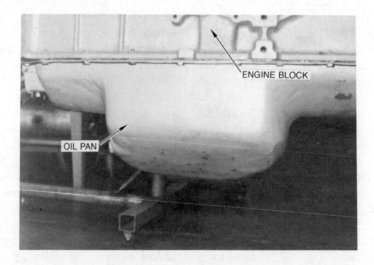

Fig. 2–5. A typical oil pan.

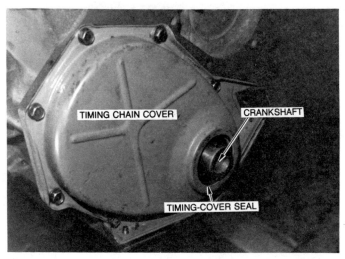

Fig. 2-6. A timing cover protects the timing gear or sprockets and chain against foreign material.

formed from pressed steel. However, in some cases, the engine manufacturer will form the cover from cast iron or aluminum because these particular covers have not only the fuel pump but also the water pump attached directly to it and have coolant flowing through special passages formed into the cover.

In addition, the cover has a machined area that accommodates the timing-cover seal. The seal prevents leakage of lubricating oil from around the area where the crankshaft protrudes through the cover to the outside of the engine. The seal itself is a lip type bonded to a steel backing that presses into the machined bore in the cover.

The detachable *flywheel or clutch cover* (Fig. 2-7) encloses and protects the flywheel and clutch assembly. This cast-iron or aluminum component also supports a portion of the clutch linkage and provides the mating-surface area to which the transmission attaches.

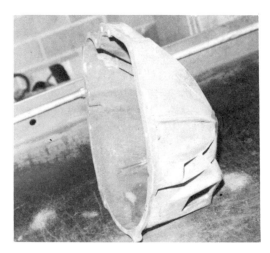

Fig. 2-7. A common flywheel or clutch cover.

The *ignition distributor* (Fig. 2-8) usually attaches to the block via a C-shaped clamp and a cap screw and serves two basic functions. First, it closes and opens the electrical circuit between the battery and the ignition coil. When the points

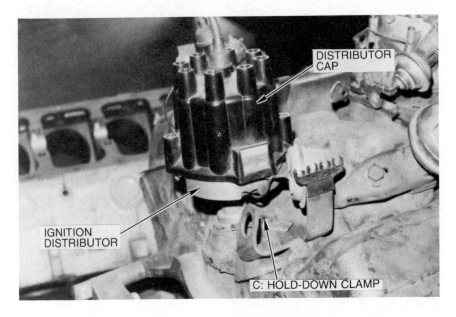

Fig. 2-8.   A typical ignition distributor.

close and completes this circuit, battery current flows into the coil and permits the coil to build up a strong magnetic field. As the points open, the circuit opens and the magnetic field in the coil collapses, which causes the coil to produce a high-voltage source of current. The second task of the distributor is then to direct each high-voltage surge to the correct spark plug at the correct instant in the engine cycle by the distributor rotor, cap, and secondary wiring.

The oil pump (Fig. 2-9) usually mounts to the upper crankcase area of the block. The camshaft usually drives both the oil pump and distributor by a spiral gear. As mentioned, the task of the oil pump is to draw lubricating oil from the pan and force it to all the moving parts of the engine.

The camshaft also activates the timing cover or block-mounted mechanical-type

Fig. 2-9.   A camshaft-driven oil pump.

fuel pump (Fig. 2-10). This pump is actually part of the fuel system. Its function is to transfer fuel from the fuel tank to the carburetor.

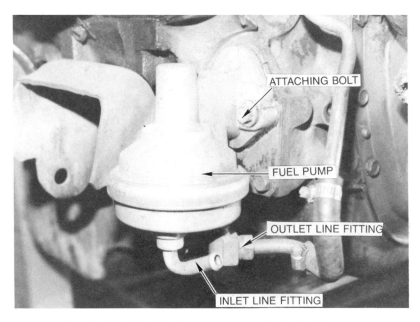

ATTACHING BOLT

FUEL PUMP

OUTLET LINE FITTING

INLET LINE FITTING

Fig. 2-10. The fuel pump is part of the fuel system.

Cylinder Head

The *cylinder head* bolts to a very flat surface above the cylinder portion of the block (Fig. 2-11). The manufacturer casts the head in one piece from iron, from iron alloyed with other metals, or from aluminum alloy. Aluminum has the advantage of combining lightness with rather high heat conductivity. This means simply that an aluminum head tends to operate cooler, other factors being equal.

Depending on the style of engine, the cylinder head serves many functions. For example, in all engine types the head forms an upper cover for the cylinders; therefore, the head forms the upper portion of the combustion chamber. All modern heads provide an access point into the combustion chamber for the spark plug.

A cylinder head of a valve-in-head (I-head) engine has other functions. For instance, this head houses both valves along with their valve springs, seats, guides, and valve ports. The *valves* are devices that open and close to allow or stop the flow of gases into or out of the combustion chamber and cylinder. All four-cycle engines will have at least two; one intake and one exhaust. The *intake valve,* on the one hand, controls the air/fuel mixture into the cylinder, while the *exhaust valve* controls the exit of exhaust gases from the cylinder. The *valve springs* are responsible for closing each valve. A *valve seat* is the surface against which a valve comes to rest, due to the action of its spring, in order to provide a seal against leakage. The valve guides are cylindrical openings in the head, where the valves are assembled and in which they move up and down. Lastly, the valve ports are the openings in

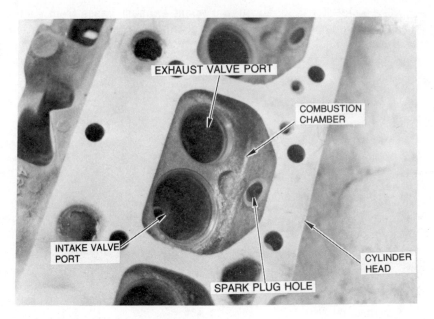

Fig. 2-11.   The combustion chamber area of a cylinder head.

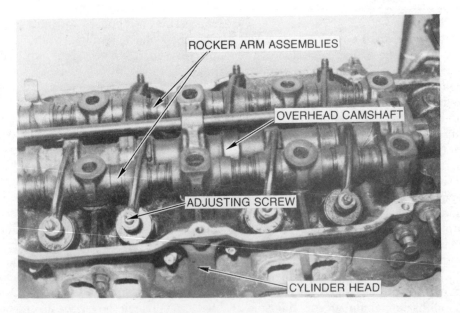

Fig. 2-12.   A rocker-arm assembly mounted on a typical cylinder head.

which the valves operate and through which the air/fuel mixture enters the cylinder or burned exhaust gases pass from the engine cylinder.

Also assembled onto the I-head is the valve-operating mechanism (Fig. 2-12). If the engine has the cam shaft supported in the block, this operating mechanism consists of a rocker-arm assembly or a set of ball-pivoted rocker arms. However, if the engine is of the overhead-camshaft design (OHC), the head supports the camshaft that will directly operate each valve, and no rocker-arm arrangement is necessary.

The final major components attached to the head are the *manifolds:* one intake and one or more exhaust (Fig. 2-13). The *intake manifold* contains passageways that carry the air/fuel mixture from the carburetor to each intake-valve port. The *exhaust manifold,* on the other hand, contains the passageways that carry the

spent exhaust gases from each exhaust-valve port to the exhaust system.

Pistons

The engine manufacturer fits a piston into each cylinder of the engine. The *piston* is a movable part or plug that receives the pressure from the burning air/fuel mixture and converts this pressure into reciprocating (up-and-down) motion (Fig. 2-14). In other words, a piston will move within the cylinder due to the force exerted on it by the pressure of the ignited air/fuel mixture.

Manufacturers form most engine pistons from aluminum, which is less than half the weight of iron. Iron pistons were common in early automotive engines. However, aluminum expands faster than iron with increasing temperatures; since

Fig. 2-13. A typical intake- and exhaust-manifold installation.

Fig. 2–14. A common automotive piston.

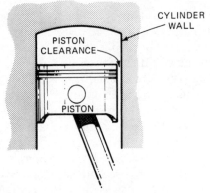

Fig. 2–15. Piston clearance is usually in the neighborhood of 0.001 to 0.004 inch.

the block is iron, in most cases, the manufacturer must provide special provisions in the piston to maintain the proper piston-to-cylinder wall clearance at engine-operating temperature.

Piston Clearance

Piston clearance is the distance between the outer circumference of the piston and the cylinder wall itself. This clearance varies somewhat with different engine designs, but it is usually in the neighborhood of 0.001 to 0.004 inch (Fig. 2–15). In operation, oil fills this clearance so that the piston moves on films of lubricating oil.

If this clearance is too small, for whatever reason, several problems can develop. For instance, the engine will lose power due to excessive friction. Also, severe wear and possible seizure of the piston to the cylinder wall can occur in an engine with tight pistons. Of course, piston seizure will result in complete engine failure.

On the other hand, excessively large clearance can result in *piston slap*—a sudden tilting of the piston in the cylinder as the piston starts down on the power strokes. The piston itself actually shifts from one side of the cylinder to the other, with sufficient force to produce a distinct noise, the piston slap. Usually, this problem occurs in older engines with worn cylinder walls or worn or damaged pistons.

Piston Expansion

The piston itself operates many degrees hotter than the adjacent cylinder wall and therefore expands more. Manufacturers must control this expansion in order to avoid the loss of adequate piston clearance. Such a loss could lead to serious engine problems. This expansion problem is also more acute with the aluminum piston, because aluminum expands more rapidly than iron with increasing temperature.

Expansion Control of Aluminum Pistons

The manufacturer controls piston expansion in its skirt area in several ways. One method is to keep heat away from the

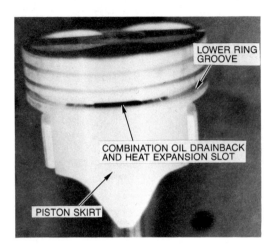

Fig. 2-16. A piston with a horizontal slot cut into the oil-control ring groove.

lower part of the piston as much as possible by cutting horizontal slots in the piston in or below the lower oil-control ring groove (Fig. 2-16). These slots reduce the direct path for the heat moving from the piston head to the skirt. Therefore, the skirt does not heat up as much and will not expand so much. Furthermore, some full-skirt pistons have a vertical slot cut into the skirt, which allows for metal expansion in the skirt area without appreciable increase in piston diameter (Fig. 2-17).

Still another method of reducing heat travel to the skirt section is the use of a *heat dam* (Fig. 2-18). The dam simply consists of a groove cut into the metal near the top of the piston head. This dam also reduces the size of the path that the heat can travel from the head of the piston to its skirt. The skirt therefore operates cooler and will not expand as much.

Many manufacturers finish their pistons so that they have a slightly oval shape when cold. Manufacturers classify

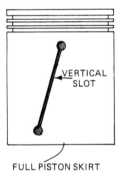

Fig. 2-17. A piston with a vertical slot machined into its skirt.

this piston design as cam-ground (Fig. 2-19), because the piston itself is finish-ground on a machine that utilizes a cam to move the piston toward and away from the grinding wheel as the piston revolves.

In operation, as a cam-ground piston warms up, it becomes round. Its contact area with the cylinder wall therefore increases. *Contact area* does not, of course, mean actual metal-to-metal contact. Some clearance must exist between the piston

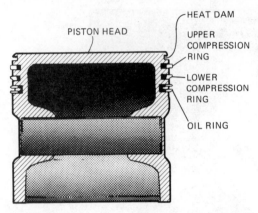

Fig. 2-18. An automotive piston with a heat dam.

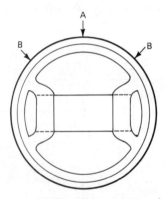

Fig. 2-19. A typical cam-ground piston. When this piston is cold, there is more clearance in shoulders B than A. As the piston temperature rises, the piston becomes nearly round, and the operating clearance is more uniform around the piston skirt.

and the cylinder wall. When the piston is cold, its oval shape permits normal clearance in only a small designated area and excessive clearance elsewhere. However, as the piston warms up, the area of normal clearance increases (Fig. 2-20).

Another common method of controlling piston expansion is to use struts, bands, or belts cast into the piston itself (Fig.

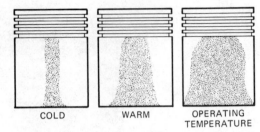

Fig. 2-20. The actual contact area of a cam-ground piston increases as the piston warms up.

2-21). These devices cause the outward thrust of an expanding piston head to be carried more inward toward the piston-pin bosses rather than toward the thrust faces of the piston skirt. This effect, in fact, is similar to that of a cam-ground piston.

Piston Rings

Some operating clearance must exist between the piston and the cylinder wall; however, some form of seal is necessary between the piston and the cylinder wall to prevent blowby. *Blowby* describes the escape of unburned and burned gases from the combustion chamber, past the piston, and into the crankcase. The manufacturer cannot fit a piston to a cylinder close enough to prevent blowby. Consequently, pistons have machined grooves, which accommodate piston rings used to provide the necessary seal to eliminate blowby and to control oil consumption.

Automotive-type pistons have two kinds of rings; compression and oil control. The *compression rings* (Fig. 2-22), which fit into the upper two ring grooves, primarily seal against the loss of air/fuel mixture as the piston compresses it and also the combustion pressure as the mixture burns. However, some compression

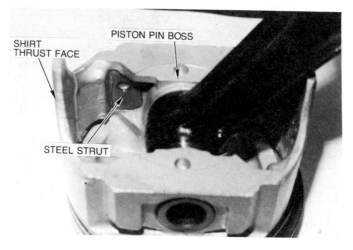

Fig. 2-21. A steel strut cast into a piston.

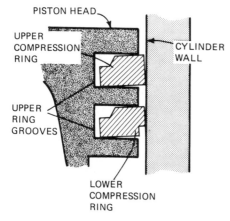

Fig. 2-22. Compression rings primarily seal against the loss of gas pressure between the piston and cylinder wall.

rings also assist in controlling the amount of oil reaching the combustion chamber.

Manufacturers basically produce compression rings in one piece from cast iron. However, some compression rings have coatings to accelerate the break-in or wear-in period. The coatings generally used are phosphate, graphite, and iron oxide. These materials are relatively soft substances that will wear off rapidly during the break-in period, but they have good oil-absorbing power for improved ring lubrication, which prevents ring-scuffing, metal-to-metal contact.

Manufacturers also form the compression ring so that it is relatively easy to install and functions automatically. The ring is split, which permits the mechanic to expand the ring and to slip it over the piston head and down into its recessed groove cut into the piston. The ring is also somewhat larger in diameter than the cylinder into which it fits. Consequently, when installed, the ring must compress until the two split ends (joints) almost come together. This compression of the ring gives it an initial tension on the cylinder wall. In other words, the ring automatically presses tightly against the cylinder wall.

The oil control ring usually fits into the

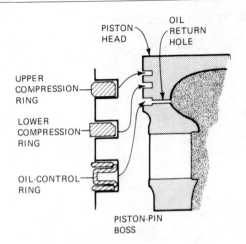

PISTON HEAD

OIL RETURN HOLE

UPPER COMPRESSION RING

LOWER COMPRESSION RING

OIL-CONTROL RING

PISTON-PIN BOSS

Fig. 2-23. An oil ring fits into the lower ring groove of the piston.

lower ring groove (Fig. 2-23). Its function is to prevent excessive amounts of oil from working up into the combustion chamber. When an engine is operating, a great deal of lubricating oil deposits on the cylinder walls due to throw-off of oil from the connecting-rod bearings. Under most circumstances, more oil deposits on the wall than necessary to lubricate the piston and rings. Consequently, the oil-control ring must scrape off most of this oil and return it to the oil pan, or the engine will burn excessive amounts of lubricating oil.

Three types of oil-control rings are used: the one-piece, slotted, cast-iron type; the one-piece, pressed-steel type; and the three-piece, steel-rail type with an expander. The one-piece, cast-iron ring (Fig. 2-24) has holes or slots between its upper and lower cylinder wall contact surfaces. The oil, scraped off the cylinder wall by

OIL SLOTS

CHANNEL

CONTACTING SURFACES

Fig. 2-24. A one-piece, cast-iron oil-control ring.

the ring contact surface, passes through these openings and through holes or slots in the back section of the oil-ring groove in the piston. From this point, the oil drains back to the oil pan. Furthermore, the slots or holes in this ring tend to distribute the oil all around the cylinder wall, thus preventing damage to any cylinder wall area due to oil starvation.

The one-piece, pressed-steel, oil-control ring has a segmental-type construction (Fig. 2-25). This construction gives the ring a three-way spring effect, providing pressure against the upper and lower sides of the ring groove as well as against the cylinder wall. In contrast, the one-piece, cast-iron ring can only seal against one side of the ring groove in the piston at a time; this leaves a path open through which oil can pass upward toward the combustion chamber. Therefore, the pressed-steel, one-piece ring not only works very well in new engines but is very useful in controlling oil consumption in engines with worn cylinder walls.

The three-piece, rail-type with expander (Fig. 2-26) acts much like the one-piece, pressed-steel ring. But in this case, the expander spacer or spring forces the two rails not only outward into contact with the cylinder but also against both the

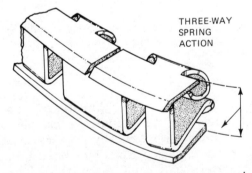

THREE-WAY SPRING ACTION

Fig. 2-25. A typical one-piece, pressed-steel oil-control ring.

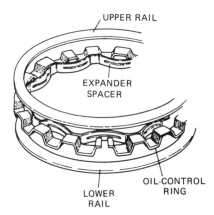

Fig. 2–26. A three-piece oil-control ring consists of two rails, an expander spacer and the oil-control ring.

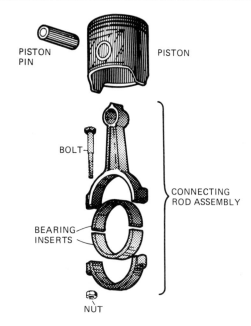

Fig. 2–27. A piston and connecting rod assembly.

upper and lower sides of the ring groove. The expander spacer itself also has openings in it to permit the excess oil to drain back to the oil pan.

Connecting Rods

As mentioned earlier, the piston moves up and down in the cylinder, in a reciprocating motion. In order to rotate the drive wheels, a connecting rod and crankshaft must change reciprocating motion to rotary. The *connecting rod* itself (Fig. 2–27) attaches at one end to the piston and on the other end to the crankpin section of the crankshaft.

The piston end of the rod (the small end) fastens to the piston itself by means of a round piston pin. The piston pin passes through both the piston and rod; a bearing surface in either the piston, connecting rod, or both permits the rod to swing back and forth in relation to the piston. Lastly, manufacturers use several methods or locking devices to prevent the piston pin from working out after the mechanic installs it.

The big end of the rod attaches to the crankpin by means of a rod cap and bolts. In addition, a split-type precision bearing fits between the crankpin, rod, and cap. With this arrangement, the larger end of the rod can rotate freely on the crankpin.

Finally, the connecting rod must be very strong and rigid but at the same time be as light as possible. The rod must be strong and rigid because it carries the power thrust from the piston to the crankpin. However, the rod also has an eccentric motion, so to minimize vibration and bearing loads, it must be as light as possible.

Crankshaft

The *crankshaft* is the main rotating member, or shaft, of the engine (Fig. 2–28). Its function, along with the con-

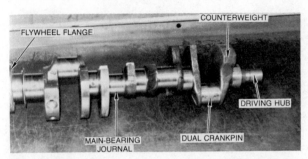

Fig. 2-28. A typical automotive crankshaft and its related parts.

necting rod, is to change the reciprocating motion of the piston to rotary. In addition, the crankshaft is responsible for driving the camshaft through timing gears or a timing chain and sprockets, plus operating the accessories via a system of belts and pulleys. Lastly, the crankshaft carries the total torque—turning or twisting effort—produced by the engine and delivers it to the flywheel. From the flywheel, the torque then passes either to the friction clutch assembly or to the torque converter.

In order to perform these functions, the crankshaft must possess considerable mechanical strength, but it also must have a design that permits it to operate in balance. To provide the crankshaft with the required strength to take the downward thrusts of the pistons without excessive distortion, manufacturers cast or forge the crankshaft in one piece from heat-treated alloy steel.

Designed into the one-piece crankshaft are areas for main bearing journals, crankpins, counterweights, flywheel flange, and driving hub. The *main bearing journals* are places on the shaft that permit the shaft to turn in the main bearings, supported in the lower section of the block. The *crankpin* is a part of the crankshaft that is offset from the centerline of the shaft; it is at the crankpins that the con-

necting rods attach. The *counterweights* are located on the crankshaft opposite to each of the offset crankpins. These weights provide the crankshaft with balance by eliminating the undue vibration, resulting from the weight of the offset crankpins. The *flywheel flange* is the area at the rear end of the crankshaft, where the flywheel attaches; and the *driving hub* is the extended section, at the front end of the crankshaft, where the vibration damper mounts.

Flywheel

The *flywheel* is a comparatively heavy wheel, bolted to the flange on the rear end of the crankshaft. Its function is to keep the engine running smoothly between power strokes. In all engines, even those with overlapping power strokes, there are times when more power is available to the crankshaft than at other times. This tendency makes the crankshaft speed up and then slow down.

However, the flywheel combats this tendency. Its inertia tends to keep the flywheel rotating at a constant speed. In other words, the flywheel absorbs energy as the crankshaft tries to accelerate and returns energy back as it attempts to slow down.

The flywheel also has several other functions. For example, the flywheel has gear teeth around its outer circumference. These teeth mesh with teeth located on the starting motor drive pinion in order to crank the engine over. In addition, the rear surface of the flywheel serves as the driving member of the clutch assembly on vehicles so equipped.

Vibration Damper

Manufacturers usually install a combination vibration damper and fan-pulley assembly onto the drive end of the crankshaft (Fig. 2-29). This damping device controls torsional vibrations. *Torsional vibration* is a negative force set up in the crankshaft by the power impulses. When a piston moves down on its power stroke, it thrusts through the connecting rod against the crankpin with a force that may exceed 3 tons. This force tends to twist or drive the crankpin ahead of the

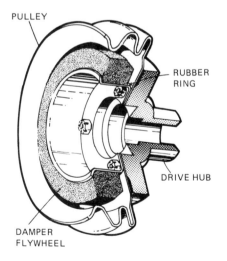

PULLEY

RUBBER RING

DRIVE HUB

DAMPER FLYWHEEL

Fig. 2-29. Partial cutaway view of a torsional vibration damper.

rest of the crankshaft. Then, in a moment, the termination of the power stroke relieves the force on the crankpin. The pin now tends to untwist or snap back into its original relationship with the rest of the crankshaft. This twist-untwist tendency repeated with every power stroke can set up an oscillating motion in the crankshaft, known commonly as torsional vibration. If not controlled, these oscillations can build up so much that a crankshaft may actually break at certain speeds.

A typical *vibration damper* is shown in Fig. 2-29. It consists basically of two parts—a damper flywheel and a pulley—bonded to one another by a rubber insert. The pulley itself mounts to the drive end of the crankshaft. When the crankshaft attempts to speed up or slow down, causing the twist-untwist action, the damper flywheel imposes a dragging effect on the pulley due to its inertia. This action slightly flexes the rubber insert, which tends to hold the pulley and crankshaft to a constant speed. The effect tends to control the twist-untwist, or torsional vibration, of the crankshaft, which relieves the stresses in the shaft.

Camshaft

The *camshaft* is another rotating shaft within the engine; it serves usually three functions (Fig. 2-30). First, the camshaft has a series of *cams*—devices that can change rotary motion to straight-line motion—which cause the intake and exhaust valves to open. The camshaft will have one cam for each valve, or, in most engines, two cams per cylinder. Second, the camshaft has an eccentric, or special cam, designed to operate the fuel pump. Finally, the camshaft has a gear that

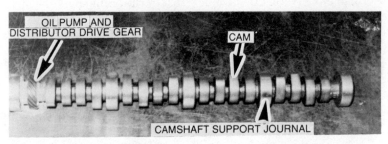

Fig. 2–30. A camshaft from a V-8 engine.

drives the oil pump and ignition distributor.

The crankshaft drives the camshaft by means of two sprockets and a chain or by two gears (Figs. 2–31 and 2–32). The camshaft sprocket or gear has twice as many teeth on it as the sprocket or gear on the crankshaft. This design provides a 1:2 gear ratio between the camshaft and the crankshaft; the camshaft turns at half the speed of the crankshaft. Therefore, every two revolutions of the crankshaft produce one revolution of the camshaft and one opening and closing of each valve in the four-cycle engine.

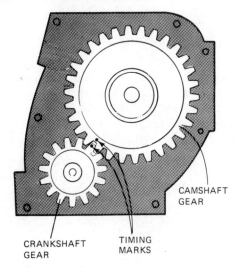

Fig. 2–32. Crankshaft and camshaft gears of a typical engine.

Cam Contour

The shape or *contour* of the individual cams controls when and how fast the valves open and close. It will also determine how far the valves open and how long they stay open. Consequently, cam contour has a greater effect on the engine's breathing efficiency (the actual amount of air/fuel mixture drawn into the cylinders) than any other component of the valve train (Fig. 2–33).

The cam contours are different for mechanical lifters than for hydraulic

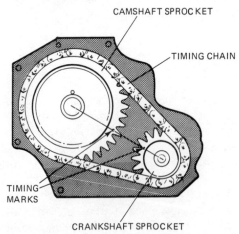

Fig. 2–31. A typical crankshaft and sprocket arrangement with a timing chain connecting the two sprockets.

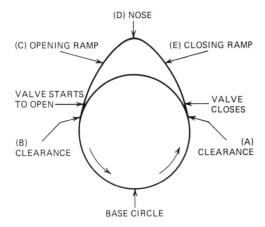

Fig. 2-33. Cam contour for a mechanical valve lifter.

lifters, which are in contact with the cam lobes. A mechanical lifter requires a cam shape that provides a clearance area beginning at point A when the valve closes (Fig. 2-33). The cam, after rotating a few degrees off the base circle (heel), again takes up this clearance at area B. At this point, then, the valve begins to open. Also, the opening ramp C has curvature that reduces valve-train acceleration. After the nose section of the cam D passes under the lifter, the valve starts to close. The closing ramp E also has curvature to slow down the valve, so that it does not hammer down onto the valve seat. Finally, clearance in the valve train again reappears at A and continues as long as the base circle passes under the lifter. This clearance is necessary to compensate for heat expansion of the valve stem.

However, the hydraulic lifter requires no clearance area in order for it to compensate for heat expansion. In addition, the opening and closing ramps are shorter. This shape permits the valve to open and close faster with less overlap. Finally, the nose portion is more rounded because of this particular ramp curvature.

Valve Timing—Duration

Duration is the length of time a valve is open. The measurement of this open period is not in units of time, like minutes or seconds, because the actual time a valve remains open varies with engine speed. Therefore, this measurement is in *degrees of crankshaft rotation,* which does not change with speed. For example, the average engine will have an intake valve duration of 248 degrees, but intake duration for a high-performance engine may easily be as high as 290 degrees.

Overlap

To lengthen the time and to accelerate the air/fuel mixture flow into the cylinders, both the intake and exhaust valves must be open at the same time for a short period. Referring to Fig. 2-34, note that the intake valve begins to open 12 degrees before top dead center (TDC), a position where the piston is in its uppermost posi-

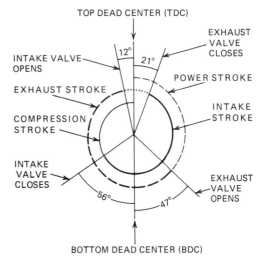

Fig. 2-34. An intake- and exhaust-valve timing chart.

tion in the cylinder. However, the exhaust valve remains open for 21 degrees of crankshaft rotation into the intake stroke.

Manufacturers provide overlap in order to take advantage of the inertial forces in the escaping exhaust gases that peak as the piston is slowing down at the end of its exhaust stroke. These gases create strong suction as they rush out of the combustion chamber. In order to take advantage of this suction, the intake valve opens at 12 degrees before TDC.

This overlap period basically permits the incoming air/fuel mixture to gain speed before the intake stroke of the piston actually begins. The suction created by the escaping exhaust gases causes the speed of the air/fuel mixture to build rapidly so that its inertial force can be at its peak throughout the entire intake stroke. A small amount of the air/fuel charge may be lost through the exhaust valve, but it ensures exhaust scavenging and assists in cooling the very hot exhaust valve.

Note also that the piston passes bottom dead center (BDC) and begins its compression stroke before the intake valve closes. This extended valve-open period permits the air/fuel mixture to continue to crowd into the cylinder, due to its inertia, even though the piston is moving upward. Only when the piston reaches 56 degrees after BDC does the intake valve close. The total duration for the intake of an air/fuel charge is 248 degrees, which does not greatly reduce the effective compression of the engine.

Finally, note when the exhaust valve begins to open, 47 degrees before BDC on the power stroke; it stays open 21 degrees after TDC on the intake stroke. The additional time that the exhaust valve is open permits a greater quantity of the spent ex-

haust gas to leave the cylinder. This extended duration is possible because by the time the piston reaches 47 degrees before BDC on the power stroke, the combustion pressure has dropped considerably; little power is lost by giving the exhaust gases a little extra time to exit the cylinder. Therefore, the total exhaust-valve-open period or duration is also 248 degrees of crankshaft rotation.

Timing the Valves

The actual timing of the valve in relation to piston position in the cylinder is due to the shape of the lobe on each cam *and the relationship between the gears or sprockets and chain on the camshaft and crankshaft.* The manufacturer machines a cam lobe into a given shape that produces a given amount of valve-open duration and overlap. Furthermore, meshing the gears or installing the chain onto the sprockets at a specific place (designated usually by timing marks) will time the valves to open and close at the proper moment in the engine's cycle (Fig. 2–32).

Altering the relationship between the drive and driven gears or sprockets changes the timing when the valves open and close. For instance, if an engine has a very loose timing chain or a mechanic did not align the timing marks on the gears, the valve timing would be too early or late. Further, suppose that for whatever reason the gear or sprocket alignment was off by one tooth, and this moved the valve action ahead 15 degrees. The intake valve would open at 27 degrees before TDC and close at 41 degrees after BDC (Fig. 2–34). The exhaust valve action would, in like manner, be too early. This valve-action advance would seriously reduce the performance of the engine. Furthermore, in some engines that use very small clearances between the valves and piston heads, the possibility exists that a valve head can strike a piston. This problem, of course, could severely damage the engine.

Lifters

A *lifter* is a cylindrical part within an engine that rests on a cam of the camshaft. As the camshaft rotates, the cam raises the lifter, and the lifter in turn opens a valve. The lifter may be in direct contact with the tip of the valve stem, or it may bear against a push rod that functions along with a rocker-arm assembly to open a valve. In either case, there are two types of lifters: mechanical and hydraulic.

Mechanical Lifters

A *mechanical lifter,* sometimes known as a tappet or cam follower, operates on a cam lobe, shaped to compensate for a given clearance in the valve train when the valve closes (Fig. 2–35). Remember this clearance is necessary to compensate

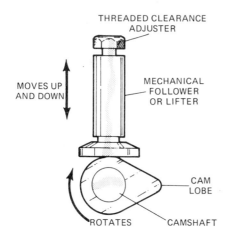

THREADED CLEARANCE
ADJUSTER

MOVES UP
AND DOWN

MECHANICAL
FOLLOWER
OR LIFTER

CAM
LOBE

ROTATES   CAMSHAFT

Fig. 2–35. A simple cam and mechanical lifter.

for heat expansion of the valve stem, and it appears between the tip of the valve stem and the lifter or between the valve tip and rocker arm. In either situation, some method must be available to adjust this clearance if it becomes too great or small.

Excessive clearance is usually due to wear on certain valve-train components and usually causes several problems. First, the valve train will begin to produce a distracting hammering-type sound, and the hammering itself can damage valve tips, rocker arms, or lifters. Second, the engine will lose power because a valve with excessive clearance will not open as far as it should.

Clearance less than specifications is usually the result of the stretching of valve-train components. This will usually cause an engine to idle poorly and can lead to valve burning because the valve cannot seat properly. Naturally, valve clearances will require adjustment whenever a mechanic performs engine maintenance that disturbs the valve train.

Over the years, manufacturers have employed several methods to adjust clearances in valve trains that have mechanical lifters. One method employs the use of an adjuster that threads into the lifter itself (Fig. 2–35). Another method incorporates an adjustment device mounted on the rocker arm itself (Fig. 2–36). Finally, in the case of stud-mounted rocker arms, the arms themselves are moved up or down to adjust clearance.

Hydraulic Lifters

This type of lifter, used in many engines, is very quiet in operation. This unit (Fig. 2–37) operates on a cam lobe, ground without a clearance area; and the lifter, when in operation, assures zero

Fig. 2-36.   An adjustment screw installed in a rocker arm.

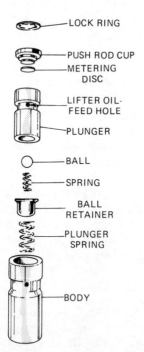

Fig. 2-37.   The components of a typical hydraulic lifter.

valve clearance in the valve train. In other words, the hydraulic lifter adjusts itself to compensate for variations due to wear in the system or temperature changes; consequently, the lifter requires no adjustment in normal service.

A typical hydraulic lifter consists of a body; plunger; metering disc and push rod cup; ball, spring, and ball retainer; and a plunger spring. The *body* of the lifter houses the remaining lifter components. The body also operates in a bore in the engine with its base in contact with the cam lobe.

The *plunger* is nothing more than a small, hydraulic piston that operates inside the body. Its function is to assure zero clearance in the system by automatically moving to a position that compensates for wear or temperature changes in the valve system.

The *metering disc* fits under the pushrod cup. It is nothing more than a round, thin piece of metal with a calibrated hole in its center. This orifice controls the quantity of oil moving up through the hole in the push-rod cup to the push rod itself. The push-rod cup has a rounded seat that fits under the push rod. If the engine has hollow pushrods, lubricating oil passes through this cup to the push-rods.

The *ball, spring, and ball retainer* fit beneath the plunger between its base and the bottom of the body. Its function is that of a one-way check valve, allowing lubricating oil to pass from inside the plunger to the cavity below the plunger's base but preventing the return of the oil to this area.

The *plunger spring* sits under the ball retainer with its tension imposed on the retainer together with the plunger and also against the bottom of the body. Its job is to keep the valve train free of clearance by forcing the plunger upward in its bore in the body.

Lifter Operation

When the engine is running, the oil pump feeds oil to the lifter through an oil gallery (passage) that runs the length of the engine (Fig. 2–38). As the valve closes, oil moves into the valve lifter through the oil holes in the lifter body and plunger. Inside the lifter, the plunger spring expands and moves the plunger upward, preventing any clearance from developing in the system.

At the same time, the oil inside the plunger forces the check-valve open, compressing its spring. With the valve open, oil enters the space under the plunger and fills the cavity. This action replenishes any oil lost from the cavity during the valve-open cycle.

As the cam nose moves under the lifter, the pressure of the valve spring attempts to force the plunger downward within its bore in the body (Fig. 2–39). This action

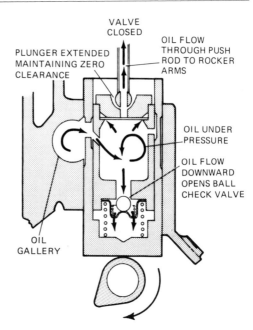

Fig. 2-38. *Lifter operation with a valve closed.*

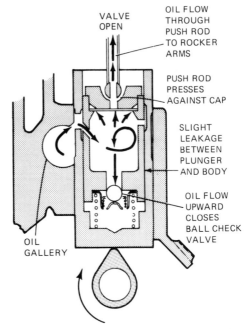

Fig. 2-39. *Lifter operation as the camshaft opens the valve.*

produces a sudden increase in pressure within the oil contained in the cavity below the plunger; this pressure closes the ball-check valve. At this point, the oil trapped beneath the plunger supports it, and the lifter becomes a solid unit that begins to open the valve.

However, the design of the lifter is such that it permits a small amount of oil to *bleed by* the sides of the lifter. This small loss of oil allows the lifter plunger to compensate for any heat expansion of valve-train components. Then, when the valve closes, the required amount of oil will once again fill this cavity, and the cycle begins again.

Valve Design

Modern engines have cylinder heads that contain *valves.* These valves open and close ports to allow or stop the flow of gases into or from the combustion chamber. Each cylinder requires at least two: an intake and an exhaust.

Figure 2–40 illustrates the design of a typical poppet valve, showing its head,

margin, face, radius, stem, retainer lock grooves, and tip. The *valve head* is the large, flat, circular surface on the end of the stem. This head always faces toward the inside of the combustion chamber.

The *margin* is the area between the edge of the head and the beginning of the valve face. This area must be a specific thickness in order to reinforce the valve head. If not, the valve head can overheat (especially an exhaust-valve head) and burn out.

The *valve face* is the angled surface, starting at the edge of the margin and terminating at the beginning of the radius. When the valve is in the closed position, this face makes contact with an angled seat in the head to close off a port. In other words, the face is half of the valving mechanism; the other half is the seat.

Two factors determine the design (shape) of the radius. First, some valves have a radius that is quite thick (Fig. 2–41). This design strengthens the radius area where the valve-head assembly attaches to the stem. This helps to prevent valve-head distortion or loss of the valve head from the stem on exhaust valves

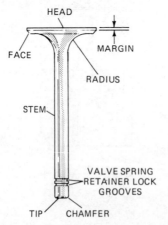

Fig. 2–40. *The design of a typical poppet valve.*

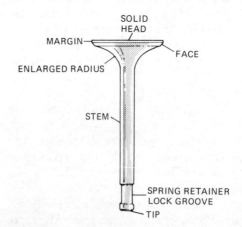

Fig. 2–41. *An exhaust valve with a thick radius.*

that operate under severe temperature conditions.

Second, radius design also implements the flow of gases around an open valve. For instance, most intake valves (Fig. 2-40) have a reduced radius area compared to the one already mentioned. In the case of an intake valve and many exhaust valves, this design is a compromise between valve head-to-stem strength and the volume of gas flow required for excellent engine performance.

The *stem* is the long rodlike shank attached to the underside of the valve head. This stem fits into and operates in a precision opening in the cylinder head, called a *guide*. The stem and guide together maintain the alignment between the valve seat and valve face, required for positive port sealing.

Machined into an area near the end of the valve stem are one or more *retaining-lock grooves*. These grooves accommodate a ridge machined into the retainer locks or keepers. The locks themselves keep the valve spring and its retainer in position over the valve stem.

The *valve tip* is the very flat end of the stem. Depending on the style of engine, the tip is in direct contact with a lifter, cam lobe, or rocker arm that will apply force to the tip to open the valve. The tip also has a chamfer machined into it. This angled ring serves to reduce the natural tendency of the metal to spread (mushroom over) due to the hammering force applied to the tip by the lifter, cam lobe, or rocker arm.

Valve Materials

The metal used in the production of a valve depends on its use in an engine. For example, an exhaust valve receives more punishment than an intake valve because of the corrosive effect and high temperature of exhaust gases. The head of the exhaust valve may reach 1,500° F., and at this temperature, the flowing exhaust gases tend to act as a cutting torch attempting to etch or cut pathways through the metal. For this reason, manufacturers usually forge exhaust valves from a combination of expensive steel alloys such as chromium and nickel with the addition of small amounts of carbon, manganese, silicone, and molybdenum.

On the other hand, intake valves receive less stress in operation. Although the intake valve receives combustion heat, the incoming fuel/air charge absorbs much of this high temperature as it blows over the intake valve on its way to the combustion chamber. In practice, the temperature of an intake valve head in most engines seldom exceeds 800°. Therefore, manufacturers make most intake valves from a mild steel that costs less and performs satisfactorily.

Sodium-Cooled Valves

To help cool the valves in many engines, manufacturers produce valves with hollow stems partially filled with sodium (Fig. 2-42). *Sodium* is a metal substance that melts at 208° F. When the engine is running, with the valves traveling up and down, the sodium changes into a liquid that easily moves up and down inside the stem. First, the liquid sodium travels toward the hot valve head, where it absorbs part of the heat. Then, as the valve changes direction, the sodium moves into the stem, where it gives off heat to the valve guide. This sodium circulation may reduce valve temperature by as much as 200° F., which lengthens valve life.

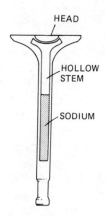

Fig. 2-42. Sectional view of a sodium-cooled valve.

Note: Sodium is a very dangerous material. For instance, sodium causes severe burns if it gets onto the skin. Also, if dropped into water, sodium bursts into flame. However, when tightly sealed inside the valve stem, sodium is safe enough, but a sodium-cooled valve with a broken or cracked stem is potentially very dangerous. Always bury discarded sodium-cooled valves deep underground or dispose of them according to governmental regulations. Do not just throw them in a trash container. Finally, sodium valves are not always marked as such but usually are recognizable by the thickness of their stems.

Other Valve-Train Components

Along with the camshaft with its gears or sprockets and chain; mechanical or hydraulic lifters; and valves, valve seats, and valve springs, some valve trains have several other components: the push rods and rocker arms. In the over-head-valve (I-head) engine, the *push rod* is a metal rod that fits between the lifter and the rocker arm (Fig. 2-43). Its function is to transmit cam-lobe lift from the camshaft to the rocker-arm assembly. Some pushrods are hollow, to permit lubricating oil to pass through the tube to the rocker arms.

The *rocker arm* is nothing more than a precision-designed lever. Its function is to convert the upward motion of a push rod into downward motion that compresses the spring and opens the valve. Because the rocker arm is a lever, it can provide a mechanical advantage that increases valve lift. In other words, the rocker arm will cause the valve to open further than the actual lift of the cam lobe.

Manufacturers produce rocker arms in a variety of ways and from different types of materials. For instance, rocker arms can be forged, cast, or stamped. A forged-steel rocker arm is stronger than a cast-

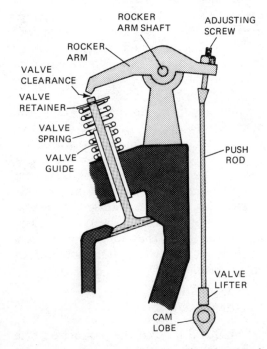

Fig. 2-43. A simple I-head rocker-arm and push rod arrangement.

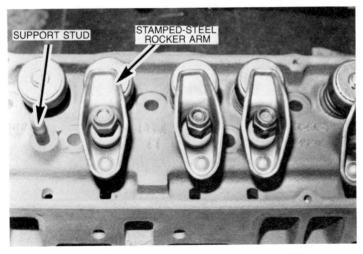

Fig. 2-44.   A common ball-pivoted, stud-mounted rocker arm.

iron rocker arm, which is somewhat cheaper to produce. A stamped-steel rocker arm is lighter than forged-steel or cast-iron and is stronger than an aluminum arm.

Manufacturers support and attach these rocker arms to the cylinder head at their pivot points. Some rocker arms pivot on a single support shaft that attaches to the cylinder head, while still others operate separately on their own support studs (Fig. 2-44).

Review

This section will assist you in determining how well you remember the material in this chapter. Read each statement carefully. If you can't complete the statement, review the section in the chapter that covers the material.

1. The engine _____ is the main framework of an engine.
   a. crankcase
   b. cylinder
   c. head
   d. block

2. The device that circulates coolant between the water jackets and the radiator is the _____.
   a. thermostat
   b. water pump
   c. water jackets
   d. fan belt

3. The device that stops oil from leaking past the front end of the crankshaft is the _____ _____.
   a. timing-cover seal
   b. head gasket
   c. main seal
   d. timing cover

4. The _____ opens and closes the circuit between the battery and the coil.
   a. distributor
   b. rotor
   c. cap
   d. camshaft

5. The engine with the camshaft mounted over the head is a _____-type.
   a. T
   b. L

c. OHC

d. F

6. The _____ moves within the engine due to the force exerted on it by the burning air/fuel mixture.

   a. valve

   b. piston

   c. rod

   d. ring

7. The piston that is oval when cold is the _____ type.

   a. horizontal-slot

   b. vertical-slot

   c. T-slot

   d. cam-ground

8. The term given to the escape of gases around the piston and into the crankcase is _____ _____.

   a. gas flow

   b. air flow

   c. blowby

   d. bleedby

9. The device that prevents excessive oil consumption is the _____.

   a. oil-control ring

   b. compression ring

   c. valve guide

   d. expander spacer

10. The portion of the crankshaft where the connecting rod attaches is the _____.

    a. flange

    b. crankpin

    c. counterweight

    d. journal

11. The device that controls torsional vibrations is the _____ _____.

    a. heavy flywheel

    b. hydraulic lifter

    c. connecting rod

    d. vibration damper

12. The gear ratio between the camshaft and the crankshaft is _____.

    a. 1:5

    b. 1:4

    c. 1:3

    d. 1:2

13. _____ is the length of time a valve is open.

    a. term

    b. moment

    c. period

    d. duration

14. The device that automatically compensates for heat expansion or wear in the valve train is the _____ _____.

    a. hydraulic lifter

    b. cam lobe

    c. timing gear

    d. mechanical lifter

15. The part of the hydraulic lifter that rests against the cam lobe is the _____.

    a. plunger

    b. body

    c. spring

    d. disc

16. The portion of the hydraulic lifter that moves to assure zero clearance in the valve train is the _____.

    a. plunger

    b. body

    c. spring

    d. disc

17. Modern engines use _____-type valves.

    a. rotary

    b. reed

    c. slide

    d. poppet

18. The portion of the valve that reinforces the valve head is the _____ _____.

a. face
b. stem
c. margin
d. tip

19. Intake valves are usually made from
   _____ _____.
   a. mild steel
   b. chromium alloy
   c. nickel alloy
   d. hard steel

20. Valves with hollow stems are filled
    with _____.
    a. air
    b. graphite
    c. sodium
    d. lead

For the answers, turn to the Appendix.

The internal combustion engine operates on certain scientific principles. These principles relate to how this engine induces fuel into its combustion chamber and then converts the energy contained in the fuel into heat energy during the combustion process. *Energy,* as used here, is the ability of the fuel or heat to perform work or the actual moving of the vehicle. In order to comprehend fully what really takes place during the operating cycle of an engine, the reader needs a basic understanding of these scientific principles. With this in mind, let's examine some of these principles, beginning with the physical makeup of matter and continuing with a few laws relating to its behavior under certain conditions.

Structure of Matter

Matter is anything that has weight and occupies space. For example, the air that we breathe, the food that we eat, and the chair or sofa on which we sit are all forms of matter—that is, they all have weight (mass) and occupy space. The actual differences between the appearance or forms of matter depend basically on two things: the composition of the molecule and its physical arrangement within the object itself.

Molecule

A *molecule* is the smallest particle in which any substance (matter) is divisible while still retaining its original physical properties. For instance, if a scientist divided a grain of salt in two and then divided each subsequent grain again until

Chapter 3

ENGINE OPERATING PRINCIPLES

he finished the division as finely as possible, the smallest particle still retaining all the properties of salt would be a salt molecule. This molecule would be almost one-millionth of an inch in diameter and need to be enlarged about one hundred times before it could be seen in a microscope. However, each of these molecules contains at least two different types of atoms.

Atom

The *atom* is a very tiny particle or building block that can exist alone or in combination can form millions of different molecular substances. An atom that exists alone is known as an element; scientists are aware of over one hundred of these atoms or elements. To signify all of these elements, each one has assigned letter(s) to represent them, such as H for hydrogen and O for oxygen.

If, on the other hand, two or more of these elements chemically combine, this action forms a molecule. For example, if two atoms of hydrogen (H_2) combine with one atom of oxygen (O), they form water (H_2O). When one atom of sodium (Na) unites with an atom of chlorine (Cl), the result is a molecule of common table salt (NaCl).

Three States of Matter

Science also divides matter by its molecular arrangement into three classifications or states: solids, liquids, and gases. In a *solid* form of matter such as a piece of steel (Fig. 3–1), the molecular structure is rigid. All molecules are very close to each other and have a strong attraction for one another. This molecular arrangement resists any attempt to change the steel object's shape physically. For this reason, solid substances, for practical purposes, are not compressible.

In a *liquid* such as water (H_2O), the molecular structure is not as rigid as in solid material. The molecules in this case do move somewhat in relation to one another or have less attraction for each other. This particular property allows a liquid to conform to its container's shape. Furthermore, the distance between the molecules in a liquid substance remains relatively close; consequently, the liquid is also not compressible by normal means.

A *gas* such as steam has molecules that are far apart and move about at high speeds. These molecules can move freely in relation to one another and tend to repel each other. These factors give a gaseous substance its limited expansion quality,

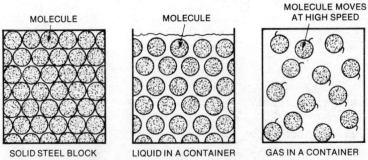

Fig. 3–1.   *The three classifications of matter: solids, liquids, and gases.*

yet the substance is compressible by normal means because of the distance between the molecules.

Gas Is Compressible

The fact that a gas is compressible so as to build up pressure is a very important principle. This principle makes possible, for example, the operation of both the gasoline and diesel engines. Figure 3–2 illustrates this principle through a simple experiment of blowing up a toy balloon.

As the person forces more and more air into the balloon at A, the pressure inside the balloon gradually increases, causing the balloon to inflate or expand. This pressure increase inside the balloon is due to the ever-increasing number of molecules bombarding all the inner surfaces of the balloon. But eventually, the rubber is no longer able to withstand any further increase in pressure, so the balloon bursts (B in Fig. 3–2).

Now let's see what will happen when we compress the air in a container that is strong enough to withstand the pressure. In order to demonstrate this, a steel pipe, closed at one end, and a fairly snug-fitting plunger are necessary (Fig. 3–3). Consider the inside of the pipe to be the cylinder of an engine and the plunger to be a piston.

As the plunger begins to move down-

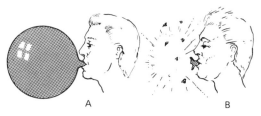

Fig. 3–2. Compressed air inflates balloon until it bursts.

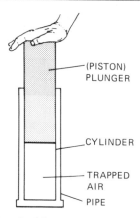

Fig. 3–3. Building up pressure in a closed container by compressing air.

ward inside the pipe, its movement seems unrestricted. However, as the plunger moves further toward the base, more resistance to movement becomes apparent due to the plunger compressing the trapped air into a smaller space. The more the plunger travels downward, the greater the resistance and air pressure become due to the increased bombardment of molecules against all sides of the sealed chamber.

If the plunger is released while the trapped air is under compression, the plunger will bounce back very nearly to its original position. In other words, the compressed air, due to its increased pressure, forces the plunger upward in the pipe. If the plunger does not return to its original position, some air has probably leaked out from under the plunger.

What applies to air, in this respect, also applies to other forms of gas. Air is a gas in the same sense as hydrogen, oxygen, and the gaseous air/fuel mixture used in an engine. Even though these various gases differ from each other in their chemical makeup, they are all compressible.

Compression Increases Temperature

When the plunger (piston) compresses the air into a smaller area (Fig. 3-3), not only is there a pressure increase but an increase in gas temperature as well. This phenomenon results from the plunger forcing the molecules closer together, which causes them to bump into one another more often. The resulting increase in molecular movement brings about an increase in gas temperature.

Depending upon the amount of compression, the gas temperature may go quite high. For example, a given diesel engine compresses air to as little as $1/16$ of its original volume. This action raises the temperature of the air to as much as 1,000°F. At this temperature, the air is hot enough to ignite a fuel charge, injected into the combustion chamber of the diesel engine.

However, the heat, produced by the compressing action, will dissipate from the air very quickly. The heat, in this situation, passes into its container (cylinder) and then dissipates into the surrounding air. In other words, the hot air will lose heat until its temperature falls to that of the cylinder, its surrounding medium.

Expansion of a Gas

Another important fact about a gas substance is that it expands when heated. A simple demonstration of this phenomenon is shown in Fig. 3-4. The drawing shows two soft-drink bottles with their openings placed slightly below the surface of the water contained in two dishes.

The heat of the hand, applied to the bottle at A, causes the air trapped in the

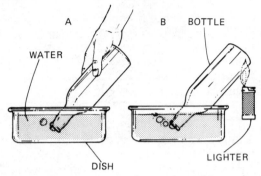

Fig. 3-4. Heat causes air to expel from the bottle.

bottle to expand sufficiently to expel some of it from the opening in the bottle. This expansion effect results from more rapid molecular motion that tends to push the molecules farther apart, so that they must spread out and take up more room. The result is, of course, the expulsion of some air from the opening, where it then rises to the surface of the water in the form of bubbles.

B of Fig. 3-4 shows the heat of a flame applied to a bottle. In this situation, the bubbles appear more frequently. This demonstrates that an increase in temperature increases the expansion of air molecules within the bottle.

If after a moment the flame is extinguished and the bottle begins to cool, water will rise in the bottle to take the place of the expelled air. This action is due to the fact that as the bottle cools, the air molecules come closer together, which reduces the air pressure inside the bottle. Under these circumstances, the higher air pressure above the water in the dish forces the water into the opening until the air pressure inside the bottle is the same as that above the surface of the water in the dish.

What applies to the air in the bottle in this case also applies to other gases. In other words, all gases expand greatly when heated. This expansion of gases when heated is another very important factor that makes it possible for an engine to produce power.

Atmospheric Pressure

The atmosphere, or the blanket of air in which we live, exerts a definite pressure on our bodies and everything else that exists around us (Fig. 3–5). This pressure is the result of the weight of the air itself. At sea level, for example, a cubic foot of air weighs about 0.08 pound, or 1.25 ounce. This does not seem to be very much; however, the blanket of air, our atmosphere, is over 50 miles thick. There are, in fact, many thousands of cubic feet of air stacked on top of one another, all adding their weight to the total.

The total weight, or downward push, of the atmosphere results in a pressure of 14.7 psi (pounds per square inch) at sea level, or about 2,160 pounds on every square foot. This pressure exerts itself at the same point equally in all directions—downward, sideways, and upward. On the human body, with a surface area of several square feet, the total pressure would be several tons.

It would appear that this tremendous pressure would crush the body. But because the natural internal pressures inside the body balance the outside pressure, the body adjusts itself to the atmospheric pressure. Therefore, we are not collectively aware of the pressure on us at all times.

From sea level upward to plateaus and mountains, atmospheric pressure decreases. This pressure reduction is due to a reduction in the volume of air at higher altitudes. Consequently, the total weight of the air decreases and so does atmospheric pressure. Figure 3–5 illustrates the approximate atmospheric pressure at various elevations above sea level.

Vacuum

A *vacuum* is the partial absence of air or any other matter from a given area. In other words, whenever air is removed from any container, the container has been evacuated, and a vacuum exists inside the container. A vacuum then is merely a condition wherein there is less

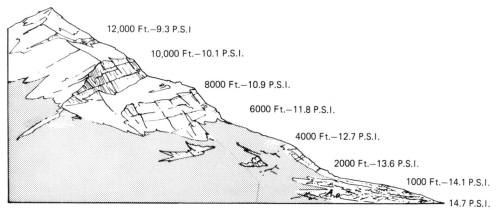

12,000 Ft.—9.3 P.S.I

10,000 Ft.—10.1 P.S.I.

8000 Ft.—10.9 P.S.I.

6000 Ft.—11.8 P.S.I.

4000 Ft.—12.7 P.S.I.

2000 Ft.—13.6 P.S.I.

1000 Ft.—14.1 P.S.I.

14.7 P.S.I.

Fig. 3–5.   The weight of the air produces atmospheric pressure.

pressure inside the container than outside, or a difference in pressure exists between the atmosphere and the inside area of this container. However, if someone opens the container, atmospheric pressure will cause air to rush in and equalize the pressure between the inner and outer surfaces of the container.

In the automotive engine, the movement of the piston in the cylinder can create a difference in pressure, or a vacuum. In order to understand how these components reduce air pressure, observe Fig. 3-6. Here we have a typical cylinder fitted with a movable piston. The cylinder is closed at one end, trapping a given volume of air inside the cylinder between the piston head and the end of the cylinder.

When the piston is in the cylinder as far as possible, a small space exists between the cylinder base and the piston head. For now, let us say this chamber is full of air at a pressure of 14.7 psi (normal air pressure at sea level). In other words, the trapped air molecules are bombarding all the inner surfaces of the chamber, producing this pressure of 14.7 psi.

If we move the piston away from the closed end, the air molecules cannot be

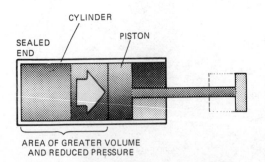

AREA OF GREATER VOLUME
AND REDUCED PRESSURE

Fig. 3-6. Moving the piston within a sealed cylinder causes the pressure in the cylinder to lower.

replaced (assuming both the chamber and piston have an absolutely tight seal). The space that a given amount of air once occupied is now larger, but the total amount of air remains the same. Since the same amount of air now occupies a larger space, air pressure is lower because the same number of molecules have a greater area in which to move around. Therefore, the molecules do not bombard the area with the same intensity, and air pressure decreases. In other words, there is a difference in pressure (vacuum) between the inside of the cylinder and the atmosphere.

This pressure difference would cease if the cylinder were again open to the atmosphere. The atmospheric pressure would force enough air molecules into the cylinder to balance the chamber pressure with that of the atmosphere. This is basically what takes place when an intake valve opens.

Combustion Process

During part of the engine's operating cycle, combustion takes place within the cylinder. *Combustion,* or fire, is a very common chemical reaction in which the gas, oxygen, combines with other elements such as carbon and hydrogen. In the gasoline engine, a mixture of compressed air and gasoline is set on fire. The air is approximately 20 percent oxygen; gasoline is mostly hydrogen and carbon. Therefore, during engine combustion, the chemical reaction is between atoms of oxygen, hydrogen, and carbon.

This chemical reaction produces water (H_2O) and carbon dioxide (CO_2). In order for this to occur, two hydrogen atoms (H_2) combine with one oxygen atom (O) to form H_2O, or water. Similarly, one carbon atom

(C) unites with two oxygen atoms (O_2) to form a molecule of CO_2, carbon dioxide gas. Therefore, during the combustion process, oxygen in the atmosphere combines with the carbon and hydrogen within the gasoline to form water vapor and carbon dioxide. During combustion, temperatures within the combustion chamber reach as high as 6,000°F; the water in vapor form along with the gas, carbon dioxide, leaves the engine through the exhaust system.

Under ideal conditions, all the hydrogen and carbon convert to H_2O and CO_2. In the engine, however, ideal combustion does not occur. Consequently, some hydrocarbons are left over. Also, the incomplete combustion produces some carbon monoxide (CO) instead of CO_2; these hydrocarbon and CO emissions contribute to the air pollution problem.

Four-Stroke Engine Cycle

With these scientific principles in mind, let's examine the four-stroke engine cycle. Before beginning a detailed description of this cycle, let's examine the definitions of a few terms to be used in the discussion—stroke, cycle, top dead center (TDC), and bottom dead center (BDC).

Stroke refers to piston stroke, the actual distance the piston moves from its uppermost position in the cylinder to lowermost, or back again.

Cycle is any series of events that repeat themselves continuously. In the engine cycle to be described, four strokes of the piston together constitute a cycle.

TDC and BDC are terms used to designate piston position within the cylinder. *TDC* for example, means that a piston is

at its uppermost position in the cylinder, or top dead center. *BDC*, on the other hand, signifies that a piston is in its lowermost position, or bottom dead center.

Intake Stroke

The intake stroke of a four-cycle engine begins with the piston at TDC. Activating the starter causes the crankshaft to begin rotating in a clockwise direction. The crankshaft, through the connecting rod, forces the piston to move downward (Fig. 3–7). As described earlier in this chapter, this downward movement of the piston creates a vacuum, a difference in pressure, in the space above the piston.

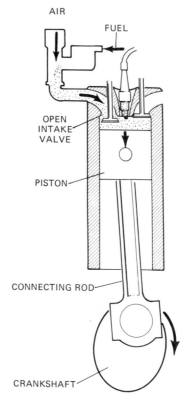

Fig. 3–7. *The intake stroke of a four-cycle gasoline engine.*

The engine manufacturer times the intake valve action so that it opens automatically at or slightly before the piston starts down. Therefore, a mixture of gasoline and air rushes through the intake manifold and into the engine cylinder, pushed by the atmospheric pressure outside the engine. In other words, atmospheric pressure forces the air/fuel mixture into the cylinder in an attempt to raise and stabilize the pressure in the cylinder.

The arrows in Fig. 3–7 illustrate this inrushing air/fuel mixture. Also, notice that the exhaust valve remains closed during this downward stroke of the piston. This valve closure prevents the entering air/fuel charge from escaping through the exhaust port.

After the piston reaches the bottom of its first stroke, the cylinder is practically full of an air/fuel charge. The drawing of an air/fuel charge into the cylinder in this manner, during the downward movement of the piston, constitutes the intake stroke of the piston. The crankshaft, by this time, has now rotated 180 degrees.

Compression Stroke

After the piston reaches BDC, it moves upward again as the starter continues to turn the crankshaft in a clockwise direction (Fig. 3–8). As the piston starts moving upward, the intake valve closes, and the exhaust valve remains closed. Since both valves are closed, the piston compresses the air/fuel mixture to a pressure of about 100 to 150 psi in the small space between the top of the piston and the cylinder head. The actual compression pressure will vary somewhat from one engine design to another.

As the piston reaches TDC again during its upward travel, the compression stroke

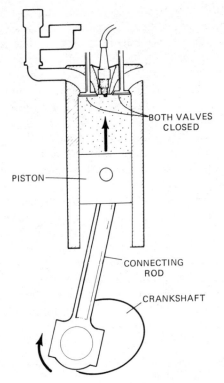

Fig. 3–8. *The compression stroke of a four-cycle gasoline engine.*

of the piston is over; the crankshaft has rotated 360 degrees from its starting point. The air/fuel charge is now under compression so that it will produce a great deal of power when the spark plug ignites it.

Power Stroke

Just as or slightly before the piston reaches TDC on the compression stroke with the air/fuel mixture fully compressed, a timed electrical spark appears at the spark plug (Fig. 3–9). This spark ignites the compressed air/fuel charge. The burning mixture begins to expand; almost immediately, the pressure in the combustion chamber above the piston increases

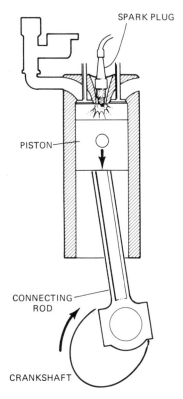

SPARK PLUG

PISTON

CONNECTING ROD

CRANKSHAFT

Fig. 3–9. The power stroke of a four-cycle gasoline engine.

The reader should also be aware that a violent, sudden explosion does not take place in the engine cylinder. Actually, the air/fuel mixture burns progressively, but it does so in a very short period of time. This assures that the expansion of the gas is also progressive and thereby applies more of a pushing force to the piston head instead of a hammering-type blow. This *push* is more effective in producing power than would a sudden sharp blow. Also, it does not have the damaging effect on engine parts as a sudden heavy blow would have.

Exhaust Stroke

Near the end of the downward movement of the piston on the power stroke, the camshaft opens the exhaust valve, but the intake valve remains closed (Fig. 3-10). By this time, the crankshaft is approaching 540 degrees of total rotation since the cycle began but is turning due to the force applied to the piston by the burning air/fuel mixture.

Although much of the gas pressure has expended itself driving the piston downward, some pressure still remains when the exhaust valve opens. This remaining pressurized gas flows comparatively freely from the cylinder through the passage (port) opened by the exhaust valve. Then, as the piston again moves up in the cylinder, it drives any remaining gases out of the cylinder, past the open exhaust valve. In other words, while the exhaust valve is open, the upward movement of the piston provides an effective method for expelling all waste gases from the engine cylinder and combustion chamber.

As the crankshaft nears the end of its second complete revolution, or 720-degree

to around four times compression pressure before ignition. This results in a pressure of between 400 to 600 psi in an average engine cylinder, with the total force thus applied to the top of the piston around 2 tons.

Notice also in Fig. 3–9 that both valves remain closed during the power stroke. This assures that the total force of the expanding gas applies itself to the head of the piston. This tremendous force pushes the piston downward on the power stroke, causing the connecting rod to rotate the crankshaft. In other words, the force resulting from the expansion of the burning air/fuel mixture, not the starter motor, is turning the crankshaft.

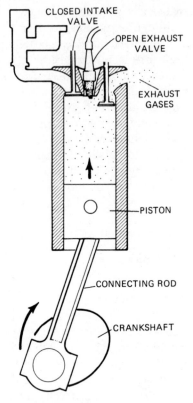

CLOSED INTAKE
VALVE

OPEN EXHAUST
VALVE

EXHAUST
GASES

PISTON

CONNECTING ROD

CRANKSHAFT

Fig. 3-10. The exhaust stroke of a four-cycle gasoline engine.

rotation, the piston again approaches the TDC position. At this point the exhaust valve is closing and the intake valve starts to open. Both valves are open together for a short period of time in order to accelerate the fresh fuel/air charge as it starts to flow into the cylinder. As the piston travels through the TDC position and starts downward again in the cylinder, a new operating cycle begins.

Need for a Flywheel

The engine cycle has only one power stroke where the piston is actually driving the crankshaft. During the other three strokes, the rotating crankshaft is moving the piston up or down in its cylinder. Thus, during the power stroke, the crankshaft tends to speed up; during the other three strokes, it tends to slow down.

To keep the crankshaft turning smoothly between successive power strokes, a heavy wheel, the *flywheel*, attaches to the end of the crankshaft (Fig. 3–11). This wheel resists any effort to change its speed of rotation. When the crankshaft tends to speed up or slow

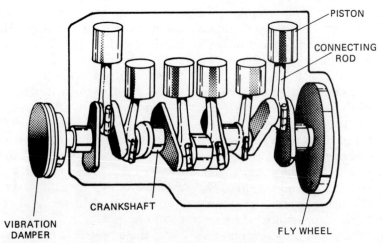

PISTON

CONNECTING
ROD

CRANKSHAFT

VIBRATION
DAMPER

FLY WHEEL

Fig. 3-11. The engine flywheel.

down, flywheel inertia resists it. In effect then, the flywheel absorbs power from the crankshaft during the power stroke and returns it to the crankshaft during the remaining three piston strokes of the engine cycle.

Multiple-Cylinder Engines

The single-cylinder engine just described provides only one power stroke during every two crankshaft revolutions or delivers power only one-fourth of the time. To provide a more even and continuous flow of power, automobiles have engines with four, six, or eight cylinders (Fig. 3–12). These engines have power strokes arranged so as to follow one another closely or overlap one another. For example, a four-cylinder engine has a power stroke in a cylinder every 180 degrees of crankshaft rotation. A six-cylinder engine has a power stroke every 120 degrees of crankshaft rotation, and an eight-cylinder engine fires an air/fuel charge in a given cylinder every 90 degrees of crankshaft rotation. The power strokes in the four-cylinder engine follow each other, one after another. However, the six- and eight-cylinder engines have power strokes that actually overlap one another.

Diesel Four-Cycle Engines

Although manufacturers have used diesel engines to power trucks, buses, ships, and many types of industrial and agricultural machinery for many years, domestic car makers did not install them until recently into passenger vehicles. Several factors relating to the design, operating characteristics, and fuel usage of the diesel have brought about this change. First of all, the diesel engine is somewhat less complex in design because

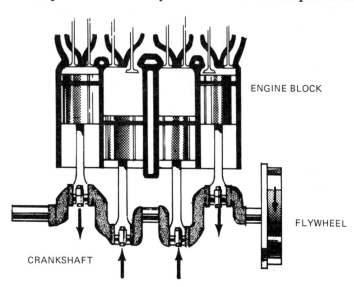

ENGINE BLOCK

FLYWHEEL

CRANKSHAFT

Fig. 3–12. A four-cylinder engine has a power stroke every 180 degrees of crankshaft rotation.

it does not require an ignition system to ignite the fuel charge. Along with this, since no ignition system is necessary, there is no need for the periodic ignition tune-ups that gasoline engines require. Second, a diesel engine compared with the same size gasoline engine produces somewhat greater torque or is more efficient and produces less harmful exhaust emissions. Finally, the diesel engine operates on a somewhat less expensive fuel; in these days of rising fuel costs, this factor has motivated many people to purchase diesel-powered automobiles.

Although the four-stroke diesel engine appears similar to the gasoline engine, there are some differences in design and the way in which the diesel operates. For instance, air alone enters the cylinder during the intake stroke; consequently, no carburetor is necessary. In addition, the piston compresses the air until it becomes hot enough to fire a fuel charge. This action eliminates the requirement for an ignition system. Finally, at the end of the compression stroke, a fuel-injection system injects or sprays a calibrated amount of diesel fuel into the combustion chamber, where the heated air ignites it.

Intake Stroke

With these facts in mind, let's briefly review the four strokes of the diesel engine: intake, compression, power, and exhaust. The *intake stroke* begins with the piston at TDC. By activating the starter, it causes the crankshaft to begin rotating in a clockwise direction. The crankshaft through the connecting rod forces the piston to move downward (Fig. 3–13). This downward movement of the piston creates a vacuum in the space above the piston.

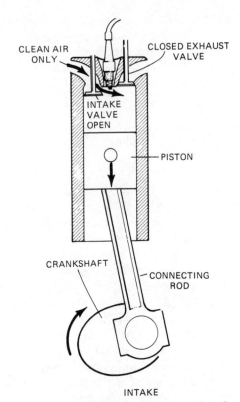

Fig. 3–13. *The intake stroke of a four-stroke diesel engine.*

The engine manufacturer times the intake valve action so that it opens automatically at or slightly before the piston starts down. Therefore, a quantity of *clean air* rushes through the intake port and into the cylinder, pushed by atmospheric pressure outside the engine. In other words, atmospheric pressure forces the air into the cylinder in an attempt to raise and stabilize the pressure in the cylinder.

The arrows in Fig. 3–13 illustrate this inrushing air charge. Also notice that the exhaust valve remains closed during the downward stroke of the piston. This valve closure prevents the entering air charge from escaping.

After the piston reaches the bottom of its first stroke, the cylinder is practically full of air. The drawing of this air charge into the cylinder in this manner, during the downward movement of the piston, constitutes the intake stroke of the piston. The crankshaft by this time has rotated 180 degrees.

Compression Stroke

After the piston reaches BDC, it moves upward again as the starter continues to turn the crankshaft in a clockwise direction (Fig. 3-14). As the piston starts upward, the intake valve closes; and the exhaust valve remains closed. Since both

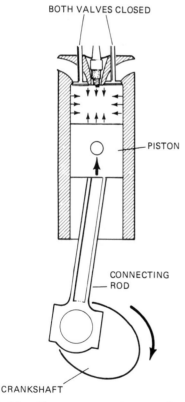

BOTH VALVES CLOSED

PISTON

CONNECTING ROD

CRANKSHAFT

Fig. 3-14. The compression stroke of a four-stroke diesel engine.

valves are closed, the piston compresses the air to a pressure of about 400 to 500 psi at a temperature of well over 1,000°F. in the small space between the top of the piston and the cylinder head. This actual compression and the resulting combustion pressure will vary somewhat from one engine design to another.

As the piston reaches TDC again during its upward travel, the compression stroke of the piston is over; the crankshaft has rotated 360 degrees from its starting point. The air charge is under compression and is hot enough to ignite a fuel charge.

Power Stroke

Just as or slightly before the piston reaches TDC on the compression stroke, the injection system begins to spray a calibrated amount of diesel fuel into the combustion chamber (Fig. 3-15). The red-hot air immediately ignites this fuel charge, and the burning mixture begins to expand. Almost immediately, the pressure in the combustion chamber above the piston increases.

Notice also in Fig. 3-15 that both valves remain closed during the power stroke. This assures that the total force of the expanding gas applies itself to the head of the piston. This tremendous force, approximately 900 to 1,000 psi, pushes the piston downward on the power stroke, causing the connecting rod to rotate the crankshaft. In other words, the force resulting from the expansion of the burning mixture, not the starter motor, is turning the crankshaft.

Exhaust Stroke

Near the end of the downward movement of the piston on the power stroke, the camshaft opens the exhaust valve, but

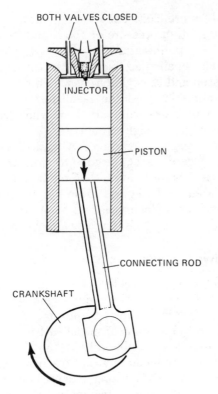

Fig. 3-15. The power stroke of a four-stroke diesel engine.

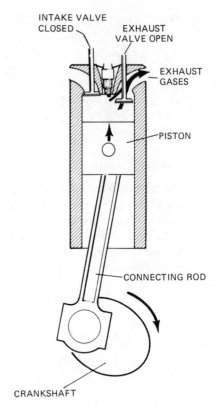

Fig. 3-16. The exhaust stroke of a four-stroke diesel engine.

the intake valve remains closed (Fig. 3-16). By this time, the crankshaft is approaching 540 degrees of total rotation since the cycle began but is now turning due to the force applied to the piston by the burning fuel charge.

Although much of the gas pressure has expended itself driving the piston downward, some pressure still remains when the exhaust valve opens. This remaining pressurized gas flows comparatively freely from the cylinder by way of a passage (port) opened by the exhaust valve. Then, as the piston moves up again in the cylinder, it drives any remaining gases out of the cylinder, past the open ex-

haust valve. In other words, while the exhaust valve is open, the upward movement of the piston provides an effective method for expelling all waste gases from the engine cylinder and combustion chamber.

As the crankshaft nears the end of its second complete revolution or 720-degree rotation, the piston approaches the TDC position. At this point the exhaust valve is closing, and the intake valve begins to open. As the piston travels through the TDC position and starts downward again in the cylinder, a new operating engine cycle begins.

Engine Classification

For identification purposes, manufacturers classify automobile engines by their cylinder arrangement, valve arrangement, and type of system used to cool the engine. Engine manufacturers basically use three distinct ways to arrange the cylinders in an engine: in-line, V-shape, or opposed. In-line engines, for example, use a single row of cylinders, one behind the other (Fig. 3-17). Most four- and six-cylinder engines have this design.

A V-type engine has two rows or banks of cylinders with the cylinders of each bank situated one behind each other (Fig. 3-18). Also, the cylinders, at their centerlines, usually have an inclination of 60 or 90 degrees. Although some V-4 engines have been built, most automotive V-type engines have six or eight cylinders.

Horizontally opposed (pancake) engines have two banks of cylinders 180 degrees apart (Fig. 3-19). Corvairs, Porsches, and many Volkswagens use this type of space-saving air-cooled engine. In addition, the

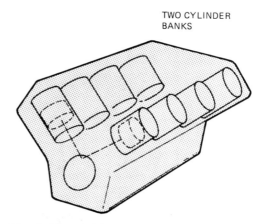

TWO CYLINDER BANKS

Fig. 3-18. A V-type engine has two rows of cylinders, usually inclined 60 or 90 degrees.

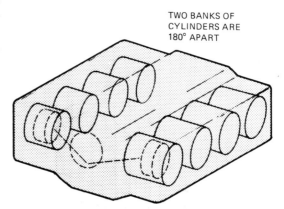

TWO BANKS OF CYLINDERS ARE 180° APART

Fig. 3-19. The horizontally opposed engine has two rows of cylinders 180 degrees apart.

Subaru uses a horizontally opposed, four-cylinder engine, but this engine has a water-type cooling system.

Classification by Valve Arrangement

Automobile engines also have their valves arranged in one of three ways. For example, in an L-head engine (Fig. 3-20),

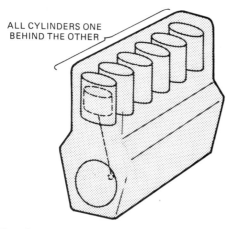

ALL CYLINDERS ONE BEHIND THE OTHER

Fig. 3-17. An in-line engine has a number of cylinders placed one behind the other.

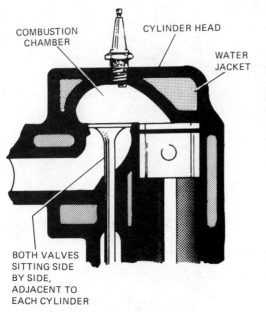

Fig. 3-20. The L-head engine has both valves located in the block.

the valves are in the block, sitting side by side, adjacent to the cylinder. Most people refer to this engine design as a *flathead* because the cylinder head itself is somewhat flat, containing only the combustion chambers, spark plugs, and water jackets. This engine design was at one time very common, but because of its limited compression ratio, manufacturers have not used this design since the early 1960s.

The F-type engine has one valve in the cylinder head and one in the engine block (Fig. 3-21). The intake valve operates in the head, while the exhaust valve is in the engine block. Although this engine type offered a slightly higher compression

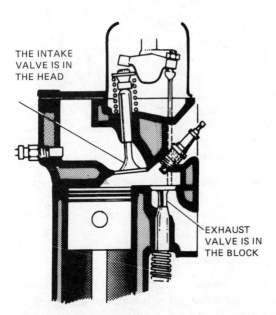

Fig. 3-21. The F-head engine has the exhaust valve in the block and the intake valve in the head.

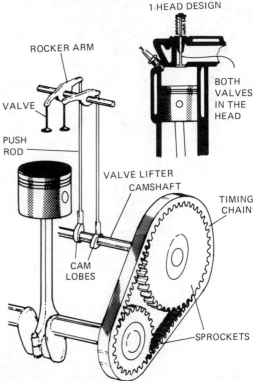

Fig. 3-22. The valve mechanism of an I-head engine with the camshaft located in the block.

ratio than the L-head engine, the last production vehicle to use it was a jeep in 1971.

Modern automotive engines therefore utilize the third type of valve arrangement, with both valves in the cylinder head (Fig. 3–22). With the overhead, or I-head, arrangement, the manufacturers can raise or lower the compression ratio to fit operating requirements. Furthermore, this engine can have the camshaft located either in the block or above the cylinder head.

When a manufacturer installs the camshaft in the block of an I-head engine, the valves require more components to open them than in any other engine style. The valve-opening mechanism of this engine design will consist of a camshaft, lifters, pushrods, and rocker arms (Fig. 3–22). However, this engine has more problems

with valve action at higher engine rpm than either the L- or F-type engines due to inertia on the additional valve-train components.

To compensate for inertia on valve-train components, many manufacturers install the camshaft above the cylinder head, over or to one side of the valves (Fig. 3–23). The valves themselves open directly with valve lifters (cam followers) or sometimes rocker arms. But at least the pushrods and sometimes the rocker arms are eliminated; this improves valve action by reducing valve train inertia at high engine rpm.

Classification by Type of Cooling

Manufacturers also classify engines as being either air- or water-cooled. The Cor-

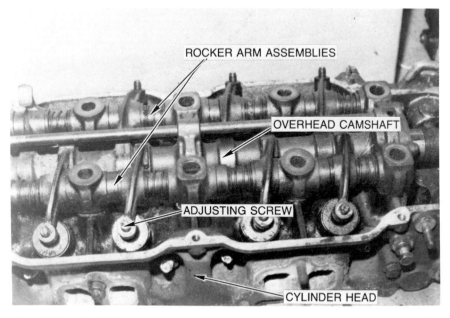

Fig. 3–23. In OHC engines, the camshaft operates over or to one side of the valves.

Fig. 3-24.   An air-cooled engine uses air to remove heat from the engine.

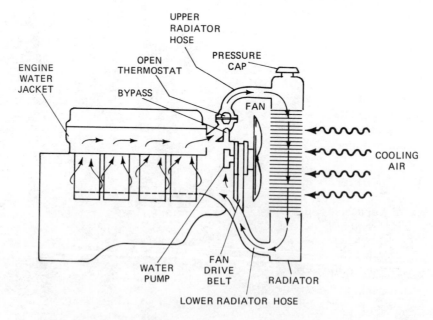

Fig. 3-25.   The water-cooled engine uses a liquid to remove heat from the engine.

vair, Porsche, and many Volkswagens are good examples of vehicles using air-cooled engines (Fig. 3–24). In these air-cooled engines, the cylinders are individual barrels equipped with metal fins. This design provides a large radiating surface from which the heat generated inside the cylinder can easily pass to the surrounding air. Also, to increase and direct the air flow around all the cylinders and other hot areas for improved cooling, these engines have a belt-driven blower and a series of metal-cooling shrouds.

A liquid-cooled engine (Fig. 3–25) uses a liquid coolant as the medium to remove heat from the engine. With this system, the engine has the water jackets in the block and head, which surround the cylinders and combustion chambers and through which coolant circulates freely. This coolant enters the engine from the bottom of the radiator and circulates throughout the engine, where it absorbs heat. Then it exits from the upper water jackets and pours into the upper portion of the radiator. As the coolant passes through the radiator, it picks up the heat contained in the coolant and passes this heat to the air flowing around the radiator passages or tubes. Thus, the coolant leaving the lower tank is cool and ready to flow through the engine again.

Review

This section will assist you in determining how well you remember the material in this chapter. Read each statement carefully. If you can't complete the statement, review the section in the chapter that covers the material.

1. Anything that has weight and occupies space is _____.
   a. space
   b. nothing
   c. matter
   d. visible

2. The substance that has molecules far apart is a _____.
   a. gas
   b. solid
   c. liquid
   d. vacuum

3. A gas substance _____ when heated.
   a. contracts
   b. compresses
   c. expels
   d. expands

4. Atmospheric pressure at sea level is _____ psi.
   a. 14.7
   b. 12.2
   c. 10.5
   d. 8.7

5. A(n) _____ is a difference in pressure.
   a. molecule
   b. vacuum
   c. atom
   d. reaction

6. Incomplete combustion causes _____.
   a. water
   b. carbon dioxide
   c. carbon monoxide
   d. oxygen

7. When the piston has reached BDC on the intake stroke, the crankshaft has rotated _____ degrees.
   a. 180
   b. 360
   c. 540
   d. 720

8. The _____ keeps the crankshaft turning smoothly between power strokes.

a. piston
b. rod
c. crankshaft
d. flywheel

9. A(n) _____ engine produces a power stoke every 90 degrees of crankshaft rotation.
   a. six-cylinder
   b. eight-cylinder
   c. four-cylinder
   d. one-cylinder

10. In the diesel engine _____ is compressed during the compression stroke.
    a. air/fuel
    b. gasoline
    c. air
    d. oil

11. When the piston has reached BDC on the power stroke of a diesel engine, the crankshaft has rotated _____ degrees.
    a. 720
    b. 180
    c. 360
    d. 540

12. Modern automobile engines have a(n) _____-head valve arrangement.
    a. L
    b. I
    c. F
    d. T

For the answers, turn to the Appendix.

The last chapter presented the scientific principles upon which the automobile engine operates. It is time to expand on the topic of engine operation by exploring the many factors that influence engine performance. Some of these factors are design features of every engine and are used to compare all engines as to their power output and efficiency. These factors include bore, stroke, displacement, compression ratio, compression pressure, volumetric efficiency, thermo efficiency, and mechanical efficiency.

This chapter will also cover a few negative factors that adversely affect the normal combustion process and can cause power loss and serious engine damage. These factors are, of course, detonation and surface ignition, problems with which every tune-up technician must deal from time to time.

Bore

The bore of an engine is a measurement taken inside the cylinder. Actually *bore* is the diameter of the cylinder itself (Fig. 4-1); the unit of measurement for cylinder

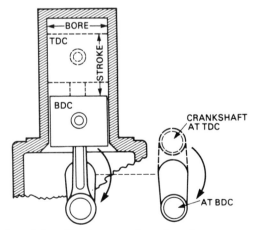

Fig. 4-1. *The bore and stroke of an engine cylinder.*

Chapter 4

ENGINE MEASUREMENT AND PERFORMANCE CHARACTERISTICS

bore is inches or millimeters. The larger the cylinder bore, of course, the more powerful will be the power stroke because a bigger piston has more area on which the high-pressure combustion gases can push down.

Stroke

Stroke is also a basic cylinder measurement. However, in this case, the measurement is that of the actual piston travel within the cylinder as it moves from TDC to BDC or back again (Fig. 4–1). As with cylinder bore, the unit of measurement for stroke is inches or millimeters.

When discussing bore and stroke, you will usually hear the terms *square* and *oversquare* in relation to engines. A *square* engine is one that has a bore and stroke of the same dimension; whereas, an *oversquare* engine has a bore greater than its stroke. For example, an engine with a 4-inch bore and stroke is square, while the same engine with a 4-inch bore and a 3.5-inch stroke is oversquare.

Manufacturers build many engines oversquare for a good reason. With a shorter stroke, the piston and rings do not move as far in the cylinder. Consequently, the engine has less wear and loss of power due to friction.

Displacement

Manufacturers commonly use displacement to indicate engine size; this specification is really a measurement of cylinder volume (Fig. 4–2). In other words, when the piston moves up from BDC to TDC, it displaces or pushes away a given volume of gases. Of course, the number of cylinders that an engine has, will determine

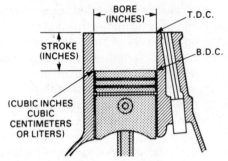

Fig. 4–2. Piston displacement is the volume of gas that the piston pushes away as it moves from BDC to TDC.

total engine displacement. Therefore, engine displacement is always equal to the piston displacement of one cylinder multiplied by the number of cylinders in the engine.

To calculate total engine displacement, you must first determine the piston displacement of one cylinder by using the formula, displacement equals $\pi \times r^2 \times L$. π is the symbol for pi or 3.1416; r^2 is the radius of the cylinder squared or multiplied by itself. To calculate cylinder radius easily, just divide the bore of the cylinder by two. Finally, L refers to length or the stroke of the piston.

With these facts in mind, let's calculate the total displacement of an eight-cylinder with a 4-inch bore and a 3.5-inch stroke. Individual cylinder displacement equals $\pi \times r^2 \times L$, or $3.1416 \times 4 \times 3.5$, or 43.98 cubic inches. In order to find the total displacement, just multiply cylinder displacement (43.98) by the number of cylinders (8). The total engine displacement is therefore 351.84 cubic inches, usually rounded to 350 cubic inches.

When written in English system values, displacement is given in cubic inches with the abbreviation for an engine's displacement being cu. in. or cid. But the metric system values for displacement can be either cubic centimeters (cc.) or liters (1 liter equals 1,000 cc.). To change engine displacement specifications from one value to another, use these formulas:

1. To convert cubic centimeters to cubic inches, multiply by 0.061 (cc. × 0.061 = cu. in. or cid).

2. To change cubic inches to cubic centimeters, multiply by 16.39 (cu. in. or cid × 16.39 = cc.).

3. To change over liters to cubic inches, multiply by 61.02 (liters × 61.02 = cu. in. or cid).

For example, the 350-cid engine previously mentioned is also a 5736.5-cc. engine (350 × 16.39 = 5736.5). If expressed in liters, the displacement of the engine would be rounded to 5.7 liters (1 liter equals 1,000 cc.).

Compression Ratio

Another design feature of an engine that determines the total power output of an engine is compression ratio (Fig. 4–3). *Compression ratio* is a measure of the cylinder volume in cubic inches above the

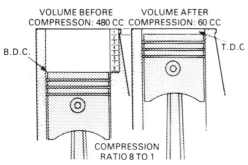

VOLUME BEFORE COMPRESSON: 480 CC VOLUME AFTER COMPRESSION: 60 CC

B.D.C.

T.D.C

COMPRESSION RATIO 8 TO 1

Fig. 4–3. Compression ratio is the ratio of the total cylinder volume to the clearance volume.

piston when it is at TDC (its clearance volume) compared to the cylinder volume above the piston when it is at BDC. When considering this statement, total cylinder volume appears to be the same thing as piston displacement, but it is not. Total cylinder volume is equal to piston displacement plus combustion chamber volume. The combustion chamber volume, with the piston at top dead center (TDC) is commonly known as *clearance volume.*

Compression ratio is nothing more than the total volume of a cylinder divided by the clearance volume. The formula for finding compression ratio is then $\frac{\text{total volume}}{\text{clearance volume}}$. If, for instance, the clearance volume is 5 cubic inches and the total cylinder volume is 40 cubic inches, the compression ratio is $\frac{40}{5}$ or 8:1. In other words, the clearance volume is 1/8 the size of the total volume, giving the engine the 8:1 compression ratio.

In theory, the greater the compression ratio is, the more power an engine will develop from a given amount of fuel. In other words, higher compression ratios are supposed to produce an engine that has more power and acceleration and obtains better mileage or fuel economy. The reason is that because the piston compresses the gas into a smaller area, the fast-moving molecules are packed or squeezed into a smaller area, thus increasing combustion pressure. For example, the engine with an 8:1 compression ratio has a compression pressure of about 150 psi and a combustion pressure of 600 psi; whereas, an engine with a 7:1 compression ratio will produce a compression pressure of about 125 psi and a combustion pressure of 500 psi. So, you can see that higher compression ratios do produce an overall higher combustion pressure.

However, there are two practical reasons to limit how high an engine's compression ratio can be. First, high compression ratios, approximately 14:1 or higher, can cause serious engine damage due to detonation. This chapter will cover this particular problem in detail. Second, higher compression engines, about 9:1 and up, must burn a high-octane leaded fuel, which creates high combustion-chamber temperatures. These high temperatures, in turn, cause a primary air pollutant—nitrogen oxide (NOx). Consequently, since 1970, manufacturers have lowered compression ratios to an average of 8:1. This ratio permits the engine to operate without damage on a lower octane, low-lead, or unleaded fuel, which reduces NOx formation.

Compression Pressure

Manufacturers can change compression pressure by altering the compression ratio or by using a supercharger. The compression ratio itself can be changed in several ways. First, to raise the compression ratio and pressure, the manufacturer or engine machinist can reduce the clearance volume by installing high-dome (high-compression type) pistons and/or machining off some material from the combustion chamber side of the cylinder head or from the top of the block. In this situation, the volume of the cylinder itself remains unchanged.

The second or alternate method of raising the compression ratio is by increasing the volume of the cylinder itself. In order to accomplish this, the engine manufacturer or mechanic will enlarge the cylinder's bore and install a crankshaft with a crankpin throw of a greater length, which increases engine stroke.

To lower the compression ratio and pressure, the process just described is reversed. In other words, the manufacturer will increase clearance volume without altering cylinder volume or will reduce cylinder volume (bore and stroke) and leave clearance volume unchanged.

The other method of raising compression pressure and power output without altering the basic engine design is through the use of a supercharger. This device forces the air/fuel mixture into the combustion chamber under pressure, which accomplishes two objectives. First, the additional pressure somewhat increases the total cylinder pressure at the end of the compression stroke, which naturally will produce additional power from the fuel. Second, when the air/fuel mixture is under pressure, it tends to mix together thoroughly before entering the cylinder. Therefore, the higher pressure and the thorough mixing of a well-proportioned charge of fuel raise not only the compression pressure slightly but also engine power output.

Before considering any further aspects of engine efficiency, it is important that the reader understands a few terms relating to engine performance, namely, *energy, work, power, torque, brake horsepower, indicated horsepower,* and *frictional horsepower.*

Energy

Energy is the capacity or ability to perform work. For example, the heat energy contained in a burning air/fuel mixture has the capacity to perform work by pushing a piston in its cylinder bore; the piston, in turn, through the connecting rod causes the crankshaft to rotate. The unit of measurement for energy is pounds-feet (kilogram-meters) and in heat units of Btus (joules).

Work

Work then is the moving of an object against an opposing force. If, in our example on energy, the rotating crankshaft through the drive train is able to set a vehicle in motion, the engine has produced a given amount of work and has expended a given amount of energy. The measurement of work is in terms of distance and force, namely, foot-pounds or kilogram-meters.

Power

Power is the rate at which work is done. The most common unit of measure for power is the horsepower which is equal to the movement of 33,000 pounds 1 foot in 1 minute, or 33,000 foot-pounds per minute.

Torque

Torque is a twisting or turning effort. The reader, however, must not confuse torque with work or power. Torque is a turning effort, which may or may not result in motion. Power is something else; in order to measure the rate of useful work, something must move against an opposing force. Referring again to our examples of energy and work, the piston moving down on the power stroke applies torque to the crankshaft through the connecting rod (Fig. 4–4). The harder the push on the piston by the combustion pressures, the greater the amount of torque. But unless the crankshaft is ac-

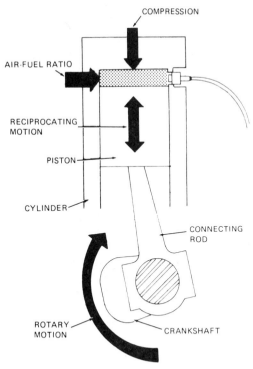

Fig. 4-4. The piston moving down on the power stroke applies torque to the crankshaft through the connecting rod.

tually propelling the vehicle, the crankshaft is turning but not performing work, so that there can be no measurement of power.

The unit of measurement for torque is the pound-foot, not foot-pounds as for work. The device commonly used to measure engine torque along with horsepower is the dynamometer. As mentioned in Chapter 1, most tune-up shops use the dynamometer for checking engine performance under varying load conditions.

The torque that an engine does develop varies with engine speed (rpm). At intermediate rpm, torque reaches its maximum amount (Fig. 4–5). This high torque

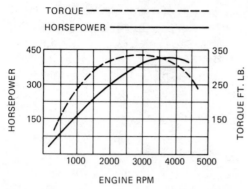

Fig. 4-5. The torque and horsepower curves of a typical automotive engine.

is due mainly to high volumetric efficiency during this phase of engine operation. *Volumetric efficiency* is basically the ability of the engine to induce an air/fuel charge. This particular subject is dealt with in detail later in this chapter.

Notice also in Fig. 4-5 that torque begins to diminish at higher rpm. This is a direct result of poor volumetric efficiency at high engine rpm. In other words, the engine does not receive an efficient air/fuel charge; consequently, combustion pressures drop off and so does torque.

Brake Horsepower

Brake horsepower (bhp) is one of the terms used in the measurement of engine output. For example, when an engine has a rating of 300 horsepower, brake horsepower is actually meant. This is the amount of power that this engine can produce at a given speed at wide-open throttle.

The word *brake*, as used before the term *horsepower*, refers to the braking device, the electrical or hydraulic portion of the dynamometer, used to hold the engine speed down while instruments on the dynamometer measure the horsepower.

But unlike the chassis dynamometer mentioned in Chapter 1, the one used to measure bhp is an engine unit that tests an engine removed from the vehicle.

The bhp curve of an engine is considerably different from its torque curve. In Fig. 4-5, bhp starts at low rpm and increases steadily with speed until it reaches a maximum amount at a high rpm. As engine speed continues to increase, bhp drops off. This dropoff of bhp is due not only to reduced torque at higher speed but also to increased friction.

Indicated Horsepower

A manufacturer may also evaluate an engine in terms of indicated horsepower (ihp). *Indicated horsepower* of an engine is the theoretical horsepower that the engine should produce, based on the power actually developed inside the engine's cylinders by the combustion process. The formula for determining ihp of a given engine is $ihp = \dfrac{PLANK}{33,000}$. *PLANK* represents the following factors:

1. *P* represents the mean effective cylinder pressure in pounds per square inch. *Indicated mean effective pressure* is the actual pressure that, when applied to a piston's area during the power stroke, will produce the total power output for a particular cylinder during one complete cycle. In other words, it is the pressure arrived at by subtracting the average pressure of the three other strokes from the average pressure of the power stroke.

2. *L* is the stroke in inches.

3. *A* is the cross-sectional area of a cylinder.

4. *N* represents the number of power strokes per minute.

5. *K* represents the number of engine cylinders.

However, the actual horsepower available from an engine is less than ihp because of the friction of the moving engine parts.

Frictional Horsepower

Frictional horsepower (fhp) is a measurement of the actual frictional losses in an engine. In other words, fhp represents the amount of indicated horsepower used up in the engine to overcome friction. A common method to determine fhp is to drive an engine with an electric motor while measuring the amount of horsepower required to rotate the engine. During this test, the engine is at operating temperature, but there is no fuel in the carburetor, and the throttle is in the wide-open position.

Figure 4-6 shows fhp in a typical engine at various speeds. At low test rpm, friction is low, but as speed increases, fhp

FRICTION HORSEPOWER ————

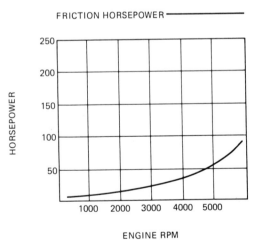

Fig. 4-6. The frictional horsepower curve of a typical engine at various speeds.

goes up rapidly. For example, at 1,000 rpm, the fhp is only about 5 hp. At 4,000 rpm, it is about 40 hp.

One of the major causes of fhp losses in an engine is piston-ring friction. Under certain conditions, piston-ring friction in the cylinder will account for 75 percent of all frictional losses within the engine itself. For instance, Fig. 4-6 points out a fhp of 40 hp at 4,000 rpm. It may very well be that 75 percent, or 30 hp, is due to piston-ring friction.

Relating BHP, IHP, and FHP

The relationship between the three horsepower measurements is $bhp = ihp - fhp$. Brake horsepower (bhp) is the actual power delivered *from* an engine. Indicated horsepower (ihp) is the actual power developed *within* the engine. Frictional horsepower (fhp) is the amount of power lost due to friction. In other words, the actual horsepower delivered by an engine [bhp is equal to the developed horsepower (ihp) minus the frictional power losses (fhp)].

Road Horsepower

Road horsepower is the actual amount of power at the drive wheels. Road horsepower is considerably less than the engine's bhp for one basic reason. Bhp is usually measured with an engine dynamometer with most or all of its driven accessories — water pump, alternator, power-steering pump, air-conditioning compressor, along with the air cleaner and exhaust system disconnected. However, when a technician uses a chassis dynamometer on a vehicle to measure road horsepower, all these items along with the drive-train components are operational.

All these accessories and systems along with the drive-train components reduce the engine's useful power. These losses can range from about 35 percent to as high as 70 percent. For example, an engine may have a bhp of 375 but, when installed in a vehicle, will produce a road horsepower of 175.

Volumetric Efficiency

Volumetric efficiency is a term used to describe the actual air flow by volume that enters an engine compared to the engine's displacement, the maximum volume that it could take in under ideal conditions. In other words, volumetric efficiency in any automotive-type engine has to do with inducing the greatest possible charge of air/fuel mixture (by weight) into the cylinder, then expelling the spent gases (during the exhaust stroke) with the least possible back pressure against the piston. Volumetric efficiency, or the engine's breathing ability, is normally expressed in percentage, with 100 percent representing perfect breathing efficiency.

But the average engine is not able to take in a 100 percent fill on each intake stroke due to variables dealing with engine design and operating condition, engine speed, temperature, and atmospheric pressure. The design factors, for example, that influence volumetric efficiency are the size and shape of intake and exhaust valves and ports; size, shape, and length of manifold passages; and valve timing. Also, an engine in poor operating condition, with gum or varnish restricting manifold passages; burned, sticky, or out-

of-adjustment valves; or a loose timing chain, will lose its ability to breathe efficiently.

The operating speed (rpm) of an engine also greatly influences volumetric efficiency. For instance, a given engine operating at 3,000 rpm will only have half the time for the air/fuel charge to enter and fill the cylinders as it would at 1,500 rpm. Thus, volumetric efficiency drops as engine rpm increases. As a consequence, engine torque also decreases (when engine speed exceeds a certain range) because the engine has less air/fuel mixture to compress and burn, which weakens the power strokes.

The temperature of the induced air is important to volumetric efficiency. Cooler air is more dense (heavier by volume) and contains more oxygen molecules per cubic foot. Consequently, cooler air passing through the carburetor carries a greater amount of fuel by weight into the manifold at a given throttle opening than it would otherwise at a higher temperature. However, a cool air/fuel charge does not vaporize well to provide good combustion. Consequently, manufacturers provide the carburetor or intake manifold with a heating device to raise the temperature of the combined air/fuel charge in order to vaporize it completely before the mixture enters the cylinders.

An atmospheric pressure below sea level (14.7 psi) also reduces volumetric efficiency. For example, an engine operating in an area 5,000 feet above sea level will have less volumetric efficiency than the same engine at sea level simply because of the reduction of atmospheric pressure at the 5,000-foot elevation. Since, in fact, atmospheric pressure forces the air/fuel mixture into the cylinder, it should be obvious that any decrease in atmospheric pressure will cause a corresponding decrease in volumetric efficiency, as the altitude at which an engine operates increases.

An average automobile engine may have a volumetric efficiency of 75 to 80 percent at an rpm producing the highest torque output, but this engine could achieve 100 percent volumetric efficiency at the same rpm through the use of a supercharger. A supercharger forces the air/fuel mixture into the combustion chamber under pressure; therefore, the engine does not have to depend on atmospheric pressure as the prime mover of the air/fuel mixture into the combustion chamber. The supercharged engine then will have a constantly higher volumetric efficiency regardless of the altitude at which the vehicle operates.

Thermo Efficiency

Basically the internal combustion engine is a heat engine. A *heat engine* is nothing more than a machine that converts the heat energy contained in the fuel to mechanical energy in order to propel the vehicle. *Thermo efficiency* itself is a rating of just how well an engine makes this conversion, with 100 percent representing perfect efficiency.

Anyone who has been around a hot engine realizes that the engine has not converted all the heat from the gasoline into mechanical power. If it had, the engine block and the exhaust manifolds would not be so hot to the touch. In fact, only a small portion of the total potential energy in gasoline (approximately 19,000 Btu, British thermo units per pound) ever reaches the drive wheels of a vehicle (Fig.

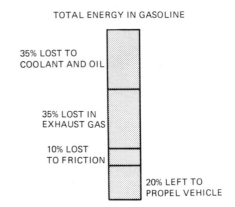

TOTAL ENERGY IN GASOLINE

35% LOST TO COOLANT AND OIL

35% LOST IN EXHAUST GAS

10% LOST TO FRICTION

20% LEFT TO PROPEL VEHICLE

Fig. 4-7. The average heat energy losses from the cylinder to the wheels.

4-7). For example, roughly 35 percent of it is lost through the exhaust. Another 35 percent of the heat absorbs into the coolant and the oil, from where it dissipates into the atmosphere. Some 10 percent is lost to friction. This leaves only 20 percent of the original 19,000 Btus per pound of gasoline to produce power to propel the vehicle.

Mechanical Efficiency

Another method of rating the efficiency of an engine other than its thermo efficiency is by how much energy is really lost due to friction of all moving parts or its mechanical efficiency. In Fig. 4-7, the loss to friction was 10 percent. However, this figure is just an approximation.

To calculate the true mechanical efficiency of a given engine at a given speed, divide bhp by ihp. For example, with an ihp of 180 and a bhp of 153, an engine would have a mechanical efficiency of $\frac{153}{180}$, or 85 percent, and a frictional loss of 7 horsepower, or 15 percent.

Detonation

Detonation is a common problem often encountered by a technician performing an engine tune-up. Detonation, commonly referred to as a *spark knock* or *ping*, results from an uncontrolled second explosion in the combustion chamber after the spark plug fires the air/fuel mixture. This spontaneous combustion of the remaining compressed air/fuel charges causes a pinging noise.

To understand how this phenomenon occurs, let's examine normal combustion and then observe what goes wrong. Normally a spark occurring at the spark plug starts the air/fuel mixture burning in the combustion chamber (Fig. 4-8). After the mixture ignites, a wall of flame spreads out in all directions from the initial spark. The air/fuel mixture does not explode; however, the flame rapidly travels through the compressed mixture until the flame consumes all the charge. The term given to the speed with which the flame travels is the *rate of flame propagation.*

During normal combustion, pressure increases several hundred pounds per square inch. Remember, the burning of the air/fuel charge raises combustion chamber pressure to a value about four times higher than it was at the end of the compression stroke. This increased pressure could exceed 800 to 900 psi in a high-compression engine.

When detonation occurs, the last portion of the compressed air/fuel charge, the end gas, explodes before the normal flame front reaches it (Fig. 4-9). This explosion results from the increasing pressure on the unburned mixture and the flame that moves through the combustion chamber; both increase the temperature of the end gas. If the increased temperature gets high enough, the end gas explodes before the flame front arrives.

This explosion causes high-frequency pressure waves. These waves impinge or hit on the combustion chamber walls and cause a vibration noise or knock. The effect on the piston head is almost the same as a heavy hammer blow.

Effects of and Testing for Detonation

There is no question that detonation has a detrimental effect on not only engine parts but engine performance as well. Top cylinder wear, piston damage, cracked connecting rod bearings, and oval crankpin journals are some good examples of engine damage attributable to detonation. Detonation, audible or not, also causes a loss of power, rough engine operation, and a tendency for an engine to overheat.

A tune-up specialist usually tests an engine for detonation by placing the vehicle on a chassis dynamometer and operating the engine under varying loads for

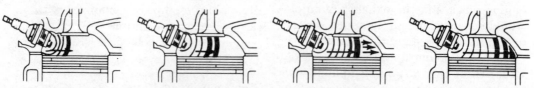

Fig. 4-8.   The normal combustion is a fast-moving wall of flame that moves across the combustion chamber.

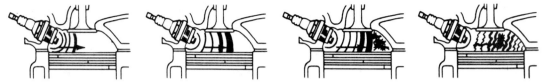

Fig. 4-9. When detonation occurs, the last portion of the compressed air/fuel charge, the end gas, explodes.

several minutes. By observing the engine temperature, speed, and horsepower during the tests, the technician can usually control detonation, obtain the best overall engine performance, and normalize engine temperature by such steps as varying the ignition timing or recommending to the customer, when possible, a change in fuel to one that has a higher antiknock value.

Causes of Detonation

Two simple causes of detonation are incorrect ignition timing and use of a fuel with too low an antiknock value. High compression pressure also has a major effect on whether an engine detonates on a given fuel. If an engine has a high compression ratio design or has large quantities of carbon deposits in the combustion chamber, compression pressures will be high. High compression does produce more power; however, it also causes high combustion pressure and temperature, which cause detonation.

Engines designed with a high compression ratio will function normally on fuels with high antiknock properties. But this same fuel may not prevent detonation in the same engine with increased compression due to carbon deposits. In this case, the only way to correct the detonation problem would be to clean out the carbon deposits either chemically or by removing the cylinder heads and decarbonizing the combustion chambers.

Surface Ignition

Another abnormal combustion condition is surface ignition. *Surface ignition* is a broad term that indicates any source of ignition other than the spark plug. The effect of this problem, because it produces a secondary ignition source, is to complete the combustion process faster than normal. Once again, this results in maximum pressure occurring at the wrong time in the engine cycle, causing the engine to lose power.

Surface ignition is usually thought of as a service problem within the engine itself. For example, one source of secondary surface ignition is hot spots, formed on spark plug electrodes, protruding gaskets, and sharp valve edges. These projections can become so hot during normal engine operation that they can and do form a second source of ignition. As long as an engine has proper maintenance, these sources of surface ignition seldom occur in modern engines.

Another very common cause of secondary ignition is combustion chamber deposits. Deposit ignition results from a hot deposit flake that ignites one charge, and then the exhaust gases carry it from the engine. This type of surface ignition is *wind ping*. In many cases, the hot flake remains attached to the combustion chamber wall. When this happens, the flake ignites several successive charges until combustion consumes the deposit or engine-operating conditions are changed. This form of ignition is known as *deposit ignition.*

Deposits that can and do cause wind ping and deposit ignition usually result from either the type of fuel or lubricating oil used in an engine or the type of engine operation. Fuel and lubricant suppliers have done extensive research to produce products that minimize deposit ignition; therefore, deposit ignition seldom occurs in modern engines using the specified grade of fuel and motor oil. However, some deposit problems may still continue to exist in engines used only for low-speed or short-trip driving.

The industry has given specific names to certain abnormal combustion conditions caused by surface ignition. If the surface ignition occurs before the spark plug fires (Fig. 4-10), the abnormal condition is known as *preignition.* Preignition may be audible or inaudible, and it may be

a wild ping or a continuous, runaway deposit ignition. Finally, *run-on* is a term given to deposit ignition that causes an engine to continue running after the operator turns the ignition key off.

Continuous surface or deposit ignition can cause several problems. The first is *rapid engine damage,* usually in the form of holes burned through the piston head. The second problem is engine rumble. *Rumble* is a low-frequency vibration of the lower part of the engine that occurs when combustion pressure reaches its maximum too early in the engine's operating cycle.

Review

This section will assist you in determining how well you remember the material contained in this chapter. Read each item carefully. If you can't complete the statement, review the section in the chapter that covers the material.

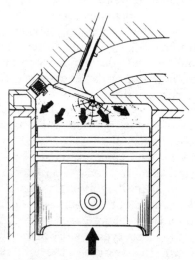

Fig. 4-10. *Preignition occurs when the fuel mixture ignites before the spark plug fires it.*

1. The actual travel of the piston in the cylinders is known as its _____.
   a. cycle
   b. bore
   c. stroke
   d. efficiency

2. Total cylinder volume is not the same thing as _____.
   a. displacement
   b. bore
   c. stroke
   d. compression ratio

3. High compression can cause an engine to _____.
   a. rumble
   b. overheat
   c. stall
   d. detonate

4. A twisting effort not always accomplishing work is _____.
   a. horsepower
   b. torque
   c. power
   d. energy

5. _____ horsepower is the theoretical horsepower an engine should produce.
   a. Frictional
   b. Road
   c. Brake
   d. Indicated

6. _____ horsepower is the actual amount of power at the drive wheels.
   a. Road
   b. Frictional
   c. Brake
   d. Indicated

7. _____ *efficiency* is a term referring to the breathing ability of an engine.
   a. *Thermo*
   b. *Mechanical*
   c. *Volumetric*
   d. *Flow*

8. A _____ increases an engine's breathing ability.
   a. fan
   b. supercharger
   c. carburetor
   d. filter

9. _____ efficiency is a rating of just how well an engine converts heat energy to mechanical force.
   a. Conversion
   b. Volumetric
   c. Mechanical
   d. Thermo

10. An uncontrolled second explosion in the combustion chamber is _____ _____.
    a. detonation
    b. surface ignition
    c. preignition
    d. run-on

11. Surface ignition produces a _____ _____ source of ignition.
    a. primary
    b. secondary
    c. backup
    d. both *a* and *c*

12. If surface ignition occurs before the spark plug fires, the engine is said to have a _____ problem.
    a. ping
    b. detonation
    c. preignition
    d. run-on

For the answers, turn to the Appendix.

As mentioned in Chapter 1, one of the first objectives of any well-trained tune-up technician should be to determine if an engine is mechanically sound enough to benefit from a tune-up. The mechanic can make this determination in one of several ways: a power check with diagnostic equipment or a compression, leakage, or vacuum test. Engine diagnostic equipment (Fig. 5–1) cannot pinpoint the cause of a mechanical problem. However, by power testing each cylinder with this equipment, the technician can spot a weak cylinder—one that is not firing or producing as much power as the rest. The technician then must perform one or more engine mechanical condition tests to locate the cause of the weak cylinder.

Although the engine may have a weak or malfunctioning cylinder due to problems in the ignition or fuel systems, this chapter concentrates only on the testing procedures used to locate the sources of mechanical problems. These tests include compression, leakage, vacuum, and noise detection. Along with these tests, this chapter covers valve adjustment, a procedure that the mechanic may have to perform as part of a normal tune-up pro-

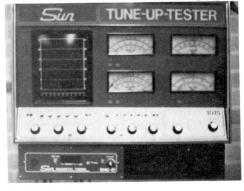

Fig. 5–1. A typical engine analyzer capable of power-checking engine cylinders.

_____ Chapter 5

ENGINE MECHANICAL TESTS AND VALVE ADJUSTMENT

cedure or as a service measure to correct a malfunction.

Compression Tests—Purpose

The efficient combustion and power output of any piston engine depend on the compression pressure generated within its cylinders. The amount of compression pressure depends directly upon how well sealed the cylinder is by the piston rings, valves, cylinder-head gasket, and the area around the spark plug (Fig. 5-2). If any one of these points leaks, cylinder compression pressure is lost and combustion efficiency and power output drop off.

A compression test then measures the amount of compression pressure in each cylinder and points out any variations in pressure between all engine cylinders. By testing how well each cylinder builds and holds its compression pressure, a tune-up specialist can easily isolate a weak cylin-

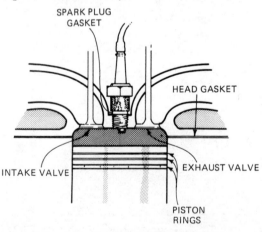

Fig. 5-2.   In order for the piston to produce a good compression, the piston and combustion chamber must have adequate sealing at the points shown.

der and locate the source of the pressure loss. However, the compression test results are only valid if the mechanic follows the proper test procedure and uses good equipment.

Specifications

The technician should always compare compression test results with the specifications. Each manufacturer supplies compression-pressure specifications for its own engines. These specification tables may state the allowable variation in compression readings for an engine in several different ways, either by a percentage or minimum figure. One percentage listing, for example, states that the compression pressure should be 160 pounds per square inch (psi) plus or minus 10 percent (160 psi ± 10%). This plus or minus tolerance is an important portion of the specification because it limits the permissible variation between cylinder pressures. Using the same idea, another percentage specification for a different engine specifies that the lowest compression reading of any cylinder must be no lower than 75 percent of the highest reading cylinder. In other words, if the highest reading is 160 psi, the lowest reading must be at least 120 psi (120 is 75 percent of 160).

When the manufacturer provides a specification with a minimum figure for all compression readings, it usually also contains a specified figure for the allowable pressure variation between cylinder readings. For instance, the minimum compression reading for a certain engine is 140 psi with a variation of no more than 30 psi. Therefore, the compression reading in each cylinder is satisfactory as long as it is at least 140 but no more than 170 psi.

Compression Gauge

The mechanic utilizes a special compression gauge when performing a compression test on an engine. This type of gauge is able to measure very high pressure up to 300 psi for gasoline engine usage (Fig. 5–3). Diesel engines, of course, usually require a gauge that measures even higher pressures. The best gauge design is one with a threaded adapter that fits into the spark plug opening. A hose connects the adapter to the gauge itself. Some compression test gauge sets utilize a quick-disconnect coupling between the gauge hose and a short adapter hose. This type of arrangement makes it easier for the technician to thread the adapter into the spark plug hole.

Another type of gauge set comes with tapered and stepped rubber tips, which fit

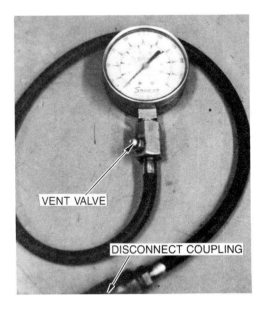

Fig. 5–3. A typical compression gauge and connector hose.

on the end of a metal stem threaded into the gauge. These tips make this gauge set universal in that the tips fit any size of spark plug hole found on automotive engines. Also, many sets have several stems of different lengths and shapes. These stems are necessary to clear the gauge of various obstructions that the mechanic may encounter while performing a compression check.

This particular gauge design is harder to use and may not be as accurate as the one mentioned earlier. In order to take a reading, the mechanic must hold the gauge firmly into position, with the rubber tip in the spark plug opening, against the force of compression. This can be a difficult task, especially on high-compression engines.

Both of these gauges have vent valves. This valve traps the compression pressure reading in the gauge until the mechanic opens the vent valve. This arrangement makes it easy for the technician to take note of the compression readings.

Remote Starter Switch

A remote starter switch (Fig. 5–4) is one of the most useful devices ever invented for the automotive mechanic. This switch may be a single tool in itself or incorporated into a compression gauge assembly. In either case, the switch itself permits the mechanic to crank the engine from under the hood area for checking compression, adjusting valves, setting ignition points, and timing. This eliminates the need for a second person inside the vehicle, activating the starter switch, while the mechanic performs these tasks.

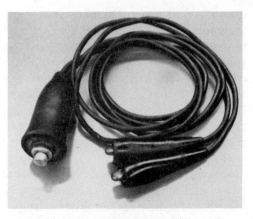

Fig. 5-4.   A remote starter switch may be a separate unit or built into a compression tester assembly.

Compression Test Procedures

To prepare a typical engine for a compression test, follow this procedure.

1. Warm up the engine until it reaches normal operating temperature.

2. Stop the engine. Then, carefully disconnect the spark plug cables from all the plugs.

3. Using compressed air, blow all foreign materials out of the spark plug wells.

4. Remove all the spark plugs. Place the plugs on a clean work bench in the cylinder order in which you removed them. This technique will make it easier for you to identify the cylinder from which a plug came, after analyzing all the plugs' condition and noting a problem.

5. Make certain to remove all the spark plug gaskets or tubes from the cylinder head.

6. Remove the air cleaner from the car-

buretor. Then, with a long screwdriver or suitable tool, block the choke and throttle plate in the wide-open position (Fig. 5-5).

7. Disable the ignition system by removing the coil's high-tension wire from the distributor cap and grounding it securely. This procedure not only prevents electrical shocks or a fire but also keeps the coil from discharging high-voltage surges, which can overheat it.

8. Connect a remote starter switch to the starter relay or solenoid. The switch will operate the starter if you connect one of its leads to the positive battery terminal and the other to the s-terminal located on the relay or solenoid (Fig. 5-6).

Performing a Dry Compression Test

Depending on the type of equipment available, connect a compression gauge to number-one cylinder, using one of the following methods.

1. Thread the gauge adapter into the spark plug hole fingertight. Next connect the compression gauge to the adapter, or insert the tapered or stepped rubber tip of the compression gauge into the spark plug opening. Be sure to hold the compression gauge firmly in place during the test.

2. While watching the compression gauge needle, turn the engine over continuously for at least four compression strokes (Fig. 5-7).

3. Record the *first* and *fourth* gauge readings.

4. Zero the gauge needle by opening the gauge vent valve.

5. Disconnect the compression tester

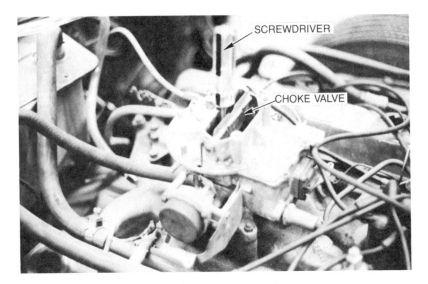

Fig. 5-5. Blocking the choke and the throttle plate wide open during the compression test.

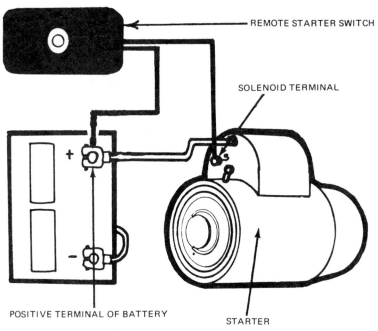

Fig. 5-6. Connecting the remote starter switch to the starter relay or solenoid.

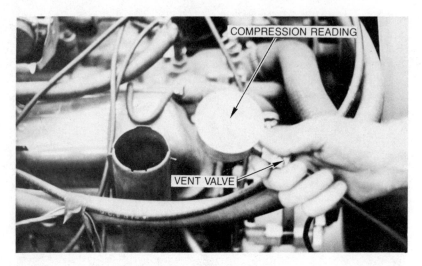

Fig. 5–7. Crank the engine over for at least four compression strokes when testing compression.

from its adapter and then remove the adapter from the spark plug opening.

6. Repeat steps 1 through 4 for each remaining cylinder.

Results of the Dry Compression Test

After completing the dry test, compare the results with the following.

1. If any gauge reading is low on the first stroke but builds up with each following stroke without reaching the specified amount, the piston rings in this particular cylinder are probably worn excessively.

2. If any gauge reading is low on the first stroke and builds up only slightly during the following strokes, a valve may be sticking or burned.

3. If any two adjacent (side-by-side) cylinders have equally low pressure readings, the head gasket is most likely leaking between the two cylinders.

4. The cylinder probably has excessive carbon deposits if the total gauge reading is higher than normal.

5. Cylinder compression is good if the gauge reading rose steadily with each successive compression stroke with a final reading within factory specifications.

6. Proceed with a wet compression on any cylinders with a low reading.

Performing a Wet Compression Test

To determine whether the rings or valves are causing the loss of compression in a particular cylinder, you should perform a wet compression test before tearing down the engine for inspection and repair. This test procedure basically consists of squirting an ounce or two of medium oil through the spark plug hole onto the top of the piston, turning the engine over several times to allow the oil to work down around the rings (this additional oil will temporarily improve the piston-ring seal on the cylinder wall), and retesting the cylinder. This test procedure will not be very accurate on horizontally opposed cylinder engines like the Volkswagen or Corvair. For this type of engine, a leakage test is the best way to locate the source of low compression.

To perform a simple wet test on a cylinder with low compression

1. Squirt an ounce or two of oil into the test cylinder (Fig. 5-8).

2. Crank the engine over several revolutions.

3. Connect a compression gauge to the test cylinder as described for dry test procedures, and perform the wet compression test.

Results of a Wet Compression Test

Compare the wet compression test results to the dry test results for any cylinders with low compression. If the compression readings are more nearly normal with the rings temporarily sealed with oil, the rings, pistons, or cylinders require service. If, on the other hand, the compression did not increase at all during the wet test, then the compression leakage is through the valves or head gasket. Lastly, a partial improvement in compression during the wet test generally indicates that both the rings and valves require attention.

Cylinder Leakage Test

Experience and research have established that in many cases a compression test alone may not show up excessive amounts of combustion chamber (compression) leakage. The cylinder leakage test, on the other hand, provides an accurate method of testing engine condition.

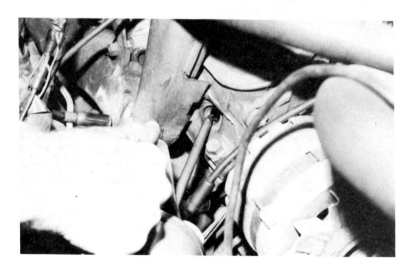

Fig. 5-8. Adding oil to the test cylinder just prior to performing a wet compression test.

This test points out, for example, in percentage terms any leakage in the valves, rings, or head gaskets. Even the smallest leak is detectable using this testing procedure.

This test procedure requires the use of a special leakage gauge (Fig. 5-9). The technician installs this gauge between a compressed air source and a sealed cylinder. Then, the gauge needle accurately indicates just how much of the calibrated amount of air allowed to enter the engine has leaked out.

The gauge of the leakage tester has a scale marked off in divisions ranging from 0 to 100 percent (Fig. 5-10). A reading of 0 percent indicates a perfectly sealed cylinder with no leaks. However, a reading of

Fig. 5-10.   The scale of the leakage tester has divisions ranging from 0 to 100 percent.

100 percent indicates that the cylinder is not holding any pressure at all. In order that the scale displays an accurate reading, the technician must calibrate the gauge before each test.

Tester Calibration

Before testing a cylinder for pressure loss, calibrate the tester following this procedure.

1. Turn the control regulator knob counterclockwise until it rotates freely.

2. Connect the shop's air supply to the tester's input air connection. The air supply must be 70 to 200 psi.

3. Turn the control regulator knob clockwise until the gauge reads zero. Momentarily connect and disconnect a test adapter to the cylinder connection fitting on the tester. The pointer on the gauge should rise to 100 percent and then return to zero. If not, readjust the control regulator knob and recheck the adjustment.

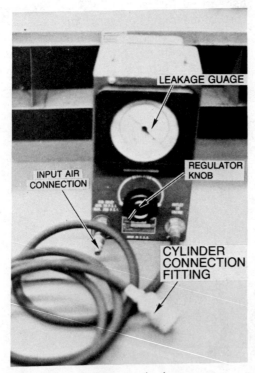

LEAKAGE GUAGE

INPUT AIR CONNECTION

REGULATOR KNOB

CYLINDER CONNECTION FITTING

Fig. 5-9.   A common leakage tester.

Preparation of the Engine for a Leakage Test

In order to prepare a typical engine properly for a cylinder leakage test, follow this procedure.

1. Operate the engine until it reaches the normal operating temperature.

2. Stop the engine. Then, carefully disconnect the spark plug cables from the plugs.

3. Using compressed air, blow all foreign materials from the spark plug wells.

4. Remove all the spark plugs, gaskets, or tubes, if used.

5. Remove the air cleaner from the carburetor. Then, with a long screwdriver or suitable tool, block the choke and throttle plate in the wide-open position (Fig. 5–11).

6. Disconnect the PVC hose from the crankcase.

7. Carefully remove the radiator pressure cap. If the coolant level is low, fill it to the prescribed level.

Test Procedure

When leakage testing an engine, always begin the test at number one cylinder. To set the number one piston at its TDC (test) position:

1. Select the proper test adapter and then install it into the number-one spark plug hole. Next, attach the whistle that accompanies the tester to the adapter (Fig. 5–12).

2. Using a wrench on the crankshaft pulley nut or bolt, rotate the engine in the normal direction of rotation until the whistle sounds. Continue to rotate the engine slowly until the engine's timing mark (TDC) on the crankshaft pulley aligns with the engine-timing pointer on

Fig. 5–11.   Blocking the choke and throttle plate wide open during a leakage test.

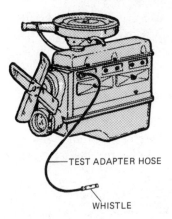

Fig. 5-12.   A test adapter and whistle connected to an engine's number-one cylinder.

the timing-chain cover. Then, remove the whistle from the adapter.

3. Remove the distributor cap from the distributor, and connect the coil-to-distributor secondary cable to ground, using a jumper lead.

4. Mount the TDC indicator (Fig. 5-13) onto the distributor shaft. Then, using a piece of chalk, mark a suitable reference point on an adjacent surface of the engine that aligns with the applicable cylinder marking on the TDC indicator. The indicator itself has markings, one for each cylinder, for any four-, six-, or eight-cylinder engine.

5. Connect an indicator light to the ignition system by attaching one of its leads to the *distributor's* primary terminal on the coil and the other lead to a good ground. Then, turn the vehicle's ignition switch on.

6. Connect the tester hose from the gauge to the adapter (Fig. 5-14) and note the percentage of leakage showing on the gauge scale. If the reading is more than 20 percent, listen for air escaping through the carburetor, tailpipe, and crankcase, and check for the appearance of air bubbles in the radiator. Note the results.

7. Disconnect the tester hose from the adapter. Then, with a wrench, rotate the engine slowly until the next applicable cylinder mark on the TDC indicator aligns

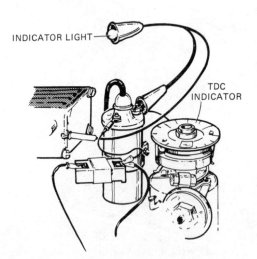

Fig. 5-13.   A TDC indicator and light in position in readiness for the leakage test.

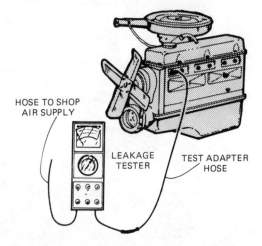

Fig. 5-14.   The leakage tester connected to the adapter hose leading to number-one cylinder.

with the chalk mark on the engine. At this point, the indicator light should glow, indicating that the piston is in its firing position.

8. Remove the test adapter from the cylinder previously tested, and install it in the spark plug hole of the next cylinder in the *engine's firing order* because the piston in this cylinder is at top dead center (TDC).

9. Repeat steps 6, 7, and 8 until you have tested all cylinders of the engine. Note the results.

Results and Indications

Use the following percentage table when interpreting the results of the test:

0–10%	good
10–20%	fair
20–30%	poor
30% and above	definite problem

All gauge readings should be comparatively even and less than 20 percent. If any cylinder reading is above 20 percent, you can determine the *cause* of the excessive leak from your notations of the area from which the air escaped.

1. Air escaping through the carburetor indicates an intake valve is leaking.

2. Air escaping from the exhaust pipe means that an exhaust valve is leaking.

3. A high percentage of leakage on adjacent cylinders points to a leaking head gasket or a crack in the block or head.

4. Air bubbles in the radiator also indicate a leaking head gasket or a crack in the block or head.

5. A high percentage of leakage at the crankcase opening indicates worn rings or cylinder walls, stuck or broken rings, or a cracked piston. But analyze the ring and

cylinder wall condition with consideration of the case history and the mileage of the engine. For example, when you note a high percentage of crankcase leakage on an engine with comparatively low mileage, occasionally the piston rings may be stuck or just not seated as yet. In this situation, it is advisable to treat the engine with a good additive or break-in oil for a period of time and then retest before recommending that the engine be disassembled for major repair.

Comparing Compression and Leakage Test Results

By comparing some typical results of both a compression and cylinder leakage test, you should be able to see why in some cases it is important to use both tests when trying to analyze a mechanical condition causing poor engine performance. The following sections describe a few combinations of such cases and what they indicate.

Good Compression but Excessive Leakage

If an engine, for example, has even compression readings within factory specifications but also has excessive cylinder leakage readings with the air escaping from the crankcase opening, it is probably just a worn, high-mileage engine. This engine will typically have excessive blowby, a lack of power, and poor fuel economy. The good compression readings in this situation usually are the result of heavy carbon deposits in the combustion chambers. These deposits raise what would otherwise be lower readings to a series of higher, more normal ones. Consequently, these compression readings create an illusion that this particular engine is a good mechanical engine, which it obviously is not.

Bad Compression but Minimal Leakage

Another engine with cylinders that have lower than normal compression readings but minimal cylinder leakage has some form of valve-related problem such as a valve or valves that do not open at the correct time, do not open completely, or do not open at all. The wrong camshaft installed in the engine, improper installation of the timing chain or gears, or a loose timing chain will cause an engine to have overall poor compression pressures but minimal cylinder leakage.

This difference in test results is due to the fact that the valves will not open and close at the correct time in the engine cycle. Worn camshaft lobes, incorrect valve adjustment, or broken or worn pushrods or rocker arms can cause an engine to have valves that do not open far enough or not at all. But regardless of what problem each engine had, the important thing is that neither test by itself located the cause, which again proves the necessity of using both tests when diagnosing *difficult* or *unusual* mechanical engine malfunctions.

Vacuum Testing

An engine vacuum test is one of the most important, useful, and quick mechanical tests that a mechanic can perform on an engine to detect and locate the cause of engine problems. A vacuum test itself provides a quick analysis of an engine's condition through the vacuum effect inside the engine's intake manifold

without removing the spark plugs and checking either cylinder compression or leakage. In other words, the vacuum test results provide a good indication of the compression within the cylinders, which may be good or bad, depending on the condition of the rings, valves, or head gaskets.

Like the other two tests, the vacuum test *alone* may not always be able to pinpoint the exact cause of a particular problem. For example, a reading taken during the vacuum test points to a defective valve, but the gauge reading cannot pinpoint which valve is bad. A leakage test is necessary for this. In other words, the vacuum test provides fast information as to the general mechanical condition of this engine, but the technician must use either or both a compression and leakage test to locate the *exact* cause of a malfunction.

Vacuum Gauge

The vacuum gauge required for this test procedure may be a separate instrument or incorporated into an engine analyzer (Fig. 5–15). In either case, this gauge has a scale with divisions marked off in inches of mercury (Hg) ranging from 0 to 30 inches of Hg (0 to 76 millimeters of Hg). The movement of the needle on this scale actually indicates the difference in pressures between what is in the intake manifold and the atmospheric pressure outside the engine. As a result, all gauge readings are dependent upon altitude; therefore, the readings must be adjusted for altitudes above sea level. For instance, with every 1,000 feet (305 meters) above sea level, the vacuum gauge will read low by 1 inch (25.4 millimeters) Hg. Consequently, the mechanic must add 1 inch of Hg to the gauge reading.

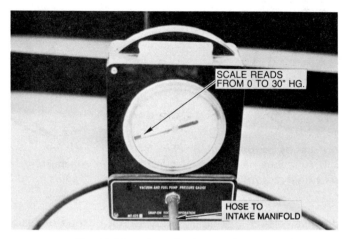

Fig. 5–15. A typical vacuum gauge.

Engine Vacuum Test Procedures

To perform an accurate vacuum test, follow this prescribed procedure.

1. Connect the vacuum gauge, using a sufficient length of hose, to a nonrestricted port on the intake manifold, where the gauge will measure the total vacuum in the manifold. The length of the hose, about 3 feet in length, should be long enough to dampen excessive vibrations from the gauge needle. However, under certain conditions, it may be necessary to dampen the pointer action further by placing a small clamp around the hose in order to restrict its passageway slightly.

2. Operate the engine until it reaches normal operating temperature.

3. Except where specified, perform all vacuum tests on the engine while it operates at idle rpm.

Test Results and Indications

The following points out the results of vacuum tests performed on engines of varying mechanical conditions and what these readings indicate.

1. A vacuum gauge needle that remains constant between 16 to 21 inches of Hg indicates the engine to be in good mechanical condition (Fig. 5–16). *Note:* The gauge reading will be lower or unsteady if the engine is brand-new or recently overhauled and not yet broken in, is a late-model engine with a high lift cam providing additional valve overlap, or an engine with certain emission-control equipment.

2. A low but steady gauge reading, between about 12 to 16 inches of Hg, indi-

Fig. 5–16. With the engine at idle, the gauge needle should hold steady between 16 to 21 inches of Hg.

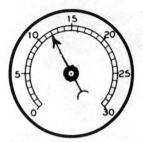

Fig. 5–17.   A low but steady gauge reading between about 12 to 16 inches of Hg indicates either defective rings or late valve or ignition timing.

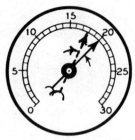

Fig. 5–19.   A stuck valve, maladjusted carburetor, or an intermittent spark plug miss can cause an irregular needle drop of 1 to 2 inches of Hg.

cates this engine has either leakage around the piston rings, late ignition timing, or late valve timing (Fig. 5–17).

3. A gauge needle that oscillates slowly, then rapidly, between about 12 to 18 inches of Hg, is a good indication that the ignition timing is too far advanced or the carburetor idle mixture is too lean (Fig. 5–18).

4. A needle reading with an irregular drop of 1 to 2 inches of Hg points to a possible sticky valve, a carburetor that is out of adjustment, or an intermittent spark plug misfire (Fig. 5–19).

5. A reading with a regular needle drop in vacuum of between 1 to 2 inches of Hg

indicates a burned or leaking valve or a spark plug in one cylinder that is not firing (Fig. 5–20).

6. If the vacuum gauge reading is normal and steady at idling speed but the pointer vibrates excessively at higher engine speeds, the valve springs are weak (Fig. 5–21).

7. If the gauge needle vibrates excessively at idling speed but steadies with increasing engine rpm, this points to the possibility of excessive wear of the valve guides (Fig. 5–22). *Note:* You can check valve-guide condition by removing the valve covers and squirting motor oil at the tops of the valve guides with the engine operating at idle rpm. If a large cloud of blue smoke comes out the exhaust pipe

Fig. 5–18.   A slow, oscillating reading between about 12 to 18 inches of Hg is a good indication that the ignition timing is too far advanced or the carburetor mixture is too lean.

Fig. 5–20.   A regular needle drop of 1 to 2 inches of Hg indicates a defective valve or spark plug.

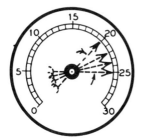

Fig. 5-21. A vibrating pointer at high engine speeds only indicates weak valve springs.

Fig. 5-23. The head gasket has a leak if the gauge needle vibrates excessively at all engine rpm.

and the vacuum gauge pointer steadies, the valve guides are excessively worn.

8. If the needle of the gauge vibrates excessively at all engine speeds, check the engine for a leaky head gasket (Fig. 5-23). Perform a compression or a leakage test to determine exactly where the leak is.

9. If the gauge needle fluctuates constantly from 3 to 9 inches of Hg below normal, a leak has developed somewhere in the intake system (Fig. 5-24). The most common causes of a leak of this nature are defective intake manifold or carburetor mounting gaskets. You can test for vacuum leaks at these particular gaskets by squirting noncombustible cleaning solvent along the gasket joints with the engine operating at idle. If the vacuum on the gauges increases and the idle speed

smoothes out, you have found the leak. Also, if the leak is large enough, you will see the vacuum pulling the solvent through the gasket joint.

Checking the intake manifold gaskets with solvent will not always find the source of a leak because the lower edges of these gaskets on V-type engines and on some in-line engines are not accessible. For example, the joints between the lower edges of the intake manifold and the cylinder heads of V-type engines are inside the lifter valley, where a leak of this type commonly occurs. The best approaches to confirm this type of leak are to check the exhaust for the presence of excessive smoke (a sign that manifold vacuum is sucking engine oil from the valley into the combus-

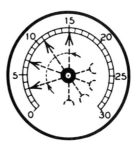

Fig. 5-22. A vibrating needle at idle engine rpm points to a possibility of worn valve guides.

Fig. 5-24. A gauge needle that fluctuates constantly from 3 to 9 inches of Hg below normal indicates a vacuum leak in the intake system.

tion chambers) and to eliminate all other possible causes of the gauge fluctuations.

Vacuum Testing the PCV System

To perform a test of a positive crankcase ventilation (PCV) system and check the amount of cranking vacuum, attach a vacuum gauge to the intake manifold, as previously explained, and follow this procedure.

1. Operate the engine until it reaches its normal operating temperature.

2. Stop the engine and then disable the ignition system by grounding the coil's secondary lead securely or disconnecting the HEI system's primary harness connector from the distributor.

3. Back out the curb idle adjustment screw on the carburetor so that the throttle valve closes completely.

4. Attach a remote starter button and then crank the engine over. Note the vacuum gauge reading; the needle should rise very quickly to the normal zone, between 16 to 21 inches of Hg. If the reading stays around 3 to 13 inches of Hg, the throttle is failing to close, leaks exist in the intake system, or the PCV valve is stuck wide open.

5. Wait a few minutes for the starting motor to cool down. Then pinch the PCV hose closed with a pair of pliers while cranking the engine over for the second time. Note the reading on the vacuum gauge.

6. Compare the readings taken in steps 4 and 5. The step 5 reading should be higher than the step 4 reading. If not, the PCV valve or hose requires service or replacement.

Vacuum Testing the Exhaust System for Restrictions

You can check the exhaust system of an engine for a restriction using a vacuum gauge. To perform this particular test:

1. Connect a vacuum gauge to the engine as described under the section on general, engine vacuum testing.

2. Connect a tachometer to the engine.

3. Warm up the engine until it reaches normal operating temperature.

4. Slowly accelerate the engine until it reaches 2,000 rpm.

5. Note the reading on the vacuum gauge. The needle should drop slightly and then rise quickly to a reading that is 3 to 5 inches of Hg higher than the normal idle vacuum.

6. Quickly close the throttle; the gauge needle should return normally to the idle reading just as rapidly as it rose.

Results and Indications

If the gauge needle at first reaches a normal reading at idle and at 2,000 rpm, but it begins to drop toward zero and then rise slowly to a below normal reading at 2,000 rpm, some form of restriction exists in the exhaust system. In this case, inspect the system for a frozen manifold heat control valve, a clogged or damaged muffler, or a damaged restricted tailpipe.

In the case of some large displacement engines, it may be necessary to perform this test while actually driving the vehicle until it reaches the road speed where the engine loses power. In order to perform this test under actual driving conditions:

1. Connect a vacuum gauge to the intake manifold with a long enough hose so that you can position the gauge itself inside the vehicle.

2. Connect a tachometer to the engine and route its wires so that this gauge is also inside the vehicle.

3. Drive the vehicle through the road speed range where engine performance begins to drop off.

4. Note the readings on both gauges. The tachometer reading will most likely be different than the figure mentioned earlier due to the size of the engine, size of the restriction, and the actual load on the engine. But regardless of the actual reading, it should be about the same each time a loss of power occurs if a restriction exists within the exhaust system. The vacuum gauge needle will react normally at first, but as the engine begins to lose power, *it will begin to drop off toward zero.* The amount of needle deflection toward zero will depend on the amount of restriction. In some cases, the needle will never reach zero but remains at a very low figure until the driver reduces engine load.

Vacuum Testing for a Loss of Compression

You can also make a vacuum test for a loss of compression due to a leakage around the pistons. This particular condition can result from stuck or worn piston rings, worn cylinder walls, or worn pistons. However, this type of test will have no real value if the engine did not produce normal readings on all the other engine vacuum tests listed earlier. To perform this test:

1. Check the level and condition of the engine oil. The level must be full and in good condition. Any diluted or worn-out oil can cause an incorrect vacuum reading, indicating a loss of compression where there is no real mechanical reason to create such a leak.

2. Connect a vacuum gauge to the intake manifold.

3. Attach a tachometer to the engine.

4. Accelerate the engine quickly until its rpm reaches 2,000. Then, quickly close the throttle.

5. Note the action of the gauge needle. As the throttle closes, the pointer will jump 5 or more inches of Hg. over the normal reading if the rings, cylinder walls, and pistons are in good condition. A reading increase of less than 5 inches of Hg is a good indication of a compression loss. To confirm the problem, perform either a leakage or compression test.

Engine Noise Diagnosis

The ability to diagnose engine noises with a fair degree of accuracy may be a vital part of the tune-up specialist's job. For instance, it may be necessary for a technician to recognize and locate the cause of noises that may develop due to normal engine wear and tear over long periods of use or may appear because of failure of one or more engine parts. The parts that produce some characteristic noises are loose pistons, excessively worn rings or ring lands, loose piston pins, worn connecting-rod bearings, worn main bearings, loose vibration damper or flywheel, or worn or loose valve-train components.

When properly interpreted, these noises are a definite aid in any diagnosis of engine mechanical difficulties. But there are many sources and varieties of engine noises; careful interpretation of these sounds is necessary for several reasons. First, a careful diagnosis of an engine noise can often prevent the expense of tearing down an engine. In this regard, a technician should *always* make a noise analysis before engine repair begins so that only the needed and correct operations are made with no extra work or charges to the customer. Second, a careful interpretation of abnormal engine sounds can prevent the engine from requiring extensive and costly repair work after continued usage has ruined it.

Stethoscope

All moving mechanical engine parts create some form of sound waves of various pitches, frequencies, qualities, and intensities. Most people can hear many of these sound waves without the assistance of a listening device. On the other hand, some sounds are impossible to hear unless magnified; even if some sounds are audible, they are frequently difficult to localize and locate. Consequently, most technicians utilize some form of sounding rod or stethoscope when diagnosing engine sounds.

A *stethoscope, or sound scope,* aids in locating the source of engine knocks and noises by magnifying their sound waves (Fig. 5-25). This instrument makes use of a metal prod, about 8 inches long and 1/8 inch in diameter, that passes through a rubber bushing and terminates against a metal diaphragm held in a plastic housing. Furthermore, two ear tubes carry the sound from this diaphragm chamber to the listener's ears.

The value of the sound-detecting and -amplifying stethoscope is, of course, to help the technician distinguish the difference between normal and abnormal sounds and to find the location and cause of the latter. Even an engine in good operating condition will make noises that the mechanic will be able to hear with a

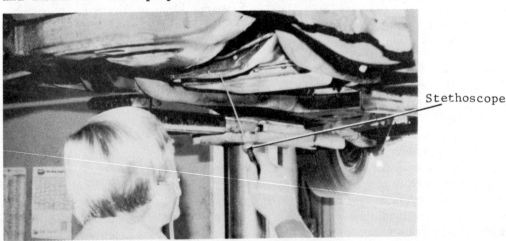

Fig. 5-25.   A stethoscope is a device that magnifies sound.

stethoscope. Being familiar with these sounds will be very helpful when the mechanic attempts to pinpoint the location and cause of any abnormal noise due to excessive wear, damage, or maladjustment of engine parts.

Sound Tracing with the Stethoscope

The best way to trace any type of noise is to follow a systematic procedure. First, for example, always use a stethoscope or other sounding device to amplify the sound. Second, with the listening device, attempt to localize and identify the noise. You can trace both unfamiliar and familiar sounds to the portion of the engine where they originate by following the sound with the prod of the stethoscope until the noise reaches its maximum intensity. After you locate this spot, a knowledge of engine construction and operation will be your best guide as to the most likely cause of the sound.

Abnormal Engine Noises and Their Causes

Common examples of abnormal engine noises follow. Along with a description of the sound itself, this listing will also point out the most common causes of sound itself and what must be done to eliminate them.

1. *Piston slap* is a very common noise most noticeable when an engine is cold. A piston that slaps against the cylinder wall produces a hollow, muffled, bell-like sound, quite audible when an engine is operating under load at low rpm. This sound, in many cases, can become more intensified and more frequent as the engine accelerates. You can sometimes quiet this type of noise by shorting out the spark plug of the affected cylinder or by feeding a quantity of oil through the carburetor.

Piston slap results from worn pistons or cylinders, collapsed piston skirts, excessive piston-to-cylinder wall clearance, misaligned connecting rods, or a lack of lubricating oil. Therefore, in order to correct piston slap, it will be necessary to replace or resize the pistons, rebore the cylinder or replace the sleeves, replace or realign the rods, or add oil to the engine.

2. An abnormal sound originating from some form of piston-ring problem is audible during engine acceleration. The best way to describe a *ring noise* is that it has a high-pitched clicking, rattling, or chattering sound that originates in the upper portion of a cylinder. You cannot usually deaden this sound out by shorting out the spark plug. *Note:* To short out a plug that has a wire with an uninsulated plug terminal, just place the shank of an insulated screwdriver against the terminal with its blade tip touching any metal surface. If the plug wire has an insulated cover over the plug terminal, you can deaden the cylinder by carefully removing the plug wire, using insulated pliers over the terminal cover.

Ring noise can result from a number of problems such as broken rings or piston-ring lands, worn rings or cylinders, in addition to weak ring tension against the cylinder walls. To correct the cause of ring noise, it may be necessary, therefore, to replace the rings, the pistons, or the sleeves or rebore the cylinders.

3. A sound not frequently heard in an engine is that of a piston ring striking the ring ridge at the top of the cylinder. This particular problem causes a very distinct

and high-pitched, metallic rapping or clicking noise audible at all engine speeds but particularly on deceleration. Also, you cannot reduce the intensity of this sound by shorting out the spark plug to each individual cylinder.

Although this sound originates from the same thing, that is a ring striking the ring ridge, the primary reason for the ridge interfering with the ring's travel may not be the same. For example, if the mechanic who installed a set of new rings did not remove the old ridge, the new top rings will make contact with this ridge and make a sound. On the other hand, if the piston has a very loose piston pin or the connecting rod has a loose or burned-out bearing, the piston can thrust up high enough in the cylinder for the top ring to make contact with the ridge. Therefore, to repair the cause of this sound, it will be necessary to remove the old ring ridge and replace the piston pin or connecting rod bearings.

4. A *piston-pin knock* is noticeable most of the time when an engine is idling. The sound itself originates from the upper cylinder portion of the engine and resembles a sharp, light, metallic rap that may seem more of a rattle if all the pins are loose. Shorting a spark plug out at idle speed sometimes will cause a double knock as the pin strikes the piston boss twice, once with the piston at TDC and the second time with the piston at BDC.

Piston pin noise is usually the result of a worn piston pin, piston-pin boss, pin bushing, or a lack of oil. To correct this problem, install oversize pins, replace the bushings and pins, or service the engine with oil.

5. An abnormal noise that is audible when the engine is running at speeds above 35 miles per hour (mph) without a load is usually the result of loose connecting-rod bearings. Loose rod bearings cause a light to heavy knock or pound, depending on how badly the bearings are worn. You can locate a loose rod bearing by shorting out the spark plug to the affected cylinder. This action reduces the intensity of the noise. However, if the bearing is completely burned out, the shorting procedure will have no effect on the noise.

Connecting-rod bearing noise can be due to a worn bearing, crankpin, misaligned rod, or lack of oil. To correct the noise, it will be necessary to replace the bearings, service or replace the crankshaft, realign or replace the rod, or service the engine with oil.

6. An abnormal noise that is audible upon engine acceleration under load is usually the result of a loose crankshaft main or thrust bearing. A loose main bearing produces a consistent, dull, heavy metallic knock; whereas, a loose thrust bearing causes a heavy thump at irregular intervals. In addition, the thrust bearing noise may be only heard on a very hard acceleration or when the driver operates the clutch.

Main or thrust bearing noise is usually the result of worn bearings, crankshaft journals, or a lack of oil. To correct this noise, it will be necessary to replace the bearings, crankshaft, or service the engine with oil.

7. A loose vibration damper or flywheel can also cause abnormal engine noises. A loose damper produces a deceptively heavy rumble or thump in the front of the engine. Also, this sound is more noticeable during engine acceleration from idle under load or at an uneven idle, but it is less apparent at higher engine rpm or during smoother engine operation.

A loose flywheel, on the other hand, sets

up either a heavy thump or a light knock at the back of the engine, depending upon the amount of play the flywheel has and the type of engine. You can detect a loose flywheel by shutting off the ignition switch at idle and then turning it on again just before the engine stops rotating. Also, operating the clutch pedal, at the same time the noise is audible at running speeds, will vary the sound enough so that it is easier to identify and then locate its source.

8. Excessive clearance in the valve train produces a noise that is usually more apparent during engine idle rpm than at any other time. *Tappet noise,* as it is commonly called, has a light, regular clicking sound. You can locate the source of the clearance problem and the noise by inserting a feeler gauge strip between each lifter and valve or between each rocker arm and valve tip until the noise diminishes.

Valve-train noise is brought about by improper valve adjustment, worn or damaged parts, dirty hydraulic lifters, or lack of clean lubricating oil. In order to correct the cause of the noise, it will be necessary to adjust the valves, replace worn or damaged parts, clean or replace the lifters, or service the engine's lubrication system.

9. The one abnormal sound unrelated to worn, damaged, loose, or maladjusted engine parts is *detonation knock.* People refer to this noise by such names as detonation knock, carbon knock, fuel knock, spark knock, or just plain ping. But whatever name it is called, the noise is most noticeable during acceleration with the engine under load and operating at normal temperature. Excessive detonation is very harmful to the engine, and you should do everything possible to correct the cause as soon as possible.

Detonation knock in an engine is usually the product of advanced ignition timing, excessive carbon buildup in the combustion chambers, or use of too low an octane fuel. To correct this malfunction, check the distributor's advance mechanisms, check and reset the ignition timing, decarbonize the engine, or recommend a change in fuel to one with a higher octane rating.

Valve Adjustment— Purpose

Many foreign and domestic engines have valve trains with mechanical-type valve lifters; these engines require a valve adjustment as part of a complete tune-up for several reasons. First, over time, wear on some valve-train parts creates excessive clearances in the valve train itself (Fig. 5–26). A valve train with excessive clearance is quite noisy; this noise is the result of a hammering-type blow to the valve tip by the rocker arm or by the lifter itself as the excessive clearance rapidly disappears during the valve-opening period. This hammering causes not only a noise but also increased wear on the affected components. Furthermore, the excessive clearance retards the valve timing slightly and reduces the actual distance

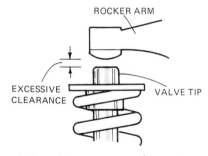

Fig. 5–26. *Wear on valve-train components can cause excessive valve clearance.*

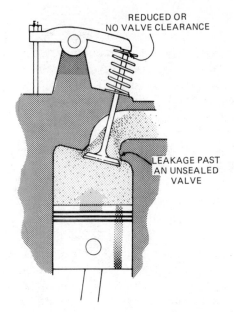

REDUCED OR
NO VALVE CLEARANCE

LEAKAGE PAST
AN UNSEALED
VALVE

Fig. 5-27.   Reduced valve clearance can cause rough engine idle and valve burning.

that the valve lifts off its seat. This, of course, reduces overall engine efficiency and can create an excessive amount of exhaust emissions.

The second reason valve adjustment is important is to check the valve train for less than specified clearance (Fig. 5-27). A reduced clearance in the valve train can be the direct result of valve-stem stretch or other component expansion that occurs from time to time. But no matter what the cause, a reduction in valve clearance can bring about a rough idle and lead to premature valve burning. Also, in this situation, the affected valves will open too soon in the engine cycle, which reduces engine efficiency and causes increased exhaust emissions.

Methods of Valve Adjustment

Engine manufacturers employ one of three different methods to alter valve clearance; they can utilize either an adjustable rocker arm, adjustable tappet, or adjustment discs or shims. Overhead valve engines with the camshaft in the block have adjustment devices on the rocker arm itself. This device can be in the form of an adjustment screw on the arm itself, or the rocker arm itself is adjustable up or down on its support stud (Figs. 5-28 and 5-29). When the rocker

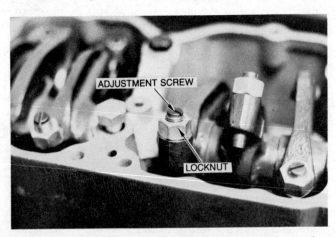

ADJUSTMENT SCREW

LOCKNUT

Fig. 5-28.   A typical adjustment screw and locknut on the pushrod end of a rocker arm.

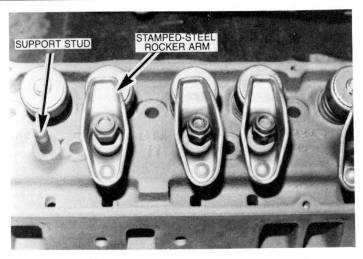

SUPPORT STUD

STAMPED-STEEL
ROCKER ARM

Fig. 5-29.   A typical adjustable stud-mounted rocker arm.

arm has an adjustment screw, it can be one of two types: a single, self-locking capscrew or an adjusting screw with a locknut.

Adjustable tappets or cam followers are not new to the automotive industry. These units were found in almost every L-head engine (Fig. 5-30). In this installation, the tappet sat on top of the cam lobe,

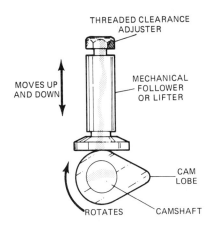

THREADED CLEARANCE
ADJUSTER

MOVES UP
AND DOWN

MECHANICAL
FOLLOWER
OR LIFTER

CAM
LOBE

ROTATES   CAMSHAFT

Fig. 5-30.   An adjustable tappet was very common in early-model L-head engines.

with the adjusting device directly beneath the valve tip. With this arrangement, the mechanic could alter valve clearance by turning the adjustment one way or the other.

Some overhead-cam (OHC) engines also have an adjustment screw in the tappet or cam follower (Fig. 5-31). In the installation shown, the screw has a tapered and a flat side; the flat side of the screw rests against the valve tip, while the tapered side fits beneath the underside of the follower. Threading this screw into or out of the follower increases or decreases the gap between the surface of the cam lobe and the top of the follower. With this design, the mechanic must adjust the screw one complete turn at a time in order to keep the flat side of the screw against the valve tip. If the mechanic cannot obtain the proper clearance, it may be necessary to install a different size adjustment screw.

Another design of an OHC engine utilizes an adjustment disc or shim between the surface of the cam lobe and the fol-

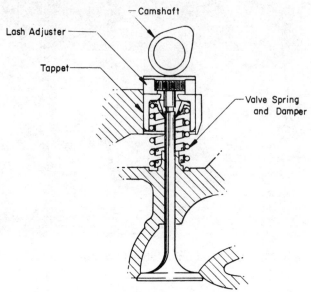

Fig. 5-31.   An OHC engine utilizing a cam follower with a tapered adjusting screw.

lower to control valve-train clearance (Fig. 5-32). With this type of installation, the mechanic must use a special tool and magnet to change the discs or spacers in order to adjust the clearance. If excessive clear-ance exists between a given lifter and cam lobe, the technician will install a thicker shim, whereas correcting a reduced clearance condition requires installing a thinner shim.

Specifications for Valve Clearances

All engine manufacturers recommend given valve clearances for their particular engines; this clearance refers to the gap in inches or millimeters between the camshaft lobe and the follower or tappet of OHC engines or between the tip of the valve and the rocker arm of the standard I-head engine. In either case, the clearance must appear in these areas with the valve completely closed.

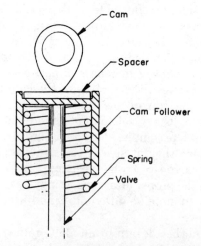

Fig. 5-32.   An OHC engine using adjusting discs or spacers to control valve clearances.

The manufacturer will also specify that the technician perform the clearance check and adjustment with the engine cold or hot. If the specifications call for the engine to be cold for the valve adjustment, the clearances are generally greater than hot clearances for the same type engine. If the technician is to set the valves cold, the engine coolant should be at or as near to ambient air temperature as possible.

On the other hand, when using a hot specification, the mechanic must warm up the engine to its normal operating temperature. Also, if the clearance check and adjustment are in process when the engine is hot but not running, the technician may have to reinstall the valve covers halfway through the job and operate the engine for a few minutes to ensure that it stays warmed up. This is a necessary step because valves and rocker arms cool off rapidly with the valve covers off, even though the temperature of the coolant remains high.

Valve clearances may be different for the intake and exhaust valves. For example, an intake valve of a given engine has a specification of 0.004 inch (0.10 millimeter) *H*, while the exhaust valve of the same engine is 0.008 inch (0.20 millimeter) *H*. The letter *H* behind the actual specification informs the mechanic that the clearance listed is for a hot (warmed-up) engine. The differences between the two specifications are due to the fact that the exhaust valve expands more in operation and consequently requires a greater clearance in this particular engine type.

Checking Valve Clearances

You can check valve clearances with the engine shut down, either cold or hot, or with it operating at its normal temperature. In all cases, a feeler gauge is necessary to make the check and adjustment. Different types of feeler gauges are available for valve clearance checks. But the feeler gauge with the strips bent near their ends is easier and safer to use around hot manifolds (Fig. 5–33). The stepped feeler gauge is also convenient to use in some cases. This gauge has strips with two dimensions. The thinner section is one size, while the thicker is another. When in use for checking clearances, you utilize the thin section to measure a certain gap while the thick section acts as a no-go gauge. If the no-go strip also passes between the gap, the clearance is too great and will require adjustment.

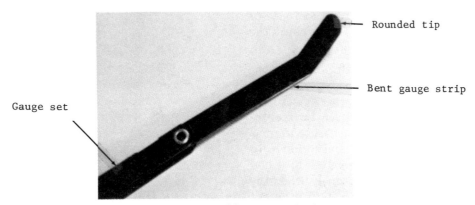

Rounded tip

Bent gauge strip

Gauge set

Fig. 5–33. A typical bent-type feeler gauge.

Valve Adjustment Procedure— Engine Running

You can check and adjust the valve clearances of a standard, I-head pushrod engine using the following procedure. However, it may be necessary to add or delete some steps when performing this task, due to the design of the engine and its accessories.

1. Install fender covers on both fenders to protect their surfaces from scratches and discoloration from oil and grease.

2. Start the engine and operate it at fast idle until the engine's coolant reaches normal operating temperature.

3. Stop the engine and then remove the valve covers. On some engines, you must first remove the air cleaner, PCV hoses, and other accessory components before you can remove the covers.

4. Inspect the valve springs for broken coils, and the valve stems for broken seals. Also, be sure that the oil-drain passages in the cylinder heads are open, and check the amount of sludge built up on the visible valve-train components.

5. Look up the valve clearance specifications in the appropriate service manual. Then, select the proper type and size of feeler gauge strips necessary to check the valve clearance.

6. Start the engine. Beginning either at the front or rear of the valve train, start checking each valve for proper clearance. Using either a front-to-rear or rear-to-front pattern will make it harder to miss any valves. Some mechanics prefer to check and set the intake valves first and then all the exhaust, especially when the intake and exhaust valves have different specifications.

7. Insert the feeler gauge strip of the proper thickness between the end of the rocker arm and the valve tip (Fig. 5–34), with the engine operating at its slowest idle rpm. The gauge strip should pass through the clearance gap with a slight drag. If it is necessary to force the strip or the engine begins to miss with the strip in place, the clearance is too tight. If, on the other hand, the gauge strip slips through the gap too easily or if there is a choppy, jerking feeling in the strip as you pass it through the gap, the clearance is too large. You can double-check for excessive clearance by using a stepped feeler gauge or by inserting another feeler gauge strip, a few thousandth inches larger, between the gap. If the larger strip of either set now drags as you move it through the gap, the valve requires adjustment.

8. If a valve's clearance requires adjustment, turn its adjustment screw in or out as required to obtain the slight drag

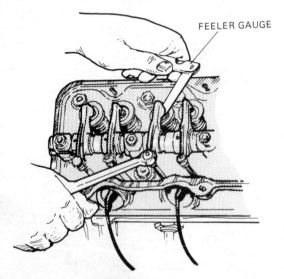

FEELER GAUGE

Fig. 5–34. Checking the clearance between the end of the rocker arm and valve tip with a feeler gauge.

on the feeler gauge strip as you pass it through the gap. If the adjusting screw is threaded into the pushrod end of the rocker arm, you can reduce the whipping action on your wrench, screwdriver, or socket extension by keeping it securely in place over the adjusting screw and maintaining the screwdriver and extension in line with the pushrod. Also, in some cases, you will find it helpful to use a universal socket on the extension to assist in cushioning rocker-arm movement.

9. If the adjusting screw has a separate locknut, be sure to recheck the clearance after tightening the locknut.

10. Replace the valve covers, using new gaskets.

11. Replace the air cleaner, PCV hoses, and other accessory components that you removed.

12. Operate the engine and check the valve covers for oil leakage. Finally, check the level of lubricating oil and service the engine with oil as necessary.

Valve Adjustment Procedure with Stationary Engine

Checking or adjusting the valve clearance of any stationary engine presents a few additional problems not encountered when doing the same task on a running engine. First, if the specification calls for the engine to be cold, the engine must not be operated for some time between a few hours to a full day, depending on how long it takes to bring the coolant or engine temperature down to about 70°F. If the engine must be at normal operating temperature, it may also be necessary for the mechanic to operate the engine periodically in order to keep the valves at normal operating temperature during the adjustment procedure.

Second, since the engine will not be running, the technician must spot each piston at its TDC position on the compression stroke in order to assure that the valves are fully closed. The easiest way to do this on any engine is to turn the engine over by hand and use the whistle and TDC indicator from the leakage tester set mentioned earlier to determine piston position. With these facts in mind, you can perform a stationary engine valve clearance check and adjustment following this procedure.

1. Install fender covers on both fenders to protect their surfaces from scratches and discoloration from oil and grease.

2. Look up the valve clearances and firing order in the appropriate service manual.

3. If the engine must be at normal operating temperature for the clearance check, start and operate the engine at fast idle until it warms up.

4. Remove the valve covers. On some engines you must first remove the air cleaner, PCV hoses, and other accessory components before you can remove the covers.

5. Remove the number one spark plug, and install into its opening in the head the adapter along with its hose and whistle (Fig. 5–35).

6. Using a wrench on the crankshaft pulley nut or bolt, rotate the engine in the normal direction of rotation until the whistle sounds. Continue to rotate the engine slowly until the engine's timing mark (TDC) on the crankshaft pulley

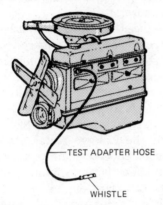

Fig. 5–35. The adapter, hose, and whistle installed into the number-one spark plug hole.

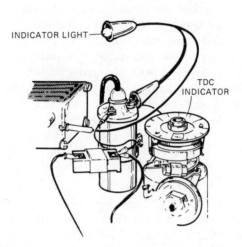

Fig. 5–36.   The TDC indicator mounted on top of the distributor and the indicator light connected to the distributor's primary terminal and ground.

aligns with the engine-timing pointer on the timing-chain cover.

7. Remove the distributor cap from the distributor, and connect the coil-to-distributor secondary lead to ground, using a jumper lead.

8. Mount the TDC indicator (Fig. 5–36) onto the distributor shaft. Then, using a piece of chalk, mark a suitable reference point on an adjacent surface of the engine that aligns with the applicable cylinder marking on the TDC indicator. The indicator itself has markings, one for each cylinder, for all four,- six,- and eight-cylinder engines.

9. Connect the indicator light to the ignition system by attaching one of its leads to the *distributor's* primary terminal on the coil and the other lead to a good ground. Then, turn the vehicle's ignition switch on.

10. Insert the correct feeler gauge strips between the gaps of both the intake and exhaust valves of number-one cylinder, and adjust them as necessary until

the strip has a slight drag on it as you move it in and out of the gap.

11. If the adjusting screws have locknuts, be sure to recheck the clearances after tightening the locknuts.

12. With a wrench, again rotate the engine slowly until the next applicable cylinder mark on the TDC indicator aligns with the chalk mark on the engine. At this point, the indicator light should glow, indicating that the piston *of the next cylinder in the firing order* is at its TDC position.

13. Perform steps 10 and 11 on the valves of this cylinder.

14. Crank the engine over again by hand until the next cylinder in the firing order is at TDC, and check and set its valves.

15. Continue the process until all the pistons have been spotted at their TDC positions, and you have checked and adjusted all the valves.

16. Remove the adapter, along with its hose and whistle from the number-one spark plug hole, and reinstall the spark plug. Also, remove the TDC indicator and light from the distributor, and reinstall the cap and secondary wire into the coil.

17. Replace the valve covers using new gaskets.

18. Replace the air cleaner, PCV hoses, and other accessory components that you removed.

19. Operate the engine and check the valve covers for oil leakage. Finally, check the level of lubricating oil, and service the engine with oil as necessary.

Note: If the valves are still noisy after the adjustment or if you are unable to achieve consistent measurements when adjusting the valves with the engine running, the rocker arms may have excessive wear above the valve tip (Fig. 5–37). You can sometimes adjust the clearances in this situation by using a feeler gauge strip that is slightly narrower than the diameter of the valve tip. But be careful to insert the strip exactly into the worn area, over the tip and in line with the rocker arm. If this procedure does not quiet the valves, you must remove, resurface, or replace the worn rocker arms. *Never tighten the clearance on any valve in order*

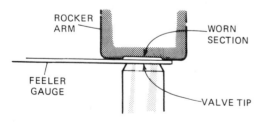

Fig. 5–37. When the end of a rocker arm is worn, a wide feeler-gauge strip will give an inaccurate reading.

to quiet it; this can cause a rough idle and lead to valve burning.

Review

This section will assist you in determining how well you remember the material contained in this chapter. Read each item carefully. If you can't complete the statement, review the section in the chapter that covers the material.

1. Efficient combustion and power output of any piston engine depends on the _____ generated within its cylinders.
   a. suction
   b. flow
   c. compression
   d. detonation

2. A gasoline engine compression tester will have a scale that reads from 0 to _____ psi.
   a. 300
   b. 250
   c. 200
   d. 150

3. It is necessary to remove the _____ _____ _____ when performing a compression test.
   a. intake manifold
   b. battery cables
   c. valve cover
   d. air cleaner

4. If during the compression test two adjacent cylinders have equally low compression, the _____ _____ is probably leaking.
   a. intake valve
   b. head gasket
   c. exhaust valve
   d. intake manifold

5. A _____ _____ will detect even the smallest leak in a combustion chamber.
   a. compression test
   b. leakage test
   c. vacuum test
   d. pressure test

6. When leakage testing an engine, always begin the test at cylinder _____.
   a. 1
   b. 2
   c. 4
   d. 6

7. An engine is in fair shape if it has between _____ ____ _____ percent leakage.
   a. 0 to 10
   b. 20 to 30
   c. 30 to 40
   d. 10 to 20

8. The test that provides the mechanic with a quick analysis of engine condition without removing the spark plugs is the _____ test.
   a. compression
   b. leakage
   c. vacuum
   d. pressure

9. A vacuum gauge has a scale marked off in inches of _____.
   a. oxygen
   b. mercury
   c. hydrogen
   d. nitrogen

10. A good indication of a burned valve is a regular _____ ____ _____ inches of Hg drop in a vacuum gauge reading.
    a. 1 to 2
    b. 2 to 3
    c. 3 to 4
    d. 5 to 6

11. You can check the _____ system for restrictions using a vacuum gauge.
    a. cooling
    b. vacuum
    c. intake
    d. exhaust

12. If the vacuum gauge needle drops back slowly or unevenly toward a zero vacuum reading with the accelerator pedal held at the 2,000-rpm position, the exhaust system is _____.
    a. restricted
    b. open
    c. closed
    d. normal

13. You should always make a noise diagnosis _____ an engine is torn down for repair.
    a. after
    b. before
    c. when
    d. either *a* or *c*

14. The _____ aids a technician in distinguishing the difference between normal and abnormal noises.
    a. stethoscope
    b. prod
    c. diaphragm
    d. both *b* and *c*

15. A piston-pin knock is most noticeable when an engine is _____.
    a. both *b* and *c*
    b. decelerating
    c. accelerating
    d. idling

16. An abnormal noise usually audible when an engine is running without a load at speeds above 35 mph is due to a loose _____ _____.
    a. main bearing
    b. rod bearing

c. vibration damper

d. piston pin

17. The one abnormal noise unrelated to worn or loose parts is _____ knock.

    a. detonation
    b. preignition
    c. emission
    d. lifter

18. Valve clearance appears in the valve train when the valve is _____ .

    a. fully opened
    b. partially open
    c. completely closed
    d. partially closed

19. It is more difficult to adjust the valves on any engine when it is ____ . _____ .

    a. both b and d
    b. accelerating
    c. idling
    d. stationary

20. You should use a _____ indicator as an aid in locating the pistons, in their proper place, when adjusting the valves on an engine that is not running.

    a. advance
    b. timing
    c. BDC
    d. TDC

For the answers, turn to the Appendix.

Function

All automobiles have some form of fuel supply system. The purpose of this system is to store and then to supply a clean, continuous, and adequate amount of fuel under sufficient pressure to the carburetor. Moreover, the system must perform these functions regardless of the outside temperature, altitude, and speed of the vehicle.

Components of the Fuel Supply System

Fuel Tank

A typical fuel-supply system consists of a fuel tank assembly, fuel lines, fuel pump, and outlet filter. The fuel tank stores a supply of fuel, usually between 12 to 25 gallons, that permits the vehicle to operate a considerable distance without refueling.

The actual capacity and design of a given fuel tank are a compromise between the available space, filler-well location, control of fuel movement within the tank, and space within the tank for fuel expansion. For example, manufacturers of many late-model vehicles limit tank capacity by extending the filler tube neck into the tank low enough to prevent complete filling (Fig. 6-1). With this design, about 10 percent of the available tank space will not fill up with fuel. This air space prevents the loss of fuel due to its expansion on a hot day.

Manufacturers form the fuel tank itself in two half-sections, using a corrosion-resistant, thin-steel plating. The exposed half-section is usually constructed of a heavier steel than the unexposed section

_____ Chapter 6

FUEL SUPPLY SYSTEM

for protection against road damage and corrosion. In addition, each section has a series of formed ribs, which provide the tank with additional strength. Finally, before welding the two sections together to form the completed tank, the manufacturer usually inserts a vertical baffle plate (Fig. 6-1). This plate has a series of openings that control the free flow of fuel from one side of the tank to another. This design prevents the fuel from sloshing around in the tank as the vehicle moves.

Some vehicles have an auxiliary as well as a main fuel tank. This two-tank combination provides the vehicle with a greater driving range without the need for refueling. The main, factory-installed tank, has an all-steel construction, whereas many add-on auxiliary tanks are made from polyethylene plastic.

The location and mounting of the fuel tank vary among different styles of passenger vehicles. For example, except for station wagons, most domestic automobiles utilize a horizontally mounted fuel tank. The manufacturer usually suspends this tank below the rear of the trunk pan, below the frame rails, and

behind the rear axle (Fig. 6-2) and holds the tank in place with hanger straps attached with hook studs and nuts. Many station wagons have a vertically mounted tank located on one side of the vehicle between the inner and outer rear fender panels. Finally, vehicles with a rear-mounted engine usually have the fuel tanks mounted horizontally within the forward section of the vehicle.

Filler Tubes

Regardless of its size, shape, and location, the main fuel tank must have all the following: a filler tube, a ventilation system, fuel pickup tube and filter, plus a gauge-sending unit. The filler tube (Figs. 6-1 and 6-2) is a tube that runs from the tank itself to a fuel service entrance on the outside of the vehicle. The tube itself can be made as one piece and attached rigidly to the tank, or the filler tube can be a separate piece attached to the vehicle body and connected to the tank by means of a neoprene hose.

Regardless of the style of construction of the filler tube, all late-model vehicles requiring unleaded fuel have a special filler tube. This type of tube has a restriction placed at the opening of the tube that prevents the entry of the larger leaded-fuel delivery nozzles at the gasoline pumps (Fig. 6-3). Also, to designate the vehicle fuel requirements further, the manufacturer installs a decal reading "unleaded fuel only" beside the filler cap and usually on the instrument panel.

Fuel-Tank Ventilation System

The fuel tank of any motor vehicle must have some form of ventilation system. This system vents the tank to the at-

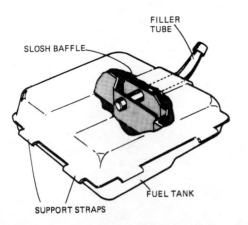

Fig. 6-1. The location of the filler tube prevents complete filling of the tank.

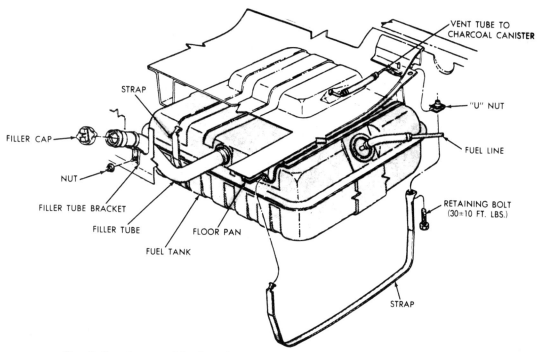

VENT TUBE TO
CHARCOAL CANISTER

STRAP

"U" NUT

FILLER CAP

FUEL LINE

NUT

FILLER TUBE BRACKET

RETAINING BOLT
(30±10 FT. LBS.)

FILLER TUBE   FLOOR PAN

FUEL TANK

STRAP

Fig. 6–2.   A typical fuel-tank installation. (Courtesy of Chrysler Corp.)

mosphere to assist in the rapid filling of the tank, to compensate for the expansion and contraction of the fuel due to temperature changes, and to maintain a constant pressure in the tank over the fuel, regardless of the fuel level. This latter function is necessary to prevent one form of vapor lock: a stoppage of fuel flow caused by an insufficient amount of atmospheric air pressure inside the tank. The atmospheric pressure must act in conjunction with the vacuum produced in the fuel pump in order for it to deliver fuel to the carburetor.

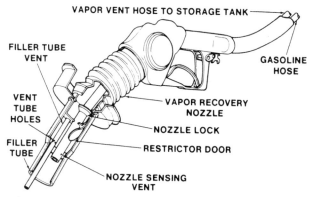

VAPOR VENT HOSE TO STORAGE TANK

FILLER TUBE
VENT

GASOLINE
HOSE

VENT
TUBE
HOLES

VAPOR RECOVERY
NOZZLE

NOZZLE LOCK

FILLER
TUBE

RESTRICTOR DOOR

NOZZLE SENSING
VENT

Fig. 6–3.   A restriction placed in the filler pipe that only allows the smaller unleaded fuel nozzle to enter. (Courtesy of Chrysler Corp.)

Before 1970, manufacturers vented the fuel tank in one of two ways: either through the fuel cap or a separate vent line. If the tank has a vented fuel cap, it uses a seal that prevents gasoline from sloshing out the filler neck as the vehicle moves. However, the cap also has an atmosphere vent that permits air pressure to enter the tank over the level of the fuel.

If the tank uses a vent line, it attaches into the filler neck or tube, thereby opening the filler neck and tank to the atmosphere. With this type of construction, the tank utilizes a nonvented cap. This is, the cap completely seals the opening at the end of the filler neck.

The two ventilation systems just described add pollution to the atmosphere by passing fuel vapors into the air. To reduce these emissions, manufacturers have installed vapor control devices on all late-model automobiles. This text covers these devices later, in the chapter on vapor emission controls.

Furthermore, because modern fuel tanks no longer vent directly to the atmosphere, the manufacturer must provide the tank with some way of compensating for fuel expansion and contraction resulting from temperature changes. One way to do this is to limit the fuel capacity of the tank by the angle in which the filler tube enters the tank (Fig. 6-1). Since the tank cannot fill completely, this leaves an air space that allows room for fuel expansion. Other methods of providing expansion space are the use of a dome in the top of the tank (Fig. 6-4) and the use of a separate expansion tank inside the main tank assembly (Fig. 6-5). Both these units compensate for changes in fuel volume within the tank due to variations in temperature.

Fuel Pickup Tube and Filter

A *fuel pickup tube* that is the same diameter as the main fuel line running to the fuel pump enters the tank to carry off the fuel necessary for engine operation (Fig. 6-6). Manufacturers generally locate the end of this tube about one-half inch from the inside bottom of the tank. This location permits room for some water and sediment to collect in the bottom of the

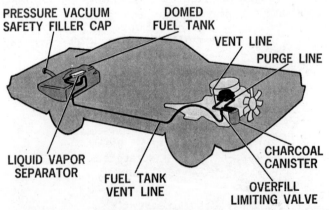

PRESSURE VACUUM
SAFETY FILLER CAP

DOMED
FUEL TANK

VENT LINE

PURGE LINE

LIQUID VAPOR
SEPARATOR

FUEL TANK
VENT LINE

CHARCOAL
CANISTER

OVERFILL
LIMITING VALVE

Fig. 6-4.   A typical tank with an expansion dome. (Courtesy of Chrysler Corp.)

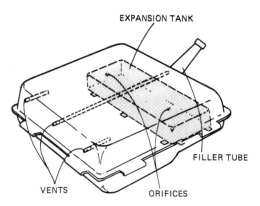

EXPANSION TANK

FILLER TUBE

VENTS

ORIFICES

Fig. 6-5. This fuel tank has an expansion tank that allows for changes in fuel volume due to variations in temperature. (Courtesy of Chrysler Corp.)

tank without the fuel pump drawing either out with the fuel.

On the end of the majority of all pickup tubes is a filter (Fig. 6-6). Manufacturers form this filter of sintered (oclite) bronze, small particles of bronze pressed into a porous mass or from a woven plastic (Saran). No matter which design it has, this filter prevents sediment and water that settled to the bottom of the tank

from entering the line to the fuel pump. However, if enough water somehow gets into the tank, some of it passes through the filter with the fuel.

Over time, accumulated water and sediment can clog the pickup filter. Water accumulates into the tank as a result of condensation when the tank is partially full or from contaminated fuel. In either case, the water is heavier than gasoline, so that it sinks to the bottom of the tank. The sediment is a natural formation of rust caused by the water acting on the inner tank surfaces along with dust and dirt. These latter two contaminants enter the tank in the fuel and enter the fuel during its handling between the refinery and the vehicle tank.

The accumulations of water along with this sediment form a jellylike mass on the outside of the filter. If and when this occurs, the fuel pump cannot pull enough fuel from the tank through the filter to operate the engine. As a result, the engine begins to malfunction, usually first at high vehicle speeds. But as the filter becomes more restricted, the malfunction occurs at even lower speeds until the engine no longer runs at all. Other than

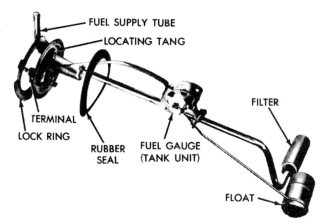

FUEL SUPPLY TUBE

LOCATING TANG

FILTER

TERMINAL

LOCK RING

RUBBER SEAL

FUEL GAUGE (TANK UNIT)

FLOAT

Fig. 6-6. Fuel pickup tube, filter, and tank unit assembly. (Courtesy of Chrysler Corp.)

the replacement of the filter to correct this condition, it requires no other service.

Tank Unit and Fuel Gauges

Thermostatic Type

The pickup tube and filter are usually part of an assembly that also incorporates a *fuel-tank unit* (Fig. 6–6). The tank unit electrically operates in conjunction with a dash gauge to indicate to the driver the level of the fuel in the tank. Two general types of *fuel indicating systems*, which consist of tank unit and dash gauge, are used: the thermostatic type and the balancing coil type.

The *thermostat-type* fuel-indicating system consists of voltage regulator unit along with the tank unit and gauge (Fig. 6–7). The *voltage regulator* has a design that maintains an average value of 5 volts (see Chapter 12) at the dash gauge. Also, this unit is temperature-compensated so that the system can function accurately at any temperature extreme. Finally, many regulators have an adjuster to alter the

rate at which its contact points open and close, which in turn controls the voltage supplied to the system.

The tank unit itself mainly is a *variable rheostat*. The rheostat is nothing more than a length of resistor wire (see Chapter 12) upon which a sliding contact moves. The sliding contact connects to a hinged arm with a float that moves up or down with the level of the fuel. The float is made of cork or wood, treated with a fuel-resistant varnish. Finally, the action of the sliding contact varies the amount of electrical resistance within the gauge circuit in relation to the amount of fuel in the tank.

The dash gauge consists of a heating coil and a bimetallic arm. As electricity passes through it, the coil heats up in proportion to the amount of electrical current flow. As the coil heats up, it causes the bimetallic arm to deflect. This action moves the gauge needle.

System Operation

When the driver turns the ignition switch on, the system begins to function. If the fuel tank is very low on fuel or empty, current (see Chapter 12) from the battery flows through the heating coil within the dash gauge and through the resistance wire in the tank unit. Since the tank is very low or empty, the grounded sliding contact (Fig. 6–7) is at the end of the resistance wire of the rheostat. With all the electrical resistance in the gauge circuit, only a small amount of current flows through the heating coil of the gauge. Consequently, the bimetallic arm does not deflect very much, if any, and the needle reads low or zero fuel level in the tank.

If on the other hand the tank is full of

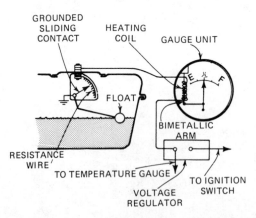

Fig. 6–7. A schematic of a thermostat-type fuel-level indicating system.

fuel, the float and its arm moves up in the tank. This action moves the grounded contact toward the beginning of the resistance coil. As a result of decreased electrical resistance at the rheostat, more current flows through the heating coil to the ground. This causes the coil to heat up sufficiently to cause full deflection of the bimetallic arm. Then, the gauge needle moves over to register a full fuel tank.

Balancing-Coil Type

A balancing-coil type of fuel-level indicating system consists of a tank unit and a dash gauge (Fig. 6-8). The *tank unit* of this system also contains a sliding contact hinged to the float arm. This contact slides back and forth on a resistor as the float moves up and down in the fuel tank. When the float moves all the way up, the contact arm moves over the coil to a position that places maximum resistance between the gauge and the ground at the tank unit. As the tank empties, the float drops; the sliding contact moves over on the coil to a position that reduces resistance.

The *dash gauge* contains two coils, placed 90 degrees apart. At the intersection of the center line of these two coils are an armature and pointer, which pivot back and forth. Finally, to prevent vibration of the pointer during system operation, the armature has a dampening device.

System Operation

If the fuel tank is very low or empty with the ignition key on, the tank unit offers little or no resistance between the "empty" gauge coil and ground (Fig. 6-9). Electrical current then passes only through the "empty" coil of the dash gauge because the "full" coil offers a higher resistance between itself and its ground. The "empty" coil, therefore, creates a strong magnetic field (see Chapter 12) that pulls the armature and pointer toward the low or zero side of the gauge.

If the tank is full with the ignition

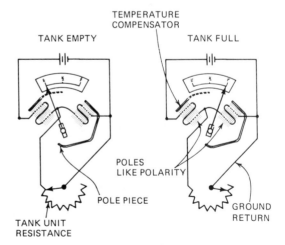

Fig. 6-9. *Operation of a balancing-coil-type fuel-level indicating system. Left illustration shows circuit conditions if the fuel tank is empty. The right-hand illustration shows what occurs in the system when the tank is full.*

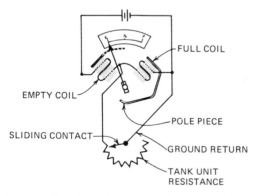

Fig. 6-8. *A schematic diagram of a balancing-coil fuel-level indicating system.*

switch on, the float is all the way up (Fig. 6-9). This upward position of the float positions the contact arm on the resistor so that there is considerable resistance between the dash-gauge coils and the ground in the tank unit. As a result, the current moving through the "empty" coil also flows through the "full" coil and then through its ground and back to the battery. This action creates a stronger magnetic field in the "full" coil that pulls the armature to the right so that the pointer is on the full side of the dial.

When the fuel tank begins to empty again, the float moves down, and the sliding contact moves on the resistor, lowering the total resistance between the tank unit and ground. More of the current flows through the "empty" coil than the "full" coil. Since less current flows through the "full" coil, its magnetic pull

on the armature is less. Consequently, the armature begins to move to the left, and its attached pointer begins to indicate a lower fuel level. Finally, along with any of the fuel-level indicating systems mentioned, some vehicles have a low-level warning light circuit that warns the driver when the fuel tank gets low.

Fuel Lines

Manufacturers connect the many components of the fuel system together with lines and hoses (Fig. 6-10). These lines and hoses carry the fuel from the tank to the fuel pump, from the pump to the carburetor, return excess fuel to the tank, and carry fuel vapors. Depending on the type of installation, these lines can be either rigid or flexible.

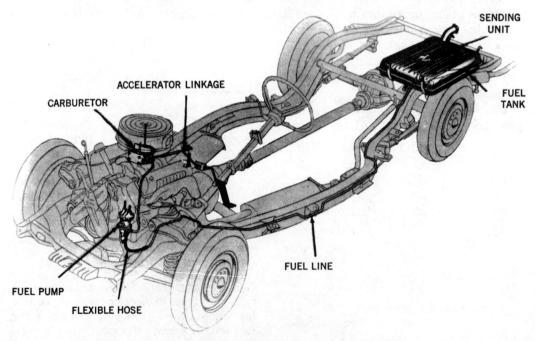

Fig. 6-10. Typical fuel line installation. (Courtesy of Chrysler Corp.)

Rigid Lines

Manufacturers form the fuel lines that fasten to the vehicle body, frame, or engine from seamless steel tubing. In addition, some lines may have a steel spring covering at certain points for protection against damage. The tubing is held in place by clips and positioned in areas that afford maximum protection against road hazards such as flying stones, where vibration is least likely to harden it, and away from the exhaust system in order to minimize the possibility of creating a vapor lock.

A *vapor lock* is a condition that can occur anywhere in the fuel lines, pump, or carburetor if one of these components is close to too much heat. For example, the gasoline passing through a heated line can get hot enough to boil. This is especially true in the case of the fuel-tank-to-pump line. The higher temperatures along with the vacuum created by the pump cause the fuel to boil at a lower temperature. *Note:* Liquids boil at lower temperatures when the pressure on them decreases. For example, water boils at 212° F. (100° C.) at 14.7 psi but boils at 198° F. (92.2°C.) at 10 psi. Thus, large bubbles develop in the fuel lines, or the fuel completely vaporizes. As a result, the bubbles stop or restrict normal fuel delivery to the pump, or by the pump to the carburetor, or the carburetor only receives fuel vapors that pass into the carburetor and out its vent without the engine receiving any fuel.

In order to keep the fuel line as far away as possible from the exhaust system heat, manufacturers route it from the tank to the pump a given way. For example, on single-exhaust-system vehicles, the line runs along the frame on the opposite side of the exhaust system components. If a vehicle has a dual exhaust system, the line runs along the center of the vehicle, often through the drive-shaft tunnel.

When a rigid line requires replacement, you should use only new steel tubing. Never use copper or aluminum tubing as a substitute for steel lines. These materials cannot withstand normal vehicle vibration without breaking.

Flexible Lines

In all sections of the fuel system where flexibility is necessary, manufacturers install a section of synthetic rubber hose (Fig. 6–10). These hoses along with their clamps connect two rigid lines or connect a rigid line to some other component within the fuel system. The diameter of a flexible fuel delivery hose is $5/16$ to $3/8$ inch while a fuel return or vapor hose is usually $1/4$ inch.

The design of fuel hoses is such that their material is fuel resistant. Ordinary rubber hose, such as vacuum hose, is not and, therefore, deteriorates rapidly when exposed to gasoline. Similarly, vapor vent hoses are made from a material that resists deterioration by fuel vapors. Consequently, when replacing either a fuel or vapor hose, make sure that you use the correct size and type. To assist in identifying fuel hoses, many manufacturers mark them to designate their function such as *EVAP* for vapor vent hoses.

Fuel Pumps—Function

Every fuel-supply system has some sort of pump. The function of this pump is to deliver fuel from the tank to the carburetor (Fig. 6–11). In operation, the

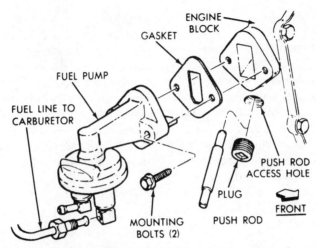

Fig. 6-11. The fuel pump delivers fuel from the tank to the carburetor. (Courtesy of Chrysler Corp.)

pump moves the fuel, using a mechanical action that creates a low-pressure area or vacuum at the pump inlet. Since a fuel line connects the inlet side of the pump to the tank's pickup tube, a vacuum exists below the level of the fuel. Consequently, atmospheric pressure above the fuel level in the tank forces fuel into the pump. The pump then applies a force to the fuel within the pump, which delivers it to the carburetor.

Mechanical-Type Pumps

A motor vehicle can have one of the two basic types of fuel pumps: mechanical or electrical. The most common type of fuel pump, used on both foreign and domestic automobiles, is the *single-action, diaphragm-type mechanical pump* (Fig. 6-12). This pump design operates by means of an *eccentric* (an off-center section) on the engine camshaft. The eccentric may be part of the camshaft itself or may bolt to it. In either case, the action of

the eccentric produces one pump stroke for each revolution of the camshaft.

The fuel-pump component that the eccentric actually contacts and moves is the *rocker arm*. In most cases, the eccentric rests directly against the rocker arm, while in some engines a pushrod fits between the eccentric and rocker arm. Lastly, a follower spring keeps the end of the rocker arm in firm contact with the eccentric or pushrod.

Depending on the design of the engine, the manufacturer can mount the fuel pump in several different locations on their respective engines. For example, in-line engines usually have the fuel pump mounted on the side of the engine blocks. In some V-type engines, the pump bolts to the area between the two cylinder banks. However, most modern V-type engines have the fuel pump on the side of the block at the front of the engine (Fig. 6-11).

The pumping mechanism of a typical single-action pump consists of a pump housing, diaphragm, and spring, plus an inlet and outlet valve. The housing in Fig.

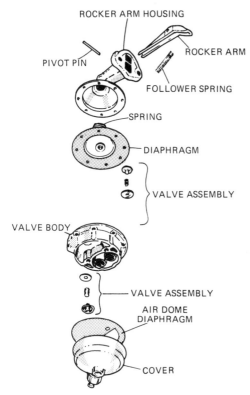

ROCKER ARM HOUSING
ROCKER ARM
PIVOT PIN
FOLLOWER SPRING
SPRING
DIAPHRAGM
VALVE ASSEMBLY
VALVE BODY
VALVE ASSEMBLY
AIR DOME
DIAPHRAGM
COVER

Fig. 6-12. A common mechanical fuel pump.

6-12 consists of three sections: rocker-arm housing, valve body, along with a cover and diaphragm. The *rocker-arm housing* supports the rocker arm by means of a pivot pin. This design permits the rocker arm to pivot back and forth within the housing. Also, the housing flange has two bolt holes, which act as guides for the mounting bolts that hold the pump assembly to the engine.

The *valve body* fits between the rocker-arm housing and the cover. This unit houses the inlet and outlet valves and has two passages: one leading to the outlet port in the cover and the other to the inlet port within the body. Finally, the area of

the body sealed by the main diaphragm forms the pumping chamber of the fuel pump.

The *cover* along with its combination air-dome diaphragm and gasket serves two functions. First, these units seal the valves and passages from external leakage. Second, these components of this pump form an *air dome*. The air dome dampens out pulsations in the stream of fuel delivered by the pump to the carburetor.

A portion of the cover area below the air-dome diaphragm (Fig. 6-12) provides an air pocket. As the pump applies force to the fuel during its delivery stroke, pressurized fuel moves the diaphragm into this space in the cover, compressing a certain volume of air. Then, as the pump begins to deliver fuel to the carburetor, the air pushes on the diaphragm. The diaphragm, in turn, also pushes on the discharging fuel. This action tends to smooth out the pulsations in the fuel stream by minimizing flow pressure variations and increases pump output.

Stretched across and clamped between the rocker-arm housing and the body are the *pump diaphragm and spring*. The diaphragm itself is made from a fuel-resistant material and acts as a flexible piston that creates a vacuum during one part of the pump's cycle and causes fuel flow during another. The spring exerts pressure on the diaphragm that is responsible for moving the diaphragm during its delivery phase of operation.

The diaphragm connects to the rocker arm by means of a slip link. As the rocker arm moves across the high point of the eccentric, it causes the diaphragm to move upward. When the rocker arm is on the low side of the eccentric, the diaphragm spring pushes the diaphragm downward.

Thus, the diaphragm moves up and down as the rocker arm moves around the eccentric.

Both the inlet and outlet valves fit into bores in the valve body. Each valve is nothing more than a spring-loaded, disc-type, one-way check valve serving several particular functions. An *open inlet valve,* for instance, allows fuel to flow from the tank into the pump chamber; when closed, it prevents a back flow of fuel from the chamber to the tank. An *open outlet valve,* on the other hand, permits fuel to flow from the chamber to the carburetor, thereby keeping a constant pressure on the outlet line to the carburetor. Once this pressure drops, the valve closes, thus preventing fuel from flowing back into the pump chamber.

Mechanical-Pump Operation

As soon as the engine starts, the fuel pump begins to operate (Fig. 6–13). As the highest portion of the eccentric on the camshaft comes around against the tip of the rocker arm, it pushes on the rocker arm. The rocker arm, through the slip link,

pulls the diaphragm up, increasing the tension on its return spring. As the diaphragm moves up, it creates a vacuum in the fuel chamber below the diaphragm. This vacuum opens the inlet valve and closes the outlet valve. Next, atmospheric pressure above the level of the fuel in the tank pushes the fuel through the screen and pickup tube, through the fuel line, and finally past the open inlet valve and into the pump chamber.

When the low side of the eccentric comes around, the follower spring keeps the tip of the rocker arm against the eccentric; and the diaphragm return spring forces the diaphragm down. This action creates a pressure on the fuel in the chamber ahead of the moving diaphragm. The pressure closes the intake valve and opens the outlet valve. Fuel under pressure moves past the open outlet valve, through the fuel line, and enters the carburetor.

The units of measurement for the output of a fuel pump are pressure and volume (the amount of fuel it delivers over time). The diaphragm return spring determines delivery pressure, which is in

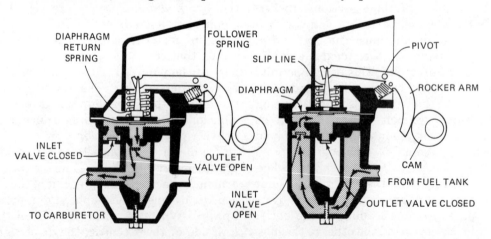

Fig. 6–13.   Operation of a single-action mechanical fuel pump.

pounds per square inch (psi). The carburetor controls flow rate or volume, in which the unit of measure is usually pints per minute.

The delivery rate by the fuel pump is proportional to the fuel usage of the engine, as controlled by the carburetor. The mechanism in the carburetor that controls the flow rate from the pump is the *needle valve* (Fig. 6–14). Any time this needle valve is open, fuel flows from the pump, through the line, and into the float chamber of the carburetor. When the needle valve closes, due to the float chamber being full, no fuel flows through the line.

The needle valve, therefore, maintains a constant level of fuel in the float chamber. When the needle valve closes, fuel cannot enter the bowl, and pressure builds up in the fuel line between the carburetor and pump chamber. As the pressure increases in the chamber, the pressure resists the action of the diaphragm return spring and prevents the diaphragm from taking a complete stroke. This action reduces the flow of fuel.

Within the pump itself, the diaphragm stays in one position, even though the rocker arm continues to move up and down. In other words, the end of the rocker arm that activates the slip link just moves up and down inside the slot in the link. As a result, the slip link and diaphragm remain stationary as the rocker arm pivots back and forth. The fuel pump, therefore, delivers no fuel to the carburetor until the fuel level goes down sufficiently in the float chamber to open the needle valve.

When the needle valve does open again, pressure drops rapidly in the main fuel line and fuel chamber within the pump. This reduced pressure permits the diaphragm to begin moving again, which causes fuel flow to the carburetor.

During different operating phases of the engine, the fuel level in the carburetor's float chamber varies. Consequently, the actual position of the needle valve varies between fully open and fully closed. The rate at which fuel flows from the carburetor into the engine controls the opening of the needle valve; it, in turn, regulates the rate of fuel flow from the pump.

When an engine using a mechanical-type pump is not running, the diaphragm

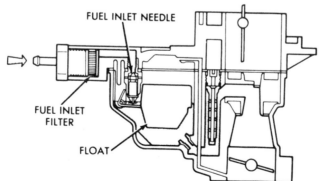

Fig. 6–14. A needle-valve arrangement within a typical carburetor. (Courtesy of Chrysler Corp.)

spring maintains fuel pressure in the fuel line and pump chamber. If underhood temperatures are high enough, the heat can expand the fuel in the line to the carburetor, causing the increased pressure to push the needle valve open. This permits excess fuel to enter the carburetor and cause a flooded condition. A flooded condition is one in which the engine will not restart easily due to excessive amounts of fuel in the intake manifold.

Also, since fuel expands when it gets too hot, the liquid fuel may turn into a vapor. This can cause a vapor lock in the fuel pump and lines. Over the years, manufacturers have used four ways to prevent carburetor flooding and vapor lock.

1. Many older pumps had a special air chamber on the outlet side of the pump. This chamber separated the vapor from the liquid fuel and directed the vapor back to the tank via a separate line. Also, this device permitted excess fuel produced by the pump to return to the fuel tank. This excess fuel, in constant circulation, kept the fuel pump cool, which helped to prevent vapors from forming.

2. Manufacturers installed a vapor separator can between the pump and the carburetor. With this installation, fuel for the carburetor comes from the bottom of the separator can while the vapor at the top of the can returns through a line to the tank.

3. Some air-conditioned vehicles have a *vapor-bypass filter*. This unit combines a vapor separator and fuel filter into a single unit (Fig. 6–15). This unit consists of a sealed can, filter screen or element, inlet and outlet fitting, along with a metered orifice or outlet for the return line to the fuel tank. Any fuel vapors formed in the line pass through the filter and enter

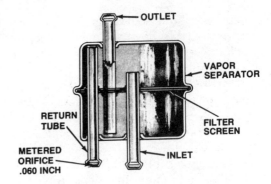

Fig. 6–15. A typical vapor-bypass filter. (Courtesy of Chrysler Corp.)

the vapor separator along with the fuel. The bubbles of the vapor rise to the top of the unit, where fuel pressure forces the vapor through the orifice and back to the fuel tank through a return line. In the tank, the vapors condense into liquid fuel.

4. Many modern pumps have a very small bleed-down hole drilled through each of the pump valves. These holes permit excess pressure in the outlet fuel line to bleed back to the inlet fuel line.

Electrical-Type Fuel Pumps—Advantages

Electrical-type fuel pumps offer certain advantages over the mechanical fuel pump. For example, fuel is available at the carburetor as soon as the operator turns the ignition switch on. Also, the electrical-type pump can deliver more fuel than the engine requires even under maximum operating conditions. Consequently, the engine never starves for fuel. Finally, electrical fuel pumps eliminate, in many cases, the problem of vapor locking that can be a problem for engines with mechanical fuel pumps.

Impeller Type of Electric Fuel Pumps

Over the years, manufacturers have used several types of electrically operated pumps. The latest version of this pump consists of an *impeller* or turbine, driven by a small electric motor (Fig. 6–16). This pump, when in operation, pulls fuel through its inlet pipe and then pushes the fuel out through the outlet pipe, through a fuel line, and finally into the carburetor. This pump design has no valves; therefore, the pump delivers fuel in a steady flow rather than a pulsating motion like the flow from a mechanical pump.

Impeller Pump Locations

The impeller pump is primarily a pusher unit; that is, it pushes the fuel through the fuel line to the carburetor. Since this pump design does not rely on the engine camshaft to drive it, the manufacturer could install it in the fuel line almost anywhere on the vehicle. However, its usual location is within the fuel tank (Fig. 6–17).

The reason for an in-tank installation is rather simple when you consider the pump's structure. Since the pump itself has no valving, it is most efficient when installed at or below the level of the fuel in the tank. This type of installation permits the force of gravity to feed the fuel into the pump's inlet instead of the need for the pump to produce a strong vacuum for this purpose.

In addition, in-tank installation eliminates the problem of a vapor lock in the fuel supply line to the carburetor in all but the most severe operating conditions. When the pump mounts within the tank, the pump pressurizes the entire fuel-supply line to the carburetor. Regardless of how hot the fuel line gets, it is very unlikely that enough fuel vapors can form in the line to interfere with the normal fuel flow. Furthermore, installing the pump in or close to the tank permits the pump to stay cooler because it is far away from the heat of the engine. Consequently, the pusher pump is less likely to overheat during hot weather.

Control of Impeller Pump Operation

A pressure switch installed into the lubrication system of the engine controls the operation of most factory-installed electric fuel pumps. This switch performs two functions. First, this switch opens the

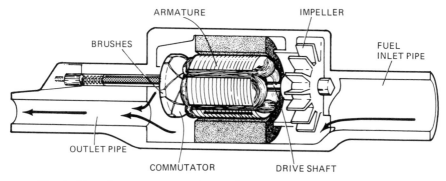

Fig. 6–16. Cutaway view of a tank-mounted electric fuel pump.

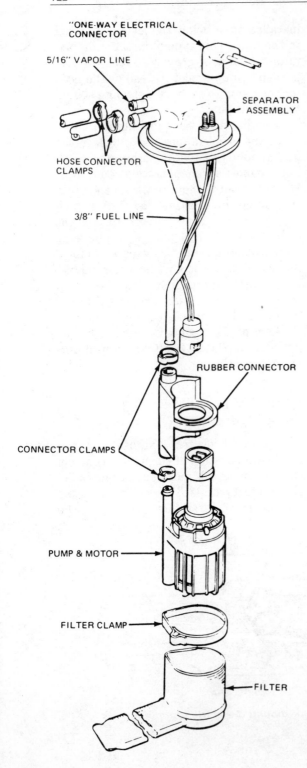

electrical circuit to the pump motor when the engine is not running. Second, it controls pump operation when the driver starts the engine and while it is operating.

The pressure switch, shown in Fig. 6–18, has two sets of electrical contact points. One set that is normally closed permits electrical current from the battery to flow through the starter relay or solenoid to the fuel pump. The other set of points is normally open. But when closed, it allows current from the battery to flow through the ignition switch to the fuel pump.

As the driver turns the ignition switch to the start position, battery current energizes the pump motor through the normally closed contact points (Fig. 6–18). With the engine operating, the pump motor receives its current flow

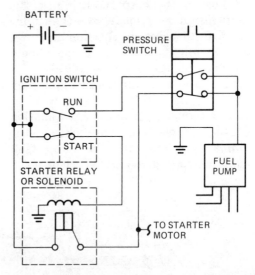

Fig. 6–18. A schematic of an electrical fuel-pump circuit during engine cranking.

Fig. 6–17. Location of an electrical pump in the fuel tank. The pump itself mounted onto the fuel-gauge, tank-unit assembly. (Courtesy of Ford Motor Co. of Canada Ltd.)

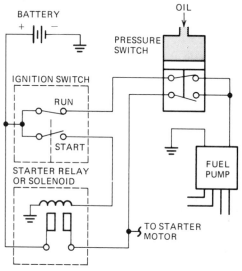

Fig. 6–19. A schematic of an electrical fuel-pump circuit with the engine running.

the *bellows-type pump* (Fig. 6–20). This unit contains an inlet and an outlet valve and a bellows operated by an electromagnet. The *spring-loaded inlet valve* permits fuel flow from the tank to the pump chamber but prevents a back flow. The *outlet valve* is also a spring-loaded, one-way check valve. It permits fuel flow from the pumping chamber to the carburetor, which maintains a constant pressure in the fuel line, but it blocks fuel return from the carburetor to the pump.

The *flexible bellows* is responsible not only for producing the vacuum necessary to draw fuel into the pump but also for pressurizing the fuel. The armature section of the electromagnet extends the bellows during one portion of the pump stroke. A return spring collapses the bellows during another.

through the normally open contact points, which oil pressure has closed (Fig. 6–19).

Engine oil pressure, acting on the pressure switch, opens the normally closed points and closes the otherwise open contacts in order to keep the pump supplied with current flow. If the operator turns off the ignition switch at any time, the electrical circuit to the pump is open. In addition, if the engine oil pressure falls below a specified amount, usually about 2 psi, the pressure switch opens the circuit between the battery and the pump motor, which stops fuel pump operation immediately. By doing so, the pressure switch acts as a safety device that protects the engine from damage due to low oil pressure.

Operation of a Bellows-Type Electrical Fuel Pump

When the driver turns on the ignition switch, battery current flows to the electromagnet inside the pump. The magne-

Bellows-Type Electrical Fuel Pumps

The type of electrical fuel pump, usually mounted in the engine compartment and above the level of the fuel in the tank, is

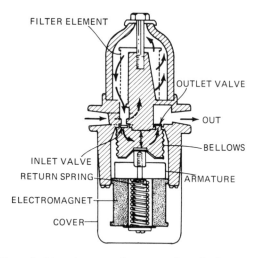

Fig. 6–20. Sectional view of a bellows-type electrical fuel pump.

tism created by the magnet pulls down the armature, which extends the bellows. This action produces a vacuum inside the bellows. Fuel from the tank enters the bellows through the inlet valve.

As the armature reaches its lower limit of travel, it opens a set of contact points. This action opens the electrical circuit between the battery and the electromagnet. The return spring forces the armature upward; that, in turn, collapses the bellows. This action forces the fuel from the bellows, past the outlet valve, and through the line to the carburetor.

As the armature reaches the upper limit of travel, it closes the contacts. This action again energizes the electromagnet, and it pulls the armature down. These actions repeat continuously as long as the switch is on and the carburetor float chamber is low on fuel. When the chamber is full, the bellows remain in a given position until the fuel pressure drops. Then, it continues discharging fuel until it and the armature reach the position that closes the contact points. Next, the electromagnet pulls the armature down, and the bellows again pulls in fuel from the tank, beginning a new pump cycle.

Outlet Fuel Filters—Function

In addition to the filter within the tank, the fuel supply system also has another filter or two on the outlet side of the fuel pump. This filter has a design that prevents small solid particles and water that may have passed through the tank filter from entering the carburetor. This material would otherwise clog small jets and calibrated openings within the carburetor.

Manufacturers form outlet filters from diferent types of materials. For example, the filter element itself may be on a fine copper-mesh screen, treated paper, fiber, ceramic, or sintered bronze. But with all designs, the element must be porous enough to pass all the fuel required by the engine, yet it must not pass any sediment or water.

Filter Types

Fuel-Pump Outlet Filters

Manufacturers may install an outlet filter in three locations: in the fuel pump, in the fuel line, or in the carburetor. Some vehicles have a filter in the outlet side of the pump (Fig. 6–21). This filtering element may be in the form of a screen but usually is a throwaway paper element.

In-Line Filters

In-line filters, used in some vehicles, are in the fuel line between the fuel pump and

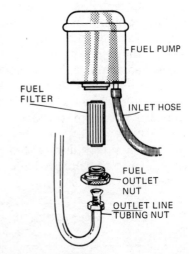

Fig. 6–21. Some fuel pumps have a filter installed in the outlet side of the pump.

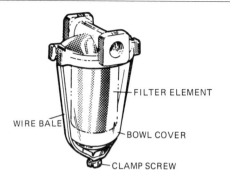

Fig. 6-22. An in-line filter element contained within a sediment bowl.

the carburetor. In some older domestic and foreign automobiles, this filter was inside a sediment bowl (Fig. 6-22). The bowl itself contains a treated paper, ceramic, fiber, or metal filter element. The bowl cover is held in place by a clamp screw and wire bail and therefore is removable for filter cleaning or replacement. The technician can clean and reuse both the ceramic and sintered bronze filters; however,

paper and fiber filters require replacement when dirty.

Other vehicles have an in-line filter element inside a plastic or metal container (Fig. 6-23). This filter assembly contains a treated, pleated paper element that is not replaceable. Consequently, when the filter is dirty, the mechanic replaces the entire assembly.

The technician must also install this type of filter in a certain way. On the outside of the container is an arrow indicating the direction of fuel flow. This arrow must point toward the inlet fitting on the carburetor. If the arrow points in the opposite direction, the filter restricts fuel delivery to the carburetor. Finally, some throwaway in-line filters are part of a combination filter and vapor separator.

Carburetor Inlet Filters

Many vehicles have the filter located at the inlet to the float chamber. This filter

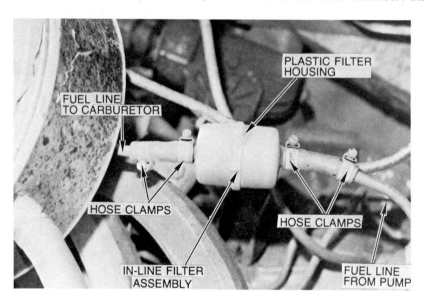

Fig. 6-23. An in-line filter element contained within a metal or plastic container.

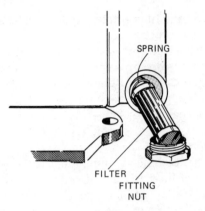

Fig. 6-24. An in-line filter element inside the entrance to the float chamber of the carburetor.

element may be inside the entrance to the float chamber (Fig. 6-24) or be part of a throwaway assembly, threaded into the float-chamber housing (Fig. 6-25). The element inside the housing may be the serviceable type, ceramic or bronze; in the case of late-model vehicles, it is a throwaway paper element.

The spring shown in Fig. 6-24 permits the filter to move off its seat due to pump pressure, if particles clog it. This action permits normal fuel delivery to the carburetor; however, the fuel does not receive

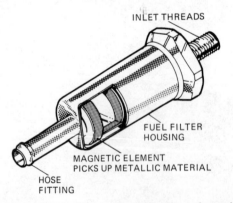

Fig. 6-25. A filter assembly that threads into the entrance to the float chamber of the carburetor.

filtering before entering the float chamber. Filter elements on some 1976 and later vehicles also contain a rollover check, which this chapter discusses later.

The filter assembly that fits onto the outside of carburetor housing (Fig. 6-25) has a filter-screen or treated-paper-type element enclosed in a metal housing. In some cases, the filter also has a magnetic washer to trap metal particles. One end of this throwaway-type filter threads into the float chamber inlet, and the fuel-pump line hose clamps over the opposite end.

Rollover Leakage Protection

All 1976 and later automobiles have one or more devices to prevent fuel leaks if the vehicle should turn over. The devices may be in the form of a check valve, float valve, or redesigned fuel-tank filler caps. Figure 6-26 shows a *rollover check valve* built into the carburetor inlet filter. This valve is nothing more than a spring-loaded plastic check valve. In operation, fuel pressure pushes the valve off its seat; its spring seats the valve when the engine is shut off. This prevents a fuel leak from the float chamber if the fuel line should break when the vehicle rolls over.

Other check valves similar in design and operation may also be found in the fuel vapor control system, discussed later in this text. Manufacturers install these devices in the return vent line from the fuel filter to the tank, in the vent line between the charcoal canister and tank, and sometimes in the fuel return line at the carburetor.

Figure 6-27 shows a rollover device that uses a float valve. This unit has a spring-loaded float valve enclosed in the vapor-separator housing. With this de-

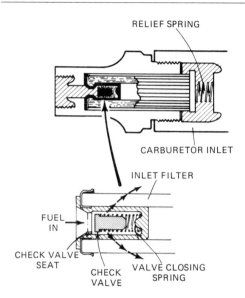

Fig. 6-26. A fuel inlet filter with a rollover check valve.

sign, the float valve closes off the orifice opening whenever the vehicle rolls over 90 degrees or more. This prevents fuel from leaking into the vent line.

Later fuel caps also required modification to prevent leakage if the vehicle turned over. This modification included a device to prevent leakage of fuel through the cap's pressure relief valve. Earlier caps may fit on a given vehicle but should

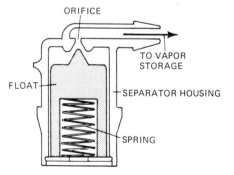

Fig. 6-27. An orifice-type vapor separator with a spring-loaded float valve for rollover protection.

not be used as a replacement because they offer no fuel-leakage protection.

Review

This section will assist you in determining how well you remember the material contained in this chapter. Read each item carefully. If you can't complete the statement, review the section in the chapter that covers the material.

1. Manufacturers make the fuel tank in _____ main sections.
   a. two
   b. three
   c. four
   d. five

2. Fuel tanks that store unleaded fuel have a special _____ _____.
   a. slosh baffle
   b. sending unit
   c. pickup tube
   d. filler tube

3. Water can enter the fuel tank due to _____.
   a. rain
   b. condensation
   c. pressure
   d. vacuum

4. The component in the fuel supply system that has a variable resistor is the _____ _____.
   a. fuel pump
   b. pickup tube
   c. tank unit
   d. outlet filter

5. The balancing-coil fuel gauge contains _____ coil(s).
   a. three
   b. no
   c. one
   d. two

6. Rigid fuel lines are made of seamless
   _____.
   a. copper
   b. aluminum
   c. steel
   d. iron

7. The portion of the mechanical fuel pump that contacts the eccentric is the _____ _____.
   a. rocker arm
   b. diaphragm spring
   c. inlet valve
   d. air-dome cover

8. The component within the carburetor that controls the flow rate of fuel from the fuel pump is the _____
   _____.
   a. float chamber
   b. needle valve
   c. throttle valve
   d. idle jet

9. The component in the fuel pump that controls the amount of fuel pump pressure is the _____ _____.
   a. slip link
   b. rocker arm
   c. diaphragm spring
   d. inlet valve

10. The device that controls the operation of most factory-installed electric fuel pumps is a _____ _____.
    a. mechanical switch
    b. pressure switch
    c. vacuum switch
    d. hydraulic switch

11. The type of electric pump usually found in the engine compartment is the _____ type.
    a. bellows
    b. impeller
    c. rotor
    d. diaphragm

12. An outlet filter may be in the fuel pump, in the fuel line, or inside the
    _____.
    a. dome
    b. manifold
    c. tank
    d. carburetor

13. After 1976, automobiles have _____ _____ devices to prevent fuel leakage after an accident.
    a. collision
    b. relief
    c. rollover
    d. pressure

For the answers, turn to the Appendix.

As a tune-up technician, you will perform many types of service to the fuel-supply system. You do some repairs or replacements as part of a routine tune-up procedure while others are necessary to correct a specific malfunction. These repair procedures include service to the fuel tank, fuel lines, fuel pump, and outlet filters.

Fuel Tank Service

As a general rule, the fuel tank itself seldom requires any maintenance. However, over time, water and sediment can build up in the bottom of the tank, restricting fuel flow through the pickup filter and tube. In addition, continuous road vibration, over a long period, can cause leakage in a tank seam, or a vehicle accident will damage the tank itself. All these situations, along with the replacement of the tank unit on some vehicles, require the removal and later reinstallation of the tank.

Fuel Tank Removal

To remove a typical fuel tank safely:

1. Remove the excess fuel from the tank. *Note:* Before attempting to drain the tank, always remove the negative cable from the battery, place "no smoking" signs and a CO_2 fire extinguisher near the work area, and wear safety glasses. The absence of a fuel-tank drain plug on late-model vehicles makes it necessary to siphon or pump the fuel from the tank.

Figure 7–1 illustrates a piece of equipment that will safely remove and store highly flammable and explosive gasoline.

Chapter 7

SERVICING THE FUEL SUPPLY SYSTEM

Fig. 7-1. A piece of equipment used to remove and store gasoline safely. (Courtesy of Chrysler Corp.)

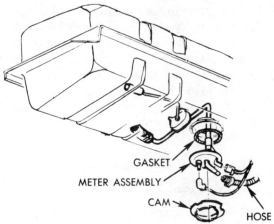

Fig. 7-2. Location of the wiring and hose connections on a typical tank unit or meter assembly.

In this situation, the unit is pulling the fuel from the tank through the filler tube. Later, the technician will use this device and the fuel, if not contaminated, to refill the tank. *Note:* Due to an extended filler tube or a restriction, it is sometimes difficult to remove the fuel adequately from the tank through the filler tube. In this situation, you must drain the fuel through the fuel feed line to the pump.

2. If you have not already done so, remove the ground cable from the battery.

3. Remove the fuel cap.

4. Raise the vehicle on a hoist, or raise the rear of the vehicle with a floor jack high enough to work under it. Then, lower the vehicle on jack stands for safety.

5. Disconnect the electrical lead at the tank unit (Fig. 7-2).

6. Disconnect the fuel line hose or the tank unit pickup line.

7. Remove the vent hoses from the tank or tank unit fittings.

8. Remove the tank unit's ground wire at its screw at the underbody floor pan, if so equipped.

9. Remove the nuts that secure the

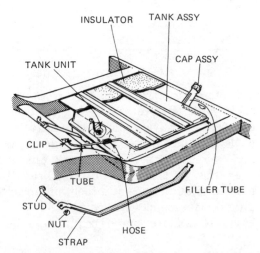

Fig. 7-3. Removing the fuel tank straps and hardware.

ends of the tank hold-down straps (Fig. 7–3) to the body or frame; and lower one end of the tank far enough to disengage the filler tube from the vehicle body. Then, lower and slide the tank out from under the vehicle.

Removing the Tank Unit

In many cases, you need not remove the fuel tank in order to change the tank unit. However, if necessary, drain and remove the tank as described earlier, or remove the tank unit, following these instructions.

1. Disconnect the wire and hoses from the tank unit.

2. Drain the fuel from the tank.

3. Using the tool shown in Fig. 7–4, loosen and remove the cam lock, holding the unit onto the tank.

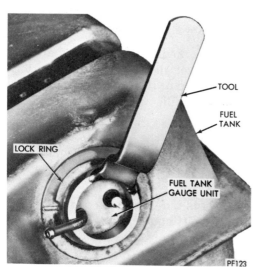

Fig. 7–4. Removing or installing the cam lock, using a special tool. (Courtesy of Chrysler Corp.)

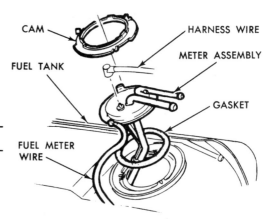

Fig. 7–5. Parts breakdown of a tank unit or meter assembly installation to the fuel tank.

4. Remove the tank unit and gasket (Fig. 7–5). *Caution:* Remove the tank unit carefully to avoid damage to the pickup screen.

5. Replace the pickup filter or the entire unit as necessary, or clean the strainer screen by blowing it out with compressed air.

Installing the Tank Unit

When replacing or reinstalling a tank unit (Fig. 7–5), always use a new gasket and follow this procedure.

1. Install the tank unit and new gasket into the tank. *Caution:* Install the unit carefully to avoid damaging the pickup screen.

2. With the tool shown in Fig. 7–4, reinstall the cam lock. *Note:* When installing the cam lock, you may have to press down on the tool in order to compress the gasket. However, once you start the cam

lock into its retaining tangs, release the pressure.

3. Reinstall the electrical lead, lines, and fuel tank as outlined later in this text.

Cleaning the Fuel Tank and System

If the tank shows signs of damage or internal rusting, you should replace it. However, if the problem requiring tank removal is due to contaminated fuel or foreign material that collected inside the tank, you can usually clean these contaminants out of the inside of the tank by using this procedure.

1. Locate the tank away from heat, flame, or other source of ignition. Remove the tank unit, as described earlier, and inspect the condition of the filter. If you cannot clean this filter, replace it before reinstalling the tank unit.

2. As necessary, complete the draining of the tank by rocking it back and forth and allowing the remaining fuel to run out of the tank unit opening and into a container.

3. Clean out the fuel tank itself with steam or hot running water for at least 5 minutes. Then, pour the excess water out through the tank unit opening. Rock the tank back and forth to assure the complete removal of the water. Finally, permit the inside of the tank to air dry or blow it dry, using compressed air. *Caution:* This procedure will not remove fuel vapors from the tank. Therefore, do not attempt any repair work on the tank or filler neck that requires heat or a flame.

4. Remove the fuel inlet filter at the carburetor, the in-line filter, or the outlet filter on the pump, and inspect the filters for contamination. If contamination has plugged the filters, replace them. However, for the present, leave the fuel line, from the pump to the carburetor, disconnected at the carburetor.

5. Disconnect the inlet fuel line at the pump; use air pressure to clean this fuel line and, if so equipped, the fuel return line. *Note:* Always apply the air pressure in the normal direction of fuel flow within the line. On tanks with a liquid separator, blow out its lines with *low* air pressure. Also, check to make sure that the restrictor located on the pipe end is open and not restricted.

6. Clean out the pipes on the tank unit, using *low* air pressure.

7. Reinstall the tank unit as outlined earlier in this section.

Tank Installation

To install a new, cleaned, or repaired tank, follow this procedure.

1. Raise and position the fuel tank under the vehicle. It may be necessary to raise one end of the tank first in order to engage the filler neck into the vehicle body.

2. Position the hold-down straps around the tank, and install the nuts over the retaining studs. Tighten these nuts to specifications.

3. Install the vent hoses on the tank or tank unit fittings.

4. Connect the fuel-line hose to the tank unit fitting.

5. Connect the electrical lead to the tank unit.

6. If so equipped, install the tank unit's ground wire under its screw at the under-

body floor pan. Tighten this screw securely.

7. Lower the vehicle to the shop floor.

Servicing the Tank,
Purging the Fuel Pump

1. Connect a fuel drain hose at the disconnected line at the carburetor. Then, insert the other end of this hose into a 1-gallon fuel can.

2. Disconnect the primary (+) wire at the ignition coil, and tape its terminal.

3. Reconnect the battery ground cable of the battery.

4. Pour at least 6 gallons of clean fuel into the tank.

5. Operate the starter long enough to pump at least 2 quarts of fuel into the fuel can from the carburetor line. This action will purge the fuel pump.

6. Remove the drain-off hose from the carburetor fuel line, and connect the line to the carburetor. Tighten the fuel-line fitting, using two wrenches.

7. Untape and connect the primary wire onto the coil.

8. Start the vehicle and check all line connections for fuel leakage.

Purging the Fuel Tank
of Vapors

If it is necessary to remove the fuel vapors from a removed tank in order to repair it, purge the tank using this procedure.

1. Remove the tank unit and all the remaining fuel from the tank.

2. Visually inspect the inside cavity of the tank; if any remaining fuel is evident, drain the tank again.

3. Move the tank to the wash rack.

4. Pour a fuel-emulsifying agent and water solution into the tank. Then, agitate this mixture for 2 to 3 minutes, making sure that it wets all interior surfaces.

5. Fill the tank completely with water and agitate again.

6. Empty the contents of the tank into the floor drain.

7. When empty, refill the tank to overflowing with water to completely flush out the remaining mixture; then empty the tank.

8. If any fuel vapor is still present in the tank, repeat steps 4 through 8. Repeat as many times as necessary until there is no evidence of fuel vapors. Also, if the tank has an integral fuel separator, check the liquid separator pipe for fuel vapor. If any vapors exist, repeat the procedure.

9. Dry the tank with compressed air and perform the necessary service work.

Leak Testing a
Fuel Tank

In order to test a fuel tank for leaks, follow this recommended procedure.

1. Plug all the tank outlets as follows.

a. Install a known, good filler cap over the filler tube opening.

b. Install the tank unit, and plug its fuel line, using a capped piece of short fuel hose.

c. If the tank has more than one vent opening, plug all but one of these openings with short, capped pieces of fuel-line hose.

d. Install another short piece of open fuel-line hose on the remaining vent tube.

2. Apply air pressure to the tank through the end of the hose, attached to the remaining open vent tube. Use extreme caution to prevent air from rupturing the tank. When you hear air escaping from the tank cap, the pressure valve in the cap has opened at about 1 to $1\frac{1}{2}$ psi. At this point, pinch off the fuel line hose to retain this pressure in the tank. *Caution:* If you are leak checking an old-style tank with a sealed cap, it will be necessary to regulate the air pressure going into the tank to about 2 psi so that the tank does not rupture.

3. Test the tank for leaks with a soap solution or by submerging it in water. If you note a leak, make a repair and retest the tank.

Fuel Line Service

Rigid Line Replacement

If upon inspection you find a rigid fuel line that has kinks, dents, or leaks, replace the line using this procedure.

1. Disconnect the fuel hoses or fittings attached to each end of the line. *Note:* When disconnecting a line fitting, always use two wrenches, one on the line fitting and one over the carburetor or pump fitting.

2. Where used, loosen and remove all the screw and clamp assemblies that hold the line to the frame or underbody.

3. Remove the line from the vehicle. *Caution:* Be careful not to distort the old line during removal.

4. Select a length of seamless-steel tubing of the correct diameter but slightly longer than the original line. *Note:* Under no conditions should you use copper or aluminum tubing as a replacement for steel tubing.

5. Using the old line as a guide and a tubing bender, form the new line, as closely as possible, into the same shape as the old line.

6. Using a tubing cutter, trim off the ends of the new pipe so that it now is not more than about one-half inch longer than the original pipe.

7. Using a flaring tool, like the one shown in Fig. 7–6, double-flare each cutoff end of the tubing. This flare is necessary along with a fitting in order to seal the pipe against leakage, or the flare will prevent the fuel hose from slipping off the line after the hose clamp is tight.

8. Install the new line into its proper position, and install its hold-down clamps and screws. Tighten the screws securely.

9. Using two wrenches, reconnect the fuel-line fittings to the carburetor and pump, or reinstall the fuel-line hoses over the ends of the line. Tighten the hose clamps securely.

Repairing a Pinhole Leak in a Rigid Line

You can repair a small pinhole leak in a rigid fuel line by using a connector fitting or a piece of fuel hose. To repair a line using a connector (Fig. 7–7):

1. Using a tubing cutter (Fig. 7–8), trim away the damaged area of the line. If the damaged area of the line is longer than the distance inside the connector, where the cutoff end of each tube will bottom

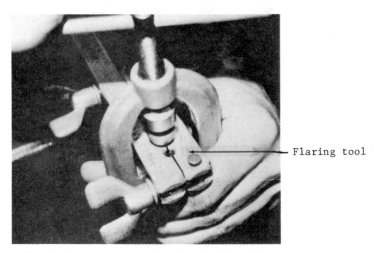

Fig. 7–6.   Using a tool to double-flare the ends of a line.

in the connector, replace the line or use a fuel hose to repair the damage. Otherwise, the fuel line will no longer be the correct length.

2. Install a nut and ferrule over each cutoff end of the tubing.

3. Install one of the tubing ends into the connector, making sure to push it in as far as possible. Then slide the ferrule against the connector, and run the nut down on the connector's threads finger-tight.

4. Using two line wrenches, tighten the nut securely. Position one of the wrenches on the connector and the other on the nut while tightening the nut (Fig. 7–9). This action prevents damage to the line or fitting.

5. Repeat the same process on the other portion of the line.

To repair a leak in a fuel line using a piece of fuel hose:

1. Using a tubing cutter, trim away the damaged section of the line.

2. With a flaring tool (Fig. 7–6), double-flare each cutoff end of the line. The flare prevents the hose from slipping off the line after its clamp is tight.

Fig. 7–7.   You can repair a pinhole leak in a fuel line with a connector similar to this one.

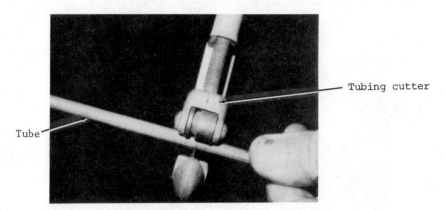

Tubing cutter

Tube

Fig. 7-8.   Using a tubing cutter to trim away the damaged section of a line.

3. Install a hose clamp loosely over each end of the line.

4. Cut a piece of fuel hose to a length approximately 2 inches longer than the piece of the damaged pipe.

5. Insert each end of the hose over the double-flared ends of the line. Make sure to push about 1 inch of hose over each line end.

6. Slip the clamps over the ends of the hose, and tighten each down securely about $\frac{1}{4}$ inch from the end of the hose.

7. Operate the engine and check the repair for signs of fuel leakage.

Replacing Flexible Hoses

If on inspection you locate a cracked, brittle, hard, or leaking fuel-line hose, replace it, following these steps.

1. With a screwdriver or hose-clamp pliers, loosen the hose clamps; and then move the clamps off the hose and onto the line.

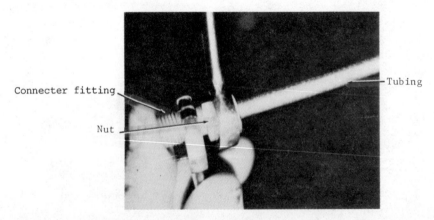

Connecter fitting

Nut

Tubing

Fig. 7-9.   Using two wrenches to secure the nut to the connector fitting.

2. Work the old hose back and forth until you can free it from the line or fitting.

3. Using the old line as a guide, cut a new line from a roll of the proper type and diameter hose.

4. Install the new hose over each end of the line or fitting.

5. Position a hose clamp over each end of the hose, about $\frac{1}{4}$ inch from each end. If it is a screwtype clamp, tighten it securely.

6. Operate the engine and check the line for leaks.

Pump

Pump Service

Engine performance at all speeds requires that a sufficient supply of fuel at the correct pressure and volume be available to the carburetor. This requirement can be met only if the fuel pump is operating properly. Faulty fuel-pump operation can cause two very common problems: incorrect pressure and low pump capacity. Both troubles affect engine performance. For example, low fuel-pump pressure causes a lean mixture within the cylinders at high engine rpm; whereas, a high pump pressure causes excessive fuel consumption and carburetor flooding. Low pump capacity, like low pump pressure, causes insufficient fuel delivery to the cylinders at high engine rpm. In other words, the engine does not receive enough fuel at high rpm to continue operating properly or stops running altogether.

Therefore, it is important that you test the pump on the engine as part of every complete tune-up. These tests include checking pump pressure and capacity.

The pump pressure test indicates at what pressure (psi) the pump delivers fuel. Whereas, the capacity test tells the pumping capacity (the amount of flow) from the pump in pints per minute.

Pressure Test

To perform a pressure test with the fuel-pump tester shown in Fig. 7–10, proceed as follows.

1. With the engine inoperative, disconnect the fuel inlet line at the carburetor.

2. Using the proper adapter fitting, insert the gauge assembly fitting into the carburetor inlet fitting. Then, tighten the knurled thumb screw on the tester finger-tight.

3. Using the proper adapter fitting, thread the inlet fuel line fitting into the gauge line fitting, and tighten the line fitting fingertight.

4. Close the shut-off clamp on the volume delivery hose.

5. Start the engine, and permit it to operate at the normal, hot-idle rpm.

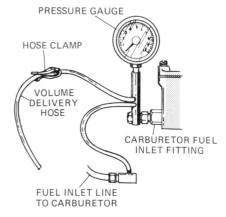

Fig. 7–10. *Testing pump pressure with a fuel-pump tester.*

6. Note the pressure on the gauge tester. The reading should be to the manufacturer's specifications, generally between 3.5 to 6.5 psi, depending on the type of engine on which you are working.

Results and Indications

1. Pressure within specifications is a good indication that the pump and outlet filters are satisfactory.

2. If the pressure is not up to specifications and an outlet filter is in the system, remove the filter or element, and take another pressure reading as explained. If after the filter or element has been removed the test indicates that pump pressure is within specifications, then the fuel filter has a restriction and requires replacement.

3. If the pressure is still low after you remove the filter, the fuel pump is defective and requires overhaul or replacement.

Capacity Test

You should only perform the capacity test after ascertaining that pump pressure is up to specifications. To perform this test, using the equipment shown in Fig. 7-11, follow these steps.

1. Attach the tester assembly to the carburetor inlet and line fitting as outlined under pump-pressure test procedures.

2. Start the engine and permit it to operate at its normal, hot-idle rpm.

3. Insert the volume hose into the graduated container, and open the shut-off clamp. When the fuel reaches the 4-ounce level in the container, submerge the end of the hose in the fuel. Then, observe the fuel for the presence of air

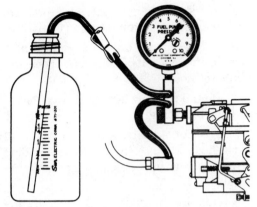

Fig. 7–11.   Testing pump capacity with a fuel-pump tester and graduated container. (Courtesy of Sun Electric Corp.)

bubbles. Air bubbles can only originate from an air leak in a mechanical pump or in the tank-to-pump fuel-line connections.

4. Using the second hand on your watch dial, note the time required to pump 1 pint, or the amount specified by the manufacturer, of fuel into the container. Then, close the tester shut-off clamp securely.

5. Compare the delivery time with the specifications for fuel-pump delivery.

6. Remove the test equipment, and reconnect the fuel inlet line to the carburetor; tighten its fitting, using two line wrenches.

Results and Indications

1. If the pump volume is within specifications, the pump and fuel lines are in satisfactory condition.

2. If pump volume is low, the pump is defective, or there is a restricted filter or leaky line.

3. Air bubbles during the volume test indicate a leak in the fuel pump or suction fuel line.

4. Other causes of both low fuel pump volume and pressure may be:

a. Worn or broken fuel-pump rocker arm, pushrod, or diaphragm linkage. Replace the pump or pushrod and repeat the tests.

b. Water or sediment restricting the pickup screen within the fuel tank. Remove the tank-filler cap and suction line at the fuel pump. Then, blow through the line with compressed air. Repeat the test. If pump volume and pressure improve, remove the tank assembly for cleaning.

c. Restricted or leaking fuel lines or hoses. Open all the lines or hoses and inspect them. Then, blow the lines out with compressed air or replace them as necessary.

d. Broken or worn fuel-pump eccentric on the camshaft. After checking that all the lines and filters are clear, install a pump that you know is good; then repeat the tests. If the volume and pressure are still low, the eccentric is probably worn out.

Mechanical Fuel-Pump Replacement

Most domestic mechanical fuel pumps are no longer repairable by an average repair shop. Consequently, when a pressure or volume test indicates a defective pump, you have no alternative but to replace it with a new or rebuilt unit.

The actual procedure for removing and replacing a mechanical fuel pump are nearly the same, regardless of the type of vehicle. Consequently, the major difficulty in replacing a mechanical pump is the lack of adequate work space. Manufac-

turers usually install this type of fuel pump in an area low on the engine where it is hard to work.

Pump Removal (Figure 7–12)

1. Disconnect the ground cable from the battery.

2. Using two wrenches, disconnect the outlet fuel-line fitting at the pump. *Note:* The best type of wrench to use for this purpose is a line wrench (Fig. 7–13).

3. With a screwdriver or hose-clamp pliers, loosen and remove the inlet hose clamp.

4. Remove the inlet hose by twisting it back and forth until it slides off the pump fitting.

5. Loosen the fuel pump attaching bolts about three complete turns each.

6. While holding the pump in place, slowly turn the engine over, with a wrench on the crankshaft pulley, until the low point on the fuel-pump eccentric rests against the rocker arm or pushrod.

7. With the tension removed from the rocker arm, remove the attaching bolts, and slide the pump off the engine.

8. If so equipped, remove the pushrod that fits between the camshaft eccentric and pump rocker arm. Check this rod for wear and then alignment, using a straight edge.

9. Clean off all the old gasket from the fuel pump mounting flange on the engine.

Pump Installation

1. Apply a thin coat of oil-resistant gasket sealer to both sides of a new gasket. Then, install the gasket onto the fuel-pump mounting flange. Make sure

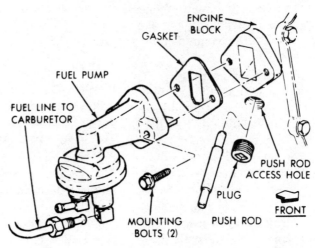

Fig. 7-12.   Removing and replacing a mechanical fuel pump. (Courtesy of Chrysler Corp.)

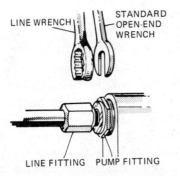

Fig. 7-13. Use two line wrenches to remove and tighten line fittings.

that the holes in the gasket align with the mount bolt holes in the flange (Fig. 7-12).

2. If so equipped, reinstall the pushrod into its bore and against the pump eccentric. Before installation, coat the rod with heavy grease on its camshaft end. The grease holds the rod in position for a moment while you install the pump.

3. Insert the pump's rocker arm into the mounting hole so that it bears against either the pushrod or camshaft eccentric. *Caution:* If you install the rocker arm incorrectly, the pump or the camshaft may sustain damage when the engine starts.

4. While holding the pump in place against its mounting surface on the block, install the attaching bolts. Tighten these bolts alternately and evenly to the manufacturer's specifications.

5. Connect the outlet line to the pump. If you find it difficult to start the threads of the outlet line fitting into the pump, use two wrenches to loosen the upper end of the fuel line at the carburetor about three turns. This action makes it easier to at-

tach the line to the fuel pump. Then, tighten the fittings on both ends of the line, using two wrenches.

6. As necessary, install a new clamp over the inlet fuel hose, and position the hose over the inlet fitting on the pump. Tighten the hose clamp securely.

7. Reconnect the battery ground cable.

8. Start the engine and check all the pump lines and fittings for fuel leaks.

Fuel-Filter Service

All outlet filters require service at regular intervals, usually about every 12,000 miles of vehicle operation. This service may involve removing, cleaning, and reinstalling the element or replacing the entire filter assembly or element. In any case, if this service work is not done, sediment eventually clogs the filter and restricts the fuel flow to the carburetor.

Replacing a Fuel-Pump Outlet Filter

To replace the outlet fuel pump filter shown in Fig. 7–14:

1. Plug or clamp off the inlet fuel-line hose to the pump to prevent a loss of fuel during the procedure.

2. Using two line wrenches, one on the outlet nut and the other on the tubing nut, loosen and remove the outlet line.

3. Loosen and remove the outlet nut.

4. Remove and discard the outlet filter. *Caution:* Be careful not to permit the filter seating spring to drop out of the pump housing.

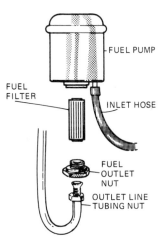

Fig. 7-14. Removing and replacing a typical outlet fuel filter.

5. Position a new filter element into the outlet nut with its open end down inside the nut.

6. Install a new metal gasket over the outlet nut. Then, thread the outlet nut into the fuel-pump housing. Tighten this fitting to specifications.

7. Reconnect the outlet fuel line to the outlet fitting, and tighten this fitting using two line wrenches.

8. Unplug or remove the clamp from the inlet fuel hose.

9. Start the engine and check the line and fittings for leakage.

Servicing or Replacing an In-line Filter— Sediment Bowl-Type

1. Loosen the screw in the bale wire at the base of the sediment bowl (Fig. 7–15).

2. Slip aside the bale wire, and remove the sediment bowl.

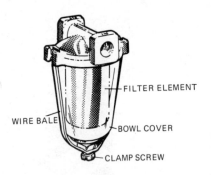

Fig. 7–15. *Removing and replacing an in-line sediment-bowl filter.*

3. Remove the filter element.

4. Remove the bowl gasket from the housing.

5. If the filter is the replaceable type, discard it; and insert a new one in place within the filter housing.

6. Or, wash the ceramic or metal element in acetone or a good carburetor-cleaning solution. Then, blow it dry with compressed air.

7. Insert the cleaned element into position within the housing.

8. Install a new bowl gasket in place in the filter housing.

9. Clean and dry the sediment bowl. Next, install the bowl in position on the housing.

10. Slide the bale wire under the sediment bowl, and tighten its retaining screw. *Caution:* Be careful not to over-tighten this screw because this can break the bowl or distort the housing.

11. Start the engine and check the filter for leaks.

Replacing an In-Line Disposable Filter

To change this type of filter (Fig. 7–16):

1. With a screwdriver or hose clamp pliers, remove the hose clamps on each end of the filter and vent hose, if so equipped. Then, slide the clamps over the metal lines.

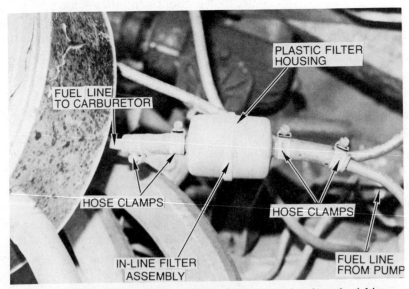

Fig. 7–16. *Removing and replacing a typical in-line fuel filter.*

2. Twist each hose back and forth until it slides off the line nipples on the filter.

3. Install a new filter over the end of the hose, on the line leading to the carburetor. Make sure that the arrow on the filter housing points toward the normal direction of fuel flow to the carburetor.

4. Insert the line hose over the other end of the filter. *Caution:* Do not push too hard on the filter housing when installing any hose because this can buckle the thin plastic or metal housing. If buckling occurs, the filter may leak or the element inside the housing may become restricted.

5. If removed, install the vapor hose over its nipple on the filter.

6. Install and tighten all clamps over their respective hoses.

7. Start the engine and check the filter and hoses for leaks.

Servicing or Replacing a Carburetor Inlet Filter

To replace this style of filter (Fig. 7-17):

1. Using two line wrenches, loosen and remove the inlet fuel line at the carburetor.

2. Loosen and remove the inlet fitting and both gaskets.

3. Remove the filter and spring.

4. If the filter element is ceramic or metal, clean it in acetone or a good carburetor-cleaning solution, and blow it dry with compressed air.

5. Install new gaskets on the inlet fitting, one on the inside and one over the threaded area of the fitting.

6. Install the cleaned or a new filter along with its spring into the carburetor

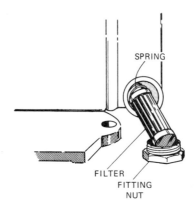

Fig. 7-17. Servicing or replacing a typical inlet filter at the carburetor.

inlet. *Caution:* Make sure that the open end of the filter faces outward or toward the fitting. If you install the filter backward, this will restrict the normal flow of fuel into the carburetor.

7. Thread the inlet fitting into the housing, and tighten it to specifications.

8. Reinstall the inlet fuel line into the inlet fitting; tighten its fitting, using two line wrenches.

9. Start the engine and check the fuel line and fittings for leakage.

Review

This section will assist you in determining how well you remember the material in this chapter. Read each item carefully. If you can't complete the statement, review the section in the chapter that covers the material.

1. One of the main reasons for taking off the fuel tank is to remove _____.
   a. pressure
   b. sediment
   c. lines
   d. filters

2. The component that secures the tank unit in place on the fuel tank is the
_____ _____.
   a. clamp screw
   b. unit strap
   c. cam lock
   d. line clamp

3. The fuel tank is held in place by _____
_____ _____.
   a. holddown straps
   b. cam locks
   c. threaded bolts
   d. bale wires

4. You should use a fuel _____
_____ to purge a fuel tank of vapor before attempting to repair it.
   a. and water
   b. soap detergent
   c. -cleaning solvent
   d. -emulsifying agent

5. When replacing a rigid fuel line, always use a piece of new seamless
_____ tubing.
   a. iron
   b. copper
   c. steel
   d. aluminum

6. You can use a _____ to repair a pinhole leak in a rigid fuel line.
   a. adapter
   b. connector
   c. union
   d. splice

7. During a tune-up, you should test the capacity and _____ of a fuel pump.
   a. pressure
   b. vacuum

   c. flow
   d. both b and c

8. If bubbles appear in the fuel container during the capacity test, there is a leak in the pump or _____
_____.
   a. carburetor inlet
   b. outlet filter
   c. tank line
   d. outlet line

9. The main problem in changing a mechanical fuel pump is the lack of adequate _____ _____.
   a. special tools
   b. work space
   c. service manuals
   d. hand tools

10. All fuel outlet filters should be serviced or changed at every _____ vehicle miles.
   a. 12,000
   b. 24,000
   c. 30,000
   d. 36,000

11. The bowl of a sediment bowl-type filter is held in place by a _____
_____.
   a. clamp screw
   b. retaining screw
   c. screw strap
   d. bale wire

12. The opening of a carburetor inlet fitting must face toward the _____
_____.
   a. line fitting
   b. float chamber
   c. fuel pump
   d. needle valve

For the answers, turn to the Appendix.

Function of the Air Cleaner

Every automotive engine comes factory-equipped with some form of air cleaner, situated on the atmosphere side of the carburetor (Fig. 8–1). This air cleaner serves three functions. It filters dust and grit from the air; it silences the noise produced by air velocity; and it acts as a flame arrester.

A great quantity of air moves through an engine as it is operating. As mentioned, this air mixes with fuel in the carburetor, and this combined mixture passes into the engine combustion chambers, where it ignites and burns. However, there are design limitations as to the proportions or ratios of air and gasoline. For example, 8 parts of air to 1 part of gasoline (8:1 ratio) is the richest mixture that will fire regularly in an engine. A mixture of 18.5 parts of air to 1 part of gasoline (18.5:1 ratio) is the leanest mixture that will fire without causing a miss in the engine.

During ideal operating conditions, the carburetor supplies a mixture ratio of about 15:1, that is, 15 pounds of air for each pound of gasoline. As a result, each

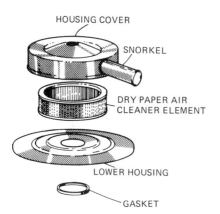

HOUSING COVER

SNORKEL

DRY PAPER AIR CLEANER ELEMENT

LOWER HOUSING

GASKET

Fig. 8–1. A typical air-cleaner housing and filter element.

Chapter 8

AIR CLEANERS AND THE PRINCIPLES OF CARBURETION

gallon of gasoline needs as much as 1,200 cubic feet of air for normal combustion within the engine. The end result is that the engine consumes as much as 100,000 cubic feet (2,831.7 cubic meters) of air every 1,000 vehicle miles (1,609.3 kilometers).

At this point, the reader may wonder why the need for so much air in the mixture. The answer is simple when you consider the actual makeup of the air from our atmosphere. The air that we breathe and the air used in the automobile engine have a mixture of 21 percent oxygen, 78 percent nitrogen, and 1 percent other gases. However, the *oxygen* in the air alone supports the combustion of the fuel. Consequently, the engine must take in a great deal of air along with the fuel, so that enough oxygen is available for complete combustion.

This is a great quantity of air, and it is very likely to contain large quantities of floating dust, grit, and, in areas, carbon particles. These contaminants cause serious damage to the engine components if permitted to enter the combustion chambers. The main problem that they cause is excessive piston-ring and cylinder-wall wear. But from the cylinders, the contaminants work their way down into the oil pan, where the oil circulates them around until the particles are caught in the oil filter. By this time, the abrasives have also damaged bearings and bearing surfaces. To prevent all this damage, each vehicle manufacturer installs on the engine an air cleaner that filters these particles from the air before they mix with the fuel in the carburetor.

The amount of abrasives in the air also varies from one region to another. For example, dust, dirt, and grit particle content in the air increase in agricultural and construction areas. In large metropolitan areas, where there is constant bumper-to-bumper traffic, the air contains large quantities of abrasive carbon particles from other vehicles' exhaust. This high concentration of contaminants in these areas clogs the air cleaner quite rapidly. As a result, the air cleaner requires frequent service to protect the engine properly from excessive wear and keep it operating properly.

The air cleaner due to its passageway design, silence chambers, or silencing pads muffles air noise. This noise results from the air moving at high speeds through the carburetor, intake manifold, and past the open intake valves. Without the air cleaner, this air noise could become quite noticeable at times and very annoying to the driver.

The air cleaner, due to its design, also functions as a flame arrester in case the engine backfires through the carburetor. Backfiring happens at certain times as a result of ignition of the air/fuel charge in the combustion chamber before the intake valves close. When this occurs, there is a momentary flash back through the intake manifold and carburetor. The air cleaner stops the resulting flame from erupting from the carburetor, where it could ignite fuel fumes outside the carburetor.

Air Cleaner Designs

Dry-Paper Type

There are five types of air-filtering devices or cleaners in use on passenger automobiles. Manufacturers classify each type of air cleaner by its filtering medium or element; these elements are dry paper, oil-wetted paper, oil bath, oil-wetted mesh, and oil-wetted polyurethane.

The *dry-paper filter* element is probably the most common filtering medium used inside the two-piece air-cleaner housing found on late-model automobiles (Fig. 8–2). The manufacturer constructs this element type from a chemically treated paper stock that contains tiny passages in the paper fibers. In addition, the paper is pleated to provide as much filtering area as possible. With this design, the air flow must take an indirect path through the various passages in the pleats in order to reach the entrance to the carburetor. As a result, the air passes through several fiber surfaces, each trapping microscopic particles of dust, grit, and carbon.

The manufacturer also forms the pleated element into a circle with the top and bottom edges sealed with a heat-resistant plastic or rubber gasket. These gaskets provide a leakproof seal between the ends of the element and the upper and lower components of the filter housing. Inside the circular element there may also be a fine wire screen that reduces the possibility of the element catching fire from an engine backfire. Also, on the outside of the filter ring may be a similar but coarser wire screen to reinforce the element and keep the oil fumes from ruining the relatively fragile dry-paper element.

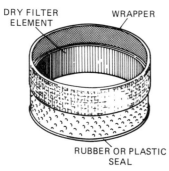

DRY FILTER ELEMENT   WRAPPER

RUBBER OR PLASTIC SEAL

Fig. 8–2. A common dry-paper filter element.

Oil-Wetted-Paper Type

The *oil-wetted-paper element* is quite similar in design to the dry-paper filter. In this case, however, the manufacturer uses an oil-wetted paper stock instead of dry paper. The light oil coating on the paper helps prevent the contaminants from working their way through the paper and increases the dust- and grit-holding capacity of this filter over an equal-size filter made from plain paper. Furthermore, some oil-wetted paper filters have an outer wrapper of polyurethane to increase the filtering capacity of the element.

Oil-Bath Type

The *oil-bath air cleaner* has been in use on motor vehicles for many years. This filter offers several advantages over any other type of air cleaner but also has several disadvantages. First of all, the mechanic can repeatedly clean and service the entire assembly without the customer having to buy additional parts. Over a long time, this saves the vehicle owner some money. Second, at higher engine speeds, this type of air cleaner provides two mediums for trapping contaminants in the air: an oil bath and a filter element. The only real drawbacks to the use of this filter are its initial cost and its overall size. The latter is a real design problem that eliminates this filter's use on most late-model vehicles with low-profile hoods. Also, this device has some negative operating characteristics, which are covered later in this chapter.

A typical oil-bath air cleaner (Fig. 8–3) consists of a reservoir and a filter assembly. The oil reservoir is part of the lower air-cleaner housing that usually fits directly over the carburetor. The reservoir

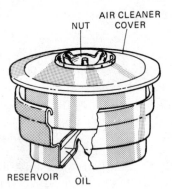

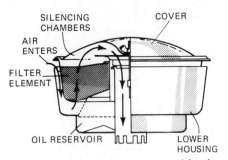

Fig. 8-3. The design of an oil-bath air cleaner.

Fig. 8-4. Operation of an oil-bath air cleaner.

holds a quantity of light engine oil, which traps particles as the air passes over the sump and provides an oil film for the element.

The air-cleaner cover contains several important components: the filtering element and the silencing chamber or pads. The filter itself may be steel wool, copper gauze, loosely packed fibers, or even curled animal hair. In any case, the manufacturer forms the filter into the structure of the cover, and the technician cannot remove it as a single unit. Consequently, when the filter requires cleaning, the mechanic must wash it out, being careful not to get solvent into the silencing chambers.

The cover also has some type of silencing device to muffle the sound of the air flow. This device may be in the form of a metal silencing chamber or a silencing pad, usually made of felt.

Oil-Bath Air-Cleaner Operation

When the engine is running, engine vacuum draws air into the air-cleaner housing (Fig. 8-4). As the air enters the cleaner, it moves down the area between the inside surface of the lower housing and the outer surface of the cover toward the surface of the pool of oil in the reservoir. Then, the air makes a U-turn over the pool of oil and goes up into the filtering element that sits slightly above the oil pool.

When the air flow makes this first U-turn, centrifugal force throws out some of the contaminants, which the pool of oil traps. If the air is moving fast enough, it also picks up some of the oil in mist form and carries it into the filter element, where the air leaves the oil mist and finer particles embedded. The oil then drains back into the reservoir from the filter, carrying some of the trapped particles with it, in a self-cleaning action.

After the air passes through the element, it passes through the upper portion of the cover. Then, the air rams into the silencing chamber or silencing pad and makes a second U-turn where the air finally enters a passage leading to the carburetor.

There are two negative operating characteristics of this type of filter. First, because the spacing between the metal, fiber, or hair strands is variable, some particles can penetrate the element, especially at low engine rpm, where the air flow is lower. Second, the two U-turns that the air flow must take within the assembly cause a lot of restriction that is not found in other filter designs.

Oil-Wetted Mesh Type

An *oil-wetted mesh element* is probably the least effective filtering medium. This filter fits inside a two-piece housing (Fig. 8–5). The lower housing mounts over the carburetor and supports the filter element. The housing cover that fits over the element and lower housing contains a silencing chamber or pad.

The manufacturer may form this circular element from several types of materials such as steel wool or copper gauge. Then, the element receives a very thin coating of light engine oil. The oil assists the filter in trapping large contaminants.

There are several advantages and one major disadvantage to using this type of filter. The oil-wetted filter assembly has the advantages of taking up very little under-the-hood space and being serviceable. However, since the element has rather large spacing between its strands, smaller abrasive particles can easily slip through the element and enter the engine.

Oil-Wetted Polyurethane Type

Oil-wetted polyurethane, sometimes called a *foam filter,* is usually interchange-

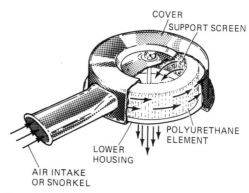

Fig. 8–6. An air-cleaner assembly with a polyurethane filter element over a metal support screen.

able with a dry-filter element. In other words, the same model vehicle comes from the same factory with either type of element installed in the same style of housing (Fig. 8–6). Each filter does as good a job as the other. However, the polyurethane element is serviceable, while the dry filter is not.

The polyurethane element consists of a polyurethane wrapper stretched across a metal support screen. The polyurethane material contains thousands of pores and interconnecting strands that create a mazelike particle trap, while still permitting air to flow through the material. The filter can function satisfactorily when dry or when lightly oiled. Finally, polyurethane elements are not as common on late-model vehicles as factory equipment, but some manufacturers still produce and sell them as after-market equipment.

Air-Cleaner Inlet Ducts

The main source of air to the carburetor is through the *air ducts* in the air-cleaner housing. In the oil-bath air cleaner (Fig. 8–3) and the wetted-mesh filter (Fig. 8–5),

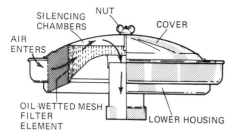

Fig. 8–5. A wetted-mesh–type air-cleaner assembly.

the air duct was the area formed between the cover and lower housing. However, most other filter designs use some form of extended *air intake* or *snorkel* made into the cover assembly (Fig. 8–6).

This snorkel serves several functions other than just being the air intake for the carburetor. First, the snorkel increases the velocity of the air flow entering the air cleaner. Second, the location of the snorkel is such that cooler air can enter the air cleaner and carburetor than without an extended air duct. This action is extremely important when temperatures in the engine compartment exceed 200°F. (93°C.) on a hot day because this hot air can thin out and heat the air/fuel mixture enough to cause detonation. Permitting the engine to consume cooler air prevents this situation.

The air intake snorkel shown in Fig. 8–6 is usually open to the air flow near the front of the engine and the fan. In other installations this snorkel attaches to a cold air duct or induction tube. This duct or tube runs from the snorkel itself to a fresh

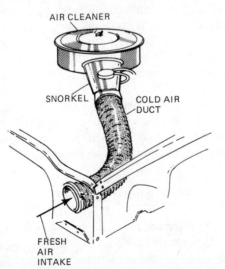

AIR CLEANER

SNORKEL   COLD AIR DUCT

FRESH AIR INTAKE

Fig. 8–7. Some snorkels attach to a fresh air intake.

air intake at the front of the vehicle (Fig. 8–7), in the cowl, or in the rear area of the hood. This air intake is usually open at all times, although it usually has some type of screen over it to prevent insects and other foreign material from entering the air cleaner.

Thermostatically Controlled Air Cleaners

It would seem that an engine should operate at all times on air that is as cool as possible; however, this is not the case. Engineers have found that by controlling air intake temperatures within certain limits a vehicle warms up faster, the automatic choke opens sooner, the air/fuel mixture does not vary as much when the outside air temperature raises and lowers, and the problem of carburetor icing minimizes.

For these reasons, beginning in 1957 some automobiles came from the factory with some type of thermostatic control on their air cleaners to regulate intake air temperature. However, since these devices maintain a more precise air/fuel mixture during all phases of engine operation, an air-temperature control mechanism is part of the air cleaner assembly found on all late-model automobiles to form a part of its exhaust emission control system. This text covers these controls in the chapter on exhaust emission control devices.

Principles of Carburetion

Up to this point, this text has covered the manner by which the fuel system stores the fuel, filters the fuel, delivers the fuel to the carburetor, and cleans the air entering the carburetor. Now we turn our attention to the carburetor and explain how this unit functions to convert the liquid gasoline into a highly combustible mixture.

A *carburetor* is a metering device that mixes fuel with air in the correct proportion and delivers this mixture to the intake manifold, where it delivers the air/fuel mixture to the various combustion chambers. *Metering*, in this situation, means that components within the carburetor accurately measure and control the flow of fuel and air passing through the various carburetor systems.

The engine must have some form of metering device when its source of fuel for power is gasoline. In a liquid state, gasoline is of very little use to the engine. Contrary to popular belief, gasoline in a liquid state is not combustible; only gasoline vapor burns. Therefore, the carburetor or another metering device must combine the gasoline properly with the correct amount of air in order for the combustion process to release the energy in the gasoline.

Functions of the Carburetor

The function of any carburetor found on a gasoline engine (Fig. 8-8) is to meter, atomize, and distribute the fuel throughout the air flow passing into the engine. The manufacturer designs the carburetor in such a way that it carries out all of these functions automatically over a wide range of operating conditions such as varying engine speeds, loads, and operating temperatures.

The carburetor also must regulate the amount of this air/fuel mixture that flows

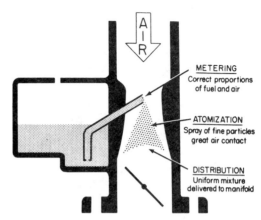

Fig. 8-8. The three basic functions of the carburetor. (Courtesy of General Motors Corp.)

into the intake manifold. This regulation gives the driver the necessary control of the speed (rpm) of the engine.

Metering

As stated, good combustion requires the correct mixture ratio between the air and fuel, commonly known as the *air/fuel ratio*. This ratio is necessary for the combustion process to release all the possible energy contained in the gasoline. An excessive proportion of fuel in the ratio results in a "rich" mixture; whereas, too little fuel brings about a "lean" mixture. The metering task of any carburetor then is to furnish the correct air/fuel ratio for all operating conditions, so that the operation of the engine is not excessively lean to meet its power requirements or too rich for economy while still meeting the prime requirements of low emission. (See Figure 8-9.)

Atomization

The carburetor must not only meter the amounts of air and fuel entering the engine but also atomize the fuel. *Atomiza-*

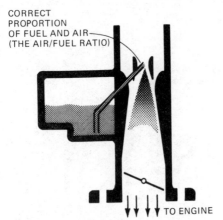

Fig. 8–9. *The carburetor must provide the correct proportion of fuel and air to the engine.*

tion simply means the breakdown of the liquid into very small droplets or particles so that it can easily mix with air and vaporize. As the carburetor breaks the fuel into these small droplets, this action permits additional air contact with the liquid fuel. The greater the air contact, the easier the fuel turns into a vapor inside the intake manifold.

Atomization occurs within the carburetor in several ways. For example, Fig. 8–10 shows air being bled into the liquid fuel as it travels through a given carburetor passage or circuit. The entrance of this air into the liquid fuel creates a turbulence that breaks the solid stream of fuel into smaller droplets.

Figure 8–11 illustrates fuel discharging

from a carburetor fuel nozzle. This nozzle is at a point in the carburetor, where the air flow reaches its greatest velocity. In this situation, the velocity of the air stream actually tears the fuel apart, which forms it into a fine spray of droplets. The resulting atomized air/fuel mixture then moves into the intake manifold.

Distribution and Vaporization

For excellent combustion and smooth engine operation, the carburetor must thoroughly mix the air and fuel together, and the intake manifold must uniformly distribute this mixture in equal quantities to all the engine's combustion chambers. Adequate distribution of the mixture requires good vaporization. *Vaporization* is the act of changing a liquid, such as gasoline, into a gas, and *this change of state only occurs when the liquid absorbs sufficient heat to boil.*

A gaseous air/fuel mixture travels much more easily around corners in the manifold and engine while liquid particles, being relatively heavy, attempt to continue in one direction and collide with the walls of the manifold itself or move on to

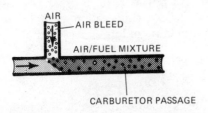

Fig. 8–10. *Atomization of liquid fuel in a carburetor passage.*

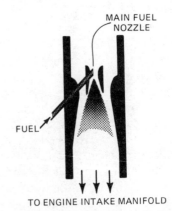

Fig. 8–11. *Atomization of fuel at a fuel nozzle.*

another cylinder. For example, consider the action within a half of the intake manifold of a six-cylinder engine shown in Fig. 8–12. In this illustration, the carburetor (not shown) mounts on the center of the intake manifold to the left of cylinder 4. The air/fuel mixture for cylinders 4, 5, and 6 initially moves toward the rear of the engine.

If cylinder 5 is on its intake stroke, its vacuum draws the air/fuel mixture sharply around a corner and into the cylinder, at a right angle to the mixture's original direction. Any large droplets of gasoline cannot make such a sharp turn and therefore continue in their normal direction to the rear of the manifold, where the vacuum from cylinder 6 will probably draw them in during its intake stroke. As a result, cylinder 5 receives a leaner mixture and cylinder 6 receives a richer mixture than they should.

It should be very obvious, then, that the air/fuel mixture must be in a complete vapor form for even and adequate distribution to all the cylinders. This vaporization process takes place in the intake manifold (Fig. 8–13) due to several factors. First, since the pressure within the intake manifold is far less than that of the atmosphere, this lower pressure considerably reduces the boiling point of gasoline.

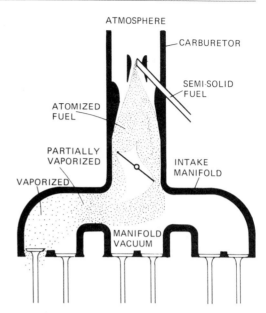

Fig. 8–13. Fuel as it moves through the carburetor is atomized and then vaporized in the intake manifold.

Second, the existing temperature of the air particles along with a heated manifold floor produces sufficient heat to boil and vaporize the gasoline faster at this lower pressure. This text covers how the intake manifold floor receives heat.

Because complete fuel vaporization is the result of many factors such as outside air temperatures, fuel temperatures, manifold vacuum, and intake manifold temperatures, it should be quite apparent that anything that reduces any one of these factors will adversely alter the vaporization process and therefore reduce engine power and fuel economy plus increase harmful exhaust emissions. Some of the conditions that interfere with proper vaporization are cold weather, inoperative heat-riser valve, high overlap camshaft, and heavy throttle demands.

The effects from lower outside temperatures and an inoperative heat-riser valve should be obvious—a reduction in the

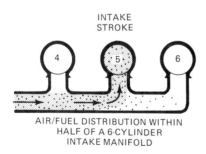

Fig. 8–12. Fuel distribution within a portion of a six-cylinder engine intake manifold.

temperature of air and fuel particles not only as they enter the intake manifold but during the distribution process. Equally detrimental to proper vaporization is the reduction of manifold vacuum either by valve timing or heavy throttle accelera- tion. These conditions produce higher pressures within the intake manifold and consequently a higher boiling point for the fuel. As a result, the amount of fuel vapor- ization that does occur, by the time the air/fuel charge enters the combustion chamber, is lower. The mixture, not vapor- ized at the time of induction, exhausts in an unburned state from the combustion chamber and causes high hydrocarbon ex- haust emissions, a reduction in power, and a lowering of fuel economy.

Air-Fuel Requirements

As stated, the carburetor must provide an air/fuel mixture within the range of 8:1 and 18.5:1 in order for an engine to run. For the sake of efficiency, the engine should utilize a ratio that produces peak power output, minimum emissions, and peak fuel economy. Unfortunately, no *single* air/fuel ratio permits an engine to meet all these conditions (Fig. 8–14). For instance, tests have proven that the best engine power output comes from using a 12:5 to 13.5:1 mixture; whereas, the best fuel economy results from using a 15 to 16:1 mixture. Since no single fuel ratio is satisfactory, the carburetor must quickly match the varying engine load require- ments with the best possible air/fuel mix- ture in order to achieve the most efficient operating conditions. This simply means that the carburetor not only must provide a ratio to meet power demands, caused by such things as light-speed variations and changing engine load conditions, but also

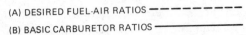

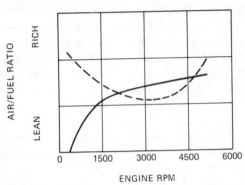

Fig. 8–14. *The carburetor must provide varying air/fuel ratios to meet the engine load requirements, achieve minimum emis- sions, and provide reasonable fuel econ- omy.*

provide reasonable fuel economy and min- imum exhaust emissions.

One of the main reasons why the car- buretor must vary the air/fuel ratios is the imperfect conditions within the combus- tion chambers. For example, exhaust gases remaining in the combustion cham- bers dilute the incoming fresh air/fuel charge. In addition, there are times when the carburetor does not properly mix the air and fuel together. As a result, tiny droplets of unvaporized fuel move into the combustion chamber, carried along by the mixture of air and evaporated fuel. Fi- nally, the intake manifold itself does not always deliver equal air/fuel mixtures to all the cylinders.

Power Versus Economy

If the engine is to produce maximum power, it is necessary to burn all the oxy- gen contained in the air/fuel mixture.

Since the power-production ability of an engine has design limitations, due to the amount of air it can take in, the carburetor must add additional fuel to the mixture to ensure that each oxygen molecule has sufficient fuel for its complete combustion. Therefore, the air/fuel ratio for maximum power usually falls into the range from 12 to 13.5:1. This, of course, is "richer" in gasoline content than the theoretical ratio of 15:1 for good performance and economy.

On the other hand, for maximum fuel economy along with the least harmful emissions, the engine must burn as much of the fuel from the mixture as possible, thereby extracting as much energy as possible from it and leaving minimum residue. But due to the various poor combustion chamber conditions, additional air is necessary in the mixture to ensure that each molecule of fuel has sufficient oxygen to burn efficiently. Consequently, the actual air/fuel ratio for maximum economy (about 16 to 17:1) tends to be somewhat "leaner" in gasoline content than the 15:1 ratio calculated for chemically perfect combustion.

The best air/fuel mixture for any given operating range varies from engine to engine. This is due to the differences in intake manifold design, combustion chamber design, valve timing, ignition timing, and other design factors. The best way to determine the optimum mixture for an engine is to operate it on a dynamometer, where engine power, speed, and fuel consumption are measurable over a wide range of operating conditions.

Dynamometer tests, performed at speeds throughout the engine's operating range, reveal that the air/fuel ratio for maximum power remains nearly the same at all except low rpm (Fig. 8-15). At low rpm, slightly additional enrichment of the

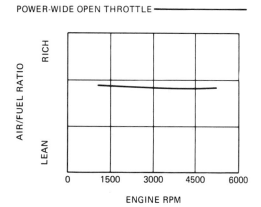

Fig. 8-15. *The air/fuel ratio during full or wide-open throttle operation.*

mixture is necessary for two reasons: (1) the effect of exhaust-gas dilution of the air/fuel mixture within the combustion chamber and (2) the inadequate mixing and distribution of the air/fuel mixture due to the reduced velocity of the air flow into the engine.

In a similar way, leaner air/fuel ratios at part-throttle operation that are necessary for maximum economy are essentially the same throughout most of this operating range (Fig. 8-16). Again, enrichment of

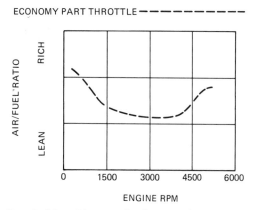

Fig. 8-16. *The air/fuel ratio during part-throttle engine operation.*

POWER-WIDE OPEN THROTTLE ————————
ECONOMY PART THROTTLE — — — — — — — —

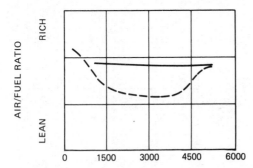

Fig. 8-17. A comparison of the air/fuel ratios at both full- and part-throttle engine operation.

the air/fuel ratio is necessary at idle and low engine rpm. During idle rpm, the air/fuel ratio usually is in the range from about 11:1 to 12.5 to 1. Also, richer mixtures are necessary at high operating speeds and loads, where the engine must produce additional power. Finally, carburetors are set up in such a manner that the engine achieves its best fuel mileage during normal cruising at part throttle. The engine achieves maximum power when the driver opens the throttle for acceleration or top speed (Fig. 8-17).

Cold Starting

This chapter has covered the engine's need for both a vaporized mixture and the various ratios necessary for efficient combustion. This leaves only one question requiring clarification. That is, why are richer fuel mixtures necessary for cold engine starting?

If you recall, it is necessary that the fuel vaporizes completely in order for it to reach and be burned easily in the combustion chamber. One of the main factors necessary for proper fuel vaporization is heat, especially in the intake manifold. However, when the driver starts a cold engine, this heat is not yet available. Consequently, the fuel entering the combustion chambers is not in a vaporized state or is only partially vaporized.

To offset this problem, the carburetor has a *choke* (Fig. 8-18). This device restricts the air flow through the carburetor to the intake manifold, thereby enriching the air/fuel mixture. This enriched fuel charge is necessary so that the total resultant fuel vapor reaching the cylinders will be rich enough to create a combustible mixture.

Many people assume that this richer mixture actually burns completely during cold-engine operation, but this is definitely not the case. Although the air/fuel ratio varies during the different phases of engine operation, the fuel itself always burns at 15:1 ratio. While this combustion ratio seems contrary to the actual air/fuel mixture supplied to the engine by the carburetor, the key to ideal combustion and this 15:1 ratio is vaporization. Since only

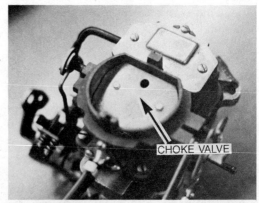

Fig. 8-18. The choke valve restricts the air flow through the carburetor, thereby enriching the air/fuel mixture.

vaporized fuel burns, any condition of engine operation, like cold starting, that reduces adequate vaporization makes it necessary for the carburetor to supply an enriched mixture. This mixture then contains sufficient vapors to get the cold engine started.

For the most part, the unused fuel that did not vaporize passes out of the engine during the exhaust cycle. While this represents a considerable waste of fuel and creates exhaust emission problems, an overly rich mixture is necessary to provide a combustible fuel mixture until the engine warms up.

Principles of Carburetor Operation

Practically speaking, there are tremendous differences between carburetors designed for various automobile models. In addition, the linkages, assist devices, and various controls on all carburetors can vary widely, even between two automobiles of the same make and model but with different engines. Yet all carburetors work on the same basic principles. Therefore, once the basic operating principles of one carburetor type have been mastered, the reader can apply this information and be able to understand all other types of carburetors.

Carburetors of all designs operate on the basic principle of a pressure differential. In this case, *pressure differential* refers to the difference in air pressure between the atmospheric and some other unit. For example, a pressure differential exists between the atmosphere and the intake manifold when the engine is operating. As this chapter explains, a difference in pressure can also exist between the at-

mosphere and the venturi inside an operating carburetor.

Any pressure lower than the atmosphere is known as a *vacuum* or *low-pressure area*. When a person sucks on a straw (Fig. 8-19), this action removes the air from the straw. This in turn creates a low-pressure area or vacuum on the end of the straw.

Atmospheric pressure above the liquid in the container is greater than on the discharge end of the straw. The weight, or pressure, of the outside air on the surface of the liquid in the container forces the liquid up the straw in order to fill the void or vacuum. The most important thing to understand is that the vacuum does not pull the fluid up the straw. Instead, the atmospheric pressure pushes the liquid into the void or low-pressure area.

The same action occurs in a gasoline engine. As the piston moves down on its intake stroke with the intake valve opened, this action creates a vacuum in the intake manifold. Atmospheric pressure pushes air through the carburetor, intake manifold, and past the open intake valve in an

ATMOSPHERIC
PRESSURE APPLIED
TO TOP OF LIQUID

LOW PRESSURE
(VACUUM) DEVELOPED
INSIDE MOUTH

Fig. 8-19.   The vacuum principle.

attempt to fill this vacuum or void with air.

A vacuum gauge, with a scale calibrated in inches of mercury (Hg), is necessary to measure engine intake-manifold vacuum. The higher this gauge reading is, the less air pressure exists in the intake manifold. As a result, there is a greater pressure differential between the atmosphere and the inside of the intake manifold. This pressure difference is the force that causes the fuel and air to pass through the carburetor circuitry because the fuel and air always travel from the high- to the low-pressure area.

Venturi Principles

The carburetor requires another device to reduce air pressure during times of reduced engine vacuum. This device is known as a venturi (Fig. 8–20). The *venturi* is nothing more than a curved, hourglass-shaped restriction placed at the inner diameter of the carburetor throat. The *carburetor throat* is the area through which the air enters and passes through the carburetor on its way to the intake manifold. With this design, all incoming air must pass through the venturi on its way to the manifold and combustion chambers.

The venturi then forms a restriction to the path of this air flow. This reduction in area forces the speed of the air to increase as it moves through the venturi. Since the same volume of air molecules flows through all sections of the throat at the same speed, the air molecules must speed up and separate in order to get through the venturi.

Since the air molecules not only speed up but also separate as they move through the venturi, this action reduces the pressure of the air or creates a low-pressure area. The greatest low-pressure area or vacuum is at the point of maximum restriction within the venturi.

At this point of greater pressure drop, the manufacturer installs the tip of a *fuel nozzle* (Fig. 8–21). The other end of the nozzle is in a *fuel reservoir*, the float chamber of the carburetor. This chamber is open to the atmosphere.

With a low-pressure area or vacuum at the tip of the nozzle and atmospheric pressure over the fuel in the bowl, fuel moves through the nozzle. This fuel movement is due to atmospheric pressure pushing the fuel through the nozzle in an attempt to fill the void or low-pressure area in the venturi. The more air that flows through the carburetor throat, the greater is the vacuum in the venturi. The higher the vacuum, the greater is the fuel flow up to design limitations.

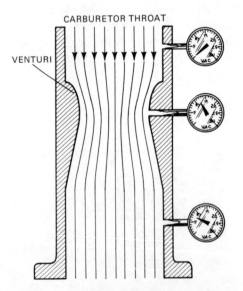

CARBURETOR THROAT

VENTURI

Fig. 8–20. The venturi principle. Note how the amount of vacuum varies through the different sections of the carburetor throat.

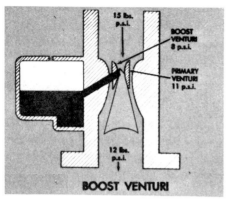

Fig. 8-21. The location of the main fuel nozzle is in the area within the venturi, where vacuum will be the greatest. (Courtesy of General Motors Corp.)

To be most effective, the venturi must have a design of certain curvature and length. The manufacturer can design a venturi to provide fuel flow under any condition of air flow. However, a small venturi restricts high rpm engine operation, while a large venturi does not produce sufficient pressure differential for low-speed operation. The production venturi size then is usually a compromise design that provides adequately for both low- and high-speed operation.

Most modern carburetors utilize a primary as well as one or more boost venturies (Fig. 8-21). Manufacturers usually locate the boost venturi over the primary venturi, with the discharge end of the boost within the low-pressure area of the primary. The function of the boost venturi is to reduce further the air pressure at the nozzle. The additional venturi(es) are necessary for finer control of the pressure drop at the fuel nozzle, thereby making the fuel delivery at the nozzle more active at lower engine rpm.

In addition, the boost venturies tend to create an airstream that holds the dis-

charging air/fuel mixture from the nozzle away from the throat walls, where it would slow down and begin to condense. This action reduces a tendency for icing on the throat walls and around the throttle valve and creates an air turbulence that results in improved mixing and finer atomization of the fuel. However, additional venturies tend to restrict the air flow to the engine at high engine rpm.

Basic Carburetor Systems

All carburetors perform a comparatively simple task but must do so under various conditions. Therefore, the carburetor must have many systems to alter its functions to adjust to the various operating conditions of the engine. Although some carburetors only have five, most units contain six basic systems: the float system, idle system, main metering system, power system, pump system, and choke system.

Float System

The *float system* is perhaps one of the most important systems in the carburetor. The float system is responsible for storing and supplying an adequate amount of clean fuel to the various other operating systems of the carburetor. In doing so, the float system also regulates the fuel flow output from the fuel pump.

While performing all of these tasks, the float system must maintain the fuel level in the float chamber at a precise, nearly constant level. This level is very critical since it determines the fuel level in all the other passages or circuits within the carburetor. A fuel level too high in the float chamber can produce an overly rich air/fuel mixture. On the other hand, a level that is too low can produce, at times, an overly lean air/fuel mixture.

Remember that the main fuel nozzle (Fig. 8-21) fits between the center of the venturi and the base of the fuel chamber or bowl. Since liquids (like fuel) seek their own level in any container, the fuel in the nozzle is at the same level as the fuel within the bowl. If this level is too high, liquid fuel can splash or siphon into the carburetor throat, or venturi vacuum will cause premature or excessive fuel movement from the fuel chamber to the tip of the nozzle. Whereas, a low fuel level results in insufficient amounts of fuel delivery from the fuel nozzle.

Float-System Design

The float system (Fig. 8-22) consists of a bowl, float, needle and seat, along with a float-bowl vent. The *float chamber* or *bowl* is cast as part of the main carburetor housing. This bowl is nothing more than a

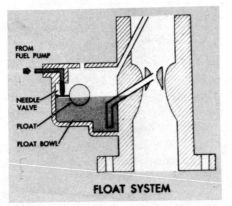

FLOAT SYSTEM

Fig. 8-22.   The float system components of a typical single-barrel (throat) carburetor. (Courtesy of General Motors Corp.)

chamber or reservoir that stores the fuel necessary to feed the other carburetor circuits. Also, some fuel bowls have *baffles,* which keep the liquid fuel from sloshing around in the chamber when the vehicle is on rough roads or makes sharp turns. Excessive fuel movement can cause premature fuel delivery through the nozzle tip.

Late-model carburetor bowls also have a device to curb evaporation losses. When an engine is shut off, its heat can cause some of the fuel in the bowl to evaporate. This was not a big problem before the advent of vapor emission control devices because these fuel vapors just vented into the atmosphere. However, with the installation of a vapor canister, a component of the vapor control system, the amount of evaporation from a large fuel bowl can quite easily overload the canister. To offset this problem, many late-model carburetors have a somewhat smaller capacity bowl. In addition, some carburetors utilize a molded plastic fuel bowl, which reduces heat evaporation due to the fact that plastic is not as good a heat conductor as metal. Finally, other installations use an *insulator* (Fig. 8-23) between the intake manifold and carburetor in order to reduce heat transfer between the two units.

Operating inside the fuel bowl is the *float assembly.* The purpose of this device is to apply force to the *needle valve* (Fig. 8-22). The float portion of the assembly attaches to a linkage arm that pivots in the float bowl on a hinge pin. The linkage arm acts as a lever to increase the force of the float on the needle valve. Because the float is a hollow metallic, plastic, or wood object sealed with a fuel-resistant compound, it has sufficient buoyancy to float in the fuel. As a result, the float assembly

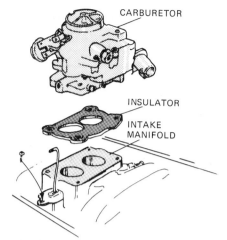

CARBURETOR

INSULATOR

INTAKE
MANIFOLD

Fig. 8-23. An insulator between the intake manifold and carburetor reduces heat transfer between the two units.

moves up or down on its hinge pin as the fuel level changes; this, in turn, alters the force on the needle valve.

Some carburetors have only a single float while others use a double-pontoon float assembly. The double float provides, along with the needle valve, a more positive control of the fuel level in the carburetor whenever a vehicle is operating off its normal axis such as on a steep, banked curve. With the dual-float arrangement, at least one float is always in the fuel to maintain the correct level in the bowl. Finally, many float assemblies have some springs, which keep them from bobbing up and down in the fuel as the vehicle travels over rough roads.

The needle and its seat form the *inlet valve* for the float system. The needle usually has a point machined on one end that bears against a machined mating area in the seat. The opposite end of the needle rests on the float arm. As the float itself moves up or down within the fuel,

the needle moves up into or away from its seat. When the needle is against the seat, no fuel enters the bowl; whereas, when the needle moves away from the seat, fuel enters the bowl in proportion to the clearance between the two.

Manufacturers usually produce the needle and seat from stainless steel or brass. In older vehicles, the needle was steel while the seat was brass. Some steel needles also had a rubber tip, or the seating area was rubber instead of all brass.

However, steel often attracted metallic particles from the fuel. The particles would collect between the needle point and its seat and create a leak. The addition of rubberized tips and seats helped this particular problem but did not eliminate it completely. Consequently, many of the modern needles and seats are brass with the needles often having plastic tips that, like the rubber ones, conform to any rough spots on the seat while still providing a good seal when the valve closes.

Float System Operation

As the engine starts, the carburetor begins to deliver fuel from its circuits, and the fuel level in the bowl drops. As the fuel level goes down, the float assembly also moves downward on its hinge pin. This action releases the force on the base of the needle valve. As a result, fuel pump pressure pushes the valve off its seat, and fuel enters the bowl through the opening between the needle tip and seat.

As the level in the bowl rises, the buoyant action of the float causes it also to move upward. When the float assembly reaches a predetermined level, it applies sufficient force on the base of the needle to seat it. This action cuts off the fuel flow to the bowl from the pump.

When the engine is constantly operating, there is a given amount of fuel always leaving the bowl area. In this situation, the float assembly drops enough to unseat the needle a slight amount. Now, the fuel pump supplies the bowl with the same amount of fuel that the engine is consuming at this particular point.

Float-Bowl Ventilation

The float bowl, above the level of the fuel, must have a vent to the atmosphere. Atmospheric pressure is necessary over the fuel to provide the high pressure necessary to push the fuel into the venturi and other low-pressure areas. Most carburetors have two types of vents: internal and external.

The *internal vent* or *balance tube* opens the fuel bowl to the air from an area of the carburetor above the choke valve (Fig. 8–24). The function of this vent is to equalize the effects of a clogged or restricted air cleaner. For instance, suppose that some dust and grit have clogged the

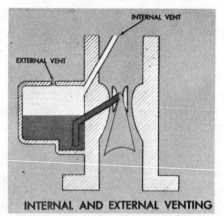

INTERNAL AND EXTERNAL VENTING

Fig. 8–24. A float system with two vents: one internal and the other external. (Courtesy of General Motors Corp.)

air cleaner element; this restricts the air flow through the element. As a result, a partial vacuum develops in the throat of the carburetor, which adds to the vacuum developed by the venturi. This action causes excessive fuel flow from the nozzle.

However, the internal vent also applies this same partial throat vacuum to the fuel bowl. Consequently, the atmospheric pressure in the bowl pushes some air through the vent to fill this void or vacuum. This action results in a reduction in air pressure above the fuel level in the bowl. Therefore, the fuel flow from the nozzle is more normal because the internal vent has balanced the air pressures between the top of the carburetor throat and the fuel bowl.

The *external vent*, as its name implies, permits atmospheric pressure outside the carburetor to enter the fuel bowl. But at the same time, it allows gasoline vapors (hydrocarbons) to escape from the fuel bowl. This adds harmful pollution to the atmosphere. However, an external carburetor vent is necessary to prevent fuel percolation. *Percolation* is the build up of vapor pressure due to heat expansion or boiling of the fuel in the bowl as a result of heat radiation from the engine. This vapor pressure (percolation) can force raw fuel from the bowl through the fuel nozzle and into the intake manifold. The result is a flooded engine and an empty fuel bowl, either of which causes hard starting.

In some older carburetors, an antipercolator valve controlled the opening of the external vent. When the engine was shut off or idling, carburetor linkage opened the valve. This allowed fuel vapors to escape to the atmosphere. As a result, there were fewer vapors entering the intake manifold, and the engine would start and idle better. Finally, during above-idle operating speeds, carburetor linkage closed the valve, and the internal vent took over the task of supplying air pressure to the float bowl.

Since 1970, the majority of automotive carburetor external vents connect into a vapor control system. This system still permits the admittance of atmospheric pressure over the fuel level and prevents fuel percolation by allowing vapor pressure to escape from the bowl. But in the latter case, the vapor system stops the hydrocarbons from reaching the atmosphere. This text covers this system in detail in another chapter.

Idle and Low-Speed System

Function

All automotive carburetors require some form of idle and low-speed system. This system is necessary to provide the proper air/fuel ratios required to operate the engine at idle and during low-speed operation. During these phases of engine operation, air flow through the carburetor is very slight due to the nearly closed position of the throttle valve (Fig. 8–25). The *throttle valve* is a round disc in the lower carburetor casting that when rotated admits more or less air flow through the carburetor throat, thereby controlling engine speed. With the throttle valve nearly closed, air flow through the venturi is insufficient to cause the main nozzle to deliver fuel.

Design

The idle and low-speed system consists of an idle tube, idle passages, idle air bleeds, off-idle discharge ports, idle-mixture–adjusting needle or screw, and the idle discharge port or hole. The *idle tube* fits into the main fuel well within the carburetor. This well connects by a passage to the fuel bowl; therefore, it has the same level of fuel as the bowl. The idle tube itself is nothing more than a calibrated tube or passageway into which the fuel from the main well enters and proceeds to the other passages of the idle system. Since the tube is a form of restriction, it limits the quantity of liquid fuel entering the system.

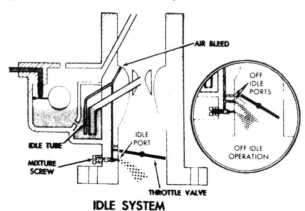

IDLE SYSTEM

Fig. 8–25. The idle and low-speed system of a typical carburetor. (Courtesy of General Motors Corp.)

The *idle passages* carry the liquid and atomized fuel from the idle tube to the *off-idle* and *idle-discharge ports*. These passages also index with the upper air bleed. An *air bleed* is an opening into any fuel passageway through which air can pass or bleed into the gasoline as it moves through the passage. The entrance of air into the fuel breaks the fuel into droplets or bubbles containing both air and gasoline, and is the first step toward completely atomizing the fuel.

The idle and low-speed system usually has two or more air bleeds. In Fig. 8–25, the carburetor has two: the top as well as the off-idle ports. The air bleed supplies air to the idle passage during both idle and low-speed (off-idle) operation. The off-idle ports only serve as an additional air bleed to the passage during idle operation.

The off-idle ports act for a time as an air bleed, but they also are discharge ports for the air/fuel mixture. These ports discharge atomized fuel as the driver accelerates the engine past idle rpm by depressing the throttle pedal. This action, by means of linkage, cracks the throttle valve open slightly.

The *mixture screw* or *needle* regulates the quantity of the fuel mixture discharged from the idle discharge port or hole. As the mechanic turns the screw in, the quantity of fuel flow from the port reduces, which leans out the total air/fuel mixture entering the intake manifold. As the screw is turned outward, flow increases from the idle port and the total mixture is therefore richer. Finally, this adjustment screw has no effect on the quantity of fuel flow from the off-idle ports.

However, the overall travel on this adjustment screw now has certain limits. After flow-testing the carburetor, the manufacturer limits the adjustability of the mixture by installing limiter caps over the adjustment screw. The reason for this action is to maintain a lean idle air/fuel mixture in order to reduce harmful exhaust emissions. Consequently, the technician should never remove the caps unless necessary to service the carburetor *or when additional adjustment is necessary to correct excessive exhaust emissions.*

Operation

In the idle position, the throttle valve is only slightly open. This permits only a small amount of air to pass between the wall of the carburetor throat and the edge of the throttle valve. Since at this point there is insufficient air flow for venturi action, fuel flow within the idle system is the result of intake manifold vacuum acting directly on the idle-discharge port, through the idle system, and on the fuel in the fuel bowl.

This low pressure (vacuum) below the throttle valve and atmospheric pressure above the level of the fuel in the bowl force the liquid gasoline through the idle tube and into the idle passage. Near the top right side of the passage (Fig. 8–25), the fuel mixes with air from the top air bleed. This action constitutes the first stage of fuel atomization. The mixture then continues down the passage, past the off-idle port, where the mixture picks up additional air that further breaks up the mixture. The mixture finally flows past the tip of the mixture screw and sprays into the carburetor throat, where the passing air carries it into the intake manifold.

As the driver depresses the accelerator pedal past the idle position, the throttle valve opens; and additional air flows through the carburetor. Since the air flow at this point is still insufficient to cause a fuel discharge from the venturi nozzle, the increased air velocity results in an excessively lean mixture. To compensate for this problem, atomized fuel must begin to discharge from the off-idle or low-speed port (Fig. 8–25).

Moving the throttle slightly open, past the idle position, exposes the off-idle discharge ports to intake manifold vacuum. At this point, the ports stop acting as additional air bleeds and begin to discharge atomized fuel. Thus, the off-idle or low-speed port openings have a dual purpose. At idle they act as an air bleed; but during low-speed operation, these ports discharge an atomized fuel mixture into the passing air flow.

Both the idle and off-idle ports are necessary to provide the smooth transition between engine idle and cruising speed. Depending on carburetor design, this cruising speed may be between 25 to 40 mph for passenger automobiles. At these approximate vehicle speeds, the throttle opening and resulting air flow are great enough to permit the main metering system to begin functioning.

The point at which atomized fuel begins to flow from the main nozzle is the transfer point shown in Fig. 8–26. At this point, the carburetor is passing from the idle to the main-metering system. However, fuel discharge, from the idle and off-idle ports, does not completely cease at this particular point but rather diminishes as discharge from the main nozzle increases. As a result, the two systems interact to produce a very smooth air/fuel flow during these vehicle speeds.

Main-Metering System

The *main-metering system* is responsible for supplying an air/fuel mixture for high-speed engine operation. During this particular phase of engine performance, the engine is not under heavy loads and therefore can operate on an economically lean air/fuel mixture. The carburetor components of this system are the main jet, main well, main nozzle, and the air bleed (Fig. 8–27).

The *main jet* fits between the fuel bowl and the main well. This main jet is a very accurately machined orifice (restriction) that controls the quantity of liquid fuel

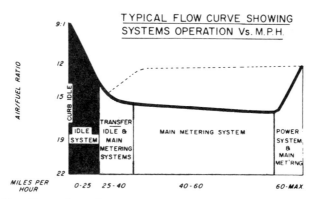

Fig. 8–26. Typical carburetor system operation at various vehicle speeds. (Courtesy of General Motors Corp.)

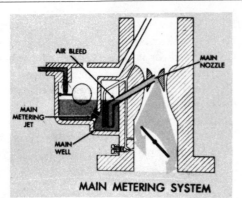

Fig. 8-27. The main-metering system of a typical single-barrel carburetor. (Courtesy of General Motors Corp.)

flow from the fuel bowl into the main well. In some carburetors, the size of the opening in the jet alone controls the fuel flow rate. However, in the carburetor shown in Fig. 8-28, a tapered metering rod passes through the opening in the jet. In this installation, the rod, by being inside the jet opening, provides a restriction to fuel flow. The movement of this metering rod up or down alters the jet restriction and therefore changes the amount of fuel flow.

The *main well* forms the working fuel reservoir for the main-metering system.

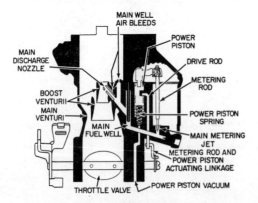

Fig. 8-28. The power system of a typical single-barrel carburetor. (Courtesy of General Motors Corp.)

Fuel entering this well must first pass through the main jet. Consequently, the main jet controls the quantity of usable fuel in the well when the main system is in operation. The result is that only a given, maximum amount of fuel is available in the main well and therefore is the controlling factor regarding the *total* fuel available for delivery by the main nozzle.

The *main nozzle* discharges an atomized air/fuel mixture into the throat of the carburetor. The discharge tip of this nozzle is located at the point in the venturi of greatest restriction. The opposite end of the nozzle fits into the main well. With this design, the fuel only travels a short distance between the well and the tip of the nozzle.

The *air bleed* adds air to the liquid fuel to atomize it partially. In the system shown in Fig. 8-27, the air bleed is the calibrated opening in the nozzle, slightly above the main well. Atmospheric pressure forces air through this opening anytime there is a decrease in pressure at the nozzle tip.

Operation

As the driver opens the throttle to a point where the main-metering system begins to function—the transfer point shown in Fig. 8-26—air velocity through the venturi increases, which in turn decreases the pressure in the venturi at the tip of the main fuel nozzle. As a result, atmospheric pressure over the fuel in the bowl pushes additional liquid fuel through the main jet and into the main well, where it rises in the main well passage leading to the nozzle (Fig. 8-27).

Then, the liquid fuel begins to enter the main nozzle, where it mixes with air coming through a calibrated hole in the lower portion of the nozzle. The air assists in breaking up the liquid fuel (partial atomization) for improved distribution and total atomization later as the fuel leaves the nozzle.

The partially atomized fuel then continues through the nozzle until it sprays from its tip. The atomized mixture then enters the air stream at the boost venturi. At this point, the air/fuel mixture mixes with the incoming air that carries it past the throttle valve and into the intake manifold for distribution to the engine cylinders.

The quantity of the air/fuel mixture flow and the resulting engine speed are factors determined by air velocity and jet size. For example, to alter engine speed, additional air/fuel flow is necessary. This means that the throttle valve must be open further, which in turn permits more air flow through the venturi. As a result, there is a greater reduction in pressure at the tip of the fuel nozzle in the venturi and greater fuel flow. Consequently, the engine accelerates.

However, there is a limit to how far the engine can accelerate on this system. This limitation is due to the size of the main jet opening. In other words, the jet limits the liquid fuel flow into the system. By so doing, the jet sets a limit to the quantity of atomized mixture exiting from the nozzle tip. When the engine reaches the rpm where this flow reaches its maximum, it can no longer accelerate.

Power System

Function

The main-metering system provides the leanest air/fuel mixture of any of the other carburetor circuits; a richer mixture is necessary not only for extended high-speed operation but also for maximum engine power. For maximum engine power, a rich fuel mixture is mandatory in order for the combustion process to consume all the oxygen in the air entering the combustion chamber. To accomplish this action, the carburetor has some type of power system used to supplement the main-metering system. This *power system* provides an increase in fuel mixture flow from the nozzle tip, according to the amount of throttle opening and engine load. In other words this additional system functions to enrich the total air/fuel mixture during any phase of main-metering system operation, depending on throttle position and engine-load requirements.

Design

The power system of the carburetor shown in Fig. 8–28 consists of the main-metering system, metering rod, power piston, and power-piston spring. The *metering rod* is a restriction placed into the opening of the main jet. This rod restricts the open area of the main jet, thereby reducing the amount of fuel flow through it. The rod provides the greatest restriction during light load or the economy phase of operation of the main-metering system. When extra fuel flow is necessary for full power, the rod moves upward in the jet to decrease the restriction and increase the fuel flow.

Since the rod does not completely move out of the jet, it has a special design feature that gradually increases fuel flow through the jet as the rod moves upward. This feature is in the form of a stepped or tapered end that, when moved to various positions in the jet, increases or decreases the jet restriction. Finally, the metering rod activates either through mechanical linkage connected to the throttle linkage or through a power piston.

The *power piston* (Fig. 8–28) connects through a special piece of linkage to the end of the metering rod. The power piston is responsible for maintaining the metering rod in its lowest position in the main jet. To accomplish this function, the piston itself moves within a special bore in the carburetor housing. This bore has a passage that supplies intake manifold vacuum to the bore and power piston. The vacuum keeps the power piston pulled down in its bore and therefore maintains the attached metering rod in its lowest position in the main jet.

Under the power piston is a calibrated power piston spring. The function of this spring is to raise or push up the power piston under low-vacuum conditions. This action, of course, moves the metering rod upward.

The actual tension of this spring varies among the various carburetors according to the size of the power piston and under what vacuum conditions the manufacturer desires the metering rod to move upward. For example, the spring of a typical carburetor has a calibrated tension that allows the piston to begin its upward movement at a vacuum of 8 to 9 inches Hg (mercury). Full upward movement of the piston and metering rod occurs at 4 to 6 inches Hg.

Operation

When the engine is operating under light load or moderate speed conditions, engine vacuum is high. In this situation, the high vacuum holds the power piston all the way down in its bore. This action maintains the largest diameter area on the end of the metering rod inside the main jet opening. The metering rod now sufficiently restricts fuel flow through the jet for the normal lean operation of the main-metering system.

However, when there is a demand for greater speed or engine power, the driver must open the throttle valve. As this valve opens, engine vacuum drops rapidly. With a reduction in vacuum acting on the bottom of the power piston, the spring begins to move it upward in its bore. This also forces the metering rod upward so that a smaller area of the rod is inside the jet. As a result, there is an increase in fuel flow through the main jet to the main nozzle.

While this particular system is always operational at vehicle speeds and loads requiring wide-open throttle, sudden throttle openings at slow and mid-range engine rpm also cause the momentary lifting of the metering rod due to the decrease in manifold vacuum. The main two factors to remember about this system are that (1) its only function is to produce an enriched mixture while the main metering system is in operation and (2) the actual drop in engine vacuum determines just how much of the metering rod moves out of the jet.

Finally, there is another style of power system on many carburetor types. This system does the same thing as the one just described; however, it uses a separate power valve instead of metering rods (Fig. 8–29). The power valve in this system, when open, bypasses fuel around the main jet to enrich the main-metering system. To control the operation of this power valve, manufacturers use engine vacuum, which acts against either a diaphragm and spring or a piston and spring. In either case, engine vacuum closes the valve and the spring opens it.

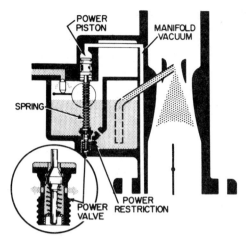

Fig. 8-29. A power valve operated by a vacuum-controlled piston and spring. (Courtesy of General Motors Corp.)

Pump System

Function

When the driver opens the throttle valve rapidly, from a closed or nearly closed position, in order to accelerate the vehicle, engine vacuum rapidly drops; but the air flow through the carburetor throat increases instantly. Due to the great difference in weight between air and fuel, the flow of fuel from the carburetor circuits lags behind the increase in air intake. As a result, the engine experiences a momentary leanness, which causes a brief engine hesitation, stumble, or flat spot.

The *pump system* provides the additional fuel flow necessary to overcome this leanness and maintains smooth engine operation during rapid low-speed acceleration. To accomplish this task, the system discharges additional fuel into the venturi air stream whenever the throttle valve initially opens. However, this system does not function beyond the point where the throttle valve is approximately half open.

Design

A typical pump system, shown in Fig. 8-30, consists of a pump plunger, duration spring, return spring, inlet valve, outlet valve, and pump jet. At its upper end, the *pump plunger* connects to a pump lever that fastens to a link attached to the throttle valve shaft. When the throttle valve opens, this link pulls the pump lever down, which in turn also causes the pump plunger to move downward into its bore. Conversely, if the throttle closes, the link pushes the lever and its attached plunger upward. This action pulls the pump plunger upward.

On the opposite end of the plunger from the lever is the *pump cup* or *seal*. This cup forms a piston that applies the force to the fuel necessary to push it through the pump passages and past the pump jet. Also, as it moves upward, the piston cup creates a slight difference in pressure that brings liquid fuel from the fuel bowl into the pump's bore or well.

The *duration spring* also moves the

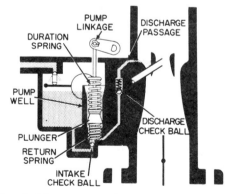

Fig. 8-30. A typical pump system. (Courtesy of General Motors Corp.)

plunger and cup downward in the well as the throttle opens. By using a calibrated spring for this purpose, along with a mechanical connection, the manufacturer controls the duration of the pump's discharge. This is a necessary consideration if or when the driver quickly opens the throttle valve in order to prevent the system from discharging all its fuel too rapidly, which can cause engine stumble during rapid engine acceleration.

The duration spring itself fits over the plunger, between a flange and washer above the piston cup and a curved washer bearing against a shoulder on the plunger shaft. With this arrangement, any lengthy upward movement of the plunger, such as when the throttle valve closes, causes the curved washer to bear against the top of the carburetor casting. As upward plunger movement continues, the duration spring compresses between the curved washer and the piston cup.

As the driver opens the throttle valve, the pump link begins to move the plunger down, and the duration spring begins to expand. This action pushes the piston cup downward in the pump well. If the well contains fuel, the pump cup applies force to it and begins pushing it through the pump system passages. The spring continues to expand and force the plunger downward until the cup reaches the bottom of the well. The spring action during this time lengthens the time period for plunger travel in the pump well and therefore lengthens the duration of the fuel discharge from the system.

Also, there must be some form of mechanism built into the plunger, duration spring, or linkage arrangement for additional throttle valve movement, once the plunger bottoms in the well. In the carburetor shown in Fig. 8–30, this mechanism consists of a plunger made in two sections, which cannot separate but telescope over one another. The tension of the duration spring keeps both plunger sections extended or apart, which provides normal plunger length during the intake phase and the beginning of the discharge phase of pump operation.

However, once the plunger cup bottoms in the well, the upper plunger section continues to move downward with the further travel of the throttle valve and linkage. As a result, the upper section telescopes over the lower section, which compresses the duration spring. In other carburetor styles, manufacturers achieve the same result by either slotting the end of the plunger where it attaches to the pump lever or permitting the end of the plunger to telescope inside the pump lever.

The carburetor illustrated in Fig. 8–30 has a *pump return spring;* however, some carburetors do not have this device. When used, this spring assists the mechanical linkage in moving the plunger to the up position as the throttle closes.

The *inlet valve* fits between the main fuel bowl and the pump well. Its function is to permit fuel to flow from the bowl to the well during the pump's inlet stroke. But this one-way valve prevents a backflow of fuel from the pump well to the fuel bowl during the pump stroke. This valve may be in the form of a metal ball located in the passage from the well to the bowl or be part of the plunger assembly. In this latter case, the cup itself moves up or down on the plunger head to form a valve. When the plunger moves upward, the flat area on top of the cup unseats from the flat on the plunger head. This action allows free movement of fuel, fed into the well above the cup, through the inside of the cup to the bottom of the well. However, as the plunger moves down, the cup moves upward, trapping the fuel in the well.

The *pump discharge* or *outlet ball valve* is also a one-way check valve. This device permits fuel to move from the pump well, through the discharge passage, and out the pump jet during the pump's delivery stroke. During the inlet stroke of the pump, the spring holds the valve closed. This action prevents any air from entering the discharge passage, which would reduce the efficiency of the plunger cup in drawing fuel into the well.

The *pump jet* is nothing more than a calibrated opening in the wall of the carburetor throat. In the carburetor pictured in Fig. 8-30, the jet opening is above the entrance to the primary venturi. With this location, the jet discharges fuel into the air flow between the primary and boost venturies.

Operation

Whenever the throttle valve closes, the plunger moves upward in the pump well, creating a slight difference in pressure between the well area below the plunger cup and the atmospheric pressure above the fuel in the float chamber or bowl. As a result, fuel from the float bowl enters the pump well through an inlet check valve or through the slot in the top of the pump well (Fig. 8-30). In the latter case, the fuel then flows past the pump cup seal and into the bottom of the pump well. At the same time, the discharge check valve seats in order to prevent air from leaking into the system.

When the driver opens the throttle valve, its connecting linkage along with the duration spring begins to force the plunger downward. The pump cup seats itself against the plunger head and begins to force fuel through the pump discharge passage. By seating the pump cup or seating the inlet check valve, if so equipped, the pressurized fuel cannot return to the float bowl. Instead, the fuel passes on through the discharge passage, through the open outlet valve to the pump jet, where it sprays into the venturi area.

Although the driver may immediately move the throttle valve wide open, the plunger does not bottom in the pump well instantly. Because this plunger has two sections that telescope over one another, the resistance of the fuel flow to movement within the pump passages forces the lower section momentarily to stop its travel while the upper section continues to move down over it. Then, the duration spring continues to move the lower plunger section and the cup down. This action permits fuel delivery by the pump plunger cup for a short period of time *after* the throttle linkage movement ends.

During high-speed engine operation, the vacuum formed at the pump nozzle in the carburetor throat may be sufficient to unseat the outlet check valve and siphon fuel from the pump system. In some carburetors, this additional fuel is part of the normal main-metering system air/fuel mixture calibration. However, in other carburetors it is not, so this fuel siphoning creates an overly rich mixture at higher speeds.

To stop this siphoning effect, manufacturers can modify the pump system in one of three ways. First, the system may have an air bleed machined to the discharge passage. Second, the weight of the discharge check valve or the tension of its spring may be increased. Finally, the pump plunger itself may contain some form of antisiphon check valve.

Choke System

When starting a cold engine, the factors necessary for good fuel vaporization are missing or inadequate. For this reason, it is necessary to provide extremely rich mixtures from the carburetor, 2:1 to 1:1, in order to provide sufficient combustible mixtures to all the cylinders for quick starting. The carburetor obtains this enrichment by the addition of a choke valve in the carburetor throat above the venturi and main nozzle. This choke valve, during cold engine starting, starts fuel to flow through the main system prematurely.

Design

The choke system illustrated in Fig. 8-31 consists of a choke valve, vacuum break assembly, fast-idle cam, choke unloader, and a thermostatic coil. The *choke valve* is an offset plate, which pivots on a shaft located near the top of the carburetor throat. The function of this choke valve is to restrict the normal air flow through the carburetor throat. By doing so, intake manifold vacuum imposes its effects on the idle as well as the main-metering system. The result is, of course, an extremely rich mixture.

The *vacuum break assembly* contains a diaphragm that attaches through linkage to the choke valve. When the engine is running, this diaphragm has intake manifold vacuum applied to it on one side and atmospheric pressure on the other. This causes the diaphragm to move and open the choke valve partially. This action prevents the started engine from stalling due to an overly rich mixture. *Note:* On other carburetor styles, this device has a vacuum piston instead of a diaphragm, and the entire unit is contained in the same housing as the bimetallic coil (Fig. 8-32).

During engine warm-up, it is very necessary to increase engine idle rpm to prevent the engine from stalling; this is the function of the *fast-idle cam* (Fig. 8-33). This cam connects by a rod to a lever on the choke valve shaft. The cam itself has graduated steps upon which the idle screw or tang on the throttle lever contacts. As the choke closes, the lever rotates the cam so that its largest step is controlling idle speed that, in this case, is much higher than the normal hot idle speed. When the engine is fully warm and the choke valve is wide open, the fast idle cam rotates so that the idle screw rests on the low step on the cam. Then, the engine operates at normal curb idle. Finally, from the point where the choke valve is fully closed until it is wide open, the cam rotates gradually, allowing one step at a time to engage the idle screw. This action permits a gradual reduction in idle rpm as the engine warms up.

A *choke unloader* mechanism is necessary if the engine becomes flooded during cold starting (Fig. 8-33). This device partially opens the choke valve to increase the air flow through the carburetor when the driver depresses the accelerator pedal to the floor. The extra air leans out the fuel mixture sufficiently so that the engine will start.

The unloader mechanism consists of a projection on the throttle lever and the fast idle cam. When the driver depresses the gas pedal down all the way, the throttle-lever projection contacts the edge of the fast idle cam. This action forces the cam to rotate, which in turn forces the choke lever rod to turn the choke lever and shaft; and the choke valve partially opens.

The *thermostatic coil* assembly may be

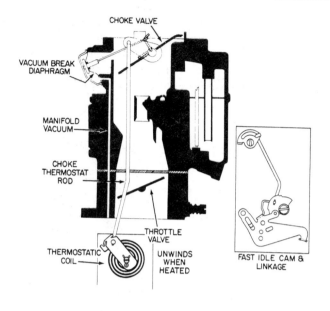

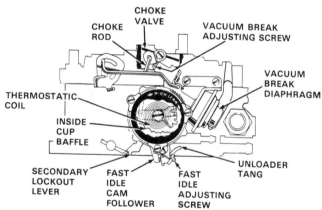

Fig. 8-31. The choke system of a typical carburetor. (Courtesy of General Motors Corp.)

a remote unit attached to a heated well on the intake manifold (Fig. 8-31) or inside a round housing on the carburetor housing near the choke valve. In the latter case, this bimetallic coil receives its heat from the exhaust manifold or from hot coolant from the cooling system; and the housing also contains the vacuum break piston (Fig. 8-32). Regardless of the location, the bimetallic coil is responsible for closing the choke when the engine is cold.

Operation

A combination of intake manifold vacuum, off-set choke valve, action of the bimetallic coil, atmospheric temperature, and exhaust manifold heat controls the

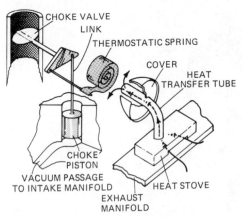

CHOKE VALVE
LINK
THERMOSTATIC SPRING
COVER
HEAT
TRANSFER TUBE
CHOKE
PISTON
VACUUM PASSAGE
TO INTAKE MANIFOLD
HEAT STOVE
EXHAUST
MANIFOLD

Fig. 8-32. When a piston-type brake is used, it is in the same housing as the bimetallic coil.

operation of the choke system shown in Fig. 8-31. For example, before the driver starts a cold engine, atmospheric temperature causes the bimetallic coil to wind up; this action through its control rod closes the choke valve. With the choke valve closed, the carburetor supplies a very rich

mixture to the engine combustion chambers as the engine turns over for starting.

Once the cold engine starts, two factors initially cause the choke valve to open slightly to prevent the engine from stalling. First, because the choke valve is offset in its support shaft, air velocity causes the valve to open slightly against the torque of the thermostatic (bimetallic) coil. Second, intake manifold vacuum, applied to the diaphragm or piston of the brake unit, pulls the choke valve open to a given position. The choke valve remains in this position until the engine begins to warm up.

As the engine warms up, the application of exhaust manifold heat causes the bimetallic coil to relax or unwind. This action gradually decreases the torque on the choke valve until it is fully open. The full opening of the choke valve also is the end result of two factors: heat and air velocity. Manifold heat on the coil causes it to unwind, releasing its hold on the choke

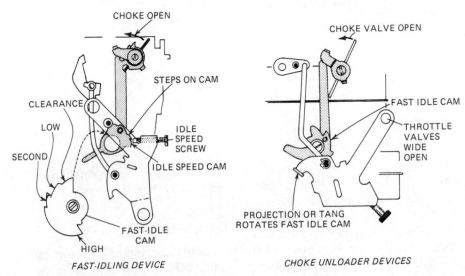

CHOKE OPEN

STEPS ON CAM

CLEARANCE

LOW

IDLE
SPEED
SCREW

SECOND

IDLE SPEED CAM

FAST-IDLE
CAM

HIGH

FAST-IDLING DEVICE

CHOKE VALVE OPEN

FAST IDLE CAM

THROTTLE
VALVES
WIDE
OPEN

PROJECTION OR TANG
ROTATES FAST IDLE CAM

CHOKE UNLOADER DEVICES

Fig. 8-33. The fast-idle cam and choke unloader mechanism of a typical carburetor.

valve. With no torque to hold the valve toward the closed position, the air flow past the offset choke valve forces it fully open.

If the driver accelerates the engine during the warm-up period, intake manifold vacuum drops. As a result, the vacuum brake becomes temporarily inoperative and closes the choke valve slightly. The amount of closure depends upon the amount of air velocity past the choke valve and how far the choke coil has relaxed. In any case, the result is a richer mixture for acceleration during the warm-up period.

Review

This section will assist you in determining how well you remember the material contained in this chapter. Read each item carefully. If you can't complete the statement, review the section in the chapter that covers the material.

1. The ideal air/fuel ratio is about _____:1.
   a. 9
   b. 11
   c. 13
   d. 15

2. The most common type of air-filtering element is the _____ _____.
   a. wetted mesh
   b. oil bath
   c. dry paper
   d. wetted paper

3. The component in an oil-bath air cleaner that reduces air noise is the _____.
   a. chambers
   b. reservoir
   c. element
   d. cover

4. The type of filtering element that is usually interchangeable with the dry-paper type is the _____.
   a. oil-wetted mesh
   b. polyurethane type
   c. oil bath
   d. oil-wetted paper

5. The device that meters the air/fuel mixture to the engine is the _____.
   a. fuel filter
   b. air cleaner
   c. carburetor
   d. fuel pump

6. The breaking of liquid fuel into droplets is known as _____.
   a. distribution
   b. evaporation
   c. vaporization
   d. atomization

7. The fuel must be in a _____ form for even and adequate distribution to all the engine cylinders.
   a. vapor
   b. atomized
   c. liquid
   d. bubble

8. For maximum engine power, it is necessary to burn all the _____ contained in the air/fuel mixture.
   a. nitrogen
   b. oxygen
   c. hydrogen
   d. carbon

9. The carburetor choke restricts _____ _____ to the intake manifold.
   a. float
   b. air flow
   c. filter
   d. jet

10. Any pressure lower than that of the

atmosphere is known as a _____
_____.
a. vacuum
b. void
c. both *a* and *b*
d. calm

11. The device in the carburetor that creates a vacuum at the fuel nozzle is the
_____.
a. float
b. choke
c. throat
d. venturi

12. The carburetor system designed to store and supply fuel is the _____.
a. float
b. choke
c. idle
d. power

13. The mechanism that controls the amount of fuel entering the bowl is the _____ _____.
a. metering rod
b. needle and seat
c. power valve
d. vacuum diaphragm

14. Many of the modern needles and seats are made of _____.
a. aluminum
b. iron
c. brass
d. steel

15. The device that allows air to enter a carburetor passage is the air _____.
a. passage
b. tube
c. bleed
d. port

16. The device that regulates the amount of mixture flow from the idle port is the _____ _____.
a. adjusting screw

b. regulator needle
c. flow needle
d. mixture screw

17. The main _____ controls the amount of liquid fuel entering the main well from the fuel bowl.
a. nozzle
b. jet
c. tube
d. passage

18. The _____ _____ controls the amount of air velocity through the venturi during main system operation.
a. needle valve
b. power valve
c. choke valve
d. throttle valve

19. The device that restricts fuel flow through the main jet is a _____
_____.
a. power piston
b. adjustable orifice
c. power valve
d. metering rod

20. The _____ system adds additional fuel to the engine during low-speed acceleration.
a. float
b. choke
c. pump
d. acceleration

21. The component of the pump system that extends the duration of fuel delivery by the system is the _____
____ _____.
a. pump spring
b. duration spring
c. throttle linkage
d. outlet valve

22. In the pump system, the _____
_____ controls the fuel flow be-

tween the fuel bowl and the pump well.

a. inlet valve
b. outlet valve
c. plunger valve
d. pump jet

23. The component of the choke system that restricts air flow through the carburetor throat is the _____.

a. choke valve
b. choke unloader
c. fast-idle cam
d. vacuum break

24. The device that increases engine idle after a cold start is the _____ _____.

a. choke unloader
b. fast-idle cam
c. vacuum break
d. choke rod

25. The device that uses engine vacuum to open the choke valve slightly is the _____ _____.

a. fast-idle cam
b. choke unloader
c. brake assembly
d. bimetallic coil

For the answers, turn to the Appendix.

Function of Multiple-Barrel Carburetors

The last chapter covered the design and theory of operation of a single-throat (barrel) carburetor. This type of metering device provides sufficient air and fuel flow to operate satisfactorily the majority of four- and six-cylinder engines used in automobiles. However, for V-type engines, this unit cannot provide adequate carburetion at all engine speeds. Consequently, manufacturers install multiple-barrel carburetors on all V-type engines and in many cases, four and six-cylinder in-line engines.

Multiple-barrel carburetors have two throats or barrels (a dual carburetor) while others have four (a quad carburetor). The overall purpose of these additional barrels is to improve engine breathing, particularly at high speeds. That is, the additional barrels allow more air and fuel to enter the engine.

Of course, if air were the only consideration, a single large-diameter barrel unit would be adequate. However, with only a single, large barrel, venturi action would be poor, which would result in improper air/fuel ratios for varying operating conditions of the engine. Venturi size must be a compromise. That is, the device must restrict air flow sufficiently to create a low-pressure area at the nozzle tip for adequate fuel flow from the main-metering system. But at the same time, the venturi restriction cannot be so large as to choke off air flow to the engine at high rpm.

Single-Stage Dual Carburetors

A single-stage dual carburetor (Fig. 9–1) is essentially two single-barrel carbu-

Chapter 9

MULTIPLE-BARREL CARBURETORS, CARBURETOR-ASSIST DEVICES, AND INTAKE MANIFOLDS

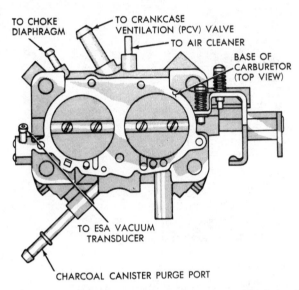

Fig. 9-1. A typical single-stage dual carburetor in which both throttle valves open and close together. (Courtesy of Chrysler Corp.)

retors in a single assembly. Each barrel has its own idle system, main-metering system, and throttle valve. However, both throttle valves attach to a common throttle shaft *so that both valves open and close together.* Also, this carburetor has a common power system, pump system, float system, and choke system. That is, these systems perform their functions simultaneously on both barrels.

Idle System—Design and Operation

Figure 9-2 illustrates a typical idle system for one barrel of a dual carburetor; the other barrel has exactly the same design. The system shown includes a main jet, main well, idle tube, idle passage, idle adjusting screw, idle port, and off idle ports. These components serve the same functions as those described in the previous chapter on single-barrel carburetion.

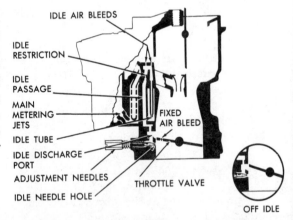

Fig. 9-2. The idle system of a common dual carburetor. (Courtesy of Pontiac Motor Division)

When the engine with a dual carburetor is idling, both throttle valves are slightly open, and a small amount of air passes between the edge of the valves and the lower throats of the carburetor. During this time, intake manifold vacuum imposes itself on the idle ports, which causes a difference in pressure between the idle ports and the fuel bowl.

Atmospheric pressure above the level of fuel in the bowl pushes *additional* fuel into each main well. Fuel is already in these main wells because fuel naturally seeks its own level. Therefore, the level in the wells is the same as in the bowl even when the engine is not operating.

However, atmospheric pressure is forcing additional fuel into the wells; this additional fuel moves through the fixed orifice on the base of the idle tubes. Then, the fuel travels up the idle tubes and mixes with air that comes through the idle air bleeds. Next, this partially atomized air/fuel mixture moves down the idle passages, past the off-idle discharge holes, around the tip of the adjusting screws, and finally through the idle discharge holes. The off-idle discharge holes act as air bleeds during this time, while each adjusting screw determines just how much of this atomized air/fuel mixture enters each throat (barrel) of the carburetor.

As the driver slightly opens the throttle valves for low-speed acceleration, engine vacuum acts on the off-idle ports. As a result, these ports stop acting as air bleeds and begin to discharge an air/fuel mixture. The off-idle and idle ports continue to discharge fuel until the main-metering system is functioning well enough to supply the engine with an adequate mixture.

Main-Metering System— Design and Operation

Each barrel has its own main-metering system. Figure 9–3 shows this complete system for one barrel of the carburetor. Note that the system has a main jet, main well, main well tube, main-system pas-

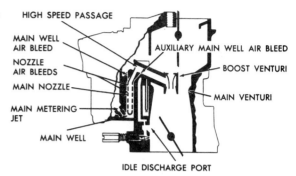

Fig. 9–3. The main-metering system of a dual carburetor. (Courtesy of Pontiac Motor Division)

sage, air bleeds, and fuel discharge nozzle.

As the driver opens the throttle valve past the low speed range, the air velocity through both barrels is sufficient to cause a low-pressure area in each boost venturi at the tip of the fuel nozzles. As a result, additional fuel moves through the main jets and into the main wells. This fuel enters the main well tubes, where it mixes with air from the air bleeds. The air enters the tubes by means of a series of holes machined into each of the tubes. The partially atomized fuel then moves up the passages and enters the main-discharge nozzles, from which the fuel discharges into the carburetor throats.

Power System— Design and Operation

The carburetor shown in Fig. 9–4 has a single power system that serves both barrels. This system consists of a power valve and a power piston. The *power valve* itself, at certain times, permits an additional amount of liquid gasoline to bypass the main jets and enter both the main wells.

The *power piston* and *spring* control the operation of the power valve. The power piston moves within a bore, acted upon by intake manifold vacuum. When vacuum is

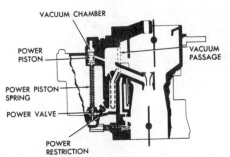

Fig. 9-4. A typical power system of a dual carburetor. (Courtesy of Pontiac Motor Division)

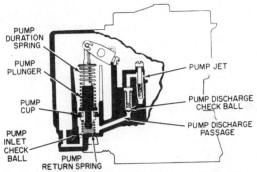

Fig. 9-5. The single-pump system of a dual carburetor. (Courtesy of Pontiac Motor Division)

high, the piston moves upward in its bore. When vacuum is low, the piston spring pushes the piston down.

On one end of the piston is a plunger. This plunger makes contact with the stem of the power valve. Consequently, any movement of the piston and plunger affects the position of the power valve.

High engine vacuum causes the power piston and plunger to move upward, overcoming the tension of the piston spring. Since the plunger is up, the spring, under the power valve itself, can close the valve. As a result, fuel cannot bypass the main jets and enter the wells.

When the engine is running hard or at very high speeds, intake manifold vacuum is low. This reduced vacuum cannot hold the power piston and plunger up against spring tension. Thus, the spring pushes the piston and attached plunger downward, and the plunger pushes the power valve open. Now, additional fuel bypasses both main jets and enters the main wells for delivery through each of the main-discharge nozzles.

Pump System—Design

The carburetor shown in Fig. 9-5 also has a *single-pump system*. This pump system is necessary to provide the engine

with an extra supply of fuel when the driver suddenly opens the throttle valve. The engine will run without the pump system, but the driver would not be able to accelerate the engine quickly through its rpm range.

The pump system illustrated in Fig. 9-5 includes an intake ball check, pump well, pump plunger, duration and return springs, discharge ball check, plunger ball check, and two pump jets. The only differences in components within this system and the ones mentioned in the last chapter, are the *plunger ball check* and the two *pump jets*. The plunger ball check is necessary to control the release of gas vapors from the pump well, resulting from percolation. The two pump jets are in the system so that each barrel receives fuel from the system.

Pump System Operation

When the throttle closes, the linkage and spring action move the plunger upward; this creates a void in the pump well. As a result, atmospheric pressure pushes fuel through the pump screen, through the open intake ball check valve, and into the pump well. The return spring seats the discharge ball check valve during this time.

As the driver pushes down on the accelerator pedal, the throttle valve linkage and the duration spring cause the pump plunger to move downward. The plunger piston or cup applies a force to the fuel in the pump well, and the resulting pressure closes the intake ball check valve and opens the discharge check ball. Fuel then passes out around the discharge ball, through the two pump jets, and into the airstream within the two barrels.

All the gasoline in the pump well is not pushed out by the plunger cup all at once. Instead, the cup forces the fuel out over a short period of time in an even flow. This delayed action is the result of the duration spring acting on the split or telescoping plunger.

Float System

The float system of the dual carburetor pictured in Fig. 9-6 stores and supplies the fuel for the idle, main-metering, power, and pump circuits for both barrels. This system consists of a single fuel bowl, float assembly, needle, and seat. These components have about the same design features and function the same way as those described earlier in the single-barrel carburetor. The only exception is the size

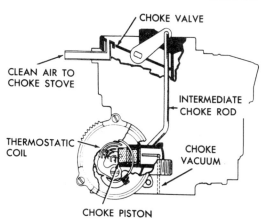

Fig. 9-7. The choke valve of a dual carburetor operates over the air entrance to both barrels. (Courtesy of Pontiac Motor Division)

of the fuel bowl; it is usually larger in the dual carburetor in order to store sufficient fuel for the additional barrel.

Choke System

The dual carburetor uses an automatic choke system quite similar in design to the system described in the last chapter. In other words, the carburetor has a choke valve, bimetallic spring, choke piston, fast-idle cam, and a choke unloader. The main difference in design in the system used in the dual carburetor is that the choke valve operates over the air entrance to both barrels (Fig. 9-7).

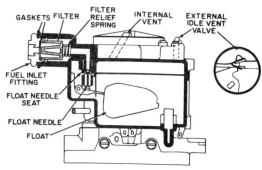

Fig. 9-6. The float system of a dual carburetor. (Courtesy of Pontiac Motor Division)

Two-Stage, Dual-Barrel Carburetors

The two-stage dual-barrel carburetor is a relatively recent development in carburetor design, brought about by emission control requirements. Domestic manufac-

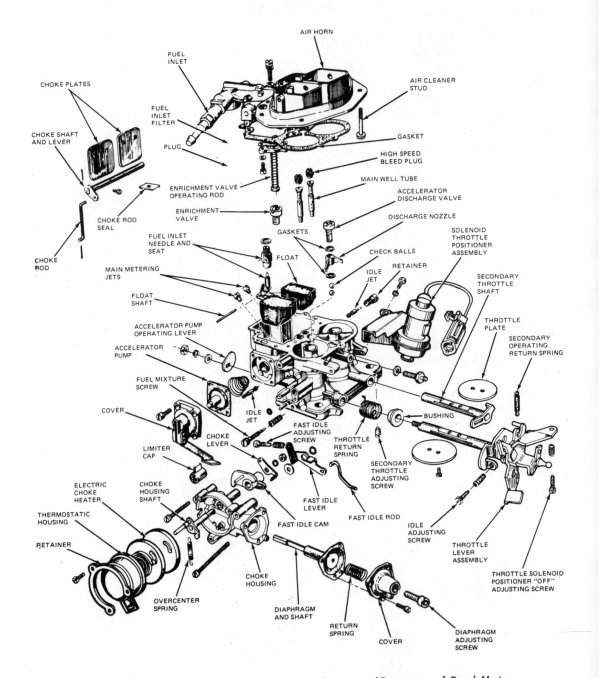

CHOKE PLATES

FUEL INLET

AIR HORN

AIR CLEANER STUD

CHOKE SHAFT AND LEVER

FUEL INLET FILTER

PLUG

GASKET

HIGH SPEED BLEED PLUG

MAIN WELL TUBE

CHOKE ROD SEAL

ENRICHMENT VALVE OPERATING ROD

ACCELERATOR DISCHARGE VALVE

ENRICHMENT VALVE

DISCHARGE NOZZLE

CHOKE ROD

FUEL INLET NEEDLE AND SEAT

GASKETS

FLOAT

CHECK BALLS

SOLENOID THROTTLE POSITIONER ASSEMBLY

MAIN METERING JETS

IDLE JET

RETAINER

SECONDARY THROTTLE SHAFT

FLOAT SHAFT

THROTTLE PLATE

ACCELERATOR PUMP OPERATING LEVER

SECONDARY OPERATING RETURN SPRING

ACCELERATOR PUMP

FUEL MIXTURE SCREW

BUSHING

COVER

IDLE JET

FAST IDLE ADJUSTING SCREW

THROTTLE RETURN SPRING

CHOKE LEVER

SECONDARY THROTTLE ADJUSTING SCREW

LIMITER CAP

ELECTRIC CHOKE HEATER

CHOKE HOUSING SHAFT

FAST IDLE LEVER

FAST IDLE ROD

IDLE ADJUSTING SCREW

THERMOSTATIC HOUSING

FAST IDLE CAM

THROTTLE LEVER ASSEMBLY

RETAINER

CHOKE HOUSING

THROTTLE SOLENOID POSITIONER "OFF" ADJUSTING SCREW

OVERCENTER SPRING

DIAPHRAGM AND SHAFT

RETURN SPRING

COVER

DIAPHRAGM ADJUSTING SCREW

Fig. 9–8. A two-stage dual-barrel carburetor. (Courtesy of Ford Motor Co. of Canada Ltd.)

184

turers use this unit (Fig. 9–8), primarily on four-cylinder and a few six-cylinder engines.

This carburetor differs from the typical single-stage dual carburetor in several respects. First of all, this unit has two throttle valves—*which operate independently of one another*—a primary and a secondary. The *primary valve* controls venturi air flow through the primary venturi, while the *secondary valve* controls the air flowing through the secondary venturi. Second, the primary barrel is somewhat smaller than the secondary. The primary barrel is responsible for meeting the air/fuel requirements of the engine during low-to-moderate engine loads and speeds. The secondary barrel supplies an additional air/fuel mixture to handle heavier load requirements. The opening of the secondary throttle valve and subsequent operation of the secondary barrel is done through a form of progressive mechanical linkage. This linkage prevents the secondary throttle valve from opening until the primary valve reaches a predetermined open position.

Each barrel *does not* have all the individual operating systems as did the single-stage carburetor just described. For instance, the primary barrel of the carburetor, shown in Fig. 9–8, has an idle and low-speed (transfer) system, pump system, main-metering system, and power system. Whereas, the secondary barrel will only have a transfer system, main-metering system, and power system. However, the systems of both barrels receive their fuel from a common fuel bowl, and both barrels have their own choke valve. But these valves operate together on a single shaft, activated by a single choke system.

Four-Barrel (Quad) Carburetors—Design

The four-barrel or quad carburetor, used on V-8 engines, consists in effect of two single-stage, dual carburetors combined into a single assembly (Fig. 9–9). The carburetor assembly has four throats or barrels, each with its own venturi, throttle valve, and main fuel nozzle. One pair of barrels forms the primary dual carburetor while the other set makes up the secondary carburetor.

The primary carburetor is responsible for delivering an air/fuel mixture to the engine under most operating conditions. In order to do this, the primary carburetor or *primary side* has a full complement of systems including float, idle and low speed, main-metering, power, pump, and choke systems. Finally, since the primary side is in fact a single-stage, dual carburetor, its throttle plates operate in unison so that each barrel supplies the same amount of air/fuel mixture to four cylinders of the engine.

The secondary carburetor or *secondary side* operates as the primary throttle valves move toward their wide-open position for engine acceleration or full-power operation. The secondary side, during this time, provides an additional air/fuel mixture to that entering the engine cylinders from the primary carburetor. This combination of individual sides permits the carburetor to provide a satisfactory mixture for starting, idle, and low speed, in addition to economical part-throttle operation, while at the same time allowing greater amounts of air/fuel mixture to enter the engine for high-speed, full-power performance.

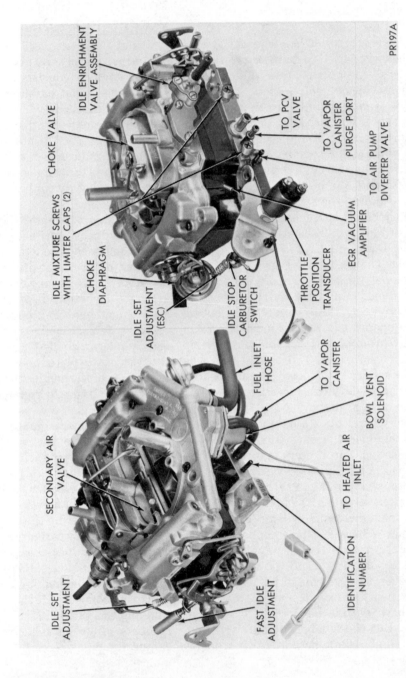

Fig. 9-9. A four-barrel carburetor is used on a V-8 engine to improve engine breathing at high rpm. (Courtesy of Chrysler Corp.)

CHOKE VALVE

IDLE ENRICHMENT VALVE ASSEMBLY

TO PCV VALVE

TO VAPOR CANISTER PURGE PORT

TO AIR PUMP DIVERTER VALVE

IDLE MIXTURE SCREWS WITH LIMITER CAPS (2)

CHOKE DIAPHRAGM

IDLE SET ADJUSTMENT (ESC)

IDLE STOP CARBURETOR SWITCH

THROTTLE POSITION TRANSDUCER

EGR VACUUM AMPLIFIER

SECONDARY AIR VALVE

FUEL INLET HOSE

TO VAPOR CANISTER

BOWL VENT SOLENOID

TO HEATED AIR INLET

IDLE SET ADJUSTMENT

IDENTIFICATION NUMBER

FAST IDLE ADJUSTMENT

PR197A

The secondary side of most four-barrel carburetors, depending on design, has from two to five operating systems. All four-barrel units have, for example, on its secondary side a main-metering and usually a power circuit. A few units have a primary as well as a secondary float system, but many carburetors use one float system for both sides. In addition, some of the older four-barrel carburetors also had an idle system on the secondary side. However, this system had a calibrated flow rate and therefore no adjustment screw. Finally, certain four-barrel units have two pump systems, one in the primary and the other in the secondary.

Over the years, two methods were used to open the secondary throttle valves: a vacuum diaphragm or mechanical linkage. Figure 9–10 illustrates a *vacuum diaphragm* assembly connected to the secondary throttle valves. The diaphragm in this unit reacts to a vacuum signal produced in one of the primary boost venturies. This signal increases proportionally with primary-venturi vacuum as the throttle valve opens. When the vacuum signal reaches a predetermined amount, it acts on the diaphragm that, in turn, starts to open the secondary throttle plates against the tension of the diaphragm spring.

Manufacturers more commonly use progressive *mechanical linkage* to open and close the secondary throttle valves (Fig. 9–11). With this arrangement, the primary throttles connect through linkage to the secondary valves. However, the design of this linkage is such that the primary valve must be open a given amount *before* the secondary valves begin to open. In other words, the primary valves must open usually 50 to 60 degrees before the secondary valves start to open; *both sets of valves reach the wide-open position together.* Of course, when both sets of valves are wide open, the passage for the air/fuel mixture to enter the intake manifold is twice as large (from two to four barrels). This permits greater amounts of air/fuel

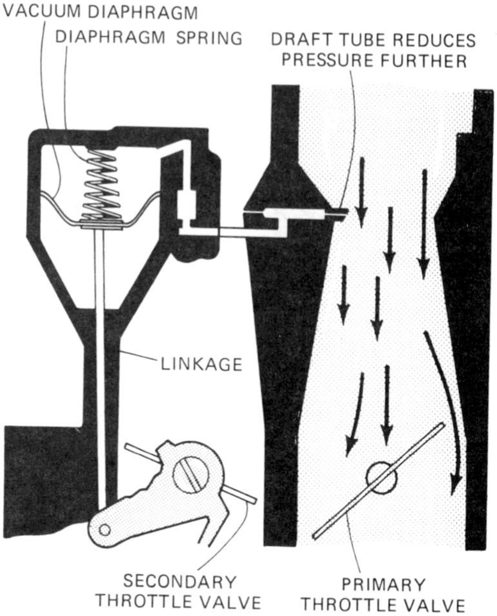

VACUUM DIAPHRAGM
DIAPHRAGM SPRING   DRAFT TUBE REDUCES
PRESSURE FURTHER

LINKAGE

SECONDARY   PRIMARY
THROTTLE VALVE   THROTTLE VALVE

Fig. 9–10. Some secondary throttle valves open by a vacuum diaphragm assembly.

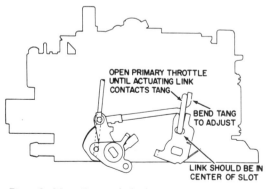

OPEN PRIMARY THROTTLE
UNTIL ACTUATING LINK
CONTACTS TANG

BEND TANG
TO ADJUST

LINK SHOULD BE IN
CENTER OF SLOT

Fig. 9–11. Typical linkage arrangement used to open the secondary throttle valves. (Courtesy of Pontiac Motor Division)

Fig. 9–12. *A typical air-valve arrangement over the secondary barrels.*

mixture to enter the engine for improved high-speed, full-power performance.

In addition to the throttle valves, the secondary side of a four-barrel unit may have a set of velocity or air valves (Fig. 9–12). These air valves appear much like large choke valves, located in the top sec-

tion of the secondary barrels. These offset valves open as air rushes into the secondary barrels due to atmospheric pressure attempting to fill the void or balance out the low-pressure area created by the opening secondary throttle valves. The valves usually close through the action of a calibrated spring.

Other than controlling venturi air flow, the air valves may have design features that perform other functions. For example, the manufacturer may contour the lower edge of each valve in such a manner that it acts *as a venturi* itself to increase air velocity at the tip of the fuel nozzle (Fig. 9–13). This occurs whenever the air velocity through the secondary barrels is high and the lower edges of the air valves approach the secondary main nozzles. This provides the secondary side with a form of variable venturi that reduces the air restrictions produced by a conventional fixed venturi.

In other carburetors, the air valves con-

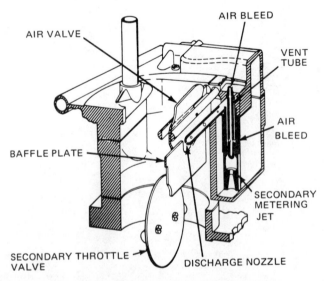

Fig. 9–13. *An air valve used as a variable venturi. (Courtesy of General Motors Corp.)*

nect to a pair of metering rods that are part of the secondary main-metering and power systems. With this design, the metering rods move up out of the secondary jets in proportion to the actual opening of the air valve. The metering rods maintain the correct air/fuel ratio throughout the operation of the secondary main-metering system.

Four-Barrel Carburetor Operating Characteristics

Float System

With these design features in mind, let's review the operating characteristics of the systems used in a four-barrel unit. This unit may have a single large fuel bowl, controlled by a single needle and seat, as in both the single- and dual-barrel carburetors. Or, the secondary side may have its own float system. In either case, the systems function in the same manner to store and supply fuel to the remaining operating systems.

Idle-System

Most four-barrel carburetors have only one idle system. This system is within the primary side of the unit, and it supplies the proper air/fuel mixture to operate the engine during engine idle and low-speed (transfer) operation. However, some four-barrel units have an idle or transfer system on its secondary side. This system has a fixed flow rate and therefore requires no external adjustment screw.

Main-Metering System

Four-barrel carburetors have a main-metering system on both the primary and secondary sides. The primary system alone produces the necessary air/fuel mixture to operate the engine from the transition point of the idle circuit to a point where the primary throttle valve is approximately halfway open. Then, the secondary main-metering system *begins* to function. By doing so, the secondary system supplements the air/fuel mixture produced by the primary for high-speed and full-power operation of the engine.

Power System

As pointed out, both sides of a four-barrel carburetor usually have a power system. This system may be in the form of a vacuum-operated power valve or a vacuum- or mechanically operated metering-rod arrangement. In either case, the power system enriches the air/fuel mixture of the two main-metering systems during heavy acceleration or wide-open throttle valve operation.

Pump System

As a general rule, the primary side of the four-barrel carburetor has the *only* pump system. The reason for this is that the pump system only functions between closed throttle to a point where the primary throttle valve is about halfway open. After this point in a four-barrel unit, both the power system and the secondary main-metering systems enrich the air/fuel mixture from the primary side for high-speed acceleration.

A few of the older four-barrel units had a pump system on both sides. However, the secondary pump system was found to be not really necessary for high-speed acceleration and did cause excessive fuel consumption. As a result, modern factory-equipped four-barrel carburetors usually do not have a secondary pump system.

Choke System

The four-barrel carburetor has only one choke circuit, found on the primary side, because the engine starts, idles, and operates on the mixtures produced by the primary side most of the time. This system may look a little bit more complicated than the basic system already discussed; however, it is really the same basic system.

The only real design difference is that a four-barrel choke unit needs additional rods and levers to help control the operation of the secondary throttle valves or the air valves. *The rods and levers form the secondary lockout mechanism, which prevents the throttle valves or air valves from opening until the choke valve is open.* This action is necessary since there is no choke on the secondary side, and the opening of the secondary throttle valves or air valves during heavy acceleration would lean out the rich mixture required for cold operation.

Figure 9-14 shows a typical secondary lockout mechanism, which consists of a trip lever and a lockout lever. The trip lever connects via a piece of linkage to the choke-valve shaft. Therefore, as the choke valve opens or closes, the linkage moves the trip lever up or down. As this lever moves, it in turn raises or lowers the lockout lever. As long as the choke valve remains even partially closed, the position of the trip lever is such that the secondary throttle-shaft tang indexes with the slot in the lockout lever; so the secondary throttle valves can't open. However, when the engine is warm and the choke opens,

Fig. 9-14. A secondary lockout device used to prevent the secondary throttle valves from opening when the engine is cold. (Courtesy of Pontiac Motor Division)

the movement of the choke linkage and trip lever pulls the lockout lever slot clear of the tang, so that the primary linkage can open the secondary throttle valves for full throttle performance.

Carburetor-Assist Devices

Up to this point, this text has covered the design and operation of single, dual, and four-barrel carburetors. Any of these carburetor styles has one or more add-on assist devices to either improve engine operation under various conditions or reduce emission levels. This chapter covers the assist devices that deal with improved engine operation and discusses those that deal with emission control later.

Hot-Idle Compensator Valve

During long periods of idling, especially on a hot day, the engine has a tendency to heat up sufficiently to cause a fuel percolation in the carburetor fuel bowl. The fuel vapors caused by this percolation enter the carburetor barrels by the internal bowl vents. As a result, the air/fuel mixture becomes too rich; the engine idles rough or stalls. To compensate for this additional fuel due to percolation, a *hot-idle compensator valve* admits additional air into the intake manifold.

A typical hot-idle compensator is shown in Fig. 9–15; this device consists of a passage and a thermostatically controlled

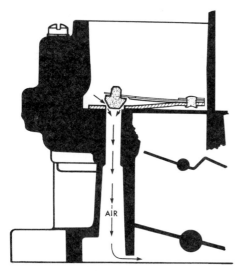

Fig. 9–15. *The hot-idle compensator permits additional air to enter the intake manifold. (Courtesy of Pontiac Motor Division)*

valve. The passage in this particular carburetor runs from an opening above the venturi to the throttle body, below the throttle valve. The function of this passage, when uncovered by the valve, is to permit additional air to bypass the throttle valve during hot engine idle.

The thermostatically controlled valve is simply a pad attached to a bimetallic strip. The pad itself forms the valve that opens or closes the opening in the air passage. A *bimetallic strip* is nothing more than two different types of metals fused together. One may be spring steel for tension, and the other could be brass or copper. Both metals have different rates of expansion and contraction.

At a given temperature the strip is straight; that is, both strips are the same length. However, as the temperature of the strip rises, the copper portion expands more than the steel; consequently, the bimetallic strip bends. When the strip cools down again, the copper section contracts (shrinks) more than the steel portion, and the bimetallic strip straightens out.

When serving as part of the fast-idle compensator valve assembly, the strip is straight at normal operating temperature. This position seats the pad over the air-passage opening. When engine temperature rises to a certain point, the bimetallic strip bends and lifts the pad off its seat; and extra air enters the intake manifold. The valve pad stays off its seat until engine temperature drops to the normal level.

There are two other locations for this valve assembly other than the barrel of the carburetor. It may be inside a chamber on the rear of the carburetor, covered by a dust cover, or the compensator valve may be part of an assembly inserted into the positive crankcase ventilation hose near the carburetor.

Dashpots

Manufacturers have installed *dashpots* on vehicles for many years. When used on vehicles with automatic transmissions, this device was primarily necessary to prevent engine stalling due to an overly rich mixture on rapid engine deceleration. In other words, if the driver rapidly opened, then closed, the throttle valve, the engine would receive a rich mixture before its air flow was cut off. This situation created an unbalanced condition in which there was too much fuel and insufficient air; therefore, the engine stalled.

On vehicles with a standard transmission, this doesn't happen because this transmission provides a direct connection between the drive axles and the engine, so that the momentum of the vehicle keeps the engine running. However, the engine does produce high hydrocarbon (HC) exhaust emissions at this time.

The dashpot takes care of both problems by controlling the rate in which the throttle valve closes. In other words, the dashpot prevents the throttle valves from closing immediately after the driver releases the accelerator pedal. Then, the engine receives sufficient air to consume the rich mixture without stalling or producing excessive HC emissions.

Although manufacturers have used hydraulic and magnetic dashpots, the most common one consists of a spring-loaded diaphragm inside a housing (Fig. 9–16). A rod attached to the front of the diaphragm extends from the metal housing and contacts the throttle-valve arm. When the

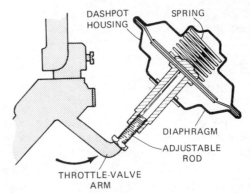

Fig. 9–16.   A typical throttle return dashpot.

throttle valve opens during vehicle acceleration, the arm moves away from the rod; the diaphragm spring forces the rod from the housing as far as possible.

As the spring moves the diaphragm and rod outward, air enters the housing behind the diaphragm through an air-bleed hole. Then, when the throttle valve closes during deceleration, the throttle arm contacts the rod again. However, in order to permit the throttle valves to close all the way, the arm must force the rod back into the housing.

In order for this to occur, the arm must overcome two obstacles: the tension on the spring and the air in the housing. The force of the spring is easy enough to overcome because only a small spring tension is necessary to extend the rod. However, a greater force is necessary to cause the rod and attached diaphragm to push the air out of the housing through the small bleed hole. This hole acts as a restriction, so the air escapes slowly. This action retards the movement of both the arm and throttle rod, which in turn slows the closing action of the throttle valves.

Antidiesel Solenoid

Many vehicles utilize an *antidiesel solenoid* to reduce the effect of run-on or dieseling. *Dieseling* in a gasoline engine is a condition in which extreme combustion-chamber heat continues to ignite excess fuel after the driver turns off the ignition switch. As a result, the engine wants to keep running.

Dieseling of late-model engines is the direct result of higher overall operating temperatures, lean idle air/fuel mixtures, and retarded ignition timing at idle. All of these factors bring about very high combustion-chamber temperatures—high enough at times to ignite an air/fuel mixture.

In addition, due to the leaner air/fuel mixture, late-model engines must idle faster, so that the throttle valve is open slightly for curb-idle operation. As a result, engine vacuum can continue to pull a fresh charge of air/fuel mixture from the carburetor's idle ports, even with the ignition switch off. Consequently, the high temperatures within the combustion chambers ignite this mixture, and the engine continues to run.

The antidiesel solenoid (Fig. 9–17) overcomes this condition by allowing the throttle valve to close beyond the normal curb-idle position. To do this, the solenoid provides the normal stop position for the throttle lever or adjusting screw during the curb-idle condition. In other words, when the driver turns on the ignition switch, it energizes the solenoid, and the solenoid plunger moves out to contact the lever or idle-speed adjusting screw on the throttle shaft. This action holds the throttle open slightly for normal curb idle.

When the driver turns off the ignition, the solenoid receives no electrical current. Consequently, the plunger retracts and allows the throttle lever or screw to move toward the closed position until it strikes

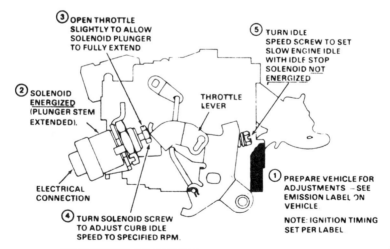

IDLE SPEED ADJUSTMENT - WITH SOLENOID

Fig. 9–17. An antidieseling solenoid allows the throttle valve to close farther when the engine is shut off. (Courtesy of General Motors Corp.)

the closed throttle stop. This action completely closes the throttle valve that blocks air flow into the intake manifold. As a result, the engine stops running due to a lack of air flow.

Air-Conditioning Idle Solenoid

Many automobiles with air conditioning have a special idle solenoid (Fig. 9–18). This device looks much like the antidiesel solenoid, but it operates at a different time and for a different reason. The *air-conditioning idle solenoid* energizes as the driver turns *on* the air conditioner. The plunger of this solenoid then moves forward to contact a special bracket on the throttle valve shaft. This action raises the normal curb-idle speed to prevent the engine from stalling due to the increased load of the compressor.

When the driver turns the air-conditioning system off, the solenoid de-energizes. The solenoid plunger then retracts, allowing the engine to return to its normal curb-idle rpm. Actually, the engine rpm is nearly the same in both situations. However, the solenoid plunger must open the throttle valves a little more, when the air conditioner is on, in order to compensate for the increased compressor load and thereby maintain a fairly stable engine idle at all times.

Intake Manifolds— Function

Gasoline engines require an *intake manifold* between the carburetor and the intake-valve ports; this device performs two basic functions. First, the manifold provides an environment that promotes vaporization of the atomized air/fuel mix-

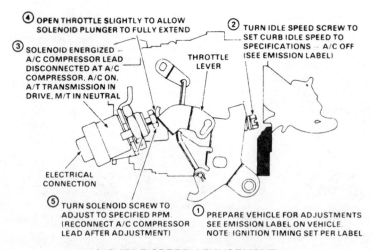

④ OPEN THROTTLE SLIGHTLY TO ALLOW SOLENOID PLUNGER TO FULLY EXTEND

② TURN IDLE SPEED SCREW TO SET CURB IDLE SPEED TO SPECIFICATIONS – A/C OFF (SEE EMISSION LABEL)

③ SOLENOID ENERGIZED – A/C COMPRESSOR LEAD DISCONNECTED AT A/C COMPRESSOR, A/C ON, A/T TRANSMISSION IN DRIVE, M/T IN NEUTRAL

THROTTLE LEVER

ELECTRICAL CONNECTION

⑤ TURN SOLENOID SCREW TO ADJUST TO SPECIFIED RPM. (RECONNECT A/C COMPRESSOR LEAD AFTER ADJUSTMENT)

① PREPARE VEHICLE FOR ADJUSTMENTS SEE EMISSION LABEL ON VEHICLE. NOTE: IGNITION TIMING SET PER LABEL.

A/C IDLE SPEED ADJUSTMENT

Fig. 9–18.   An air-conditioning solenoid increases normal engine idle when the driver turns on the air conditioner. (Courtesy of General Motors Corp.)

ture. Second, the intake manifold distributes the gaseous air/fuel mixture into each intake-valve port.

Problems in Fuel Distribution

These may seem like very simple jobs; however, the composition of the fuel and the varying operating phases of the engine create certain problems. For example, if all the hydrocarbons in gasoline vaporized at the same rate, the task of the intake manifold would be easy. However, this is not the case, since various hydrocarbon compounds are necessary to form the liquid gasoline, and these different compounds vaporize at different temperatures. As a result, not all the fuel vaporizes completely at the same rate, even under ideal conditions. Consequently, when the engine is operating, fuel particles of different weights move through the intake manifold and into the valve ports. This varies the quality of the fuel mixture that reaches each combustion chamber. Therefore, some cylinders develop more power than others, and some cylinders have a greater tendency to detonate than others.

To assist in maintaining the necessary balance in fuel quality between cylinders, manufacturers provide a mechanism to heat the intake manifold in order to improve vaporization. The heat tends to keep all the different compounds that form gasoline vaporized so that the manifold distributes fuel particles of more uniform weight. However, since heat expands air, the heating of the air/fuel mixture has a tendency to reduce the volumetric efficiency (breathing ability) of the engine and therefore engine power. Consequently, the amount of heat applied to the manifold must be carefully controlled. In other words, the amount of manifold heat must be a compromise between what is necessary to reduce the number of heavier fuel particles and adequate volumetric efficiency.

While incomplete vaporization reduces mixture quality, other factors reduce both quality and quantity of the fuel particles entering the combustion chambers. For instance, any heavier fuel particles have a greater inertia than the lighter particles. Therefore, the heavier particles tend to move past a branch opening in a manifold leading to an intake port. As a result, the cylinder supplied by this particular branch does not receive its full quota of such heavier particles but receives an excess of lighter particles. This action tends to vary the air/fuel ratio among the various engine cylinders (Fig. 9–19).

Along with this factor, the position of the throttle and choke valve affect fuel particle distribution because they both control air flow. While the engine is operating, the carburetor delivers finely atomized fuel droplets into the incoming air in a given combustible ratio. These particles begin to evaporate (vaporize) as soon as they leave the carburetor. Under efficient operating conditions, only about 60 percent of the liquid fuel particles completely vaporize by the time they reach the combustion chamber. This simply means that some of the heavier liquid fuel particles remain in suspension in the moving charge within the manifold.

These heavier particles remain in suspension during periods of high mixture velocity, such as when the choke and throttle valves are wide open. At this time, the mixture velocity may be as high as 300 feet per second. Consequently, the heavier particles, not impeded by the

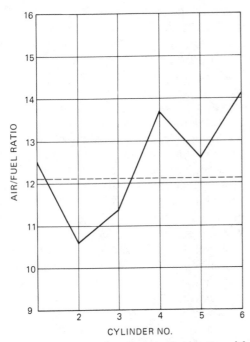

Fig. 9-19.   Note that the air/fuel ratios differ in the various cylinders, with cylinder 2 receiving a very rich mixture while cylinders 4 and 6 receive lean mixtures.

manifold obstructions, are easily swept into the intake ports, carried along by the smaller particles and the air flow. As a result, the engine receives a somewhat more uniform mixture of heavier and lighter fuel particles.

However, when the throttle or choke valve is partially to fully closed, mixture velocity in the manifold decreases. If and when the mixture velocity drops below about 50 feet per second, the heavier particles begin to separate from the air and lighter particles. This action occurs, for example, at idle speeds where intake velocity is usually below this value. As a result, the carburetor must supply additional fuel to the mixture in order to deliver a combustible mixture to the cylinders at low engine speeds.

At this point, the reader may wonder what happens to the heavier fuel particles that do not vaporize completely. All particles eventually pass into the combustion chamber. However, any fuel particle that is not in a combustible form (sufficiently vaporized) may not burn completely or at all during the combustion process. Instead, these hydrocarbon particles either work their way into the crankcase through the blowby gases or enter the atmosphere via the exhaust gases.

Finally, due to these variations in fuel mixture quality and quantity, the combustion pressures vary among cylinders in an operating engine. In a particular six-cylinder engine operating at a given rpm, for example, this pressure may vary from a low of 125 psi to a maximum of 310 psi. Cylinders 3 and 4 of this engine develop the minimum pressure, while cylinders 5 and 6 develop the maximum, and cylinders 1 and 2 produce approximately 280 psi. Enriching the air/fuel ratio to improve the combustion pressure in cylinders 3 and 4 results in an overly rich mixture in cylinders 1 and 2, which reduces their combustion process.

In order to improve this situation in any engine, engineers are striving to improve intake manifold design. Changes include better control of manifold heating and the routing of manifold passages. Redesigned passages either provide a more direct path or have longer and more sweeping curves in the various branches leading from the base of the carburetor to the intake-valve ports. This latter feature provides fewer restrictions, therefore more even distribution of fuel particles. The result is improved volumetric efficiency in all cylinders and consequently an improvement in engine performance.

Intake Manifold Design

Manufacturers usually form intake manifolds from either cast iron or aluminum. The manifold itself has a series of passages or runners, which actually carry the air/fuel mixture from the carburetor to the intake ports (Fig. 9–20). In some intake manifolds, one runner supplies the mixture to two adjacent cylinders. However, most modern engines have separate runners to each intake port. This permits a more equal runner size and shape, which aids in equalizing the air/fuel mixture distribution to each cylinder.

The actual size of these runners must be a compromise. The runners must have large enough openings to permit adequate mixture flow for maximum power, yet small enough to maintain sufficient mixture velocity. This maintains the heavier fuel particles in suspension, as required for equal mixture distribution. Automobile engine manifolds usually have a design that provides economy at light-load, part-throttle operation. These manifolds, therefore, have much smaller openings in their runners than a racing-type engine. However, a smaller size is adequate to handle the mixture velocities

throughout the normal operating range of the automobile engine.

The air/fuel mixture flow through the manifold is also dependent upon runner shape and the smoothness of the interior wall of the runner. A runner with a sharp bend, for example, tends to increase fuel particle separation. Air is lighter than the fuel particles; consequently, it can make sharp turns much easier and quicker than the heavier fuel particles.

The cross-sectional shape of runners may also differ among various manifold designs. A runner with a completely rounded appearance has a larger open area than most other runner designs with about the same wall surface area, but in a manifold, this is not always the most desirable contour. Most intake manifold runner floors are flat (Fig. 9–21), so that any heavier fuel particles that drop out of the mixture can spread out in a thin layer on the runner floor and rapidly vaporize.

The intake manifold must also have a design to keep the main manifold floor, under the carburetor, level with the engine installed in the vehicle. This is necessary

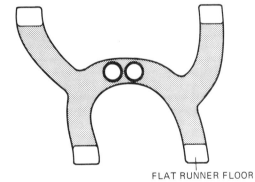

Fig. 9–21. A flat runner floor permits any heavier fuel particles that drop out of the mixture to spread out so that they can rapidly vaporize.

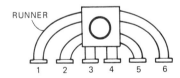

Fig. 9–20. The intake manifold has a series of passages or runners, which carry the air/fuel mixture from the carburetor to the intake ports.

because the rear of the installed engine is somewhat lower than the front, for improved drive-shaft positioning. If the main floor were not level, any condensed liquid fuel on the floor would flow to the low point. This, of course, would unbalance fuel distribution in the runners, causing some cylinders to be overly rich on start-up. This would result in an engine being somewhat harder to start, especially when cold. Finally, manifolds often have *ribs,* or *guide vanes,* positioned in the main floor. These devices aid in the equal distribution of the mixture to the cylinders runners, even though some of the fuel may still be in liquid form.

The smoothness of the interior runner surfaces also affects fuel distribution. For example, rough interior runner surfaces add a drag and turbulence to mixture velocity. This causes some of the heavier fuel particles to drop out of the mixture, which upsets mixture distribution.

Intake Manifold Types

Today three types or classifications of intake manifolds are used: single-barrel, two-barrel, and four-barrel. The type used on a given engine depends on the number of cylinders, cylinder arrangement, and type of carburetor. For example, four- and six-cylinder in-line engines usually use a manifold for single-barrel carburetors. However, as noted, some in-line engines use dual-barrel carburetors for improved engine breathing and improved emission control.

Figure 9–20 shows a typical single-barrel manifold used on a six-cylinder engine. Note that this manifold has six runners, one for each intake port. Also, each runner has a long, sweeping, curved design, which provides a more equal dis-

tribution of the air/fuel mixture into each cylinder.

As far as supplying an adequate air/fuel mixture, a single-barrel carburetor and manifold perform exceptionally well on four- and six-cylinder in-line engines. The reason for this is simple if you consider the period of the intake stroke in relation to the entire four-stroke cycle. In the four-stroke cycle of an engine, the inlet stroke occurs only about one-fourth of the total cycle. On a one-cylinder engine, the carburetor would only function on the intake stroke or about one-fourth of the time.

A four-cylinder engine could, therefore, operate on a single-barrel unit. Manufacturers accomplish this by timing each of the intake strokes so that it takes a different quarter of the 720 degrees of the four-stroke cycle. By doing this, one single-barrel carburetor can satisfy the requirements of all four cylinders just as well as it can one.

On a six-cylinder engine, the single-barrel carburetor must work a little harder. In the six-cylinder, the intake strokes of two cylinders overlap one another. Therefore, the single-barrel carburetor is supplying fuel to two cylinders at the same time. To overcome this problem in the six-cylinder in-line engines, the manufacturer enlarges the carburetor barrel size over that used on a four-cylinder engine.

Figure 9–22 illustrates a dual-carburetor manifold used on a V-8 engine. This manifold has two independent sections, each supplying four cylinders of the engine. In other words, the opening in each section indexes with four runners. Therefore, when a dual-barrel carburetor is in operation, one of its barrels supplies the air/fuel mixture to one opening and four runners; the other barrel provides the mix-

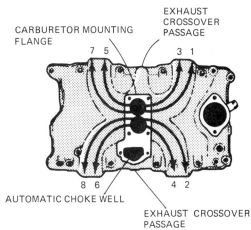

Fig. 9–22. In a dual-barrel manifold, each carburetor barrel supplies an air/fuel mixture to four cylinders.

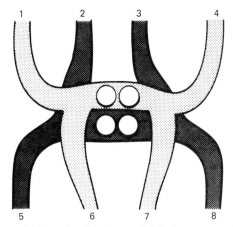

Fig. 9–23. A dual-manifold design with upper and lower runners.

ture to the second opening and its runners. In a fashion similar to the four-cylinder engine, the V-8 engine timing is such that only one cylinder at a time draws a mixture charge from each carburetor barrel.

In the dual manifold (Fig. 9–22), each carburetor barrel feeds a mixture to all four cylinders on one side of the engine while the other barrel does likewise to the opposite four cylinders. However, this is not the case in all V-8 manifold designs. Figure 9–23 shows a dual-carburetor manifold in which each barrel supplies an air/fuel mixture to the two end cylinders of one bank and the two center cylinders of another bank.

The actual design or positioning of the runners in a V-8 manifold must match the engine's firing order. To accomplish this, the manufacturers of many V-8 manifolds form its runners on two levels in order to fit them all between the cylinder heads. As a result, the carburetor barrels feed the successive firing cylinders alternately from an upper and then a lower runner.

Figure 9–23 illustrates very well this particular practice. The upper runners transport the air/fuel mixtures to cylinders 1, 4, 6, and 7. The lower runners service cylinders 2, 3, 5, and 8. The firing order for this engine is 1–5–4–2–6–3–7–8. Consequently, cylinder 1 feeds first from an upper runner off one carburetor barrel; cylinder 5 feeds next, off a lower runner that indexes with the other carburetor barrel. This process continues until the manifold supplies all the cylinders, in the firing order, with a combustible mixture.

The design of the V-8 manifold runners may be such that it also improves manifold efficiency. For example, runner design may be the *log type*, which provides the largest possible runner cross-sectional area for maximum air flow (Fig. 9–24). Many other manifold runners form an *H pattern*, which provides a compromise between maximum performance and the best use of all the available manifold space. Some manifolds have tuned runners. *Tuned* runners have a designed length that takes advantage of the inertia effect of the incoming air/fuel charge. The manufacturer times the intake valves of

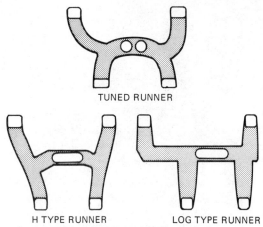

TUNED RUNNER

H TYPE RUNNER   LOG TYPE RUNNER

Fig. 9–24. *Runner designs also vary to improve manifold efficiency.*

an engine with this type of manifold, so that they open just as the fuel mixture reaches the cylinders. This action allows the charge to enter each cylinder with a ram effect.

V-6 intake manifolds are very similar in design to the V-8 manifold. The main difference is that one manifold opening along with one carburetor barrel feeds three cylinders instead of four. Consequently, each carburetor barrel is only responsible for supplying an air/fuel mixture to three runners and three intake ports during the engine's operating cycle.

Four-Barrel Manifolds

Generally speaking, a four-barrel intake manifold is nothing more than a two-barrel manifold with two additional openings (Fig. 9–25). These secondary openings may be slightly larger than the primary ones, but each secondary opening indexes into the exact same runners fed by the primary opening in front of it. Therefore, when the secondary barrels of a four-barrel carburetor function under heavy acceleration, they supply addi-

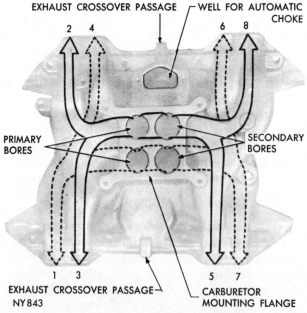

EXHAUST CROSSOVER PASSAGE   WELL FOR AUTOMATIC CHOKE

2   4   6   8

PRIMARY BORES

SECONDARY BORES

1   3   5   7

EXHAUST CROSSOVER PASSAGE
NY 843

CARBURETOR MOUNTING FLANGE

Fig. 9–25. *A typical four-barrel manifold.*

tional fuel to the same runners serviced by the primary barrels.

Manifold Heat

As mentioned, some heat is necessary in the intake manifold so that as many fuel particles as possible will vaporize. The actual method used to transfer heat to the intake manifold's main floor depends on the type and design of the engine. For example, on six-cylinder in-line engines, the manufacturer usually places the intake manifold directly above the exhaust manifold (Fig. 9–26). Surrounding the center section (the main floor) of the intake manifold, directly below the carburetor, is a heater jacket or heat stove. This stove indexes with passages leading to the exhaust manifold.

A *heat-riser valve* controls the flow of exhaust gases around the heat stove. During the engine warm-up period, this valve is in its closed position (*A* of Fig. 9–26).

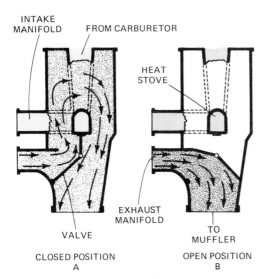

Fig. 9–26. The manifold heat control system of a six-cylinder in-line engine. (Courtesy of Chrysler Corp.)

This action forces the engine exhaust gases to pass around the heat stove before passing into the exhaust system. As a result, the manifold floor inside the stove heats up to improve fuel vaporization.

When the engine reaches about normal operating temperature, the heat-riser valve opens (*B* of Fig. 9–26). This valve position prevents exhaust-gas circulation around the stove. This prevents excessive heating of the air/fuel charge.

Excessive heating causes the mixture to expand excessively in the manifold area. This reduces the overall mass of the mixture charge available to the cylinders, thus reducing the volumetric efficiency and power of the engine. Furthermore, an overheated charge can bring about detonation and preignition. Consequently, it is important that the intake manifold not receive excessive amounts of heat, once the engine reaches normal operating temperature. By this point, normal heat radiation from the engine is sufficient to maintain sufficient heat in the intake manifold to vaporize the fuel.

In V-type engines where the intake manifold fits between the two cylinder heads and away from the exhaust manifold, the intake manifold has a special passageway known as the exhaust crossover (Fig. 9–27). This crossover passage indexes with ports in the cylinder heads that lead to the exhaust manifolds. With this design, the crossover carries the hot exhaust gases during the warm-up period around a heat stove that is very close to the main manifold floor, providing it with the necessary heat.

Again, a heat-riser valve controls the direction of exhaust gas flow. For instance, during the warm-up period, the valve closes. This action causes the exhaust gases from one cylinder bank to flow from

AIR-FUEL MIXTURE PASSAGES
FROM CARBURETOR

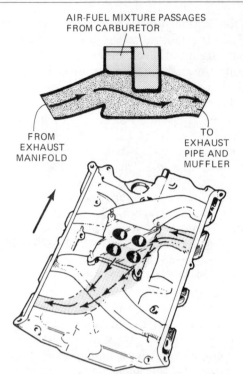

FROM
EXHAUST
MANIFOLD

TO
EXHAUST
PIPE AND
MUFFLER

Fig. 9-27. *The exhaust gas circulation through an intake manifold of a V-8 engine.*

the exhaust port in the cylinder head, through the crossover passage, around the heat stove, out the other side's manifold, and into the exhaust port in the opposite head. From this point, the exhaust gases pass into the exhaust system.

As the exhaust manifold temperature increases, the heat-riser valve opens. The exhaust gases from both cylinder banks can pass into the exhaust system. When the engine is operating at normal temperature, heat radiation and a very small flow of exhaust gases keep the manifold stove and floor hot enough for adequate vaporization.

In some engines, heated engine coolant instead of exhaust gases provides the necessary heat to the intake manifold. Manufacturers employ this source of heat in engines where mechanical design makes it difficult to utilize exhaust heat and where a uniform temperature is desirable. In the system shown in Fig. 9-28, hot coolant from the water-pump bypass outlet circulates through passageways in a special detachable heat stove during engine warm-up. This stove fits between the base of the carburetor and the main floor of the intake manifold.

When the engine reaches normal operating temperature, the thermostat opens. Consequently, no coolant, or very little, flows through the water-pump bypass and through the heat stove. As a result, this system only supplies a great deal of heat to the manifold during the warm-up period.

Choke Heat

Many automatic-choke bimetallic coils receive heat via the exhaust system. In some applications, this heat passes to the coil through a tube inserted into a special heat stove in the exhaust manifold. An alternative method uses a pocket in the intake manifold in which the coil rests (Fig. 9-25). This pocket is above the exhaust

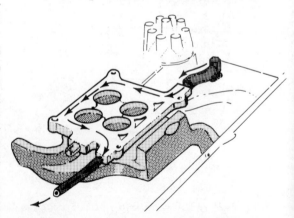

Fig. 9-28. *A coolant circulation type system, used to heat an intake manifold.*

crossover passage within the manifold; consequently, the coil senses the exhaust temperature in the crossover passage.

Review

This section will assist you in determining how well you remember the material contained in this chapter. Read each item carefully. If you can't complete the statement, review the section in the chapter that covers the material.

1. A dual-barrel carburetor has two _____ systems.
   a. idle
   b. choke
   c. float
   d. pump

2. The dual-barrel power system, discussed in this chapter, consists of a _____ _____ and a power piston.
   a. power valve
   b. metering rod
   c. mechanical linkage
   d. vacuum valve

3. The function of the plunger ball check in the pump system of the dual carburetor is to _____ any gas vapors from the pump well.
   a. eliminate
   b. pump
   c. force
   d. release

4. A quad carburetor is found on _____ engines.
   a. four-cylinder
   b. six-cylinder
   c. V-8
   d. V-6

5. All quad carburetors on the secondary side have a _____ system.

   a. choke
   b. main-metering
   c. pump
   d. float

6. In a four-barrel carburetor, the _____ _____ _____ controls the operation of the metering rods.
   a. power piston
   b. air valves
   c. throttle valves
   d. power valve

7. A _____ _____ mechanism prevents the air or secondary throttle valves from opening when the engine is cold.
   a. secondary lockout
   b. vacuum assist
   c. fast-idle cam
   d. choke unloader

8. The _____ _____ valve prevents rough idle or stalling when the engine gets hot.
   a. dashpot
   b. hot-idle compensator
   c. bowl antipercolator
   d. secondary throttle

9. The device sometimes used to retard the closing of the throttle valves is the _____ _____.
   a. secondary lockout
   b. choke unloader
   c. dashpot
   d. fast-idle linkage

10. The _____ _____ prevents engine run-on after the driver turns off the ignition switch.
    a. hot-idle compensator
    b. dashpot
    c. air-conditioning solenoid
    d. antidiesel solenoid

11. Under ideal conditions only about _____ percent of the total fuel par-

ticles vaporize before they reach the combustion chambers.

a. 50
b. 60
c. 70
d. 80

12. The variation in fuel mixture quality and quantity received by the cylinders causes a difference in all the cylinder _____ pressures.

a. compression
b. combustion
c. exhaust
d. intake

13. The floor of the intake manifold sometimes has _____ to aid in the distribution of the mixture to the cylinder runners.

a. guides
b. vents
c. ribs
d. partitions

14. Single-barrel manifolds are found on _____ engines.

a. V-6
b. V-8
c. in-line
d. opposed

15. In a V-6 engine, each barrel of the dual carburetor feeds _____ cylinders.

a. six
b. one
c. two
d. three

16. A _____ _____ valve controls the flow of exhaust gases around the intake manifold stove.

a. heat-riser
b. flow control
c. exhaust gas
d. gas regulating

For the answers, turn to the Appendix.

As a tune-up technician, you very frequently inspect and service the various types of air-cleaner assemblies. The inspection or type of service required on each unit depends on the type of element and the basic design of its housing. The most common elements in use are the dry paper, oil-wetted paper, oil bath, oil-wetted mesh, and the oil-wetted polyurethane.

Inspection and Service Intervals

Under normal operating conditions, the vehicle owner should have the air-cleaner element inspected and serviced at the interval period specified by the manufacturer. This interval, depending on the type of engine, is usually between 12,000 to 24,000 vehicle miles. However, operation of a vehicle in dusty areas causes rapid clogging of the filter element, resulting in the enrichment of the carburetor mixture. Under these conditions, it is necessary to service the element more often.

Therefore, as part of a preventive maintenance program, a technician services or changes an air-cleaner element at a given mileage interval. However, the technician should always inspect the element as part of the tune-up procedure, even if it is not due for servicing at the same time as the tune-up. The reason for this inspection is twofold. First, the owner may have forgotten to have the filter serviced at the last interval; second, the dusty or dirty driving conditions may have prematurely clogged the filter.

Chapter 10

AIR-CLEANER AND CARBURETOR SERVICE

Dry-Paper Element Service

Removal

To remove a typical dry-paper element (Fig. 10–1):

1. Loosen and remove the housing cover retaining wing or hex nuts.

2. Remove the housing cover.

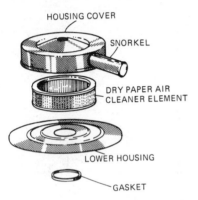

HOUSING COVER

SNORKEL

DRY PAPER AIR CLEANER ELEMENT

LOWER HOUSING

GASKET

Fig. 10–1. Servicing the dry-paper air-cleaner assembly.

3. Lift and remove the element from the lower housing above the carburetor.

4. Disconnect any vacuum signal hoses from connections on the lower housing. Then, remove the housing and gasket.

Dry-Paper Element Inspection

You can quickly inspect the cleanliness of this type of element with a droplight (Fig. 10–2) by following these instructions.

1. If so equipped, remove the polyurethane band from around the element.

2. Position the droplight on the inside of the element with its bulb facing outward or toward you.

3. Rotate the element around the droplight until you have inspected the entire filtering area of the element.

Results and Indications

1. If there is very little or no light penetration through the element, replace it.

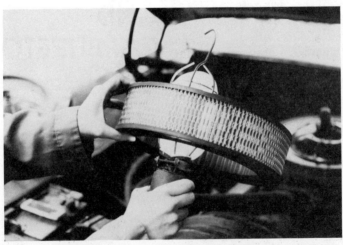

Fig. 10–2. Inspecting a dry-paper element with a droplight.

2. If the light penetrates the majority of the surface area of the element, it is still reusable. However, you may want to remove any accumulated dust and dirt particles by lightly tapping the element against the edge of a bench. Then, carefully remove any remaining particles with low-pressure compressed air. When doing this, always direct the air blast from the inside to the outside of the element.

Note: Many technicians feel that if a dry element requires cleaning, they should just replace it. This is probably the best rule to follow in the long run in order to reduce comebacks, especially when the mileage on the filter is not known.

Fig. 10-3. Cleaning a polyurethane band. (Courtesy of General Motors Corp.)

Cleaning a Polyurethane Band

Each time a dry element with a polyurethane band requires replacement, service the band as outlined.

1. If not already done, remove the band from the paper filter.

2. Inspect the polywrap band for tears, and replace it if necessary.

3. If not torn, wash the band in kerosene or mineral spirits, then squeeze out the excess solvent to dry the band as much as possible (Fig. 10-3). *Note:* Never use a hot degreaser or any other solvent containing acetone or similar solvent to clean this type of band. Also, never shake, swing, or wring out the band to remove excess solvent, as this action may tear the polyurethane material.

4. Dip the band into a bath of light engine oil, and then carefully squeeze out the excess oil.

5. Install the band carefully around the outer surface of the paper filter (Fig. 10-4).

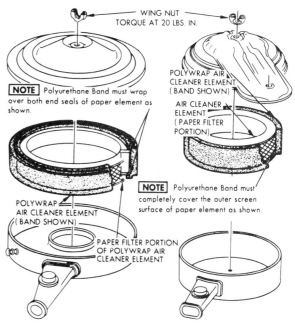

Fig. 10-4. Replacing a polyurethane band over a dry-paper element. (Courtesy of General Motors Corp.)

Dry-Paper Element Installation

To reinstall a serviceable or new element follow these steps (Fig. 10–1).

1. Clean the lower housing and air-cleaner cover with a clean rag dipped in solvent. Then, blow both components dry with compressed air.

2. Inspect the air-cleaner cover and lower housing for cracks or distortion. Replace damaged parts as necessary.

3. Install a new gasket over the air-cleaner mounting flange on the carburetor, and position the lower housing over the new gasket.

4. Reconnect removed vacuum hoses onto their respective fittings on the lower housing, and if so equipped, align the heat-stove tube into its inlet in the housing.

5. Install the paper element into the lower housing. *Note:* In most cases, you can position either end of the filter up. However, certain filter designs require that a given side of the element face upward or toward the cover. In these situations, the filter design allows it to go into the housing only one way, or the elements have markings as to which end must face upward.

6. Install the air-cleaner cover and its attaching nuts. *Caution:* Do not overtorque these nuts, especially the one over the center of the cover. Excessive torque on this wing nut and its stud can warp the carburetor air horn (upper section of the carburetor throat) and cause the choke valve to stick.

Oil-Wetted Paper Element Service

The inspection and service techniques for wetted-paper elements are the same as those for a dry element, with one exception. You must never wash, tap, or blow out with air an oil-wetted paper element, because it is so fragile. Therefore, service is limited to element inspection and replacement.

Oil-Bath Air Cleaner Service

To service a typical oil-bath air cleaner:

1. Loosen the screw through the clamp that holds the air-cleaner assembly to the carburetor. Also, if so equipped, remove any and all strap brace screws from the filter housing.

2. Disconnect and remove the crankcase ventilation hose.

3. Remove the filter assembly from the carburetor.

4. Remove the wing nut from the cleaner cover (Fig. 10–5) and separate the cover from the reservoir.

5. Empty the contents of the reservoir in a waste-oil container. Then, wash the reservoir and lower housing in clean solvent. Blow the assembly dry with compressed air. *Note:* If the reservoir section also contains a silencing chamber, read the caution under item 7 of this procedure.

6. Fill the reservoir with the proper weight of fresh oil to the measured line inside the reservoir.

7. Take the cover assembly, which in-

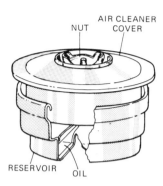

Fig. 10-5. Servicing the oil-bath air cleaner.

cludes the silencing chamber and filter, in both hands, and begin dipping the *filter section only* up and down in clean solvent. Continue this process until the filter element is clean. Then, wipe the cover and silencing chamber with a rag soaked in solvent. Permit the assembly to air dry. *Caution:* Never use compressed air to blow dry this filter element. Also, never submerge the silencing chamber in solvent. The chamber will fill up, but you cannot pour out all the solvent. As a result, the engine can run extremely rich for about a week until all the solvent evaporates.

8. Reinstall the cover over the reservoir and install the wing nut. Tighten the wing nut fingertight.

9. Install the air-cleaner assembly over the air horn, and tighten its holddown clamp screw to specifications.

10. Reinstall any removed strap braces, tightening their attaching screws to specifications.

11. Reconnect the crankcase ventilation hose if so equipped.

Oil-Wetted Mesh Element Service

To clean and service this type of element, follow this recommended procedure (Fig. 10–6).

1. Loosen the clamp screw that holds the filter assembly to the carburetor air horn.

2. If so equipped, remove the crankcase ventilation hose from its fitting on the filter housing. Then, lift the filter assembly off of the carburetor.

3. Loosen and remove the wing nut that secures the cover to the lower filter housing. Then, separate the unit into three sections: the cover, filter element, and lower housing.

4. Wipe the cover and lower housing with a rag soaked in solvent. Blow dry both units with compressed air.

5. Dip the filter element up and down in solvent until it is clean. Then, permit the element to drip dry.

6. Re-oil the element, all the way around, with drops of engine oil. *Do not soak this element with oil.*

7. Reinstall the element into the lower housing. Next, install the cover, along

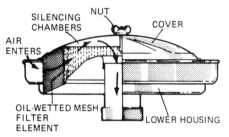

Fig. 10-6. Servicing the oil-wetted mesh filter.

with its wing nut, over the housing. Tighten the wing nut fingertight.

8. Position the assembly over the carburetor air horn, and tighten its clamp screw to specifications.

9. Reinstall the ventilation hose over its housing fitting, if so equipped.

Polyurethane Element Service

The polyurethane filter element fits over a steel mesh support. To service this type of element:

1. Remove and disassemble the filter assembly as you would any other dry-paper element assembly.

2. Carefully separate the polyurethane element from its support screen.

3. Wash the element using the same procedure and the same type of solvent as for polyurethane bands (Fig. 10-7).

4. Dip the element in light engine oil, and carefully squeeze out the excess oil.

Fig. 10-7. *Servicing the polyurethane element.*

5. Carefully reinstall the element over its support screen,.

6. Clean the cover and lower housing with a rag soaked in solvent. Blow both units dry with compressed air.

7. Reassemble the housing, filter, and cover over the carburetor air horn, following the same procedure as for a dry-paper filter.

Carburetor Service

The following sections outline the steps necessary in reconditioning a typical carburetor. Because of the large number of carburetor types found in automobiles, it is impossible to cover each type here. However, the service techniques presented here apply to any carburetor model. Therefore, with the mastery of these service tips, along with a service manual, a technician can recondition any automotive carburetor.

Parts Ordering

Before actually removing the carburetor for overhaul, it is a good idea first to order the carburetor overhaul kit. This will save you time, especially if the kit is not in stock and has to be ordered.

To order the proper kit, first remove the air cleaner and locate the identification tag on the carburetor (Fig. 10-8). This tag has the part number necessary to order the proper repair kit and obtain the correct adjustment specifications for the model of carburetor being serviced. In other words, this number identifies this carburetor model for use on a particular engine. It is very important that you use this number because of the many varia-

Fig. 10-8. A typical identification tag attached to a carburetor.

tions necessary to fit a given carburetor type to many engine configurations. Finally, because of the tag's importance, *always replace it after reassembling a carburetor.*

Carburetor Removal

These procedures include all the usual and necessary steps for carburetor removal. However, the exact sequence in which you perform these steps may vary according to the type of carburetor installation. To remove a typical carburetor:

1. If not already done, disconnect all air-cleaner hoses and vacuum lines, and remove the air cleaner.

2. Disconnect the throttle linkage by removing the necessary clips or connections, and place the linkage to one side.

3. If so equipped, disconnect the linkage from the well-type bimetallic coil assembly. If the choke assembly is an integral type with hot-water connections, disconnect these hoses at the choke housing. If the integral choke has a hot-air tube instead, disconnect it. If the choke has an electrical heating element, remove any electrical connections from the choke cover.

4. Using two line wrenches, disconnect the fuel line from the carburetor.

5. Remove and mark all vacuum lines connected to the carburetor. Use masking tape, colored golf tees, or clothespins on the end of each line to identify each connection. This procedure takes a little more time but makes it easier for you later to reinstall these lines in their proper location.

6. Disconnect all electrical solenoid connectors.

7. Loosen and remove all the carburetor attaching capscrews or nuts. Then, carefully lift the carburetor straight up and off the manifold.

8. If the carburetor sticks to the manifold flange gasket, tap the throttle flange lightly from side to side, using a plastic or rubber mallet. *Caution:* Do not pry on the carburetor body or flange with a screwdriver.

9. Insert a clean rag into each manifold flange opening to prevent foreign material from entering the engine. Then, carefully remove all traces of the old gasket from the manifold flange with a gasket scraper. Carefully remove all traces of old gasket material or cement from the base of the carburetor.

Carburetor Disassembly

Before discussing the actual teardown procedures of a carburetor, this is an appropriate time for a few tips that can save a great deal of time and energy. Although you can completely strip most carburetors for overhaul, with every nut, bolt, and lever removed, this is an unnecessary task because it complicates the reassembly and readjustment process.

The most efficient way to disassemble

any carburetor is to tear it down only as far as necessary. For example, if you don't remove the throttle valves, throttle linkage, or adjustment screws on this linkage, major adjustment may not be necessary during carburetor reassembly. Only minor adjustments, such as idle speed and mixture, are necessary due to previous adjustments to compensate for a dirty carburetor.

You should remove all carburetor jets for cleaning and inspection. Because these jets sometimes seize in their mounting threads, it may require much effort to loosen them. Consequently, always use the correct-size screwdriver or jet-removal tool to avoid damaging their screw slots. Depending on the function of a particular jet, even a minor change in the screw slot or face of the jet can result in turbulence in the fuel as it passes through the jet; and turbulence affects engine performance.

After removal, main jets require close inspection and special handling. Since most fuel flowing through a carburetor passes through the main jets, erosion can eventually cause wear. Therefore, carefully inspect each main jet; and replace any that is worn, chipped, or scored.

On four-barrel carburetors, mark all jets after removal for their relative position in the carburetor in order to prevent mixing them up. Although the primary and secondary main jets may have the same thread sizes, their jet openings are usually different. Therefore, if they are interchanged, the engine will operate too rich at some speeds and too lean at others. In addition, if the main jets have metering rods, keep all the rods and their respective jets together. Each rod, acting in its respective jet, produces a given wear pattern; switching them may create problems.

Do not attempt to remove the choke valves unless absolutely necessary. The manufacturer usually peens over the ends of the screws that hold these valves to the shaft, so that they cannot loosen and fall out. Therefore, if you try to remove them, you will usually strip out the screw slot or ruin the threads in the choke shaft.

Finally, on disassembly, always make note of or mark the position of all automatic choke and accelerator pump linkages. These linkages may have different adjustment slots or holes into which they fit. Marking or noting their positions saves time when reassembling the carburetor.

With these facts in mind, let's turn our attention to the actual disassembly process of a typical single-barrel carburetor, a YF Carter. You may have to add or delete some of these procedures even for this particular model due to year-to-year factory changes or modifications made to the carburetor so that it will operate satisfactorily on a particular engine.

To disassemble this unit for cleaning:

1. Loosen and remove the two screws from the air-cleaner bracket, and then remove the bracket (Fig. 10-9).

2. Loosen and remove the choke cover screws and brackets. Then, take off the cover, gasket, and baffle plate (Fig. 10-10).

3. Remove the two dashpot or solenoid bracket screws (Fig. 10-11), and remove the bracket. But leave the throttle linkage connected.

4. Remove the retaining clip from the fast-idle cam link (Fig. 10-12). Then, slide this link from its slot in the choke lever.

5. Disconnect and remove the fast-idle link from the fast-idle cam (Fig. 10-13).

Fig. 10-9. Removing the air-cleaner bracket screws.

Twist the link slightly to remove it from the fast-idle cam slot.

6. Remove all the remaining air-horn attaching screws (Fig. 10-14). If the air horn does not come loose at this point, tap it *lightly* with a small rubber or plastic mallet.

7. Lift the air horn off the main body (Fig. 10-15). Remove the gasket, but save it until you match it up with the new one.

8. Position the air horn upside down on a workbench. Then, pull the float retaining pin from its bracket and remove the float (Fig. 10-16). Check the brass float seam, at this point, for pinhole leaks.

9. Remove the fuel inlet needle from

Fig. 10-10. Removing the choke housing, gasket, and baffle.

Fig. 10-11.   *Removing the dashpot or solenoid bracket screws.*

the valve seat. Next, using a wide-blade screwdriver or jet tool, unscrew and then remove the valve seat and its gasket (Fig. 10-17). *Note:* The valve seat usually has an attached filter screen, and the inlet needle valve is a three-piece assembly. The spring fits between the two brass sections (Fig. 10-18).

10.   By tilting the main body over or using a pencil magnet, remove the pump dis-

charge check ball and weight from the discharge passage (Fig. 10-19).

11.   Loosen the screw that secures the throttle shaft arm to the throttle shaft (Fig. 10-20).

12.   While holding the accelerator pump plunger down in the main body, remove

Fig. 10-12.   *Removing the fast-idle link retaining clip.*

Fig. 10-13.   *Disconnecting the fast-idle link from the fast-idle cam.*

Fig. 10-14. *Removing the air-horn attaching screws.*

the throttle-shaft arm and pump link (Fig. 10-21).

13. Depress and then remove the upper pump spring retainer (Fig. 10-22) from the accelerator pump shaft. Next, remove the upper spring.

14. Lift the metering-rod assembly (Fig. 10-23) from the main body. The

spring-loaded screw on the metering-rod arm is factory preset and *should not be removed.*

15. Remove the antirock plate from the pump lifter link before lifting it from the main body (Fig. 10-24). Check the link for distortion.

16. Disconnect the plastic connector hose, if used, and remove the pump base attaching screws to remove the accelerator pump (Fig. 10-25).

17. On the bench, remove the pump diaphragm spring retainer and spring. Then, separate the pump diaphragm from the diaphragm housing (Fig. 10-26).

18. With a wide-blade screwdriver, loosen and then remove the low-speed jet (Fig. 10-27). *Caution:* Since this jet seats flush with the body casting, be careful not to damage the casting during the removal process.

19. Using a screwdriver, loosen and then remove the main-metering jet (Fig.

Fig. 10-15. *Lifting the air horn from the main carburetor body.*

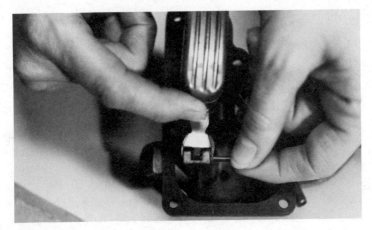

Fig. 10-16.   Removing the float from its mount bracket.

Fig. 10-17.   Removing the valve seat and gasket.

10-28). *Caution:* Since there is limited access space for jet removal, be careful not to damage the casting.

20. Remove the main body and throttle-body flange attaching screws. Then, separate the two assemblies (Fig. 10-29). Finally, remove the gasket and clean the gasket surfaces on both units.

21. Pry off the limiter cap from the idle-mixture adjusting screw. Then, counting the turns, thread the screw in lightly until it seats. Finally, unscrew and remove the adjusting screw completely (Fig. 10-30).

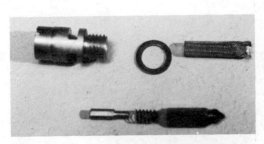

Fig. 10-18.   A disassembled inlet needle valve and seat assembly.

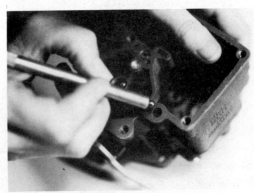

Fig. 10-19.   Using a pencil magnet to remove the pump check ball.

Fig. 10–20. Loosening the throttle-shaft arm attaching screw.

Fig. 10–22. Removing the upper spring retainer from the accelerator pump shaft.

Carburetor Cleaning

To clean the disassembled carburetor quickly and thoroughly, a special cleaning agent and equipment are necessary. The best cleaning agent to use for this job is a good grade of commercial carburetor cleaner. This cleaning solvent is very strong and quickly dissolves all the dirt, gum, and varnish from the metal carburetor components.

However, carburetor cleaner is a very strong chemical; consequently, treat it with caution. When working with this

Fig. 10–21. Removing the throttle-shaft arm and link.

Fig. 10-23. Lifting the metering-rod assembly from the main body.

Fig. 10-25. Removing the accelerator pump from the main body.

chemical, keep it away from your face and eyes. If possible, keep the cleaner off your hands, and wash your hands thoroughly after handling freshly cleaned parts. This chemical is toxic and can be absorbed through the skin to make you ill. Carburetor cleaner will ruin certain carburetor parts. For example, never soak gaskets, rubber, leather, or even some plastic parts. Also, never place dashpots, sole-

noids, vacuum diaphragm units, electrical choke housings, or other nonmetallic parts directly into the cleaner. Instead, wipe any reusable part with a clean shop towel. If the part is really dirty, clean it with a towel moistened with carburetor cleaning spray. Finally, do not use gasoline to clean carburetor parts. It is also toxic and a fire hazard. Kerosene and other commercial solvents are not so vola-

Fig. 10-24. Removing the antirock plate and pump lifter link from the main body.

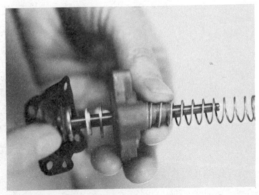

Fig. 10-26. Separating the accelerator pump diaphragm from its housing.

Fig. 10–27.   Removing the low-speed jet.

Fig. 10–29.   Separating the main body from the throttle-body flange.

tile, but like gasoline they do not always dissolve gum or varnish from carburetor parts.

The pieces of equipment necessary to use with the cleaner are a large and small cleaning basket (Fig. 10–31) and an agitator. The large carburetor parts and castings fit into the large basket that hangs from a rod lowered into the can or barrel of cleaner. The small basket, which you can also hang by a rod in the solvent or place it inside the large basket, room permitting,

Fig. 10–28.   Removing the main-metering jet.

holds the springs and other small parts. This keeps the smaller parts from being lost at the bottom of the cleaner can or barrel.

Many shops will have carburetor cleaning equipment that has a manual, air-operated, or electrically operated agitator. This device, by agitating the cleaner, speeds up its cleaning action through the constant circulation of the agent around all the parts. But a great many shops still use the two basket method and soak the parts clean in a carburetor cleaner can or barrel. This, of course, requires a longer time.

The length of time necessary for a thorough cleaning job depends on how dirty the carburetor parts are, how fresh the cleaner is, and whether the equipment agitates the cleaner. Therefore, the cleaning time can range from 30 minutes to 2 hours or more. However, you can usually tell quickly from the appearance of the parts if they are clean enough. If the solvent has removed or loosened all traces of dirt, gum, or varnish from the outer surfaces of all parts, you can assume that all the internal passages are clean enough.

Fig. 10-30.   Removing the idle-mixture adjusting screw.

At this point, the parts are ready for the rest of the cleaning process. This includes rinsing all the parts in water or a cold solvent, depending on the recommendations of the carburetor cleaner manufacturer, and blowing off all parts and *all* passages

Fig. 10-31.   A small metal basket used to hold the carburetor parts in the carburetor cleaner.

with compressed air. If this process does not remove all traces of the carburetor cleaner, repeat this procedure until all traces are gone.

Never use nails, wire, drill bits, or other hard objects to clean jets or other calibrated holes or passages. These objects can enlarge these openings and ruin the calibration or settings of the carburetor. Also, never use a wire brush, sandpaper, or steel wool to remove the stubborn dirt or carbon from the outside of aluminum castings. This can destroy the protective coating or anodizing on the carburetor casting, which will result in rapid corrosion of these surfaces.

Carburetor Repair Kit

After all parts are clean and dry, spread them out on a very clean workbench. Then, open the carburetor repair kit. This kit usually includes new gaskets, needle and seat, accelerator pump or pump diaphragm, check balls, float-setting gauge, and instruction sheet. An idle-mixture adjusting screw, metering rods, and jets are not included in the kit. Since the gaskets for several variations of this carburetor are also in the kit, the best way to locate the right new ones is to match them with the old gaskets. Also, check the new pump or pump diaphragm, needle and seat, along with the check ball, against the old parts. Once this is done, discard all the old gaskets and these parts.

Carburetor Reassembly

To reassemble the carburetor follow this procedure:

1. Reinstall the idle-mixture adjusting screw into the throttle-valve flange (Fig. 10-30). Run the screw in lightly until it bottoms out. Then, back it out the number of turns noted under item 21 of the disassembly procedure. Do not yet install the limiter cap. This will be done after the carburetor is on the engine and the mixture adjusted to specifications.

2. Install a new gasket beween the main body and throttle flange (Fig. 10-32). Then, assemble the body to the flange and install their attaching screws. Tighten these screws to specifications.

3. Install the main-metering jet into the carburetor body. Then, using a screwdriver, tighten the jet snugly (Fig. 10-28). *Caution:* Because of the limited work space, be careful not to damage the casting during the tightening procedure.

4. In the main body, install the low-speed jet. Then, with a wide-bladed screwdriver (Fig. 10-33), tighten the jet snugly. *Caution:* Since this jet seats flush with the body casting, be careful not to damage the casting during the tightening process.

Fig. 10-32. Installing a new gasket between the body and flange.

5. On the bench, assemble the new pump diaphragm into the diaphragm housing (Fig. 10-34). Then, install the pump diaphragm spring and retainer.

6. Install the diaphragm assembly into the main body. The diaphragm housing has a notch so that it fits into the body only one way. Next, install the pump

Fig. 10-33. Tightening the low-speed jet with a screwdriver.

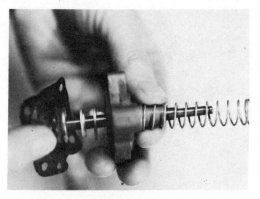

Fig. 10-34. Installing the pump diaphragm into its housing.

Fig. 10-36. Positioning the metering-rod arm over the antirock plate.

housing attaching screws (Fig. 10-35); tighten them to specifications. Finally, reinstall the plastic connector hose, if removed.

7. Reinstall the pump lifter arm over the accelerator pump diaphragm plunger and into its slot in the main body.

8. Install the antirock plate over the lifter arm with its tangs facing upward.

Next, position the metering-rod arm over the antirock plate so that its tangs index on either side of the rod arm (Fig. 10-36); and the metering rod itself goes into the main jet.

9. Install the upper spring over the metering-rod arm. Then, while depressing and holding the upper spring down, install the spring retainer (Fig. 10-37).

10. While holding the accelerator pump plunger down in the main body, in-

Fig. 10-35. Installing the pump housing attaching screws.

Fig. 10-37. Installing the upper spring retainer.

Fig. 10-38.   Installing the throttle-shaft arm and link.

stall the throttle-shaft arm and link (Fig. 10-38).

11. Tighten the screw that secures the throttle shaft arm to the throttle shaft (Fig. 10-39).

12. To check or adjust the metering-rod position, back out the idle-speed adjusting screw until you can close the throttle valve tight in the throttle bore. Then, press down on the upper end of the accelerator-pump shaft until the diaphragm bottoms in its chamber (Fig. 10-40). At this point, the metering rod should just contact the bottom of the metering-rod well; and the metering rod should contact the lifter link at its outermost end, nearest the springs, and at the supporting lug.

If adjustment is necessary for carbure-

Fig. 10-39.   Tightening the throttle-shaft arm locking screw.

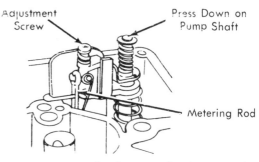

Fig. 10-40.   Checking and adjusting the metering rod. (Courtesy Echlin Manufacturing Co.).

tor models equipped with a metering-rod adjustment screw, turn the adjusting screw until the metering rod just bottoms in the body casting. For a final adjustment, turn the adjusting screw one additional turn (clockwise). Finally, if the carburetor has no metering-rod adjustment screw, make this adjustment by bending the lip of the metering-rod arm to which the metering rod attaches up or down as required.

13. Using a pencil magnet, install the pump discharge check ball and then the weight into the discharge passage within the main body (Fig. 10-41).

14. Fit a new gasket onto the fuel inlet seat (Fig. 10-42). Then, using a wide-blade screwdriver or jet tool, install and then tighten the valve seat into its threaded opening in the air horn.

15. Assemble the inlet fuel needle assembly with its spring between the brass components. Next, install the needle assembly into the seat with the needle tip facing inward (Fig. 10-43).

16. Position the float arm tangs over the float bracket, and slide the float retainer shaft in place (Fig. 10-44).

Fig. 10-42.　Installing the inlet seat into its threaded bore in the air horn.

17. To check or adjust the float level, invert the air-horn assembly. Then, check the clearance from the top of the float to the base of the air horn with the float-level gauge from the kit (Fig. 10-45). Hold the air horn at eye level while gauging the float level. The float arm (lever) should be resting on the needle-valve pin. *Caution:*

Fig. 10-41.　Installing the pump discharge check ball into the discharge passage.

Fig. 10-43.　Installing the needle into its seat.

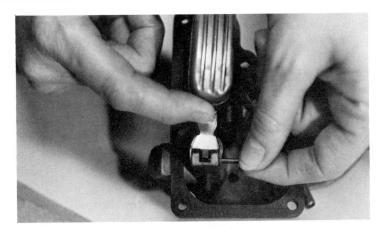

Fig. 10–44. Installing the float and its retainer shaft.

Never load the needle valve when checking or adjusting the float level because this can damage the needle tip. Next, bend the *float arm* as necessary to adjust the level. Never bend the tab at the end of the float arm because this can prevent the float from striking the bottom of the fuel bowl when it is empty.

18. Make a float drop check by holding the air horn upright and measuring the maximum clearance from the top of the float to the bottom of the air horn with a float-drop gauge from the kit or a ruler (Fig. 10–46). To adjust float drop, bend the tab at the end of the float arm in order to obtain the specified setting from the specification table supplied with the kit. The table lists this specification, along with others mentioned later in this chapter, across the page from the part number listed on the carburetor identification tag.

19. Install a new gasket into position over the main body (Fig. 10–47). Next, position the air horn over the main body and align its attaching screw holes.

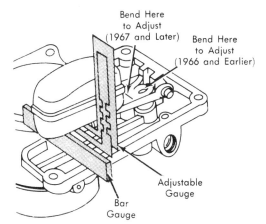

Fig. 10–45. Checking and adjusting float level. (Courtesy Echlin Manufacturing Co.).

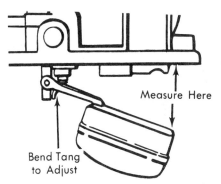

Fig. 10–46. Measuring float drop. (Courtesy Echlin Manufacturing Co.).

Fig. 10–47.   Positioning a new gasket over the main body.

20. Replace a few attaching screws loosely to hold the air horn in position while you install the tag and bracket.

21. Reinstall the dashpot or solenoid bracket, and replace its attaching screws. Also, be sure to reinstall the identification tag under its screw as shown in Fig. 10–48. Finally, tighten all air-horn attaching screws to specifications.

22. Insert the fast-idle cam link into its slot in the fast-idle cam (Fig. 10–49).

23. Insert the upper end of the fast-idle link into its slot in the choke outer lever.

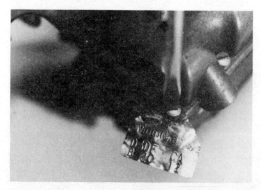

Fig. 10–48.   Reinstalling the identification tag under an air horn screw.

Fig. 10–49.   Inserting the fast-idle cam link into its slot in the fast-idle cam.

Fig. 10-50. Installing the fast-idle link's retaining clip.

Then, install the link's retaining clip (Fig. 10-50).

24. To make a choke valve pulldown adjustment, bend a 0.026 inch-diameter wire gauge at a 90-degree angle, approximately $\frac{1}{8}$ inch from one end. Insert the bent end of this gauge between the choke piston slot and the right-hand slot in the choke housing (Fig. 10-51). Then, rotate the inner choke-piston lever counterclockwise until

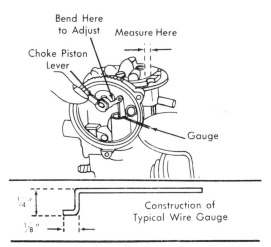

Fig. 10-51. Checking and adjusting choke-valve pulldown. (Courtesy of Echlin Manufacturing Co.)

the gauge is snug in the piston slot. Next, exert a light pressure on the choke lever in order to hold the gauge in position.

Place a drill, with a diameter equal to the specified pulldown clearance from the table, between the lower edge of the choke valve and the carburetor throat in order to check the exact clearance. If the clearance is not to specifications, bend the inner choke piston lever as necessary to obtain the specified setting.

25. Install the baffle plate and new choke-cover gasket into position within the air-horn housing (Fig. 10-52). Then, hook the choke lever into the loop of the bimetallic coil, and reinstall the choke cover. Install the choke-cover attaching screws and brackets. Next, turn the cover so that the line or index mark on the cover itself lines up with the designated mark on the air-horn choke housing. The table of specifications from the kit will designate which mark is correct for this carburetor configuration. Finally, *be sure that the screw brackets are installed properly over the choke cover* before tightening all the cover attaching screws.

26. Install the air-cleaner bracket into position on the air horn. Then, reinstall the bracket attaching screws (Fig. 10-53) and tighten these screws to specifications.

27. Check or adjust the choke unloader linkage by holding the throttle valve wide open and permitting the choke valve to close as far as possible without forcing it. Then, insert a drill of the diameter specified in the table of adjustments and specifications from the kit, between the edge of the choke valve and the air horn (Fig. 10-54). If the clearance is not within the specified amount, adjust it by bending the arm on the choke trip lever, which is part of the throttle lever. Bending this arm

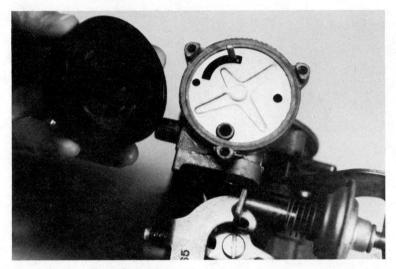

Fig. 10–52.   Installing the baffle plate and gasket into position.

downward will decrease the clearance, while bending it upward will increase the clearance.

28. Check or adjust the fast-idle cam linkage by positioning the idle-speed adjusting screw on the second step of the fast-idle cam and against the shoulder of the highest step. Using a drill of the size mentioned in the specification table from the kit, check the clearance between the lower edge of the choke valve and air horn bore. To adjust the clearance, bend the connector rod as required (Fig. 10–55).

Fig. 10–53.   Installing the air-cleaner bracket attaching screws.

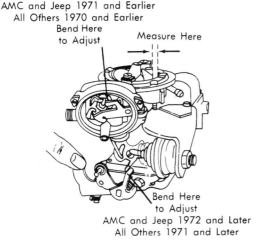

AMC and Jeep 1971 and Earlier
All Others 1970 and Earlier
Bend Here
to Adjust
Measure Here

Bend Here
to Adjust
AMC and Jeep 1972 and Later
All Others 1971 and Later

Fig. 10-54. Checking and adjusting the choke unloader. (Courtesy of Echlin Manufacturing Co.)

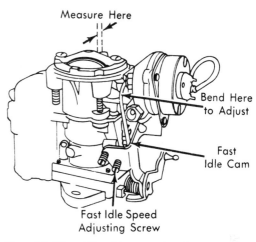

Measure Here

Bend Here
to Adjust

Fast
Idle Cam

Fast Idle Speed
Adjusting Screw

Fig. 10-55. Checking and adjusting the fast-idle cam linkage. (Courtesy of Echlin Manufacturing Co.)

Carburetor Installation

To reinstall the carburetor, follow these steps.

1. Remove the rag from inside the carburetor flange opening. Then, install a new gasket over the flange.

2. Position the carburetor over the new gasket and carburetor flange; install the carburetor attaching capscrews or nuts. Tighten these to specifications.

3. Connect all solenoid connectors.

4. Reconnect all vacuum lines into their respective fittings on the carburetor.

5. Reconnect the fuel line to the carburetor; and using two line wrenches, tighten the line fitting securely.

6. Connect the linkage, water connections, hot-air tube, or electrical connector to the automatic choke assembly.

7. Reconnect the throttle linkage to the carburetor, and install any necessary clips or connections.

Carburetor Adjustments on the Engine

After a reconditioned carburetor is installed on the engine, it requires some additional adjustments before the engine will operate properly. These adjustments include idle speed, idle mixture, antidiesel solenoid, air-conditioning solenoid, and dashpot. However, all carburetors may not require all of these adjustments because they may not have any of the solenoids or the dashpot.

Idle-Speed and Mixture Adjustments

The idle-speed and mixture adjustment procedures can be quite complicated, depending on the year of the automobile, types of accessory equipment, types of smog equipment, and type of transmission. Consequently, this text does not attempt to cover all the various factory-recommended procedures but presents an overview of the most common steps. However, you should always look up any specifications or special procedural steps in the service manual or on the underhood decal before actually setting these adjustments. By doing this and following the specifications, the engine should then operate according to factory specifications and meet both federal and state emission control standards.

Idle-Speed Adjustment Procedure

To make the idle-speed adjustments, perform the following steps.

1. Connect a tachometer to the engine, following the manufacturer's recommended procedure.

2. Set the parking brake and block the drive wheels.

3. Start and operate the engine until it reaches normal operating temperature. *Note:* After a carburetor overhaul, it may be necessary to adjust the idle-speed adjusting screw somewhat before the engine will idle well enough to continue with this procedure.

4. Make sure that after the engine warms up, the choke is open and the idle-speed adjusting screw is off the fast-idle position on the cam.

5. Following the manufacturer's recommendations, disconnect and plug the vapor hose to the carbon canister on vehicles with an evaporation emission control system; remove the air cleaner; turn the headlights and air conditioner on or off; and place the automatic transmission in drive or neutral, if so equipped.

6. Set the idle-speed to the rpm specified by the manufacturer, using the idle-speed adjusting screw or the anti-diesel solenoid. This chapter discusses how to adjust this solenoid.

Idle-Mixture Adjustment Procedure

Tachometer

Four methods are commonly used by the industry to adjust carburetor idle mixture. These include mixture adjustment through the use of a tachometer, infrared analyzer, lean-drop method, and propane enrichment. The type of procedure utilized depends on the year of the vehicle, type of emission control equipment, manufacturer's specifications, and state or federal emission control regulations.

To adjust the idle-mixture with a *tachometer:*

1. With the engine idling at normal temperature, turn the adjustment screw in (clockwise) until the engine begins to slow down as indicated by the tachometer needle.

2. Slowly adjust the screw outward (counterclockwise) to regain the highest steady engine rpm on the tachometer.

3. Readjust as necessary the idle speed to specifications.

4. A dual or four-barrel carburetor has two idle mixture adjusting screws (Fig. 10–56). Adjust each screw as you would in a single-barrel carburetor. Adjust one mixture screw as outlined above, and then set the other one. *Note:* These idle-mixture screw adjustments can affect one another because the intake manifold or carburetor throttle flange may have balance pas-

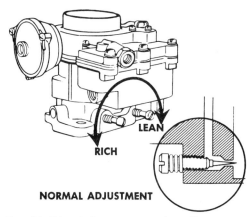

NORMAL ADJUSTMENT

Fig. 10–56. When setting the idle mixture on an engine with a two or four-barrel carburetor, both mixture screws must be adjusted. (Courtesy of United Delco)

sages between the two carburetor bores. Consequently, you may have to repeat the adjustment on both mixture screws to achieve a balanced condition between the two idle systems.

Infrared Analysis

To meet current emission control regulations, an infrared analysis of the exhaust gas is necessary during idle-speed and mixture adjustments on most engines. The infrared analyzer (Fig. 10–57) measures the amount of hydrocarbons and carbon monoxide in the exhaust during and after the adjustment procedure. A description of this machine and its use in adjusting engine idle speed and mixture is covered in Chapter 24.

Lean-Drop Method

In some cases, the manufacturer suggests the lean-drop method of adjusting idle mixture as an alternative to using the infrared analyzer. To adjust the mixture, using this method:

1. Adjust the idle speed and mixture, as mentioned earlier, with a tachometer.

Fig. 10–57. A typical portable infrared analyzer.

2. Turn the mixture screw slowly in again until the idle speed drops down as specified by the manufacturer. Then leave it there. For instance, suppose the manufacturer's specifications call for 650 rpm at a regular idle-speed and mixture setting, but then the specifications require a lean-drop setting of 630 rpm. To accomplish the lean-drop setting on a single-barrel carburetor, you must turn the adjusting screw in (clockwise) until the engine speed drops 20 rpm. However, on two- or four-barrel units, turn one mixture screw in to drop the idle speed 10 rpm, and then adjust the other one in to lower the engine speed another 10 rpm. In both situations, leaning out the mixture reduced the engine speed to 630 rpm; as a result, the leaner mixture produces less harmful emissions.

Propane Enrichment

Many late-model engines require propane enrichment in order to set the idle mixture correctly. The air/fuel ratio supplied to these engines by the idle system of the carburetor is so lean that it is very hard to use the lean-drop method to adjust idle mixture. This lean mixture is necessary for the engine to meet state and federal emission standards.

A lean mixture is also a requirement if the engine's exhaust system has a catalytic converter. However, the converter reduces the engine's emissions of hydrocarbons and carbon monoxide so that even an infrared analyzer cannot detect carburetor maladjustment unless the converter has an access plug (Fig. 10-58). This plug permits the insertion of the infrared analyzer probe in the exhaust pipe in front of the converter, so that the anal-

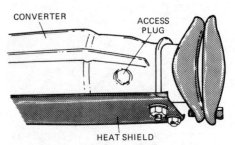

Fig. 10-58. Some catalytic converters have an access plug that permits the insertion of an infrared analyzer probe ahead of the converter.

yzer can read the engine's emissions before they enter the converter.

If you don't use propane enrichment when required, the idle air/fuel ratio may be set too rich. If the carburetor provides the engine with an overly rich idle mixture, the catalytic converter can produce an offensive, rotten-egg smell in the exhaust at the tailpipe. Once the mixture is set correctly, the smell disappears.

A further discussion of the equipment necessary and the procedure for performing the propane-enrichment, idle-mixture adjustment is covered in Chapter 24. However, this is a good time to remind you that after the reconditioned carburetor has had its idle mixture set, by any of the procedures mentioned in this chapter, install the new limiter caps (Fig. 10-59). Install the caps so that the tangs rest against the full-rich stop. This prevents

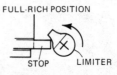

Fig. 10-59. Install the new limiter caps as shown after the idle-mixture adjustment is complete.

any further outward movement of the adjustment screw, which would enrich the air/fuel mixture at idle.

Idle-Solenoid Adjustment— Antidiesel

Several types of antidiesel and air-conditioning solenoids are in use. Consequently, their adjustment procedure can vary somewhat from one manufacturer to another. However, some general steps that you can use in most cases follow.

1. Check the manufacturer's specifications for both curb-idle and shutdown idle rpm.

2. Following the manufacturer's recommendations, disconnect and plug the hoses to the carburetor from the vapor canister, EGR valve, and vacuum advance. Also, if the vehicle has a vacuum-release parking brake, disconnect and plug its hose.

3. Connect a tachometer to the engine, following the manufacturer's instructions.

4. Set the parking brake and block the drive wheels.

5. Start the engine and permit it to reach its normal operating temperature.

6. Following the manufacturer's recommendations, place the automatic transmission in drive or neutral and turn on the air conditioner or headlights.

7. With the engine operating at curb idle, be certain that the solenoid energizes and its plunger extends fully. *Note:* In most cases, it is necessary to open the throttle slightly off its idle position in order to permit the plunger to extend.

8. Check the idle speed on the tachometer. As necessary, adjust the curb-idle rpm by:

a. Turning the solenoid plunger adjusting screw in or out (Fig. 10-60)

b. Adjusting a hex nut on the plunger at the rear of the solenoid itself

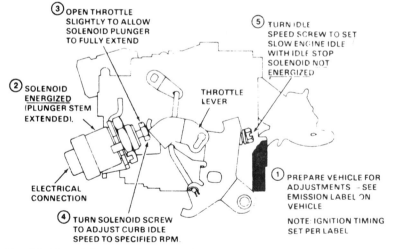

Fig. 10-60. Adjusting the curb idle by turning the solenoid plunger screw in or out. (Courtesy of General Motors Corp.).

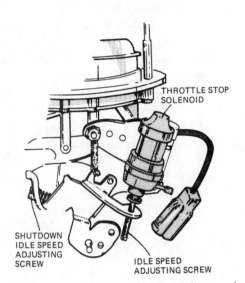

Fig. 10–61.   *Adjusting the curb idle rpm by turning a throttle linkage screw in or out.*

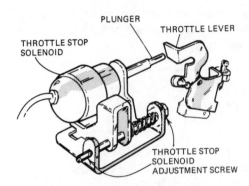

Fig. 10–62.   *Setting the curb idle by moving the solenoid mount bracket.*

12. Reconnect all hoses that you removed in step 2.

Air-Conditioning Solenoid Adjustment

c. Setting a throttle-linkage adjusting screw that makes contact with the solenoid plunger (Fig. 10–61)

d. After loosening the solenoid locknut, rotating the solenoid body in its mounting bracket

e. Or, adjusting the movable bracket upon which the solenoid mounts (Fig. 10–62)

9. Disconnect the solenoid electrical lead wire to de-energize the solenoid and retract the plunger.

10. Check and then adjust as necessary the shutdown-idle rpm by turning the shutdown idle-speed adjusting screw on the throttle linkage.

11. Reconnect the solenoid lead and then return the throttle valve to the curb-idle position. Recheck the curb-idle rpm and readjust it as necessary.

To check or adjust a typical air-conditioning solenoid:

1. Start the engine and permit it to reach normal operating temperature.

2. Set the air-conditioner temperature control to maximum cooling, and then turn the air-conditioner fan switch on.

3. Accelerate the engine slightly past the idle position to permit the air-conditioning solenoid to extend. *Note:* This action is necessary because the solenoid does not have enough power in most cases to open the throttle valve by itself.

4. Check the idle rpm on the tachometer. If the reading is not to specifications, turn the adjustment screw on the plunger in or out, until the engine speed reaches the specified amount.

5. Disconnect and remove the tachometer.

Dashpot Adjustment

To check or adjust a typical dashpot:

1. With the engine at its normal-operating temperature, adjust both the idle speed and mixture to specifications.

2. Hold the throttle valve in the curb-idle position, and then depress the dashpot plunger (Fig. 10-63).

3. Measure the clearance between the throttle lever and plunger tip of the dashpot.

4. If this clearance is not to specifications, loosen the dashpot locknut; turn the dashpot in or out as necessary to achieve the specified measurement.

5. Tighten the locknut to secure the adjustment.

6. Reinstall the air cleaner and all its attaching lines or hoses.

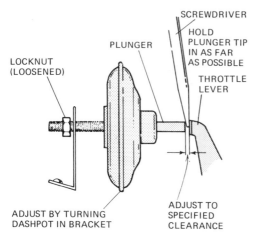

Fig. 10-63. *Checking and adjusting a typical dashpot.*

Review

This section will assist you in determining how well you remember the material in this chapter. Read each item carefully. If you can't complete the statement, review the section in the chapter that covers the material.

1. The mechanic can check a dry-filter element with a _____.
   a. droplight
   b. mirror
   c. air
   d. gauge

2. Clean a polyurethane band or element in mineral spirits or _____.
   a. oil
   b. acetone
   c. gasoline
   d. kerosene

3. Never submerge the _____ _____ of any air-cleaner assembly in solvent.
   a. attaching screws
   b. oil reservoir
   c. silencing chamber
   d. hold-down straps

4. A polyurethane filter element usually fits over a steel mesh _____.
   a. bracket
   b. support
   c. cover
   d. screen

5. Before ordering a parts kit, you must locate the carburetor part number from the _____ _____.
   a. body casting
   b. identification tag
   c. flange casting
   d. service manual

6. On carburetor disassembly, never remove the _____ _____ unless absolutely necessary.
   a. choke valves
   b. metering rods
   c. main jets
   d. mixture screws

7. When disassembling a carburetor, always save the old _____ to match them up with the new ones.
   a. linkages
   b. screws
   c. gaskets
   d. jets

8. You should be careful when using carburetor cleaner because it is _____ _____.
   a. all of the below
   b. corrosive
   c. toxic
   d. volatile

9. New _____ will not be in the carburetor repair kit.
   a. pump
   b. diaphragm
   c. gaskets
   d. jets

10. When removing and installing jets, use a wide-blade screwdriver or a _____ _____.
    a. socket wrench
    b. flat punch

c. slotted tool
d. jet tool

11. You should use a _____ or the gauge from the repair kit to check float drop.
    a. ruler
    b. drill
    c. micrometer
    d. caliper

12. Always make idle-speed and mixture adjustments, following the instructions in the service manual or on the _____ _____.
    a. underhood decal
    b. instruction sheet
    c. door post
    d. drivers manual

13. A(n) _____ analyzer measures the amount of hydrocarbons and carbon monoxide in the exhaust gases.
    a. vacuum
    b. compression
    c. infrared
    d. engine

14. _____ enrichment is necessary on some engines to set idle mixture properly.
    a. Kerosene
    b. Propane
    c. Diesel
    d. Gasoline

For the answers, turn to the Appendix.

Fuel induction systems that use carburetors all operate on the same basic principle and therefore have the same inherent problem. This is the problem of fuel distribution—the delivery of the exact air/fuel mixture to each cylinder. The problem itself is the result of the fact that air travels easily through all the passages, bends, ports, and various runner lengths of the intake manifold casting.

However, the heavier gasoline particles have more difficulty moving through the bends and sharp corners of the manifold. As a result, some of the fuel particles continue moving in a straight line to the end of the manifold. This action tends to enrich the mixture moving into the end cylinders, while leaning out the others. Finally, while the problem affects all gasoline engine types to some extent, the in-line engine, due to its manifold design, has the greatest distribution difficulties.

A fuel injection system solves the intake manifold distribution problem. The fuel injection system sprays fuel under pressure directly into the intake manifold port, close to the open intake valve (Fig. 11-1), or into the cylinder itself (Fig. 11-2). The fuel spray enters either one of these areas through a nozzle. Each nozzle sprays the same amount of fuel into the same quantity of air entering every cylinder. Therefore, for all practical purposes, the combustion chamber of each cylinder gets the same air/fuel mixture. As a result, the injection system prevents uneven air/fuel mixtures; fuel condensation in the intake manifold; and poor performance, especially during the engine's warm-up period.

Other than improving air/fuel mixture distribution to all the cylinders, the injection system offers other advantages:

Chapter 11

FUEL INJECTION AND SUPERCHARGERS

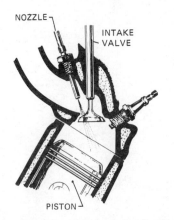

Fig. 11-1. The injection of the fuel spray into the intake port, close to the open intake valve.

1. Fuel injection permits a more efficient design of the intake manifold. This improved design increases engine breathing and volumetric efficiency. Also, with the redesigned intake manifold, the manufacturer can lower the hood height of the vehicle. Finally, with fuel injection, the intake manifold requires no special heating; therefore, engines equipped with this system have no manifold heat-control valve.

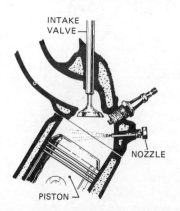

Fig. 11-2. The injection of the fuel spray directly into the combustion chamber.

2. Fuel injection systems can precisely match fuel delivery to engine requirements under all load and speed conditions. This action reduces fuel consumption by the engine without any loss of engine performance.

3. Throttle response is much quicker on a fuel-injected engine because the fuel is under pressure at all times. All that is necessary for acceleration is to open the injector nozzle, and fuel sprays out instantly.

4. Fuel injection systems eliminate part of the fuel-vapor emission-control system. Since the system has no carburetor, a float-bowl vent to the charcoal canister is no longer necessary, and the size of the canister itself can be smaller.

5. Engines with fuel injection produce less harmful exhaust emissions of hydrocarbons and carbon monoxide. This reduction is due to the system providing a more even air/fuel flow distribution and maintaining a precise air/fuel ratio according to engine requirements.

Categories of Injection Systems

Over the years, the automotive industry has designed and produced several different types of fuel injection systems. One of the main differences between the various systems is the area into which the nozzle sprays the fuel. For example, one system uses *direct injection* (Fig. 11-2) where the nozzle sprays the fuel directly into the cylinder. For the most part, manufacturers use this type of system in diesel-type engines.

The other general category of systems is known as *port injection* in which a nozzle sprays the fuel at the intake port of each cylinder (Fig. 11-1). In this latter system, manufacturers employ two different methods of fuel discharge: *timed fuel injection* and *continuous fuel injection*. *Timed fuel injection is a method where the fuel injects for a controlled-time interval every time it is needed. Whereas, continuous-fuel injection is a method in which the fuel injects continuously into the port area at a controlled flow rate.*

Another way to differentiate the various injection systems is by their mode of operation: either mechanical or electronic. Manufacturers have used *mechanical injection systems* for many years in diesel engines but not for most gasoline engines. The early systems used on gasoline engines were not very accurate or reliable and very expensive to produce.

Mechanical Fuel-Injection Systems

Recently, however, Robert Bosch has developed and manufactured a *mechanically operated fuel injection system* that has proven to be reliable; easy-to-maintain; and relatively inexpensive to produce for some passenger-car engine usage. This Bosch system (Fig. 11–3) is a hydraulically controlled, mechanically operated, and continuous-port injection system (CIS). Although this CIS system operates mechanically, the engine does not directly drive any of its components.

When in operation, an air-flow sensor, installed in front of the throttle plate, measures the volume of air intake. Then, based on the volume of air measured, a fuel distributor meters the fuel to the individual cylinders in order to produce the proper air/fuel mixture necessary to meet the power requirements of the engine, provide reasonable fuel economy, and reduce exhaust emissions. Next, this precisely metered amount of fuel moves to the injection valves, which continuously spray the finally atomized fuel in front of the intake valves.

Design of the Mechanical CIS System

The Bosch CIS system (Fig. 11–3) consists of a fuel pump, fuel accumulator, fuel filter, mixture-control unit, auxiliary air device, thermo-time switch, start valve, injector valves, and a warm-up regulator. The *pump* of this system is a roller-cell type, driven by an electric motor. The function of the pump itself, when operating, is to pressurize the fuel so that it moves through the various components of the system and into the engine.

The *fuel accumulator* is in the line between the pump and the fuel filter. The function of the accumulator is to hold the fuel pressure constant for an extended length of time after the engine is shut off. This action prevents the formation of fuel-vapor bubbles that would otherwise cause difficulty in starting a hot engine.

The *fuel filter* fits in the line between the accumulator and the fuel distributor. The purpose of this filter is to trap dust, dirt, or other particles that would otherwise cause a malfunction in or damage to the fuel distributor and nozzles.

The *mixture-control unit* is the heart of the CIS system and consists of an air-flow sensor along with the fuel distributor. The air-flow sensor (Fig. 11–4) includes an air funnel and the air-flow sensor plate that mounts onto a lever, supported at its fulcrum (pivot point). A counterweight on the end of the lever balances the combined

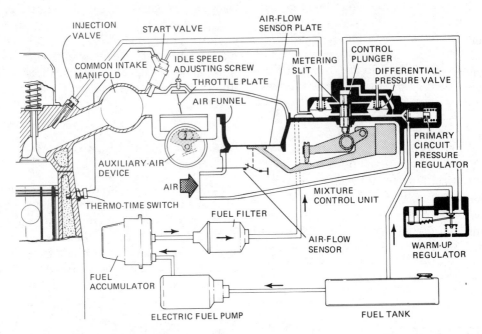

Fig. 11-3. The Bosch continuous fuel injection system (CIS), used on some imported automobiles.

weights of the air-flow sensor plate and the lever itself.

When the engine is running, the air-flow sensor plate and lever move. The actual lifting of the sensor plate is due to the force of the air flow acting against the base of the plate; the amount of force applied is in proportion to the quantity of air

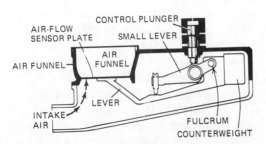

Fig. 11-4. The air-flow sensor of the Bosch CIS system.

flow controlled by the position of the throttle plate. In any case, when the sensor plate does lift, the attached lever moves a smaller lever, which in turn forces the control plunger upward in its bore in the fuel distributor.

The fuel distributor consists of a control plunger, fuel barrel, differential valves, and primary-circuit regulator. The control plunger is a hydraulic spool valve that operates inside the fuel barrel. The valve itself has two lands and one groove. The two lands act as valves to control the opening and closing of the two ports (Fig. 11-4), while the groove forms a passageway through the valve to carry pressurized fuel from one circuit to another.

The two forces control the movement of the control plunger. On top of the plunger is fuel pressure, which attempts to move the plunger downward in its bore. This force transmits through the plunger and lever to the air-flow sensor plate. As a result, the fuel pressure on top of the plunger is trying to push the sensor plate down.

Figure 11-5 shows the actual circuit that the pressurized fuel takes before it acts on the control plunger; the five arrows indicate the force of this pressure on top of the control plunger. The pressurized fuel from the pump enters the open lower port opening in the fuel barrel, passes through the groove, and enters the primary pressure circuit. From here, the fuel moves through a restriction and enters a passage leading to the dampening restriction and warm-up regulator circuit. The total amount of force applied to the plunger is in proportion to the fuel pressure allowed to enter the dampening restriction by the warm-up regulator. The fuel pressure that does pass through the restriction provides the force necessary to oppose the push of the airflow on the air-

flow sensor plate (shown as a single arrow below the plunger in the illustration).

Opposing the force of the fuel pressure is the effect of the air flow. The intake air flowing through the intake funnel lifts the air-flow sensor plate upward. This movement continues until the force of this air flow and the opposing force of the fuel pressure on the plunger are equal.

A given position where these forces are equal is shown in Fig. 11-6. In this illustration, the plunger has moved to a specific point in its bore, the fuel barrel. Its horizontal control edge of the upper land has opened the upper port opening a given amount. As a result, pressurized fuel can flow from the lower port, through the groove, out the upper port, to the injector valves.

Figure 11-7 illustrates the fuel barrel that fits inside the mixture-control unit. This barrel, which acts as the bore for the control plunger, has as many metering slits (slot-shaped port openings) as there are engine cylinders. As the control plunger moves up and down inside the barrel, it opens a more or less slit area for fuel flow.

Figure 11-8 is a diagram of a control plunger inside the barrel. In this drawing, the control plunger is in its down position

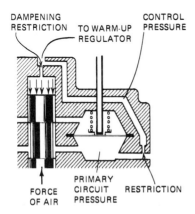

Fig. 11-5. The control-plunger, pressure-signal circuit.

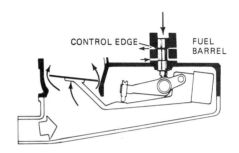

Fig. 11-6. A particular control plunger position where the forces of air flow and fuel pressure are equal.

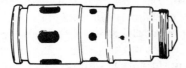

Fig. 11-7. A typical fuel barrel with its metering slits.

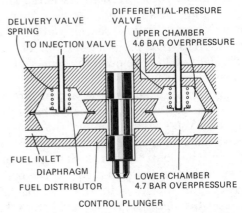

Fig. 11-9. Two differential-pressure valves located in the fuel distributor.

where the control edge blocks the metering slits. In this valve position, pressurized gasoline cannot move through the slits to the injector valves.

Also inside the fuel distributor are a number of differential pressure valves—one for every fuel injector valve on the engine. The function of the differential-pressure valves is to regulate the pressure across the metering slits to keep it as constant as possible, regardless how much the slit is open.

Figure 11-9 shows two of these differential-pressure valves. Each valve consists of a calibrated spring fitted over a diaphragm. The diaphragm is made of steel, is very small in diameter, and can only move a few hundredths of a millimeter. As indicated in Fig. 11-9, the pressure has dropped 0.1 bar (about 1.5 psi) by the spring in the upper chamber above the diaphragm. A *bar* is the international measurement for pressure. For practical

purposes, 1 bar is equal to about 14 psi or 1 atmosphere of pressure. This 0.1-bar drop is the difference between the 4.7-bar overpressure (about 66 psi) on the bottom of the metal diaphragm and the 4.6-bar overpressure, about 64.5 psi, on the top of the diaphragm and the outside of the slit in the barrel.

Figure 11-10 illustrates the flexing of the diaphragm. In view *A*, the metering slit is open; the diaphragm flexes down to permit a greater flow while maintaining the same pressure on both sides of the slit. View *B*, on the other hand, shows the metering slit nearly closed. Now, the diaphragm flexes back up again to decrease the flow and equalize the pressure.

The last component inside the fuel distributor is the primary-circuit pressure regulator (Fig. 11-11). This regulator holds the primary-circuit pressure in the system constant. The regulator itself consists of a plug, piston-type valve, and calibrated spring. The valve controls the opening of a port leading to the fuel tank, and the spring maintains the valve in the closed position until fuel pressure reaches a predetermined amount.

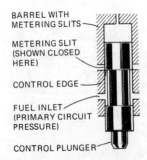

Fig. 11-8. The control plunger controlling the slit openings inside the barrel.

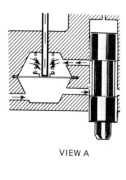

VIEW A

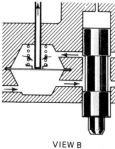

VIEW B

Fig. 11-10. Operation of the diaphragm to control fuel pressure across the metering slits.

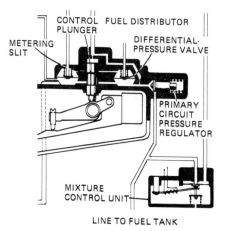

Fig. 11-11. The primary circuit pressure regulator holds fuel pressure constant in the primary circuit.

The *auxiliary air device* is a valving mechanism that fits into a bypass channel in the common intake manifold (Fig. 11-12). This channel, when open, permits air to bypass the throttle valve. The auxiliary air device opens the channel during engine warm-up to permit additional air to flow to the engine. Then, an electrically operated bimetallic strip causes the valving mechanism to close the bypass channel.

The *thermo-time switch* and *start valve* (Fig. 11-13) function together to supply additional fuel to the engine during cold-starting. The thermo-time switch electrically opens the start valve when the engine is cold, but it closes the valve above a certain temperature limit. The start valve itself, when open, sprays additional fuel directly into the common intake manifold to enrich the mixture for cold-engine starting.

Each cylinder of the engine has an *injector valve* installed into its intake-valve port (Fig. 11-14). These valves are open continuously after the engine starts and spray a precisely metered atomized spray of gasoline into the intake ports. From this point, the air moving through the intake port from the common intake manifold, carries the fuel past the open intake valve and into the cylinder.

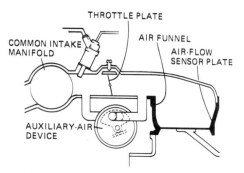

Fig. 11-12. A diagram of an auxiliary air device.

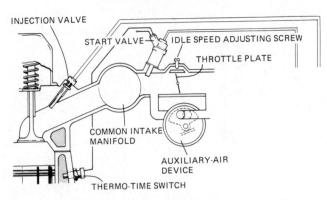

Fig. 11–13.   The thermo-time switch and the start valve are in the system to supply additional fuel to the system during cold-engine starting.

The last component in the Bosch CIS system is the *warm-up regulator* (Fig. 11–15). This regulator operates during the engine warm-up period to control the pressure acting against the control plunger. When the driver starts a cold engine, the regulator reduces the pressure on top of the control plunger. This action permits the control plunger to open the metering slits a greater amount than usual, with a given air flow in order to produce a richer mixture. When the engine reaches its normal operating temperature, an electrically heated bimetallic strip switches the regulator off, and the pressure above the control plunger increases. As a result, the plunger cannot open the metering slits as far with a given airflow, and less fuel flows to the nozzles. This action leans out the total mixture.

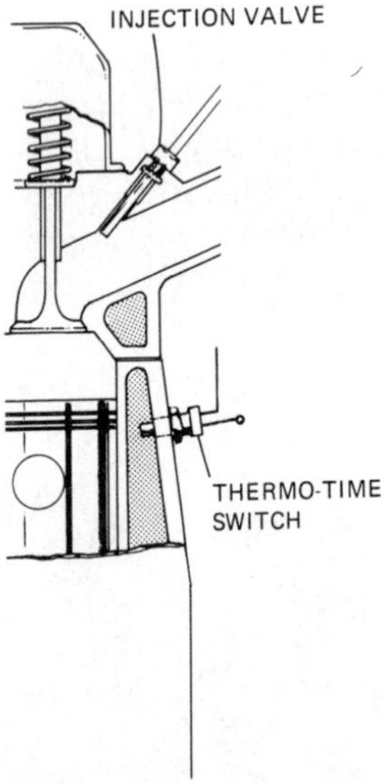

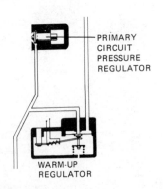

Fig. 11–14.   Each cylinder has its own injector valve.

Fig. 11–15.   The warm-up regulator of the CIS system.

Electronic Fuel Injection Systems

As mentioned, mechanical fuel injection systems are not very efficient on all engine types. However, with the development of solid-state electronics, such as transistors and diodes, manufacturers have developed and produced electronic fuel injection systems that function well on engine types previously limited to carburetor-type induction systems. These systems began to appear on automobiles in the late 1960s with a design that not only reduced exhaust emissions but also conserved fuel and improved engine performance.

There are three basic types of electronic systems on the market. Robert Bosch designed two of these systems, which have a number of similar features. These are the manifold-pressure-sensitive type (EFI-D) and the air-flow–sensitive type (EFI-L). The third system is the Bendix EFI system used by General Motors. This latter system is quite similar to the Bosch EFI-D system; therefore, this chapter discusses only the Bosch EFI-L and the Bendix systems.

Bosch EFI-L Fuel Injection System

The Bosch EFI-L system (Fig. 11–16) is a timed-port injection system. The system itself can be split into three sections: the fuel delivery system, the detecting sensor element, and the electronic control unit. The fuel delivery system has the responsibility for fuel delivery, pressure genera-tion, pressure regulation, and fuel filtering. The detecting sensor elements collect all the engine's operating information necessary to calculate its fuel needs. The electronic control unit processes the data from all the sensor elements, determines the duration of injection, and controls the operation of the injector valves.

EFI-L Fuel Delivery System—Fuel Pump

The EFI-L fuel delivery system consists of a fuel pump, fuel-pressure regulator, fuel filter, injector valves, and start valve. The fuel pump for this system is the electrical, roller-cell type similar to the one used in the CIS system. The function of this pump is also to draw fuel from the tank and deliver it under pressure to the injector nozzles.

Figure 11–17 illustrates a sectional view of a roller-cell pump. When the pump is in operation, fuel flows into the suction side inlet, to the roller-cell pump, around the electric motor, through the nonreturn valve, to the pressure side outlet. The excess pressure valve allows fuel to return to the inlet when or if the pressure in the pump becomes too high. Finally, there is never a danger of an explosion in this pump because of an insufficient amount of air mixed with the fuel.

Figure 11–18 shows the pump rotor mounted inside the pump housing. When the pump is operating, the rotor turns as an eccentric inside the pump housing. This action causes the metal rollers to move outward due to centrifugal force. As a result, the rollers bear against the inside surface of the pump housing and act as a rotating seal.

Because the rotor mounts in an offset position within the housing, there is more

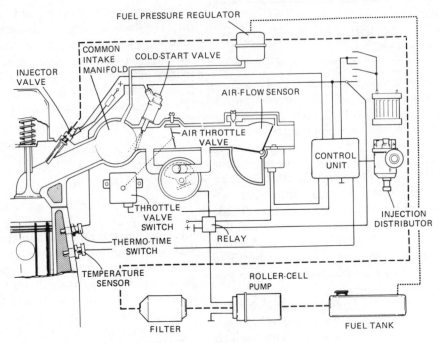

Fig. 11–16. *A diagram of the Bosch EFI–L fuel injection system.*

clearance between it and the housing on one side than the other. The area of greatest clearance is at the suction inlet while the area of decreased clearance is at

the pressure-side outlet. Also, the rollers separate these various clearance areas into individual pumping chambers (cavities) of different volumes.

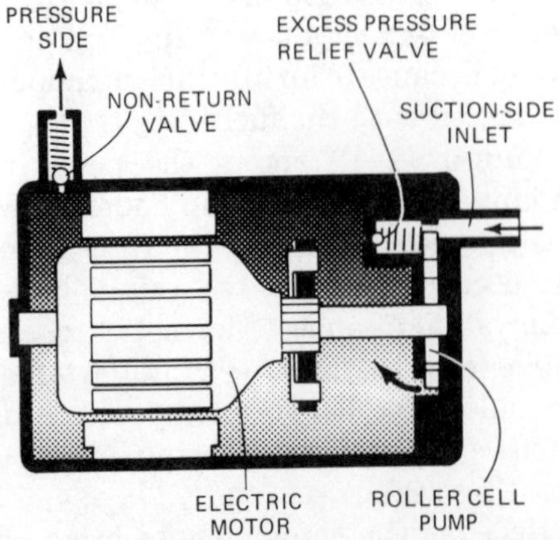

As the largest pumping chamber indexes with the suction-inlet port, fuel flows into this chamber due to the action of atmospheric pressure pushing fuel into an area of lower pressure. As this chamber continues to move toward the pressure side, its area decreases. This squeezing action applies a force on the fuel and expels it out of the pressure-side outlet. This process is continuous as each subsequent pair of rollers and cavities move from the suction inlet to the pressure-side outlet.

Fuel-Pressure Regulator

The EFI-L system has a nonadjustable, variable-pressure regulator (Fig. 11–19). With this type of regulator, fuel pressure

Fig. 11–17. *Sectional view of a roller-cell fuel pump.*

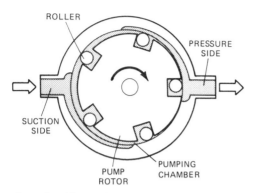

Fig. 11-18. Schematic of the roller-cell pumping mechanism.

enters through the fuel connections and pushes the diaphragm down against the force of the pressure spring. At a given fuel pressure, the diaphragm moves down far enough so that the valve opens. Now, excess fuel returns through the return line to the fuel tank.

If the pressure spring alone resisted the fuel pressure acting on the diaphragm, the regulator valve would keep the fuel pressure at a set amount. However, this is not the case in the EFI-L regulator because

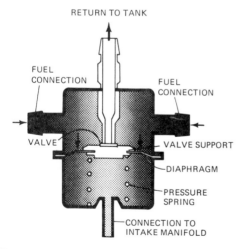

Fig. 11-19. Cross-sectional drawing of an EFI-L fuel-pressure regulator.

manifold vacuum is brought into the spring chamber via the connection to the intake manifold below the diaphragm. With this arrangement, the changing intensities of the manifold vacuum react against the lower side of the diaphragm. As a result, the vacuum assists the fuel pressure in moving the diaphragm downward against spring tension. This varies the fuel pressure in the supply lines to the nozzles in proportion to engine loads and throttle positions. If engine vacuum is low, fuel pressure is high. Conversely, when vacuum is high, fuel pressure is low.

With this design, the regulator holds constant the differences between the vacuum signal from the intake manifold and the fuel pressure to the injector valves. This provides an equal pressure drop across each of the injector valves for any engine load condition and throttle position. By doing so, this regulator design helps to reduce exhaust emissions and conserve fuel.

Fuel Filter

The *fuel filter* is in the line between the electric fuel pump and the fuel-pressure regulator. The filter traps particles of dust, dirt, or other contaminants so that they cannot clog or damage the regulator, start, or injector valves.

Injector Valves

The EFI-L fuel injection system utilizes electrically activated injector valves, one for each cylinder (Fig. 11-20). This injector consists of a solenoid coil, solenoid armature, nozzle valve and seat, plus a filter. The *solenoid coil* itself receives electrical impulses from the control unit (Fig. 11-16). This causes the winding of the solenoid coil to produce an electrical-magnetic field.

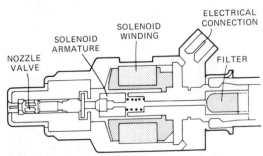

Fig. 11-20. An electrically operated fuel injection valve.

The *solenoid armature* along with its spring fits into the air core of the solenoid coil. When electrical current energizes the solenoid coil, its magnetic field pulls the armature into the air core, compressing the spring. As the control unit breaks the electrical circuit to the solenoid windings, the spring pushes the armature out.

The *nozzle valve* attaches to the armature; consequently, any armature movement causes the nozzle valve to travel either off of or onto its seat. For example, as the solenoid coil energizes and pulls the armature in, the attached nozzle valve moves away from its seat. Fuel can flow past the filter, through the center of the unit, and into the manifold. On the other hand, when the control unit de-energizes the solenoid coil, the armature spring pushes the armature out. It in turn moves the nozzle valve against its seat, cutting off fuel flow into the manifold.

Compared to the injectors of the earlier Bosch electronic fuel injection system, the EFI-L injector has a smaller nozzle-valve opening. This smaller opening is a necessary design feature because all the injectors together form a single group, which operates at the same time. However, with this arrangement, the nozzles inject one-half of the required fuel for an operating cycle twice during each camshaft rotation.

For instance, during one injection cycle, half of the cylinders receive fuel for combustion on or near their intake stroke, while the intake manifold stores the fuel for the remaining cylinders until their intake cycle occurs. Then during the next injection cycle, the nozzles inject the other half of the fuel charge *on or near the intake cycle of the second half of the cylinders first,* while the manifold stores the fuel charge for the first half.

No appreciable loss of engine performance results from the storage of a fuel charge in the intake manifold. This point is easy to understand if you consider that the whole action takes place in a small fraction of a second. At cruising speed, for example, the time between injection of fuel into the manifold for storage and the opening of the intake valve averages only about one-hundredth of a second.

Start Valve

In a carburetor-type fuel induction system, the choke is responsible for increasing the amount of fuel delivered to a cold engine during start-up. In the EFI-L system a cold-start valve (Fig. 11-21) performs the same function. This valve, located near the air-throttle valve, sprays finely atomized fuel into the air inside the

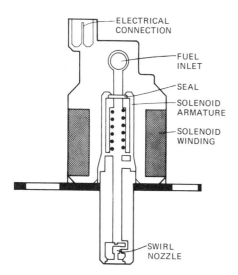

Fig. 11–21. Sectional view of an EFI–L cold-start valve.

intake manifold. However, the start valve only sprays fuel when the starting motor is on and the thermo-time switch is in the closed position.

The cold-start valve operates in a similar way as the injector valve. When the engine is cold, the thermo-start switch allows an electrical current to flow through the windings of the start valve's solenoid coil. This current flow produces a magnetic field that pulls the solenoid armature in, against the force of the pressure spring. This armature movement, in turn, pulls open the valve seal. As a result, fuel passes through the start valve and sprays from the swirl nozzle.

As the thermo-start switch opens at a given temperature, it breaks the electrical circuit to the start-valve solenoid coil. Consequently, the force of the pressure spring pushes the armature out, which closes the valve seat. At this time fuel can no longer pass through the start valve to the swirl nozzle.

Detecting Sensor Elements—Thermo-Time Switch

The detecting sensor elements of the EFI-L system include the thermo-time switch, temperature sensor, auxiliary air device, injection distributor, air-flow sensor, and throttle-valve switch. The *thermo-time switch* (Fig. 11–22) electrically controls the operation of the start valve. This switch basically consists of a bimetallic strip, heater winding, and set of electrical contacts. The bimetallic strip attaches on one end to the switch housing; mounted on its opposite end is one of the contacts. This strip reacts to heat and will raise the attached contact at a predetermined temperature.

During switch operation, the bimetallic strip reacts not only to engine temperature but also to the heat produced by current flowing through the heater windings. When the driver starts a cold engine, the bimetallic strip is straight and maintains the contacts in their closed position. As a result, the start valve opens and delivers additional fuel to the engine. How long the start valve remains open then depends on the period of time necessary for engine heat and the heat from the winding to bend the bimetallic strip sufficiently to open the contacts.

The heater windings supply heat to the

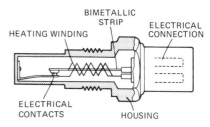

Fig. 11–22. A sectional view of an EFI–L thermo-time switch.

bimetallic strip. When the engine operates, electrical current flows through
these windings to produce heat. However,
it does require a period of time for the coil
to generate enough heat to cause the bimetallic strip to bend.

The contact points themselves open and
close the electrical circuit between the
start valve and ground. When the contacts close, the circuit is complete, and the
start valve solenoid energizes. As the contacts open, the ground circuit is also open,
and the solenoid inside the start valve de-
energizes.

Temperature Sensor

Along with a thermo-time switch, the
EFI-L system also has a *temperature sensor* (Fig. 11-23). This sensor reports
engine temperature to the control unit so
that this unit can adjust the amount of
fuel enrichment to match varying engine
temperatures. This type of enrichment
control is especially necessary during engine warm-up after the thermo-time
switch has de-energized the start valve.
The temperature sensor shown in Fig.
11-16 threads directly into the engine
water jacket and senses coolant temperature. In an air-cooled engine, the unit
threads into the cylinder head to sense its
operating temperature.

Auxiliary Air Device

Figures 11-16 and 11-24 illustrate the
auxiliary air device. This device at certain
times provides a controlled amount of air

Fig. 11-23.   A typical temperature sensor.

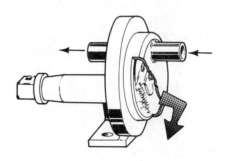

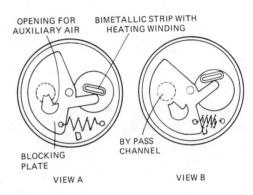

OPENING FOR   BIMETALLIC STRIP WITH
AUXILIARY AIR   HEATING WINDING

BLOCKING   BY PASS
PLATE   CHANNEL

VIEW A   VIEW B

Fig. 11-24.   An auxiliary air device.

flow that bypasses the throttle valve to
create a fast idle. This action is necessary
when either or both the start valve and
control unit enrich the mixture during
cold-engine starting and warm-up to prevent engine stalling.

The air device shown in Fig. 11-24 does
not operate on engine heat but has its own
heating element, the heater winding.
When the driver starts a cold engine, the
bimetallic strip with its heater winding is
cool and has moved the blocking plate to
the position shown in *A* of Fig. 11-24. The
auxiliary air opening in the blocking plate
aligns with the bypass channel, and a
quantity of air flows around the throttle
valve to increase engine idle.

After a period of time, current flowing through the heater winding produces sufficient heat to move the bimetallic strip once again. This action permits the spring to pull the blocking plate to the position shown in *B* of Fig. 11-24. At this point, the auxiliary air opening in the plate no longer aligns with the bypass channel; and air no longer flows around the throttle valve. As a result, the engine returns to its normal idle.

Injection Distributor

The *injection distributor* of the EFI-L system (Fig. 11-16) serves several functions. First of all, this unit performs the regular functions of an ignition distributor. That is, it closes and opens the primary circuit to the ignition coil at the proper times, and it distributes the resulting high-voltage electrical surges from the ignition coil to the proper spark plugs.

Second, the primary ignition points that open and close the coil's primary circuit also signal the control unit when to open the injector valves. The control unit receives a signal every time the contact points open. Consequently, the control unit takes in four, six, or eight signals during each distributor shaft rotation (depending on the number of engine cylinders). Then, the control unit divides these signals by two, three, or four in order to obtain the two electrical pulses necessary to open the injector valves. Finally, the point open signals provide the control unit a method of counting engine rpm.

Air-Flow Sensor

Figure 11-25 is a cross-sectional drawing of an *air-flow sensor*. This device generates an electrical signal in proportion to the amount of air drawn into the engine, as controlled by the throttle valve.

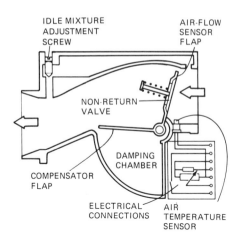

Fig. 11-25. A cross-sectional view of an EFI-L air-flow sensor.

This signal and the information from the distributor on engine speeds are the main data inputs to the control unit. The control unit, in turn, uses this information to regulate the actual duration of the fuel injection period.

In operation, the air flow through the sensor pushes against a spring-loaded sensor flap. A potentiometer (a variable resistor), acted upon by the varying positions of the sensor flap, produces an electrical current signal in proportion to flap movement. In addition, a compensation flap, attached to the air-flow–sensor flap, works together with the dampening chamber to eliminate oscillations caused by air pressure pushing against the back of the sensor flap. Finally, an adjustment screw regulates the air flow and therefore the mixture during the idle operating range.

Throttle-Valve Switch

The *throttle-valve switch* (Fig. 11-26) directly attaches to and is activated by the movement of the throttle-valve shaft.

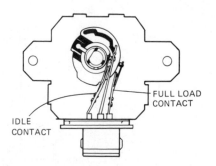

Fig. 11-26. The throttle-valve switch used in the EFI system.

The function of this switch is to signal the control unit whenever the throttle valve is in the closed or wide-open position. To accomplish this task, the switch has two contacts; the idle contact and the full-load contact. The *idle contact* signals the control unit when the throttle-valve closes, and the engine requires an idle mixture. The *full-load contact,* on the other hand, signals the control unit whenever the throttle valve is wide open, and the engine is in need of enrichment to compensate for heavy load.

Electronic Control Unit

The *electronic control unit* (Fig. 11-16) is the "brain box" of the EFI-L system. This unit contains a large number of electronic components working together to process the signals from the various engine sensor elements. The control unit then processes this information and produces the electrical pulses that operate the injector valves for the necessary injection duration under all engine conditions.

This control unit receives battery voltage from a relay when the driver turns on the ignition switch. The same relay directs current to activate the electric fuel pump, start valve, temperature-time switch, and auxiliary air device.

Although the control unit uses integrated circuits (circuits in which the manufacturer miniaturizes and assembles the components together in such a way as to reduce the number of parts in the circuit), it contains about 80 electrical components. The control unit is therefore very complex, and the mechanic should not attempt to repair it. Instead, when it is defective, the technician should replace the unit or send it to an authorized repair shop.

Bendix EFI Fuel Injection System

The last fuel injection system to be discussed is the Bendix EFI system, a timed-port injection system (Fig. 11-27) used by General Motors. In this particular system, *intake manifold pressure* along with engine speed controls the injection of fuel into the engine. The main subsystems involved in the Bendix arrangement are the fuel delivery, air induction, sensor, and electronic control.

Bendix Fuel Delivery Subsystem

The fuel delivery subsystem consists of the fuel tank, two electrical-type fuel pumps, filter, fuel rails (or tubes) with eight injectors, fuel-pressure regulator, supply, and return lines (Fig. 11-28). Inside the fuel tank is a special "bath tube" type–reservoir that fits directly under the in-tank fuel booster pump. This design ensures adequate fuel pickup by the booster pump at all times.

This subsystem utilizes two pumps: the boost pump and the main pump. The in-tank *boost pump* is responsible for drawing fuel from the tank and delivering it to

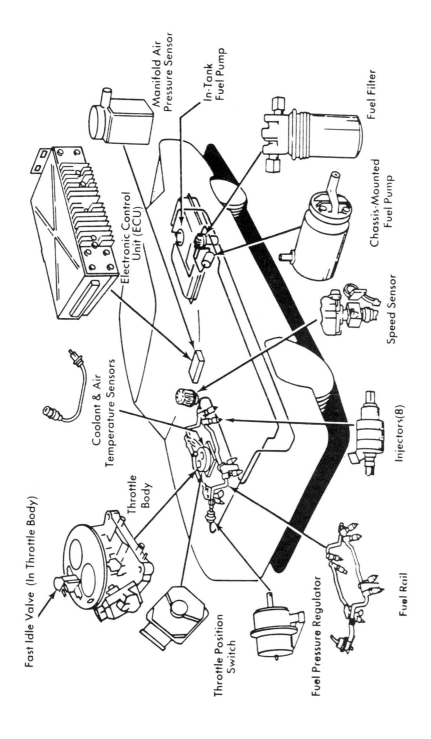

Manifold Air Pressure Sensor

In-Tank Fuel Pump

Fuel Filter

Electronic Control Unit (ECU)

Chassis-Mounted Fuel Pump

Speed Sensor

Coolant & Air Temperature Sensors

Injectors (8)

Throttle Body

Fast Idle Valve (In Throttle Body)

Throttle Position Switch

Fuel Pressure Regulator

Fuel Rail

Fig. 11-27. The Bendix EFI system. (Courtesy of General Motors Corp.)

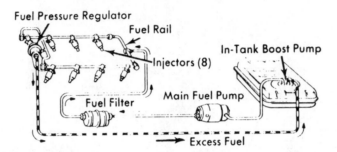

Fig. 11-28.   The Bendix EFI fuel delivery subsystem. (Courtesy of General Motors Corp.)

the main pump. This action prevents a vapor lock from forming on the vacuum side of the main pump.

The *main pump* mounts on the vehicle chassis, under the body and ahead of the rear wheels. This pump is a constant-displacement type responsible for pushing the fuel through the filter and into the fuel rails at a pressure above that in the intake manifold.

The main pump contains two valves: a check and an internal-relief valve. The *check valve* prevents a back flow of fuel, thus maintaining fuel pressure in the system when the pump is off. The *relief valve*, on the other hand, protects the pump and subsystem components from excessive pressure buildup by bypassing excess fuel internally to the intake side of the pump. Finally, the manufacturer wires both of these pumps in parallel with the electronic control unit (ECU) that controls their operation.

The *fuel filter* is responsible for trapping foreign particles within the fuel, thus preventing them from reaching the fuel rails and injectors. The fuel filter assembly either mounts on the chassis near the main fuel pump or on the engine in place of the mechanical fuel pump. In either case, the assembly has a casing that contains a throwaway paper filter element.

The *fuel rail* connects to each of the eight injectors, one for each cylinder. The rail itself is nothing more than a fuel manifold. That is, the rail stores and supplies each injector with fuel under pump pressure.

The *injector valves* are solenoid-operated and similar in construction and operation to the Bosch EFI-L injectors. These units also spray a fine mist of fuel into the intake manifold, near the intake port and just ahead of each intake valve (Fig. 11-29). The electronic control unit, using electrical signals, triggers the pulse (opening and closing) of the injector valves. The pulse width, the length of time electrical current flows to the injector during each operating period, is regulated by the ECU according to the needs of the engine at any particular time.

When used in a particular V-8 engine, the manufacturer forms all eight injector valves into two groups containing four injectors each. Injectors for cylinders 1, 2, 7, and 8 form one group, while the injectors for cylinders 3, 4, 5, and 6 make up the other group. With this arrangement, all four injectors in each group open and close at the same time; and the two groups operate alternately, once during every camshaft revolution.

The *fuel-pressure regulator* attaches

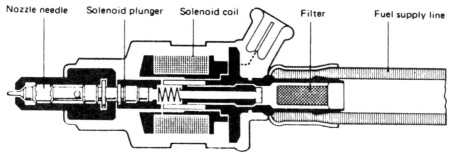

Fig. 11-29. The Bendix EFI injector valve. (Courtesy of General Motors Corp.)

into the fuel rail near the front of the engine (Fig. 11-28). This device has air and fuel chambers separated by a spring-loaded diaphragm (Fig. 11-30). The air chamber connects to the throttle body via a hose. Consequently, pressure within the air chamber is the same as that in the intake manifold. The fuel chamber contains pressurized fuel from the fuel rail, which acts against the diaphragm and spring.

Changes in intake manifold vacuum cause the diaphragm valve in the regulator to open or close the fuel-chamber orifice. For example, when engine vacuum is high, the diaphragm moves toward the left due to the action of fuel pressure on

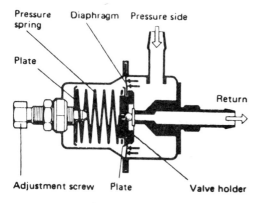

Fig. 11-30. The Bendix EFI fuel-pressure regulator. (Courtesy of General Motors Corp.)

one side and vacuum on the other. This moves the diaphragm valve away from the orifice. But when vacuum drops, the diaphragm spring moves the diaphragm to the right against fuel pressure and seats the diaphragm valve against the orifice. This opening and closing of the orifice maintains a constant pressure differential of about 38 to 40 psi (262 to 276 kilopascals) across the injectors no matter what the position of the throttle valve. Any excess fuel from the regulator returns to the bathtub reservoir in the fuel tank.

This subsystem has supply as well as a return fuel line. The *supply line* is in several sections and is responsible for carrying the fuel from the tank, to the main pump and filter, and finally to the fuel rail. The *return line* transports the excess fuel from the regulator back to the fuel tank.

Bendix Air Induction Subsystem

This particular subsystem controls the air flow to the combustion chamber during all phases of engine operation; it consists of a throttle body, fast-idle valve, and intake manifold. The *throttle body* (Fig. 11-31) contains two bores with a throttle valve in each one. These valves

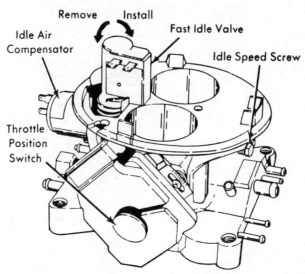

Fig. 11–31. The Bendix EFI throttle-body assembly (Courtesy of General Motors Corp.)

connect to the accelerator pedal linkage and are responsible for controlling the primary airflow rate through the throttle body, the intake manifold, and into the cylinders.

However, the throttle body does have an idle bypass air passage, controlled by an adjustment screw in front of the throttle body. This passage and screw allow a regulated amount of air to bypass the throttle valves to provide an adjustable idle speed.

An electrically operated *fast-idle valve* on top of the throttle body connects into the fuel pump circuit of the control unit. This valve permits additional air to bypass the throttle valve whenever the driver starts a cold engine and during the warm-up period. The additional air is necessary to compensate for the fuel enrichment from the injectors. The ECU provides this enrichment automatically whenever the temperature sensors on the engine signal that it is cold.

The fast-idle valve contains a temperature-sensitive (thermostatic) element, plunger valve, and spring, along with an electric heater (Fig. 11–32). When the engine is cold, the thermostatic element permits the spring to open the plunger valve to allow some air to bypass the throttle valves. This action produces a fast idle.

The heater in the valve warms the thermostatic element, which expands with the additional heat. This element expansion closes the plunger valve against spring tension. As a result, the closed valve stops the flow of additional air; engine rpm

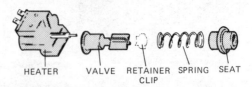

HEATER   VALVE   RETAINER   SPRING   SEAT
                           CLIP

Fig. 11–32. The components of the fast-idle valve.

drops to the normal idle speed. Finally, the warmer the air temperature is, the faster the valve plunger closes to reduce engine speed.

The *intake manifold* has about the same appearance as any two-plane manifold used on a carbureted engine. However, the manufacturer of this type of manifold locates the injectors within the individual ports of the manifold above each cylinder. This allows the installed injectors to spray the fuel directly toward the top of the intake valve in each cylinder.

Bendix Sensor Subsystem

This subsystem contains a number of engine sensors that electrically connect to the electronic control unit. All these sensors operate independently, with each sensor sending a signal to the control unit, relaying to it a particular engine-operating condition. The ECU then analyzes all these signals and sends the appropriate commands to all of the injector valves.

The sensors within this subsystem include the manifold absolute pressure sensor, throttle position switch, two temperature sensors, and speed sensor. The *intake-manifold absolute pressure* (MAP) *sensor* fits inside the ECU and connects to the throttle body by means of a vacuum line (Fig. 11–27). This device monitors the changes in the vacuum within the intake manifold that result in variations in engine speed and load, barometric pressure, or altitude. The information on these particular pressure changes passes into the ECU in the form of electrical signals.

These signals to the control unit either increase or decrease the length of injection with changes in vacuum. For instance, as the driver opens the throttle valve for engine acceleration, intake manifold vac-

uum decreases. In this situation, the engine requires additional fuel, and the MAP electrically signals to the ECU to increase the pulse width time of the injectors. This action results in an increase in injection, so that the engine can receive more fuel, necessary for acceleration.

On the other hand, if the driver closes the throttle and manifold vacuum increases, the engine requires less fuel. The MAP signals the ECU to decrease the pulse width. As a result, the ECU reduces the duration of injection, and engine rpm decreases.

The *throttle position switch* (Figs. 11–27 and 31) mounts onto the throttle body and connects directly to the throttle-valve shaft. With this arrangement, any accelerator pedal movement causes the throttle-valve shaft to rotate. This, in turn, moves the throttle position switch. Consequently, the switch senses shaft movement and position and directs an electrical signal to the ECU. The ECU then processes this signal to determine the fuel requirements for the engine for any given throttle position.

There are two *temperature sensors* in this subsystem: a coolant and an air (Fig. 11–33). Both sensors are identical and interchangeable. Each consists of a coil of nickel wire sealed into an epoxy case. The

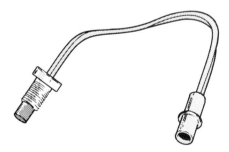

Fig. 11–33. A Bendix temperature sensor.

manufacturer molds this case into a brass housing with two wires and a connector extending from it.

With this design, the electrical resistance (see Chapter 12) of the wire changes with the variation in either coolant or air temperatures. For example, low temperature results in low electrical resistance, whereas high temperatures increase the total resistance in the wire. Consequently, the ECU that connects to both sensors monitors the voltage drop (see Chapter 12) across each sensor.

The air temperature sensor attaches into the intake manifold. This sensor then reads the air temperature inside the manifold. The coolant temperature sensor fits into a coolant passage and monitors coolant temperature. Both devices have the same effect on engine performance. That is, they signal the ECU to alter air/fuel mixture enrichment according to the engine-operating temperature. When the engine is cold, the mixture is enriched, but it is leaned out as the engine warms up to its normal operating temperature.

The *speed sensor* is part of the ignition distributor assembly (Fig. 11–34). This

device has two main functions. First, it directs signals to the ECU to time the correct injector group operation with the intake valve timing of the engine. Second, the switch also signals engine rpm information to the ECU so that it can determine fuel needs at the various engine speeds.

To accomplish these tasks, the speed sensor consists of a combination external-internal unit. The external component is nothing more than a plastic housing that contains two reed switches. This assembly attaches to the distributor-shaft housing. The internal unit is a rotor with two magnets that attach to the distributor shaft.

Whenever the distributor shaft rotates, the rotor with its attached magnets causes the reed switches to open and close. This action creates the signals that time the appropriate injector group opening and closing to coincide with the engine's valve timing. Also, the signals supply the engine's rpm information to the ECU.

Electronic Control Unit Subsystem

The ECU (Fig. 11–27) is a programmed analog computer consisting of a number of electronic circuits housed in a steel case. The ECU receives its electrical power from the vehicle's battery and various signals from the engine's sensors. This unit then processes these signals to determine the air/fuel requirements for all driving conditions. Also, this unit has a given calibration for each vehicle body style and equipment package; therefore, it is not interchangeable among the various vehicle configurations with the Bendix EFI system.

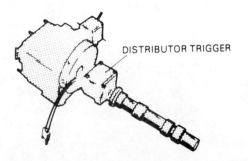

DISTRIBUTOR TRIGGER

Fig. 11–34. The speed sensor is part of the ignition distributor (Courtesy of General Motors Corp.)

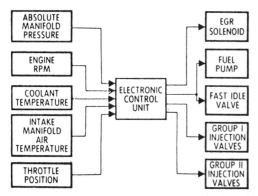

Fig. 11-35. A schematic diagram showing the various signals to and from the ECU. (Courtesy of General Motors Corp.)

Figure 11-35 shows the various signals entering and leaving the ECU. The left side of the block diagram shows the number of signals coming into the control unit from the various sensors. These include absolute manifold pressure, engine rpm, coolant temperature, intake manifold air temperature, and throttle position.

The right side of the same diagram points out the output signals from the ECU that regulate the operation of the various units in the system. These signals then either turn off or on the EGR solenoid, fuel pump, fast-idle valve, Group I injector valves, or Group II injector valves.

The design of the ECU provides the desired air/fuel mixture for various driving and atmospheric conditions. As the unit receives the many sensor signals, it processes them and computes engine fuel requirements for different conditions. Then, the control unit sends signals to the injector valves to open them for a specific time duration. This duration or width of pulse varies with engine fuel needs; but no matter what the duration actually is, all the injectors' valves in one group open at the same instant on command from the ECU.

Operation of the Bendix EFI System

The Bendix EFI system begins its operation as the driver turns on the ignition switch. With this switch on, the following components become energized:

1. The ECU.

2. All engine sensors. These components begin at once to send signals to the control unit.

3. Both fuel pumps. These pumps operate for only about 1 second, unless the engine is either cranking over or running.

4. The electrically heated fast-idle valve. This valve connects to the electrical fuel pump circuit; consequently, it also only operates for about 1 second, unless the engine is cranking over or operating.

5. The EGR solenoid. This solenoid is an electrically operated switch in the vacuum line that operates the exhaust gas recirculation (EGR) valve. These components are part of the nitrogen oxide emission control system to be covered in a later chapter.

Once the engine is running, the following events occur within the system.

1. The ECU activates both fuel pumps for continuous operation.

2. The heater element of the fast-idle valve energizes for continuous operation.

3. With the throttle valve closed, the throttle body air bypass controls the air flow to the intake manifold. When the

driver depresses the accelerator pedal, the throttle valve opens, creating enough air flow for engine acceleration.

4. The fuel-presure regulator maintains the correct fuel pressure within the fuel rail and returns any excess fuel to the fuel tank.

At this same time, the ECU receives and processes the following signals:

1. Intake manifold air temperature
2. Engine coolant temperature
3. Intake manifold absolute pressure
4. Engine rpm and firing position
5. Throttle position changes

With this data, the ECU directs signals alternately to each injector group. These signals precisely control injector opening and closing time (pulse width) to deliver the proper amount of fuel to each cylinder of the engine during all phases of engine operation.

Electronic Fuel Injection Service

Because of the complexity and variety of fuel injection systems on the market, it is not possible to cover in detail all individual service techniques in this text. However, the manufacturers of these various systems publish this type of information; no attempt should ever be made to service a particular system without the proper equipment, manufacturer's specifications, instructions, and diagnostic charts. Table 11-1 is a typical chart used to trouble-shoot the Bendix EFI system just described.

Superchargers/ Turbochargers

Function

Engines using conventional carburetion depend upon the effect of atmospheric pressure to push an air/fuel mixture into the combustion chamber toward the vacuum produced by each of the pistons moving down on the intake stroke. Engines using this method for the induction of fuel are known as *normally aspirated engines.* Each piston then compresses this air/fuel mixture before the point of ignition in order to increase the force of the burning, expanding gases.

The higher the compression pressure is at the end of the compression stroke, the greater the power is from the combustion process. One way to increase this compression pressure is to raise the compression ratio of the engine. A higher compression ratio has two major benefits. First of all, a higher ratio improves volumetric efficiency because the piston pulls in a larger percentage of the total cylinder volume on each intake stroke than in a low-compression engine. Second, due to the fact that the temperature increases as cylinder pressure goes up, thermo efficiency is higher within a high-compression engine.

However, since about 1971, emission control requirements have forced the compression ratios of passenger-car engines down to the range of 8:1 or 8.5:1. This was necessary because high-compression engines tend to emit too much nitrogen oxide. In addition, a lowering of the compression ratio has also been necessary due to a reduction in the lead content in gasoline.

Table 11–1. Bendix EFI Diagnostic Chart

Problem	Cause	Correction
Engine cranks but does not start.	1. Blown fuel pump fuse. 2. Open circuit in fuel pump feed line. 3. Open circuit at temperature sensor or speed sensor. 4. Inoperative fuel pump. 5. Throttle position switch inoperative. 6. Restricted fuel flow.	1. Replace fuse. 2. Locate and correct as needed. 3. Locate and correct as needed. 4. Test and correct or replace. 5. Correct or replace as needed. 6. Locate restriction and correct as required.
Engine stalls.	1. Idle air compensator operation faulty. 2. Poor connection in feed to ECU unit. 3. Poor connections at coolant or distributor sensors. 4. Coolant sensor faulty.	1. Correct or replace as needed. 2. Correct as required. 3. Correct as needed. 4. Replace if not up to specifications.
Hard starting.	1. Inadequate fuel supply or pressure. 2. Throttle switch faulty.	1. Test pressure and delivery of fuel and correct as needed. 2. Disconnect switch and start engine. If engine starts, replace switch.
Rough idle or hesitation.	1. Coolant sensor short circuit. 2. Poor electrical connections at injectors. 3. Induction triggering of injectors. 4. Vacuum leak in manifold air pressure sensor hose.	1. Test with ohmmeter. Replace if it does not meet specifications. 2. Clean and tighten or replace connections. 3. Check and correct speed sensor wiring too close to high tension wires. 4. Locate leak and correct or replace as needed.
Poor high-speed performance.	1. Inadequate fuel supply. 2. Throttle position switch misalignment. 3. Malfunction of injector triggering system.	1. Check fuel supply and pressure and correct as needed. 2. Check throttle position switch for proper alignment at wide open throttle position. 3. Check speed sensor and wiring. Correct connections as needed. Replace sensor if needed.
Excessive fuel consumption.	1. Vacuum leak. 2. Shorted air temperature sensor and connections.	1. Locate vacuum leak and correct as required. 2. Test sensor resistance. Replace sensor if resistance is below specifications. Correct shorted connections.

An alternate way to increase the total compression of the air/fuel mixture is with a supercharger. A supercharger delivers the air/fuel charge to the cylinders at a pressure greater than atmosphere. The end result is nearly the same as having a high-compression ratio, but the manufacturer can control the supercharged effect during idle and deceleration in order to avoid high, harmful emission levels.

The purpose of the supercharger basically is to pressurize the incoming air or air/fuel mixture to an amount greater than the atmosphere. The total amount of this pressurization above normal atmospheric pressure is known as *boost*. This boost pressure is measurable in the same way as atmospheric pressure, namely, in psi. Normally, atmospheric pressure at sea level is 14.7 psi; many superchargers have design capability of doubling this pressure, providing 12 to 16 psi *above* the normal atmospheric pressure.

Depending on its usage, the supercharger can double or even triple the horsepower of a normally aspirated engine. On passenger vehicles where reliability and driveability are of more concern, the normal horsepower increase is usually about 50 percent. For instance, a given V-8 engine with a two-barrel carburetor has about a 40 percent increase in horsepower with the addition of a turbocharger (a form of supercharger). The same engine with a four-barrel carburetor attains about a 60 percent horsepower increase when turbocharged.

A *supercharger* is a device mechanically driven by the engine; it pressurizes the incoming air. The engine drives this device either through gears, shafts, chains, or belts at speeds between 50,000 to 90,000 rpm. However, these mechanical driving devices use up a lot of power from the engine; consequently, the engine-driven supercharger has never been extensively utilized for passenger-car engines.

The main differences between the typical supercharger and a *turbocharger* are the methods used to drive the pump itself and what the pump compresses. The engine mechanically drives the traditional supercharger and it pressurizes air. On the other hand, the velocity of the engine exhaust gases drives the turbocharger, and this unit compresses the air/fuel mixture before it enters the intake manifold, or it compresses the air before it enters the carburetor.

The main advantage of the turbocharger over the supercharger is that the turbocharger does not drain power from the engine. For example, in the normally aspirated engine, roughly 35 percent of the potential heat energy in the gasoline is lost through the exhaust. Another 35 percent of this heat energy absorbs into the engine's coolant and lubricating oil, from where it dissipates into the atmosphere. Some 10 percent of energy is also lost to friction; this leaves only about 20 percent of the original amount of heat energy from the gasoline to produce power to propel the vehicle. The mechanically driven supercharger uses up a part of this remaining heat energy, but a turbocharger receives its driving energy from the exhaust gases. Therefore, the turbocharger converts more of the fuel's heat energy into useful mechanical energy.

Turbocharger Design

The turbocharger is a centrifugal pump that consists basically of an exhaust-driven turbine (finned wheel) that connects to a compressor or blower by a shaft (Fig. 11–36). The turbocharger mounts onto the engine in such a way that exhaust gases pass over the vanes of the turbine. The velocity and expansion of the exhaust gases force the turbine wheel to rotate at speeds in proportion to the total force of the gas on the vanes. The compressor or

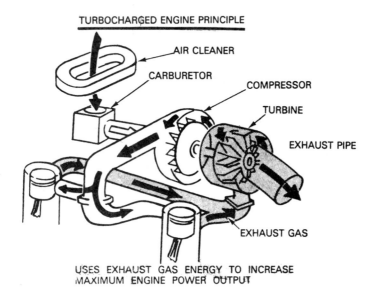

TURBOCHARGED ENGINE PRINCIPLE

AIR CLEANER

CARBURETOR

COMPRESSOR

TURBINE

EXHAUST PIPE

EXHAUST GAS

USES EXHAUST GAS ENERGY TO INCREASE
MAXIMUM ENGINE POWER OUTPUT

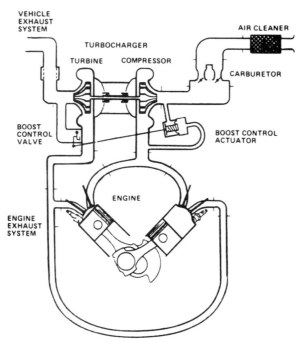

VEHICLE EXHAUST SYSTEM

AIR CLEANER

TURBOCHARGER

TURBINE   COMPRESSOR

CARBURETOR

BOOST CONTROL VALVE

BOOST CONTROL ACTUATOR

ENGINE

ENGINE EXHAUST SYSTEM

Fig. 11–36. The basic components and flow of a turbocharger. (Courtesy of General Motors Corp.)

blower wheel that connects to the turbine, therefore, turns at turbine rpm, which can be at a very high rate.

Turbocharger Installation

A typical turbocharger installation is shown in Fig. 11–36. In this installation, the compressor fits into the induction system between the carburetor and the intake manifold. With this design, as the compressor turns, it pressurizes the air/fuel mixture, thereby increasing the amount of mixture delivery to the engine's cylinders.

There are a few drawbacks to this type of installation. First, since the air and fuel mix first in the carburetor and the turbocharger compresses the mixture, the particles of fuel can easily separate before reaching the combustion chambers. Second, because the manufacturer must mount the carburetor further away from the engine, this can cause some problems in starting and warm-up in cold weather.

The exhaust gases pass from the top left-hand exhaust manifold to the turbine (Fig. 11–36). The right-hand exhaust pipe connects to the left-hand manifold by means of a crossover pipe. After passing through the turbocharger, the exhaust gases enter a single, large-diameter exhaust pipe that runs to the vehicle's exhaust system.

The air cleaner used with this turbocharger system does not mount directly on the carburetor. Instead, it sits forward of the engine, near the vehicle's grill, and the assembly connects to the carburetor by flexible tubing and a metal shroud. This type of installation permits the manufacturer to lower the hood line of the vehicle.

Turbocharger Controls

Turbocharger installations require a given number of controls so that the engine will not detonate. These controls regulate the mixture temperature, ignition timing, and maximum boost pressure. Consequently, the engine does not develop excessive combustion chamber temperatures and pressure, which can cause detonation of the air/fuel mixture. Detonation not only wastes engine power but also can cause severe engine damage.

Three controls are used on the turbocharger system: a coolant-operated plenum, spark-retarding mechanism, and waste gate. The *plenum* (Fig. 11–37) is a special chamber casting that attaches to the compressor inlet and upon which the carburetor mounts. This casting has coolant passages connected through hoses to the engine's cooling system. With this arrangement, coolant flows through these plenum passages when the engine is operating. This coolant flow has two effects. First, the air/fuel mixture passing through the plenum chamber picks up heat from the coolant, which is an aid to the fuel vaporization. This action is especially helpful as the engine is warming up. Second, the coolant flow reduces the temperature of the air/fuel mixture as outside and underhood temperatures increase. This avoids the overheating of the mixture and assists in the prevention of detonation.

The second control device used with this turbocharger design is a *spark-timing control system*. This system senses detonation within the engine when it begins and retards the ignition timing around 20 degrees in order to control this problem. The system contains two main components: a detonation sensor and the electronic spark control.

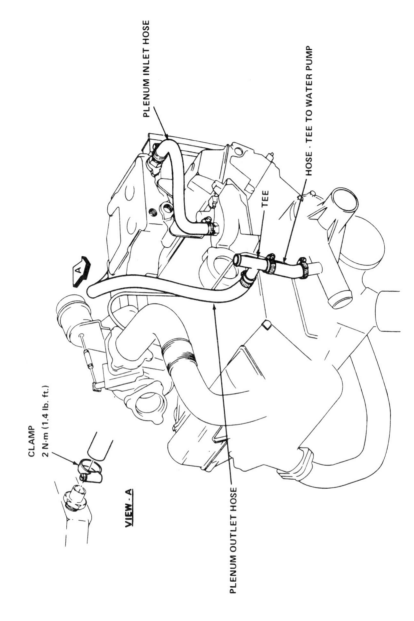

PLENUM INLET HOSE

HOSE - TEE TO WATER PUMP

TEE

A

CLAMP
2 N·m (1.4 lb. ft.)

VIEW - A

PLENUM OUTLET HOSE

Fig. 11-37. A plenum chamber is necessary on some turbocharger installations to control mixture temperatures. (Courtesy of General Motors Corp.)

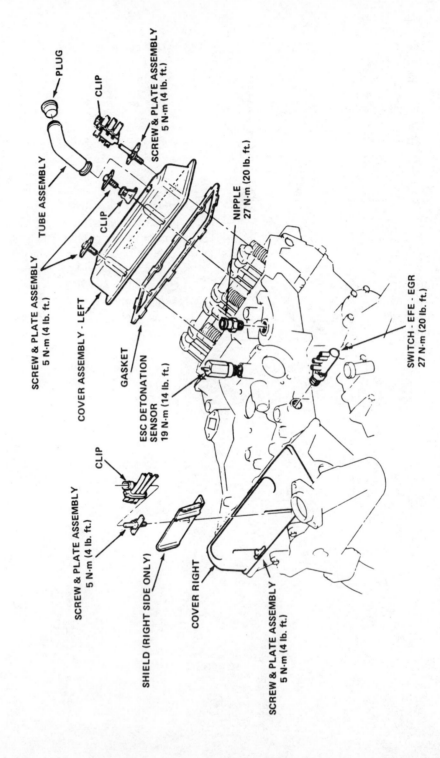

PLUG

CLIP

SCREW & PLATE ASSEMBLY
5 N·m (4 lb. ft.)

TUBE ASSEMBLY

CLIP

SCREW & PLATE ASSEMBLY
5 N·m (4 lb. ft.)

COVER ASSEMBLY - LEFT

GASKET

ESC DETONATION
SENSOR
19 N·m (14 lb. ft.)

NIPPLE
27 N·m (20 lb. ft.)

SWITCH - EFE - EGR
27 N·m (20 lb. ft.)

CLIP

SCREW & PLATE ASSEMBLY
5 N·m (4 lb. ft.)

SHIELD (RIGHT SIDE ONLY)

COVER RIGHT

SCREW & PLATE ASSEMBLY
5 N·m (4 lb. ft.)

Fig. 11–38.   The location within the intake manifold of the ESC detonation sensor.

On the engine shown in Fig. 11–38, the *detonation sensor* threads into the intake manifold. This sensor is an accelerometer (a device for detecting and measuring vibrations), which responds to any shock waves caused by detonation. If the engine begins to detonate, the sensor sends a signal to the electronic spark control.

The *electronic spark control* is the heart of this system. The ESC electrically connects with the distributor pickup coil hookup to the electronic-ignition control module. The ESC processes the signals from the detonation sensor and compares them with the signals coming from the pick-up coil. Then, the ESU directs a timing delay signal back to the ignition module, to retard the timing if and when detonation occurs. The ignition timing re-turns to its normal setting in relation to the engine's speed and load condition within about 20 seconds after detonation stops.

The last control unit used by this turbocharger system is the *waste gate*. The waste gate regulates the flow of exhaust gases to the turbine within the turbocharger, as necessary. In operation, the waste gate can permit maximum exhaust gas flow into the turbine, or it can route all or part of this exhaust gas flow into the exhaust system of the vehicle. As a result, the waste gate controls the speed of the turbine and compressor, thereby limiting, as necessary, boost pressure to reduce engine detonation.

The waste gate illustrated in Fig. 11–39 is nothing more than a diaphragm-oper-

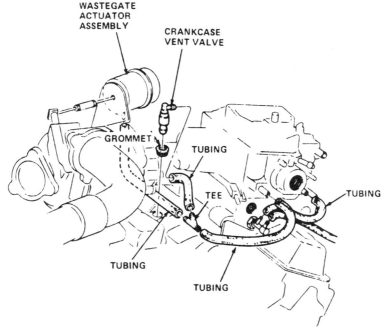

Fig. 11–39. A typical waste gate and actuator installation. (Courtesy of General Motors Corp.)

ated bypass valve in the exhaust passages within the turbocharger. The waste gate attaches to the actuator assembly via a rod. Inside the actuator assembly are a spring and diaphragm that react to an intake-manifold vacuum signal that enters the actuator assembly by a hose.

Upon acceleration, vacuum in the intake manifold drops. At a given vacuum, the spring pushes the diaphragm over within the actuator assembly. The rod attached to the diaphragm forces the waste gate to open, permitting all or part of the exhaust gases to bypass the turbine. The amount of valve opening depends on the actual vacuum drop in the intake manifold.

As vacuum increases again in the intake manifold, the diaphragm retracts within the actuator assembly, compressing the spring. The diaphragm rod closes the waste gate, and all the exhaust gases flow through the turbine. At this point, the turbocharger can produce maximum boost if the engine is operating at a high enough rpm.

Turbocharger Service

At this time, several foreign and one domestic passenger vehicles are equipped with turbochargers. Because of their differences in design and service requirements, it is not possible to cover in detail all the required maintenance on these units. However, Table 11–2 is a diagnostic chart providing an overview of what should be done if a given problem occurs in the General Motors turbocharger system described in this chapter.

Table 11–2.   Diagnostic Chart—Turbocharger

Problem	Cause	Correction
Detonation.	1. EGR system defect. 2. Actuator allows too much boost. 3. Internal turbocharger defect.	1. Diagnose and correct as needed. 2. Check linkage and hoses. Defective waste-gate. 3. Refer to internal inspection of turbocharger.
Low power.	1. Air inlet restriction. 2. Exhaust system restriction. 3. Heat-riser valve defect. 4. Turbocharger defect.	1. Locate and correct. 2. Locate and correct. 3. Check and repair. 4. Check for exhaust leaks. Collapsed plenum coolant hose. Defective waste gate. Perform internal inspection of turbocharger.
Engine surges.	1. Loose turbocharger bolts on compressor side.	1. Diagnose and correct.
Black exhaust smoke.	1. Carburetor defect.	1. See carburetor section.
Engine noise.	1. Loose exhaust system or leak. 2. Restricted turbocharger oil supply. 3. Internal turbocharger defect.	1. Correct as needed. 2. Locate and correct. 3. Inspect turbocharger.
Oil consumption.	1. Leak at turbocharger oil inlet. 2. Turbocharger oil drain hose leaks or is stopped up. 3. Turbocharger defect (internal).	1. Locate and correct. 2. Correct as needed. 3. Inspect turbocharger.

Review

This section will assist you in determining how well you remember the material in this chapter. Read each item carefully. If you can't complete the statement, review the section in the chapter that covers the material.

1. A fuel injection nozzle can spray fuel directly into the combustion chamber or into the _____ _____.
   a. intake manifold
   b. exhaust manifold
   c. air cleaner
   d. throttle body

2. The continuous port injection system discussed in the chapter is the _____ _____ _____ system.
   a. General Motors
   b. Bosch EFI-L
   c. Bosch EFI-D
   d. Bosch CIS

3. The heart of the mechanical fuel injection system covered in this chapter is the _____ _____.
   a. injector valves
   b. fuel accumulator
   c. mixture-control unit
   d. fuel pump

4. The _____ _____ in the CIS regulates the pressure across the metering slits to keep it as constant as possible.
   a. control plunger
   b. fuel barrel
   c. differential-pressure valves
   d. auxiliary air device

5. The timed-port injection system discussed in this text is the _____ _____.
   a. Bosch EFI-D
   b. Bosch EFI-L

   c. Bosch EFI-E
   d. both *a* and *c*

6. The type of electric pump used in the EFI-L system is the _____ type.
   a. roller-cell
   b. gear
   c. rotor
   d. diaphragm

7. All the injectors in the EFI-L system operate _____ _____ _____.
   a. in two pairs
   b. in staggered sequence
   c. in a group
   d. in progressive sequence

8. The device that reports engine temperature to the EFI-L control unit is the _____ _____.
   a. injection distributor
   b. thermo-time switch
   c. temperature sensor
   d. thermo sensor

9. The device in the EFI-L system that generates an electrical signal in proportion to the amount of air flow through the engine is the _____ _____.
   a. sensor flap
   b. air-flow sensor
   c. dampening chamber
   d. air switch

10. The electronic control unit of the EFI-L system has about _____ electrical components.
    a. 80
    b. 60
    c. 40
    d. 20

11. There are _____ electrical fuel pumps in the Bendix EFI system.
    a. 3
    b. 0

c. 1
d. 2

12. When the driver starts a cold engine, using the Bendix EFI system, the _____ valve increases engine idle.
   a. speed
   b. rpm
   c. fast-idle
   d. air

13. The speed sensor within the Bendix EFI system is part of the _____ _____.
   a. ECU
   b. distributor
   c. throttle body
   d. coil

14. The device that receives all the signals from the Bendix EFI sensors is the _____.
   a. ECU
   b. computer
   c. EGR
   d. EFI

15. The device that can double or even triple the horsepower of an engine is the _____ system.
   a. EFI
   b. turbocharger
   c. supercharger
   d. both *b* and *c*

16. Turbocharger controls help prevent _____ of the engine.
   a. overspeeding
   b. dieseling
   c. detonation
   d. preignition

17. The device that controls the speed of the turbocharger is the _____ _____.
   a. waste gate
   b. governor valve
   c. speed sensor
   d. detonation sensor

For the answers, turn to the Appendix.

According to historical records, the Greeks knew about electricity in static form 2,500 years ago; but it was not until the last century that anything was done to develop its usefulness. In 1831 Michael Faraday discovered electromagnetic induction, whereby magnetic lines of force generated electricity. This discovery made it possible to develop the present vast amount of electrical power and its many applications for commercial use. Moreover, Faraday's discovery is the basis for almost all automotive electrical equipment.

When working with all automotive electrical equipment, most people accept certain general statements regarding the operation of various devices. For example, it is an accepted fact that a storage battery converts chemical energy into electrical energy; a generator or alternator converts mechanical energy into electrical energy; and a starter converts electrical energy into mechanical energy. These are true statements, but unless the reader has learned the underlying fundamentals, it is impossible to get a clear mental picture of each action.

In addition, the technician who thoroughly understands the fundamental actions associated with the flow of electrical current, is ready to make an analysis of new equipment when it appears in the field. This technician will find that these new devices merely employ adaptations and arrangements of already familiar principles, and the technician is thus able to understand their operation quickly.

Electricity is an invisible force that behaves according to definite rules and produces predictable results and effects. Although people have learned to produce, store, use, and measure electricity, no one knows exactly what electricity is. How-

Chapter 12

PRINCIPLES OF ELECTRICITY AND MAGNETISM

ever, in recent years, scientists have developed a theory, the electron theory, that explains the nature of electricity fairly well. This new theory explains more thoroughly than any other theory the behavior of electricity and magnetism. However, it is difficult to understand because electrons can't be seen or easily illustrated.

Structure of Matter

To comprehend the electron theory, it is first necessary to review the structure of matter, as covered in Chapter 3. This chapter discusses the fact that all matter is made up of tiny particles, called *molecules;* these molecules, in turn, are formed of two or more still smaller particles known as *atoms.* For example, a molecule of water (H_2O) (Fig. 12-1) has a composition of two atoms of hydrogen and one atom of oxygen. Both are gases, which

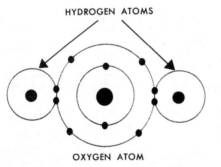

HYDROGEN ATOMS

OXYGEN ATOM

Fig. 12-1. A molecule of water. (Courtesy of Delco Remy)

form a liquid compound under proper conditions.

Structure of the Atom

According to the electron theory, the atom itself is further divisible into even smaller particles known as *protons, neutrons,* and *electrons* (Fig. 12-2). These particles are the same in all matter; and the different properties of matter such as hardness, softness, toughness, fragility, solidity, conductivity, or nonconductivity occur only because of the number and arrangement of these particular particles.

The particles have a definite placement within the atom. For instance, the proton and neutron form the center or nucleus in the atom, much as the sun does in our solar system (Fig. 12-3). The electron, on the other hand, turns in an orbit around the nucleus, much as the earth, Venus, Mars, and other planets rotate around the sun.

Both protons and electrons have a type of electrical charge. For instance, the proton has a positive charge. The electron has a negative charge. However, the neutron has no electrical charge but adds weight to the atom.

Any substance made up of only one kind of atom is known as an element. Hydrogen, copper, and gold are good examples of elements. There are over a hundred known elements on the atomic scale, and each element differs from the one preced-

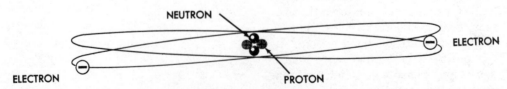

Fig. 12-2. The composition of the atom. (Courtesy of Delco Remy)

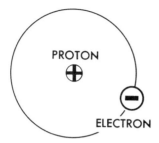

Fig. 12-3. The placement of the proton, neutron, and electron in the hydrogen atom. The neutron is not shown but is assumed to be in the nucleus. (Courtesy of Delco Remy)

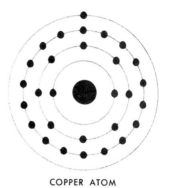

COPPER ATOM

Fig. 12-4. The structure of a copper atom. (Courtesy of Delco Remy)

ing it on the scale by the addition of one protron and one electron. Hydrogen, for example, is one of the simplest of all atoms; it is number 1 on the atomic scale. It consists of one proton and one electron. Copper, on the other hand, is number 29 with, therefore, 29 protons and 29 electrons.

Electron Theory

The electron theory states that a flow of electricity or current flow is the movement of electrons between atoms within a conductor. To understand this statement, it is necessary first to explain the differences between a good conductor and an insulator, or a nonconductor. For purposes of explanation, let us examine the make-up of a good conductor, the copper atom (Fig. 12-4). Within this atom are four orbital paths for the electrons. In the innermost orbit, closest to the nucleus, are 2 electrons. The second orbit contains 8 electrons; the third orbit has 18 electrons; and the fourth orbit accommodates 1 electron, commonly known as a *free* electron.

This particular electron is a very important one because it can become lost from its orbit easily. If and when this occurs, the atom takes on a more positive polarity because it has more protons (29) than electrons (28). Before the electron was lost, the atom was electrically neutral, having the exact same number of protons and electrons.

An insulator, like glass and hard rubber, is said to have *bound* electrons. These substances have more than four electrons in their outer orbits, and these electrons are bound, which means that they cannot easily be dislodged from their orbits. Consequently, these materials cannot normally carry a current of electricity.

In order for electrons to flow between atoms in a conductor, something must force the free electrons from their orbit. Friction, heat, magnetism, or chemical activity are all examples of forces that can expel electrons from their orbital paths. In the automotive electrical system, electron movement is due to the action of the battery or the alternator, which induces electron flow by producing voltage, a difference in electrical potential.

For the present, we will use the battery as the device that causes electron flow in the conductor. The battery, as the next chapter explains in detail, has two terminals, a positive and a negative. The positive (+) terminal, through chemical action, has a net positive charge (an abundance of protons) while the negative (−) terminal has an excess of electrons or a negative charge. In other words, the battery chemically produces a difference in electrical potential or voltage.

If you connect a copper wire, which contains billions of atoms per square inch, between the two terminals of a battery, electrons will flow from negative to positive. Figure 12–5 shows this action within the copper conductor. Although this conductor contains billions of copper atoms, all having free electrons, the diagram only shows a few atoms with only a single electron in all their outer orbits.

The electron closest to the positive terminal of the battery moves out of orbit and passes into the net positive charge of the battery. This action results because *unlike electrical charges attract one another.* This particular atom, therefore, has a net positive charge because it has one less electron. As a result, this atom attracts an electron from an adjacent atom. This action, in turn, attracts an electron from the next atom and so forth. In addition, at the negative end of the conductor, the negative battery terminal applies a push on the first atom because *like electrical charges repel each other.*

The result of both this attracting and repelling action is the forced movement of electrons through the wire from the negative end toward the positive end. This flow of electrons (current) continues as long as the unlike positive and negative charges remain at the two terminals of the battery.

Electrical Current, Voltage, and Resistance

When discussing electricity, we deal with three basic factors: current, voltage, and resistance. These terms are basic to the understanding of electricity and its effects within the complex electrical system of the automobile.

Current

The flow of electrons in a conductor is known as a *current* of electricity; its measurement is *amperes.* One ampere is an electric current of 6.28 billion, billion electrons passing a certain point in a conductor in 1 second (Fig. 12–6). Thus, current is the rate of electron flow and is measurable in amperes or electrons per second. It is this current flow through a conductor that performs the work of operating the electrical units such as the starter motor, headlights, and ignition system.

Current flow is comparable to the flow of water in a pipe. In fact, comparing current flow to water flow is undoubtedly the easiest and quickest way to explain this and all factors dealing with electricity. Current flow is the movement of electrons

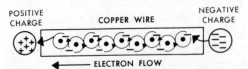

Fig. 12-5. *The flow of electrons in a copper conductor. (Courtesy of Delco Remy)*

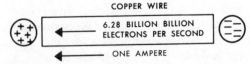

Fig. 12-6. *The measurement of current flow. (Courtesy of Delco Remy)*

through a conductor (wire) just as water flow is the movement of this liquid through a pipe (Fig. 12–7). In regard to current flow, amperage is the electrical unit of measure, while gallons per minute is the measurement for the rate of water flowing through a pipe.

Voltage

Voltage is the electrical force, measured in volts, that causes the flow of current in a conductor. The amount of this force or pressure depends on the difference in the charges existing at each end of the conductor. At one end of the conductor, there must be a net positive charge while at the other end there must be a net negative charge.

In the automobile, two devices provide these differences in electrical charges: the battery and the alternator. The *storage battery* produces voltage through chemical action while the *alternator* mechanically generates voltage, using magnetic induction.

Voltage is a potential force and can exist even when there is no current flow within a circuit. A storage battery, for example, may have a potential of 12 volts between its positive and negative terminals; this potential is there even if there are no current-consuming devices connected directly across its terminals. Consequently, voltage can exist without current flow, but current flow cannot occur without the push of voltage.

In one regard, a storage battery and a water tower have something in common—they all provide pressure (Fig. 12–8). The battery is a source of electrical pressure due to its internal chemical action; while on the other hand the water tower provides water pressure due to the action of gravity on the weight of the water in the tank. In other words, battery voltage is simply electrical pressure; it is this voltage or pressure that pushes the electrons through the wire in a complete circuit, just as the pressure at the outlet of the

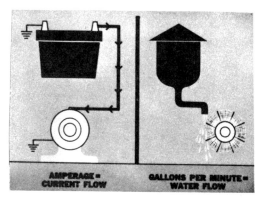

Fig. 12–7. *Amperage and gallons per minute both measure flow. (Courtesy of Chrysler Corp.)*

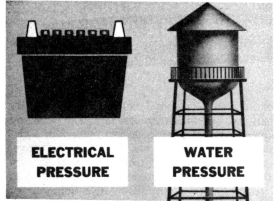

Fig. 12–8. *Both a battery and a water tower provide pressure. (Courtesy of Chrysler Corp.)*

water tower forces the water through the pipes in a plumbing system.

When dealing with electrical voltage, you must understand this one particular point. In order to have voltage between two points, there must be a positive charge existing at one point and a negative charge on the other (Fig. 12-9). The greater the charges are at each point (like the terminals of a battery) the greater the voltage. In other words, the greater the *lack* of electrons at the (+) terminal and the greater the *excess* of electrons at the (−) terminal, the higher the voltage is.

Resistance

Electrical resistance is just that—resistance to the flow of electrons. All electrical conductors offer some resistance to the flow of current (Fig. 12-10). This resistance is the result of each atom resisting removal of its electrons due to its attraction toward the nucleus, and collisions of countless electrons as they move through the conductor. These collisions cause resistance and create heat in the conductor.

Several other factors increase or decrease resistance. For example, the size of the wire also affects resistance. A small wire causes more resistance to current flow than a larger wire of the same material, in much the same way as a small pipe in a water system offers more resistance to water flow than a large pipe. In addition, the length of the wire and the material from which the manufacturer makes the

Fig. 12-9. *Voltage exists between two unlike electrical charges. (Courtesy of Delco Remy)*

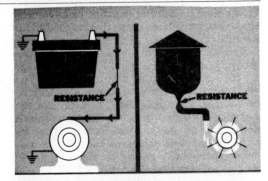

Fig. 12-10. Resistance reduces flow. (Courtesy of Chrysler Corp.)

wire affect resistance. Shorter wire offers less resistance than long wires, and good conductor materials provide less resistance than poor conductors. Manufacturers use metals like copper, aluminum, and silver for conductors because they offer low resistance.

Resistance, therefore, is the only real difference between good conductors and good insulators. Any material that is an extremely poor conductor is usually a good insulator. In other words, an insulator is a material that offers enough resistance to prevent the flow of current.

The basic unit of measurement for resistance is the *ohm*. One ohm is the resistance that will allow only 1 ampere to flow in a circuit with a pressure of 1 volt.

Ohm's Law

Ohm's law is the most fundamental equation in electrical science. This law very definitely defines the relationship between volts, amps, and ohms. Ohm's law states that voltage equals amperage times resistance in ohms. This simply means that 1 volt will push 1 ampere of current through 1 ohm of resistance (Fig. 12-11).

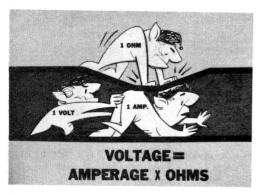

**VOLTAGE =
AMPERAGE X OHMS**

Fig. 12–11. Ohm's law defines electrical behavior. (Courtesy of Chrysler Corp.)

Since Ohm's law is an equation, you can write it three different ways. Consequently, if you know two facts about a circuit, you can calculate the third or unknown by using one of the following equations (Fig. 12–12).

1. Amperes equals volts divided by ohms.

2. Volts equals amperes times ohms.

3. Ohms equals volts divided by amperes.

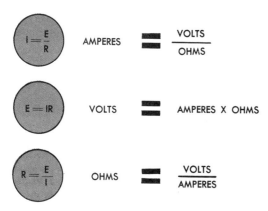

$I = \dfrac{E}{R}$ AMPERES $=$ $\dfrac{\text{VOLTS}}{\text{OHMS}}$

$E = IR$ VOLTS $=$ AMPERES X OHMS

$R = \dfrac{E}{I}$ OHMS $=$ $\dfrac{\text{VOLTS}}{\text{AMPERES}}$

Fig. 12–12. The three equations derived from Ohm's law. (Courtesy of Delco Remy)

Electrical Circuits

Batteries and alternators apply electrical pressure and cause electrical current to flow through a circuit from the high-pressure side to the low-pressure side or from negative to positive. However, there must be a complete circuit or pathway, made up of wires or other conductors, or the current cannot flow. If for some reason a wire is broken or disconnected, the current flow stops.

Automotive circuits are not all alike, and electricity does not behave exactly the same in different types of circuits. Therefore, it is important that the technician understand the basic kinds of circuits found within the automobile and how volts, amps, and ohms behave in these individual circuits.

Simple Circuit

The easiest way to explain the basic circuits is through the use of a battery, some wire, and electrical lamps or other devices that serve as resistance units. In the simplest type of circuit, current flows from the battery through the lamp or resistor and back to the battery to complete the circuit. However, most automotive circuits have more than one lamp or resistance unit and *use the vehicle body and frame as the circuit from the resistance unit to the negative side of the battery.* This forms a single-wire system.

There are two ways to describe current flow in any circuit, using either the conventional theory or the electron theory (Fig. 12–13). In the conventional theory, current flows from the (+) terminal of the battery, through the circuit, and to the (−) terminal of the battery. The electron

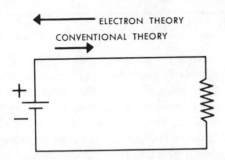

ELECTRON THEORY

CONVENTIONAL THEORY

Fig. 12-13. The two theories of current flow in a circuit. (Courtesy of Delco Remy)

theory states that current flow is from the (−) terminal of the battery, through the circuit, and to the (+) terminal of the battery.

Either theory is usable. However, *this text utilizes the conventional theory in its remaining explanation of electrical circuits, coils, and other magnetic devices basically because it is more popular and easier to use on automotive single-wire circuitry.*

Series Circuit

In a series-type circuit, two or more lamps or resistance units connect in such a way that there is only one continuous path for current flow (Fig. 12-14). Since

CURRENT SAME EVERYWHERE IN CIRCUIT

Fig. 12-14. A series circuit means only one path for current to flow. (Courtesy of Chrysler Corp.)

within a series circuit all the current must flow through each resistance unit, the current flow is always the same everywhere within the circuit. This is always true regardless of the number of resistance units connected in series into the circuit. The important thing to remember about this type of circuit is that there is only one path for current to flow. If you remember this, you will have no trouble recognizing a series circuit when you see it on a wiring diagram.

Voltage Drop within a Series Circuit

Resistance in an electrical circuit always reduces electrical pressure (voltage). This reduction in electrical pressure is known as voltage drop. *Voltage drop* is simply the difference between the voltage at one point in a circuit and the voltage at another point in the circuit.

Here are a few important facts to remember about voltage drops.

1. The voltage drops across each resistance unit will be different if the resistances have differing values.

2. The sum of the voltage drops always equals the source of voltage. As in Fig. 12-15, the voltage drop across the one re-

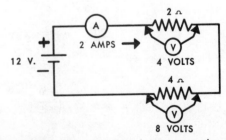

Fig. 12-15. The voltage drop across the resistors in a series circuit. (Courtesy of Delco Remy)

sistor is 4 volts and across the second is 8 volts. The sum of these two voltage drops is 12 volts, battery voltage.

You can apply Ohm's law to determine the current flow, resistance, and voltage drop across a series circuit. In the series circuit shown in Fig. 12–15, the voltage is 12 volts and the resistors in the circuit have a *sum* of 6 ohms. In order to find the current flow, use the application of Ohm's law where current (I) equals $\dfrac{\text{voltage } (E).}{\text{resistance } (R)}$ In this case, I is equal to $\frac{12}{6}$ or 2 amperes.

In a series circuit, the total resistance is always equal to the sum of all the resistors. Within the circuit shown in Fig. 12–16, the total resistance therefore is 1 plus 2, or 3 ohms. Consequently, the current flow in this circuit is $I = \frac{E}{R} = \frac{12}{3}$, or 4 amperes.

It is also easy to figure the voltage drop across each resistor, using Ohm's law. For example, in Fig. 12–15, the voltage across the 2-ohm resistor is $E = 1 \times R = 2 \times 2 = 4$ volts. For the 4-ohm resistor, voltage drop equals $E = 1 \times R = 2 \times 4$, or 8 volts. These values are known as *voltage drops;*

the sum of the voltage drops in the circuit must equal the voltage source, the battery. Finally, as shown in Fig. 12–15, an ammeter connected into the circuit reads 2 amperes, while a voltmeter connected across each resistor reads 4 volts and 8 volts, respectively.

Parallel Circuits

In a parallel circuit, the lamps or resistance units connect in such a way that there is more than one path for current flow (Fig. 12–17). This simply means that part of the current flows through one lamp and part of it flows through the other lamp. Also in this type of circuit, the voltage drop across each resistor is equal to the voltage of the battery since there is a separate path for current to flow through each resistor. This means:

1. The voltage across each resistor is the same.

2. The current through each resistor is different if the resistance values are not the same.

3. The sum of the separate currents equals the total current flow within the circuit.

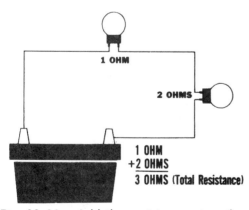

Fig. 12–16. Add the resistances together to obtain total series resistance. (Courtesy of Chrysler Corp.)

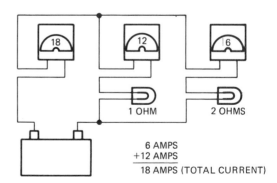

Fig. 12–17. Current flow in a parallel circuit. (Courtesy of Chrysler Corp.)

In the parallel circuit shown in Fig. 12–17, there is a 1-ohm and a 2-ohm resistor, connected to a 12-volt battery. These two resistors are in parallel with each other since the battery voltage of 12 volts flows across each resistor. Using Ohm's law, we can figure the current flow through each resistor or branch. For example, branch 1 with the 1-ohm resistor has a current flow equal to $I = \frac{E}{R} = \frac{12}{1}$, or 12 amperes. For branch 2 with the 2-ohm resistor, current flow equals $I = \frac{E}{R} = \frac{12}{2}$, or 6 amperes. The total current in the entire circuit is therefore 6 + 12 amperes, or 18 amperes of current.

The total resistance in a parallel circuit is always *less* than that of the smallest resistor in the circuit. This is explainable by the fact that there is less resistance to current flow when two paths are in a circuit to provide current flow, than with only one path.

There is a simple way to calculate the total resistance in a given parallel circuit. To do this, all you need to do is to multiply the resistances together, and then divide this product by the sum of the same resistances. For example, if we multiply the two resistance values shown in Fig. 12–18 together, the product is 8. Then, if we divide the sum of these same two resistances (6) into the product, the total circuit resistance equals $1\frac{1}{3}$ ohms, which is a smaller resistance value than either of the resistors in the whole circuit.

Series-Parallel Circuits

The last circuit that this chapter discusses is a series-parallel circuit (Fig. 12–19). Note in this diagram that a 2-ohm resistor is in series with a parallel combination (the 3- and 6-ohm resistors). In this situation, the total current in the circuit is

TOTAL RESISTANCE $\frac{2 \times 4}{2 + 4} = \frac{8}{6} = 1\frac{1}{3}$ **OHMS**

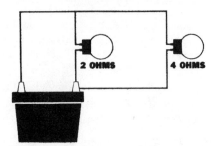

Fig. 12–18.   Finding the total resistance in a typical parallel circuit. (Courtesy of Chrysler Corp.)

equal to the total voltage divided by the total resistance ($I = \frac{E}{R}$).

You can determine the total resistance in the parallel circuit using the formula just given for parallel circuits. In other words, the total resistance offered by the two parallel branches is equal to $\frac{6 \times 3}{6 + 3}$, or 2 ohms. To find *total* circuit resistance, you must add these 2 ohms to the other 2-ohm resistor because they are in fact in series. This gives us a total circuit resistance of 4 ohms. The total current flow, therefore, is $I = \frac{E}{R} = \frac{12}{4}$, or 3 amps.

To find the voltage drops across the resistors in a series-parallel circuit, first determine the voltage drop across the series-connected resistor. With 3 amperes flowing through the 2-ohm series-connected resistor nearest the battery (Fig. 12–19), the voltage drop across it is equal to $E = I$

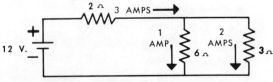

Fig. 12–19.   A typical series-parallel circuit. (Courtesy of Delco Remy)

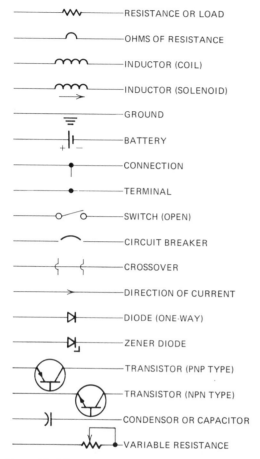

RESISTANCE OR LOAD

OHMS OF RESISTANCE

INDUCTOR (COIL)

INDUCTOR (SOLENOID)

GROUND

BATTERY

CONNECTION

TERMINAL

SWITCH (OPEN)

CIRCUIT BREAKER

CROSSOVER

DIRECTION OF CURRENT

DIODE (ONE-WAY)

ZENER DIODE

TRANSISTOR (PNP TYPE)

TRANSISTOR (NPN TYPE)

CONDENSOR OR CAPACITOR

VARIABLE RESISTANCE

Fig. 12–20. Common symbols used on electrical diagrams.

$\times R = 3 \times 2$, or 6 volts. This leaves 6 volts across the two parallel 6- and 3-ohm resistors. Remember that in a parallel circuit the voltage across each resistor is the same. Consequently, each resistor will show a voltage drop of 6 volts.

To determine the current flow through the parallel branches, first figures the current flow through each branch. For example (Fig. 12–19), the current flow through the 6-ohm resistor is $I = \frac{E}{R} = \frac{6}{6}$, or 1 ampere. The current flow through the 3-ohm

resistor is equal to $I = \frac{E}{R} = \frac{6}{3}$, or 2 amperes. The total current flow then in the entire parallel circuit is the sum of these two values, or 3 amperes.

The current flow in the entire series parallel circuit is equal to $I = \frac{E}{R}$. However, in the series-parallel circuit, the total resistance is 2 ohms in the series portion plus the resistance of the parallel branches. The resistance in the parallel circuit is $\frac{6 \times 3}{6 + 3}$, or 2 ohms. Consequently, the total resistance in this entire circuit is $3 + 2$, or 5 ohms. The total current flow then in this entire series-parallel circuit is equal to $\frac{12}{5}$ or 2.4 amperes.

In order to read electrical diagrams, the technician must know certain symbols (Fig. 12–20). These symbols are graphic representations used by draftsmen to simplify electrical diagrams. These symbols represent certain electrical components and can be seen readily on most any vehicle electrical diagram, no matter what make or model.

Semiconductor

Conductors have less than four electrons in their outer orbits while insulators have more than four electrons. A *semiconductor* is an element that has *just* four electrons in its outer orbit. These elements are neither good conductors nor good insulators. The most common of these semiconductors are silicon and germanium. The basic usage for semiconductors in the automobile is for diodes and transistors.

Before examining a diode or transistor, let us first examine how these basic elements work. A silicon crystal for a semiconductor is made by covalent bonding

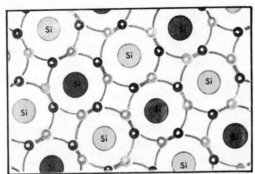

Fig. 12-21. Silicon crystal formed as a semiconductor by covalent bonding. (Courtesy of Deere & Company Technical Services)

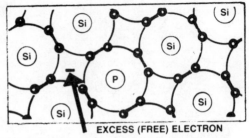

EXCESS (FREE) ELECTRON

Fig. 12-22. The use of phosphorus to "dope" silicon leaves an electron left over. (Courtesy of Deere & Company Technical Services)

(Fig. 12-21). This simply means that the electrons in the outer orbit of one silicon atom join the electrons of other silicon atoms so that the atoms share electrons in all their outer rings. As a result, each atom really has eight electrons in its outer orbit as shown. This action creates a very good insulator since there are now more than four electrons in each atom's outer ring.

However, the manufacturer then "dopes" the silicon crystal by adding other materials. The two common elements used to "dope" the silicon are phosphorous and antimony. Both these particular elements have five electrons in their outer orbit.

During the covalent bonding process, one electron is left over (Fig. 12-22). This particular electron is a free electron that can be made to move through the material very easily. Any material having an extra electron is known as an N-type material, because it already has excess electrons and will repel additional negative charges.

Manufacturers also use two other elements commonly to "dope" silicon crystals; these are boron and indium. The par-

ticular elements have only three electrons in their outer orbit. Therefore, during the covalent bonding process, there is a shortage of one electron for complete bonding. This resulting void is known as a *hole* (Fig. 12-23). Engineers consider this hole as a positive charge of electricity. Consequently, materials lacking this electron and having this hole are known as *P*-type material because the hole attracts a negative charge.

Semiconductor Operation

To understand the operation of a semiconductor, consider this hole in the P material as a positive (+) charge and the extra electron in the N material as a negative (−) electrical charge. The hole can move

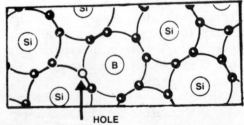

HOLE

Fig. 12-23. The use of boron to "dope" a silicon creates a "hole" in the atom's outer orbit. (Courtesy of Deere & Company Technical Services)

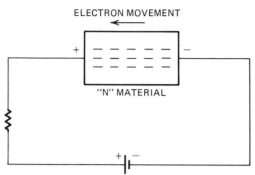

ELECTRON MOVEMENT

"N" MATERIAL

Fig. 12–24. Electron flow in a circuit with N-type material. (Courtesy of Deere & Company Technical Services)

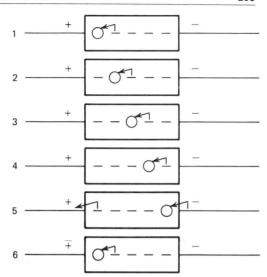

Fig. 12–26. The movement of holes within a P-type material. (Courtesy of Deere & Company Technical Services)

from atom to atom in the same way as an electron can move from atom to atom.

Figure 12–24 shows the current flow in an N-type material. By connecting a battery (the voltage source) to the material, a current flows through the circuit. This current flow is the movement of the excess of free electrons through the material, and this is very similar to what occurs in a good conductor, a copper wire.

The current flow in a P-type material is shown in Fig. 12–25. However, in this instance, the flow results from movement of positively charged holes. Figure 12–26 also illustrates this hole movement. Notice how the positive battery terminal in diagram 1 attracts the negative electron in the material (unlike charges attract one

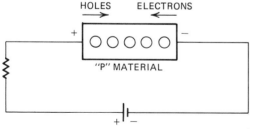

HOLES   ELECTRONS

"P" MATERIAL

Fig. 12–25. The movement of holes within the circuit with P-type material. (Courtesy of Deere & Company Technical Services)

another). Similarly, the negative battery terminal repels the electrons. As a result, the electron from one of the covalent bonds moves to the left toward the positive terminal; this electron fills one of the holes near the terminal.

This movement of an electron leaves behind a hole. As a result, the positively charged hole then has moved to the right toward the (–) battery terminal. This process continues and the hole keeps moving to the right until it nears the (–) terminal of the semiconductor, At this time (diagram 5), an electron that leaves the (–) terminal of the battery fills the hole; the positive battery terminal removes an electron from the semiconductor at the opposite end. Then, the process is ready to repeat itself.

The continuous movement of holes from the (+) terminal to the (–) terminal is considered to be current flow in the P-type material. Of course, this activity only occurs when the battery voltage causes the electrons to shift around in the covalent bonds. This hole movement happens *only in the semiconductor itself* while the electrons flow through the entire circuit. Finally, this hole movement theory will assist you in understanding how diodes and transistors operate.

Diodes

Function and Structure

A *diode* (Fig. 12–27) is an electrical device that permits current to pass through itself in one direction only. Manufacturers form diodes by joining two semiconductor materials, one of which is N-type material while the other is P-type material. In diodes, the N material is usually phosphorus-doped silicon while the P material is usually boron-doped silicon.

Figure 12–28 illustrates the basic structure of the diode. In this structure, the N and P materials attract one another but the positive and negative ions on each side keep them stabilized. An *ion* is an atom with a shortage or an excess of electrons. These ions are responsible for "pulling

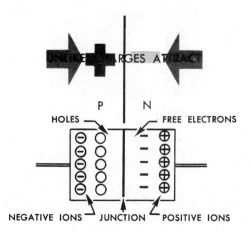

Fig. 12–28. The basic structure of the diode. (Courtesy of Deere & Company Technical Services)

back" on the free electrons and the holes to prevent them from crossing the junction. As a result, the diode has a stabilized condition with a lack of electrons and holes at the junction area.

Operation

Figure 12–29 shows a diode activated by a battery. Now, the negative battery terminal repels the electrons in the N material while the positive battery terminal repels the holes in the P material. With adequate battery voltage, electrons move from the (−) battery terminal, across the junction, to the (+) battery connection to create a current flow. In addition, the positive holes move through the P material and through the junction as shown.

Battery voltage maintains this current flow. However, for current to flow in the direction shown through the diode, there must be holes at the junction into which electrons can move.

Figure 12–29 also shows a forward bias connection of the diode, the (−) terminal to the N material and the (+) to the P ma-

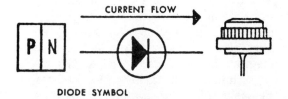

DIODE SYMBOL

ELEMENT	ATOMIC NUMBER	NUMBER OF PROTONS	NUMBER OF ELECTRONS	VALENCE RING ELECTRONS
Boron (B)	5	5	5	3
Silicon (Si)	14	14	14	4
Phosphorus (P)	15	15	15	5

Fig. 12–27. A diode. (Courtesy of Deere & Company Technical Services)

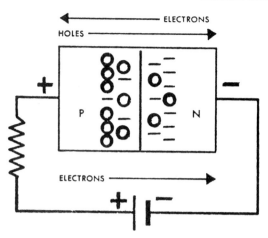

Fig. 12-29. *Diode operation. (Courtesy of Deere & Company Technical Services)*

terial. This type of hookup creates the repelling action by the battery voltage that causes both the electrons and holes to collect at the junction in vast quantities. This action is necessary for current to flow through the diode.

Figure 12-30 illustrates a battery connection that results in a reverse bias condition, which causes the diode to block current flow. In this situation, the (+) terminal of the battery attracts electrons

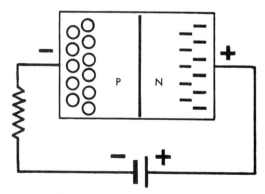

Fig. 12-30. *A diode blocking current flow due to a reverse bias connection. (Courtesy of Deere & Company Technical Services)*

away from the junction while the (−) terminal pulls the holes away from the junction. As a result, no current flows through the diode.

When a reverse bias condition occurs in a diode, a small current may flow through the diode in a reverse direction. However, this reverse current flow is very small.

If this voltage across the diode increases to a value known as the *maximum reverse voltage* of a diode, the covalent bond breaks down, and a sharp increase in reverse current occurs. If this reverse current is great enough both in magnitude and duration, the diode overheats enough to be damaged. Engineers of course select diodes with a maximum reverse voltage rating so that damaging reverse currents cannot occur during normal operation *as long as the battery connections to the circuit are correct.*

Zener Diodes

A *zener diode* has a special design that permits it to conduct current, under certain conditions, in the reverse direction (Fig. 12-31). The primary design feature of this particular diode is that its manufacturer heavily "dopes" this unit with large numbers of extra current carriers (electrons and holes). This structure permits the zener diode to conduct current,

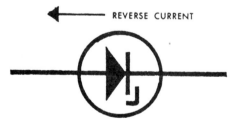

Fig. 12-31. *The zener diode symbol. (Courtesy of Deere & Company Technical Services)*

without damage, in the reverse direction if installed in the proper circuit.

What makes the zener diode very unique is that the unit will not conduct current flow in a reverse direction below a predetermined value of reverse bias voltage. For instance, a given zener diode does not conduct current flow when the reverse bias voltage is lower than 6 volts. But if the reverse bias voltage increases to 6 volts or more, the diode suddenly conducts reverse current.

Transistors

Function and Design

A *transistor* is an electrical device used in circuits to control the flow of current. In operation, the transistor controls current flow in a given circuit.

Manufacturers usually form a transistor by the addition of a second section of P-type material to the PN junction used for diodes. This design results in the PNP transistor (Fig. 12–32). The P material on the left is the emitter; the N material in the center comprises the base; and the P material to the right forms the collector.

Manufacturers also build NPN transistors (right diagram of Fig. 12–32). However, the PNP transistor type is the one most commonly used in the automotive electrical circuit.

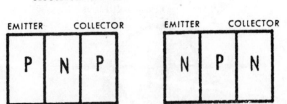

Fig. 12–32. Basic components of transistors. (Courtesy of Deere & Company Technical Services)

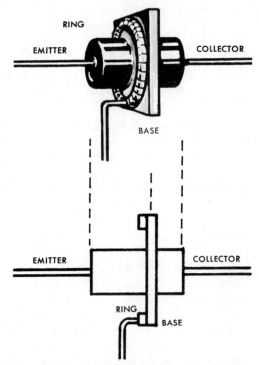

Fig. 12–33. The design of a transistor. (Courtesy of Deere & Company Technical Services)

The base section of the transistor is very thin (Fig. 12–33). Attached around this base is a metallic ring, which connects into the electrical circuit. With this design, the total distance between the emitter itself and the collector is shorter than the distance between the emitter and the base ring. This design provides the transistor with its unusual operating characteristics.

Operation

Figure 12–34 illustrates a PNP transistor connected into a series-parallel circuit with a battery as the source of voltage. In

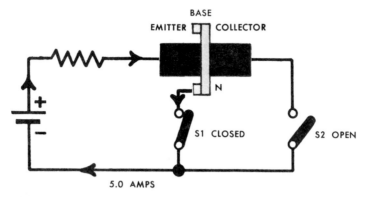

Fig. 12–34.   Transistor in a circuit with the collector inoperative. (Courtesy of Deere & Company Technical Services)

this illustration, switch S1 is closed while S2 is open. As a result, current flows through the emitter-base of the transistor. However, since switch S2 is open, the collector does not operate. The circuit shown is a simple PN junction diode (through the emitter-base), which connects to the battery in a forward bias direction.

Before proceeding with this discussion, it is a good time to review one point, the definition of current flow or the movement of electrons from atom to atom in a conductor. The electron theory states that electrons in this circuit flow from the negative battery terminal, through the base-emitter, and back to the positive side of the battery.

However, to make it easier to understand the operation of this PNP transistor, let's use the hole movement as a theory of current flow and apply it to the PNP transistor shown in Fig. 12–34. With this hole movement theory, the current flow within the transistor is the movement of holes (positive charges) through the P material to the N material. As in the conventional theory of current flow, you can assume that this movement of holes is the same thing as current flow; this theory

simplifies the explanation of how the transistor operates.

Let's assume that in the transistor circuit shown in Fig. 12–35 the emitter-base current is 5 amperes. However, when switch S2 closes, a rather startling phenomenon occurs. While the total circuit current flow remains at 5 amperes, most of the current leaves the transistor through the collector circuit. The current flow through the collector circuit is 4.8 amperes while the current through the base circuit is only 0.2 ampere.

There are several reasons for this. First, the design of the transistor is such that the emitter and the collector are closer together than the emitter and the base ring. Therefore, most of the holes take the path of least resistance, which is through the base and into the collector, impelled onward, as it were, by their velocity. Second, the negative potential at the collector terminal attracts the positive holes from the base on into the collector.

In this example, the collector current is 24 times that of the base current. This particular factor is known as *current gain* and is a significant aspect of a transistor. That is, by controlling the very small base cur-

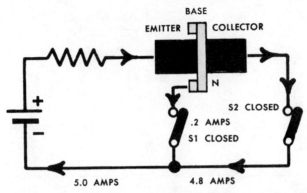

Fig. 12–35.   *Transistor operation with both the base and collector circuits operational. (Courtesy of Deere & Company Technical Services)*

rent, the much larger collector current is also regulated.

Figure 12–36 points out what occurs when switch *S2* closes and *S1* is open. In this instance, no appreciable current flows. The reason for this is that with the emitter-base circuit open, there are no holes injected into the base from the emitter. Consequently, there are no holes in the base that the negative potential at the collector terminal can attract. In addition, this negative battery potential attracts what holes there are in the collector away from the base-collector junction. As a

result, the resistance across the base-collector junction becomes very high. Although the emitter and collector join together, the opening of switch *S1* effectively shuts off the transistor so that no appreciable current can flow.

Symbols

The most common symbols for transistors are shown in Fig. 12–37. In these diagrams, the line with the arrow is the emitter; the heavier line represents the base; and the line without the arrow indicates

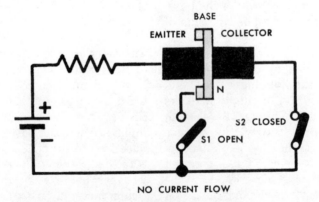

Fig. 12–36.   *Operation of the transistor with the base circuit open. (Courtesy of Deere & Company Technical Services)*

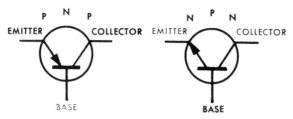

Fig. 12–37. The common symbols for transistors. (Courtesy of Deere & Company Technical Services)

the collector. Note that the arrow points in the direction of *conventional* current flow, that is, from the positive to negative within the external circuit. It is more convenient to visualize current flow in the PNP transistor as the movement of positively charged holes and in the NPN transistor as the movement of electrons. Although the electrons move against the arrow within the NPN transistor, this is not contradictory as it is much easier to visualize the emitter injecting the electrons into the base and collector.

Magnetism

The discovery of the effects of magnetism was the result of the observation of how the fragments of iron ore called lodestone attracted other pieces of iron (Fig. 12–38). It was also noticed that a long piece of this particular ore, suspended in

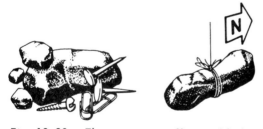

Fig. 12–38. The magnetic effects of lodestone. (Courtesy of Delco Remy)

the air on a string, would align itself so that one end always pointed at the North Pole of the earth. Consequently, this end of the iron bar or bar magnet became known as its north pole or N pole while the opposite bar end is known as the south or S pole. This principle of magnetism became the basis for the compass, used as an aid in navigation for over 1,000 years.

Magnetic Fields

Further study of the bar magnet showed that an invisible attractive force from the magnet exerted itself upon bits of iron or iron filings even though they were some distance away from it. This phenomenon makes it very clear that some form of force exists in the space close to the magnet. The force that fills this space around the magnet and into which iron filings attract is known as a *magnetic field*. This field is nothing more than invisible lines of force that come out of the N pole and enter the S pole.

You can see the effects of these magnetic lines of force by sprinkling iron filings on a piece of paper resting on top of a bar magnet (Fig. 12–39). If you lightly tap the paper by hand, the iron filings line up to form a clear pattern around the bar magnet. This pattern shows that these lines of force heavily concentrate themselves at the N and S poles of the magnet

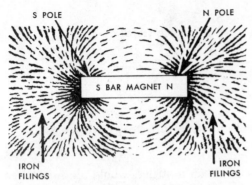

Fig. 12-39. *The effects of the magnetic field around a bar magnet. (Courtesy of Delco Remy)*

and then spread themselves out into the surrounding air between the poles. The concentration or the number of lines at each pole is equal, and the attractive force on the filings at each pole is also equal. Notice that the force of attraction of bits of metal is strongest at the point where the concentration of magnetic lines is greatest, the area next to the poles for a bar magnet.

Fundamental Law of Magnetism

There is a fundamental law that deals with magnetism. This law states that unlike poles attract one another, and like poles repel one another. Figure 12-40 demonstrates this fundamental law. In the upper portion of this illustration are

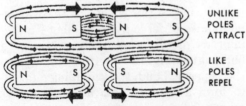

Fig. 12-40. *Fundamental law of magnetism. (Courtesy of Delco Remy)*

two magnets placed so that the N pole of one and the S pole of the other are close together. In this situation, the magnetic lines of force leaving the N pole of the right-hand magnet enter the S pole of the left-hand magnet, creating an attractive force since all lines of force are in the same direction. This action causes the adjacent N and S poles to attract each other, and this force of attraction increases as the two magnets move closer together.

The diagram of the lower two magnets, on the other hand, shows two magnets lying end to end with both S poles adjacent to one another. In this instance, the lines of force from both magnets move in opposite directions. As a result, the adjacent poles repel one another. *Note:* In understanding this magnetic principle, it is helpful to know a rule that says that lines of force never cross one another. While this statement *is not* theoretically correct, it has often been found effective in explaining this phenomenon.

Theories of Magnetism

Although no one knows exactly what magnetism is, two basic theories try to explain what it is and how it exerts a force field. Theory 1 implies that a magnet is formed of a very large number of small magnetized particles (Fig. 12-41). When a piece of iron has no magnetic properties, these particles are found to be arranged in a random manner. However, if the iron bar becomes a magnet, these particles align themselves so that their individual effects add together to form a strong magnet.

The second theory concerning magnetism deals with the electron. This theory assumes that the electron has a circle of force around it (the electron orbit), and when these orbits align in a bar of iron so

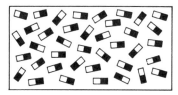

UNMAGNETIZED IRON

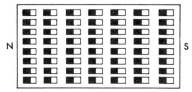

MAGNETIZED IRON

Fig. 12-41. Particles are in alignment according to the first theory of magnetism. (Courtesy of Delco Remy)

that these circles of force add together, the bar of iron becomes a magnet.

Magnetic and Nonmagnetic Materials

Iron is one of the better-known magnetic materials. However, manufacturers make most permanent magnets of hard metals composed of alloys because softer metals do not retain much of their magnetism. A few of the most common alloys are nickel-iron and aluminum-nickel-cobalt.

Some materials are nonmagnetic because they do not exhibit any magnetic properties. A few of these nonmagnetic materials are wood, paper, glass, copper, and zinc.

Formation of a Magnet

You can convert an iron bar into a magnet in a number of ways. One method is to stroke the iron bar with another piece of iron that is a magnet. The effect of in-

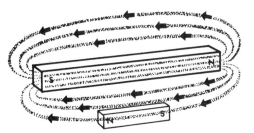

Fig. 12-42. Inducting magnetism into an iron bar. (Courtesy of Delco Remy)

ducing magnetism into the iron bar in this way is known as magnetic induction.

Another method of magnetic induction is simply to position an iron bar into a strong magnetic field (Fig. 12-42). The lines of force from the magnet itself pass through the iron bar and cause the bar to become a magnet as long as it remains in the magnetic field. If you remove the field of force and its composition is such that it retains some of the induced magnetism, the bar becomes a permanent magnet.

The most effective way of inducing a high level of magnetism in a material, in order to form a permanent magnet, is through the use of electromagnetic induction. This chapter covers this form of induction.

Electromagnetism

The discovery that a magnetic field always exists around a current-carrying conductor was responsible for most of the modern electrical equipment. Such a field of force is always at right angles to the conductor (Fig. 12-43). When you hold a compass over a wire, for example, the needle turns so that it is crosswise to the wire. Since the only thing that attracts the compass needle is a magnetic field, it is ob-

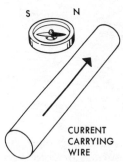

Fig. 12-43.   The magnetic field is always at a right angle to the conductor as shown by the compass. (Courtesy of Delco Remy)

vious that the current flow in the wire created a force field around itself.

This reveals a connection between electricity and magnetism. You can observe the nature of the magnetic field around the wire if you position a piece of cardboard over the wire as shown in Fig. 12-44. Then, sprinkle iron filings on the cardboard. These iron filings align themselves to show a clear pattern of concentric lines around the wire. In addition, the circles appear more concentrated near the wire than further out. Although the iron filings on the cardboard piece only show the pattern in one plane, remember that the con-

centric lines of force extend over the entire length of the current-carrying wire.

Magnetic lines have a certain direction and change this direction whenever the current flow in the conductor reverses (Fig. 12-45). When current flow within a wire is in a direction indicated by the cross, the N pole of the compass needle points in the direction shown in the upper illustration. On the other hand, when current flows in the wire in the opposite direction (toward the reader as indicated by the dot), the N pole of the compass reverses and points to the opposite direction. This action results because the compass needle always has a tendency to align itself so that the magnetic lines enter its S pole and leave its N pole.

You can determine the actual direction by which the magnetic field encircles the

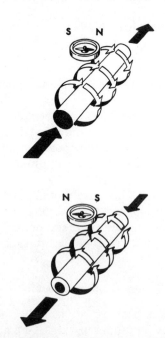

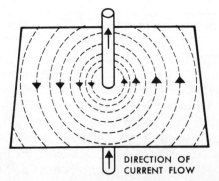

Fig. 12-44.   The shape of the magnetic field around a current-carrying wire. (Courtesy of Delco Remy)

Fig. 12-45.   The magnetic lines change direction whenever the current reverses in the conductor. (Courtesy of Delco Remy)

conductor by using the right-hand rule
(Fig. 12-46). With the right hand, grasp
the conductor so that the thumb extends
in the direction of current flow, as shown
in the illustration, and your fingers will
encircle the wire in the direction of the direction of the magnetic field. *Note:* The
use of the right-hand rule, in this case, is
necessary if you are using the conventional theory of current flow.

Force Strength

The number of lines of force (strength of
the magnetism) grows as the current
through the conductor increases (Fig.
12-47). If (as shown in the upper illustration) you move a compass a distance away
from the conductor, the compass reaches a
point where it is no longer affected by the
magnetic field. Then, however, if you increase the current flow through the conductor (note the lower illustration), the
compass needle responds to indicate the
presence of the magnetic field. This action
indicates that the number of lines of force
in the area around the conductor which

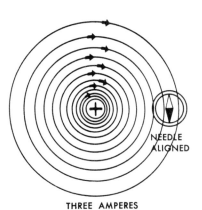

*Fig. 12-47. An increase in conductor cur-
rent flow creates a stronger magnetic field.
(Courtesy of Delco Remy)*

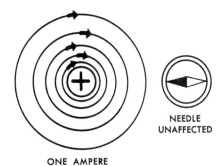

ONE AMPERE

NEEDLE
UNAFFECTED

THREE AMPERES

NEEDLE
ALIGNED

RIGHT HAND
RULE FOR
STRAIGHT
CONDUCTOR

*Fig. 12-46. Using the right-hand rule to
determine the direction of the lines of force
around a conductor. (Courtesy of Delco
Remy)*

they occupy grows as current through the
conductor increases. In other words, more
current flow creates a stronger magnetic
field around the conductor.

When two adjacent, parallel conductors
carry current in opposite directions, the direction of the field is clockwise around one
conductor and counterclockwise around
the other (Fig. 12-48). In this situation,
the lines of force concentrate themselves
between the two conductors and spread
out into space on the outside of the conductors. The lines of force between the
two wires move in the same direction; this
forms a concentration of lines or a strong
magnetic field. Under these conditions,
the two wires tend to move apart. In other

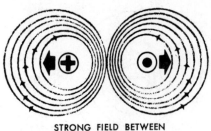

STRONG FIELD BETWEEN
CONDUCTORS

CONDUCTORS TEND TO
MOVE APART

Fig. 12–48. *A current-carrying conductor moves from a strong to a weak magnetic field. (Courtesy of Delco Remy)*

words, a current-carrying conductor tends to move out of a strong field into a weak field.

However, a different condition exists when two parallel conductors carry equal current flow in the same direction (Fig. 12–49). In this instance, a magnetic field, clockwise in direction, forms around each conductor with the magnetic line between the conductors opposing each other in direction. As a result, the magnetic field between the conductors cancels out, leaving essentially no field in this area. This action causes the two conductors to move toward one another, that is, from a strong field to a weak field.

The magnetic field around a current-carrying conductor grows in intensity as current flow increases. However, there is another way of achieving the same result. For example, two conductors lying along side each other, each carrying current in the same direction, create a magnetic field equivalent to one conductor carrying twice the current flow (Fig. 12–50). The main reason for this occurrence is that when several more conductors are side by side, the magnetic effect increases as the lines from each conductor join around all the conductors.

Electromagnetic Coils

If you form a straight, current-carrying wire into a single loop (Fig. 12–51), it has the same magnetic field surrounding it as when the wire was straight. However, in this instance, all the lines of force enter the inside loop of wire on one side and leave from the other side. These lines of force, therefore, concentrate themselves

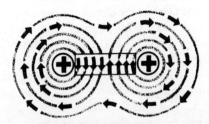

MAGNETIC EFFECTS OF LINES OF FORCE
IN OPPOSITE DIRECTION TEND TO BE
CANCELLED

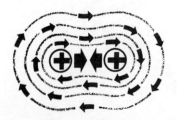

AND PRODUCE UNBALANCED FIELD. TO
RELIEVE UNBALANCE, CONDUCTORS TEND
TO MOVE TOGETHER

Fig. 12–49. *Adjacent conductors tend to move together if their current flow is in the same direction. (Courtesy of Delco Remy)*

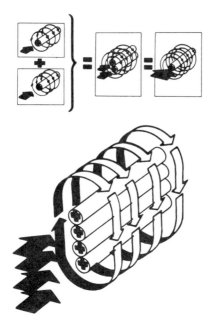

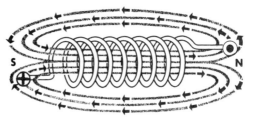

Fig. 12–52. Magnetic field of a coil grows by increasing the number of loops. (Courtesy of Delco Remy)

MAGNETIC FIELDS ADD TOGETHER

Fig. 12–50. How two or more adjacent conductors with the same current flow increase the magnetic field. (Courtesy of Delco Remy)

inside the loop. Consequently, this single loop of wire forms a basic electromagnet.

When a current-carrying conductor is wound into a number of loops or turns to

construct a coil (Fig. 12–52), the resulting magnetic field is the sum of all the single loop fields added together. This has the same effect as several conductors, side by side, carrying current in the same direction.

With the lines of force leaving the coil at one end and entering the coil at the other end, a N and S pole form at the coil ends in the same way as in the bar magnet. If the coil is wound over a material such as iron, the assembly becomes a useful electromagnet.

The strength of the magnetic field at the N and S poles increases greatly by the addition of this iron core (Fig. 12–53). The reason for this increase is that air is a very poor conductor of magnetic lines while iron is a very good conductor. Relatively speaking, the use of iron in the coil's core increases its magnetic strength by about 2,500 times over a coil with an air core.

DIRECTION OF
CURRENT FLOW

Fig. 12–51. The lines of force concentrate themselves inside the loop of wire carrying current flow. (Courtesy of Delco Remy)

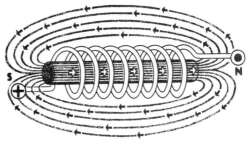

Fig. 12–53. The use of an iron core increases field strength of the coil. (Courtesy of Delco Remy)

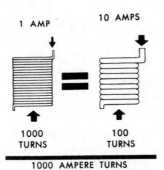

Fig. 12-54. *The total strength of an electromagnet depends on the current flow and the number of coil turns. (Courtesy of Delco Remy)*

The strength of the magnetic poles within the electromagnet is directly proportional to its current flow and the number of loops or turns of wire (Fig. 12-54). For example, both an electromagnet having 1 ampere flowing through its 1,000 turns of wire and another electromagnet having 10 amperes flowing through 100 turns have 1,000 ampere-turns, which is a measurement of their magnetic-field strength. In other words, the magnetic attraction of other magnetic materials placed within the fields of both these coils is the same.

Magnetic Resistance

In a similar way as electrical current flows through a closed circuit, so does the force field, created by a magnet, occupy a closed magnetic circuit. A complete magnetic circuit must be present for each mag-

netic field because the same number of lines that come out of a magnet's N pole must enter the S pole.

The resistance that any magnetic circuit offers to these lines of force is known as *reluctance*. This reluctance is comparable to resistance in an electrical circuit. There is an equation for figuring the effect of reluctance in electromagnetic circuits which is similar to Ohm's law for electrical circuits. This equation is, the number of magnetic lines is proportional to $\frac{\text{ampere-turns}}{\text{reluctance}}$.

Two facts related to this equation are important. First, the number of magnetic lines, the strength of the field, is in direct proportion to the ampere-turns. In the electromagnet, the more current flow through the coil, up to its design limitation, the greater is the field strength.

Second, the number of lines of field strength is inversely proportional to the reluctance; that is, if the reluctance increases, the field strength decreases. Due to the fact that most magnetic circuits consist of iron and short air gaps, the reluctance of such a series circuit is equal to the iron reluctance added to the air gap reluctance.

The effect of an air gap on the total circuit reluctance of a given magnetic circuit is very large. This is true because air has a much higher reluctance (resistance) to magnetic lines than iron. To illustrate this point, examine the magnetic circuit

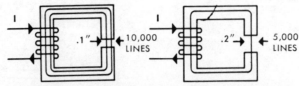

Fig. 12-55. *The effect of an air gap on the total reluctance in a magnetic circuit. (Courtesy of Delco Remy)*

shown in Fig. 12-55. The circuit on the left has a short air gap and a field strength of 10,000 lines of force. If the length of the air gap is doubled, the reluctance doubles also; and the field strength is cut to 5,000 lines of force. In other words, the air gap that represents only a very small portion of the total magnetic path really affects reluctance, as shown in the example. The increase of the air gap from 0.1 inch to 0.2 inch cut the field strength in half.

Electromagnetic Induction

When any conductor moves across (through) a magnetic field, its lines of force induce a voltage into the conductor. This basic principle is known as *electromagnetic induction*. Figure 12-56 illustrates this point very well. When the straight-wire conductor moves across (cuts through) the magnetic field of the horseshoe magnet, the attached sensitive voltmeter registers a small induced voltage. However, if the wire moves parallel with the lines of force, they cannot induce a voltage in the wire (Fig. 12-57). In other words, the conductor must cut across the lines of force in order for the field to induce voltage in the conductor.

As mentioned, voltage has polarity;

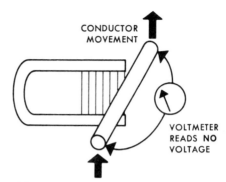

Fig. 12-57. *Moving the conductor parallel to the field induces no voltage. (Courtesy of Delco Remy)*

that is, it has (+) and (−) poles. Also, electron flow is always from the (−) to the (+) terminal, according to the electron theory, or from the (+) to the (−), according to the conventional theory. A wire cutting across a magnetic field also becomes a source of electricity, and therefore it must also have a (+) and (−) pole, just like a battery. However, unlike the battery, the wire's polarity at its ends can change. This polarity depends on the relative direction of wire movement through the magnetic field or the direction of the field itself.

Figures 12-58 and 12-59 illustrate this

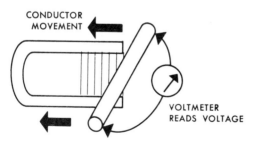

Fig. 12-56. *Moving a conductor through a magnetic field induces voltage into the conductor. (Courtesy of Delco Remy)*

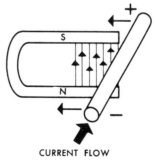

Fig. 12-58. *The voltage polarity of the wire as it moves through the magnetic field. (Courtesy of Delco Remy)*

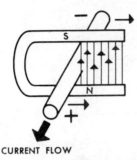

CURRENT FLOW

Fig. 12–59. The reverse polarity of the same conductor as it passes back through the field. (Courtesy of Delco Remy)

point. Figure 12–58 shows a straight wire moving to the left across the magnetic field. With this direction of wire movement, the magnetic lines strike the wire on its left side, its leading side. This induces voltage in the wire and causes current to flow away from the reader.

When the direction of the motion of the conductor reverses (Fig. 12–59) to move toward the right, the right side of the conductor becomes its leading side. Consequently, the induction of voltage reverses and the resulting current flow is toward the reader. This means that the voltage polarity of the wire ends have reversed themselves.

If instead of moving the wire to the left, as shown in Fig. 12–58, the magnetic field moves to the right across a stationary wire, the same voltage induction and current flow occur in the wire. The same holds true for moving the field to the left across a conductor because in each case the leading side of the conductor and the magnetic-field direction are unchanged. In other words, voltage induction in a conductor can occur by moving the conductor across a stationary magnetic field or moving the magnetic field across a stationary conductor. It really does not matter

which, as long as there is relative movement between the two.

Factors Determining Magnitude of Induced Voltage

Several factors determine the magnitude of the induced voltage in a conductor. These factors are:

1. The strength of the magnetic field

2. The speed at which lines of force cut across the conductor

3. The number of conductors that cut across the lines of force

If you strengthen the magnetic field, for example, by using a larger horseshoe magnet, the conductor cuts more lines of force in any given interval of time. Consequently, the induced voltage is higher.

If the relative motion between the conductor and field increases, more lines of force are cut during a given interval of time. Therefore, the induced voltage within the conductor again is higher.

If you form the straight wire into a coil and then move it across the field, the magnetic field induces a higher voltage. This results because all the loops are in series; consequently, all the voltage induced in the loops adds together to give a higher voltage.

Ways of Inducing Voltage

Basically, there are three ways to generate voltage through the principle of electromagnetism: moving a conductor through a magnetic field, self-induction, and mutual induction. A direct-current generator produces voltage by moving a

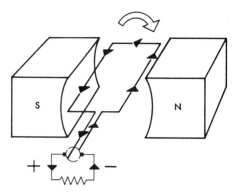

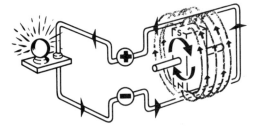

Fig. 12–61. A basic alternator. (Courtesy of Delco Remy)

Fig. 12–60. A basic d.c. generator. (Courtesy of Delco Remy)

Self-Induction

number of conductors across a stationary magnetic field (Fig. 12–60). This figure illustrates a basic type of direct current (d.c.) generator, where a single loop of wire rotates between the N and S poles of a magnetic field. In the position shown, current flows within the loop, as indicated. Due to the voltage induced in the loop, it provides voltage at the two commutator segments attached to the wire ends. The current then flows through the brushes, riding on the commutator, and out into the external circuit. *Note:* The generator, due to its design, is able to produce voltage even if no current passes out of it into the external circuit.

The alternator is another application of the principle of generated voltage (Fig. 12–61). However, in this instance, the magnetic field cuts across a stationary conductor in order to produce voltage and then current flow. The basic alternator (Fig. 12–61) has a rotating magnetic field that cuts across a stationary conductor mounted on the alternator frame. As you can see with the rotating field position, current flows through the conductor in the direction indicated, with the voltage polarities as shown.

Self-induction is the induction of voltage in a current-carrying wire when the current in the wire itself changes. In the two previous illustrations, an external magnetic field produced voltage in a conductor as it moved through the field. In self-induction, no separate field is necessary. Instead, the magnetic field created by a changing current flow in the conductor induces voltage in the wire itself. Thus, the wire's own magnetic field causes this self-induction of voltage.

This is why a voltage induces in a wire carrying a changing current value: Since the current flow creates a magnetic field in the form of concentric circles around the wire, which expands and contracts as the current flow increases or decreases, these magnetic lines cut across the conductor itself and thereby induce a voltage within the conductor. Since there is relative motion between the field and the conductor, the condition for inducing the voltage has been met.

Mutual Induction

If a magnetic field produced by a current flow in one electromagnet coil cuts across the windings of a second coil, the field induces a voltage in the second coil.

This induction of voltage in one coil because of the electromagnetism from the other coil is known as *mutual induction*. Figure 12-62 illustrates this principle of mutual induction in a circuit where a secondary winding is wound around an iron core, while the primary is wound around the secondary coil.

When the switch closes, current increases its flow in the primary coil, causing a magnetic field to expand and cut across the secondary windings, causing some voltage induction in it. Similarly, when the switch opens (Fig. 12-63), the sudden decrease in primary-coil current flow causes its magnetic field to shrink and pass through the secondary windings once more. This action again induces a voltage in the secondary windings. In either case, the secondary windings become a source of voltage and provide current to the external circuit.

Secondary-Coil Polarity

There are several ways to determine the polarity of the voltage induced into a secondary coil. One of the easiest ways is to

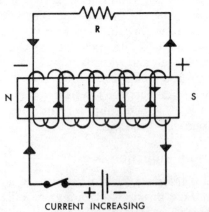

CURRENT INCREASING

Fig. 12-62. Mutual induction in a secondary coil with the primary-coil circuit closed. (Courtesy of Delco Remy)

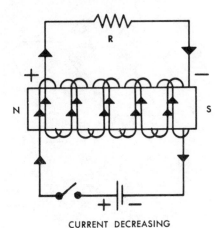

CURRENT DECREASING

Fig. 12-63. Mutual induction in a secondary coil with the primary-coil circuit open. (Courtesy of Delco Remy)

observe the direction of current flow in the primary coil, knowing that the current flow direction in the secondary must oppose any change in primary current flow. Therefore, when the primary current flow is increasing, the secondary current must flow in an *opposite* direction around the core in order to oppose the increase. This action slows the current increase in the primary windings and establishes the secondary coil polarities (Fig. 12-62).

If on the other hand, primary current flow decreases (Fig. 12-63), the current from the secondary coil must flow in the *same direction* around the core as that of the primary in order to oppose this change. This action attempts to keep the magnetic field in the core from changing and provides the secondary polarities.

The other method of determining the induced voltage polarity of the secondary coil is through the use of the right-hand rule for an induced voltage. Figure 12-64 shows a lengthwise cross-sectional view of the coil assembly as current is increasing in the primary, and its circular lines of

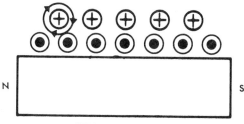

CURRENT INCREASING

Fig. 12-64. Determining polarity of the secondary coil as current flow in the primary coil increases. (Courtesy of Delco Remy)

force are expanding and striking the lower secondary windings on their top side.

By applying the right-hand rule for an induced voltage, the current flow is in the direction shown. Remember that the two coils carry current in *opposite directions* around the core when the current within the primary coil is increasing.

As the primary-coil current decreases (Fig. 12-65), the magnetic field produced by this coil begins to shrink inward. This causes the circular magnetic lines of force from the primary coil to pass once again through the secondary coil. However, this time the field enters the secondary windings from their underneath side. This direction induces a voltage and current flow into the secondary coil in the same direc-

tion as the decreasing current flow in the primary.

The determining factor as to the extent of the voltage induced within the secondary coil is the ratio of the number of turns in the secondary to those in the primary. For example, if the coil has a ratio of 100 to 1, the secondary coil has 100 turns for each single loop in the primary. With this design, a self-induced voltage in the primary as its current decreases (Figs. 12-63 and 12-65) of 250 volts would result in a secondary voltage of 25,000 volts. In other words, the secondary coil increases primary voltage 100 times.

Chapter 15 explains self- and mutual-induction as they apply to ignition coils. That chapter also explains the function, design, and operation of capacitors.

Review

This section will assist you in determining how well you remember the material in this chapter. Read each item carefully. If you can't complete the statement, review the section in the chapter that covers the material.

1. The _____ were the first to know about static electricity.
   a. Germans
   b. French
   c. Romans
   d. Greeks

2. The difference in electrical potential is known as _____.
   a. reluctance
   b. resistance
   c. current
   d. voltage

3. _____ is electrical pressure.
   a. Voltage
   b. Amperage

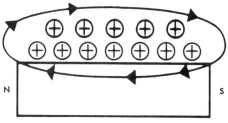

CURRENT DECREASING

Fig. 12-65. Determining secondary-coil polarity as primary-coil current flow decreases. (Courtesy of Delco Remy)

c. Resistance
d. Reluctance

4. Something that hinders the movement of electrons is known as _____
   _____.
   a. current
   b. resistance
   c. voltage
   d. inductance

5. Ohm's law states that resistance is
   equal to voltage _____
   resistance.
   a. none of these
   b. multiplied by
   c. divided by
   d. plus

6. A circuit that has only one pathway
   for the current to flow is a _____
   circuit.
   a. parallel-series
   b. parallel
   c. series
   d. series-parallel

7. The circuit that offers several pathways for current flow is a _____
   _____ circuit.
   a. parallel
   b. series-parallel
   c. series
   d. none of these

8. A semiconductor is a material with
   only _____ electrons in its outer
   orbit.
   a. four
   b. three
   c. two
   d. one

9. N-type material has an excess of ____
   _____.
   a. protons
   b. electrons
   c. neutrons
   d. holes

10. The ring of a transistor connects to
    the _____.
    a. diode
    b. collector
    c. emitter
    d. base

11. The device that permits electrical
    flow in one direction only is the ____
    _____.
    a. conductor
    b. resistor
    c. diode
    d. transistor

12. The control circuit of a transistor is
    the _____.
    a. collector
    b. base-collector
    c. emitter-base
    d. collector-base

13. The law of magnetism states that like
    poles _____ each other.
    a. attract
    b. repel
    c. neutralize
    d. cancel

14. A nonmagnetic material is _____
    _____.
    a. glass
    b. nickel-iron
    c. iron
    d. aluminum-nickel-cobalt

15. As current through a conductor in-
    creases, the magnetic field around it
    _____.
    a. decreases
    b. grows
    c. cancels
    d. neutralizes

16. Two adjacent current-carrying wires
    _____ each other if cur-
    rent in the wires is in the same direc-
    tion.

a. repel
b. attract
c. short-circuit
d. ground-out

17. The resistance to flow of magnetic lines is known as _____.
a. attraction
b. repulsion
c. reluctance
d. induction

18. If a conductor moves through a magnetic field, its lines of force induce _____ into the conductor.
a. reluctance
b. resistance
c. current
d. voltage

19. In a _____, the magnetic field cuts across the conductor to generate voltage.
a. alternator
b. generator
c. starter
d. both *a* and *b*

20. An ignition coil uses both self- and mutual _____ to generate voltage.
a. reluctance
b. induction
c. magnetism
d. none of these

For the answers, turn to the Appendix.

Function

The storage battery (Fig. 13-1) is the heart of the automotive electrical system because it plays such an important role in the operation of the starting, charging, ignition, and accessory circuits. The *storage battery* used in automobiles is an electro-chemical device for converting chemical energy, which the battery stores until connected into a circuit, into electrical energy. The storage battery then converts this chemical energy into electrical energy, which flows from one battery terminal, through the circuit, and back to the other battery terminal.

However, these actions are reversible. That is, the battery can also convert electrical energy to chemical energy, but the battery does not store up electricity at any time. The battery can only store up chemical energy.

The ability of a given storage battery to convert chemical energy to electrical energy has certain limitations. The factors limiting this conversion process are the amount of active chemical materials within its plates and the concentration of the electrolyte.

Within the automobile, the battery has three main functions: (1) to produce voltage and a source of current for starting, lighting, and ignition; (2) to help control the voltage in the electrical system; and (3) to furnish current to the various circuits when the electrical demands exceed the output of the generator or alternator.

In order for the battery to maintain these functions, the generator or alternator must replace these current withdrawals. If the "output" exceeds the "input," the battery eventually is unable to function as a source of voltage and cur-

Chapter 13

AUTOMOTIVE STORAGE BATTERIES

Fig. 13-1. A typical 12-volt storage battery. (Courtesy of Delco Remy)

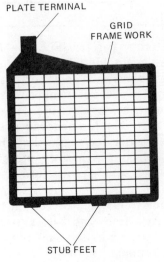

Fig. 13-2. A typical battery grid.

rent, unless a generating source makes up the deficit by recharging.

Battery Construction

Grids

The storage battery consists of grids, positive plates, negative plates, separators, elements, electrolyte, container, cell covers, vent plugs, cell connectors, terminals, and sealing compound. The *grids* form the basic framework for the battery plate (Fig. 13-2). These grids are flat, rectangular, latticelike castings with fairly heavy borders and a mesh of horizontal and vertical wires made from a lead-antimonial alloy.

The grids themselves have two main functions. First, the design of each grid is such that it holds the active materials of the plates within its borders. In other words, once the manufacturer has pasted the grid with the active materials, the grid becomes a plate. Second, the grid serves

to conduct the current to and from the active materials in the positive and negative plates.

Positive Plates

A positive plate consists of a grid filled with an active material, lead peroxide (PbO_2) (Fig. 13-3). This is a dark-brown crystalline material that consists of very small grains, or particles, disposed so as to provide a high degree of porosity in order to permit the electrolyte to penetrate freely. Lastly, after pasting the lead peroxide into the grid, the plate receives a special process that cures and transforms the pasted material into chemically active material with the potential of a net (+) charge.

Negative Plates

The manufacturer forms the negative plates in much the same way as the positive. However, the material pasted onto the grids of the negative plates is

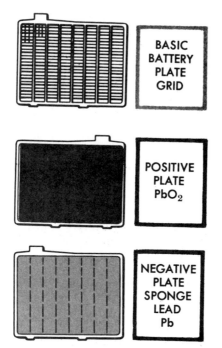

Fig. 13-3. The construction of typical battery plates. (Courtesy of Delco Remy)

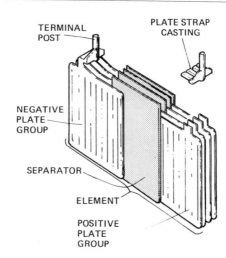

Fig. 13-4. A typical battery element with separators between the two plate groups.

sponge lead (Pb), which is gray in color. The sponge lead is nothing more than a porous mass of lead in spongy form, which electrolyte can penetrate freely. This active material also contains so-called expanders, included to prevent the sponge lead from expanding and reverting to a solid state during the life of the battery. After forming on the grid, the negative material has the potential of a net (−) charge.

Separators

During the assembly of the battery, the manufacturer inserts a *separator* between each positive and negative plate (Fig. 13-4). The separators prevent the positive plates from contacting the negative plates, which would cause these plates

within any of the cells to lose their stored energy. The separator itself is a thin sheet of nonconducting porous material such as chemically treated wood, porous rubber, porous sheets of resin-impregnated fiber, or thin sheets of polyvinylchloride.

On one side, separators have ribs, which face the positive plates. This design provides greater acid volume next to the positive plates for improved efficiency and for easier acid circulation within the cell. The ribs also minimize the contact area with each positive plate, which has a very high oxidizing effect, especially on wood-type separators. Finally, in some battery designs, fiberglass retainer mats or perforated rubber or plastic sheets are sometimes placed between the positive plate and separator to retard the loss of active material from this plate and to protect the separator itself from oxidation.

Elements

Each storage battery contains a number of elements (Fig. 13-4). The *element* itself consists of two groups of plates: positive and negative. The manufacturer forms a positive- or negative-plate group by welding a number of these individual plates to a post strap. Then, the manufacturer positions the two groups together with separators between them, with their grooved faces next to the positive plates. The post straps themselves extend up to provide terminals for connecting one element of a cell to another.

There may be any desired number or size of plates utilized in an element, depending on how much stored energy each element must provide. However, there is usually one additional negative plate per element than positives to improve battery performance. The greater the number of plates used in the element, the higher is the voltage of the battery during discharge at high rates and low temperatures.

Cells

When the element is inside the battery case and immersed in electrolyte, it becomes a *cell*. The automotive battery may contain three to six of these finished cells with each cell having an open circuit voltage of about 2.1 volts (Fig. 13–5). This cell voltage is the same no matter what the size of the cell or the number or size of the plates within its element. Finally, since all cells of a battery connect in series, total battery voltage is the sum of the voltage of all its cells.

Electrolyte

The sponge lead and the lead peroxide that fill the respective plates are the *active* materials of the storage battery. However, the materials cannot become active unless immersed in *electrolyte,* a liquid composed of water and sulphuric

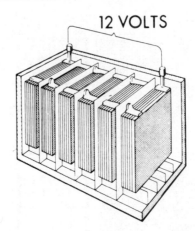

12 VOLTS

Fig. 13–5. A 12-volt battery with six 2-volt cells connected in series. (Courtesy of Ford Motor Co. of Canada Ltd.)

acid. The sulphuric acid of the electrolyte supplies the sulphate, which combines with each of the plate materials to release electrical energy. Morover, the sulphuric acid electrolyte is the carrier for the electrons inside the battery between the positive and negative plates, through the separators.

The electrolyte of a fully charged battery is usually about 64 percent water and 36 percent sulphuric acid (Fig. 13–6). This corresponds to a specific gravity of about 1.270. *Specific gravity* is the weight of a given volume of any liquid divided by the weight of an equal volume of water. Pure water has a specific gravity of 1.000, while battery electrolyte should have a specific gravity of 1.260 to 1.2680 at 80°F. (26.7°C.). In other words, the electrolyte of the battery is 1.260 to 1.280 times as heavy as water.

As the battery discharges, the specific gravity of the electrolyte decreases because the acid changes into water as the sulphate goes into the plates. Consequently, the specific gravity of the electrolyte can be a good indicator as to how

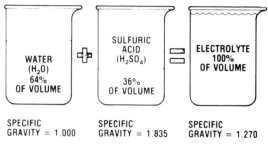

WATER (H_2O) 64% OF VOLUME	SULFURIC ACID (H_2SO_4) 36% OF VOLUME	ELECTROLYTE 100% OF VOLUME
SPECIFIC GRAVITY = 1.000	SPECIFIC GRAVITY = 1.835	SPECIFIC GRAVITY = 1.270

Fig. 13-6. The composition and specific gravity of electrolyte. (Courtesy of Chrysler Corp.)

discharged a battery is. Figure 13-7 illustrates a typical range of specific gravity readings for a cell in various stages of charge with respect to its ability to crank the engine over at 80°F. However, these values may vary slightly, according to the design factors of a particular battery.

Battery Container

The container of an automotive battery is usually a one-piece molded assembly of hard rubber or plastic. The materials used must be able to withstand the extremes of heat and cold, mechanical shocks, and the absorption of acid. In these respects, most modern automotive battery cases are made of plastic materials, which are lighter and stronger and more corrosion-resistant than rubber.

The container (case) has a number of individual cell compartments, partitioned

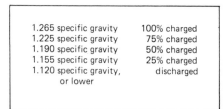

1.265 specific gravity	100% charged
1.225 specific gravity	75% charged
1.190 specific gravity	50% charged
1.155 specific gravity	25% charged
1.120 specific gravity, or lower	discharged

Fig. 13-7. A typical range of cell specific gravity readings and what they indicate.

inside the assembly, one for each cell of the battery (Fig. 13-8). In the bottom of these compartments are sediment chambers (spaces) formed underneath the element rests or bridges, upon which each of the elements sits. These sediment rests minimize the danger of a short circuit due to sediment that falls from the plates and into the sediment chambers.

However, the repeated discharging and charging of the battery (called *cycling*), of course, gradually wears it out so that, after a time, the active material from the positive plates gradually disintegrates and loses physical contact with the plates. This loosened material is free to fall off the plates and deposit into the sediment chamber between the rests, at the bottom of each cell. By the time the sediment spaces fill up to the base of the element, the life of the cell is usually over, because the shredded material gradually forms an electrical path or a short circuit between the positive and negative plates. This interferes with the normal charging and retention of the charge by the battery.

Cell Connectors

In order to join all the cells of a battery in series, a number of *cell connectors* are necessary (Fig. 13-9). As the manufacturer assembles the battery, the elements fit into the case in such a way that the positive terminal from one element is adjacent to the negative terminal of the next element and so on throughout the battery. The cell connectors attach over the protruding terminals and are welded to them in order to connect the cells in series. These cell connectors are heavy enough to carry the high current required for starting without excessive heating or voltage drop.

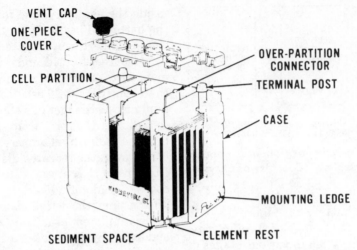

Fig. 13-8.   Typical battery case construction. (Courtesy of Ford Motor Co. of Canada Ltd.)

Cell Covers

A *cell cover*, as its name implies, incases the top of the cells. This device may be a one-piece assembly (Fig. 13-8), or there may be a number of individual covers (Fig. 13-10), one for each cell. The one-piece cover is usually made of hard rubber or plastic, while the individual covers are usually hard rubber.

In either case, the manufacturer provides the cover with a vent opening, used for several purposes. For example, the opening provides access into the cells for servicing them with electrolyte or water and permits the escape of gases formed in the cell during battery charging and discharging. Furthermore, the vent hole permits access through which the technician can check the specific gravity and voltage of the various cells.

Vent Plugs (Caps)

The *vent plugs*, or *caps*, close the openings in the cell cover (Fig. 13-8). These devices have several other functions. First, each cap covers the access hole into the cell to prevent the splashing out of the electrolyte during rapid vehicle starts and stops. Second, the vent plug, or cap, has a

Fig. 13-9.   A typical cell connector.

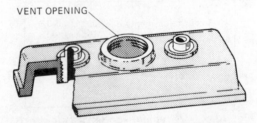

Fig. 13-10.   An individual cell cover.

special design that operates along with the vent opening to permit gases to escape but baffle these gases along with the electrolyte spray and splash, on the underside of the cover, in order to prevent the loss of acid from the cell.

Some vent caps have a design in which a transparent rod extends through its center. When the electrolyte in the cell is at the proper level, the lower tip of the rod is in the liquid, and the exposed top of the rod appears very dark. If the electrolyte level drops below the tip of the rod, the top glows. The design of the plug reveals at a glance if the cell requires water, without the need of removing the cap.

Terminals

Each battery has two external terminals: a positive (+) and a negative (−). These terminals are either two tapered posts on top of the case or two internally threaded connectors on the side. These terminals connect to either end of the series of elements inside the battery and have either a positive (+) and a negative (−) marking, depending on which end of the series they represent.

Tapered terminals have a given dimension in accordance with standards agreed upon by the Battery Council International (BCI) and Society of Automotive Engineers (SAE). This was necessary so that all positive and negative cable clamp terminals would fit any corresponding battery terminal interchangeably, no matter what company made the battery. However, the positive terminal is slightly larger, usually around $\frac{11}{16}$ inch in diameter at the top, while the negative terminal usually has a $\frac{5}{8}$ -inch diameter. This design minimizes the danger of installing the battery cables in reverse polarity.

Sealing Compound

A sealing compound is necessary to form an acidtight joint between the covers and the case. This reduces the tendency for corrosion to form on top of the battery; with less corrosion, electrical leakage is minimized between the posts themselves and between the (+) post and ground.

Battery Operation

Inside the battery, chemical reaction between the active materials of the dissimilar plates and the sulphuric acid within the electrolyte produces electrical energy. The active area and the weight of the materials in the plates along with the quantity of sulphuric acid in the electrolyte limit the manner by which the battery can produce electrical energy. After the available materials have reacted with the electrolyte, the battery can produce little or no additional energy. The battery then is said to be in a discharged state.

Figure 13–11 illustrates the chemical reaction taking place as a battery cell discharges into a completed circuit. The lead peroxide (PbO_2) within the positive plates is a compound of lead (Pb) and oxygen (O); sulphuric acid is a compound of

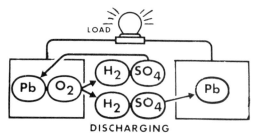

DISCHARGING

Fig. 13–11. Chemical reactions within a battery cell during discharge.

hydrogen (H) and sulphate radical (SO_4). With the battery discharging, oxygen in the positive active plate material combines with the hydrogen from the sulphuric acid to form water (H_2O). At the same time, lead in the active positive material combines with the sulphate radical (SO_4) to form lead sulphate ($PbSO_4$).

A similar reaction takes place at the negative plate. In this plate, lead (Pb) of the negative active material combines with sulphate radical (SO_4) to also form lead sulphate ($PbSO_4$). Thus, lead sulphate forms at both types of plates as the battery discharges while the chemical process uses up the sulphuric acid in the electrolyte and replaces it with water.

As the discharge continues, dilution of the electrolyte plus the accumulation of lead sulphate in the plates eventually halts the reactions. However, the process never completely exhausts the active material during a discharge. At low rates of discharge, the reactions are more nearly complete than at higher rates, since more time is available for all the materials to come into contact. When the battery finally can no longer produce the desired voltage and current flow, it is said to be in a *discharged state*. Then, in order to be returned to service, the battery must receive a suitable flow of current from an external source.

Also note in Fig. 13–11 that the material in the positive and negative plates becomes more similar chemically during discharge, as the lead sulphate accumulates. This condition accounts for the loss of cell voltage, since voltage depends on the difference between the two materials.

The chemical reactions occurring within a cell during charging are essentially the reverse of those occurring while the cell discharges (Fig. 13–12). The lead sulphate

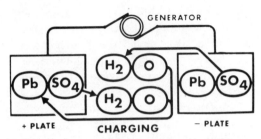

Fig. 13–12. Chemical reaction within a battery cell during charging.

($PbSO_4$) on both plates separates into lead (Pb) and sulphate (SO_4). As the sulphate (SO_4) leaves both plates, it combines with hydrogen in the electrolyte once again to form sulphuric acid (H_2SO_4). At the same time, the oxygen (O) in the electrolyte combines with the lead (Pb) at the positive plate to form lead peroxide (PbO_2). As a result, the negative plate returns to its original form of lead (Pb), and the positive plate reverts to lead peroxide (PbO_2).

These reactions demonstrate the important fact that water actually takes part in the chemistry of the storage battery. In normal operation, the battery gradually loses water from the cell due to its conversion into hydrogen and oxygen gases, which escape into the atmosphere through the vent caps. If someone does not replace the lost water, the level of the electrolyte falls below the tops of the plates. This results in a high concentration of sulphuric acid in the electrolyte and also permits the exposed material of the plates to dry and harden. Consequently, if someone does not maintain the water level, premature failure of the battery is certain. Finally, since water loss is more rapid during high-temperature operation than at low-temperature, the electrolyte level in the battery must be checked more frequently during the summer months.

Battery Voltage— Determined by Number of Cells

As mentioned, the open circuit voltage of a fully charged cell is about 2.1 volts with the specific gravity of the electrolyte at approximately 1.280. This is true no matter what the size of the cell, since it is a fixed characteristic of the chemicals utilized in the battery and the strength of the electrolyte. Consequently, a 6-volt battery has three 2-volt cells and a 12-volt battery has six 2-volt cells.

The size of the cell, the state of its charge, the rate of discharge, the design and condition of the battery, and the temperature of the electrolyte very strongly influence the voltage of a cell during discharge. The average voltage of a cell during discharge, for example, while cranking an engine over at 80°F. may be about 1.95 volts, where at 0°F., the voltage may be 1.4 volts per cell. Generally speaking, the larger the cells of a battery, the higher their available cranking voltage is under almost any given set of conditions of discharge rate and temperature. However, the cell voltage is never as high as under "open" circuit conditions.

The concentration of acid maintained in the pores of the plates also affects battery voltage on discharge. As soon as the discharge process uses up the acid within these pores, by chemically combining it with the active material of the plates, the voltage drops, unless fresh acid from outside the plate can diffuse into their pores. As the discharge process continues, the acid outside the plates becomes weaker, and sulphate saturates the plate material, until it is increasingly difficult for acid and unused plate material to combine for continued chemical activity. As a result, the voltage drops to a value no longer effective in delivering useful current to the electrical system.

In cold weather, the viscosity of the electrolyte increases and therefore slows the diffusion of the acid into the plate pores and through the separators. As a result, this slows the rate of chemical action and lowers the cell voltage, limiting the output of the battery, especially at cranking rates. Some makes of batteries suffer more from the effects of cold weather than others due to their differences in design, materials, and processing of the plates and separators.

Battery Capacity— Determined by Plates and Acid

The *capacity* of a battery, its ability to deliver a given amount of current flow over a period of time, depends upon the *number and size* of plates used in each cell as well as the amount of sulphuric acid present in the electrolyte. Therefore, the battery's starting capacity is roughly proportional to the area of its plates. Manufacturers build automotive batteries with thin plates in order to provide a larger plate area so that the acid may have quick access to as much active material as possible.

Most automotive batteries also have limitations in capacity at low rates of discharge, due to not only the quantity of electrolyte contained in the cells but also the percentage of sulphuric acid. In other words, this quantity and concentration represent a compromise between the requirements for battery performance, conservation of weight and space, and battery life. The manufacturer could increase the acid content in the electrolyte to improve battery capacity, but this higher concentration of sulphuric acid definitely reduces battery life due to its corrosive effects on the grids and other battery components.

Battery Capacity Ratings

20-Hour Rating

There are three common ways to rate the capacity of an automotive battery: the 20-hour rating, the cold rating, and the reserve capacity rating. The *20-hour rating* of a battery in ampere-hours indicates the lighting ability of the battery with a full charge at 80°F. (26.7°C.). A laboratory test determines this rating under controlled conditions. The test begins by bringing the test battery up to full charge at 80°F. (26.7°C.). Then, the battery receives a discharge at a constant rate for 20 hours; afterward the cell voltage must be 1.75 volts or above. This equates to 5.25 total voltage in a 6-volt battery, or 10.5 volts in a 12-volt battery.

A battery capable of supplying 3 amperes under these test conditions qualifies for a rating of 60 ampere-hours (3 amperes × 20 hours = 60 ampere-hours). Consequently, a 12-volt battery that is able to supply 6 amperes for this period qualifies for a 120 ampere-hour rating (Fig. 13–13). On the other hand, a 6-volt battery rated by its manufacturer at 100 ampere-hours is able to handle a discharge of 5 amperes for a period of 20 hours (Fig. 13–14) before its total cell voltage drops below 5.25 volts.

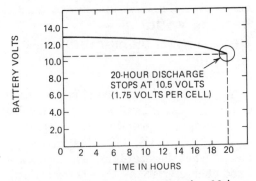

Fig. 13–13.   A chart showing the 20-hour rating of a typical 12-volt battery.

The cold rating of a typical battery is obtainable by discharging a fully charged battery at 0°F. at a rate of 150 or 300 amperes, depending on the voltage and ampere-hour rating of the test battery. Two values are considered before rating a battery in this particular way. The first is the voltage obtained after 5 or 10 seconds of discharge, while the second is the time in minutes required for the battery to indicate an end terminal voltage. For example, a 12-volt battery having a 10-second voltage value of 7.6 volts at a 300-ampere discharge rate must maintain a voltage of 7.6 volts or higher for 10 seconds. In addition, the same battery with a time value of 2 minutes must operate under these condi-

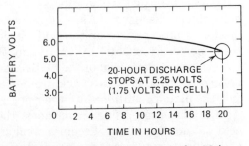

Fig. 13–14.   A chart illustrating the 20-hour rating of a 6-volt battery.

tions for 2 minutes before the terminal voltage falls to an end voltage of 5.0 volts. Therefore, the higher the 10-second voltage value and the higher the time value, the greater will be the battery's cranking capacity rating at 0°F.

Reserve Capacity

The *reserve capacity* of a battery is the length of time a vehicle can travel at night with minimum electrical load and no alternator output. This reserve capacity, expressed in minutes, is the time necessary for a fully charged battery at a temperature of 80°F. (26.7°C.) and at a constant discharge rate of 25 amperes to reach a terminal voltage of no less than 1.75 volts per cell, or 10.5 volts for a 12-volt battery. In other words, this rating defines the length of time a battery will last in a vehicle driven with an inoperative charging system. Finally, each of these tests provides a meaningful comparison between batteries *in specific group sizes,* with regard to their load-carrying and cold-cranking capacity.

Battery Voltage Comparison

Figure 13-15 is a chart comparing ratings of a typical 6- and 12-volt battery. In this chart, the 6-volt battery has a rating of 70 ampere-hours and has 11 plates (the total of all positive and negative plates) in each of three cells. The 12-volt battery also has a 70 ampere-hour rating, but it has three more identical cells.

However, there is one significant difference between the performances of the two batteries, the voltage at which the battery supplies current. Since battery power (watts) is equal to volts times amperes (Fig. 13-16), the power of the 12-volt battery is twice that of the 6-volt unit. For example, when the battery voltage is 12 volts and the discharge rate is 3.5 amperes, the power output is 42 watts (12 volts × 3.5 amperes = 42 watts). On the other hand, the 6-volt battery power output at the same discharge rate is only 21 watts (6 volts × 3.5 amperes = 21 watts). The important point to understand here is that although the

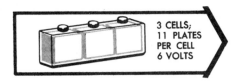
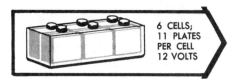

Plates Per Cell	No. of Cells	Battery Voltage	Ampere Hour Rating	20 Hour Discharge Rate in Amperes	Battery Voltage After 20 Hours
11	3	6	70	3.5	5.25
11	6	12	70	3.5	10.5

Fig. 13-15. A chart showing the comparison between the ratings of a 6- and 12-volt battery. (Courtesy of Delco Remy)

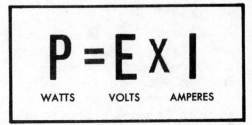

Fig. 13–16.   Battery power (watts) is equal to volts times amperes. (Courtesy of Delco Remy)

6-and 12-volt batteries have the same ampere-hour rating, the 12-volt battery is capable of producing twice the power as the 6-volt unit.

Watts Ratings

In some cases, a battery may have a *watts rating*, which is another measurement of its ability to crank an engine over at cold temperatures. A laboratory test is also necessary to determine the wattage rating of specific battery groups; the rating itself is found by multiplying the voltage by the test current flow. Each battery size receives its watts rating at a given temperature, which is usually 0°F. (−17.8°C.). Thus, by comparing the watts rating, it is easy to determine what battery is necessary to meet the electrical needs of a vehicle during starting operations at cold temperatures. The average wattage rating for most 12-volt batteries ranges between 2,000 to 4,000 watts.

Battery Selection

Manufacturers normally use optional heavy-duty batteries (units with high ratings) in automobiles with air conditioners or several other major electrical accessories and in vehicles operating in cold climates. To ensure adequate cranking power and to meet all other electrical needs, a replacement battery may have a higher rating but should never have a lower rating than the original unit. In addition, the battery must have the proper physical dimensions for the vehicle and the correct type of terminals.

To facilitate what battery fits into a given vehicle, the Battery Council International (BCI) publishes charts that list the correct battery for each automobile. These charts have a coding system (a group number) that identifies each battery by its length, width, height, terminal design, and other special features. Consequently, all the technician needs to know in order to replace a defective battery is its group number.

Battery Types

Manufacturers produce and sell two types of batteries: the wet charge and the dry charge. A *wet-charged battery* comes from the factory fully filled with electrolyte and charged. In other words, this type of battery contains electrolyte from the time of its manufacture.

Although the wet-charged battery may not be in use, a slow reaction takes place inside it between the plate materials and the electrolyte. This causes the battery to discharge slowly; this action is known as *self-discharge*.

Self-discharge occurs much more rapidly at high temperatures than at low. For example, a fully charged battery stored at room temperature of 100°F. will almost completely discharge after a standing period of 90 days (Fig. 13–17). On the other hand, the same type battery

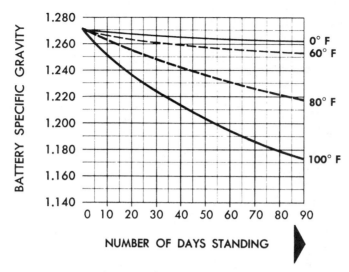

Fig. 13-17. A wet-charged battery discharges faster at higher temperatures. (Courtesy of Delco Remy)

stored at 60°F. will only slightly discharge after 90 days.

Therefore, a wet-type battery requires storage in as cool a location as possible as long as the electrolyte does not freeze. In this regard, a discharged battery with a specific gravity of 1.100 will freeze at 18°F. (Fig. 13-18). Whereas, a fully charged battery with a specific gravity of 1.260 is never in danger of freezing because this would require a temperature

Value of Specific Gravity	Freezing Temp. Deg. F.	Value of Specific Gravity	Freezing Temp. Deg. F.
1.100	18	1.220	−31
1.120	13	1.240	−50
1.140	8	1.260	−75
1.160	1	1.280	−92
1.180	−6	1.300	−95
1.200	−17		

Fig. 13-18. If the electrolyte specific gravity drops low enough, it may freeze. (Courtesy of Delco Remy)

of 75°F. below 0 to freeze the electrolyte.

The storage of a wet-type battery for long periods of time may permanently damage the unit. This damage results from the oxidation of the positive-plate grid wires and the formation of lead sulphate crystals in the plates, which become very hard and dense. If the sulphate crystals are not too dense and hard, you may be able to restore the battery to normal service by applying a slow-charge rate for a longer than normal period. However, if the sulphate crystals are extremely hard and dense, you will never be able to restore the battery to normal operating conditions, regardless of the rate of charge or the length of charging time.

Consequently, a wet-type battery should be brought up to a full charge every 30 days by charging it at a slow rate. Before doing this, you should always check and bring the electrolyte level up to that specified by the manufacturer, by the addition of water to each low cell. In addition, you should not use a trickle charger to maintain a battery in storage because its very low charging rate for a long period of time can cause permanent damage to positive-plate grid wires.

Dry-Charged Batteries

A *dry-charged battery,* as its name implies, is a completely charged unit that contains no electrolyte until someone activates it for service in a vehicle. The elements in this particular battery are the same as in the other type of battery. However, during the construction of the dry-charged battery, the manufacturer immerses each element in electrolyte and "forms" the plates by charging the element with electrical current. Then, the newly formed element is thoroughly washed, completely dried, and installed into the case to complete the manufacturing process.

The dry-charged battery remains in this fully charged condition as long as moisture does not enter the cells. The presence of moisture and air in the cells causes the negative plates to oxidize and lose their charge. Therefore, it is very important that this type of battery be stored in a dry place.

A technician can place a dry-charged battery into service simply by adding electrolyte to all its cells. The next chapter details this procedure.

The dry-type battery offers several advantages over the wet type. For example, you can store a dry-type battery indefinitely in almost any kind of environment as long as it is dry. Also, the need for periodic addition of water to the cells and recharging of the unit is not necessary. Finally, you can deliver this type of battery in a factory-fresh condition by simply activating the unit with electrolyte.

Maintenance-Free Batteries

Many battery manufacturers produce sealed *maintenance-free* units. A battery of this design does not need someone to add water to its cells during its lifetime. In other words, a maintenance-free battery receives its electrolyte at the factory, but the unit is then sealed so that no one can later add additional water.

A maintenance-free battery differs in design from the conventional wet or dry battery in two ways. The first and most important difference is the material used for the plate grids. The typical battery has antimony as a main ingredient of the grid alloy. The replacement of the antimony with a calcium alloy reduces the battery's internal heat, which is the principle reason for water loss from the cells. The heat itself is the end result of the charging current. In addition, calcium-alloy grids require less charging current than the antimony-alloy grids; therefore, there is less heat and water loss.

Second, the maintenance-free battery has a greater electrolyte capacity. Manufacturers accomplish this, in many cases, by the use of special separators that form a porous plastic envelope around each positive plate. These envelope-separators trap active materials that tend to flake off the positive plates during the discharge and charging processes. As a result, the envelope-separators permit the plate group installation on the bottom of the case rather than on rests or bridges. This allows an increased electrolyte capacity above the tops of the plates, which is sufficient for a great deal of service time.

The antimony-free grids also provide the maintenance-free battery with other important characteristics. For example, the maintenance-free battery has less corrosion buildup at its terminals. This is basically due to less water loss in this battery type, which is a major cause of terminal corrosion. However, this battery has small vents in the top or in the case to relieve the small amount of gas pressure. Therefore, the unit is not really completely sealed.

In addition, as a standard-type battery ages, antimony from the grids moves into the active material of the negative plates. This action makes a battery less able to resist an overcharge with its resulting increase in heat and water loss. However, this is not the case with the maintenance-free battery that has no antimony within its grids.

Finally, maintenance-free batteries usually have about a 20 percent higher cold-cranking watts rating than a comparably sized standard battery. This is the direct result of *not* using antimony in the grids. Nonantimony lead alloys provide a greater conductivity and therefore reduce internal battery resistance.

The Battery and the Charging Circuit

The battery supplies electrical energy produced by chemical action to the automobile's electrical accessories (upper illustration, Fig. 13–19). The battery alone performs this function when the engine is not operating. However, as the battery continues to supply this current, the resistance units eventually use up the battery's chemical energy, and it will become discharged. Consequently, in order to supply additional current, the *generator* or *alternator* must restore the chemical energy to the battery.

The generator or alternator restores this chemical energy to the battery by directing current through the battery in a direction opposite to its flow during normal discharge (lower illustration, Fig. 13–19). This charging current reverses the chemical action within the battery and therefore restores it to a charged condi-

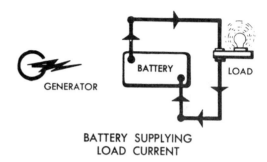

BATTERY SUPPLYING
LOAD CURRENT

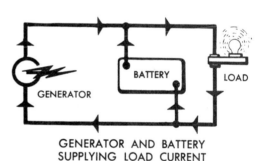

GENERATOR AND BATTERY
SUPPLYING LOAD CURRENT

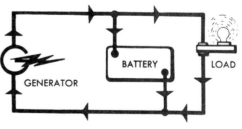

GENERATOR SUPPLYING LOAD
CURRENT AND CHARGING BATTERY

Fig. 13–19. The charging circuit can recharge the battery as well as supply current to the automobile's electrical units. (Courtesy of Delco Remy)

tion. However, the voltage regulator, which is part of the charging circuit, limits the charging voltage to a safe value so that the battery does not receive an overcharge at high generator or alternator speeds.

The total current output from the battery and the generator or alternator therefore varies at different engine speeds. For instance, when the engine is shut off, the battery alone supplies current flow, as necessary, for starting, ignition, and accessories. However, at low engine rpm, both the battery and the generating device may supply current flow (center diagram, Fig. 13-19). Finally, as the speed of the generator or alternator increases, it alone supplies current to operate all the resistance units and also charge the battery (lower diagram, Fig. 13-19). Additional information on this process is explained in more detail in Chapter 20.

Factors Determining Battery Life

All storage-type batteries have a limited service life, but some conditions can shorten its life even more. These conditions include electrolyte level, corrosion, overcharging, undercharging and sulphation, cycling, temperature, and vibration. Although all these conditions can and do reduce the life of the battery, periodic service on the battery will reduce the effects of many of these conditions, while, in contrast, neglect and battery abuse will increase their effects and shorten the battery's life.

Electrolyte Level

Normally, water is the only portion of the electrolyte lost from the battery. This loss of water is the result of two factors: (1) evaporation, especially in hot weather, and (2) gasing while the battery is charging. Consequently, keeping up the level of the electrolyte in each battery cell is the most basic step in battery life.

In this respect, when adding water to a battery, make sure that you use distilled water if available. Otherwise, use any clean, soft water. Never use water with a high mineral content because the minerals will set up a reaction within the cells that shorten battery life.

When servicing a battery with water, it is possible to underfill or overfill the cells. If the cell has insufficient electrolyte (underfilled), this causes a greater concentration of sulphuric acid, which deteriorates the plates' grids more rapidly. This low level also exposes the tops of the plates, which causes the active materials to harden and become chemically inactive.

Overfilling the battery can be just as harmful. The additional water weakens the concentration of sulphuric acid (reduces the electrolyte's specific gravity), which reduces the efficiency of the battery. Moreover, any overflow of electrolyte causes corrosion around the battery terminals, increasing resistance to current flow.

Corrosion

Battery *corrosion* is the result of spilled electrolyte or electrolyte condensation from gasing. In either case, the sulphuric acid from the electrolyte corrodes, attacks, and can destroy not only connectors and terminals but hold-down straps and the carrier box as well.

Corroded connections increase the resistance at the battery terminals. This resistance reduces the applied voltage to the vehicle's electrical system. The corrosion on the battery cover can also create a current leakage path that can allow the battery slowly to discharge. Finally, corrosion can lead to mechanical failure of the hold-down straps and carrier box, which can result in physical damage to the battery.

Overcharging

A battery can receive an *overcharge* either from the automobile's charging system or from a battery charger. In either case, there is a violent chemical reaction within the battery. For example, overcharging causes a loss of water in the cells by separating the electrolyte into hydrogen and oxygen gas bubbles, which can push active materials off the plates. This permanently reduces the capacity of the battery. Overcharging can also cause excessive heat, which can oxidize the positive-plate grid material and even buckle the plates. This, of course, results in a loss of cell capacity and early battery failure.

Undercharging and Sulphation

The charging system of the automobile may not fully recharge the battery due to excessive battery output, stop-and-go driving, or a fault in the charging system. In either case, the battery operates in a partially discharged condition. A battery in this condition will become sulphated. A *sulphated battery* is one in which the sulphate normally formed in the plates becomes dense, hard, and chemically irreversible. This, of course, occurs because the sulphate has been allowed to remain in the plates for a long period.

Sulphation of the plates causes two problems. First, it lowers the specific gravity levels and makes the battery more likely to freeze. Second, in cold weather a sulphated battery often fails to crank the engine because of its lack of reserve power.

Cycling

A *cycle* of storage battery simply consists of a discharge and a recharge. If operating conditions subject the battery to a heavy and repeated cycling, its useful life will be less. This is the result of the fact that cycling causes the positive-plate active material to shed and fall into the sediment space in the bottom of the battery box. This action reduces the capacity of the battery and can cause premature short-circuiting of the cells.

Vibration

If the battery hold-down strap or cover is loose, the battery can bounce around or *vibrate* within its carrier case or box. This shock or vibration can shake the active materials off the plates and severely shorten a battery's life. Also, vibration can loosen the plate connections to the plate strap or damage other internal connections. Lastly, severe shock or vibration can even crack a battery case or loosen cable connections.

Review

This section will assist you in determining how well you remember the material in this chapter. Read each item carefully. If you can't complete the statement, review the section in the chapter that covers the material.

1. The symbol for lead peroxide in a positive plate is _____.
   a. Pb
   b. PbO_2
   c. H_2SO_4
   d. H_2O

2. An element immersed in electrolyte is known as a _____.
   a. plate
   b. cell
   c. separator
   d. battery

3. Each cell has a voltage of about _____ volts.
   a. 4.1
   b. 3.1
   c. 2.1
   d. 1.1

4. _____ join the cells in series.
   a. Connectors
   b. Plates
   c. Elements
   d. Terminals

5. During battery discharge _____ forms on all battery plates.
   a. $PbSO_4$
   b. Pb
   c. PbO_2
   d. H_2O

6. If a cell is completely discharged, the electrolyte becomes mostly _____.
   a. SO_4
   b. H_2SO_4
   c. H
   d. H_2O

7. The size and number of plates determine a battery's _____.
   a. resistance
   b. voltage
   c. capacity
   d. both a and b

8. A 100 ampere-hour battery can provide _____ amperes for 20 hours.
   a. 1
   b. 5
   c. 10
   d. 20

9. The type of battery that will self-discharge is the _____ type.
   a. wet
   b. dry
   c. activated
   d. none of these

10. The type of battery placed into service by the addition of electrolyte is the _____ type.
    a. maintenance-free
    b. wet
    c. dry
    d. both a and b

11. A maintenance-free battery uses a _____ alloy grid.
    a. calcium
    b. antimony
    c. lead
    d. copper

12. Electrolyte spillage and gasing cause _____.
    a. cycling
    b. corrosion
    c. sulphation
    d. all of these

13. Undercharging causes _____ of the plates.
    a. oxidation
    b. corrosion
    c. buckling
    d. sulphation

For the answers, turn to the Appendix.

As a tune-up technician, you must perform many types of battery checks and services. This maintenance is necessary not only to prolong the life of the battery but also to prevent a battery malfunction that could cause an electrical failure within the vehicle.

As a general rule, battery maintenance is divisible into two categories: in-vehicle service and maintenance on a battery removed from the automobile. *In-vehicle battery maintenance* includes such items as battery inspections; cleaning the battery, terminals, and carrier; battery replacement; battery testing; and battery recharging. *Bench service* of a battery may include many of these. However, in this category, this chapter only discusses activating a dry-charged battery.

Safety Precautions

Before discussing the inspection of a storage battery, let's take a moment to review some safety rules dealing with general battery maintenance or working on any other part of the electrical system or engine.

1. To avoid injury from a spark due to a short circuit, always disconnect the battery's ground cable when working on a part of the electrical system or engine. This action also prevents the accidental starting of the engine.

2. Disconnect the battery ground cable before fast-charging the battery in the vehicle. This is especially important if the vehicle has an alternator instead of a generator; if you have improperly connected the charger cables to the battery terminals, the reverse current flow damages the alternator.

Chapter 14

BATTERY MAINTENANCE

3. When removing a battery, always disconnect the battery ground cable first. When installing the battery, connect the ground cable last.

4. Never attempt to polarize an alternator after reconnecting a battery. No polarization of this unit is necessary, and any attempt to do so may damage the alternator, regulator, or circuits.

5. Never, in any situation, reverse the polarity of the battery connections. Generally speaking, all automobiles use a negative ground. Reversing this polarity damages the alternator and possibly some of the wiring in the system.

6. If you use a boost battery to help start the engine, make certain to connect it properly. Connect the negative (−) terminal of the booster battery to the (−) terminal of the vehicle's battery, and connect the positive (+) terminals to each other. *Caution:* To prevent a possible fire or explosion:

   a. Use equipment with a switch in the line connecting the booster battery to the vehicle's battery.

   b. Connect the booster battery's (+) cable to the (+) terminal of the battery first. Then connect the (−) cable of the booster battery to a good ground on the vehicle's engine or frame.

   c. Always rock the connector clips to make sure that they are secure.

   d. If you are using jumper cables between two vehicles, always connect the cables to the vehicle with the low battery first; then attach the other two clips to the booster battery, being very careful to connect them in the proper polarity.

   e. When disconnecting jumper cables or the leads from a portable booster battery, always break the negative connection at the vehicle's engine or frame first. Then, when using jumper cables, disconnect the clip at the (−) terminal of the booster battery.

7. Never use a fast-charger as a boost to start the engine.

8. Never lay metal tools or other objects across a battery, as this may create a short circuit.

9. To prevent a possible fire or explosion when connecting a fast-charger to a battery, always disconnect the battery's ground cable *and make sure that the charger is off.*

10. Gases from the battery can explode. Therefore, keep all sparks and fires away from the battery.

11. When the battery is charging, the process creates hydrogen gas more rapidly; consequently, make sure that the room or shop has good ventilation.

12. Battery acid is harmful if it contacts the skin or most materials. If the acid spills, follow these first aid tips to minimize the damage.

   a. Immediately remove any clothing upon which acid spills.

   b. If you get acid on your skin, rinse the affected area with running water for 5 minutes or more. Then, if available, put baking soda on the affected area.

   c. If acid splashes into your eyes, force the lids open and flood the eyes with running water for at least 5 minutes. *Then, see a doctor at once.*

   d. Acid from the battery can also damage the paint and metal surfaces of the vehicle as well as shop equipment. To neutralize any spilled acid, use one of the following mixtures:

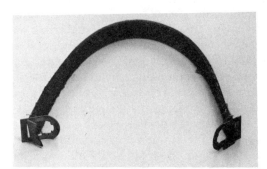

Fig. 14-1. A battery strap enables you to handle a battery safely.

(1) One pound of baking soda in a gallon of water

(2) One pint of household ammonia in a gallon of water

13. Batteries are quite heavy and can be awkward to handle. If you happen to drop a battery, electrolyte may spill out of it or the case may break open. Consequently, always use a battery carrier or lifting strap (Fig. 14-1) to make the moving of batteries easier and safer.

14. Before boost starting or charging a dead battery in winter, always check the electrolyte in the cells for signs of freezing. If ice or slush is visible or you cannot see the electrolyte level, allow the battery to thaw at room temperature, around 70°F., before charging. If you do not do this and pass current through a frozen battery, it may rupture or explode.

Battery Inspection

With these facts on battery safety in mind, let's examine the items you should inspect the battery for as part of the tune-up procedure (Fig. 14-2).

1. Inspect the battery cover and case for dirt or grease, which can cause an electrical pathway to ground.

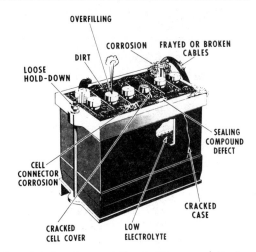

Fig. 14-2. Inspect the battery and its installation for the defects shown.

2. Check the battery itself for cracks, loose terminal posts, and signs of other physical damage. A battery with any of these types of damage requires replacement.

3. Check for missing or damaged cell caps or covers. Replace any that are missing or broken.

4. Inspect the battery's electrolyte level (Fig. 14-3). The level must be above the top of the plates in each cell or at the

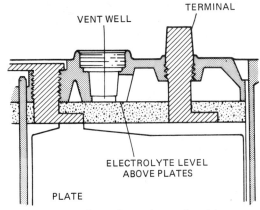

Fig. 14-3. The electrolyte should completely cover the battery plates.

level specified by the manufacturer. If the level is low, add distilled or a good, mineral-free drinking water.

5. Check both battery cables for frayed or broken wires, worn insulation, and loose or damaged connectors (Fig. 14-2). Replace the cables and connectors as necessary.

6. Inspect the cable connections at both terminals for looseness, corrosion, or dirt.

7. Check the carrier box and hold-down straps or cover for corrosion, damage, looseness, or missing components.

8. If installed, check the battery heat shield for proper installation.

Battery Cleaning

Before removing the battery connectors or the battery for cleaning or other service, it is a good idea first to neutralize the accumulated corrosion on the outer por-

tions of the connectors, hold-down straps or cover, and the top of the battery. You can accomplish this task easily with a brush and a solution of baking soda and water or an ammonia solution (Fig. 14-4). However, be careful not to allow any of the soda solution to enter any of the battery cells; and do not splash any of the solution or corrosion on yourself, painted surfaces, or metal parts. Finally, as necessary, remove any stubborn amounts of heavier corrosion with a stiff bristled brush (Fig. 14-5).

Remove any dirt or accumulated grease with a detergent solution or with solvent. Then, after the corrosion and dirt are gone, rinse the battery and cable connection with water. Dry the components with a clean rag or with low-pressure compressed air.

To clean the inside of the battery connectors and the exterior surfaces of both battery terminals, remove the cables, beginning with the ground cable, following this procedure.

Fig. 14-4.   Using a brush and a baking soda and water solution to clean off corrosion from the battery.

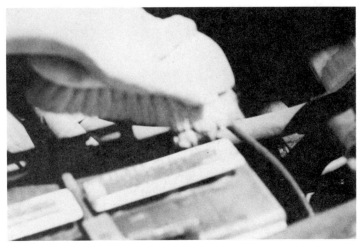

Fig. 14-5. *Remove heavier, stubborn corrosion with a stiff bristled brush.*

1. Detach the spring-ring type of cable connector by squeezing the ends of its prongs together with a pair of wide-jaw, vise-grip, channel-lock, or special battery pliers. This action expands the connector so that you can lift it off the terminal post (Fig. 14-6).

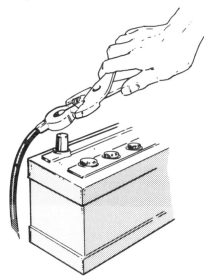

Fig. 14-6. *Using a pair of pliers to loosen and remove a spring-type cable connector.*

2. If the cable connector has a nut and bolt, loosen the nut about ⅜-inch (9.53 millimeters), using a box-end wrench or special, cable-clamp pliers (Fig. 14-7). While loosening this nut, be careful of two things.

a. Never use ordinary pliers or an open-end wrench for this procedure because the jaws of the pliers or the wrench itself may break free and swing around, breaking the cell cover.

b. Always grip the cable with your free hand while loosening the nut. This action tends to prevent the torque, necessary to break free the nut, from loosening the terminal or breaking it off where it attaches to the cell element.

3. If the connector, after its nut is loose, sticks to the battery terminal, use a connector or clamp puller (Fig. 14-8) to detach the connector from the terminal. *Never use a pry bar or a screwdriver to pry the connector loose.* Prying the connector

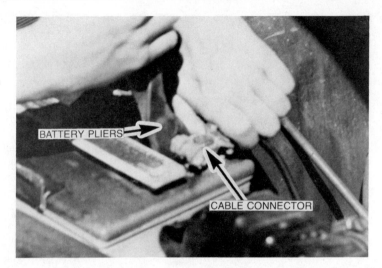

Fig. 14-7. Loosening the nut on a cable connector, using battery pliers.

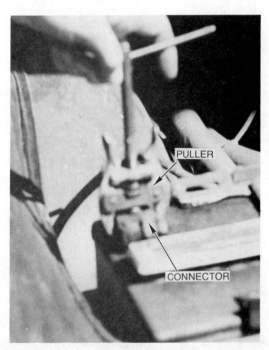

Fig. 14-8. Removing a cable connector from its terminal with a puller.

off, places a strain on the terminal post and the plates attached to it. This can cause the cell cover to break or cause the plates to break loose from the terminal, either of which would ruin the battery.

Cleaning the Terminals and Cable Connectors

To clean the battery terminals and the cable connectors themselves, follow this procedure.

1. Use a connector-spreading tool (Fig. 14-9) to open the cable connector.

2. Neutralize any additional corrosion on the cable connections by dipping them into a baking soda solution.

3. Using a combination wire brush with external and internal bristles (Fig. 14-10), clean the terminal posts and the inside of both cable connectors. Make certain that the terminals and connectors are com-

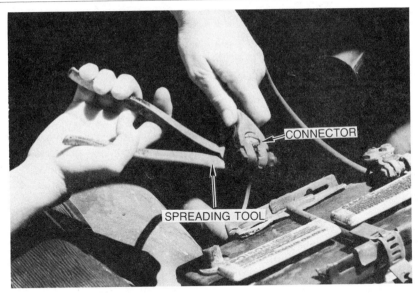

Fig. 14-9. Using a spreading tool to open the cable connector prior to cleaning and reinstallation.

pletely clean before reattaching the connectors over the terminal posts.

4. If available, install felt washers treated with a corrosion-resistant compound, over each terminal post.

Fig. 14-10. Using a combination external-internal wire brush to clean both a battery terminal and its cable connector. (Courtesy of Delco Remy)

5. Install both the cable connectors over their respective post, beginning with the positive connector. Make certain that each connector fully seats down on the terminal post (Fig. 14-11).

6. Tighten the cable connector's nut, when used, securely with a box-end wrench or battery pliers. *Caution:* Do not overtighten this nut, since this action could damage the clamp. Also, never hammer or force the cable connector down on the post since this may break the cell cover or cause internal damage that could ruin the battery.

7. Make sure that both cable connectors are good and secure on the terminals.

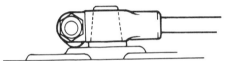

Fig. 14-11. Each cable connector must fully seat down on its terminal post.

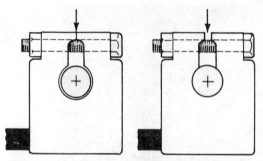

Fig. 14–12. There should be some gap between the jaws of the cable connector after its installation over the terminal.

If the jaws of the bolt- and nut-type connector come together, as shown on the left of Fig. 14–12, chances are the connector is not tight on its terminal. This can cause a starting problem later. You can correct this condition by disconnecting the connector from the post and removing some metal from the connector jaws until there is some measurable gap between the jaws after installation.

8. Coat both connector clamps with petroleum jelly or special battery anticorrosion paint or paste.

Battery Replacement

Before removing the old battery from the vehicle, mark the cable that attaches to the positive (+) terminal of the battery with masking tape or other suitable marking device. On most 12-volt electrical systems on domestic vehicles with negative-ground electrical systems, the positive cable attaches to the starter relay or motor. However, some imported automobiles and some older domestic vehicles with 6-volt systems have a positive ground. Therefore, in all cases, the marking of the cable to the (+) battery terminal prevents the reversing of cable connectors, which would change the electrical

system's polarity, after battery installation.

Another safeguard in preventing the reversal of battery polarity is the size of the terminals. For instance, on top-type terminal batteries, the positive post is larger than the negative. Also, many side-terminal batteries have different-sized connectors for the positive and negative terminals. However, it saves time in the long run if you take a moment and tape the positive cable because it is possible, in some cases, to install the positive cable connector over the negative post and secure it. However, the smaller negative connector does not fit over the larger (+) terminal post.

With these facts in mind, remove the battery following this procedure.

1. Beginning with the ground cable, disconnect both cable connectors, following the procedure outlined under terminal cleaning.

2. Loosen and remove the battery hold-down straps or cover and any installed heat shield.

3. With a carrier or battery strap, lift the battery from its carrier box.

4. Inspect and clean the carrier box, cover, or straps as necessary, using a baking soda and water solution.

5. Using a carrier or battery strap, re-install the battery into its box.

6. Install the battery cover or hold-down straps into position, and tighten their attaching bolts or nuts. *Caution:* The hold-down straps or cover must be kept relatively tight, so that the battery does not bounce around or vibrate in its box or tray. However, avoid overtightening the hold-down cover or strap's attaching nuts or bolts, since this could cause the battery case to warp, bulge, or break.

7. If so removed, install the battery's heat shield.

8. Reinstall, beginning with the positive cable, both terminal connectors, following the procedure outlined under terminal and cable connector cleaning.

Battery Testing

You can test a state of charge and the capacity of a battery in or out of the vehicle by many methods. The most common methods are the specific gravity, cadmium-probe test, high-discharge or capacity, and the 3 minute charging test. The specific gravity of the electrolyte, as mentioned in the last chapter, provides a good indication as to the relative charge of a battery cell, since the acid strength of the electrolyte varies directly with its state of charge. Therefore, the specific gravity test provides a convenient and easy method for estimating a battery's state of charge; you, of course, cannot perform it on sealed, maintenance-free batteries.

To perform the specific gravity test, a battery hydrometer is necessary (Fig. 14-13). A basic battery hydrometer consists of glass tube or barrel, rubber bulb, rubber tube, and glass float or hydrometer. The glass tube encases the float or hydrometer and forms the reservoir for the test electrolyte. The bulb, when squeezed, creates a vacuum that pulls up an electrolyte sample into the glass tube. The rubber tube attaches to a rubber tip on the opposite end of the glass barrel from the bulb. During the test, the rubber tube carries the electrolyte from the cell to the glass tube.

The sealed hydrometer floats in the electrolyte pulled into the inside of the glass tube. This hydrometer float is made of glass and is equipped with a paper scale built inside its upper, extended stem. This scale's marks must be read on a level even with the surface liquid. This reading indicates the specific gravity of the liquid (Fig. 14-14).

The depth in which the float sinks in the electrolyte indicates its relative weight

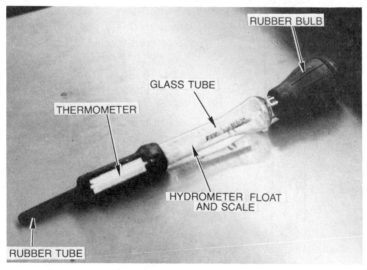

Fig. 14-13. A typical battery hydrometer.

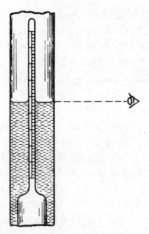

Fig. 14-14. To read the hydrometer scale correctly, sight along the level of the electrolyte until it contacts the scale. Disregard the curvature of the liquid against the stem and glass tube.

Correcting Specific Gravity Reading for Temperature

No hydrometer reading is strictly correct until you make a temperature correction. At ordinary temperatures, it is not usually necessary to correct a hydrometer reading for the temperature effect, but at extremes of temperature, this correction is important.

The hydrometer float described earlier has a calibration to indicate correctly only at one fixed temperature, 80°F. If this particular unit floats in acid at any other temperature, a correction is necessary. The reason is that the electrolyte expands when heated and shrinks when cooled.

The error due to temperature is well known. You can easily correct for it, if you know the temperature of the electrolyte surrounding the hydrometer float. In order to take care of this problem, many hydrometers have a built-in thermometer and correction scale so that the technician can easily make a temperature correction (Fig. 14-16).

This temperature correction amounts to about 0.004 specific gravity, sometimes referred to as 4 "points" of "gravity" for each 10°F. change in temperature. Figure 14-16 illustrates a thermometer and scale that shows the corrections for hydrometer readings when the electrolyte temperature (not the air temperature) is above or below 80°F. Battery manufacturers adjust the acid in their batteries so that the specific gravity readings are accurate only when the electrolyte is at 80°F.

The reader should note how misleading a hydrometer reading can be at extremes of temperature, unless making a temperature correction. For example, if you take a hydrometer reading of 1.270 from a particular cell with an acid temperature of 20°F., the actual specific gravity is

compared to water. This provides us with a measure of the electrolyte's specific gravity. For example, if the hydrometer floats deep in the liquid (Fig. 14-15), the specific gravity is low. On the other hand, if the float rides shallow in the liquid, the specific gravity of the electrolyte is high.

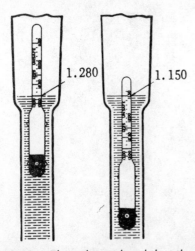

1.280   1.150

Fig. 14-15. The relative level that the float rides in the electrolyte indicates its specific gravity.

°F.

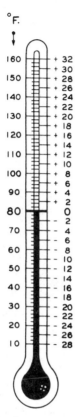

Fig. 14-16. A thermometer with a temperature correction scale, built into some hydrometers.

somewhat less. The actual gravity reading will be 1.270 minus 0.024 specific gravity, or 1.246.

At the other temperature extreme, a reading of a given cell of 1.255, at a temperature of 100°F., will actually be too low. The corrected specific gravity reading will be 1.255 plus 0.008, or 1.263. In the first example, without a temperature correction, a mechanic would consider the cell to be well charged. The reason for this, of course, is that the uncorrected hydrometer reading indicated a fully charged cell at 80°F. However, with the temperature correction, the true reading would show the cell with only about a 75 percent charge.

You may encounter the second example during very hot weather even with a new battery. The 1.255 gravity reading would indicate too low a charge. When you correct it to a 1.263 specific gravity, it is not unreasonably low. Under this condition, the tested cell is serviceable without considering whether it can function.

Sometimes a mechanic misinterprets a low gravity reading of a hot battery that is charging as a failure of the unit to take a full charge. However, the application of the temperature correction soon shows that the battery has a full charge. In a similar respect, you should never take a specific gravity reading of a battery just discharged at a high rate, such as for a prolonged engine cranking, because it will be misleading.

This type of discharge weakens the acid adjacent to the plates. Until this weak acid has had time to diffuse outwardly and mix with the remaining stronger acid in the cell, the reading taken at the top of the cell is too high, indicating a higher state of charge than exists. The acid mixes slowly if the battery stands idle for several hours; the mixing is more rapid if you charge the battery, which mixes the acid by gasing.

Taking a Specific Gravity Reading

To take a specific gravity reading from the cells of a typical battery in or out of a vehicle, follow this procedure.

1. Remove the vent caps and check the electrolyte level in each cell. If the level is too low to take a sample, add water to the affected cell. Then, charge the battery for 5 to 10 minutes at a slow-charge rate, about 5 amperes, to mix the water with the electrolyte before testing.

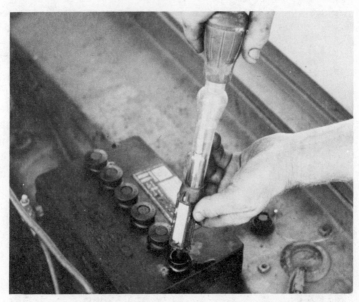

Fig. 14-17. Drawing some electrolyte into the glass barrel in order to float the hydrometer and measure the liquid's specific gravity.

2. Place the tip of the rubber tube into an end cell. Then, draw enough electrolyte into the glass tube to float the hydrometer (Fig. 14-17) without it touching the sides or top of the glass tube. *Note:* If the hydrometer has a built-in thermometer, draw the sample electrolyte into the glass tube several times in order to stabilize the temperature. Then, note the temperature reading. Next, withdraw another sample of electrolyte into the glass tube for test purposes.

3. Holding the instrument vertical with the hydrometer float at eye level, read the specific gravity on the indicator scale.

Return the sample to the cell and note the reading.

4. Take the specific gravity reading from the remaining battery cells; note all their readings.

Results and Indications

The specific gravity of the cells in a fully charged battery should be 1.260 to 1.280, with the electrolyte temperature at 80°F. The table shown in Fig. 14-18 indicates the relationship between specific gravity readings and the state of charge of a cell.

You should recharge a battery if the specific gravity drops below an overall average of 1.230. In addition, a specific

1.265 specific gravity	100% charged
1.225 specific gravity	75% charged
1.190 specific gravity	50% charged
1.155 specific gravity	25% charged
1.120 specific gravity, or lower	discharged

Fig. 14-18. A table of various specific gravity readings and their relationship to a cell's state of charge.

gravity variation of more than 50 points (0.050 specific gravity) between cells is a good indication of a defective battery requiring replacement.

Cadmium-Probe Test

The cadmium-probe test measures the open-circuit voltage of the battery's cells. You can perform this test on a battery in or out of the vehicle. As in the case of the specific gravity test, this one cannot be done on the sealed maintenance-free battery.

This particular test requires the use of a special tester with two probes connected to a voltmeter. The probe tips are cadmium tubes about 1 inch long. These tubes contain an absorbent material, which keeps the cadmium moist. When inserted into adjacent filler openings in the battery, the probes contact the electrolyte and react to it in much the same way as the active materials in the plates do. This chemical reaction creates a voltage in the tester.

The meter face has graduations to indicate the efficiency of the cell's electrolyte to create voltage in the tester. If the reading of any two tested cells vary five scale divisions or more, the battery is near the point of failure.

To perform the probe test (Fig. 14–19):

1. Remove the vent caps and check the electrolyte level in all cells. If necessary, add water to bring the level in each cell to specifications. *Note:* If it is necessary to add water, charge the battery for 5 to 10 minutes at a slow-charging rate for about 5 minutes, in order to mix the water with the electrolyte before testing.

2. Remove the surface charge by turning the headlights on for 1 minute before testing the battery. *Note:* When the automobile is operating, the battery receives a charge from the alternator. This charging process builds up what is known as a *surface charge* in the battery, which you must remove before an accurate test is possible. If the battery has not been operating in a vehicle for at least 8 hours prior to testing, step 2 is unnecessary.

3. Turn off the headlights and make sure that the ignition and accessories are also off during the test.

4. Place the red probe in the positive (+) cell [next to the (+) terminal] and the black probe in the second cell. Note the reading on the meter. If you reverse the probes, there is no meter reading at this time.

5. Move the red probe to the second cell and the black probe to the third cell. Note the reading. Then, move the red probe to the third cell and the black probe to the fourth cell, and continue the process until you have tested all the cells. Note all cell readings so that you can compare them.

Results and Indications

Compare all the meter readings to those in Fig. 14–20.

1. If the reading of any two cells varies five scale divisions or more on the top scale (A of Fig. 14–20) regardless of the colored section into which they may fall on the bottom scale, the battery is near failure and requires replacement.

2. If all the cells vary less than five scale divisions on the top scale and are in the green section on the bottom scale (B of Fig. 14–20), the battery is in good condition and in a safe state of charge.

3. If all cells vary less than five scale divisions on the top scale but any of the

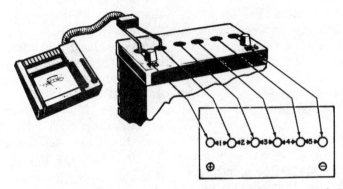

Fig. 14-19. Performing a cadmium-probe test. (Courtesy of Chrysler Corp.)

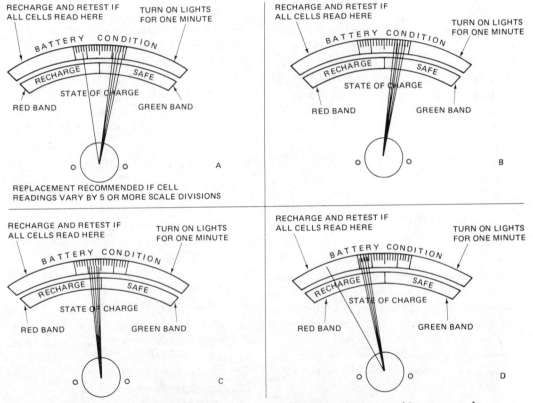

Fig. 14-20. Typical results of a cadmium-probe test. (Courtesy of Chrysler Corp.)

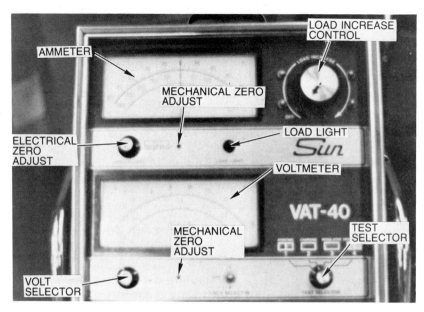

Fig. 14–21. A SUN VAT-40 is a good instrument to test battery capacity.

cells test in the red section on the bottom scale (*C* of Fig. 14–20), the battery is in good condition but is in a low state of charge.

4. If any cell readings are in the recharge-retest section of the top scale and the balance of the readings are within the first four scale divisions (*D* of Fig. 14–20), the battery has too low a state of charge for testing purposes. Consequently, you must recharge the battery and retest, making certain to remove its surface charge before retesting.

High-Rate Discharge or Capacity Test

The *load* or *capacity test* determines how well *any* type of battery functions under a load. In other words, it indicates the battery's ability to furnish starting current and still maintain sufficient voltage to operate the ignition system. This capacity test is only reliable when the battery's specific gravity exceeds 1.220 at 80°F. When the reading is below this amount, the battery requires slow-charging until it reaches full charge.

The test instrument known as a battery-starter tester, like the SUN VAT-28 or -40, is a reliable unit for this test (Fig. 14–21). Both machines consist of an ammeter, voltmeter, and variable-resistance carbon pile. The carbon pile is necessary to initiate the current draw of the starting system.

To perform the capacity test on a battery in or out of the vehicle, using a SUN VAT-40, follow these instructions.

1. Check each of the meter's mechanical zero. Adjust each as necessary.

2. Rotate the load increase control fully counterclockwise to the off position.

3. Connect the tester's load lead to the battery terminals—red to (+) and black to (−).

4. Set the volt selector to Int. 18-V.

5. Adjust the ammeter to read zero, using the electrical-zero adjust control.

6. Connect the green clamp-on amps pickup around either tester load cable, disregarding polarity (Fig. 14–22).

7. Set the tester to starting position 1.

8. While observing the red ammeter scale, turn the load increase control clockwise until the ammeter reads three times the battery's ampere-hour rating or one-half its cold-cranking rating at 0°F. *Note:* If either rating is unknown, you can estimate the test current as follows.

    a. For a battery used with V-8 engines, set the current draw to 225 to 300 amperes for large engines and 175 to 250 amperes for small engines.

    b. For a battery with a four- or six-cylinder engine, set the current draw at 200 to 275 amperes.

Note: If you cannot reach the test current load and the battery voltage drops below 9.6, the battery's performance is very poor. In this case, perform the 3-minute charge test, which this chapter explains later.

9. Maintain the load for 15 seconds and note the green voltmeter scale reading. Then, return the load control knob to off.

Results and Indications

1. If the voltage with the load applied is 10.0 or more, the performance of the battery is good. Therefore, the battery is serviceable.

2. When the voltage with the load applied is 9.6 to 9.9, the battery is probably still serviceable, but you should perform a test on the starting system to see if it is pulling excessive amounts of amperage. This text covers this test in the chapter on starters (Chapter 20).

3. If the voltage with the load applied is below 9.6 volts, the battery is either in a discharged condition or defective, and further testing is necessary. Perform the 3-minute charge test.

4. If you cannot reach the test load, perform the 3-minute charge test.

Alternate Capacity Test

If a battery-starter tester, similar to the one in Fig. 14–21, is not available, you can use the starter motor as a loading device for a *capacity test*. To perform this test:

1. Connect a voltmeter to the battery terminals with its positive lead to the (+) post and its negative lead to the (−) terminal.

2. Pull the coil's secondary lead out of the center tower, and ground it with a jumper wire.

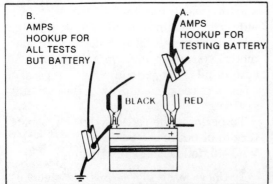

Fig. 14–22. *Connect the amps pickup around either tester load cable. (Courtesy of Sun Electric Corp.)*

3. Crank the engine over continuously for 15 seconds, and observe the voltmeter reading at the end of this period.

Results and Indications

1. If the voltmeter reading is 9.6 volts or higher for a 12-volt battery or 4.8 volts for a 6-volt battery, the battery and starting circuit are in good condition.

2. If the voltage reading drops below these figures, the battery may be in poor condition, or the starting circuit may be drawing too much current. In this situation, perform both the 3-minute charge test and the starting-system load test.

Three-Minute Charge Test

The *3-minute charge* test determines if a discharged battery is too badly sulphated to accept a charge. You can perform this test on batteries either in or out of the vehicles. However, do not perform the test on a maintenance-free battery because the test is not accurate.

A battery fast-charger is necessary for this test in order to pass a high charging current through the battery for 3 minutes. If the battery is not very sulphated, this high current dislodges the sulphate deposits from the plates. On the other hand, if this high charging current does not knock the deposits from the plates and high voltage occurs across the battery terminals, the battery is too sulphated to accept a normal charge.

If you test a battery in the vehicle, disconnect at least the negative battery cable connector in order to avoid damage to the alternator and the electrical system. Also, if you record high voltage early in the test, stop the procedure because high internal resistance due to sulphation or poor internal connections will cause excessive heat, which can boil the electrolyte.

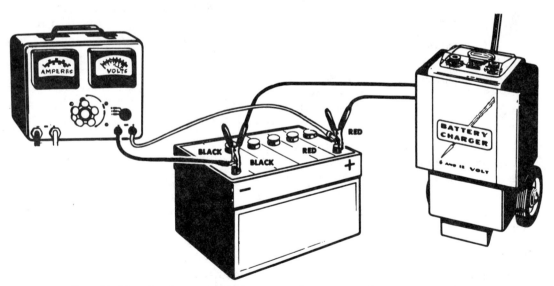

Fig. 14–23. Performing the 3-minute charge test. (Courtesy of Chrysler Corp.)

With these facts in mind, you can perform a 3-minute charge test following this procedure (Fig. 14–23).

1. Connect the battery charger's positive lead to the (+) battery terminal and its negative lead to the (−) terminal of the battery.

2. Connect a voltmeter across the battery with its positive lead to the (+) battery terminal and the voltmeter's negative lead to the (−) terminal.

3. Trip the charger's power switch to the on position. Then, turn the charger's timer switch past the 3-minute mark and then back to this mark.

4. Adjust the charger's output switch to the highest possible rate not exceeding 40 amperes for a 12-volt battery or 75 amperes for a 6-volt battery.

5. When the timer switch cuts off at the end of 3 minutes, turn the timer switch to the fast-charge position. Then, read the voltmeter indications.

Results and Indications

1. If the reading is not more than 15.5 volts for a 12-volt battery or 7.75 for a 6-volt battery, the battery is in satisfactory condition, and you can safely recharge it at its manufacturer's suggested charging rate.

2. If the voltage reading is more than the preceding values, the battery is defective and requires replacement.

Battery Charging

To charge a battery, a given charging current must pass through the battery for a period of time. For example, a 10-ampere rate for 2 hours will result in a 20 ampere-hour charging input to the battery. You can provide this input to the battery in two ways: either with a fast or slow charger.

There are, in most cases, some differences in design and operating characteristics among the various makes of fast and slow chargers. Therefore, when attempting to use one of these devices, always follow the manufacturer's operating instructions to prevent an accident or damage to the battery. Since these differences exist, this chapter does not attempt to cover all the varying operating steps of the many units but presents an overview of what these chargers do and what to watch for when using them.

Fast Chargers

A battery that is in satisfactory condition but requires recharging will accept a large amount of charging current without undesirable effects. A battery fast-charger recharges this type of battery quickly (in about an hour) at a higher rate, usually 40 amperes for a 12-volt battery and 70 amperes for a 6-volt unit. Fast chargers are the most widely used type of charger in service stations and garages (Fig. 14–24). Moreover, many of these units can recharge a battery at both a high and a low rate.

Slow Chargers

A sulphated battery does not accept a fast charge without possible damage because its sulphated condition causes high resistance to current flow within the battery. A forced flow of a high rate of charging current through this resistance creates heat, which can result in warping of the plates, boiling of the electrolyte, and eventual damage to the separators.

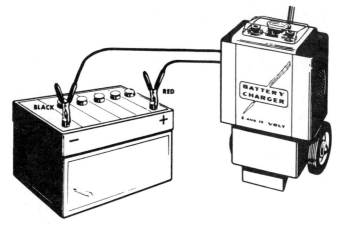

Fig. 14-24. A typical fast charger connected to a battery. (Courtesy of Chrysler Corp.)

For these reasons, you must charge a sulphated battery over a long period of time at a slow rate or through the use of a slow charger. With a slow charger, the sulphate formations on the plates gradually break down, and the battery returns to its normal charged state. Many vehicle owners have a slow-type or trickle charger that provides a low charging current, about 5 to 15 amperes, for an extended period of time.

Battery Reaction Determines Charger to Use

The reaction of the battery to the rate of charge indicates whether it will accept a prolonged fast charge without damage. Generally speaking, you can charge almost any battery at any current rate as long as excessive electrolyte gasing and spewing does not occur and the electrolyte temperature does not exceed 125°F. However, when time is available, a slow-charging rate is the best and safest to use.

Precautions When Fast-Charging a Battery

When fast-charging a battery with any type of unit, follow the safety rules outlined in the text along with these precautions.

1. When using a fast charger, always follow the manufacturer's instructions for its hookup, charging rate, and length of charging time, according to the battery's specific gravity and capacity (ampere-hour rating).

2. Never attempt to fast-charge a battery that has failed the 3-minute charge test.

3. Never fast-charge a battery that appears sulphated or has plate or separator damage.

4. Always make sure that the electrolyte level is up to specifications.

5. Watch the electrolyte temperature closely and stop charging if it rises above 125°F.

6. Whenever possible, follow a fast charge with a period of slow charging to

recharge the battery fully. *Note:* Many fast chargers have a decreasing charge rate that protects the battery from over-charging.

7. Never fast charge for more than 1 hour. If the battery does not indicate a good rise in the specific gravity of all its cells within 1 hour, slow charge the battery.

8. Check the voltage across the terminals with a voltmeter. If voltage is more than 15.5 volts for a 12-volt unit or 7.5 volts for a 6-volt battery, reduce the charging rate until the voltage drops below these values.

9. When charging a sealed maintenance-free battery, follow the manufacturer's specifications for charging rate and time. Under no conditions exceed these specifications.

10. After charging, always wash and dry the top of the battery to remove any acid resulting from electrolyte gasing.

11. After charging, check the electrolyte level and add water as necessary to bring the level up to specifications.

Precautions When Slow-Charging a Battery

When slow-charging a battery, always adhere to the safety rules already outlined in this chapter relating to battery service and fast-charging and also these special precautions.

1. Never exceed the normal slow-charging rate or time, without periodically checking the battery's state of charge. The slow-charging rate is 5 to 15 amperes while the charging time may be 12 to 24 hours.

2. Never exceed the safe charging rate for a particular battery size or condition.

You can determine the safe charging rate by using one of two methods. Using the first method, the safe charging rate would be equal to 1 ampere per positive plate per cell. By the second method, a safe charging rate would be equal to 7 percent of the battery's ampere-hour rating. However, the charging rate for a sulphated battery is one-half the normal rate and takes 60 to 100 hours to recharge the battery.

3. Stop charging the battery after three specific gravity readings, taken at 1-hour intervals, indicate the battery is fully charged. Make sure to correct the specific gravity readings to the electrolyte's temperature.

Activating a Dry-Charged Battery

The one task that you will usually perform on a battery out of a vehicle is activating the unit. This is done to prevent damage to the vehicle from spilled acid.

To activate a dry-charged battery (Fig. 14–25):

1. Remove all its vent caps, and fill all the cells over the tops of the plates with the packaged electrolyte. *Caution:* Be sure to read and follow the instructions on the electrolyte package.

2. Wait several minutes after activating the battery. Then, recheck the electrolyte level. Add electrolyte as necessary, according to the battery manufacturer's specifications. After this, the unit is now a "wet" battery, and you only need to add water during subsequent servicing.

3. You may now install the battery into the vehicle. However, for improved performance, you may want to perform the following tests.

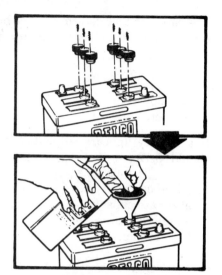

Fig. 14-25. Activating a dry-charged battery. (Courtesy of Delco Remy)

a. Check the open circuit voltage of the battery. Less than 5 volts on a 6-volt battery or 10 volts on a 12-volt battery indicates a reversed cell or an open circuit. In either case, replace the battery.

b. Check the specific gravity of all cells. If the readings, corrected to 80°F., show more than a 30 point (0.030 specific gravity) drop from the 1.265 filling electrolyte, the battery requires a charge before use. In addition, the battery requires replacement if one or more cells gas violently after the addition of electrolyte.

4. For best performance when the temperature is 32°F. or less or anytime the battery and electrolyte are not at 60°F. or above at activation, warm the battery by boost charging as follows:

a. Boost-charge 6-volt batteries and heavy-duty 12-volt batteries for a minimum of 10 minutes at 30 amperes.

b. Boost-charge all other 12-volt batteries for a minimum of 10 minutes at 15 amperes. If either boost charge does not bring the electrolyte temperature up to 60°F., continue charging until the temperature reaches that point.

5. After charging, check the electrolyte level. If it is low, add water to bring the level up to specifications.

Review

This section will assist you in determining how well you remember the material in this chapter. Read each item carefully. If you can't complete the statement, review the section in the chapter that covers the material.

1. Proper maintenance improves the _____ of the battery.
   a. voltage
   b. input
   c. life
   d. capacity

2. When fast-charging the battery, always disconnect the _____
   _____.
   a. positive cable
   b. negative cable
   c. alternator lead
   d. both b and c

3. Neutralize corrosion from battery components, using a solution of _____ _____ and water.
   a. clean kerosene
   b. cleaning detergent
   c. cleaning solvent
   d. baking soda

4. Loosen the nut of a cable connector with a box-end wrench or with special _____ pliers.

a. battery
b. channel-lock
c. vise-grip
d. wide-jaw

5. Before removing the battery, it is a good idea to mark the _____ _____.
   a. connector position
   b. charging lead
   c. negative cable
   d. positive cable

6. A _____ is necessary to measure a battery's specific gravity.
   a. charger
   b. ammeter
   c. hydrometer
   d. voltmeter

7. In order for a specific gravity reading to be accurate, you must correct it for electrolyte _____.
   a. content
   b. temperature
   c. volume
   d. gasing

8. The cadmium-probe test measures the _____ _____ of a cell.
   a. discharge rate
   b. open-circuit voltage
   c. ampere-hour rating
   d. cold rating

9. The batter is usually defective if during the cadmium-probe test the reading of any two cells vary more than _____ scale divisions.
   a. 5
   b. 4
   c. 3
   d. 2

10. The capacity test determines the battery's ability to deliver current during engine _____.
    a. idling
    b. starting
    c. shutdown
    d. acceleration

11. If a battery appears sulphated, you should perform the _____ _____ test.
    a. specific gravity
    b. alternate capacity
    c. 3-minute charge
    d. battery capacity

12. A fast charger should not be used to recharge a _____ battery.
    a. sulphated
    b. new
    c. low
    d. both *a* and *b*

13. If during a fast-charge the voltage of a 12-V battery exceeds _____ volts, reduce the charging rate.
    a. 7.5
    b. 10.5
    c. 13.5
    d. 15.5

14. The normal slow-charging rate is _____ amperes.
    a. 30 to 40
    b. 40 to 60
    c. 5 to 15
    d. 10 to 20

For the answers, turn to the Appendix.

Function

All gasoline engines require some form of *ignition system*. The purpose of this system is to supply to the spark plugs, within the engine combustion chambers, high-voltage surges. Furthermore, the ignition system must provide these surges or sparks to the correct cylinder of the engine at the proper time in its operating cycle for most efficient combustion. The result of these sparks, of course, is ignition of the air/fuel mixture within each of the combustion chambers.

Types

Two types of ignition systems are used: the standard system and the electronic system. The *standard battery-ignition system* has been used on automobiles for over 60 years. This chapter and the next cover this type of system in detail.

Manufacturers began to use electronic ignition systems on high-performance vehicles in the 1960s. However, solid-state systems did not appear on many domestic passenger vehicles until early in the 1970s. These systems are now the rule instead of the exception, due to stricter emission control standards and the need for improved fuel economy. This text covers the electronic ignition systems in Chapters 17 and 18.

Primary Circuit

Battery

To assist the reader in understanding the standard system, this chapter divides the system into two circuits: the primary circuit and the secondary circuit. The

---

Chapter 15

STANDARD IGNITION SYSTEMS

primary circuit consists of the battery, ignition switch, ignition resistor, contact points, condenser, and primary windings of the ignition coil (Fig. 15-1). The *battery* is the heart of the total electrical system. In regard to the primary circuit, its function is to supply voltage and current flow to the primary windings of the ignition coil, in order to produce an electromagnet.

Ignition Switch

The *ignition switch* is simply an on-off switch for the current flow from the battery to the primary windings of the coil. This current can flow, in many cases, when the ignition switch is in either the start or run position. In any other switch position, it routes current to the accessory circuits or locks the steering wheel in position.

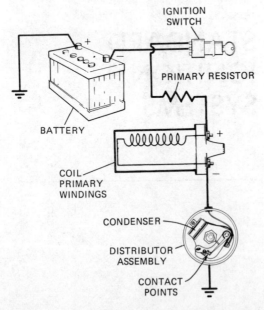

Fig. 15-1. The primary circuit of the standard ignition system.

Primary-Circuit Resistor

All 12-volt standard ignition systems require some type of *resistor* in the primary circuit. This resistor can be in the form of a resistance wire from the ignition switch to the primary windings of the coil, a part of the ignition coil itself, or a ballast resistor (Fig. 15-2). This device is nothing more than a small coil of resistance wire mounted on a ceramic block. In either case, the resistor is in series between the battery and the primary coil windings in order to keep primary-circuit voltage at a desired level, thus protecting the contact points.

In order to understand why a resistor is necessary in the primary circuit, the reader must understand a few facts concerning ignition system operation. First of all, for an ignition coil to have uniform secondary voltage capabilities over a wide range of engine speeds, the magnetic field produced by the primary coil windings must completely saturate the secondary windings. However, magnetic saturation of the secondary coil depends upon the amount of voltage applied to the primary coil, the amount of current actually flowing through its windings, and the length of time during which current flows.

But the standard ignition system does not operate with uniform voltage, current flow, or current-flow time. For instance, during engine starting, the high-current draw of the starter motor drops circuit voltage to about 10 volts. Consequently,

Fig. 15-2. A typical ballast resistor.

the ignition coil must be able to produce sufficient secondary voltage to ignite the air/fuel mixture with only 10 volts applied to the primary windings.

Moreover, at high engine speeds, the current flow to the primary coil has only a few milliseconds to flow due to the rapid opening and closing of the contact points. As a result, secondary-coil saturation must happen under extremes of low voltage with its resulting reduced current flow and shortened current-flow time. To be able to function under these conditions, manufacturers design and produce most ignition coils to operate very well on 9 or 10 volts, under most conditions.

The starter motor operation drops ignition system voltage to about 10 volts; but as soon as the engine starts, system voltage rises to 12 volts or more. At low rpm when the contact points are in the closed position for longer intervals, there is a strong possibility of excessive current flow through the contact points that would cause arcing and eventual burn-out of the points. This action is the result of the self-induction of high voltage within the primary windings. This chapter explains the effect of self-induction later.

At higher engine rpm, the contact points open more often. Therefore, there is less tendency for point arcing because this accelerated point operation reduces the time interval for current to flow through the primary windings. As a result, less voltage is self-induced in the primary windings.

Primary Resistor Operation

At lower engine rpm, current flows into the primary circuit for relatively long periods of time. This current flow heats the ignition resistor, and its resistance in-

creases. This action reduces the applied voltage at the primary coil. By doing so, the resistor reduces peak self-induced voltage of the primary coil and thus decreases current flow across the contact points, which will burn them out prematurely.

At higher engine speeds, the contact points open more frequently, and current flows for shorter periods of time. In this situation, the resistor has time to cool; its total resistance drops. As a result, the resistor permits the application of higher voltage to the primary coil. The shorter current-flow duration results in the same magnetic-field buildup by the primary coil as at low rpm.

Starting Bypass

During engine starting, it is necessary to bypass the primary resistor. This action is necessary because the starter motor operation already drops the system voltage to the desired level, about 9 to 10 volts. Any additional reduction of voltage by the resistor reduces the ignition system's efficiency in producing an arc at the spark plugs.

To bypass the resistor during starting, an additional parallel circuit is necessary. In some installations, the ignition switch controls this bypass circuit (Fig. 15-3). The resistor, in this case, connects between the run position of the ignition switch contacts and the primary coil windings. When the ignition switch is in the start position, the switch applies full battery voltage to the coil's windings.

In other systems, the *starter relay* or *solenoid* controls the bypass circuit (Fig. 15-4). With this design, the resistor again connects between the run position of the ignition switch contacts and the coil.

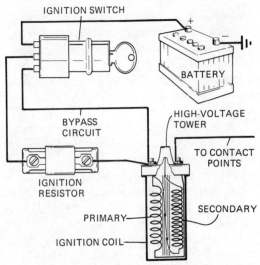

Fig. 15-3. A bypass circuit controlled by the ignition switch.

However, when the ignition switch is in the start position, current from the switch flows through the starter relay or solenoid and closes a set of contact points. As a result, battery current flows through the

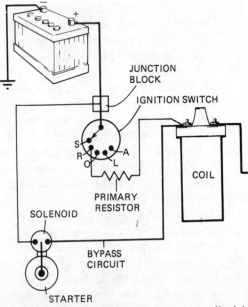

Fig. 15-4. A bypass circuit controlled by the starter solenoid.

relay or solenoid to the coil's primary windings through a parallel circuit.

In both cases, when the engine starts, the bypass circuit opens, and primary current once again all flows through the resistor. This action reduces voltage to the desired level. Finally, bypassing the resistor at any time other than starting can cause rapid burning of the contact points and can damage the coil's primary windings.

Primary Ignition Coil

The primary side of the ignition coil connects in series between the resistor and the breaker points (Fig. 15-1). The function of this coil when current passes through it is to create a very strong electromagnetic field. In other words, the coil becomes an electromagnet with N and S poles. The magnetic field from this coil, in turn, induces a voltage in the secondary windings that is necessary to cause an arc at the spark plug gap.

The primary section of the ignition coil (Fig. 15-5) consists of a number of windings, a positive, and a negative terminal. The primary coil itself has about 100 to 150 turns of relatively heavy copper wire. The manufacturer insulates these coil turns from each other by a thin coat of enamel.

The two ends of these primary windings attach to the primary terminals on top of the coil. In a negative-ground type of electrical system, the coil's positive (+) terminal connects through wiring to the positive side of the battery via the resistor and ignition switch. The negative (−) terminal connects to the (−) battery ground through the contact points. However, in a positive-ground system, the coil's pri-

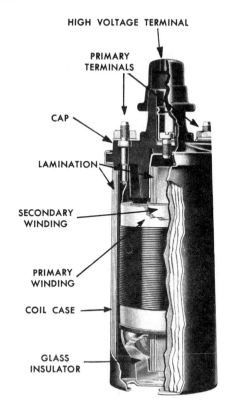

Fig. 15–5. The primary windings consist of a few hundred turns of relatively heavy wire. (Courtesy of Delco Remy)

mary connections are reversed in relationship to this hookup. In other words, the negative (−) terminal of the coil connects to the negative side of the battery while the positive (+) terminal connects to the positive (+) ground through the contact points.

Contact Points

Function

The contact points are in series usually with the negative terminal of the primary coil (negatively grounded systems). The function of the contact points is to open or close the electrical circuit between the coil's negative terminal and ground. As a result, current either flows or does not flow through the primary windings.

Contact Points Design

The *contact point assembly* (Fig. 15–6) mounts onto the breaker plate inside the distributor. This assembly includes a fixed contact point, movable contact point, movable arm, rubbing block, pivot, and spring. Manufacturers make both contact points from tungsten, an extremely hard metal with a high melting point. The *fixed contact* itself grounds through the distributor housing. The *movable contact*, on the other hand, attaches to the negative terminal of the primary coil windings and is insulated from the distributor housing. Finally, because the current flows from the movable to the fixed contact, using the conventional theory of current flow, the movable contact is known as the (+) point while the fixed contact is the (−) point (in a negatively grounded system).

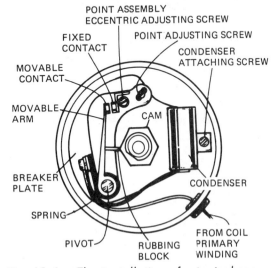

Fig. 15–6. The installation of a typical contact point assembly and condenser in a distributor.

The (+) contact point attaches to a *movable arm*. This arm also has a rubbing block, a small piece of plastic or other synthetic nonconducting material that rides on the surface of the distributor cam. As this cam rotates, its lobes or raised portions push on the rubbing block to open the arm and attached contact point. The spring moves the arm and point to the closed position when the cam lobe moves away from the rubbing block.

The *pivot* permits the movable arm to rotate back and forth due to the action of each cam lobe on the rubbing block. The spring holds the movable arm and its (+) contact point against the fixed (−) point when the rubbing block is between any two lobes on the cam.

In order to open the points mechanically, a distributor cam is necessary. This cam mounts on a shaft, driven directly or indirectly by the camshaft of the engine through a gearing arrangement. This gearing permits the distributor shaft to rotate at camshaft speed, which is one-half the rpm of the crankshaft.

During one rotation of the shaft and cam, the contact points must open as many times as the engine has spark plugs. The cam therefore has as many lobes as the engine has spark plugs. The cam in Fig. 15–6 has six lobes and therefore opens the contact points six times during one revolution of the distributor shaft and two revolutions of the crankshaft.

Dwell, or Cam-Angle, Period

When discussing the operation of the primary coil circuit, *dwell*, or *cam-angle*, is a very important factor. Dwell is the number of degrees the distributor cam rotates while the contact points remain closed (Fig. 15–7). For example, with a special cam and contact-point combination, it is possible to obtain as much as 34 to 36 degrees usable dwell on an eight-cylinder distributor.

This dwell period is important to the proper functioning of the primary coil. The purpose of the primary windings is to create a magnetic field; this magnetic field induces a high-voltage surge in the secondary coil. However, it requires time for current to pass through all the primary windings in order to create the magnetic field. This period occurs when the points close or during dwell time.

Although the dwell may not change, the length of time the contact points remain closed becomes less and less as engine speed increases. Consequently, at higher engine rpm, the primary-coil current flow does not reach its maximum value, due to a shortened period of point closure and the

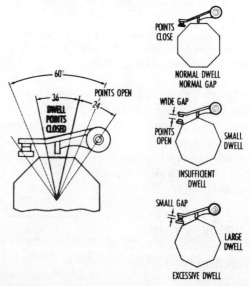

Fig. 15–7. Dwell is the number of degrees the distributor cam rotates while the points remain closed. (Courtesy of Ford Motor Co. of Canada Ltd.)

resistance in the windings themselves. Therefore, in order for the primary coil to produce a large enough field, it is important that the dwell time be correct at the start.

The point-open period is also important in the operation of the secondary system. The *point-open period,* usually measured in thousandths of an inch, is the distance that occurs between the separated contacts as the distributor cam rotates. If the dwell is properly set, the point opening most likely also is to specifications. However, in some cases, it may be necessary to measure point opening with a feeler gauge in addition to dwell to make sure the points are correctly set. The next chapter details these procedures.

Condenser or Compacitor

The last component of the primary ignition circuit is the *condenser* or *compacitor.* The manufacturer wires the condenser in parallel with the (+) breaker point (Fig. 15-6). The function of the condenser in this type of installation is to prevent excessive arcing across the points as they open, due to self-induction of high voltage in the primary windings. This arcing would prematurely burn-out the contact points.

Condenser Construction

Manufacturers form most automotive condensers from two thin foil strips, separated by several layers of insulation (Fig. 15-8). The insulating material is known as a *dielectric* and is usually paper or any similar nonconductive material.

The foil strips and separators are usually about 8 feet in length; the manufacturer rolls these components into a tight,

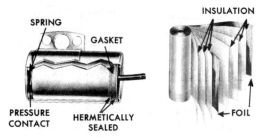

Fig. 15-8. The construction of a typical condenser.

round, cylinder-shaped bundle. However, during this process, the foil strips are offset so that the top edge of one strip protrudes past the insulation on one end of the cylinder, and the ends of the other strip extend past the insulation on the opposite end of the cylinder.

These exposed edges provide the electrical contact points for the two foil strips. The manufacturer flattens these edges before installing the cylinder into a metal canister. With this arrangement, the bottom of the canister contacts one foil edge and grounds it while the other foil provides the contact point for an insulated lead at the top of the canister. Finally, to provide additional insulation, wax or oil is drawn into the canister, and the entire unit sealed.

On most modern distributor assemblies, the condenser fits inside the distributor housing on the breaker plate (Fig. 15-6). The bracket of the condenser attaches to the breaker plate by a screw, and this installation grounds the condenser. The insulated lead from the top of the condenser attaches to the spring of the movable point arm.

Condenser Operation

When the contact points open, the induced voltage within the primary windings forces current (electrons) into the condenser via the insulated lead (Fig. 15-9). Since the electrons cannot flow through the dielectric of the condenser, excess electrons collect on what becomes the negatively charged roll of foil. At the same time, the other foil becomes positively charged because it is low on electrons.

Current continues to flow into the condenser until the voltage charge across the negative roll becomes the same as the induced voltage in the primary coil. At this time, the negative foil roll and the negative terminal of the primary coil are at the exact same negative potential. The positive roll within the condenser and the positive terminal of the primary coil are also at equal potentials.

There is now a voltage charge across the coil's terminals, and an equal voltage charge across the condenser rolls (Fig. 15-10). The circuit is in balance, and no additional current flows. An electrostatic field exists between the two foil rolls of the condenser due to their opposite charges. This field is comparable to the electromagnetic field that results from current flow in a conductor. In any case, this field stores the energy.

The condenser holds this charge until after the plug has fired. Then, the energy

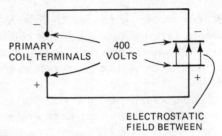

Fig. 15-10. When the condenser is fully charged, there is equal voltage across the condenser and the coil.

stored in the negative roll discharges through the primary coil until its stored energy dissipates as heat. After discharging, both plates of the condenser are again electrically neutral.

Condenser Capacity Ratings

Manufacturers rate the ability of a condenser to accept a charge in units known as *farads*. In reality, 1 farad is a very large charge. Consequently, condensers used in automotive ignition systems have a rating in microfarads; a microfarad is 0.000001 farad. A typical automotive condenser, for instance, has a rating 0.18 to 0.32 microfarads.

Many conditions affect the proper condenser capacity under operating conditions such as the type of coil, dwell, distributor shaft rpm, temperature of the units, and, in some respects, altitude. As a result, the correct condenser capacity for a given ignition system, with the engine idling at 575 rpm, is not correct for the same system with the engine running at 3,500 rpm.

In the primary ignition circuit, two forces oppose each other: inductance versus capacitance. These forces should be in "balance" at all times in order to obtain maximum coil efficiency. However, the

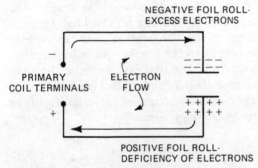

Fig. 15-9. As the condenser is charging, the primary coil's induced voltage forces electrons into the insulated roll.

voltage induction in the primary coil changes according to its period of saturation, which is a factor governed by the length of time the breaker points remain closed. On the other hand, the capacitance of the primary circuit is fixed (in the form of a condenser) and cannot be altered from one moment to another to correspond with the changes in induction. Therefore, the primary ignition circuit is "out of balance" part of the time.

In practice, these factors are dealt with by a compromise. For example, assume that a 0.28-microfarad condenser is correct for a given ignition circuit of an engine operating at 550 rpm, but a 0.22 microfarad condenser is necessary at 3,500 rpm. Manufacturers use a 0.25-microfarad condenser as a compromise with good results.

Condenser Reaction on the Contact Points

When the primary ignition system is in proper balance as to inductance and capacitance, the contact points wear down quite evenly with a minimum of pitting. However, if the condenser has the wrong average capacity, the following results are apparent at the contact points.

1. A hole forms in the negative point if the condenser capacity is too small (Fig. 15-11). The metal transfers through the arc from the negative point to the positive point, where a mound forms.

2. A hole forms in the positive point if condenser capacity is too large (Fig.

Fig. 15-11. The result of insufficient capacity.

Fig. 15-12. The result of excessive capacity.

15-12). In this case, the metal transfers from the positive to the negative point, where the mound forms.

Operation of the Primary-Coil Circuit

Figure 15-13 illustrates the action within the primary-coil circuit with the ignition switch on and the contact points closed. In this situation, current flows from the battery through the ignition switch, primary resistor, primary coil windings, the closed contacts to ground, and returns to the battery. This current flow creates a magnetic field around the primary windings.

This magnetic field does not reach its maximum intensity all at once. A moment of time is necessary in order to build up the field's strength. This basically results

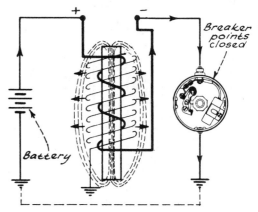

Fig. 15-13. Operation of the primary circuit with the points closed.

because the expanding field induces a momentary countervoltage in adjacent primary windings as the field expands. This countervoltage opposes the normal current flow from the battery, and it must be overcome by circuit voltage in order for current flow and field strength to increase.

This action only requires a small fraction of a second, but this buildup time (dwell) is important. For example, at high engine rpm, the distributor points remain closed for a very short time. As a result, current flow with its resulting buildup of a magnetic field has a more difficult time reaching full potential.

When the breaker cam opens the contact points (Fig. 15-14), the second phase of primary-coil circuit operation begins. As the points open, the battery current flowing through the primary windings begins to decrease rapidly. This causes the magnetic field around the windings to begin shrinking back toward the center of the coil. This collapse of the field induces a high voltage in the primary winding due to self-induction.

This induction of high voltage attempts

to keep current flowing across the separating contact points. Since the primary voltage can be as much as 400 volts, this high voltage would cause an arc across the air gap, formed between the opening points. This unwanted arc would not only consume the magnetic energy produced by the primary windings but would burn and pit the points as well, causing rapid point failure. In addition, the arc would leave an oxidized coating on the points, increasing resistance in the primary circuit.

However, the condenser is in the circuit in parallel with the insulated contact point. When the points open, the condenser receives the charge of induced current from the primary windings. This action requires a certain amount of time, about 0.1 millisecond, to charge the condenser to the peak voltage of the primary windings. By the time the current charges the condenser, the contact points have opened far enough that very little current can arc across the air gap.

Condenser Discharges

Figure 15-15 illustrates the manner by which the condenser discharges its stored energy in current form. This current does not remain in the condenser when forced there by 250 to 400 volts. It immediately "bounces" back and flows back through the primary coil until it reaches its (+) terminal, which has the same charge potential as the opposite side of the condenser. Then, the current "bounces" back again. This oscillating action continues until all the electrical energy dissipates as heat. There may be a dozen or more reversals before current flow stops; however, the complete cycle lasts only a short time.

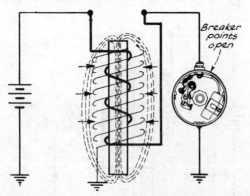

Fig. 15-14.   As the contact points open, the second phase of primary-circuit operation begins.

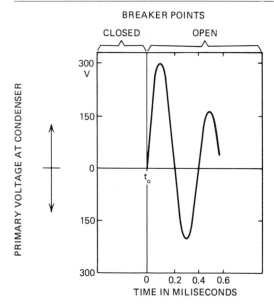

BREAKER POINTS

CLOSED   OPEN

PRIMARY VOLTAGE AT CONDENSER

300 V

150

0

t_o

150

300

0   0.2 0.4 0.6
TIME IN MILISECONDS

Fig. 15-15.   The current stored in the condenser dissipates by oscillating through the primary circuit.

Condenser Action Improves Field Collapse

Because the condenser permits the breaking of the primary circuit quickly and completely, the magnetic field of the primary coil collapses rapidly. This field collapses about 20 times faster than if there were no condenser in the circuit. The faster the field collapses, the greater is the induced voltage in the secondary winding, as this chapter explains later.

In spite of condenser action, there at times is still some arcing at the contact points. For instance, at low engine rpm, the breaker points open relatively slowly. At engine rpm with fewer than 3,000 plug firings in a minute, the primary winding's self-induced voltage is sufficient to cause a slight arcing across the slowly opening point air gap. As a result, vehicles driven mostly at low engine speeds show more

rapid point failure than those used in high speed operation.

Secondary-Ignition Circuit

Function

The *secondary ignition circuit* not only transforms the 6 or 12 volts of the battery to a voltage high enough to cause an arc at the spark plug but also delivers this high-voltage surge to the spark plugs. The automotive battery supplies either 6 or 12 volts to the primary coil windings. But the voltage necessary to jump across the spark plug air gap and ignite the air/fuel mixture can range from 5,000 to 25,000 volts or more, depending upon the engine's operating condition at any given time.

The actual voltage required to fire a spark plug depends on many factors such as engine compression ratio, engine speed, fuel mixture ratios, spark plug temperature, and the width and shape of the spark plug gap. In other words, the voltage that actually appears in the secondary circuit is the result of the actual voltage requirements of the spark plugs. Since plug requirements vary, the secondary voltage must vary, up to the maximum available as determined by the energy input to the secondary coil and other factors. *A spark plug misfire always occurs when the voltage requirement exceeds the voltage available.*

Design of the Secondary Circuit—Coil

The secondary ignition circuit itself consists of the secondary coil, the distributor cap, rotor, high-tension wires, and spark plugs. Manufacturers form the secondary (transformer) portion of the ignition coil from 15,000 to 30,000 turns of very fine insulated copper wire. These turns of secondary wire wrap around a laminated, soft-iron core (Fig. 15–16). Over the secondary windings are the primary windings.

One end of the secondary windings attaches to one of the primary coil's terminals. The opposite end attaches to the high-voltage terminal on top of the coil. These types of connections provide the secondary coil with a given polarity at the high-voltage terminal.

Surrounding the secondary windings and the core is a shell of laminated material. The manufacturer then encases the core, windings, and shell into a metal container. The container is then filled with either oil or insulating material and hermetically sealed with a coil cap. The manufacturer forms this cap from an insulating material with the two primary terminals and one high-voltage terminal molded into it.

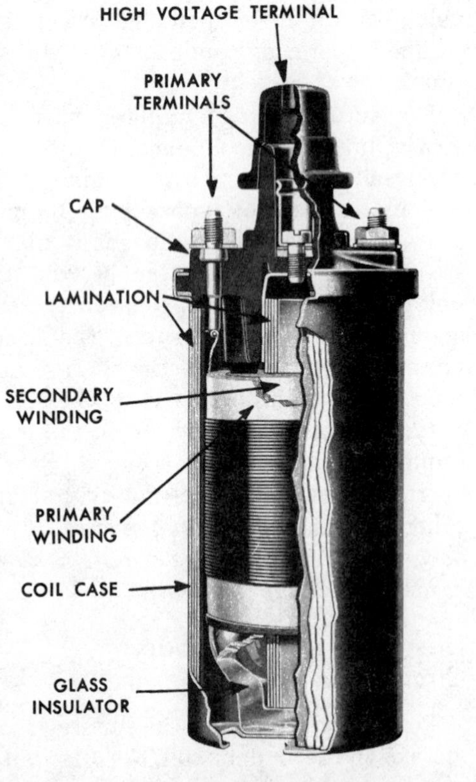

Secondary-Coil Operation

Before the engine starts, the distributor points are in the closed position (Fig. 15–17). When the driver turns on the ignition switch, current can flow through the primary-coil windings. This current begins to create a magnetic field around all the windings. From the primary winding, the current (still at low voltage) simply travels through the closed contact points and back to the battery.

Since the magnetic field caused by this

HIGH VOLTAGE TERMINAL

PRIMARY TERMINALS

CAP

LAMINATION

SECONDARY WINDING

PRIMARY WINDING

COIL CASE

GLASS INSULATOR

Fig. 15–16.   *The design of a typical ignition coil.*

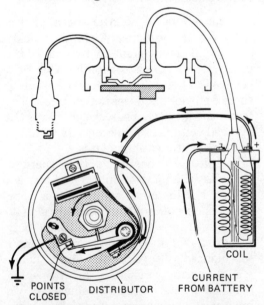

POINTS CLOSED

DISTRIBUTOR

COIL

CURRENT FROM BATTERY

Fig. 15–17.   *Operation of the secondary coil with the contact points closed.*

current flow cuts across the secondary winding during this buildup time, these lines of force induce a voltage in the secondary windings. However, since the buildup time is not very fast, the voltage induced in the secondary winding is very low and is insufficient to cause an arc across the spark plug gap.

As the distributor cam opens the contact points, the second phase of secondary-coil operation begins (Fig. 15–18). As the points open, they break the primary coil's circuit to ground. This action causes the flow of battery current through the coil to decrease. As a result, the magnetic field from the primary coil begins to collapse rapidly.

As this field begins to collapse, it begins to cut across its own windings, causing a voltage induction in the windings. This action creates a high voltage in the primary windings that attempts to keep the current flowing across the opening contact points. However, the condenser receives and momentarily stores this current flow. Without the action of the condenser, the arcing at the points would consume the energy stored in the primary coil in the form of the magnetic field. This would reduce, if not eliminate, the action of the secondary coil in producing a high voltage arc at the spark plug.

Because of the condenser's action, the magnetic field around the primary windings quickly collapses. This collapsing field passes through the secondary windings; the rapid collapse of this field induces high voltage in the secondary windings. The voltage induced in the primary may be as high as 250 to 400 volts, while the voltage may go to 25,000 or more volts in the secondary. The voltage actually used in the secondary circuit is determined by the voltage necessary to cause the arc to jump the spark plug gap; this may range from 5,000 to 25,000 volts.

The high voltage produced in the secondary windings leaves the coil through its high-voltage tower. Then it travels through the remaining secondary components until it reaches the spark plug, where it jumps the gap. After this arc begins at the plug, the energy in the coil, stored in the form of the magnetic field, begins to drain from the coil through the secondary terminal, sustaining the arc at the spark plug gap. The spark continues at the plug for several degrees of crankshaft rotation.

When the secondary coil voltage drops below the level necessary to sustain the arc at the spark plug, the spark ceases. At this point, the spark plug gap becomes nonconductive. The remaining secondary voltage oscillates back and forth through the secondary windings until it dissipates as heat. This is known as *secondary*

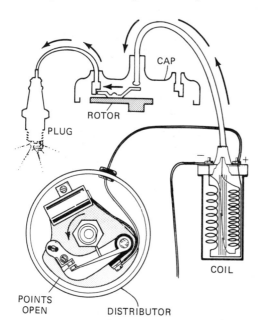

Fig. 15–18. As the contacts open, the second phase of secondary-coil operation begins.

voltage decay. Then, the primary circuit closes again, and the cycle begins again.

The remaining secondary circuit consists of the distributor cap and rotor, high tension wires, and spark plugs. These components conduct the high-voltage surges from the ignition coil to the spark plug air gaps.

Distributor Cap and Rotor

Function

The *distributor cap* and *rotor* receive the high-voltage surge from the secondary coil windings through a high-tension wire (Fig. 15-19). This surge enters the distributor cap through its center terminal,

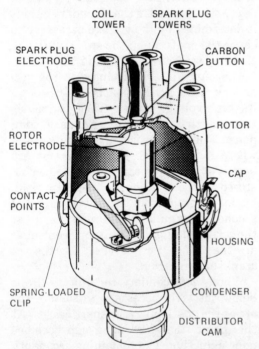

COIL TOWER   SPARK PLUG TOWERS

SPARK PLUG ELECTRODE

CARBON BUTTON

ROTOR ELECTRODE

ROTOR

CAP

CONTACT POINTS

HOUSING

SPRING-LOADED CLIP

CONDENSER

DISTRIBUTOR CAM

Fig. 15-19. A typical distributor cap and rotor.

known as the *coil tower.* The rotor carries this current from the coil tower to spark plug electrodes formed into the rim of the cap.

The rotor itself mounts on the upper distributor shaft and rotates with it. As a result, the rotor electrode moves from one cap spark plug electrode to another, following the specific firing order of the engine.

Distributor Cap Design

Manufacturers form distributor caps from silicon plastic, bakelite, or a similar material that resists chemical attack and provides protection for other distributor parts. In the center of the cap is the contact terminal (coil tower) for the high-tension wire from the coil. This terminal contains a carbon insert, which carries the current from the high-tension coil lead to the raised portion of the electrode, mounted on the rotor.

Also, spaced around the cap are the high-tension spark plug towers from which high-tension wires carry the current to the spark plugs. There is one of these towers for each spark plug, and inside each is a metal electrode, either copper or aluminum. Copper electrodes are necessary if the cap has high-tension wires with metal conductors; whereas, aluminum electrodes are necessary if the wire has a nonmetallic conductor. Finally, the cap itself secures to the distributor housing either by screws or two or more spring-loaded clips.

Rotor Design

Manufacturers make the rotor of silicon plastic, bakelite, or a similar synthetic material that is a good insulator. A metal electrode fastens to the top of the rotor and conducts current from the carbon button terminal of the coil tower to the individual plug electrodes in the distributor cap.

The rotor itself keys to the distributor shaft in order for the shaft to drive it and to maintain its proper relationship with the shaft, along with the spark plug electrodes inside the cap. The keying mechanism may be in the form of a flat or slot, machined into the top of the shaft, which mates with a similar arrangement in the rotor. While most rotors are handpressed onto the shaft, others secure into position over the mechanical advance mechanism by two screws.

Rotor Air Gap

In operation, an air gap exists between the tip of the rotor electrode and the spark plug electrode in the cap. This air gap is usually a few thousandths of an inch and is necessary to prevent the two electrodes from making contact. This action, of course, would cause both units to wear out very quickly.

Since this gap is not measurable in the assembled distributor, the technician can only check the voltage necessary to create an arc between the two electrodes. In this regard, only about 3,000 volts are necessary to create the arc across the normal air gap. However, some late-model distributors require as much as 9,000 volts. In other words, there is less of an air gap if only 3,000 volts are necessary to create the arc than on units with a 9,000-volt requirement. The larger air gaps are necessary in some systems to add additional resistance to the secondary circuit.

High-Tension Wires

Each ignition system has a number of high-tension wires or cables (Fig. 15–20). These units carry the high-voltage surges not only from the coil to the distributor but from the distributor towers to the various spark plugs.

These cables have a somewhat smaller conductor than those used in the primary-circuit wiring that carries current from the battery to the coil. But the cables have thick insulation designed to prevent leakage of the high-voltage current. In addition, this insulation must be strong enough to withstand vibration, heat, abrasion, and oil.

The high voltage carried by these wires together with atmosphere and oil conditions can cause the insulation to become brittle and crack open. If water and dust enter any minute cracks in this insulation,

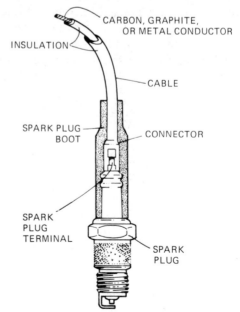

Fig. 15–20.   A common high-tension cable.

an electrical path is formed that partially grounds the high-tension voltage and thus weakens the arc at the spark plug.

Corona is another condition that deteriorates high-tension wiring. The surge of high-voltage current through this wiring builds up a magnetic field or corona around the cable's conductor. This field of energy is so strong that it breaks down the surrounding air into its constituent parts, chiefly nitrogen and oxygen. The oxygen forms ozone, which attacks rubber components in the insulation if the manufacturer does not properly protect it. Rubber subjected to ozone for a considerable length of time loses its elasticity, cracks down to the conductor, and thereby becomes useless as an insulator.

Since high resistance is not a great factor in the connections of the high-tension cables, manufacturers usually equip them with a snap-type connector. However, the design of these connectors is such that they make a physically strong contact with the coil and distributor towers along with the spark plug terminals.

High-tension cables also have special insulating boots over their connectors (Fig.

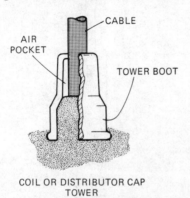

Fig. 15-21. *Over each connector of the cable is a boot.*

15-21). These boots have two purposes. First, the boots prevent the entrance of water or other foreign material into the connections, whether at the distributor tower or at the spark plug. Second, the boots provide a strong insulator for the snap connectors on each end of the cable.

Before 1960, the conductors inside the cable were usually metal such as copper or aluminum. However, in the early 1960s there was a general adoption of the so-called TVRS (television-radio-suppression) high-tension cable. Its function was to reduce interference with television and radio reception, caused by the emission of high-frequency waves from the vehicle's ignition system.

The conductor in this cable type consists of fibers, such as linen, nylon, or fiber glass, impregnated with particles of carbon or graphite. The physical contact between the carbon or graphite particles conducts the electricity.

These nonmetallic conductors cause a given amount of resistance within the cable. This resistance amounts to about 4,000 ohms per foot of cable length. This resistance provides the suppression necessary to avoid the unwanted television and radio interference and does not decrease the effectiveness of the ignition system because there is no current flowing prior to the occurrence of the arc.

Before manufacturers used this type of cable, there was no resistance at all to small current surges in the cable that resulted from the coil's induced voltage attempting to jump the spark plug's gap. There can be a whole series of these preliminary surges; at the end of the sparking cycle, the spark may stop and attempt to reform several times. The effect of all this is that the metallic wire acts as a transmitting antenna, sending out high-frequency waves that interfere with television and radio reception. However, the resistance in the nonmetallic wire tends to concentrate or hold back these surges, reducing their number, until the coil's voltage is high enough to establish and maintain the arc at the spark plug. This has the effect of reducing the high-frequency waves emitting from the cables.

As soon as the arc occurs at the plug, a few milliamperes of current flow for a brief period of time within the cable. But since the arc has already ignited the fuel/air mixture in the cylinder, the added resistance has no real effect on engine operation because more than sufficient voltage is available in the coil for good ignition.

The use of suppression cable also has another positive effect. The added resistance in this cable type also apparently reduces spark plug electrode erosion. This makes the plugs last a little longer. Consequently, the use of metallic conductor cables on a system that should have TVRS cable leads to increased plug electrode erosion and, of course, interference with nearby television and radio sets.

Also, late-model emission-controlled engines run much hotter than early-model engines with no control devices. Old-style ignition cables do not last in these high underhood temperatures. This is due to the fact that newer high-temperature cables have insulation of either hyplon or silicon materials. Therefore, you must exercise care and use the proper high-temperature secondary cable when replacing defective cables on emission-controlled engines.

Another precaution to be aware of when replacing cables is that the distributor cap electrode inserts used with TVRS cables must be aluminum. Old-model engines, with metal conductor cables, have copper inserts in the cap. The mixing of the distributor caps or cable types produces corrosion, which adds resistance to the secondary circuit.

Because of the voltage reserve built into the coil, the secondary portion of the ignition circuit can tolerate considerable resistance in its circuit—up to about 20,000 ohms without any undesirable effect. Primarily, if the total resistance becomes too high, the circuit uses up coil voltage reserve until it reaches a point where the coil can no longer produce sufficient voltage to cause an arc at the spark plug. At this point, the plug does not fire.

The suppression of television and radio interference is also obtainable by using resistor spark plugs, the early versions of which had a resistance of about 10,000 ohms. When the manufacturer used this type of plug, the spark plug high-tension cables had metallic conductors. However, the newer resistor-type spark plugs now have a total resistance of 5,000 ohms, and manufacturers do install them with TVRS cables because the total resistance of both does not affect engine performance.

Since the conductor within a TVRS cable is more fragile than the metal-type conductor, you must handle it more carefully. When removing the cable from a spark plug or distributor cap, apply a steady pull on the rubber boot rather than to the cable itself. Never jerk on the cable because rough treatment can cause a break in the conductor and a spark gap inside the insulation. The break gradually gets larger and forms an "open" in the conductor, or an "open" occurs between the conductor and its connector.

Spark Plugs

Function

A spark plug threads into each combustion chamber of the engine. These spark plugs each provide an air gap through which high-voltage current from the coil flows across in the form of an arc. This arc in turn ignites the air/fuel mixture at the end of each piston's compression stroke.

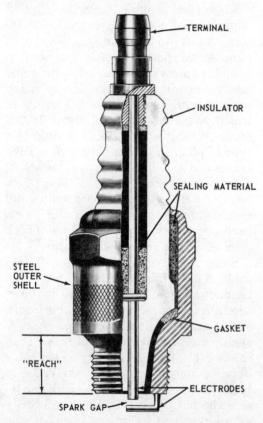

Fig. 15-22. *The design of a typical spark plug. (Courtesy of Deere & Company Technical Services)*

Design

The three basic parts of a typical spark plug (Fig. 15-22) are a ceramic core or insulator, two electrodes, and a sealed shell. The *ceramic core* performs several functions. For example, the core insulates the center electrode so that the current passing through it will not leak off to ground. In addition, the core itself acts as a conductor to transfer heat away from the center electrode.

Each spark plug will have two *electrodes* made of a special heavy wire. The center or insulated electrode extends through the insulated core, and this electrode may have a resistor built into it. The ground electrode, on the other hand, is formed into the shell of the spark plug. The manufacturer bends this electrode inward toward the center electrode.

The *metal shell* also has two main functions. First, the shell holds the core and the electrodes into a gastight assembly. Several seals or gaskets prevent leakage between these assembly components. Second, the shell also has threads for the installation of the plug into the combustion chamber.

Other Spark Plug Design Features

Reach

Manufacturers make many different sizes and designs of spark plugs to fit various engines. The most important design differences among spark plugs are reach, heat range, threads and seat, in addition to air gap. The *reach* of a given spark plug refers to the length of the shell from its contact surface at the seat to the bottom of the shell itself, including all threaded and unthreaded portions. The reach of the spark plug is important so that the plug's air gap is in proper position to ignite the air/fuel mixture in the combustion chamber effectively.

If you install a spark plug with too short a reach, the electrodes are in a pocket, and the arc at the electrodes cannot ignite the air/fuel mixture (Fig. 15-23). In addition, the exposed threads in the engine's cylinder head accumulate carbon deposits, which must be removed before you can install the correct plug.

If, on the other hand, the spark plug reach is too long (Fig. 15-24), the exposed plug threads could get hot enough to ignite the air/fuel mixture at the wrong time, causing preignition. Also, plug removal may be difficult due to the carbon deposits on the plug threads. Finally, engine damage results if the electrodes or shell interfere with the moving piston.

Heat Range

The heat range of a spark plug is the primary factor governing its performance

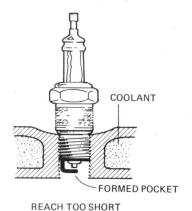

REACH TOO SHORT
INTO COMBUSTION CHAMBER

Fig. 15-23. An installed plug with insufficient reach.

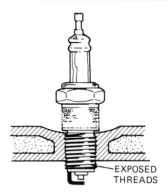

SPARKPLUG REACH TOO LONG
INTO COMBUSTION CHAMBER

Fig. 15-24. An installed plug with excessive reach.

under various operating conditions. The term *heat range* simply refers to the classification of spark plugs by how well they transfer heat from their firing end to the cooling system of the engine (Fig. 15-25).

Earlier this text pointed out that a spark plug must maintain an even flow of heat from its firing end to avoid becoming a source of preignition. At the same time, a spark plug must operate hot enough to burn off combustion deposits. Such contaminants would, if allowed to remain, cause a short-circuiting of the voltage at the plug tip, resulting in a subsequent misfire.

Basically speaking, manufacturers specify a given spark plug as being cold or hot. A *cold spark plug* (Fig. 15-25) has a short insulator-core tip that provides a shorter path for heat to travel; it permits the heat to dissipate rapidly to the cooling system, in order to maintain a lower electrode temperature. The heat actually transfers from the electrode, to the insulator, through the plug shell, and finally into the engine's cooling system.

A *hot plug* has a long insulator tip. This

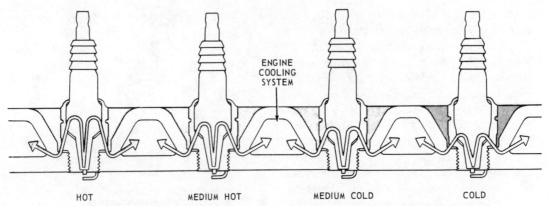

HOT   MEDIUM HOT   MEDIUM COLD   COLD

Fig. 15-25.   The heat range of a spark plug is a way of classifying how well a plug transfers heat away from its firing end. (Courtesy of Deere & Company Technical Services)

creates a longer path for the heat to travel. As a result, this maintains a higher center electrode temperature.

When replacing spark plugs, take note of the specifications for the plug type recommended by the manufacturers of the engine and plugs. This, however, does not necessarily mean that you must adhere to the recommended heat range, because they are recommendations only. The primary use of a particular engine is the controlling factor in the selection of a spark plug's heat range. For instance, continued heavy driving requires a much cooler plug than stop-and-go or idle operation.

Threads and Seats

Manufacturers of automotive spark plugs produce plugs with two different thread diameters: 14-millimeter and 18-millimeter (Fig. 15-26). The 14-millimeter plug may have a flat seat that requires a gasket or have a tapered seat that does not. However, the gasket type of 14-millimeter plug is the more common of the two found in automotive engines. On the

other hand, all 18-millimeter spark plugs have a tapered seat that matches a similar seat in the cylinder head. Consequently, no gasket is necessary.

The steel shell of the spark plug has also a hex shape above the threads. This shape accommodates a socket wrench for use in removal and installation of the plug. A 14-millimeter tapered-seat plug has a shell that accommodates a $\frac{5}{8}$-inch hex socket. A 14-millimeter spark plug using a gasket and an 18-millimeter tapered-seat plug

14mm SPARKPLUGS

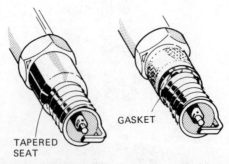

TAPERED SEAT

GASKET

Fig. 15-26.   An automotive spark plug may have a thread diameter of either 14 or 18 millimeters.

both have shells with a $\frac{13}{16}$-inch hex, for use with a $\frac{13}{16}$-inch socket wrench.

Air Gap

Another important factor that influences plug life and engine performance is the amount of spark plug *air gap*. An air gap, for example, that is too narrow increases current flow. However, this may lead to prematurely burned electrodes. A gap that is too wide requires higher voltage to create an arc. This causes a misfire if the required voltage is too great.

The typical air gaps for standard-ignition systems range between 0.030 to 0.040 inch (0.75 to 1.0 millimeter). But several of the electronic ignition systems utilize air gaps ranging from 0.045 to 0.080 inch (1.0 to 2.0 millimeters). This wider gap is necessary to fire the leaner air/fuel mixtures of late-model engines.

Manufacturers produce special spark plugs for use in electronic systems. This is necessary because the standard plug's negative electrode does not handle the larger opening without, in most cases, some damage.

Spark Plug Operation

There are two types of discharge across the spark plug air gap: *capacitive* and *inductive*. When the coil first delivers a high-voltage surge to the spark plug's center electrode, the air/fuel mixture within the air gap is not at first ready to conduct the arc. In other words, the mixture momentarily acts as an insulator. In this situation, the spark plug acts as a capacitor or condenser with the center electrode storing the negative charge and the grounded electrode storing a more positive charge—one having less electron buildup than the center electrode. The air gap acts as a dielectric insulator in much the same way as the insulating material does between the two conducting strips of a condenser.

Having the center electrode with a more negative polarity is an opposite condition from what you might expect in a normal negative-ground electrical system. However, a negative polarity at the center electrode is necessary because this decreases the voltage required for ignition. This effect is due to the high operating temperatures of the center electrode and the fact that electrodes leave a hotter surface and travel to a cooler surface at a lower voltage.

In a very short time, the secondary voltage of the coil increases, which strengthens the charges at the electrodes. This action increases the difference in potential between these two electrodes until it is great enough to ionize the spark plug gap. That is, this voltage changes the air/fuel mixture in the gap from a nonconductor to a conductor. To ionize the air/fuel mixture simply means breaking up its molecules into two or more oppositely charged ions. As a result, the dielectric resistance of the air gap breaks down, and current flows between the electrodes. The voltage level at this instant is known as *ionization voltage*. This voltage is much higher than what is necessary to maintain the arc at the air gap.

The current that flows across the arc gap at this moment of ionization is the capacitive discharge portion of the spark. It flows from the more negatively charged center electrode to the less negatively charged ground electrode. This current flow uses the energy stored in the plug itself when it acted as a condenser before ionization. Finally, this portion of the arc starts the combustion process within the combustion chamber.

This ionization voltage is usually at a lesser level than that produced in the secondary windings. The remaining voltage (the amount of voltage not necessary to force ionization) dissipates as current flows across the air gap of the spark plug. This is known as the *inductive* portion of the discharge and causes the visible flash, or arc, seen at the plug's electrodes. It actually contributes nothing to the combustion of the air/fuel mixture, but the arc is the cause of electrical interference and severe electrode erosion. The TVRS cables or resistance spark plugs suppress this inductance portion of the spark discharge.

Ignition Polarity

The center electrode must have a negative polarity to function at a reduced voltage. This negative polarity is the result of the internal wiring connections within the coil (Fig. 15–27). In this case, one end of the secondary coil attaches to the positive primary terminal. The opposite end of the coil then connects to the coil's center tower. This provides the negative polarity at the high-voltage tower and the plug's center electrode as long as the coil's primary terminals connect into the battery circuit with the correct polarity, as shown in the illustration.

If for some reason someone incorrectly connects the coil into the battery circuit or reverses the battery cables, the polarity of the coil reverses. In this instance, the voltage leaving the center tower of the coil will have a positive charge. This results in the coil having to produce between 20 and 50 percent more voltage to fire the spark

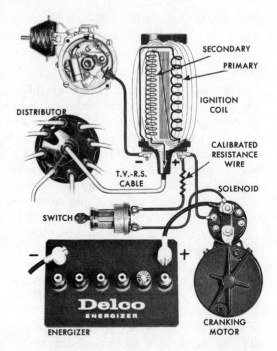

Fig. 15–27. A coil with internal connects producing a negative polarity at the spark plug center electrode. (Courtesy of Delco Remy)

plug because electrons flow much easier from a hotter center electrode to the cooler ground electrode.

Spark-Advance Mechanisms

In order for the rotor and cap of the distributor to deliver to the spark plug an arc at the correct moment in the engine's cycle under all conditions of rpm and load, most distributor assemblies have two spark advance mechanisms: a centrifugal advance and a vacuum advance. The *centrifugal advance* mechanism times the high-voltage surge so that it fires the air/fuel charge at the correct instant, as determined by engine rpm. When the engine is idling, for example, the timing of the arc usually occurs in the cylinder just before the piston reaches TDC.

At higher engine rpm, however, a shorter interval of time is available for the mixture to ignite, burn, and give up its energy to the piston. Consequently, in order to obtain the maximum power from the mixture, it is necessary at higher rpm for the ignition system to deliver the spark to the cylinder much earlier in the cycle. To illustrate this point, assume that the combustion time of a given charge of air/fuel mixture in a combustion chamber is 0.003 second. Also, to obtain full power from this combustion, the burning mixture must reach maximum pressure while the piston is 10 to 20 degrees past TDC. At 1,000 rpm, the crankshaft travels through 18 degrees in 0.003 of a second. However, at 2,000 rpm, the crankshaft moves through 36 degrees of rotation. Since the maximum pressure point is a fixed factor, it is easy to see why the spark requires delivery into the cylinder earlier in the cycle as engine speed increases, in order for the burning mixture to deliver full power.

The centrifugal advance mechanism changes the timing of the arc in relation to engine speed. In order to do this, the mechanism itself assembles onto the distributor shaft (Fig. 15–28). The mechanism consists primarily of two weights and a cam assembly. The two weights connect to the distributor drive shaft by two springs. The distributor cam along with the distributor rotor mounts on a second shaft. This second shaft fits over the drive distributor shaft like a sleeve. The motion of the distributor drive shaft transfers to the second shaft through the two weights.

When the weights move, the relative

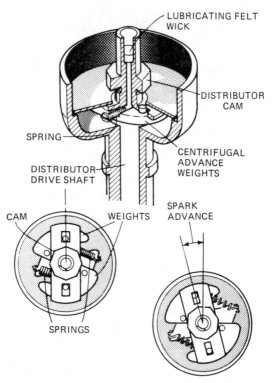

Fig. 15–28.   The design and operation of a typical centrifugal advance mechanism.

position of the driving shaft and the second shaft changes. When engine rpm increases, the driving shaft speed goes up. As a result, the advance weights move outward due to centrifugal force. This movement shifts the second shaft and cam along with its attached rotor ahead of the rotation of the driving shaft. Thus, the cam opens the ignition points earlier than at lower engine speeds, which results in the spark appearing sooner in the engine's cycle.

Each advance weight connects to the driving shaft by a control spring. The manufacturer selects the springs to permit the correct amount of weight movement and ignition advance for a particular engine. At low engine rpm, spring tension

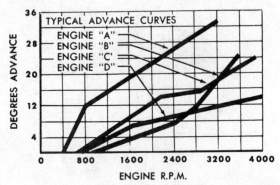

Fig. 15-29. *The typical advance curves of four different engines. (Courtesy of Delco Remy)*

holds the weights inward, which maintains the engine's basic ignition timing. But as engine speed increases, centrifugal force overcomes spring tension and the weights move outward to advance the second shaft and cam. This action permits the cam to open the points sooner.

This advancing of the timing is not a rapid change but rather a slow, gradual shift. Consequently, timing varies from no advance at idle (basic timing) to full advance at high engine speed, where the weights reach the outer limits of their travel (Fig. 15-29).

Vacuum Advance

During part-throttle engine operation, a high vacuum exists within the intake manifold, and a smaller amount of air and fuel enters the cylinder. Under these conditions, additional spark advance (over and above the advance provided by the centrifugal advance mechanism) increases fuel economy. Consequently, in order to achieve maximum power and economy, the arc at the plugs must occur still earlier in the cycle than it would using only the centrifugal advance mechanism.

To provide a spark advance based on intake manifold vacuum, most distributors have a vacuum advance mechanism (Fig. 15-30). This mechanism consists of a spring-loaded diaphragm, which fits inside a metal housing. The spring-loaded diaphragm connects by linkage to the distributor breaker plate.

The housing on the spring-loaded side of the diaphragm is airtight, but it connects by a hose or tubing to a vacuum passage in the carburetor. This opening, in most cases, is on the atmospheric side of the throttle valve. Consequently, when the throttle valve is in the idle position, no vacuum is acting on the diaphragm. The housing chamber on the other side of the diaphragm is open to the atmosphere.

With this arrangement, any throttle-valve travel past the idle position causes

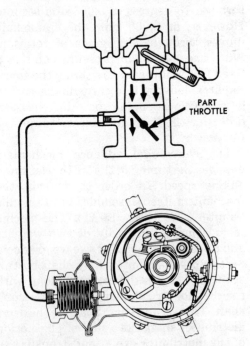

Fig. 15-30. *A typical vacuum advance mechanism. (Courtesy of Delco Remy)*

the valve to swing past the vacuum opening. Intake manifold vacuum can draw air from the airtight chamber in the vacuum advance chamber. This causes atmospheric pressure on the opposite side of the diaphragm to push it over against spring tension. This motion transmits by linkage to the distributor breaker plate assembly, causing it to rotate. The actual amount of breaker plate rotation is governed by the amount of vacuum in the intake manifold, up to the limit imposed by the vacuum-advance mechanism.

When it rotates, the breaker plate assembly and the attached contact points move around the breaker cam to an advanced position. This action causes the breaker cam to contact the rubbing block of the movable point, opening it sooner in the cycle. This provides a spark advance based on the amount of intake manifold vacuum. Thus, for varying compression pressures in the cylinder, this spark advance varies, permitting greater economy of engine operation. However, understand that this additional advance, provided by this vacuum control, is effective only in providing additional economy at or during part-throttle operation.

At any particular engine speed, a certain definite advance results from the operation of both the centrifugal and vacuum advance mechanisms (Fig. 15-31). For example, on the curve shown, an initial spark advance of 5 degrees plus a centrifugal advance of 10 degrees makes a total of 15 degrees of spark advancement at 40 mph. However, with the throttle only partially open, there may be an additional vacuum advance up to 15 degrees more, for a total of 30 degrees of advancement. But if the throttle valve is wide open, there is no appreciable vacuum in the intake manifold, so this additional ad-

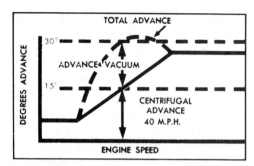

Fig. 15-31. A typical advance curve indicating that total spark advance results from vacuum plus centrifugal advance operation. (Courtesy of Delco Remy)

vance will disappear. Therefore, the centrifugal-advance mechanism alone will supply all the advance in ignition timing, based on engine speed alone.

Spark-Timing Emission Controls

Manufacturers use spark-timing control systems on late-model automobiles to reduce exhaust emissions. Specific engine-operating conditions produce certain types of air pollutants. As a result, the use of special spark-timing control systems helps reduce such things as hydrocarbon (HC) and, to some extent, oxides of nitrogen (NOx) emissions. These control mechanisms are detailed later in the chapters on emission control.

Firing Order

To permit all engine cylinders to produce power once in each 720 degrees of crankshaft rotation, manufacturers arrange the pistons and rods onto the crankshaft in a given order. This is known as *engine's firing order*, and it varies for different engine designs (Fig. 15-32). The design of firing order reduces engine rocking and imbalance caused by the power strokes of the pistons.

Manufacturers assign numbers to the engine cylinders for easy identification. But the cylinders do not produce power in the order of their numbering. In-line engines, for instance, are usually numbered from front to rear with cylinder 1 at the front.

The numbering sequence for V-type engines may be different between manufacturers. In some engines, all the odd-numbered cylinders (1, 3, 5, and 7) are on one bank and all the even on the other. On others, the right-bank cylinders, begin-ning at the front, have the numbers 1, 2, 3, and 4, and the left bank 5, 6, 7, and 8.

Cylinder 1 of all automotive engines begins the firing order. Then, the remaining cylinders fire in sequence (Fig. 15-32). As a result, the firing of the fuel charge within cylinder 1 is used as the basis for setting basic ignition timing on the engine and for checking the advance curves of the distributor.

Review

This section will assist you in determining how well you remember the material in this chapter. Read each item carefully. If you can't complete the statement, review

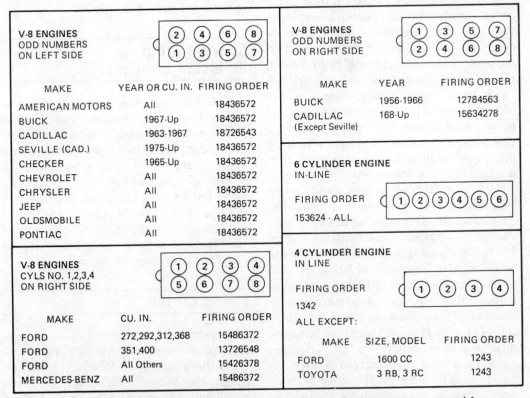

Fig. 15-32. *The numbering sequence and firing order vary among different engine designs.*

the section in the chapter that covers the material.

1. The device that maintains a desired primary-circuit voltage is the __

   _____.
   a. coil
   b. resistor
   c. points
   d. switch

2. Voltage at the primary coil during engine cranking is about _____ volts.
   a. 6
   b. 8
   c. 10
   d. 12

3. The component of the ignition system that becomes an electromagnet is the

   _____ _____.
   a. primary coil
   b. secondary coil
   c. contact points
   d. ignition resistor

4. The distributor _____ opens the contact points.
   a. cam
   b. shaft
   c. weight
   d. rotor

5. The _____ prevents excessive arcing at the points.
   a. bypass
   b. switch
   c. coil
   d. condenser

6. The unit of measurement of condenser capacity is _____.
   a. ohms
   b. amperes
   c. microfarads
   d. volts

7. The magnetic field around the primary coil collapses when the points

   _____.
   a. close
   b. open

8. The condenser discharges back through the _____ _____.
   a. primary coil
   b. secondary coil
   c. primary resistor
   d. battery circuit

9. The portion of the ignition circuit that produces the high-voltage surge is the

   _____ _____.
   a. contact points
   b. ignition condenser
   c. secondary coil
   d. primary coil

10. Voltage induced into the secondary coil may exceed _____ volts.
    a. 10,000
    b. 15,000
    c. 20,000
    d. 25,000

11. The _____ keys onto the distributor shaft.
    a. cap
    b. rotor
    c. points
    d. condenser

12. The metal used for the conductor in high-tension cable is copper or ____

    _____.
    a. aluminum
    b. lead
    c. iron
    d. steel

13. TVRS cables have graphite or ____ _____ conductors.
    a. copper
    b. aluminum
    c. carbon
    d. antimony

14. The secondary circuit can tolerate up to _____ ohms of resistance.
    a. 7,000
    b. 15,000
    c. 20,000
    d. 30,000

15. The _____ _____ of a spark plug is the primary factor governing its performance.
    a. shell reach
    b. heat range
    c. thread diameter
    d. air gap

16. In a standard ignition system, spark plug air gap ranges from 0.030 to _____ inch.
    a. 0.040
    b. 0.050
    c. 0.060
    d. 0.070

17. The center electrode requires a _____ polarity.
    a. negative
    b. positive

18. The centrifugal-advance changes ignition timing in relation to _____.
    a. vehicle speed
    b. engine vacuum
    c. engine speed
    d. engine load

19. To provide additional economy, the _____ _____ alters ignition timing.
    a. manifold vacuum
    b. throttle valve
    c. vacuum advance
    d. centrifugal advance

20. The sequence by which combustion occurs in an engine is known as the _____ _____.
    a. numbering sequence
    b. firing order
    c. firing sequence
    d. cylinder sequence

For the answers, turn to the Appendix.

A standard ignition system requires maintenance at regular intervals in order to prevent malfunctions. The frequency of the service is usually specified by the engine or system manufacturer; it varies from 5,000 to 10,000 miles. However, the type of vehicle operation influences the service life of some of the system components. For example, short-term, stop-and-go driving causes more rapid point wear and a tendency to load up the spark plugs with combustion chamber deposits. In this case, these system components usually require service more often. The best kind of vehicle operation, with regard to ignition system longevity, is for periods of extended driving under moderate loads.

Of course, the tune-up technician not only performs the preventive maintenance on this system but must work on vehicles towed into the shop due to the failure of one or more ignition system components. In this situation, the mechanic must perform a series of tests and inspections on the components in order to locate the *cause* of the malfunctions. In other words, the technician performs diagnostic as well as repair services on the system.

In regard to standard ignition system maintenance, this chapter covers the routine tests, inspection, replacement, and adjustment procedures on system components. The components involved in this discussion are the ballast resistor, ignition coil, distributor cap and rotor, spark plugs, points and condenser, and distributor advance mechanisms.

Ballast Resistor

You can test the serviceability of a ballast-type and most other primary resistors with an ohmmeter. This type of test-

_____ Chapter 16

STANDARD IGNITION SYSTEM SERVICE

ing points out if the unit has high or infinite resistance, caused by an open circuit in the conductor.

The manufacturer specifies the exact amount of resistance that should be present in the resistor, whether ballast-type or a length of resistor wire. In the latter case, it is difficult to measure the resistance in the wire type because of it being inside a wiring harness, in many cases. In addition, testing is difficult because one end of this wire attaches to the ignition coil, while the other is inside the vehicle, connected to the ignition switch. In this situation, the easiest way to test the wire accurately is the volt-drop method, explained previously.

To test a typical ballast resistor or a primary resistor within the engine compartment:

1. Disconnect the battery ground cable or make sure that the ignition switch is off.

2. Disconnect the wiring connectors from the resistor.

3. Calibrate the ohmmeter as necessary, and connect its leads to the resistor terminals (Fig. 16-1). Note the results.

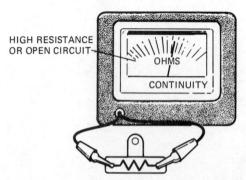

HIGH RESISTANCE OR OPEN CIRCUIT

OHMS

CONTINUITY

Fig. 16-1. Testing a ballast resistor with an ohmmeter.

Results and Indications

Compare this reading against the manufacturer's specifications (the average is 0.5 to 0.6 ohms):

1. If the reading is within specifications, the resistor is still serviceable.

2. If the meter reading is not within specifications, replace the resistor.

Ignition Coil Tests

Purpose

You can test an ignition coil on or off the vehicle using an ohmmeter, ammeter, voltmeter, or coil tester. For test purposes, the ohmmeter measures the coil for internal resistance and shorting; the ammeter measures current draw by the primary coil windings; and the voltmeter tests coil polarity. The coil tester measures a coil's efficiency in producing a secondary voltage.

Before testing an ignition coil, make sure that it is at its normal temperature (because coil resistance changes directly with increases in temperature) and inspect it for the following:

1. A cracked or burned high-voltage tower

2. A dented or cracked housing

3. Signs of oil leakage

4. Loose mounting and dirty and loose wiring connections

Resistance Test— Primary Windings

To measure the resistance in both the primary and secondary coil windings:

1. Disconnect the battery ground cable or the primary coil connections.

2. Calibrate the ohmmeter, and set it for a low-scale reading.

3. Connect one ohmmeter lead to the coil's positive (+) or battery terminal and the other lead to the negative (−) or distributor terminal (Fig. 16–2). Note the reading on the scale; disconnect the leads.

Results and Indications

Compare the reading to the manufacturer's specifications for primary winding resistance (usually about 1.5 to 1.8 ohms).

1. If the reading is satisfactory, proceed with the secondary-winding resistance test.

2. If the reading is not within specifications, replace the coil.

Resistance Test— Secondary Windings

To perform this test:

1. Calibrate the ohmmeter and set for a high-scale reading.

2. Connect one ohmmeter lead to the terminal within the high-voltage terminal

(Fig. 16–3) and the other lead to the positive (+) primary terminal (for coils used in a negative-ground battery system) or to the negative (−) primary terminal (for coils used in a positive-ground battery system). Note the reading and disconnect the leads.

Results and Indications

Compare the reading to the manufacturer's specifications for secondary winding resistance (should be about 9,500 to 11,500 ohms).

1. If the reading is satisfactory, proceed with the test for shorted windings.

2. If the reading is not within specifications, replace the coil.

Testing for Grounded Windings

To use an ohmmeter in testing a coil for grounded windings (Fig. 16–4):

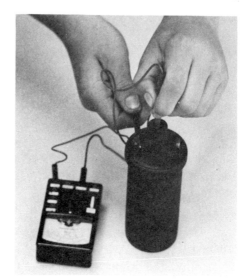

Fig. 16–3.   Testing the resistance of a coil's secondary windings.

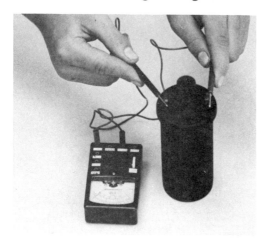

Fig. 16–2.   Testing the resistance of a coil's primary windings.

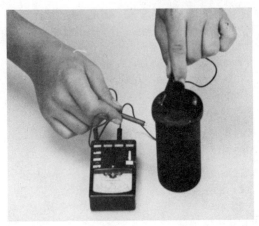

Fig. 16-4. Testing a coil for grounded windings.

1. Calibrate and set the ohmmeter for a low-scale reading.

2. Connect one ohmmeter lead to either primary terminal and the other to the metal case of the core. Note the reading.

Results and Indications

The meter must show infinite resistance (an open circuit). Any other reading than this indicates the coil has windings grounded to the case, and the coil requires replacement.

Current Test

Some manufacturers provide a current-draw specification for their ignition coil circuits. To check the amount of current draw through a typical coil circuit, using an ammeter, follow these steps.

1. Making sure that the ignition switch is off, disconnect the coil's positive (+) primary wire from the coil.

2. Connect the ammeter's positive (+) lead to the positive (+) primary wire connector and the ammeter's negative lead to

the positive (+) primary terminal of the coil (Fig. 16-5).

3. Remove the distributor cap; rotate the engine until the contact points close.

4. Turn on the ignition switch; note the ammeter reading.

5. Shut off the ignition switch; remove the ammeter leads; install the distributor cap and primary wire.

Results and Indications

Compare the ammeter reading to the manufacturer's specifications (should be around 3 amperes):

1. A zero ammeter reading indicates an open circuit in the primary circuit. In this case, the ignition system would not operate at all. Check for an open circuit in the primary resistor or insulated contact points.

2. If the reading is less than specifications, check for a discharged battery or high resistance in the primary resistor or wiring, in the coil's primary windings, or contact points.

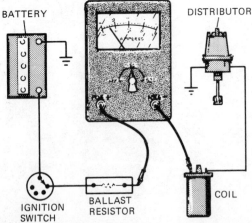

Fig. 16-5.   Checking the coil's current draw.

3. If the reading is more than specifications, check for a shorted coil or ballast resistor or for the installation of incorrect ballast resistor or coil for the vehicle.

Coil Polarity Test

As mentioned in the last chapter, the reversal of coil polarity increases the voltage requirements of the coil from 20 to 50 percent, but the engine still starts and runs. However, this condition can lead to plug misfire under some operating conditions.

If you cannot determine the proper polarity of a coil from the markings at the primary terminals, check it with a voltmeter or the visual test. If you use the voltmeter method, the meter should have a negative as well as a positive scale. That is, the zero-voltage position should be in the center of the scale. If the meter does not have this feature, it may sustain damage during the test.

Polarity Test with a Voltmeter

To perform this test:

1. Connect an adapter with an exposed terminal into any spark plug cable, either at the distributor cap or plug (Fig. 16-6).

2. Connect the voltmeter's positive (+) lead to a good engine ground and the negative (−) lead to the adapter.

3. Start and idle the engine, and note the direction the voltmeter needle moves.

Results and Indications

1. If the needle moves toward the positive scale, the coil's polarity is correct.

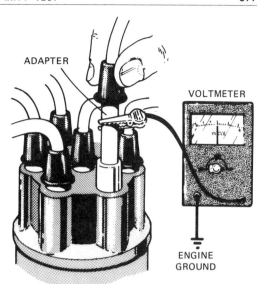

Fig. 16-6. Checking the coil's polarity with a voltmeter.

2. If the needle moves toward the negative scale, this indicates reverse coil polarity. Reversed coil polarity can result from incorrect primary-coil terminal connections or reversed cable connections at the battery. The latter, of course, would damage the alternator as well as other solid-state components.

Visual Coil Polarity Test

To check the polarity of a coil visually:

1. Remove the cable from any spark plug.

2. Hold a pencil (Fig. 16-7) between the cable terminal and the spark plug terminal.

3. Have someone crank the engine briefly with the starter motor.

4. Observe the spark at the exposed plug terminal.

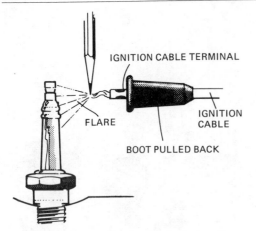

IGNITION CABLE TERMINAL

IGNITION CABLE

FLARE

BOOT PULLED BACK

Fig. 16-7. Visually checking the coil's polarity.

Results and Indications

1. If the arc flares between the pencil tip and the spark plug, coil polarity is correct.

2. If the spark flares between the pencil tip and the cable, there is a reversal in coil polarity.

Checking Coils with a Tester

Special coil testers isolate the coil from the rest of the electrical system and test it separately under normal operating conditions. The tester itself may be a single piece of equipment or part of the console of an engine analyzer. In either case, the tester evaluates the coil ability to produce a secondary voltage.

Most coil testers include an ohmmeter for measuring the resistance of the coil windings and a cathode-ray tube for viewing the coil's voltage output trace. If the tester is part of an engine analyzer, the coil trace, during the test, is visible on the large central oscilloscope screen. Separate coil testers have a small cathode-ray tube that displays only the coil trace.

High-Tension Wires —Inspection

Inspect all high-tension secondary cables for:

1. Good connections at the spark plugs, distributor cap, and coil towers. Loose cable connections corrode and increase the resistance within the secondary circuit.

2. Damaged and worn boots. The boots should be in good condition and fit tightly over the coil and cap towers in addition to the spark plug insulators. Boots that are loose where they fit over the cable permit water to enter the towers or around the spark plug electrodes, causing ignition malfunction. *Note:* To maintain proper sealing between the boots, cable, and the coil or distributor towers, do not remove the cables or boots from these areas unless the wires require testing or replacement.

3. The presence of oil, grease, or dirt. As necessary, clean the high-tension cables with a cloth moistened with a nonflammable solvent and wipe dry.

4. Frayed, burned, or cracked insulation. To check for cracked or brittle insulation, *carefully* and slightly bend each cable. Replace any high-tension cables that are brittle, cracked, burned, or frayed.

Testing High-Tension Cables—Insulation Breakdown

You can test high-tension cables for insulation breakdown and high resistance with an oscilloscope. Chapters 25 and 26 of this text will explain this procedure, along with others dealing with oscilloscope testing of the entire ignition system.

If an oscilloscope is not available, you can also test a secondary cable for insulation breakdown with the following procedure.

1. With the engine off, connect one end of a test probe (Fig. 16–8) to a good ground. You will use the free end of the tool for probing the cables.

2. One at a time, disconnect each spark plug cable at the plug itself. Insulate the plug connector from ground.

3. Start the engine, and move the free end of the test probe along the entire length of the wire. Do not touch the wire; keep the probe at least 1/16 inch away from the cable. If insulation breakdown is present, there is a noticeable arcing from the faulty area to the probe.

4. You can also test the secondary-coil wire in the same manner. However, do not ground one end of this cable; instead, remove and insulate one of the spark plug cables while running the probe along the coil cable. Replace any leaking secondary cables.

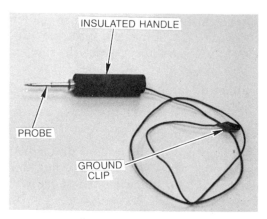

Fig. 16–8. A test probe used to check for insulation breakdown.

High-Tension Cable and Distributor Cap Removal

In order to test a cable for excessive resistance with an ohmmeter, it is first necessary to remove the cable from the spark plug and the cap from the distributor. To remove these components:

1. Grasp the cable by hand as close as possible to the spark plug (Fig. 16–9). Then, remove it by twisting it back and forth very slightly and pulling the cable outward, using a straight and steady pull. Do not use pliers and do not pull on the cable on an angle. Doing so will damage the insulation, cable terminal, spark plug insulator, or the conductor within the TVRS cable.

2. Remove the distributor cap using one of these procedures:

a. On distributor caps held in place by spring clips, unsnap all the clips using the blade of a screwdriver. Then, lift the cap straight off the distributor.

b. On distributor caps held in position by screw-type latches, turn each latch with a screwdriver about one-half turn counterclockwise. Then, lift the cap straight off the distributor.

c. In both cases, carefully remove the high-tension cable from the top of the ignition coil.

Testing High-Tension Cables with an Ohmmeter

To check a TVRS or standard cable for opens, loose terminals, or high resistance with an ohmmeter, follow these directions.

1. Calibrate the ohmmeter as necessary, and set it for a high-meter reading.

Fig. 16-9. Removing a high-tension wire from the spark plug.

2. Connect one ohmmeter lead to the cable at the spark plug terminal (Fig. 16-10), and attach the other lead to the corresponding cable electrode *inside the distributor cap*. Note the reading on the meter scale.

3. Test all spark plug cables in this manner, noting the results.

4. Test the coil high-tension cable by connecting one ohmmeter lead to the connector at the end of the cable and the other to the center carbon button in the cap. Note the results.

Results and Indications

1. If all the readings are within specifications (an average of 4,000 ohms per foot of TVRS cable), the cables are in good condition.

2. If any reading is not within specifications, remove the cable from the cap tower, and recheck the cable's resistance.

If the reading is still not to specifications, replace the cable. If the resistance in the cable is satisfactory, check the cap tower for corrosion.

3. If the needle does not move at all while testing a cable, it is open circuited. Remove the cable from the cap and retest. If the reading still indicates an open circuit, replace the cable. If the cable checks satisfactorily, inspect the cap tower for corrosion or a burned-out electrode. Remove the corrosion or replace the cap.

Replacing High-Tension Cables

To replace a set of high-tension cables, follow this procedure:

1. Beginning at the front of the engine, remove one cable from the spark plug and distributor cap following the steps outlined earlier.

2. As necessary, remove the cable from any retaining bracket on the engine.

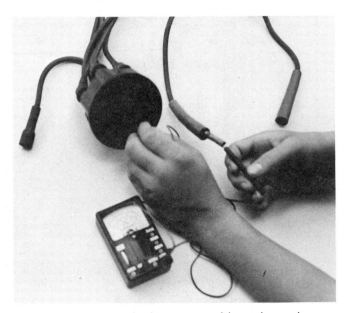

Fig. 16-10. Testing a high-tension cable with an ohmmeter.

3. Be sure that the cap tower is clean and free of corrosion. As necessary, remove accumulated corrosion from the cap tower, using the tool shown in Fig. 16-11. To perform this task, insert the small wire brush of the tool into the cap tower, and rotate it clockwise several turns. Then, remove the tool and blow out the tower, us-

Fig. 16-11. Removing corrosion from a tower in the cap.

ing low-pressure compressed air. Inspect the tower for cleanliness, and repeat the process as necessary until the tower is clean.

4. If using a universal cable set, one that fits many engine types, cut the new cable to length, using the old cable as a guide. Then, install a new boot and connector on the cap end of the wire. Make sure that the connector attaches properly to the cable and makes contact with the conductor inside the cable.

5. Insert the connector of the new universal or ready-made cable into the distributor cap tower so that its connector seats firmly into and the rubber boot seals over the tower. Then, pinch the large diameter of the boot to release trapped air between the boot and the tower (Fig. 16-12).

6. Install the spark plug end of the cable on the plug. Make sure that its connec-

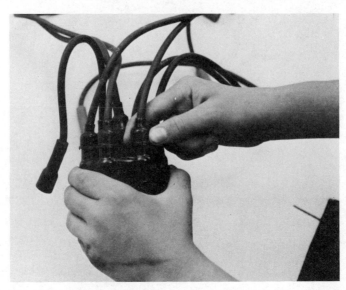

Fig. 16–12. *Removing trapped air from inside boot after installing the cable connector into cap.*

tor firmly seats on the spark plug terminal and the boot seals against its insulator.

7. Reconnect the cable to all retainer brackets.

8. Repeat these steps to install the other cables. Be sure to route all the cables as originally placed by the manufacturer in order to avoid cross firing and cable damage. In addition, secure the cables in their retaining brackets, and be certain that the cables do not touch the hot exhaust manifolds.

Distributor Cap— Inspection

Inspect the outside of the distributor cap for:

1. Cracks. Any cracks appearing on the outside of the distributor cap necessitate cap replacement.

2. Oil, grease, or dirt. Remove these contaminants with a rag moistened with a nonflammable solvent and wipe dry.

3. Carbon paths (Fig. 16–13). In this situation, replace the cap. After removing the cap from the distributor, check its interior for:

a. Cracks.

b. A worn carbon button.

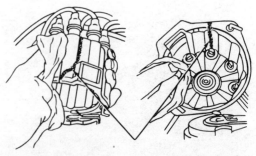

Fig. 16–13. *Carbon paths on the outside and inside of a distributor cap. (Courtesy of Deere & Co. Technical Services)*

3. Signs of carbon paths or runners (Fig. 16–13) from arcing current and moisture. Carbon paths inside the cap are usually between the spark plug electrodes or from an electrode to a grounded surface.

4. Burned or corroded spark plug electrodes.

5. Deposits of grayish-white aluminum oxide powder, caused from arcing and moisture in caps with aluminum electrodes. This oxide prematurely wears out the point rubbing block and distributor cam. Replace the cap if you find any cracks, worn carbon button, carbon paths, burned or corroded electrodes, or signs of aluminum oxide.

Distributor Cap Replacement

You can replace a distributor cap by following these steps.

1. Match up the replacement cap with the original to make sure that you have the correct part.

2. With a piece of chalk or similar marking device, locate and mark the position of the number-one spark plug cable tower on the new cap, using the old cap as a guide.

3. Beginning with the number-one cable, remove it from the old cap and install this cable into the new cap.

4. Continue this process, moving in a clockwise direction, until you have removed and installed each high-tension cable onto the new cap.

5. Following the procedure outlined under cable replacement, make sure that each cable connection seats firmly in its respective tower, and you have removed the excess air from each wire boot.

6. Reinstall the new cap onto the distributor, making certain that it seats properly, and the cap's hold-down spring clips or latches are correctly in place.

Spark Plugs—Removal

There are at least three general reasons why you must periodically remove spark plugs from the engine. First, it is necessary to remove these units to perform compression and leakage tests. Second, it is necessary, of course, to remove the plugs for routine replacement. In this regard, the spark plugs require replacement as often as every 5,000 miles or as seldom as 50,000 miles. This interval depends upon:

1. The type of ignition system
2. The type of engine design
3. The type of driving
4. The type of fuel used
5. The types of emission control devices used on the engine

Third, it is sometimes necessary to remove a spark plug before its normal replacement interval due to a misfiring condition. This may result from total plug failure or fouling of the unit due to a worn-out engine or other problems discussed later in this chapter.

No matter what the reason, the procedure for removing spark plugs is the same. To remove the spark plugs, follow this procedure.

1. As necessary, mark each cable as to which spark plug it attaches to, using a pencil and a piece of masking tape. Then, using the procedure mentioned earlier, carefully remove the cables from each spark plug.

2. Using a combination of a spark plug socket, extension, and ratchet shown in Fig. 16–14, loosen each plug one or two turns.

3. Blow the dirt away from the base of each spark plug at the cylinder head with compressed air.

4. Remove the plugs and place in a tray or holder in their installed or cylinder firing order for inspection later (Fig. 16–15).

5. On spark plug types using gaskets, make sure that the old gasket comes out of the plug seat with the removed unit. If not, remove the old gasket from the seat.

Spark Plug Inspection

After plug removal, you can diagnose a variety of engine conditions by examining the firing end of each plug. This is commonly known as *reading the plugs* and basically amounts to noting and making a diagnosis based on the type of deposits and the degree of electrode erosion.

Fig. 16–15. A tray used to hold the removed spark plugs in their installed or firing order. (Courtesy of AC Spark Plug Division of General Motors Corp.)

Normal Condition

Figure 16–16 illustrates a spark plug operating under normal engine conditions. In this case, the plug has operated at the correct temperature in a "healthy" engine. The few deposits present probably are light tan or gray in color with most regular grades of regular commercial gasoline. There is no evidence of electrode burning, and the growth in air gap averages not more than 0.001 inch per 1,000 miles of engine operation. Chances are if

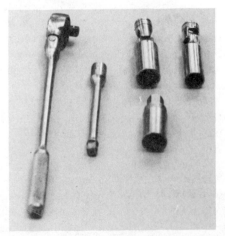

Fig. 16–14.   The various tools necessary to remove spark plugs.

Fig. 16–16.   The firing end of a spark plug that has operated under normal conditions. (Courtesy of AC Spark Plug Division of General Motors Corp.)

the plug shown in Fig. 16–16 has less than 10,000 miles of service, it is still serviceable. Consequently, you can reinstall the unit after cleaning, filing the electrodes, and regapping the electrodes to specifications.

Carbon Fouling

Figure 16–17 shows a spark plug that has carbon deposits brought about by what is known as *cold fouling*. This plug tip has a layer of dry, fluffy black carbon deposits due to an overly rich air/fuel mixture. This condition can result from a faulty choke, blocked air cleaner, improper idle air/fuel adjustment, dirty carburetor, or malfunctioning ignition system that causes plug misfiring. However, if only one or two plugs within a set indicate this type of fouling, it is a good idea to check for sticking valves. In addition, this condition can result from prolonged engine operation at idle. If this is the case and the vehicle operates extensively at idle and low speeds, you can improve plug life and service by using the next step hotter spark plug.

In any case, a fouled plug of this type is not the cause but the result of some other problem. Therefore, after eliminating the cause, you can reuse the plug after cleaning it, filing its electrodes, and resetting plug air gap.

Wet Fouling

Figure 16–18 points out a typical *wet-fouled* spark plug. In this situation, the firing tip has drowned in excess oil. If the plug has been in an old engine, suspect worn rings or excessive cylinder wear. Also, in an overhead valve engine, excessive amounts of oil may be coming into the combustion chamber past worn valve guides or defective valve-guide seals. On vehicles with automatic transmissions, the problem may be a defective vacuum modulator that allows engine vacuum to pull transmission fluid into the combustion chambers.

In such situations, the use of a hotter plug may relieve such fouling, but a hotter plug cannot take the place of an engine overhaul or the need to replace the modulator. Also, too hot a spark plug can cause preignition, which could bring about severe engine damage. Finally, a wet-fouled plug, in most cases, is reusable if cleaned and serviced properly.

Fig. 16–17. A typical cold-fouled spark plug firing tip. (Courtesy of AC Spark Plug Division of General Motors Corp.)

Fig. 16–18. A typical wet-fouled spark plug. (Courtesy of AC Spark Plug Division of General Motors Corp.)

Splash Fouling

Splash fouling of the firing end of a plug (Fig. 16–19) may occur after an overdue tune-up. In this case, red, brown, yellow, or white deposits in the combustion chamber, accumulated after a long period of misfiring, suddenly loosen when the tune-up restores normal combustion-chamber temperatures. Then, during a high-speed operation, these materials shred off the combustion chamber and cling to the hot insulator and electrode surfaces of the plug. If they happen to short out the plug, you can remove it for regular cleaning and maintenance. Next, you can reinstall the plug with good results as the engine has already scavenged itself.

Gap Bridging

A spark plug with a *bridged gap* (Fig. 16–20) is relatively rare in automobile engines. This condition also occurs due to flying deposits within the combustion chamber. In a few cases, fluffy deposits may accumulate within the plug during in-town driving. Then, when the driver places the engine under a hard load, this material can melt and bridge the gap.

Fig. 16–20. A spark plug with a bridged gap. (Courtesy of Chrysler Corp.)

This, of course, causes the plug to misfire. This plug condition is correctable by cleaning and servicing the unit.

High-Speed Glazing

Figure 16–21 illustrates a firing tip of a plug, contaminated by *high-speed glazing*. Most powdery combustion-chamber deposits have no adverse effect on plug operation as long as they remain in a powdery state. However, under high-speed operation, these deposits melt and form a shiny, yellow glaze coating on the insulator. This coating, when hot, acts as

Fig. 16–19. The firing tip of a spark plug that has splash fouling. (Courtesy of AC Spark Plug Division of General Motors Corp.)

Fig. 16–21. A plug's firing tip glazed by high-speed driving. (Courtesy of AC Spark Plug Division of General Motors Corp.)

a good electrical conductor. This permits the current to follow the deposits instead of jumping the gap, thus shorting out the spark plug.

Glazed deposits can be avoided in several ways. First, advise the driver not to apply a sudden load on the engine, such as wide-open throttle acceleration, after sustained periods of low-speed or idle operation. Second, you can install a colder plug in the engine if the driver operates the vehicle for long periods at high speeds.

It is almost impossible to remove glazed deposits effectively. Therefore, if and when they occur, just replace the spark plugs.

Overheating

A white or light-gray insulator that appears "blistered" indicates an *overheated* spark plug (Fig. 16-22). In this instance, electrode gap wear may be considerable— in excess of the 0.001 inch per 1,000 miles. Check for too hot a spark plug, overadvanced ignition timing, detonation, or cooling system malfunctions that can overheat a spark plug with the correct heat range. In addition, overheating can also result from lean air/fuel mixtures, low

octane fuel, improper installation procedures, or a stuck closed heat-riser valve. Install a new plug of the correct heat range, after correcting the cause of the problem.

Turbulence Burning

Turbulence burning of the firing tip of a spark plug (Fig. 16-23) causes the electrodes to wear away on one side. This is the direct result of normal turbulence patterns in the combustion chambers of certain engines. You can ignore it as long as normal plug life has occurred. However, if the air gap growth appears excessive, it may be due to overheating. In this case, check the same items as listed under the section on overheated plugs.

Preignition Damage

Preignition damage to the firing end of a plug is a direct result of excessive temperature (Fig. 16-24). This produces such things as melting of the electrodes or chipped, or broken electrode tips. Remember, the spark plug is like an electric fuse. When electrodes melt, they are warning you to look for the causes and also for damage inside the engine such as scuffed pistons or burned pistons or valves.

Fig. 16-22. A typical overheated spark plug. (Courtesy of AC Spark Plug Division of General Motors Corp.)

Fig. 16-23. A firing tip of a plug with turbulence burning. (Courtesy of AC Spark Plug Division of General Motors Corp.)

Fig. 16–24. A spark plug damaged by pre-ignition. (Courtesy of AC Spark Plug Division of General Motors Corp.)

In these cases, always inspect the plug for the proper heat range, for overadvanced ignition timing, loose spark plugs, burned head gasket, use of too-low octane fuel, and other general causes of engine overheating. After locating the cause of the problem, install the new spark plugs of the correct heat range.

Damage due to Reversed Coil Polarity

Figure 16–25 shows what can happen to the firing end of a plug due to reversed coil

Fig. 16–25. Negative electrode dishing due to reversed coil polarity. (Courtesy of AC Spark Plug Division of General Motors Corp.)

polarity. Note the slight dishing of the ground electrode and that the center electrode is not worn badly. The source of this condition along with misfiring and, in some cases, rough idling is the reversal of the primary coil leads and, in older vehicles, the reversal of battery polarity.

Spark Plug Cleaning

As a general rule, it is often more economical, in terms of labor costs, to install new plugs than to clean and regap

Fig. 16–26. A typical spark plug cleaner. (Courtesy of AC Spark Plug Division of General Motors Corp.)

the old ones. However, used plugs that are not excessively worn and misfired due to fouling or excessive deposits, can be cleaned for continued use.

For best results in removing carbon, oil, and oxide coating from the firing end of a spark plug, use an approved cleaner with special cleaning compound (Fig. 16-26) and this procedure.

1. Clean any oil or grease from the outside of the plug with a clean rag moistened with nonflammable cleaning solvent. If the lower end of the plug has an oily or wet deposit, brush this area with solvent. Then, dry the entire plug thoroughly with compressed air before cleaning in the machine. This action prevents gumming or caking of the cleaning compound deep within the plug.

2. Very carefully, with thin, needle-nose pliers or an electrode adjusting tool, bend back the side (ground) electrode about 0.010 inch for improved cleaning.

3. Install the correct adapter in the cleaner, and insert the plug into the cleaner (Fig. 16-27). Then, rotate the plug slowly while applying the cleaning blast to the plug.

4. Use the air blast from the machine to remove the cleaning abrasive from inside the plug. Next, inspect the inside of the plug to make sure that all the deposits are gone.

5. Use a hand-held or powered brush to clean threads of accumulated carbon or scale (Fig. 16-28). Be careful not to damage the electrodes or the insulator tip. The clean threads permit easier installation and proper seating of the plug, when you install it in the engine.

6. Because the cleaning operation does not always remove the oxide or scale deposits from the electrodes, clean the firing surfaces of the center and side electrodes with several strokes of a small, flat distributor point file or a spark plug gauge file (Fig. 16-29). This action reduces the required firing voltage of the plug.

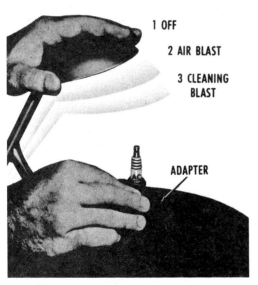

1 OFF

2 AIR BLAST

3 CLEANING BLAST

ADAPTER

Fig. 16-27. Using a cleaner to blast loose the deposits on the firing tip of a plug. (Courtesy of AC Spark Plug Division of General Motors Corp.)

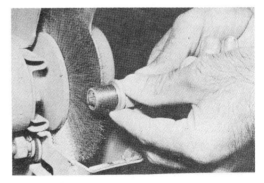

Fig. 16-28. Using a powered wire brush to clean plug threads. (Courtesy of AC Spark Plug Division of General Motors Corp.)

Fig. 16-29.   Cleaning the plug electrodes with a file. (Courtesy of AC Spark Plug Division of General Motors Corp.)

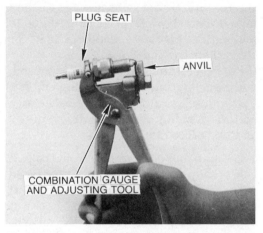

Fig. 16-30.   A combination gauge and air-gap adjusting tool.

Spark Plug Regapping

Both a new or a cleaned plug requires its air gap set to the exact limits specified by the engine manufacturer. Therefore, before attempting to regap a plug, always look up this specification in the appropriate service manual, and use an approved tool not only to measure the air gap but to *bend the side electrode* to make an adjustment.

Figure 16-30 shows a combination gauge and adjusting tool in use, regapping a plug. This tool is for use on new spark plugs only because it uses a flat gauge for the actual adjustment. The tool itself has a series of gauges mounted on it in the form of a spoked wheel. When the tool is in use, the correct size flat gauge fits between the two electrodes.

Above the gauge set is a flat anvil. This anvil rests over the top of the side electrode, and it applies force to the electrode as the technician applies pressure to the hand grips.

On the opposite end of the tool from the anvil is a curved seat. This seat performs two functions. First of all, the rest supports the spark plug shell during the regapping process. Second, the seat applies a force to the shell that attempts to move it toward the anvil when the mechanic squeezes the grips. As a result, the anvil pushes the ground electrode toward the shell. The action compresses the ground electrode against the gauge, thus setting the air gap.

Figure 16-31 illustrates the use of a

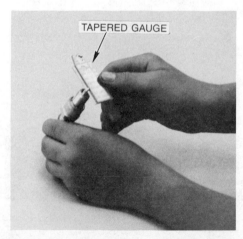

Fig. 16-31.   The design and use of a tapered-type spark plug regapping tool.

tapered-type regapping tool. This tool is nothing more than a flat, tapered piece of steel with the leading and tailing edges of two different dimensions. Between these points, the size of the gauge varies in thickness.

Above and to the right of the gauge is a scale. The scale itself indicates the thickness of the gauge at any given point. Thus, when the technician slides the gauge between the electrodes, it stops when the plug air gap size reaches the same thickness on the gauge. Then, the mechanic observes the scale reading in thousandths of an inch.

On the opposite end of the tool from the gauge are adjusting slots. The technician uses these slots to bend the ground electrode as necessary to adjust the air gap.

Figure 16–32 pictures the use of a round wire gauge to set the air gap of a new plug. However, the round gauge is necessary on a used plug due to the fact that the electrodes on such a plug are no longer flat. Consequently, the use of a flat gauge for regapping purposes would result in an inaccurate reading (Fig. 16–33).

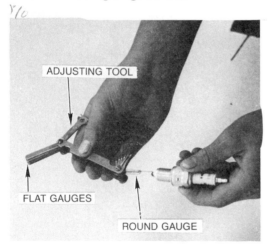

Fig. 16–32. A combination round and flat feeler-gauge set.

Fig. 16–33. Always use a round gauge on used spark plugs because a flat gauge cannot accurately measure the true width of the gap. (Courtesy of AC Spark Plug Division of General Motors Corp.)

The gauge set shown in Fig. 16–32 is several tools in one unit. For example, the tool has a series of individual wire gauges for checking plug air gaps. Also, the unit has a series of flat gauges for use in adjusting contact points. Finally, the tool has a slotted electrode-bending tool and a contact point and electrode file.

When actually setting the air gap of a spark plug with any of these tools, always follow these precautions.

1. Never assume that a new plug has the proper air gap.

2. Never tap the side electrode on a bench to reduce the air gap.

3. Never attempt to set a wide-gap, electronic ignition spark plug to a smaller gap specification. Never attempt to adjust a small-gap, standard ignition spark plug to a wide gap necessary for electronic ignition. In both cases, you would damage the electrodes.

4. Never attempt to bend the center electrode in order to adjust air gap because this will crack or break the insulation.

Spark Plug Installation

To install a cleaned or new spark plug:

1. Wipe any dirt or accumulated grease off the spark plug seat with a clean cloth moistened with a nonflammable solvent.

2. Make sure that the gaskets on plugs requiring them are in good condition and are in proper position over the plug threads. Whenever possible, install a new gasket when installing a used spark plug, and make sure that there is only one gasket on each plug.

3. On plugs used in aluminum heads, coat the threads of the plugs with anti-seize compound.

4. With a piece of heater hose over the insulator or the tool shown in Fig. 16–34, thread the spark plugs into the cylinder head until the hose or tool begins to slip. If you cannot start the plug into the threads easily in this manner, the threads in the cylinder head may require cleaning with a thread-chasing tap. Be very careful when installing a plug or cleaning the threads in an aluminum head because these threads will strip out very easily.

5. Torque all spark plugs with a torque wrench to specifications. Never over-

Fig. 16–34. A tool used to start a spark plug into its threads in the cylinder head.

tighten the spark plugs, especially in aluminum heads.

6. Reinstall the cable connectors and boots over the spark plugs, making sure that each connector seats over the plug terminal and the boot seals over the insulator.

Contact Points and Condenser Service

Inspection

To inspect the serviceability of the contact points, follow this procedure.

1. Remove the distributor cap as outlined earlier.

2. If so equipped, remove the radio-frequency-interference (RFI) shield (Fig. 16–35) from over the contact points and condenser. This shield substantially re-

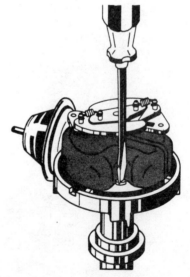

Fig. 16–35. To remove the RFI shield, loosen and remove its attaching screws. (Courtesy of Echlin Manufacturing Co.)

duces radio interference. You can easily remove it by loosening and removing its two attaching screws.

3. Remove the rotor. On the press-on-type rotor, grasp the rotor with your fingers and apply some upward force. Some rotors attach to the flyweights of the advance mechanism with two screws. To remove this type of rotor, loosen and remove its attaching screws, and the rotor will come off easily. *Note:* The tool shown in Fig. 16-36 is very handy for removing and installing attaching screws of rotors or contact points in recessed or difficult-to-reach areas. The tool driver locks onto the screw head, thus preventing the loss of the screw during either process.

4. With a small screwdriver, open the contact points and examine their condition.

Contact Wear

Contact points that have undergone several thousand miles of operation have a rough surface. However, do not interpret this as meaning that the points are worn out. If their surface area has a gray color and the roughness on both contact points matches so that there is a large contact

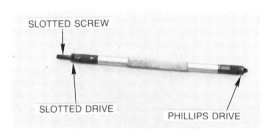

SLOTTED SCREW

SLOTTED DRIVE

PHILLIPS DRIVE

Fig. 16-36. This tool locks onto the screw head, thus preventing its loss during the removal or installation process.

area, the points can continue to provide satisfactory service.

Oily Contact Point Surfaces

An oily contact point surface indicates the presence of engine oil or other type of lubricant. Engine oil or crankcase vapors that work up into the distributor and deposit onto the contact point surfaces cause them to burn rapidly. This is easy to detect since the oil produces a smudgy line under the contact points.

There are two primary causes for the presence of oil on the points. First of all, a clogged positive ventilation control (PVC) valve permits crankcase pressure to build up and forces oil or oil vapors into the distributor. Second, overlubrication of the distributor causes the excess oil to work its way onto the point surfaces.

Point Burning

Contact points that appear mottled or black are a good indication that they are burning. This condition is due to voltage that causes an extremely high current flow through the points.

Oil on the contacts can cause this condition, but there are many other causes for this problem. For example, high voltage can result from an out-of-adjustment or malfunctioning voltage regulator, a defective condenser, and improper contact point adjustment.

High series resistance in the condenser circuit prevents normal condenser action, so the contact points burn rapidly. This resistance may be due to a loose condenser mounting or lead connection or to poor connections inside the condenser itself. In any case, you must tighten the connections as necessary or replace the condenser to correct the problem.

If the contact point opening is too small (dwell is too high), arcing occurs between the contact points. This arcing burns the points. You can easily correct this problem by replacing the contact points as necessary and setting the air gap to specifications.

Contact Point Pitting

Point pitting is the direct result of the transfer of material from one contact point to the other. This results in a spike that builds up on one contact while a pit forms in the other. A small amount of pitting, in several thousand miles of operation, is normal; and it does not affect distributor operation. However, excessive pitting such as a long, sharp spike is harmful and causes arcing and voltage loss. You should replace a set of contact points that have excessive pitting.

Excessive point pitting can result from too small a contact point opening, high primary voltage, or wrong condenser capacity. In this situation, make sure that the contact point opening is correct and locate the source of high primary voltage. In addition, check the capacity of the condenser to make sure that it is what the manufacturer specifies for the system. You can perform this check with a condenser tester as outlined later in this chapter.

In all cases where the contact point area is oily, mottled, dark in color, or pitted, the points will soon become unsatisfactory for further operation. Not only must you replace the points but check the engine and other involved components in order to eliminate the *real cause* of the problem. Unless this is done, the new points can provide no better service than the old ones.

Contact Points and Condenser Removal

You can remove the points and condenser from the distributor, in most cases, while the distributor is in the vehicle or on the work bench, following this procedure.

1. Loosen the terminal screw that secures the condenser and coil primary lead to the contact point assembly. Then, remove the lead (Fig. 16-37). *Note:* In some assemblies, there is no terminal screw. In this case, the leads fit between the contact spring and its stop. To remove the leads, push in on the spring slightly, with the tip of the screwdriver, in order to relieve tension on the leads. Next, pull them straight up and away from the stop.

2. Loosen and remove the condenser bracket attaching screw, and remove the condenser from the breaker plate.

3. Loosen and remove the contact point assembly attaching screws. Then, lift the assembly off the breaker plate.

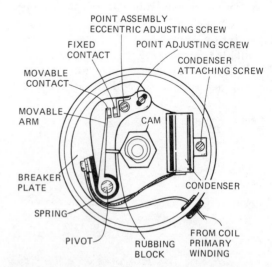

Fig. 16-37. Removing the contact points and condenser from a typical distributor.

Contact Points and Condenser Installation

Manufacturers produce two types of contact point assemblies: a preassembled set and a two-piece set. In the preassembled set of points, point alignment and spring tension are factory set. Consequently, you may not have to align the points and adjust spring tension on these assemblies, but *you should always check them to make sure that they are to specifications.*

However, this is not the case with the two-piece set. With this type of arrangement, it is necessary for you to check and, in most cases, adjust point alignment and spring tension. These checks and adjustments are explained later in this chapter.

With these facts in mind, install typical contact points and condenser following these steps (Fig. 16–37).

1. Clean the breaker plate and cam with a clean rag moistened with solvent. Then, blow these units dry with compressed air.

2. Position the preassembled contact point set over the breaker plate assembly, making sure that its alignment pin indexes with the hole in the breaker plate.

3. When installing a two-piece set, first position the lower adjustable point bracket over the breaker plate, making sure that the opening at one end fits over and pivots on the upper contacting mounting pin. Then, install the movable contact point and spring assembly over the mounting pin; engage the spring into its mounting and against the stop.

4. Install the contact point attaching screws, tightening them only fingertight.

5. Position the condenser and its bracket onto the breaker plate so that the hole in the bracket indexes with the dowel in the breaker plate when used. Then, install the condenser attaching screw, and tighten it to specifications.

6. Connect the condenser and primary lead to the terminal at the contact points, and tighten the hold-down screw, where used, to specifications.

Checking Contact Points for Alignment

To check and adjust point alignment, follow these steps.

1. Rotate the engine or the distributor shaft (if the unit is on the bench) until the point rubbing block is on the flat surface between any two lobes. This action should close the contact points.

2. Check point alignment. Both point contact surfaces should be parallel with the center of both points in line. If the points are out of alignment, use the tool shown in Fig. 16–38 to bend the stationary contact support enough to correct the alignment. *Never bend the movable contact arm.*

Fig. 16–38. A set of tools for use in bending the stationary contact point to correct point misalignment.

Checking and Adjusting Point Spring Tension

The proper amount of spring tension is very important for effective ignition and efficient engine performance. For instance, too much spring tension causes excessive wear on the distributor cam and on the contact point rubbing block. Too weak spring tension is unable to keep the points in contact with each other when they close. This is particularly true as engine speed increases, causing high-speed misfiring.

To check and adjust spring tension:

1. Hook a spring scale onto the breaker arm (Fig. 16–39).

2. Pull on the end of the scale in a straight line at a right angle to the contact point surfaces.

3. Take a reading as the contact points just begin to separate, under a slow and steady pull.

4. Spring tension should be to specifications. If the reading is outside the limits and the contact point assembly is one-piece and not adjustable, replace the contact set. If it is a two-piece set or any set with an adjustable spring, loosen the terminal screw that holds the condenser and primary wires to the spring stop. Then, slide the end of the spring in or out as necessary. Tighten the screw and remeasure the spring tension. Repeat the process as necessary until spring tension is to specifications.

Measuring Point Opening with a Feeler Gauge

To adjust the air gap opening of a properly aligned set of contact points with a feeler gauge, follow this procedure.

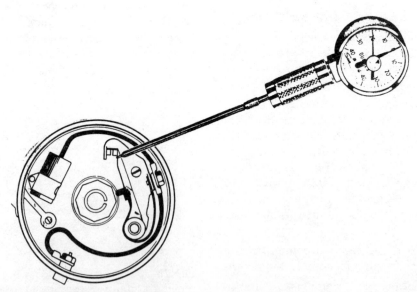

Fig. 16–39.   Checking contact point spring tension with a scale. (Courtesy of Sun Electric Corp.)

1. Check and note the manufacturer's specification for the proper contact point air gap.

2. Rotate the engine or distributor shaft until the breaker point rubbing block is exactly on a high point of the cam.

3. Slide a clean specified feeler gauge strip between the two contact points (Fig. 16–40). Adjust the gap by shifting the position of the point assembly.

a. In a contact point assembly with one attaching screw, along with an eccentric screw, make the adjustment by turning the eccentric screw with the attaching screw fingertight. A slight drag should be felt as you slide the gauge strip between the two points; however, the movable point arm should not move when the adjustment is correct. Then, tighten the attaching screw, and recheck the air gap. Repeat the adjustment as necessary.

b. On contact point assemblies with two attaching screws and a slotted adjuster (Fig. 16–41), leave both attaching screws fingertight. Then,

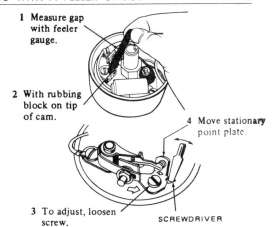

1 Measure gap with feeler gauge.

2 With rubbing block on tip of cam.

4 Move stationary point plate.

3 To adjust, loosen screw.

SCREWDRIVER

Fig. 16–41. Adjusting contact point opening, using a screwdriver in the slotted adjuster. (Courtesy of Ford Motor Co. of Canada Ltd.)

with the blade of a screwdriver positioned between the adjusting slots, move the lower contact bracket until the feeler gauges will move back and forth between the contacts with a slight drag. Next, tighten both attaching screws to specifications and recheck the setting. Repeat the procedure as necessary. Finally, after adjusting the points using either method, close the points, and pull a piece of paper through them to remove any traces of oil or grit.

c. If the contact point assembly is held in place by two screws and has an

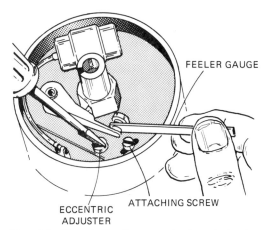

FEELER GAUGE

ECCENTRIC ADJUSTER

ATTACHING SCREW

Fig. 16–40. Adjusting contact point air-gap using the eccentric adjusting screw.

CONTACT-POINT ASSEMBLY

ALLEN WRENCH

Fig. 16–42. A contact point assembly with an allen-screw type of adjuster.

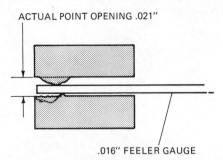

ACTUAL POINT OPENING .021"

.016" FEELER GAUGE

Fig. 16-43. Never set the air gap of used points with a feeler gauge.

allen-screw type of adjuster (Fig. 16-42), tighten the screws to specifications, and make the adjustment with an allen wrench. In most cases, the air gap of this type of points is not set with a feeler gauge. Instead, you use a meter to measure point dwell. This chapter explains this procedure later.

Do not attempt to set any used contact points with a feeler gauge. The uneven point surface makes the measurement inaccurate (Fig. 16-43). In this case, you must use a meter to set point dwell.

Checking and Adjusting Dwell

Another way of adjusting contact points is with a dwell meter. This device measures the period of time the points remain closed in relationship to the rotation of the distributor cam. The dwell meter provides a more accurate way to adjust points, especially used points. However, the distributor must be in place on the engine before performing the check and adjustment with the portable meter.

To adjust dwell on an internal-adjustment type distributor, follow these instructions.

1. Connect the test leads from the dwell meter to the coil and ground, following the manufacturer's recommendations. In most cases, one lead will be clipped to the negative (−) or distributor terminal of the coil and the other to a good engine ground. Figure 16-44 pictures an adapter clip necessary to connect the dwell meter to Ford-type standard ignition coils. The adapter fits beneath the plug-in type connector, and the dwell meter lead clips to it.

2. Set the dwell meter control knob to the corresponding number of engine cylinders.

3. Connect a remote starting button to the starter solenoid.

4. Ground the coil high-tension wire with a jumper lead.

5. Turn the ignition switch to the on position.

6. While observing the dwell meter scale, crank the engine over with the remote starter switch.

Results and Indications

1. If the reading is within specifications, no adjustment is necessary.

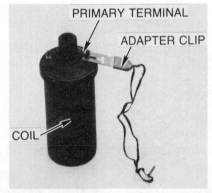

PRIMARY TERMINAL

ADAPTER CLIP

COIL

Fig. 16-44. A typical adapter clip necessary to connect a dwell meter lead to a Ford coil.

2. If the scale reading is not within specifications, adjust the point assembly as you did in items *a* and *b* under setting the points with a feeler gauge. The main difference is that instead of using a feeler gauge between the contacts, you are observing the meter reading with the engine cranking while making the adjustment.

3. After the initial adjustment has been made, tighten the contact point attaching screws and recheck the dwell. If it does not remain within specifications after tightening the screws, repeat the adjustment.

4. Disconnect the remote starter button and dwell meter.

Dwell on External-Adjustment–Type Contact Points

You can set the dwell on this type of contact points with or without the distributor cap installed, following these instructions.

1. Connect a dwell meter to the coil and ground, using the procedure mentioned earlier.

2. Set the dwell meter control knob to the corresponding number of engine cylinders.

3. Attach a remote starter button to the starter solenoid.

4. Ground the high-tension coil wire with a jumper lead.

5. Crank the engine over with the remote starter button while observing the reading on the dwell meter.

Results and Indications

Compare the dwell reading with the specifications.

1. If the dwell is within specifications, no adjustment is necessary.

2. If dwell is not within specifications, make the adjustment as follows.

a. Lift the window in the distributor cap (if installed), and insert an allen wrench into the adjustment slot in the point assembly (Fig. 16–45).

b. While observing the dwell meter, crank the engine over. Then, turn the wrench clockwise to increase the dwell or counterclockwise to decrease the dwell.

c. When the dwell is to specifications, remove the allen wrench and close the window of the cap, if installed.

Lubricating the Distributor

After the point air gap or dwell is set, lubricate the distributor as follows:

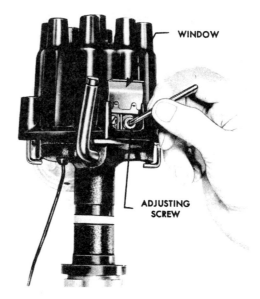

Fig. 16–45. *Adjusting the dwell on a distributor with contact points having an external adjuster. (Courtesy of Delco Remy)*

1. Add about three drops of SAE 10W oil to the oiler on the outside of the distributor housing.

2. Where used, lubricate the felt wick on top of the distributor cam with about two drops of SAW 10W oil. Do not overoil this wick.

3. Apply a light film of distributor cam lubricant over the entire cam surface. *Caution:* A thin film is all that is necessary. Do not overlubricate. Any excess oil on the cam is thrown off when the engine is running. If either of these substances strikes the points, arcing and burning of the contacts will result.

4. If so removed, reinstall the RFI shield. Then, install the rotor and distributor cap.

Distributor Service— Removal

To remove a typical distributor for bench repair or testing, follow these steps.

1. With a remote starter button or a wrench on the front pulley attaching bolt, turn the engine over until the TDC indicator on the pulley lines up with the pointer on the engine.

2. Remove the distributor cap; check to see if the rotor is pointing at the number-one spark plug electrode within the cap. If not, rotate the engine one full revolution to bring the TDC mark up again. This time the rotor should point to the number-one cap electrode.

3. With a scriber, mark the relative position of the distributor housing to the engine as an aid to the reinstallation of the distributor.

4. Disconnect all vacuum advance lines. If there are more than one, mark each with tape as to its proper connection to the advance unit.

5. Disconnect the distributor primary lead at the coil.

6. Loosen and remove the distributor hold-down attaching bolt. Figure 16-46 shows a typical wrench, suitable for loosening and tightening this bolt.

7. Remove the hold-down clamp.

8. Twist the distributor housing slightly; then, pull it straight up and out of the engine.

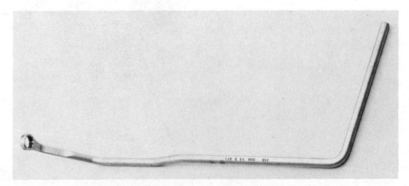

Fig. 16-46. A typical distributor wrench used to loosen or tighten the hold-down clamp bolt.

Distributor Inspection

With the distributor removed, clean its exterior surfaces with nonflammable cleaning solvent and blow dry with compressed air. Then, inspect the assembly for the following:

1. Excessive distributor shaft side clearance and end play.

2. The distributor shaft in its bearings or bushings for wear and smoothness of operation.

3. The distributor shaft gear and oil pump drive slot for damage.

4. The breaker plate bearings or bushings for wear, smoothness of operation, and lubrication.

5. The cam wick for proper lubrication.

6. The distributor cam for smoothness and proper lubrication.

7. Insulators, pigtails, and flexible internal leads for signs of damage.

8. Contact points for alignment, pitting, burning, and rubbing block wear.

9. Vacuum advance linkage for alignment, wear, or binding.

10. Centrifugal advance mechanism for binding. You can check the action of this mechanism by holding the drive end of the distributor shaft and attempting to rotate the distributor cam in the direction of normal rotation. The cam should move forward a few degrees in that direction and then spring back to its original position. If this action is not apparent, there is a binding within the mechanism. *Note:* Some older distributors do not have a centrifugal advance mechanism. Therefore, there will be no movement of the distributor cam.

Distributor Testing

The distributor tester shown in Fig. 16–47 evaluates the distributor for the following items:

1. The condenser for high-series resistance, capacity, and leakage

2. The resistance within the distributor

3. Cam-lobe accuracy

4. Contact point dwell

5. Dwell variation

6. Vacuum advance condition

7. Vacuum advance operation on the breaker plate

8. Centrifugal advance operation

To install a typical distributor in the machine (Fig. 16–47), follow this procedure.

1. Using the elevator crank, raise the crank arms high enough to permit the distributor shaft to clear the drive chuck.

2. Position the distributor into the clamp arms with the vacuum advance unit pointing to the right. Next, tighten the clamp arms securely onto the machined surfaces of the distributor housing. If the vacuum advance rotates the entire distributor, first install the proper collet onto the distributor.

3. Using the elevator crank, lower the distributor until its gear or until about $\frac{3}{4}$ inch of the distributor shaft tip enters the drive chuck or chuck adapter (if one is necessary). Do not bottom the distributor shaft in the chuck. Then tighten the chuck. *Note:* For external-adjustment-type distributors, approximately center the drive gear within its upper and lower limits of end play travel before tightening

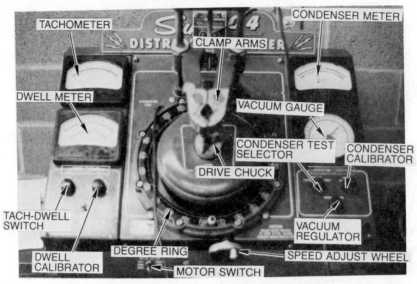

Fig. 16-47. *A Sun distributor tester.*

the chuck. *Never attempt to raise or lower the distributor after tightening the drive chuck.*

Condenser Tests

Preparations

To ensure good ignition system performance, you should check the condenser for series resistance, which affects coil output; capacity, which controls point arcing and pitting; and leakage, which determines if the condenser can stand the stress of the ignition system. Condensers failing one or more of these tests are defective and require replacement.

With these facts in mind, perform the condenser tests following this procedure.

1. Trip the motor switch to the proper direction of distributor rotation, and set distributor speed to zero rpm.

2. With the condenser test selector switch in series resistance position, con-nect the two condenser test leads together.

3. Turn the condenser calibrate control knob clockwise from the off position.

4. Allow about 30 seconds for the tester to warm up. Then, adjust the calibration knob until the condenser test meter reads on the set line.

5. Rotate the distributor shaft by hand until the cam holds the contact points open.

6. Separate the test leads, and connect one to the distributor primary wire and the other to the distributor body or vacuum unit (Fig. 16-48).

Series Resistance Test

Place the condenser selector switch in the series resistance position. The needle of the condenser meter should now be within the black bar at the right end of the scale. Otherwise, the condenser is defective.

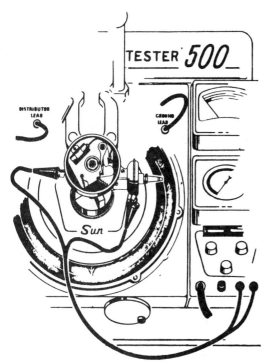

Fig. 16-48. A distributor properly mounted onto and connected to the machine in preparation for testing. (Courtesy of Sun Electric Corp.)

Capacity Test

Set the condenser selector switch in the capacity position. Note the reading on the condenser meter, and compare it with the manufacturer's specifications.

Leakage Test

Turn the condenser selector switch to the leakage position. The needle of the condenser meter should now move into the black bar at the left end of the scale. If it doesn't, replace the condenser. Then, turn the test selector to the series resistance position; place the condenser calibrator to the off position; and remove the test leads from the distributor.

Distributor Resistance Test

This particular test indicates the electrical resistance of the distributor primary circuit from the primary lead, through the points, and to the distributor housing. Excessive resistance in any portion of this circuit will prevent the coil from performing its full efficiency.

To perform this test, follow this procedure.

1. Connect the two distributor leads together.

2. Set the tach-dwell selector switch to the calibrate position, and adjust the dwell regulator until the dwell meter reads on the set line (Fig. 16-49).

3. Separate the leads, and connect the distributor lead to the distributor-to-coil wire and the ground lead to the housing.

4. Rotate the distributor shaft as necessary to close the distributor points; the needle of the dwell meter should move over into the black bar at the right end of the scale (Fig. 16-50).

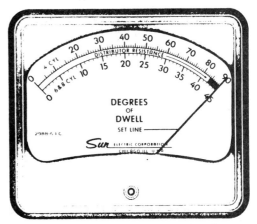

Fig. 16-49. The needle of the dwell meter positioned on the set line. (Courtesy of Sun Electric Corp.)

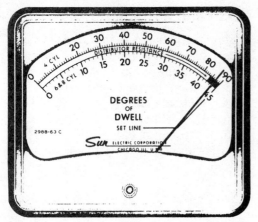

Fig. 16–50.   The needle of the dwell meter should be within the black bar if the resistance level of the distributor is satisfactory. (Courtesy of Sun Electric Corp.)

5. If the pointer of the meter registers in the blue area to the left of the black bar, excessive resistance is present in the distributor's primary circuit. To locate the source of excessive resistance, disconnect the distributor lead and move it step by step through the primary distributor circuit toward the ground lead. When the meter reading indicates less resistance than the previous reading, some measurable resistance exists between the present point of contact of the distributor lead and its previous point of contact.

Note: On distributors with two sets of contact points, test the resistance of each set of points separately by holding or blocking one set open while testing the other.

Cam-Lobe Accuracy

To conduct this test:

1. Connect the leads of the machine to the distributor as before, and turn the tach-dwell switch to the position corresponding to the number of engine cylinders (four, six, or eight) that the distributor services.

2. Adjust the distributor speed to 1,000 rpm.

3. Rotate the degree ring of the tester until the zero on the ring aligns with one of the arrow flashes.

4. Observe the relative position of the remaining arrow flashes.

5. All arrow flashes must appear evenly spaced around the degree rings at 90 degrees for four-lobe cams, 60 degrees for six-lobe cams, and 45 degrees for eight-lobe cams. Also, the flashes must be within + or − of one degree of the degree marks.

Contact Point Alignment

After performing the cam-lobe accuracy test, check contact point alignment by using this procedure.

1. Observe the slight arc appearing between the contact points. If the contact points are in proper alignment, the arcing will appear in the center of the points when viewed from above and from one side.

2. Reduce the speed of the distributor to 200 rpm.

Contact Point Dwell

After checking point alignment:

1. Observe the dwell meter and, as necessary, adjust the contact points, using one of the procedures previously outlined, until the meter indicates the specified degrees of dwell.

2. On distributors equipped with dual points, it is necessary to adjust the dwell on each individually. To isolate each set

for adjusting purposes, block the other one open by inserting a piece of cardboard between the points.

Contact Point Dwell Variation

After checking and setting the dwell to specifications, check dwell variation in this manner.

1. While watching the dwell meter, vary the distributor speed from 200 to 1,750 rpm. A dwell variation in excess of 2 degrees or the amount specified by the manufacturer indicates a worn distributor shaft or bushing.

2. Reduce distributor speed to 200 rpm.

Testing the Operation of the Centrifugal Advance Mechanism

This test determines if the centrifugal advance mechanism is providing the specific advance curve throughout all speeds of engine operation. A defective centrifugal advance unit results in the engine being out of time at certain engine rpm. This always results in a loss of engine performance and may also cause spark knock or overheating. Of course,

this particular test is not necessary on older-type distributors without the centrifugal advance mechanism.

To perform this procedure:

1. Set the zero of the degree ring in line with the arrow flash nearest you.

2. Increase distributor speed pausing at each rpm, specified by the manufacturer, to note if the amount of advance is within plus or minus one degree of the tolerance specified by the manufacturer (Fig. 16–51).

3. Momentarily exceed the highest specified speed given as a test rpm. Then, while returning the distributor rpm to zero, recheck the flashes at each test speed to see if the amount of advance at that rpm is the same as in step 2 or as specified by the manufacturer. Any inconsistency in readings requires corrections to ensure best engine performance.

4. Shut off the machine.

Results and Indications

1. If the advance curve is excessive in both steps 2 and 3, the weight springs are weak or the mechanism has the wrong springs.

2. If the advance is slow in step 2 and excessive in step 3, the weights are sticking and require freeing up.

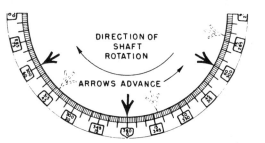 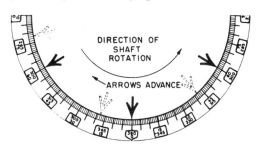

Fig. 16-51. *Regardless of which direction the distributor shaft rotates, the flashes move to a new position on the degree wheel as rpm increases, up to a specified amount. (Courtesy of Sun Electric Corp.)*

3. If the advance is insufficient both on acceleration and deceleration, the spring tension is excessive.

Vacuum Advance Diaphragm Test

This particular test indicates if the diaphragm within the vacuum advance unit is leaking. A leak within the diaphragm results in the failure of this advance unit to move the timing forward during part-throttle operation. This causes reduced performance and an increase in fuel consumption.

To perform this test:

1. Insert the proper adapter in the vacuum advance unit, and tighten it securely with a wrench to ensure a good seal.

2. Attach the vacuum hose from the machine to the adapter. Then, seal the hose closed with a metal clamp.

3. Adjust the machine's vacuum regulator until the vacuum gauge reads 15 inches of Hg. Release the hose clamp and observe the vacuum gauge.

Results and Indications

1. The gauge reading will momentarily fall to a lower reading. However, if the gauge reading returns to 15 inches of Hg within a few seconds, the vacuum diaphragm chamber is airtight.

2. If the gauge reading fails to return to 15 inches of Hg, the vacuum diaphragm or chamber is leaking, and the vacuum unit requires replacement.

Vacuum-Operated Breaker Plate Test

The breaker plate, when activated by the vacuum advance, must have a smooth and even movement, or the plate twists.

This causes a change in the relationship between the cam and the point rubbing block with a resulting alteration in dwell. Any change in dwell angle affects the ignition spark both in quality and timing.

This test only applies to distributors with centrally located breaker plate bearings. On distributors with side-pivoted breaker plates, the dwell normally varies by much more than two degrees when you operate the vacuum unit. In many cases, the manufacturer does not provide a certain specification for dwell variation on these types of distributors since the amount of dwell variation is so different with the individual distributor, depending upon the amount of maximum vacuum applied.

To perform this test procedure on a distributor with centrally located breaker plate bearings:

1. Adjust the speed control to 1,000 rpm.

2. Using the vacuum regulator knob, adjust the vacuum to zero. Then, increase meter vacuum to 20 inches of Hg while observing the dwell meter pointer for variations. Note the results, and adjust the vacuum regulator to zero vacuum.

Results and Indications

Dwell variation of more than two degrees from 0 to 20 inches of vacuum, indicates worn breaker plate bushings or bearings or intermittent distributor resistance. Note the condition of the distributor wiring, which may be broken within the insulation due to flexing.

Vacuum Spark Advance Test

The purpose of this procedure is to test the complete vacuum advance mechanism. This vacuum advance mechanism adjusts ignition timing according to the

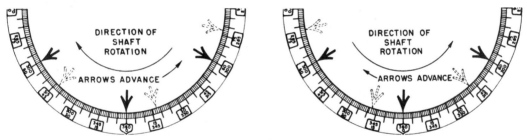

Fig. 16–52. Regardless of which direction the distributor shaft rotates, the flashes move to a new position on the degree wheel with increasing vacuum, up to a specified amount. (Courtesy of Sun Electric Corp.)

load on the engine to provide peak fuel economy at moderate loads and full power without detonation at heavier loads. During the course of this test on the vacuum advance mechanism, particularly look for improper vacuum advance calibration, sticky or erratic breaker plate action, tilting of the breaker plate, or interference of the condenser with the action of the plate.

With these facts in mind, perform this test by following these steps.

1. With zero vacuum applied to the vacuum diaphragm, set the zero on the degree ring in line with one of the flashing arrows, at about 200 rpm.

2. Adjust the vacuum regulator to apply the specified amount of vacuum for each check point in turn and note the amount of advance obtained (Fig. 16–52).

3. Momentarily exceed the highest vacuum value specified by the manufacturer. Then, reduce the vacuum and note the amount of advance obtained at each check point as you did in step 2. Note the results.

Results and Indications

1. Excessive vacuum advance during both steps 2 and 3 indicates a weak vacuum advance spring. Replace the vacuum control unit or adjust it following the manufacturer's instructions.

2. Insufficient vacuum advance during both steps 2 and 3 indicates an excessively strong spring within the control unit. Replace the control unit or adjust it following the manufacturer's instructions.

3. If the vacuum advance is insufficient in step 2, excessive in step 3, or erratic in both steps 2 and 3, the breaker plate is sticking or binding.

Installing the Distributor

The actual procedure for installing a distributor depends basically upon its type of drive. Some distributors have a slotted drive without a gear. With this design, the camshaft drives the oil pump, which in turn rotates the distributor shaft via its slotted shaft. In other designs, the camshaft drives the distributor through a gear on its shaft. The distributor shaft then turns the oil pump by a drive slot or hex.

To reinstall a distributor with a plain slotted shaft:

1. Rotate the distributor shaft until the rotor points to the number-one spark plug electrode in the cap.

2. Position the distributor into its opening in the engine. Then, rotate the rotor

slightly in one direction, then the other, until the slot in the distributor shaft engages into the oil pump drive.

3. Line up the reference marks that you made on the distributor housing and engine before removing the distributor.

4. After making sure that the distributor seats against the engine, reinstall its hold-down clamp and attaching bolt. Tighten the attaching bolt fingertight.

To install a distributor with a gear drive:

1. Rotate the distributor shaft until the rotor reaches a point about 10 or 15 degrees before the rotor aligns with the number-one spark plug electrode position in the normal direction of shaft rotation.

2. Install the distributor into its opening in the engine. As the distributor drops into place, the rotor should move while its gear engages into the camshaft drive gear. This movement should bring the rotor into alignment with the number-one cap electrode. However, if the distributor does not drop into position and the rotor is out of alignment, lift the distributor slightly out of the opening, and move the rotor back a few additional degrees. Then, repeat the installing procedure until the distributor drops fully into position.

3. Rotate the distributor housing until its locating mark, made before distributor removal, lines up with the corresponding mark on the engine.

4. Install the hold-down clamp and attaching bolt. Tighten the attaching bolt fingertight.

5. Install the distributor lead onto the coil terminal, tightening its attaching nut securely.

6. Reinstall the distributor cap.

Setting Basic Ignition Timing

This procedure varies somewhat among the various engine manufacturers. For example, some manufacturers require that the engine be operating at normal temperature, the vacuum advance lines be disconnected and plugged, and the engine be operating at a specific rpm. Consequently, before attempting this procedure on any engine, always look up the timing specifications and special instructions in the appropriate service manual.

To check and adjust ignition timing on a typical engine:

1. Locate the timing marks on the engine's crankshaft pulley or balancer. On some engines these marks are on the flywheel. Wipe the marks clean, and mark them with chalk or white paint. *Note:* It may be difficult to locate the timing marks on many late-model engines because they are often hidden behind a maze of belts and engine accessories. If you cannot reach the timing marks to clean them by hand, spray them with carburetor- or choke-cleaning spray to make them easier to see. Also the timing marks on some engines, particularly in vans, are visible only from the bottom of the engine.

2. Connect a tachometer and timing light to the engine, following the manufacturer's instructions.

3. As specified by the manufacturer, remove and plug the vacuum lines to the distributor.

4. Start the engine, and run it at the specified rpm. Permit the engine to reach normal operating temperature.

5. Aim the timing light at the timing marks and observe their position (Fig. 16-53).

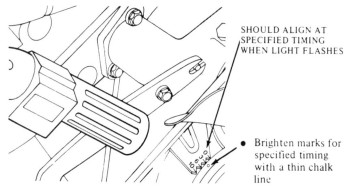

SHOULD ALIGN AT
SPECIFIED TIMING
WHEN LIGHT FLASHES

● Brighten marks for
specified timing
with a thin chalk
line

Fig. 16–53.   Using a timing light to check basic ignition timing. (Courtesy of Ford Motor Co. of Canada Ltd.)

6. If adjustment is necessary:

a. Loosen as necessary the distributor hold-down attaching bolt with a distributor wrench (Fig. 16–46) or a ratchet with an extension and universal-joint socket.

b. Advance the timing by rotating the distributor *against* normal rotor rotation. Retard ignition timing by turning the distributor in the *same* direction as rotor rotation.

c. Tighten the hold-down attaching bolt securely, and recheck the timing.

7. Reconnect the vacuum lines, and readjust the idle speed as necessary.

8. Disconnect the dwell meter and timing light from the engine.

Review

This section will assist you in determining how well you remember the material in this chapter. Read each item carefully. If you can't complete the statement, review the section in the chapter that covers the material.

1. You can test a primary ignition resistor with a (an) _____.
   a. ammeter
   b. ohmmeter
   c. voltmeter
   d. both *a* and *b*

2. The average resistance in the primary winding of a coil is _____ to _____ ohms.
   a. 1.5–1.8
   b. 1.8–2.1
   c. 2.1–2.5
   d. 2.5–2.8

3. The current draw by the primary ignition circuit is usually about _____ amperes.
   a. 6
   b. 5
   c. 4
   d. 3

4. When visually testing a coil's polarity, use a _____.
   a. ammeter
   b. voltmeter
   c. pencil
   d. ohmmeter

5. You can test for high resistance in secondary cables with an oscilloscope or a (an) _____.

a. voltmeter
b. ammeter
c. ohmmeter
d. both *a* and *b*

6. The average resistance in a secondary cable is _____ ohms per foot.
   a. 2,000
   b. 4,000
   c. 6,000
   d. 8,000

7. The interval for changing spark plugs ranges from 5,000 to _____ miles.
   a. 50,000
   b. 40,000
   c. 20,000
   d. 10,000

8. The firing tip of a wet-fouled plug has excess amounts of _____.
   a. carbon
   b. glaze
   c. soot
   d. oil

9. Preignition damage to the firing end of a spark plug is the direct result of excessive _____.
   a. carbon
   b. soot
   c. oil
   d. temperature

10. You must set the air gap of a used spark plug with a _____ gauge.
    a. round
    b. flat

11. Normally functioning contact points are _____ in color.
    a. white
    b. gray
    c. tan
    d. black

12. If it is necessary to adjust point alignment, bend the _____ point.

a. movable
b. stationary

13. One way to adjust _____ _____ is through the use of a dwell meter.
    a. used points
    b. new points
    c. preassembled points
    d. all of the above

14. Lubricate the felt wick above the distributor cam with about 2 drops of SAW _____ oil.
    a. 10W
    b. 20W
    c. 30
    d. 40

15. Always remove the distributor with the engine stopped at the _____ position.
    a. BDC
    b. TDC

16. Condenser capacity controls point _____.
    a. bounce
    b. wear
    c. pitting
    d. both *a* and *b*

17. Cam-lobe accuracy should be within the amount specified by the manufacturer or plus or minus _____ degree(s).
    a. 0
    b. 1
    c. 3
    d. 6

18. When testing the vacuum advance diaphragm for leaks on a distributor machine, apply _____ inches of Hg to the diaphragm chamber.
    a. 15
    b. 17
    c. 19
    d. 21

19. Dwell variation of a centrally mounted breaker plate should not exceed _____ degrees.
   a. 0
   b. 2
   c. 4
   d. 6

20. In most all cases, a(an) _____ _____ is necessary to set basic ignition timing.
   a. engine analyzer
   b. dwell meter
   c. timing light
   d. distributor tester

For the answers, turn to the Appendix.

Advantages

Manufacturers began to install solid-state electronic ignition systems on many domestic vehicles in the early 1970s. This action was necessary not only to meet stricter emission control standards but to increase the fuel economy of the vehicle.

Although the electronic system costs more to install than the standard system, the advantages that it offers more than outweigh the drawback of increased cost. These advantages include:

1. Greater available secondary voltage, especially at high engine rpm

2. Reliable and consistent system performance at any and all engine speeds

3. A potential for more responsive and variable ignition advance curves

4. Decreased maintenance cost of the system

To understand how an electronic system can provide all these advantages over the standard system, let's review for a moment the inherent negative characteristics of the standard system. If you recall, in order for a coil in the secondary system to produce adequate secondary voltage at all times, the contact points must remain closed for a given period of time—the dwell period. As vehicle speed increases, the points open and close much faster, and this reduces the effective time the points remain closed. Consequently, there is a reduction in the build-up time of the magnetic field around the primary coil, which is responsible for producing secondary voltage. This characteristic of the standard system permits it to produce a substantially large secondary voltage at lower engine speeds but a reduced voltage at high rpm.

_____ Chapter 17

ELECTRONIC IGNITION SYSTEMS

In addition, due to the fact that the contact points mechanically close and open (due to the action of a spring and the distributor cam), there is some arcing as the points open. This occurs despite a condenser in the circuit. This arcing results in point wear and the requirement for periodic point replacement.

In summation, standard ignition systems fail at high engine rpm to produce sufficient voltage in order to prevent misfires. These misfires cause negative exhaust emissions and decreased economy. In addition, the standard system requires frequent service on its spark plugs, due to less available secondary voltage at high rpm, especially as the plug's air gap grows larger due to high mileage. This, of course, increases emissions and reduces fuel economy.

Contact points require frequent service due to arcing. This arcing is a direct result of high primary-coil–induced voltage, which the condenser cannot handle at low engine speeds. As a result, the point air gap increases so that the dwell (buildup time of the primary coil) is cut back. This reduction in dwell affects the secondary coil's ability to produce high voltage until it reaches a point where the entire system malfunctions, unless the contact points receive service.

The electronic ignition system, on the other hand, does not depend on mechanically operated contact points (Fig. 17–1) to open or close the primary coil circuit. As a result, the system can provide overall higher voltages necessary to fire the leaner air/fuel mixtures on emission controlled engines and also bridge enlarged air gaps due to plug wear. Consequently, the electronic system reduces harmful exhaust emissions, increases fuel economy, and lowers maintenance costs.

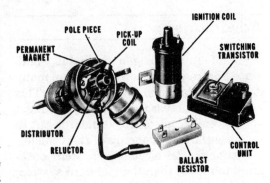

Fig. 17–1. The components of a typical electronic ignition system. (Courtesy of Echlin Manufacturing Co.)

The electronic ignition system does not use the contact points as a switching device to open and close the primary circuit. Instead, the system uses an electronic switch in the form of one or more transistors to control primary current flow. These transistors and other parts of the solid-state control circuitry are inside a sealed control unit, which this chapter discusses later .

Types of Electronic Ignition Systems

Since the early 1970s, a number of different types of electronic systems have been designed and produced by the automotive industry. Because of the quantity of the units developed and used, this chapter cannot cover them all in the space available. Instead, the text presents samples of the various types of units produced by domestic automobile manufacturers.

The two general categories used to type these systems deal with the design of the triggering devices and switching units. A *triggering device* is necessary in any electronic system in order to signal the switching (control) unit to open and close the primary circuit. The two types of triggering devices in general use are the *contact points* and the *magnetic-pulse*. The two most common designs of switching units are the *inductive* and the *capacitive*.

Triggering Devices— Contact Points

Many add-on and some of the early factory-installed solid-state electronic ignition systems adapted the control unit to the existing triggering device—the *ignition contact points* (Fig. 17–2). With this arrangement, the system uses a conventional distributor with the original contact points, but the unit *does not* require a condenser. Note in the illustration that there is a condenser in the distributor.

This installation is decided by the vehicle owner—the condenser *is not necessary* but may be used if desired in order to reduce radio interference. In some cases, the condenser connects instead to the ground terminal of the ignition coil.

In this contact-controlled system, a transistor assembly within the switching unit (the *amplifier*) takes over the traditional task of the contact points in controlling primary-circuit current flow (Fig. 17–3). In other words, the contact points in this electronic system act as an on-off switch for the *emitter-base circuit* of the transistor. The *emitter-collector circuit* of the transistor handles the current flow of the primary-coil windings to ground while the contact points carry only about 1 ampere, depending on the make and model of the system.

Observe also in this diagram and Fig. 17–2 that the ignition coil connects to ground through a separate resistor. This

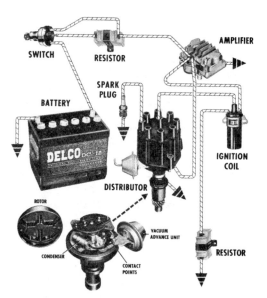

Fig. 17–2. A typical contact-point-controlled electronic ignition system. (Courtesy of Delco Remy)

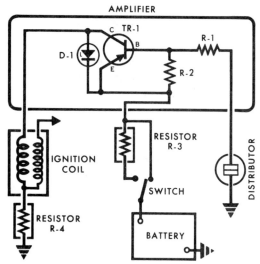

Fig. 17–3. A wiring diagram of a typical contact-controlled ignition system. (Courtesy of Delco Remy)

resistor assists the original primary-circuit resistor in controlling current flow through the entire primary circuit, under a safe limit at all times, except during starting, when it alone controls the flow.

Even if this particular type of electronic system activates by the contact points, it is much more reliable than the standard system. Remember that in the standard contact-point system about 2 to 6 amperes of current flowed through the points; this high current eventually wears out the points. However, since only a small current is necessary to trigger the transistor, this does not occur in the electronic system. The one disadvantage of the low-ampere contact-point triggering device is the periodic replacement of the points due to wear on the rubbing block, caused by friction between itself and the distributor cam.

Contact-Controlled System Operation

With the ignition switch closed, current from the battery passes through the switch, primary resistor R-3, emitter-base circuit of the transistor, resistor R-1, and to ground through the closed contact points. Resistor R-2 provides the forward bias voltage for transistor TR-1, and resistor R-1 limits the current through the emitter-base circuit (marked E and B in Fig. 17–3) of TR-1. Since the emitter-base circuit is complete, current also passes through the emitter-collector circuit, primary windings of the coil, the resistor R-4, and to ground. With current moving through the primary winding of the coil, it produces an electromagnetic field.

When the contact points open, current flow stops through the emitter-base circuit because the points open its ground circuit back to the battery. As a result, current flow also ceases through the emitter-collector, primary windings of the coil, the second resistor, and to ground. Because the current stops flowing abruptly in the primary coil windings, its magnetic field collapses immediately, inducing a high voltage in the secondary coil. This voltage potential is much higher than in a standard system due to the rapid collapse of the magnetic field and the absence of arcing at the contact points. From the coil, the high-voltage surge passes through the remaining secondary components to the spark plug. Then, the distributor points reclose, and the cycle begins over again.

There is also a zenor diode D-1 in the switching unit (amplifier). This diode protects the transistor against damage from the high primary self-induced voltage when the magnetic field collapses.

Magnetic-Pulse Triggering Devices

An electronic ignition system using a *magnetic-pulse triggering device* is similar to the contact-controlled type. However, when a magnetic-pulse triggering device is in the distributor, it switches the transistor on or off by means of an electrical charge induced through magnetism. Since this system has no contact points at all, it is known as a *breakerless electronic ignition system.* Many manufacturers utilize magnetic impulse distributors in their systems, among them Delco Remy, Chrysler, and Ford.

Delco Magnetic-Pulse System

Figure 17-4 illustrates a typical magnetic-pulse Delco system. This system resembles the contact type just described except for the design of the distributor and the switching unit (the amplifier). Externally, this magnetic pulse distributor resembles any standard distributor and mounts in the same location. However, internally the unit is entirely different. Instead of the conventional cam and contact point assembly, an iron core driven by the distributor shaft rotates inside a stationary magnetic pickup unit.

As shown in Fig. 17-4, the iron timer core of the magnetic-pulse distributor has the same number of equally spaced external vanes as the engine has cylinders. The magnetic pickup assembly consists of

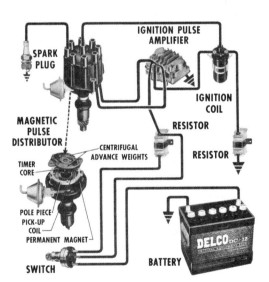

Fig. 17-4. A typical V-8 Delco magnetic-pulse electronic ignition system. (Courtesy of Delco Remy)

a permanent magnet, pickup coil, and steel pole piece with equally spaced internal teethlike projections, one for each cylinder of the engine.

The magnetic pickup assembly mounts on a plate supported by bearings within the distributor housing. This housing attaches to the vacuum advance unit that partially rotates it and the pickup assembly in a direction opposite to the normal rotation of the core. This design provides a vacuum-controlled spark advance.

The iron timer core is also made to turn slightly in the direction of its normal rotation, due to the action of the centrifugal advance mechanism. This provides an advance curve based on engine rpm.

The transistor control unit or amplifier consists essentially of transistors, resistors, compacitors, and a diode mounted on a printed circuit board, contained within a heat-dissipating metal chassis. This stationary assembly also has four connecting leads. Two of these leads connect to the pickup coil of the magnetic-pulse distributor, one to the ignition coil and one to the battery circuit.

Notice also in Fig. 17-4 that this system has two external resistors. The primary ballast resistor connects directly to the ignition switch and is bypassed during the starting period of the engine. Whereas, the other resistor always remains in series with the ground side of the primary ignition coil.

Operation of a Magnetic Pickup System

When the driver turns on the ignition switch, with the engine not operating, battery current flows through the ignition switch; primary resistor R-7; and into the amplifier. The current then flows through transistors TR-1 and TR-2; resistors R-1, R-2, and R-5; the coil's primary winding; resistor R-8 to ground; and back to the battery. With resistor R-1 providing the forward bias voltage necessary to operate the output transistor TR-1, its emitter-collector circuit is operational. As a result, battery current flows through the coil's primary winding to produce a magnetic field and also charges capacitor C-1 with a positive charge toward driver transistor TR-2. (See Fig. 17–5.)

When the driver turns over and starts the engine, the magnetic-pulse distributor provides a "triggering" pulse or small current signal to the switching transistor TR-3 as follows. As the vanes of the iron timer core, mounted on the distributor shaft, align with the teeth of the pole piece, the magnetic field produced by the permanent magnet completes its circuit through the iron core as shown in Fig.

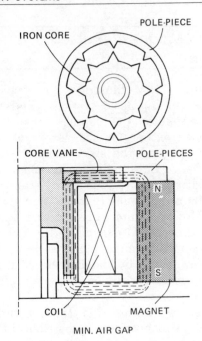

Fig. 17–6. The magnetic field from the permanent magnet expands through the pickup coil as the core vanes align with the pole teeth.

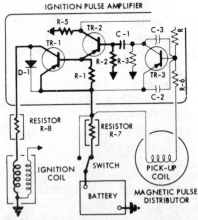

Fig. 17–5. Current flow through the ignition pulse amplifier with the ignition switch on and engine not running. (Courtesy of Delco Remy)

17-6. This is the minimum air-gap position between the vanes and the teeth.

Since this field has expanded to pass through the windings of the pickup coil, a triggering voltage signal is induced into the coil. This voltage causes a current to flow to the amplifier, where it "turns on" transistor TR-3 (Fig. 17–7). With transistor TR-3 turned on, current flows through its emitter-collector circuit to ground via resistor R-3. This causes the positive charge in this capacitor to discharge to ground through resistor R-3. This "turns off" transistor TR-2 and TR-1 momentarily, which opens the emitter-base (primary coil) circuit of transistor TR-1. As a result, the magnetic field of the primary coil collapses, producing a high

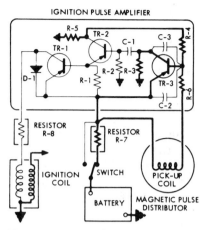

Fig. 17-7. Current flow through the ignition pulse amplifier as the spark plug fires. (Courtesy of Delco Remy)

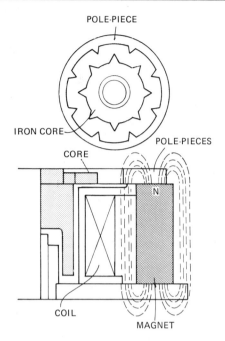

Fig. 17-8. The magnetic field from the permanent magnet collapses back toward itself as the core vanes move away from the pole teeth.

voltage in the secondary coil, which causes an arc at the spark plug.

As the distributor shaft and core rotate past the point where the vanes align with the pole teeth, the air gap increases. This causes the magnetic field to collapse (Fig. 17-8). This also induces a voltage in the pickup coil, but in this case, the resulting reversed polarity causes current flow away from the amplifier and switching transistor TR-3. Consequently, by the time capacitor C-1 has finished discharging through resistor R-3, transistor TR-3 has switched back off. This causes transistor TR-1 and TR-2 to turn back on and permits current to flow once again through transistor TR-1 to the primary coil windings. Thus, the system is ready to fire the next spark plug.

The purpose of feedback resistor R-4 is to turn off transistor TR-3 when TR-2 returns to the on condition, and the current from the pickup coil ceases its flow into the amplifier. This occurs as the core vanes move away from the pole teeth within the distributor.

The zenor diode D-1 in the amplifier (Figs. 17-5 and 17-7) protects transistor TR-1 from the high voltage induced into the coil's primary winding as its field collapses. Capacitors C-2 and C-3 protect transistor TR-3 from this same high voltage. Resistor R-6 protects transistor TR-3 from excessive current in case the pickup coil becomes grounded.

Chrysler Magnetic-Pulse System

Distributor

Figure 17-9 shows the components of a Chrysler-built magnetic-pulse electronic

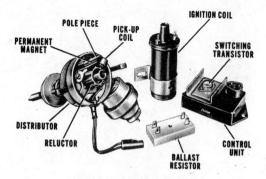

Fig. 17-9. The components of a Chrysler electronic ignition system. (Courtesy of Echlin Manufacturing Co.)

Reluctor

The *reluctor* (Fig. 17-10) attaches to the distributor shaft in the same position as the cam in a contact-point distributor. The reluctor has a shape similar to a gear, with a tooth for each cylinder. The metal reluctor is not a magnet, but it is a good conductor for magnetic lines of force. In other words, the reluctor reduces resistance to magnetic flow (reluctance) by providing a better magnetic circuit than air between the poles of the permanent magnet.

Permanent Magnet and Pickup Coil

The distributor also has a permanent magnet that rivets to a pole piece and hold-down bracket (Fig. 17-11). The magnet produces a magnetic field, which concentrates itself at the tip of the pole piece and the hold-down bracket. However, there is a large air gap between the

ignition system. This system consists basically of a magnetic-pulse distributor, control unit, ignition coil, and dual ballast resistor. The magnetic-pulse distributor has both a centrifugal and vacuum advance mechanism as in any standard distributor but incorporates a pickup coil and reluctor instead of contact points and a cam.

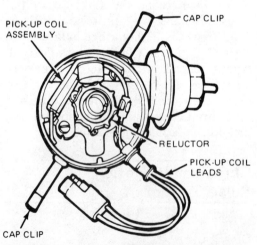

Fig. 17-10. The reluctor of a Chrysler distributor attaches to the distributor shaft. (Courtesy of Chrysler Corp.)

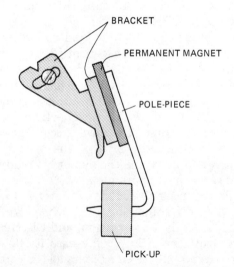

Fig. 17-11. The permanent magnet and pickup coil assembly.

tip of the pole piece and the hold-down bracket (the opposite pole of the magnet).

A pickup coil is wound around the tip of the pole piece. Consequently, the magnetic field produced by the permanent magnet passes through the coil. However, the strength of this field and its ability to induce a voltage are in proportion to the amount of air gap between the tip of the pole piece and the hold-down bracket. For example, there is a relatively weak field when there is a large air gap between the pole piece and the bracket because air does not provide a good magnetic path between the two.

The reluctor provides a better path for the magnetic lines and therefore works with the pickup coil in the production of an electrical signal. For instance, Fig. 17-12 shows a reluctor tooth as it approaches the tip of the pole piece. In this situation, the magnetic field in the pickup coil increases because there is a reduced magnetic path between the reluctor tooth

and the pole piece, and another tooth and the bracket.

The increasing field strength within the pickup coil induces a positive voltage at one terminal of the coil's windings. This voltage induction is the result of the increasing field strength and not by the movement of the magnetic field or the pickup coil. This positive voltage signal continues to build up within the pickup coil terminal until the reluctor tooth is exactly opposite the pole piece.

As soon as the reluctor tooth passes the tip of the pole piece, the air gap begins to increase (Fig. 17-13). As a result, the magnetic field strength within the pickup coil begins to decrease. This decreasing field induces a reversed or negative voltage at the same terminal of the pickup coil.

Control Unit

The induced voltage in the pickup coil is very small, but it provides a tiny electrical signal fed into the electronic control unit. The *control unit* electronically determines

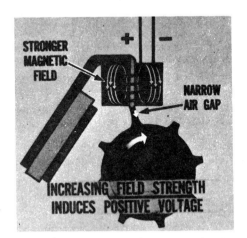

Fig. 17-12. As the reluctor tooth moves toward the tip of the pole piece, magnetic field strength increases in the pickup coil. (Courtesy of Chrysler Corp.)

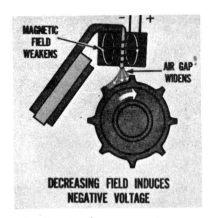

Fig. 17-13. As the air gap increases, the strength of the magnetic field decreases. (Courtesy of Chrysler Corp.)

how long the ignition coil's primary current flows before being interrupted. In other words, the control unit determines the dwell in the electronic part of the system. Since the manufacturer seals the circuitry of the control unit and it has no moving parts, the coil dwell is not changeable.

The reluctor along with the pickup coil determines ignition timing and works together with the control unit to time the interruption of the primary current flow and the firing of the plugs. For example, when the pickup coil provides a positive voltage signal to the control unit (Fig. 17-14), current flows through the ignition coil's primary windings and to ground. This current flow creates a magnetic field inside the coil. This magnetic field continues as long as the control unit remains "on" due to the application of a positive signal from the control unit.

However, when the reluctor passes the pole piece, the pickup coil voltage turns negative (Fig. 17-15). This signal turns off the control unit circuitry in a similar way as in the Delco unit. As a result, current cannot flow through the control unit

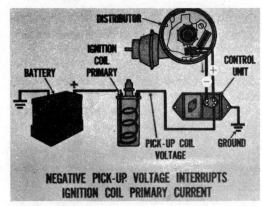

NEGATIVE PICK-UP VOLTAGE INTERRUPTS IGNITION COIL PRIMARY CURRENT

Fig. 17-15. A negative signal from the output coil turns off the control unit. (Courtesy of Chrysler Corp.)

to ground, which interrupts the current flow through the primary coil windings. This causes the collapse of the primary coil's magnetic field and the induction of high enough voltage in the secondary coil to arc across the spark plug air gap.

Ignition Coil and Ballast Resistor

The ignition coil used with this system is the same as any standard ignition coil. However, the ballast resistor in the circuit has two resistances instead of one. The 0.55-ohm side of the resistor serves the same function as any other type of primary-coil circuit. That is, it regulates primary-circuit voltage and current flow during variations in engine speed. This protects the ignition coil against high current flow at low engine speeds and raises the voltage applied to the coil at higher rpm.

The opposite side of this dual-ballast resistor has 5 ohms of resistance. This resistance protects the control unit by limiting the flow of current within its circuitry.

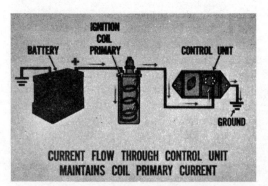

CURRENT FLOW THROUGH CONTROL UNIT MAINTAINS COIL PRIMARY CURRENT

Fig. 17-14. Current flow through the primary-coil circuit when the pickup coil is supplying a positive voltage signal. (Courtesy of Chrysler Corp.)

Ford Magnetic-Pulse System

With a few exceptions, the Ford magnetic-pulse electronic ignition system is quite similar in design and operation to the Chrysler system. For example, within the distributor (Fig. 17–16) is an armature with eight tips, or projections, instead of the reluctor in the Chrysler unit. In addition, Ford calls its pickup coil the *stator;* this unit is still wound around the extended tip of the pole piece as in Chrysler distributors. Figure 17–17 illustrates the operation of the armature, stator, pole piece, and magnet as they produce the signal necessary to turn on or off the switching transistor within the control module.

As compared to the Chrysler system, Ford does not use a standard ignition coil. Instead, Ford's coil is a special oil-filled type that is easily identified by its blue case, or tower. Also, this coil has primary terminals labeled BAT and DEC (distributor electronic control). However, in a similar manner as the Chrysler unit, this special coil requires a standard primary-circuit resistor.

The switching unit of the Chrysler unit is the control unit; Ford calls its switching unit the *control module.* This module also contains a number of electronic components that regulate dwell and function along with the triggering mechanism to time the collapse of the primary coil's magnetic field and the firing of each plug.

Other Switching Devices

Metal Detection

Other than the contact points and the magnetic-pulse generator, there have been three other breakerless triggering devices: one using metal detection, Hall effect, and light detection. The *metal detection* form of a triggering device is a variation of the magnetic-pulse system. However, in this system, the pickup coil is an electromagnet instead of coil that has voltage induced into it by a changing magnetic field produced by a permanent magnet (Fig. 17–18).

When this triggering device is in operation, the control module applies a small amount of battery current to the coil of the electromagnet. The metal teeth on the trigger wheel, as it rotates with the distributor shaft, affects the resulting electromagnetic field and the voltage within the electromagnetic coil.

The control module senses these voltage variations and opens or closes the primary coil circuit. Consequently, this form of triggering device produces a more reliable signal voltage, especially at lower engine rpm, than the traditional magnetic-pulse unit.

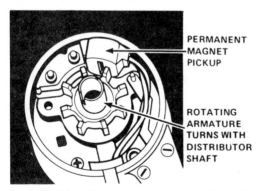

PERMANENT MAGNET PICKUP

ROTATING ARMATURE TURNS WITH DISTRIBUTOR SHAFT

Fig. 17–16. The components of Ford's solid-state ignition distributor. (Courtesy of Ford Motor Co. of Canada Ltd.)

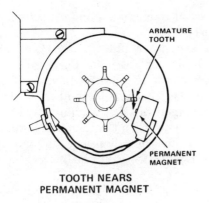

**TOOTH NEARS
PERMANENT MAGNET**

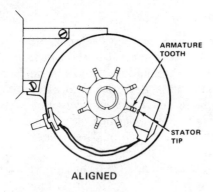

ALIGNED

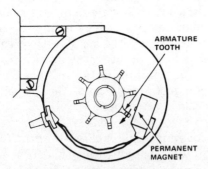

**TOOTH AWAY FROM
PERMANENT MAGNET**

A. As each tooth (pole) of the armature nears the permanent magnet, an electrical signal is generated in the pickup coil.
B. As each tooth (pole) of the armature goes away from the permanent magnet, an electrical signal of opposite polarity is generated in the pickup coil.
C. The signals generated go from positive to negative and back again as the distributor rotates.
D. This signal tells the module to turn off, producing the same effect in the primary circuit as the opening of the contacts in a conventional ignition system; it breaks the primary circuit.
E. The sudden stoppage of current to the ignition coil primary winding causes its magnetic field to collapse, inducing a high voltage in the secondary winding.
F. This high voltage surge is delivered to the correct spark plug, the one ready to fire, by the distributor rotor, cap, and secondary wiring, exactly as it happens in the distributor with contact points.
G. A timing circuit in the module turns the primary circuit on again to engage the coil for the next spark cycle. This can be compared to the conventional ignition system dwell.

*Fig. 17–17. The operation of a Ford magnetic-pulse distributor.
(Courtesy of Ford Motor Co. of Canada Ltd.)*

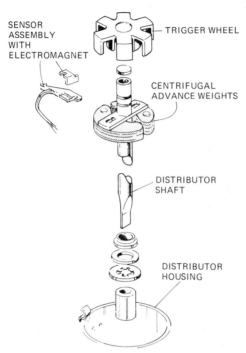

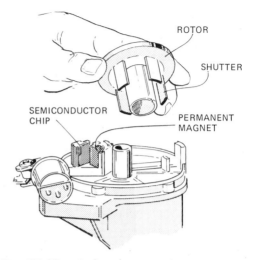

Fig. 17–19. A distributor with a triggering device using the Hall effect.

Fig. 17–18. A distributor with a metal-detection type of triggering device.

Hall Effect

A triggering assembly, using the *Hall effect,* consists of a small semiconductor chip, permanent magnet, and ring of low-reluctance shutters (Fig. 17–19). During system operation, a small amount of current passes through the semiconductor chip. This causes the chip to produce an electromagnetic field, which crosses the semiconductor at right angles and induces a voltage at the edges of the chip.

The permanent magnet is necessary in this triggering device for one purpose. That is, it provides a magnetic field that affects the field produced by the semiconductor chip during certain phases of the triggering operation.

The low-reluctance shutter blades hang below the distributor. As the blades turn, they pass between the permanent magnet and the semiconductor chip. As a result, the shutters alter the interaction between the two magnetic fields.

When the shutters rotate, they pass between the two magnetic fields. The magnetic field produced by the permanent magnet concentrates itself in the shutter blade as it passes close by. Therefore, this field does not affect the magnetic field produced by the semiconductor chip; and a voltage develops at the edges of the chip. After amplification, the voltage passes into the control unit as a signal.

When none of the shutters is close to the magnet, its magnetic field spreads out and interferes with the one produced by the chip. This action forces the chip's magnetic field to recede. As a result, the voltage at the edges of the chip disappears. In other words, the Hall-effect voltage appears and disappears in the chip edges as the position of the shutter blade changes.

Light Detection

The *light-detection* type of triggering device contains an optical device that operates on a beam of light. This device (Fig. 17–20) uses a light-emitting diode (LED) and a light sensitive phototransistor (photocell) to produce voltage signals.

Connected to the distributor shaft and rotating with it is a slotted disc: the *light-beam interrupter*. This device fits and operates between the LED and the photocell. For example, when the light from the LED passes through a slot in the light-beam interrupter, it generates a voltage in the photocell. This voltage causes a small current flow into the control unit as an on signal.

When the disc section of the interrupter is between the LED and the photocell, no voltage is generated in the photocell by the light beam. As a result, the control unit receives no signal and switches off.

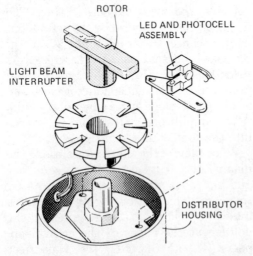

Fig. 17–20. A light-detection type of triggering device.

Switching Devices

Inductive System

As stated, there are two types of switching devices: inductive and capacitive. Up to this point, this chapter has discussed two designs of inductive switching devices in detail during its presentation of Delco contact-point and magnetic-impulse type systems.

Both of these and all other types of inductive systems operate on one basic principle. That is, a signal from a triggering device turns off a transistor in order to produce a secondary voltage surge to fire the spark plug. In other words, the inductive type of switching unit acts in the same capacity as the standard contact points to open the primary-coil circuit, thus permitting the magnetic field produced by the primary coil to induce a voltage in the secondary coil. This, of course, results in the high-voltage surge at the spark plug air gap.

Capacitive System

In a *capacitive-discharge switching device,* the control unit or module functions by first charging up an energy-storage capacitor. Then, upon a signal from a triggering device, the capacitor releases its energy to the primary side of the coil.

In the system shown in Fig. 17–21, the pulsing voltage signal from the triggering device applies itself to a silicon-controlled rectifier (SCR). This rectifier controls the operation of the capacitor of the switching unit.

The SCR, also known as *thyristor,* is a solid-state device that normally blocks

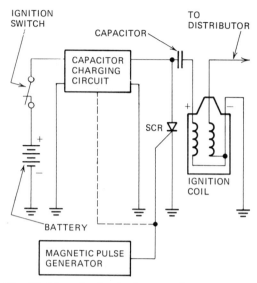

Fig. 17-21. A simple design of a capacitor-discharge switching unit connected into a primary circuit.

current flow in both directions, but it can be switched on to allow current flow in one direction while still blocking it in the opposite direction. Figure 17-22 shows an SCR connected into a typical circuit. In this situation, the SCR blocks current flow in both directions because of the open switch.

However, when the switch closes, a small amount of battery voltage applies itself on the gate of the SCR, and it begins to act as a diode (Fig. 17-23). That is, the SCR permits battery current to flow in one direction while still blocking it in the opposite direction. However, when voltage no longer is available to the gate, the SCR once again blocks current flow in both directions.

In the capacitive-discharge system, the SCR blocks all current through itself whenever the gate does not receive a signal from the triggering device (Fig. 17-24). At this time, the battery charges the capacitor; and a charging circuit raises capacitor voltage to about 300 volts.

When the triggering device sends a voltage signal to the gate of the SCR (Fig. 17-25), it permits current to flow in one direction. As a result, the 300 volts within the capacitor discharge through the coil's primary windings. This sudden increase in primary current flow and resulting magnetic field induces a high voltage in the secondary coil, which bridges the air gap at the spark plug.

In summation, the main difference be-

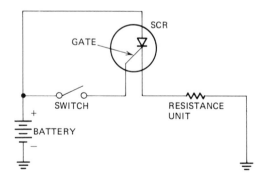

Fig. 17-22. Operation of a SCR with no voltage applied to the gate.

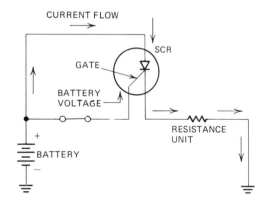

Fig. 17-23. Operation of a SCR with voltage applied to the gate.

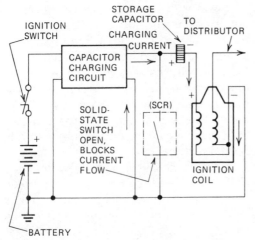

Fig. 17-24. Whenever the SCR blocks current flow, the capacitor is charged to about 300 volts.

tween the inductive and capacitive switching units is that the inductive unit shuts off the current flow through the primary-coil windings to produce a high-voltage secondary arc. Whereas, the capacitive-discharge unit very quickly increases primary-current flow to produce

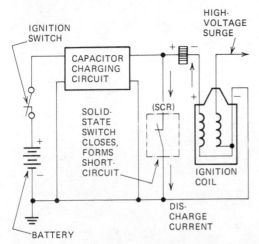

Fig. 17-25. When a triggering signal activates the SCR, the capacitor discharges through the coil's primary windings.

the secondary voltage necessary for ignition.

Advantages of the Inductive and Capacitive Systems

In the inductive system, the magnetic field around the primary coil builds slowly; and its collapse and resulting voltage induction are not as rapid as in a capacitive-discharge system. This means that the arc actually jumps the plug air gap for a longer period of time in an induction system. This helps in the ignition of the air/fuel mixture.

The capacitive-discharge system, on the other hand, offers the unusual advantage of being able to fire partially fouled spark plugs. This outstanding feature results from the extremely rapid voltage increase at the spark plug, which takes place in 1 to 2 microseconds. This compares with 80 to 130 microseconds for a standard system and 100 to 210 microseconds for the contact-point or magnetic pulse–controlled inductive-type systems.

In considering the effect of the voltage-increase time, remember that an arc cannot jump an electrode gap until the voltage reaches the ionization point of the mixture within the air gap. However, when deposits on the spark plug insulator nose form a low-resistance conductive path to ground, the high-tension voltage of the system literally bleeds away. If the electrical resistance is low enough, coil voltage never reaches a high enough value to ionize the air gap and produce an arc; therefore, the plug misfires.

However, with a capacitor-discharge system, secondary voltage builds so fast that it does not have time to leak off. Therefore, most spark plugs continue to fire even with a build up of deposits.

Unitized Electronic Ignition Systems

Up to this point, all the electronic systems discussed had a separately mounted coil and control unit in addition to a distributor cap, rotor, and high-tension wiring, which were the same or nearly the same as those found in standard ignition systems. For some time, manufacturers have produced unitized electronic ignition systems like the one shown in Fig. 17-26. In this system, all the components are in one assembly consisting of:

1. A breakerless magnetic pulse distributor

2. A distributor cap

3. An ignition coil

4. A secondary spark plug wiring harness

5. An electronic control module

The assembly is held together by two through bolts. The module itself, depending on unit design, secures to the outside of the distributor itself, or it is inside the unit near the triggering device.

Review

This section will assist you in determining how well you remember the material in this chapter. Read each item carefully. If you can't complete the statement, review the section in the chapter that covers the material.

1. An electronic ignition system does not depend on the _____ _____ to open or close the primary circuit.

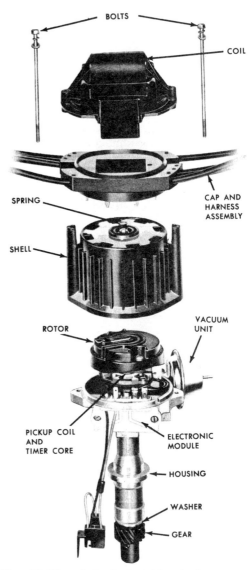

Fig. 17-26. A typical unitized electronic ignition system. (Courtesy of Delco Remy)

a. ignition switch
b. ballast resistor
c. ignition coil
d. contact points

2. In the induction switching unit, a _____ opens and closes the primary circuit.
   a. diode
   b. transistor
   c. resistor
   d. switch

3. A _____ _____ protects the switching unit compenents from damage due to high voltage induced into the primary coil.
   a. zenor diode
   b. primary resistor
   c. switching transistor
   d. bias resistor

4. The positive signal from the magnetic-pulse triggering device turns on transistor _____ in the Delco amplifier discussed in this chapter.
   a. TR-1
   b. TR-2
   c. TR-3
   d. TR-4

5. The rotating compenent of the Chrysler magnetic-impulse triggering device is the _____.
   a. magnet
   b. reluctor
   c. coil
   d. tip

6. The Chrysler ballast resistor mentioned in this chapter has _____ resistance element(s).
   a. two
   b. one

c. zero
d. three

7. The rotating member of the Ford magnetic-pulse distributor is the _____.
   a. reluctor
   b. rotor
   c. stator
   d. armature

8. The _____ type of switching units acts in much the same way as the standard contact points.
   a. reluctive
   b. capacitive
   c. inductive
   d. pulse

9. In the capacitive system, a _____ controls the operation of the capacitor within the switching unit.
   a. rectifier
   b. SCR
   c. transistor
   d. diode

10. In a _____ system, most ignition components are in one assembly.
    a. unitized
    b. standard
    c. inductive
    d. compactive

For the answers, turn to the Appendix.

Many components of certain electronic ignition systems are the same or nearly the same as those in standard ignition systems. Therefore, when testing and servicing components such as the distributor rotor and cap; the centrifugal and vacuum-advance mechanisms; the secondary high-tension cables; the ignition coil, ballast or primary resistor; and the spark plugs, follow the same procedures as outlined in Chapter 16.

However, there are many types of electronic systems—each with its own design and operating characteristics and each requiring some different testing and servicing techniques. Consequently, always follow the manufacturer's instructions and specifications when testing and servicing any electronic ignition system, in order to prevent damage to the various system components.

There is insufficient room in this chapter to discuss thoroughly all the testing and service procedures for the many systems built and installed by domestic manufacturers. Therefore, this section will present tests, inspections, and service techniques on the systems discussed in the last chapter, using the equipment commonly found in tune-up shops.

_____ Chapter 18

ELECTRONIC IGNITION SYSTEM TESTING

Testing a Contact-Point-Type System

When you are testing any type of electronic ignition system, always check the secondary circuit first, using this procedure.

1. Connect a remote starter button into the starting circuit.

2. Carefully remove the high-tension cable from any of the spark plugs.

3. Turn the ignition switch to the on position.

4. With a pair of insulated pliers, hold the end of the cable about $\frac{3}{8}$ inch (10 millimeters) from a good engine ground (Fig. 18-1).

5. Crank the engine over slowly and observe the spark. *Caution:* Permit the arc to jump to the engine ground. Do not operate the system on an open circuit.

Results and Indications

1. A hot spark is a good indication that the primary circuit, coil, and control unit (amplifier) are functioning normally. Any ignition problems such as misfiring, hard starting, or a no-start condition most likely result from conditions within the distributor cap, rotor, spark plug cables, spark plugs, or ignition timing.

2. If the spark is weak or there is no arc at all, the trouble is likely in the primary circuit, the coil, or from the coil-to-distributor high-tension cable.

Testing for an Arc From the Coil High-Tension Cable

To test the cable from the coil to the distributor for a high-voltage arc, follow this procedure.

1. Carefully remove the coil high-tension cable from the center tower of the distributor (except on Delco hi-energy ignition systems).

2. With a pair of insulated pliers, hold the end of the cable about $\frac{3}{8}$ inch (10 millimeters) from a good engine ground (Fig. 18-2).

3. With the remote starter button, slowly crank the engine over a few revolutions, and check for a good spark, arcing from the cable end to ground.

Results and Indications

If a good arc is present during this test, the cause of an ignition problem is probably in the distributor cap, rotor, spark

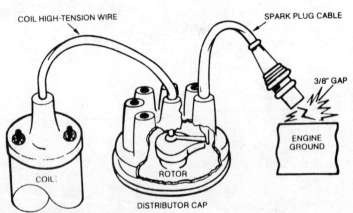

Fig. 18-1. *Testing for a good spark from a secondary spark plug cable. (Courtesy of Echlin Manufacturing Co.)*

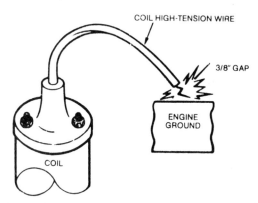

COIL HIGH-TENSION WIRE

3/8" GAP

ENGINE GROUND

COIL

Fig. 18-2. Testing for a spark from the coil-to-distributor high-tension cable. (Courtesy of Echlin Manufacturing Co.)

plug cables, or spark plugs. Always inspect the condition of these units prior to any primary tests on the ignition system. This will save you a great deal of time because problems within these parts are easy to correct.

Checking the Primary Circuit

If a hot spark did not occur at the end of the coil-to-distributor cable, remove the distributor cap and rotor, and inspect the contact points for:

1. The presence of oil or grease. The points may become contaminated by excessive or wrong cam lubricant or by oil forced into the distributor housing by crankcase pressure, developed by a faulty positive crankcase ventilation system.

2. The proper air gap. In a contact point system, the point air gap may decrease due to frictional wear on the rubbing block. If this is the case and the rubbing block is still in good condition, reset the air gap to the manufacturer's specifica-

tions. Then make sure that the cam has the proper amount of lubricant.

Checking the Distributor for Excessive Resistance

If the contact point air gap is set to specifications and the points are in good condition, the problem may be due to excessive resistance within the distributor. You can check the resistance in the distributor with a distributor tester, as mentioned in Chapter 16, or with an ohmmeter as follows.

1. Calibrate the ohmmeter as necessary, and set it for an X1 reading.

2. Rotate the engine to close the contact points.

3. Disconnect the distributor wiring harness connector.

4. Connect both ohmmeter leads to the terminals within the connector (Fig. 18-3). Note the reading on the meter.

Results and Indications

1. If the needle on the ohmmeter reads zero resistance, the contact points and wiring are all in good condition, and the problem is not within the triggering device.

2. If the meter indicates high resistance or infinity (no reading), there is high resistance in the connections or wires, or the contact points are extremely dirty.

Testing the Coil and Resistors

If the triggering unit (the contact points) passed the preceding tests, the problem may be in either the ignition coil

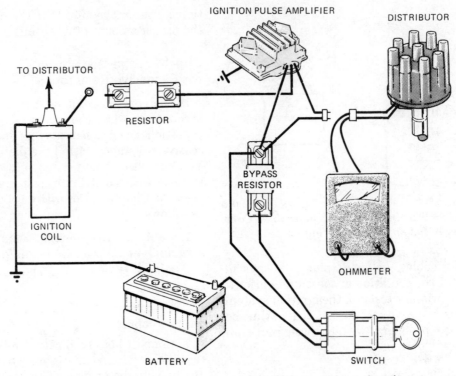

Fig. 18-3. Checking the resistance in a Delco contact point distributor with an ohmmeter.

or resistors. In either case, test these units with an ohmmeter, following the procedure outlined in Chapter 16. If the resistance in any of these components is not to specifications, replace it.

Testing the Amplifier

If there were a weak-spark or a no-spark condition from the coil, and the primary circuit passed all the preceding tests, the problem is most likely within the switching unit (amplifier). To check the amplifier for proper grounding:

1. Connect a jumper lead between the amplifier base and a good engine ground.

2. Recheck for a spark at the coil-to-dis-

tributor cable. If there is a hot spark, there is a poor ground at the amplifier base.

If after the grounding test there is still a weak or no spark at the coil high-tension cable:

1. Calibrate an ohmmeter and set it to an X1 setting.

2. Connect the ohmmeter leads to the two amplifier connector terminals. Observe the resistance reading, and then reverse the ohmmeter leads.

Results and Indications

1. If there is a low-resistance or no-resistance reading in both tests, the ampli-

fier has a defective transistor and requires replacement.

2. If there is a high reading during one test and a low reading in the other, the amplifier is in satisfactory condition.

Testing a Delco Magnetic-Pulse Nonunitized Electronic Ignition System

You will test this magnetic-pulse system for the cause of three types of conditions: no-start, misfiring, or surging. If the complaint is no-start, remove one of the spark plug cables, as mentioned earlier, and check the quality of the spark while cranking the engine with the ignition switch on. If a good spark occurs, the problem is most likely *not* in the ignition system.

If, however, a spark does not occur, check the ignition system components as follows.

1. Check all the high-tension cables with an ohmmeter as discussed in Chapter 16.

2. Check the distributor cap and rotor.

3. Test the coil and ballast resistors with an ohmmeter.

If all these parts check out satisfactorily, perform a system continuity test as follows.

1. Connect a voltmeter lead to the ignition coil positive (+) primary terminal and the other to a good engine ground (Fig. 18-4).

2. Turn the ignition switch on, and observe the voltmeter reading. The reading should be 8 to 9 volts. If the reading is battery voltage, there is an open circuit in the coil primary winding, in the resistor, or in the wiring from the coil to ground. If the reading is zero, there is an open circuit between the battery and voltmeter connections. This portion of the circuit includes the ignition switch, primary resistor, distributor, amplifier, and connector wiring. Check each of these units with an ohmmeter, and replace any defective parts.

3. Connect one voltmeter lead to the distributor side of the primary resistor and the second lead to a good engine ground (Fig. 18-5).

4. Turn the ignition switch on, and observe the meter reading. If the reading is zero, there is an open circuit in the ignition switch, resistor, or connector wiring. Use an ohmmeter to determine the cause, and replace the defective components. However, if the reading is battery voltage, there is an open within the amplifier or the connecting wiring. If the wiring is not defective, replace the amplifier.

Misfiring

If the complaint is a misfiring condition, perform the following checks in the sequence listed.

1. Inspect the fuel system for an adequate fuel supply to the engine. Pay close attention to the fuel filters and pump pressure.

2. Check ignition timing for the specified setting.

3. Remove the spark plugs. Then clean, file, and regap the old plugs, or replace worn or defective plugs in full sets.

4. Inspect all ignition system wiring—both primary and secondary. Especially check all secondary cables for brittle or

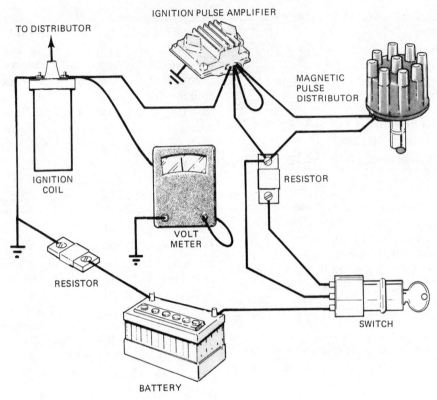

IGNITION PULSE AMPLIFIER

TO DISTRIBUTOR

MAGNETIC
PULSE
DISTRIBUTOR

IGNITION
COIL

RESISTOR

VOLT
METER

RESISTOR

SWITCH

BATTERY

Fig. 18-4.   Testing the coil and primary-circuit components for continuity with a voltmeter.

cracked insulation, loose connections, or corroded terminals. Make certain that all the cable connections seat firmly into the cap towers with all their boots securely in place.

5. Check the inner and outer surfaces of the distributor cap for cracks or carbon runners. Also inspect the rotor for wear or damage. If the cap or rotor is defective, replace it.

6. Check the pickup coil with an ohmmeter. To perform this procedure:

   a. Disconnect the distributor harness connector from the connector body.

   b. Calibrate the ohmmeter and set it to the X100 scale.

   c. Touch one ohmmeter prod to each terminal inside the connector body.

   d. Note the reading; it should be to specifications—about 550 to 750 ohms. If the meter reading is infinite (no reading), the coil is open. If the reading is low, the coil has a short circuit.

   e. Touch one of the ohmmeter prods to ground while contacting either connector body terminal or the other. The meter reading should be infinite; if not, the coil is grounded. If the coil is open, shorted, or grounded, replace it.

7. Test the ignition coil with an ohm-

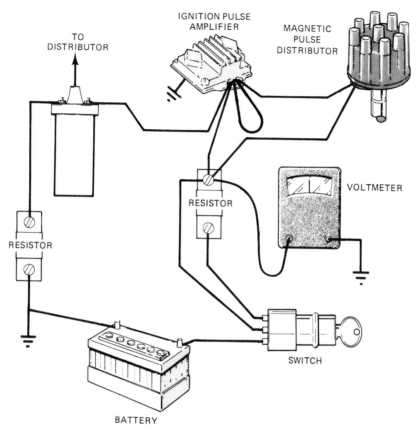

Fig. 18-5.   Testing the continuity of the ignition switch, primary resistor, and amplifier with a voltmeter.

meter or a tester approved for transistor-ignition system coils. If defective, replace the coil.

8. If all these checks or tests do not locate the cause of the trouble and the amplifier has a good ground, the amplifier is most likely defective and requires replacement.

Engine Surge

An engine power surge condition can result from reversed pickup coil leads within the connector body or an open in the pickup coil itself. To locate the cause of the problem:

1. Check the color coding of the pickup coil leads at the connector body for proper installation.

2. Check the pickup coil itself with an ohmmeter for opens, shorts, or grounds as previously outlined.

3. Test the pickup coil for opens or grounds as it moves due to the action of the vacuum advance unit. To perform this check:

a. Disconnect the vacuum-advance line, and connect either the line from a portable vacuum pump or from a distributor tester to the vacuum-advance fitting.

b. Connect the ohmmeter prods to the terminals within the connector body, and note the meter reading. It should be to specifications.

c. Regulate the applied vacuum to about 16 inches of Hg, and note the ohmmeter reading. If the reading is not the same as during step b, there is a break or short in the pickup coil wiring, and the unit requires replacement.

d. Remove one ohmmeter lead from the connector body terminal, and connect it to ground.

e. Regulate the vacuum applied to the advance unit first to 0 and then to about 16 inches of Hg, while observing the ohmmeter reading. Any reading less than infinite indicates a grounded pickup coil that requires replacement.

Testing Chrysler Electronic Ignition Systems

Precautions

When you are testing a Chrysler electronic ignition system or engine, observe the following precautions.

1. Never operate the system when the control module does not have a good ground.

2. When performing a compression or leakage test, always disconnect battery power from the system.

3. Always remove one of the battery cables before disconnecting the control module.

4. While the engine is operating, never touch the switching transistor on the control module because you may receive a high-voltage shock.

5. Never file the edges of the reluctor teeth. They must remain very sharp. If the reluctor is defective, replace it.

Specifications

When testing and servicing a Chrysler electronic system, always look up the circuit and electrical specifications for the year of the engine. This is necessary due to the variations within the system in order to permit it to function on a given engine configuration. A typical wiring or circuit diagram is shown in Fig. 18-6.

Inspecting the Distributor

If the engine will not start, first perform the secondary spark test as mentioned earlier in this chapter. If there is no spark or it is very weak at both the spark plug

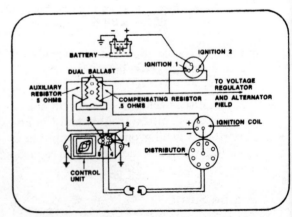

Fig. 18-6.   A typical diagram for a Chrysler electronic ignition system. (Courtesy of Echlin Manufacturing Co.)

and coil high-tension cables, inspect the distributor and its circuit as follows.

1. Check the battery and cable connections for cleanliness and security. Clean them both; tighten all clamps or connectors as necessary.

2. Remove the distributor cap and rotor. Then check the air gap between the reluctor tooth and the pickup coil. If it is not to specifications, adjust it, following this procedure.

    a. Loosen the pickup coil hold-down screw (Fig. 18–7).

    b. Insert a 0.008-inch (0.2-millimeter) nonmagnetic feeler gauge between a reluctor tooth and the pickup coil pole piece. Adjust the pickup coil so that the feeler gauge is snug. Then tighten the hold-down screw.

    c. Rotate the engine two complete turns, checking each reluctor tooth in turn for its proper distance from the pickup coil. The air gap should never be less than 0.006 inch (0.15 millimeter) or more than 0.010 inch (.25 millimeter) between any reluctor tooth and the coil.

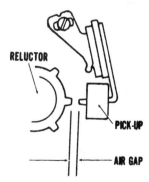

Fig. 18–7. Adjusting the pickup coil to reluctor air gap. (Courtesy of Echlin Manufacturing Co.)

3. Check the distributor cap for cracks, excess tower corrosion, or carbon tracking. If there is evidence of any of these problems, replace the cap.

4. Check the primary wires at the ignition coil and dual ballast resistor for tightness.

Primary-Circuitry Voltage Tests

If these checks or inspections do not locate the cause of the problem, the following tests will determine if other system components are defective. When performing these tests, it is necessary to connect a 10-ohm, 2-watt resistor between the circuit being tested and a ground. This resistor serves as a load on the circuit and results in a more accurate reading.

Test A—Cavity 1 Circuitry

To perform this test:

1. Remove the wiring connector from the control module in order to expose the wiring harness connector cavities. *Caution:* When you remove or install this wiring connector at the control module, make sure that the ignition switch is off, or disconnect a battery cable. Otherwise, the control module will sustain damage.

2. Connect the 10-ohm, 2-watt resistor between cavity 1 and a good ground.

3. Connect one voltmeter lead to a good ground and the other to the terminal within connector cavity 1 (Fig. 18–8). Then turn on the ignition switch.

Results and Indications

1. The available voltage at the terminal in cavity 1 should be within 1 volt of total battery voltage, with all accessories off.

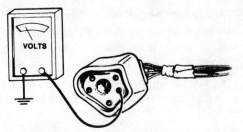

Fig. 18-8. Testing the voltage at connector cavity 1. (Courtesy of Echlin Manufacturing Co.)

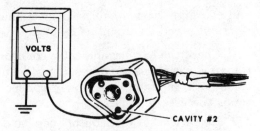

Fig. 18-10. Testing the circuitry of cavity 2. (Courtesy of Echlin Manufacturing Co.)

2. If there is more than a 1-volt difference between the reading and battery voltage, the circuit connected to cavity terminal 1 requires further checking and replacement as necessary. The heavy dark line in Fig. 18-9 outlines the circuit connected into cavity 1.

Test B—Cavity 2 Circuitry

To perform this test:

1. Connect a 10-ohm, 2-watt resistor between the terminal within cavity 2 and ground (Fig. 18-10).

2. Attach one voltmeter lead to ground and the other to the terminal in cavity 2.

3. Turn on the ignition switch, and note the voltmeter reading.

Results and Indications

1. The available voltage at cavity 2 should be within 1 volt of battery voltage, with all accessories off.

2. If the noted reading indicates more than a 1-volt difference, check the wires and connectors shown by the dark lines in Fig. 18-11. In this situation, the compo-

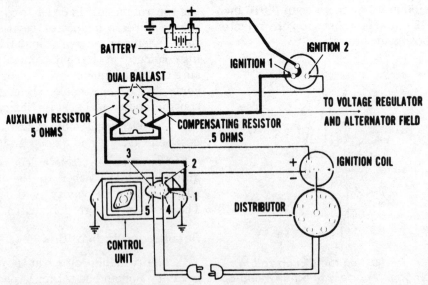

Fig. 18-9. The circuit connected to the terminal in cavity 1. (Courtesy of Echlin Manufacturing Co.)

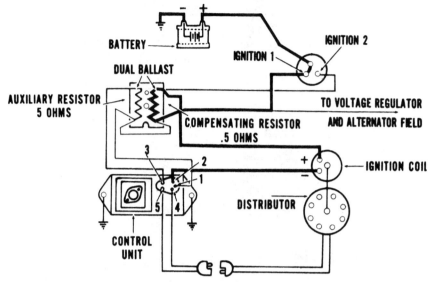

Fig. 18–11. The circuit connected to the terminal within cavity 2. (Courtesy of Echlin Manufacturing Co.)

nents that can cause ignition failure are the ignition switch, dual-ballast resistor, ignition coil, or related wires and connections. Test all these components individually, and make replacements as necessary.

Test C—Cavity 3 Circuitry

To make this particular test:

1. Attach the 10-ohm, 2-watt resistor between ground and the terminal within cavity 3 (Fig. 18–12).

2. Connect one voltmeter lead to ground and the other to the terminal inside cavity 3.

3. Turn on the ignition switch, and note the reading on the voltmeter.

Results and Indications

1. The available voltage should be within 1 volt of total battery voltage, with all accessories off.

2. If there is more than a 1-volt difference, repair the wires or connections

shown by the dark lines in Fig. 18–13. Make all repairs or replacements to correct the cause of the problem.

Testing the Coil with an Ohmmeter

You can test the coil from a Chrysler electronic ignition system with an ohmmeter. When doing so, always follow the procedure outlined in Chapter 16; compare the results with the manufacturer's specifications.

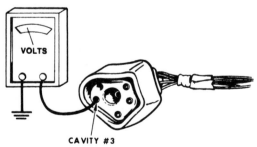

Fig. 18–12. Testing the circuitry of cavity 3. (Courtesy of Echlin Manufacturing Co.)

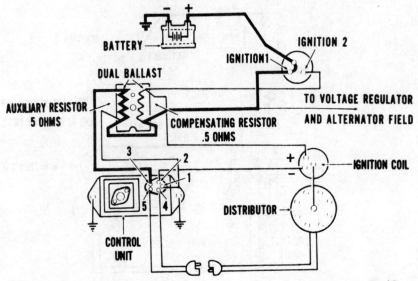

Fig. 18-13.   The circuit connected to the terminal within cavity 3. (Courtesy of Echlin Manufacturing Co.)

Testing the Ballast Resistor with an Ohmmeter

To test the dual-ballast resistor as utilized with the Chrysler electronic system, follow these steps.

1. As necessary, calibrate the ohmmeter, and then adjust it for an X1 scale reading.

2. With the ignition switch off, connect the ohmmeter leads to the two opposite terminals on the resistor, as shown in Fig. 18-14. Note the reading.

3. Switch the ohmmeter leads to the second pair of resistor terminals. Note the reading.

Results and Indications

1. The reading for the auxiliary resistor molded into the unit should be 4.75 to 5.75 ohms of resistance.

2. The reading for the wire-wound resistor should be 0.5 to 0.6 ohms. If either

resistor varies from these specifications, replace the ballast-resistor assembly.

Testing the Pickup Coil with an Ohmmeter

To test the resistance in the pickup coil, follow these directions.

1. As necessary, calibrate the ohmmeter, and set it for an X100 scale reading.

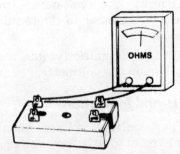

Fig. 18-14.   Testing the dual-ballast resistor with an ohmmeter. (Courtesy of Echlin Manufacturing Co.)

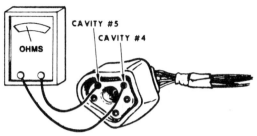

Fig. 18–15. Testing the pickup coil with an ohmmeter. (Courtesy of Echlin Manufacturing Co.)

2. With the ignition switch in the *off* position, connect the ohmmeter leads to the wire harness cavities 4 and 5 (Fig. 18–15). Note the reading.

Results and Indications

1. If the reading is 150 to 900 ohms or the amount specified by the manufacturer, the pickup coil is good.

2. If the reading is higher or lower than the specified amount, disconnect the dual-lead connector coming from the distributor (Fig. 18–16). Then connect the ohmmeter leads to the distributor terminals within the connector. If the reading is still not to specifications, replace the pickup coil assembly.

However, if the reading is within specifications, inspect the wiring harness from

the dual-lead connection back to the control module.

3. If the reading is not to specifications, also test the pickup coil for a grounded circuit as follows.

a. Connect either ohmmeter lead to ground and the other to any lead connection terminal in the distributor harness.

b. Note the reading on the ohmmeter. The reading should be infinity (no reading). If the meter shows continuity, the pickup coil is grounded and requires replacement.

Checking the Control Module

To make this test:

1. Calibrate the ohmmeter as necessary, and set it for an X1 reading.

2. Connect one ohmmeter lead to a good ground and the other lead to control module connector pin 5 (Fig. 18–17).

3. The ohmmeter should show continuity (zero resistance) between ground and the connector pin. If the meter does not show continuity, remove the module, clean the module and firewall mating surfaces, and reinstall the module. Next

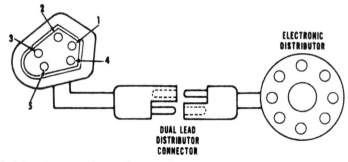

Fig. 18–16. Testing the pickup coil's resistance at the dual-lead connector. (Courtesy of Echlin Manufacturing Co.)

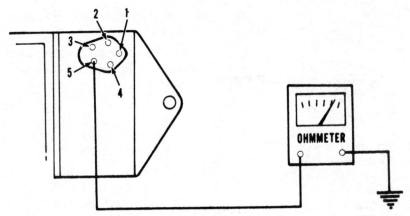

Fig. 18-17.   Testing the control module for proper grounding. (Courtesy of Echlin Manufacturing Co.)

tighten the attaching bolts to specifications.

4. Recheck for continuity. If the meter still does not indicate a continuity reading, replace the control module.

5. If all test results are to specifications and the ignition system still does not function properly, replace the control module.

Testing a Ford Electronic Ignition System

When performing any test or services involving the Ford ignition system, always follow the same precautions mentioned earlier under the test procedures for Chrysler systems. Also, be sure to look up in the manufacturer's shop manual the ignition circuit and electrical specifications for the year of the engine that you are repairing. This is necessary because electrical specifications can change from year to year.

Stator Tests—Resistance

If the secondary spark test indicates a weak- or no-spark condition, begin testing the ignition system components with the stator as follows.

1. Calibrate the ohmmeter as necessary, and adjust it for an X100 scale reading.

2. With the ignition switch off, disconnect the distributor wiring harness connector. Then connect one ohmmeter lead to the purple stator-lead terminal and the other to the orange lead terminal (Fig. 18-18). Note the reading.

Results and Indications

If the reading is not 400 to 800 ohms or the amount specified by the manufacturer, replace the stator assembly.

Stator Tests—Ground Circuit

To test the black ground wire within the distributor harness for an open circuit:

1. Calibrate the ohmmeter as necessary, and adjust it for an X1 reading.

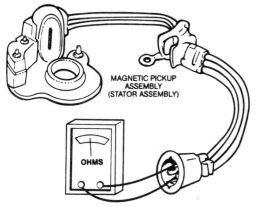

Fig. 18-18. Testing stator resistance. (Courtesy of Echlin Manufacturing Co.)

2. Connect one ohmmeter lead to ground and the other lead to the black wire's terminal in the connector (Fig. 18-19).

3. Note the reading. You should get a zero resistance (full-continuity) reading. If not, perform repairs or replacements as necessary. This wire must have full continuity because it grounds the control module.

Stator Test—Grounded Windings

To perform this particular test:

1. Calibrate the ohmmeter as necessary, and adjust it for an X1 reading.

2. Connect one ohmmeter lead to ground and the other to either the orange or purple stator-lead terminal in the harness connector (Fig. 18-20).

3. Note the reading. If the meter shows any continuity reading, the stator has become grounded and requires replacement.

Testing the Coil with an Ohmmeter

To test a Ford electronic ignition-system coil, follow these steps.

1. Calibrate the ohmmeter as necessary, and set it for an X1 scale reading.

2. Connect one ohmmeter lead to the coil terminal marked DEC and the other

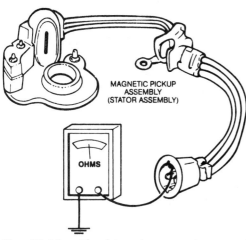

Fig. 18-19. Checking the stator's ground circuit. (Courtesy of Echlin Manufacturing Co.)

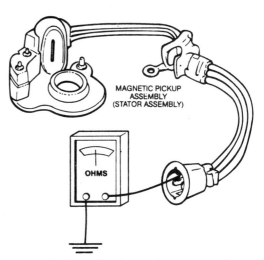

Fig. 18-20. Checking the stator for a grounded circuit. (Courtesy of Echlin Manufacturing Co.)

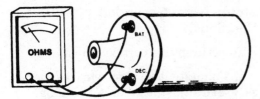

Fig. 18–21. Testing the resistance in the primary section of a Ford coil. (Courtesy of Echlin Manufacturing Co.)

to the BAT terminal (Fig. 18–21). The reading should be 1 to 2 ohms or the amount specified by the manufacturer. If the reading is not to specifications, replace the coil.

3. Adjust the ohmmeter for an X1000 scale reading.

4. Connect one of the ohmmeter leads to the DEC terminal and the other to the secondary tower (Fig. 18–22).

5. Note the reading. It should be 7,000 to 13,000 ohms or that specified by the manufacturer. If the reading is not to specifications, replace the coil.

Voltage Tests

When performing the following voltage tests, a 10-ohm, 2-watt resistor and a wiring diagram for the circuit are necessary. The resistor, when installed between ground and the test circuit, serves as a load during the test, thereby providing a more accurate reading.

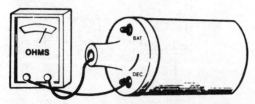

Fig. 18–22. Testing the resistance within the secondary section of a Ford coil. (Courtesy of Echlin Manufacturing Co.)

With this in mind, perform the voltage checks as follows.

1. Using the wiring diagram as a guide, check all the wires in the system to make sure that they are connected properly.

2. Check all electrical connections to be sure that they are clean and tight.

3. With the ignition switch off, unplug the control module wiring harness.

4. Using the wiring diagram as a guide, locate the power-input circuit terminal at the wiring harness connector.

5. Connect the 10-ohm, 2-watt resistor between this terminal and ground.

6. Connect one voltmeter lead to ground and the other to the power-input terminal.

7. Turn on the ignition switch.

8. Note the voltmeter reading. It should be within 1 volt of battery voltage, with the ignition switch in both the run and start positions. If not, repair or replace the battery cables, ignition switch, or related wiring.

9. Connect the 10-ohm, 2-watt resistor between the DEC terminal in the harness connector and ground.

10. Connect one voltmeter lead to ground and the other to this DEC terminal.

11. Turn on the ignition switch.

12. Note the reading. It should be within 1 volt of battery voltage. If not, the ignition coil and related circuitry require replacement or repair.

13. If the system still does not operate or its operation is unsatisfactory, replace the control module.

Testing HEI, Delco Unitized Ignition Systems

When testing a unitized high-energy ignition (HEI) system, be aware of these facts. First, the integral coil windings have two different types of connections. For example, early types have one secondary winding lead connected to the primary circuit (Fig. 18-23). On the other hand, the late designs have one secondary lead connected directly to ground (lower illustration, Fig. 18-23).

Second, always follow the precautions set forth earlier in this chapter relating to the testing of electronic ignition systems. Also, make sure that you look up in the manufacturer's shop manual the circuit being tested along with its specifications.

Voltage Tests—Battery Terminal Connector Plug

If, after checking the system for a good secondary spark at a plug cable, the arc is weak or nonexistent, begin testing the system, following these steps.

1. Remove the battery terminal connector plug from the distributor.

2. Connect a 10-ohm, 2-watt resistor between ground and the battery terminal within the plug.

3. Connect one lead of a voltmeter to ground and the other to the battery terminal (Fig. 18-24).

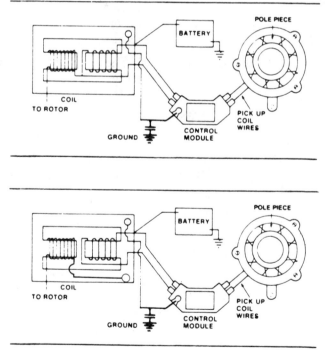

Fig. 18-23. Coil connections on early and late unitized HEI systems. (Courtesy of Echlin Manufacturing Co.)

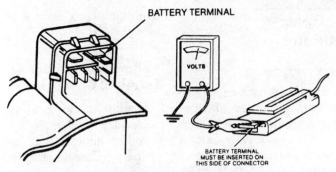

Fig. 18–24. Testing the battery terminal within the connector plug. (Courtesy of Echlin Manufacturing Co.)

4. Turn the ignition switch on.

5. Note the reading. It should be the same as battery voltage in both the run and start switch positions.

Testing Integral Coils with an Ohmmeter—Primary Side

To perform this check:

1. Remove the distributor cap and wires as an assembly.

2. Calibrate the ohmmeter as necessary, and set it for an X1 scale reading.

3. Connect one ohmmeter lead to the *battery* terminal in the distributor cap and the other to the *tach* terminal (Fig. 18–25).

4. Note the reading. If it is not 0.4 to 1.0 ohms or the amount specified by the manufacturer, replace the ignition coil.

5. Remove the ohmmeter lead from the battery terminal, and connect it to

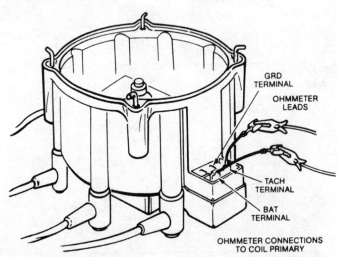

Fig. 18–25. Testing the primary side of an integral coil. (Courtesy of Echlin Manufacturing Co.)

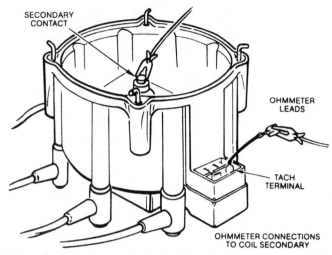

Fig. 18–26.   Testing the secondary side of an integral coil. (Courtesy of Echlin Manufacturing Co.).

ground. The reading on the ohmmeter should be infinity (no reading). If the meter shows continuity, replace the coil.

Secondary Side

To make this check:

1. Calibrate the ohmmeter as necessary, and adjust it for an X1000 scale.

2. Connect one ohmmeter lead to the coil's secondary tower contact and the other to the tach terminal on early type units or to the middle terminal of the cap connector on late types (Fig. 18–26).

3. Note the reading. It should be 16,000 to 40,000 ohms or the amount specified by the manufacturer. If the reading is too high, too low, or infinity, replace the coil.

Testing the Resistance of the Pickup Coil

To perform this particular test:

1. Calibrate the ohmmeter as necessary, and set it for an X100 reading.

2. Disconnect the pickup leads from the control module.

3. Connect one of the ohmmeter leads to each of the pickup leads at the distributor (Fig. 18–27).

4. Note the reading. It should be 500 to 1,500 ohms or the amount specified by the manufacturer. If not, replace the pickup coil.

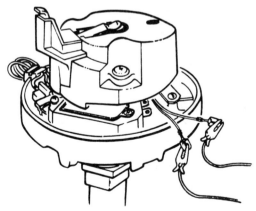

Fig. 18–27.   Testing pickup coil resistance. (Courtesy of Echlin Manufacturing Co.)

5. Wiggle and flex the pickup leads while observing the ohmmeter scale. If the reading varies at this time, the leads have sustained damage due to movement of the pickup coil assembly by the vacuum advance. In this case, replace the pickup coil assembly.

Checking the Pickup Coil for Grounds

To test the pickup coil for grounds:

1. Calibrate the ohmmeter as necessary, and adjust it for an X1 scale reading.

2. Connect one ohmmeter lead to ground and the other to either pickup coil lead (Fig. 18–28).

3. Note the reading. It should be infinite (no reading). If the meter shows continuity, replace the pickup coil.

Testing the RFI Capacitor

To check the radio frequency interference (RFI) capacitor with an ohmmeter:

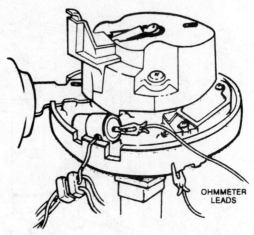

Fig. 18–29. Testing the RFI capacitor. (Courtesy of Echlin Manufacturing Co.)

1. Calibrate the ohmmeter as necessary, and set it for an X1000 scale reading.

2. Disconnect the RFI capacitor.

3. Connect one ohmmeter lead to a good ground and the other on the capacitor terminal (Fig. 18–29).

4. Note the reading. The meter needle should move slightly and then return to infinity. If there is any continuous reading other than infinity, replace the capacitor.

5. If the system still does not operate or operates unsatisfactorily and you have checked all the wiring connections and performed the preceding tests, replace the control module.

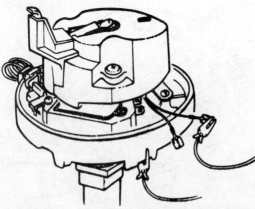

Fig. 18–28. Testing the pickup coil for grounds. (Courtesy of Echlin Manufacturing Co.)

Review

The following statements will assist you in determining how well you remember the material contained in this chapter. Read each item carefully before completing it. If you can't, review the section in the chapter that covers the material.

1. When testing any electronic ignition system, check the _____ _____ first.
   a. primary circuit
   b. secondary circuit
   c. storage battery
   d. ignition coil

2. If a contact-point type of electronic ignition system did not pass the secondary-spark test, first inspect the _____ _____.
   a. contact points
   b. ignition coil
   c. primary resistor
   d. distributor cap

3. When testing a magnetic-pulse system for continuity with a voltmeter, the reading at the coil should be _____ _____ volts.
   a. 4 to 6
   b. 6 to 7
   c. 8 to 9
   d. 10 to 11

4. The resistance in the pickup coil of early magnetic-pulse Delco systems should be _____ _____ _____ ohms.
   a. 450 to 650
   b. 550 to 750
   c. 650 to 850
   d. 750 to 950

5. While working on an operating Chrysler engine with an electronic system, never touch the _____ _____ because you may receive a shock.
   a. contact points
   b. ground cable
   c. zenor diode
   d. switching transistor

6. When performing the primary-circuit voltage tests on a Chrysler system, you will need a _____ _____ resistor.

   a. 6-ohm, 1-watt
   b. 8-ohm, 2-watt
   c. 10-ohm, 2-watt
   d. 12-ohm, 4-watt

7. When testing the various cavity terminals of a Chrysler control module wiring harness connector, the reading should be within _____ volt(s) of battery voltage.
   a. 1
   b. 2
   c. 3
   d. 4

8. The resistance of the auxiliary side of a Chrysler dual-ballast resistor should be _____ ohms.
   a. 1.75 to 2.75
   b. 2.75 to 3.75
   c. 3.75 to 4.75
   d. 4.75 to 5.75

9. The resistance within the primary side of a Ford electronic ignition coil should be _____ ohms.
   a. 0 to 1
   b. 1 to 2
   c. 2 to 3
   d. 3 to 4

10. A Delco HEI coil may have its secondary coil connected into the circuit _____ different ways.
    a. 2
    b. 3
    c. 4
    d. none of these

11. The resistance of the secondary portion of a HEI integral coil should be _____ _____ _____ ohms.
    a. 12,000 to 36,000
    b. 14,000 to 38,000
    c. 16,000 to 40,000
    d. 18,000 to 42,000

For the answers, turn to the Appendix.

System Function

When an automobile engine is operating, the design of the charging system is such that it supplies all the current required by the vehicle's electrical system and also charges the battery. The battery supplies the necessary voltage and current flow to turn the engine over for starting and the occasional extra electrical demands that exceed the capacity of the charging system. This particular condition usually occurs at idle engine speed when a large number of accessories and lights are functioning.

D.C. Systems

Before the early 1960s, the typical charging system on an automobile consisted of a belt-driven generator, regulator, and necessary electrical wiring and switches to connect these units into the vehicle's electrical system (Fig. 19-1). The generator in this system converted mechanical energy to electrical energy by rotating a series of conductors within a stationary magnetic field. This action induced a voltage into the rotating conductors on the armature; if the armature itself connected into an external circuit, direct current (d.c.) would flow. Thus, this form of charging device is known as a *direct-current generator*.

The regulator used with a d.c. generator contains three operating units: the cutout relay, voltage regulator, and current regulator. The *cutout relay* connects the generator into the battery circuit when the generator's output reaches a predetermined amount. The same relay also disconnects the generator from the system when its induced voltage falls below a given amount.

_____ Chapter 19

OPERATION AND TESTING OF THE CHARGING SYSTEM

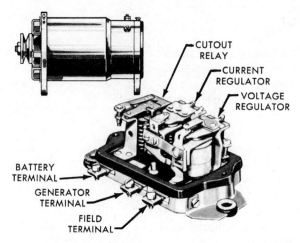

- CUTOUT RELAY
- CURRENT REGULATOR
- VOLTAGE REGULATOR
- BATTERY TERMINAL
- GENERATOR TERMINAL
- FIELD TERMINAL

Fig. 19-1. A typical d.c. generator and regulator. (Courtesy of Delco Remy)

This latter action prevents the battery from discharging through the generator when the engine is operating at low speeds or is shut off.

The *voltage regulator* within the regulator assembly prevents the generator's output voltage from exceeding a given value. This is necessary to protect the electrical units of the vehicle from damage due to high voltage that the generator can produce at high rpm.

The *current regulator* stops the generator from producing excessive current output at high engine speeds. This is necessary to protect the generator itself from overheating and prematurely burning out.

A.C. Systems

Beginning in the early 1960s, manufacturers began to install *diode-rectified alternators* (Fig. 19-2) in place of the d.c. generator for many reasons. The most important reason for this change was the fact that vehicles were beginning to have more electrically operated accessories and

these same vehicles had to operate in slow-speed driving because of greater traffic congestion. Both factors contributed to the need for a generating device that was capable of developing a higher charging rate not only at slower vehicle speeds but also at engine idle. The a.c. generator

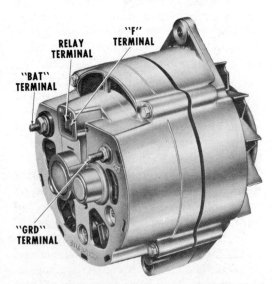

- "F" TERMINAL
- RELAY TERMINAL
- "BAT" TERMINAL
- "GRD" TERMINAL

Fig. 19-2. A typical automotive alternator. (Courtesy of Delco Remy)

(alternator) can meet this demand by delivering 6 to 10 amperes at normal engine idle speed while the d.c. generator at the same rpm may not develop enough output to close the cutout relay.

The other advantages of an alternator over the d.c. unit are that the alternator is more compact, weighs less, and rarely requires servicing. In addition, the regulating device used with the alternator has no cutout relay or current regulator.

The final advantage of the alternator is that it provides a distinct mechanical advantage over the d.c. unit. The typical d.c. generator usually operates through a belt-and-pulley arrangement at about twice the crankshaft speed. However, with this arrangement, the d.c. generator armature can easily reach speeds in excess of 10,000 rpm. Such speeds can cause the armature to throw its windings. A pulley resizing can resolve this problem by lowering armature speed, but this adversely affects low-speed generator output due to too slow an armature rotation.

The alternator due to its construction is capable of rotational speeds of 15,000 rpm without any danger of physical damage. Thus, the alternator can use a smaller pulley than the d.c. generator and therefore can produce a higher output at low rpm with no high-speed problems.

Alternator Construction

The typical alternator consists of four major components: a stator assembly, a rotor assembly, and two end-frame assemblies (Fig. 19-3). The *stator assembly,* as its name implies, is a stationary component that fits between the two end frames. This assembly has a number of conductors (wires) into which the rotor's magnetic field induces voltage.

The stator assembly (Fig. 19-4) usually

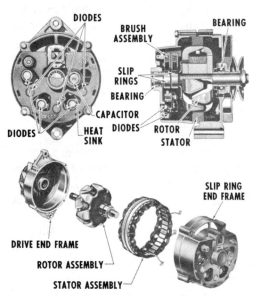

Fig. 19-3.   The components of a typical alternator. (Courtesy of Delco Remy)

consists of three conductors wound into slots in a cylindrical, laminated frame. The laminations prevent unwanted eddy magnetic currents from forming in the frame.

The manufacturer forms each of the three conductors into a number of coils spaced evenly around the frame. Each in-

Fig. 19-4.   The design of the stator assembly. (Courtesy of Delco Remy)

dividual coil has 8 to 16 turns, depending on stator design. In addition, there are as many coils in each of the three windings as there are pairs of N and S rotor poles. Finally, one end of each stator winding attaches to a separate pair of diodes, one being positive while the other is negative.

Rotor Function and Design

The *rotor* is the only moving or rotating member within the alternator (Fig. 19-5). The function of the rotor, when the alternator is in operation, is to produce a rotating magnetic field. This field, in turn, induces voltage into the stator windings.

The rotor assembly consists of a coil, pole pieces, shaft, and two slip rings. The magnetic field of the rotor is due to current flow through the rotor coil. This coil is nothing more than a number of windings wrapped around an iron core (Fig. 19-6). The strength of the magnetic field produced by this coil varies with the amount of current flow through the windings themselves. As a result, altering the current flow through the coil affects the voltage output of the alternator.

The coil itself fits between two interlocking soft-iron sections, called *pole pieces* (Fig. 19-7). Each pole piece bears

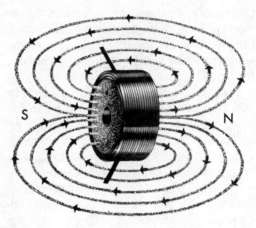

Fig. 19-6.   The structure of a rotor coil. (Courtesy of Delco Remy)

against either end of the core of the rotor coil; as current flows through the coil, the iron core becomes a magnet. As a result, the pole pieces take on the magnetic polarity of the end of the core that they touch. Consequently, one pole piece has an N polarity while the other has an S polarity.

Each pole piece also has extended segments, known as *fingers*. These fingers form the actual magnetic poles. Each pole piece then has either all N or all S poles, with a typical automotive rotor having 14

Fig. 19-5.   The rotor assembly of an alternator. (Courtesy of Delco Remy)

Fig. 19-7.   The rotor coil fits between the pole pieces. (Courtesy of Delco Remy)

poles, 7 Ns and 7 Ss. The magnetic field between the pole pieces moves from the N poles to the adjacent S poles (Fig. 19-8). This design increases the number of magnetic lines of force within the alternator and therefore the potential for voltage output.

The pole pieces, windings, and core, in addition to the slip rings, press onto the alternator shaft. Two bearings, one in each end-frame assembly, support this rotating shaft. Also, outside one end frame, a belt pulley and fan attach to the end of the shaft. A belt from the vehicle's engine passes over this pulley to turn the alternator shaft and rotor assembly.

The slip rings press onto the rotor shaft. These two slip rings have a design that provides insulation between themselves and the stator shaft. In addition, one end of the rotor windings connects to each slip ring (Fig. 19-7).

A carbon brush rides on each slip ring to carry current to and from the rotor windings (Fig. 19-9). These brushes actually connect in parallel with the alternator output circuit. Consequently, they draw some of the alternator output and route it through the rotor windings when the unit is in operation. However, before the en-

Fig. 19-9. The brushes carry current to and from the rotor windings via the slip rings. (Courtesy of Delco Remy)

gine starts, the battery supplies this initial current flow.

Field current through the brushes in the alternator is usually about 1.5 to 3 amperes. Because these brushes carry such little current, they do not require maintenance very often.

The two *end-frame assemblies* contain the bearings that support the rotor, and they enclose the support the remaining alternator components (Fig. 19-3). Furthermore, both end frames have cast-in air ducts to allow air to pass through the inside of the alternator. This air flow carries heat away from internal alternator components. The fan on the end of the rotor shaft provides this air flow.

Attached to the rear end frame is a heat sink that contains three positive diodes (Fig. 19-10). The manufacturer insulates these diodes from the end frame yet mounts them in such a manner that heat can readily dissipate from them to the passing air. Pressed in the end frame itself are the three negative diodes. All six of these diodes attach to the three stator windings.

The diode end frame also supports the holder for the two slip-ring brushes. One

Fig. 19-8. The magnetic field travels from the N to adjacent S pole in the rotor. (Courtesy of Delco Remy)

Fig. 19-10. Three positive diodes mount directly onto the heat sink. (Courtesy of Delco Remy)

of these brushes actually grounds to the end frame while the other is insulated from the frame. Two springs within this holder keep the brushes in constant contact with the slip rings.

Alternator Operation

As discussed in Chapter 12, anytime a magnetic field moves across a conductor, voltage is induced in the conductor itself. For example, consider a bar magnet with its magnetic field rotating inside a loop of wire (Fig. 19-11). With the magnet rotat-

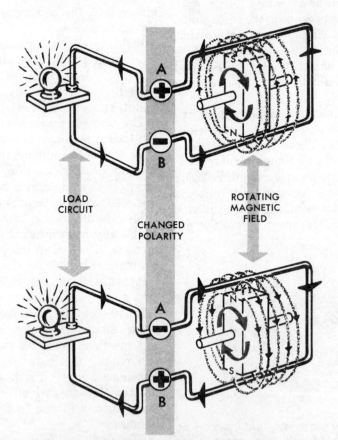

Fig. 19-11.   Operation of a simple alternator. (Courtesy of Delco Remy)

ing as shown and the S pole of the magnet directly under the top portion of the loop and the N pole over the bottom loop, the induced voltage causes current to flow in the direction indicated. Since current flows from positive to negative through the external circuit (as determined by the right-hand rule and conventional theory of current flow), the end of the loop marked *A* will have a positive (+) polarity while the end of wire *B* will be negative.

When the bar magnet moves through a half revolution, the N pole has moved directly under the top conductor while the S pole is over the bottom conductor. As a result, the induced voltage causes the current to flow in the opposite direction. The end of the loop marked *A* becomes negative (−) polarity while the wire end *B* is positive (+). Obviously, the polarity at the ends of the wire changes as the magnet rotates.

After a second half revolution, the bar magnet is back at its starting point where *A* is positive (+) and *B* is negative (−). Therefore, current flows through the external circuit first in one direction and then in the other. This is alternating current (a.c.), which the alternator develops internally.

An alternator made with a bar magnet rotating inside a single loop of wire is not very practical, since the unit could produce very little voltage and current flow. Manufacturers improve the performance of the alternator by placing both the conductor (the stator winding) and the rotating magnet (the rotor) inside an iron frame, the stator core (Fig. 19–12).

The iron frame not only provides a place into which the loops of wire are held but also acts as a conducting path for the magnetic lines of force. Without the stator frame or core, magnetism, after leaving an

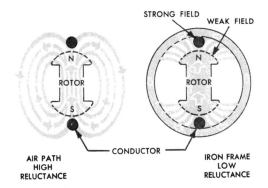

Fig. 19–12. The stator frame improves alternator performance by providing a good path for the magnetic lines of force. (Courtesy of Delco Remy)

N rotor pole, would travel through the air to get to an S pole. Because air has a high resistance to magnetism, only a few lines would come out of a N and enter a S pole.

Since iron conducts magnetism very easily, adding the stator frame greatly increases the number of lines between the N and S poles. This simply means that more lines of force cut across the stator conductors that lie between the rotor poles and the frame.

It is also important to note that a very large number of magnetic lines of force is at the center of the tip of each pole, whereas there are only a few lines of force at the leading and tailing edges of the rotor fingers. Thus, there is a strong magnetic field at the center and a weak field at the leading and tailing edges. This condition results from the fact that the air gap between the magnet and the stator frame is greater at the leading and tailing edges than at the center of the rotor finger.

As mentioned in Chapter 12, the amount of voltage induced in a conductor is proportional to the number of lines of force that cut across the conductor in a given length of time (Fig. 19–13). Conse-

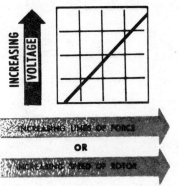

Fig. 19-13. *Increasing either the number of lines of force or the speed of the rotor raises the induction of voltage. (Courtesy of Delco Remy)*

quently, if the number of lines of force doubles, the induced voltage doubles. To increase voltage induction, the automotive alternator has a rotor with a large number of magnetic poles instead of just the N and S poles of a bar magnet used to explain simple alternator operation.

The induced voltage also increases if the rotor turns faster. This results from the fact that the total lines of force cut across the conductor in a shorter period of time.

Consequently, increasing the lines of force cutting across the conductor or the rotational speed of the rotor will produce higher induced voltages. Similarly, decreasing the lines of force or rotor speed will cause a reduction in voltage induction.

Voltage Curve

Illustrated in Fig. 19-14 are the different positions of the rotor as it turns at a constant speed. In the upper portion of this illustration is a curve showing the magnitude of the voltage generated in the conductor as the rotor revolves. This voltage curve shows generated voltage or electrical pressure measured across the ends of the conductor.

When the rotor is in position 1, there is no voltage generated in the wire loop because there are not any lines of force cutting across the conductor. As the rotor turns and approaches position 2, the rather weak magnetic field at the leading edge of a rotor finger starts to cut across the wire and begins to induce a weak volt-

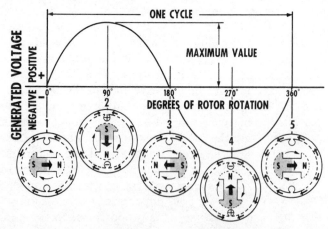

Fig. 19-14. *The induced voltage curve of an alternator with just one conductor. (Courtesy of Delco Remy)*

age. When the rotor finger finally reaches position 2, the generated voltage reaches its maximum value, as shown above the horizontal line in the illustration. The maximum voltage occurs when the center of the finger is directly under the conductor; in this position, the conductor itself is cut by the heaviest concentration of magnetic lines of force.

By applying the right-hand rule for conventional current flow to the conductor with the rotor at position 2, it is obvious that the direction of current flow within the wire is out of the top end and into the bottom end. Thus, the top end of the conductor is positive (+) and the lower end negative (−).

The voltage curve shown above the horizontal line represents the positive (+) voltage at the top end of the wire loop, generated as the rotor turns from position 1 to position 3. Note that as the rotor turns from position 2 to position 3, the voltage decreases until it reaches 0 at position 3. This is due to the magnetic field again moving away from the conductor.

As the rotor moves from position 3 to position 4, the N pole of the rotor passes under the top portion of the wire loop; the S pole travels over the bottom part. Using the right-hand rule, the top end of the wire is now negative (−) while the bottom is positive (+). This negative voltage at the upper end of the loop is shown in the illustration by the curve, which moves below the horizontal line.

The voltage again returns to zero as the rotor moves from position 4 to position 5. This is the direct result of the rotor's magnetic field moving away from the conductor and into a neutral zone.

The voltage curve shown in Fig. 19-14 represents 1 complete revolution or cycle of the rotor. If the rotor makes 60 com-

plete turns in 1 second, there will be 60 such curves—one coming right after the other. This results in 60 cycles per second. The number of cycles per second is known as *frequency*. Since automotive alternator speed varies, frequency is constantly changing.

Thus far, we have considered only the voltage induction in a single loop, or phrase, of wire in the stator, which results in a low-voltage output. Manufacturers raise the induced voltage by increasing the number of windings, or phases, in the stator. In actual practice, the automotive alternator stator has three separate windings.

Figure 19-15 shows exactly what occurs within a stator that has three separate windings spaced 120 degrees apart. To make it easier for the reader to follow the discussion on voltage induction

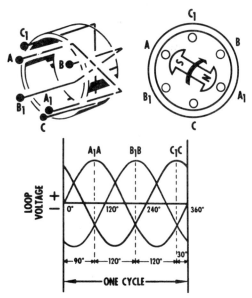

Fig. 19-15. The voltage curves of a stator with three separate windings. (Courtesy of Delco Remy)

in these windings, the loops are identified as *A1A*, *C1C*, and *B1B*.

When the S pole of the rotor moves directly under the *A* conductor, the voltage induced in *A* is maximum in magnitude and positive in polarity. As the rotor moves to the 120-degree position, its S pole is under the *B* conductor, and its induced voltage is maximum positive. Similarly 120 degrees later, the voltage induced in C is at maximum positive. This simply means that the peak positive voltages in each loop of wire *A*, *B*, and *C* occur 120 degrees apart. Also note in the illustration that peak negative voltages occur 120 degrees apart, as shown by the curves below the horizontal lines.

When the manufacturer connects the ends of these loops of wire *A*1, *B*1, and *C*1 to the ends of *B*, *C*, and *A*, this forms a basic three-phase delta-connected stator (Fig. 19–16). The three a.c. voltages available from the delta-connected stator are identical to the three voltages previously discussed. However, the induced voltages are from *B* to *A*, *C* to *B*, and *A* to *C* or more simply *BA*, *CB*, and *AC*. Finally, an alternator with a delta-connected stator winding functions well in heavy-duty applications where low voltage but a higher amperage output is necessary.

An alternate method of connecting the stator windings together is found in Y-connected units. In this case, the manufacturer connects the ends of the three windings marked *A1*, *B1*, and *C1* together at a single point (Fig. 19–17). In this illustration, the voltages available from this stator are labeled *BA*, *CB*, and *AC*.

Note in Fig. 19–17 that the voltages consist of the total voltages induced into two wires added together. For example, the voltage measured from *B* to *A* consists of the voltages in loops *B1B* and *A1A* added together. This combination yields a voltage curve *BA* similar in shape and form to the individual loop voltages

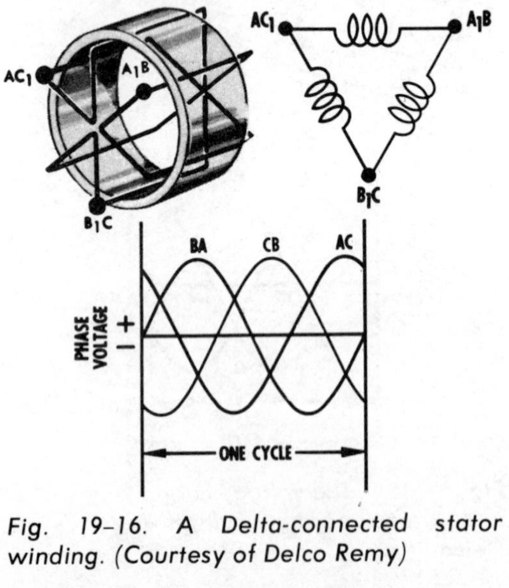

Fig. 19–16. A Delta-connected stator winding. (Courtesy of Delco Remy)

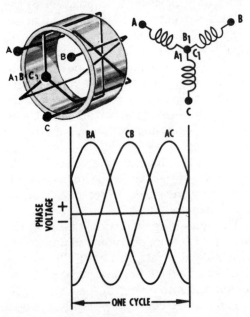

Fig. 19–17. A Y-connected stator winding. (Courtesy of Delco Remy)

shown in Fig. 19-15 except that the voltage curves are 1.7 times larger in magnitude than the individual loop voltages.

Most automobiles use an alternator with the Y-connected stator. The reason for this is that this unit produces a higher voltage output at lower speed, while still providing sufficient current flow to meet the demands of the vehicle's electrical system.

Up to this point, this section has discussed the two basic types of stator windings and how the alternator produces three separate cycles of a.c. voltage spaced 120 degrees apart for each revolution of the rotor. It is time to turn the discussion to the diodes and see how these units that connect to the stator windings change the a.c. voltages to a single d.c. voltage necessary for the automotive electrical system.

A.C. Rectification

As mentioned in Chapter 12, a *diode* is an electrical device that permits current to flow in one direction but not the other. Figure 19-18 illustrates the symbol of the diode. Note in the diagram that current flows through the diode only in the direction indicated by the arrow.

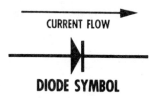

DIODE SYMBOL

Fig. 19-18.   The symbol used to designate the diode. (Courtesy of Delco Remy)

Figure 19-19 shows a diode connected to an a.c. voltage source, a coil having its ends marked A and B. In this situation, a voltage induced in the coil that creates a positive polarity at A and a negative polarity at B causes current to flow in the direction shown. With this voltage polarity, the diode responds to a forward bias condition; consequently, it conducts current flow.

When the voltage polarity at A is negative (−) and at B is positive (+), the diode reacts to a reversed bias condition. In this situation, the diode will not conduct current flow.

The current flow obtainable from this arrangement only flows half the time (Fig. 19-20). In other words, the diode provides what is known as *half-wave rectification*. Consequently, an alternator with only one diode would provide limited output.

In order to have full-wave rectification for the circuit mentioned, four diodes are

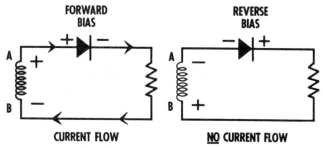

Fig. 19-19.   A single diode connected to an a.c. voltage source. (Courtesy of Delco Remy)

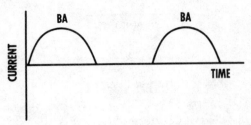

Fig. 19–20. Output curve of an a.c. voltage source with a single diode. (Courtesy of Delco Remy)

necessary (Fig. 19–21). Note in the lowermost illustration that the current is more continuous than in the system using one diode but that the current varies from a maximum value to a minimum value. Also

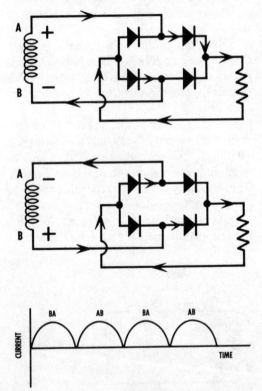

Fig. 19–21. Four diodes connected into a single a.c. voltage source. (Courtesy of Delco Remy)

note in both the upper and middle diagrams that the current flows through the external load resistor in one direction only. The a.c. voltage and current flow, therefore, have changed to d.c. voltage and current. This circuit arrangement is adequate to charge a d.c. battery, but it does not produce the highest output obtainable from an alternator because there is only the single-loop voltage source.

A three-phase stator connected to six diodes is necessary to obtain high enough voltage and current output for automotive usage. The six silicone-diode rectifiers change the a.c. output of the three-phase connected alternator to direct current. Three of these diodes mount on a heat sink that is sometimes known as a *positive rectifier assembly* (Fig. 19–10). This assembly attaches to the alternator output (BAT) terminal, but manufacturers insulate it from the alternator itself (Fig. 19–22). The other three diodes have negative polarity and ground to the alternator itself.

With the battery connected to the d.c. output (BAT) terminal, it has its electrical energy restored as the alternator provides charging current. However, the blocking action of the positive diodes prevents the battery from discharging directly through the alternator. As a result, the alternator

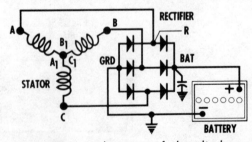

Fig. 19–22. A diagram of the diode arrangement in a typical automotive alternator. (Courtesy of Delco Remy)

does not require a cutout relay as the d.c. generator did.

In the discussion of three-phase rectification, we will use a Y-connected stator because it is the most common type found in automotive alternators. However, before attempting to explain this process, let's briefly review the three a.c. voltage curves produced in the Y-connected stator. In the first reference of the voltages induced in three single loops (Fig. 19-15), the alternator produced voltage curves $A1A$, $B1B$, and $C1C$. But in the Y-connected stator, these particular voltages do not appear across the diodes because the diodes connect only to the A, B, and C terminals of the stator. Therefore, the voltages that really appear across the diode rectifiers are the phase voltages BA, CB, and AC.

Not only are these voltages produced by the manner in which the diodes connect to the stator windings but also due to the fact that the stator windings connect. In other words, the phase voltage curves BA, CB, and AC are the result of adding each pair of loop voltages together. For example, phase voltage BA results from the addition of the voltages in $A1A$ and $B1B$. In other words, to obtain phase curve BA, the voltage from B to $B1$ and the voltage from $A1$ to A combine.

Consider the moment when the voltage curve BA is maximum in magnitude and positive in polarity, due to the movement of the rotor (Fig. 19-23). At this instant, the voltage $B1B$ is minus 8. This value added to the voltage of loop $A1A$, 8 volts, yields a maximum positive voltage of 16 volts, or curve BA. Consequently, during different periods of rotor travel, the alternator produces curves BA, CB, and AC in this same manner.

For convenience, this chapter divides

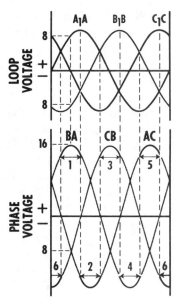

Fig. 19-23. In a Y-connected stator, the voltages produced by two phases add together to produce voltage curves with higher magnitudes. (Courtesy of Delco Remy)

the three a.c. voltage curves provided by the Y-connected stator for each revolution of the rotor into six periods, 1 through 6. Each of these periods represents one-sixth of a rotor revolution, or 60 degrees.

Figure 19-24 illustrates what occurs during period 1. The rotor induces voltage into the stator, which appears across terminal BA. This means that the current

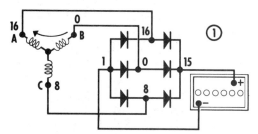

Fig. 19-24. Stator voltage rectification during period 1. (Courtesy of Delco Remy)

flows from B to A within the stator windings. Then, it passes through the upper-right positive diode to the battery and returns to the stator via the middle-left negative diode.

In order to understand more clearly why the current flows as it does during period 1, assume that the peak phase voltage developed from B to A is 16 volts. This simply means that the potential at B is zero volts, and the potential at A is 16 volts. Similarly, from the remaining curves, the voltage from C to B at this moment is minus 8 volts since the voltage from C (8 volts) to B (zero volts) represents a minus 8 volts. The voltage from A to C is also minus 8 volts because A has 16 volts and B has 8 volts, or 16 to 8, representing a potential of minus 8 volts.

Neglecting the voltage drops in the wiring and assuming a 1-volt drop in the conducting diodes, the voltage potentials are shown in Fig. 19–24. Only two of the diodes conduct current since these diodes are the only ones through which current can flow in the forward direction.

The other diodes do not conduct current because they are reverse-biased. For example, the lower right-hand diode has a reverse bias voltage of 7 volts $(15 - 8 = 7)$; the right-hand middle diode has a reverse bias of 15 volts $(15 - 0 = 15)$. It is the biasing of these individual diodes, provided by stator voltages, that determines how current flows in the stator rectifier combination.

Throughout period 1, the current flows as indicated due to the bias condition across the diodes, which does not change from that shown. Although the voltage potentials across the diodes does change in value, this variation is not sufficient during period 1 to change a diode from reverse to forward bias or from forward to reverse bias.

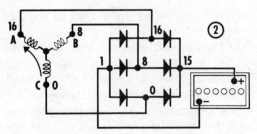

Fig. 19–25. Stator voltage rectification during period 2. (Courtesy of Delco Remy)

Figure 19–25 shows what occurs during period 2. An inspection of the phase voltages during this period of rotor travel reveals that between periods 1 and 2 the maximum voltage (being impressed across the diodes) changes or switches from phase BA to AC. This means that as the maximum voltage changes, the current flow changes from BA to CA as the rotor moves another 60 degrees.

It is important to note that the maximum voltage produced in the stator winding during phase 2 appears across winding AC; this voltage is negative from

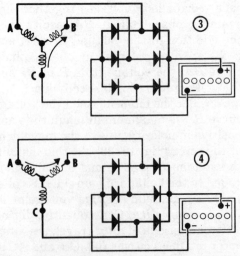

Fig. 19–26. Stator voltage rectification during periods 3 and 4. (Courtesy of Delco Remy)

A to *C*. This voltage is 16 volts—the potential being 16 at *A* and zero at *C*. (*A* to *C* or 16 to 0 is a negative 16 volts.) At this same instant, the voltage across *BA* is 8 volts and across phase *CB* is 8 volts. This means that the potential at *B* is 8 volts as shown in Fig. 19–25.

The direction of current flow during period 2 is from the *A* terminal to the upper-right positive diode. From here, the current passes through the diode, the battery, and returns to the *C* stator terminal via the lower-left negative diode.

Figures 19–26 and 19–27 illustrate alternator stator rectification during periods 3 through 6. Following the same procedures for these periods, you can determine the current flow conditions. During period 3, for example, current will flow from terminal *B* through the middle, right-hand positive diode, through the battery, and returns to terminal *C* via the lower left-hand negative diode. During period 4, current moves from the *B* terminal again through the right-hand center diode, the

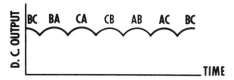

Fig. 19–28. The d.c. output curves of a three-phase alternator. (Courtesy of Delco Remy)

battery, and reenters the *A* terminal by means of the upper left-hand negative diode.

Period 5 begins with current leaving terminal *C*. Next, the current flows through the lower right-hand positive diode, the battery, and back to the *A* terminal via the upper left-hand negative diode.

During period 6 of rotor travel, current exits from the *C* terminal. Next, it passes through the lower right-hand positive diode, the battery, the center negative diode, and reenters terminal *B*.

The voltage obtained from the stator-rectifier combination, when connected to a battery, is not perfectly flat (Fig. 19–28). But it is so smooth that for all practical purposes, the output flow is considered to be nonvarying d.c. The voltages pictured in the illustration are those induced into the three phases of the stator.

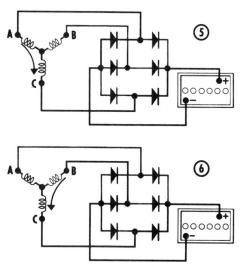

Fig. 19–27. Stator voltage rectification during periods 5 and 6. (Courtesy of Delco Remy)

Alternator Regulators

Every alternator must have some form of regulating device. While this device may have as many as three functioning units, the voltage regulator is the only unit that actually performs a controlling function. It limits the d.c. output voltage according to the external load and state of charge of the battery. This control is brought about by regulating the current flow through the rotor field coil.

A current regulator is not necessary because the alternator is capable of current self-regulation at given alternator speed and voltage output by *inductive reactance.* This occurs when the current flow through the stator coils increases, and the resulting magnetic lines of force extend outward and cut across adjacent coil windings. The direction by which these lines of force cut the adjacent windings is such that the voltage induced in the coil windings is opposite to that normally applied to the coil. This opposing voltage limits (counteracts) the normal voltage being induced in the total coil. This creates the opposition to current flow. This opposition is always present because the alternator is an alternating current source in which the current flow is always changing direction.

The speed at which the lines of force build up and collapse (frequency) also affects the amount of inductive reactance. The speed of the rotor has a direct bearing on the alternator output. As output increases with rotor speed, the inductive reactance becomes more effective in further curtailing the amount of current output.

A cutout relay is also unnecessary in the alternator regulator. This results directly because the positive diodes prevent the battery from discharging through the alternator when the engine is not operating.

Types of Alternator Regulators

Electromechanical

Two basic types of regulator assemblies are used with alternators: the electromechanical and the transistorized. Figure 19–29 illustrates a wiring schematic of a typical *electromagnetic* regulator assem-

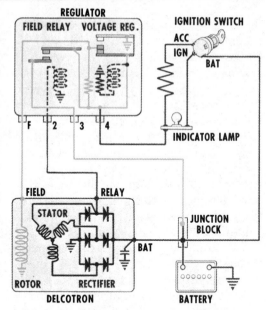

Fig. 19–29.   A wiring schematic of a two-unit alternator voltage regulator. *(Courtesy of Delco Remy)*

bly that has a voltage regulator and field relay. The voltage regulator operates to limit the alternator's output voltage to a present amount. The field relay is necessary to connect the alternator rotor field windings and the voltage regulator coil to the battery as soon as the alternator begins to produce electricity.

Two-Unit Regulator Operation

When the driver turns on the ignition switch, battery current flows through the switch to the indicator light, causing it to glow. At the same time, current also passes through the resistor connected in parallel to the light. From there, the current flow moves to regulator terminal 4. Then, the current flows through the closed voltage regulator points and to the rotor field coil via the slip ring brushes.

The current flow to the rotor coil is small because of the resistance that is now in the coil circuit. However, this current still produces a sufficient enough magnetic field to produce voltage induction in the stator windings. The induced voltage causes current to flow from the stator, to regulator terminal 2, and through the field relay coil. This action produces a magnetic field around the field coil.

When this magnetic field is large enough, it pulls the movable armature and attached point downward and into contact with the stationary point. When this happens, full battery voltage impresses itself on the rotor field coil. The current path is from the battery; through terminal 3, the closed field-relay contact points, the closed voltage regulator points; and to the field coil, via the *F* terminal and the slip ring brushes. This path produces maximum rotor field coil voltage and full alternator output. In addition, the indicator light no longer glows because the light now has system voltage on either side of the bulb.

As alternator output reaches a predetermined amount, the voltage regulator begins to function. Up to this time, spring tension has held the regulator points closed. But as the alternator voltage output increases, additional current flows in to terminal 3 of the regulator. This additional current passes through the field relay coil and also the voltage regulator coil windings. This action increases the regulator coil's magnetic field, which pulls down the armature, causing the lower contacts to separate. As a result, the flow of current to the field coil is lower because the path that it must take to the coil is through a resistor. This action reduces the alternator's charging rate.

As the alternator voltage output drops, spring tension once again closes the voltage regulator contact points. This action reestablishes full current to the field coil because the closed contact points permit field current to bypass the resistor. As a result, alternator output increases.

With a fully charged battery, a light electrical load, and high alternator rpm, a larger magnetic field develops in the voltage regulator coil, due to high current flow. This magnetic field becomes great enough, during these conditions, to pull the ground regulator point into contact with the stationary point. When this happens, both ends of the field coil have ground potential; and no current passes through the coil.

With no current in the field coil, the alternator's voltage decreases. This decreases the magnetism on the regulator coil, which permits the contact points to open. With these points open, field current again flows through the resistor circuit to the field coil. As the voltage again goes up, the upper contact points close again. The cycle repeats itself many times per second in order to limit the alternator output voltage to a preset value at higher operating speeds.

Transistorized Regulators

The other type of voltage regulator now used a great deal with alternators is the *transistorized* unit. This electronic regulator is a solid-state device with no moving parts or adjustments. Consequently, you can service it only by replacement if the unit becomes defective.

The transistorized regulator may be an integral unit built into or attached to the alternator, or it may be an external unit mounted on the vehicle's firewall. Figure

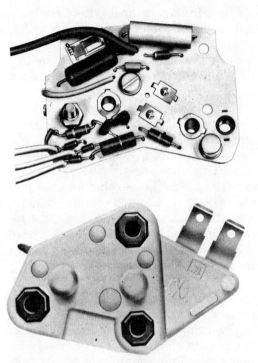

Fig. 19-30. A typical integral alternator, transistorized voltage regulator. (Courtesy of Delco Remy)

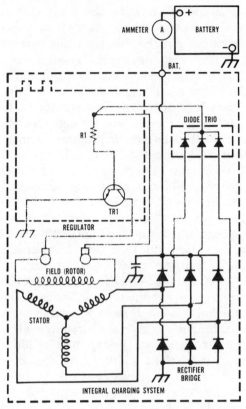

Fig. 19-31. The diode trio, resistor R1, and transistor TR1 of an integral charging circuit. (Courtesy of Delco Remy)

19-30 shows an integral voltage regulator.

In order to simplify the explanation of a transistorized regulator, we will build up a typical integral-type regulator circuit step-by-step, adding components when necessary until the circuit is complete. The construction of the basic circuit begins with an output transistor $TR1$, a resistor $R1$, and three diodes, which comprise a diode trio (Fig. 19-31).

In operation, the voltages, generated in the stator initially by residual magnetism in the rotor, impress themselves through the diode trio and across resistor $R1$ to forward-bias the emitter-base circuit of transistor $TR1$. As rotor speed increases, the output voltage goes up; and the current flows through the diode trio, $R1$, emitter-base of $TR1$, through the ground circuit, and back to the stator via the grounded diodes within the alternator. With transistor $TR1$ on, current also flows from the stator, through the diode trio, the rotor field, transistor $TR1$, the ground circuit, and back to the stator.

With current flow through the field, the rotor can now produce a strong magnetic field. This field causes the induction of high voltages in the stator that would overcharge the battery. It is now necessary then to add more components to the regulator; this will control alternator output by turning the voltage across the rotor coil on or off, thus controlling field current.

Figure 19–32 is a diagram showing the addition of a back-bias diode *D1*, a driver transistor *TR2*, and a series of resistors *R2* and *R3*. In operation, the current flowing through resistors *R2* and *R3* causes the voltage between *R2* and *R3* to apply itself to the base of transistor *TR2*. This turns on transistor *TR2*. As a result, *TR2* acts as if it has essentially zero resistance;

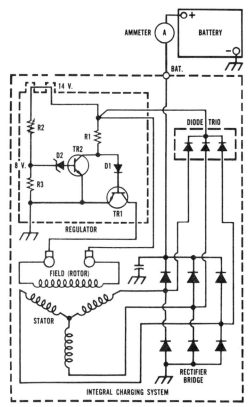

Fig. 19–32. A wiring diagram showing the addition of diode D1, zener diode D2, transistor TR2, and resistors R2 and R3 to the basic transistorized regulator circuit. (Courtesy of Delco Remy)

so the voltage of the emitter of *TR2* is the same as the voltage between *R1* and diode *D1*. This causes transistor *TR1* to turn off because its emitter-base is no longer forward-biased. Consequently, there is no current flow through the rotor field.

If current were to flow through diode *D1* and the emitter-base circuit of *TR1*, the voltage drop across *D1* would make the total voltage between *R1* and *D1* higher than that at the collector of *TR1*. However, transistor *TR1* prevents this condition.

There must be some means to turn the field voltage and current flow back on. The manufacturer accomplishes this through the addition of a zener diode *D2* (Fig. 19–32). The zener diode connects into the circuit to block current flow through the emitter-base circuit of transistor *TR2*. With *TR2* turned off, it acts like an open switch, and current flow reestablishes itself through *R1*, *D1*, transistor *TR1*, and the field.

Since the zener diode *D2* is a special type of diode that allows current flow in both directions, when the voltage across the diode reaches a given value, it does not permit current flow from between resistors *R2* and *R3* to the base-emitter of *TR1*, until system voltage reaches a certain amount. To illustrate this point, assume that the system voltage is 14 volts. With 14 volts across *R2* and *R3*, the voltage divides so that 8 volts appears between *R2* and *R3*. This same voltage impresses itself across *D2* and *TR2*, and this 8 volts is the breakdown voltage of the zener diode.

When the system voltage increases to 14 volts, zener diode *D2* conducts current. This suddenly turns on transistor *TR2* and forces transistor *TR1* to turn off. As a result, rotor field current decreases a very small amount, which reduces system voltage below 14 volts.

As system voltage drops below 14 volts, zener diode *D2* stops conducting current. This action turns off transistor *TR2*, and transistor *TR1* turns back on. As a result, the flow of field current rises slightly. Consequently, system voltage goes back up to 14 volts. Finally, this switching of *TR1* between on and off and back on again controls the field current and limits the alternator voltage to 14 volts. We now have a workable regulator—one that limits the field current and therefore the voltage induced in the stator over a very narrow range. This provides, for all practical purposes, a steady 14-volt regulator setting.

Different alternator regulators, of course, have different voltage settings, depending on voltage requirements of the system. In addition, some voltage settings vary with temperature, with the regulator functioning at a lower voltage when hot to meet the voltage requirements of a hot battery more efficiently. Other systems will not have this temperature compensation feature and therefore produce a constant voltage throughout the temperature range.

The wiring circuit illustrated in Fig. 19–33 is of a regulator with the temperature compensation feature. Note the arrow through resistor *R2*. This indicates that *R2* is a special type of resistor that decreases its resistance with increases in temperature. With this design, the hotter the regulator is, the lower the voltage output setting is.

The important thing to consider here is that the regulator operates when 8 volts appear across zener diode *D2*. Therefore, the regulator must operate to provide a constant current through resistors *R2* and *R3* in order to have 8 volts across *R3*.

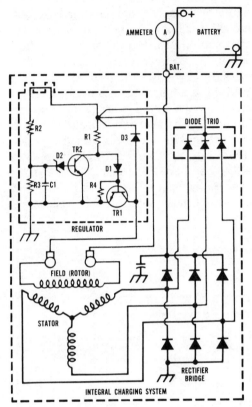

Fig. 19–33. A schematic of a complete transistorized regulator assembly. (Courtesy of Delco Remy)

However, if the resistance of *R2* decreases with temperature increases, the system voltage goes down also because there is a higher current flow through resistors *R2* and *R3*. Thus, the resulting setting might be 14 volts at 80°F. and 13.7 volts at 100°F.

Note also in Fig. 19–33 that capacitor *C1*, resistor *R4*, and diode *D3* are also in the regulator circuit. These components make the regulator more stable and prevent damage to the transistors under certain operating conditions. For example, capacitor *C1* smooths out the system voltage variations that appear across *R3*. This provides a more stable and constant voltage control.

Resistor *R4* prevents the leakage of current from the base-emitter of *TR1*. This leakage can occur at high temperatures, even though *TR2* has switched *TR1* off.

Diode 3 connects into the rotor field circuit. Its function is to prevent high induced voltages within the field as *TR1* turns the field current off. These high induced voltages could damage *TR1*, causing it to become shorted or open.

Testing the Charging Circuit Output

The actual testing procedures for a charging circuit depend, for the most part, on its design. Therefore, when attempting to test the various alternator systems, always refer to the manufacturer's in-structions and specifications. By doing so, the test provides accurate data and reduces the possibility of damage to system components.

Because of the differences in the various domestic charging systems, this chapter presents the typical alternator testing procedures, using a SUN VAT-40 and a common ohmmeter. To test a charging system with the VAT-40 (Fig. 19–34):

1. Check the condition and state of charge of the battery.

2. Check the mechanical zero of both meters; adjust each as necessary.

3. Rotate the load increase control knob fully counterclockwise to the off position.

4. Connect both tester load leads to the battery terminals with the red lead to positive and the black lead to negative.

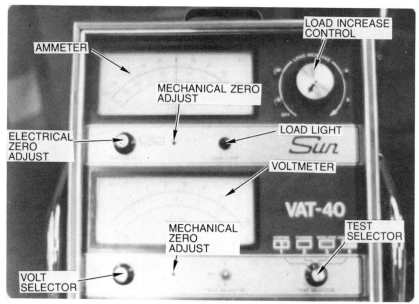

Fig. 19–34. A SUN VAT-40 starting and charging system tester.

5. Set the volt selector knob to INT. 18V.

6. Set the test selector knob to charging position 2.

7. As necessary, adjust the ammeter to read zero, using the electrical zero adjusting control.

8. Connect the green clamp-on amps pickup around a tester load cable, disregarding polarity (Fig. 19–35).

9. Turn the ignition switch to the run position, and read the rate of discharge on the ammeter. Note the results.

10. Start the engine and adjust its speed to about 2,000 rpm or the manufacturer's specified test speed.

11. Adjust the load increase control knob slowly as necessary to obtain the highest reading on the blue ammeter scale. Note the results. Do not drop the voltage lower than 12 volts. *Caution:* For charging systems rated over 100 amperes, set the test selector to starting position 1, and read the red 0- to 500-ampere scale.

12. Rotate the load increase control knob to the off position.

13. Add the ammeter readings obtained in steps 9 and 11 for the total alter-

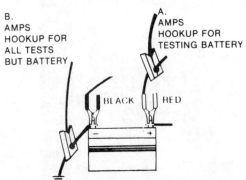

Fig. 19–35. The test connections for the ammeter. (Courtesy of Sun Electric Corp.)

nator output. Compare this total to the manufacturer's specification for the system being tested.

Results and Indications

1. If the alternator output is within 10 percent of the manufacturer's specifications, the charging system is satisfactory.

2. If the charging system output is not within 10 percent of specifications, the system is functioning poorly, and further testing is necessary. Proceed with the alternator-regulator test.

Alternator-Regulator Test

This particular test determines if the alternator or voltage regulator is defective and is only necessary if the system failed the output test. To perform the test:

1. Stop the engine and disconnect the regulator lead from the alternator field terminal. Disconnect the regulator connector plug, if the field terminal is not accessible (Fig. 19–36).

2. Using the proper lead terminal, connect the blue field test lead to the field terminal at the alternator or to the field lead in the regulator connector plug. *Caution:* Never use the blue field lead with the voltage regulator connected. Also, always refer to the manufacturer's instructions for identifying the field terminal and for bypassing the integral regulator used in some charging systems.

3. Set the test selector to charging position 2 for systems rated at less than 100 amperes or to starting position 1 for systems rated over 100 amperes.

4. Start the engine, and adjust its speed to the manufacturer's recommended rpm.

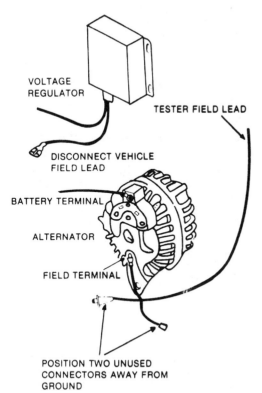

VOLTAGE
REGULATOR

TESTER FIELD LEAD

DISCONNECT VEHICLE
FIELD LEAD

BATTERY TERMINAL

ALTERNATOR

FIELD TERMINAL

POSITION TWO UNUSED
CONNECTORS AWAY FROM
GROUND

Fig. 19–36. The field lead connections for testing the alternator. (Courtesy of Sun Electric Corp.)

5. Rotate the load increase control knob clockwise until the voltmeter indicates about 2 volts less than system voltage.

6. Following the manufacturer's instructions, hold the spring loaded field selector switch in position *A* or *B*. *Note:* These positions reverse on positive ground systems—*A* becomes *B,* and *B* becomes *A*. However, no damage occurs if you use the wrong position. If you do not know which one to use, test in each position.

7. Adjust the load increase control knob as necessary to obtain a reading on

the voltmeter as specified by the manufacturer.

8. Observe the reading on the proper ammeter scale.

9. Release the field selector switch; turn off the load increase control knob; shut off the engine.

10. Add the ammeter reading observed in step 8 of this text to the reading observed in step 9 under the charging system output test. Compare this total to the manufacturer's specifications.

Results and Indications

1. If the output falls within 10 percent of manufacturer's specifications, check the vehicle wiring, replace the voltage regulator, and retest the system.

2. If the output still does not fall within the manufacturer's specifications, replace or repair the alternator, using the manufacturer's instructions. Then retest the system.

Alternator-Regulator Setting Test

To make this test, follow these steps.

1. Set the test selector knob to regulator position 3.

2. Start the engine; adjust its speed to 2,000 rpm or the speed specified by the manufacturer.

3. Note the reading on the green voltmeter scale after the needle ceases to rise—usually after the current output drops to 10 amperes or less.

Results and Indications

1. If the voltage is within the manufacturer's specifications, the regulator is satisfactory.

2. If the voltage reading is above or below the specified voltage range, replace the voltage regulator and retest the system.

Diode-Stator Test

To perform this test procedure:

1. Start the engine, and adjust its speed to about 2,000 rpm or the speed specified by the manufacturer.

2. Place the test selector knob in regulator position 3.

3. Adjust the load increase control knob as necessary to obtain a charge rate of at least 15 amperes. *Note:* If you did not obtain at least 15 amperes during the alternator-regulator test, the alternator is defective and requires replacement or repair. The diode test is not valid unless the alternator produces 15 amperes.

4. Set the test selector to diode-stator position 4.

5. Observe the red and blue diode-stator scale.

6. Turn the load control knob to the off position; return the engine speed to its normal idle rpm; shut off the engine.

Results and Indications

1. If the meter reads in the blue area of the diode-stator scale, these units are functioning properly.

2. If the meter reads within the red area of the diode-stator scale, replace or service the alternator following manufacturer's instructions. Then retest the system.

Charging System Requirements Test

To perform this test sequence:

1. With the engine off, place the test selector in position 2.

2. Turn on all the vehicle's accessories, the ignition switch, headlights (on high beam), air conditioning, windshield wipers, and rear-window defroster if so equipped.

3. Note the reading on the ammeter. This reading indicates the entire accessory load.

4. Compare this reading to the total alternator output reading obtained during the alternator-regulator test, step 8. The total alternator output reading should exceed the accessory load reading by at least 5 amperes.

Testing Internal Alternator Components with an Ohmmeter

Field Windings Test

If these previous tests indicated a defect within the alternator itself, remove the alternator from the vehicle; and disassemble it, following manufacturer's instructions. Then, test its rotor field windings as follows for shorts and opens:

1. Calibrate the ohmmeter as necessary, and set it for an *X1* scale reading.

2. Connect one ohmmeter lead to each slip ring (Fig. 19–37).

3. Note the resistance reading, and compare the reading to manufacturer's

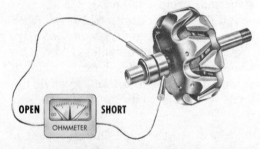

Fig. 19–37.   Checking the rotor winding for opens and shorts. (Courtesy of Delco Remy)

Fig. 19-38. Testing the rotor winding for grounds. (Courtesy of Delco Remy)

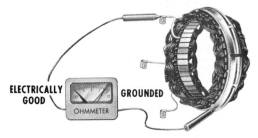

Fig. 19-40. Checking the stator for grounds. (Courtesy of Delco Remy)

specifications. If the resistance is high (infinite), the winding is open. If the resistance is too low, the coil is shorted.

4. Connect one ohmmeter lead to either slip ring and the other to the rotor shaft (Fig. 19-38).

5. Note the reading. The reading should be very high (infinite). A low reading indicates a grounded field winding.

Stator Winding Test

To check the stator winding for opens or grounds:

1. Calibrate the ammeter as necessary, and set it for an X1 scale reading.

2. Connect the ohmmeter leads to any two stator leads (Fig. 19-39). Note the reading. Then, disconnect one ohmmeter lead, and connect it to the middle stator lead. Note the results. If either reading is high (infinite), the stator winding is open.

3. Attach either ohmmeter lead to the stator frame and the other to any stator lead (Fig. 19-40).

4. Note the reading. A low reading indicates a grounded stator winding.

Diode Test

You can test each diode for shorts or opens *with their stator leads disconnected.* To perform this test:

1. Calibrate the ohmmeter as necessary, and set it for an X100 scale reading.

2. Connect one ohmmeter lead to the diode case and the other to the diode lead (Fig. 19-41). Note the reading.

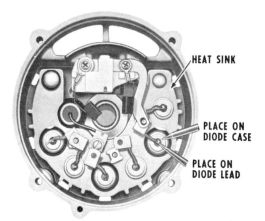

HEAT SINK

PLACE ON DIODE CASE

PLACE ON DIODE LEAD

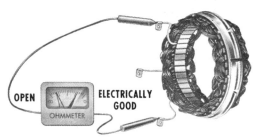

Fig. 19-39. Testing the stator for opens. (Courtesy of Delco Remy)

Fig. 19-41. Testing a diode for shorts or opens. (Courtesy of Delco Remy)

3. Reverse the ohmmeter lead connections, and again note the reading.

Results and Indications

1. If both readings are very high or very low, the diode is defective and requires replacement.

2. If one reading is low and the other one high, the diode is satisfactory.

Review

This section will assist you in determining how well you remember the material in this chapter. Read each item carefully. If you can't complete the statement, review the section in the chapter that covers the material.

1. The alternator can produce _____ amperes at idle speed.
   a. 0 to 5
   b. 6 to 10
   c. 10 to 15
   d. 16 to 20

2. The _____ of an alternator produces the magnetic field.
   a. rotor
   b. stator
   c. frame
   d. diode

3. The current flow through the rotor coil is _____ amperes.
   a. 4.5 to 6
   b. 3 to 4.5
   c. 1.5 to 3
   d. 0 to 1.5

4. The rotor has usually _____ magnetic poles.
   a. 7
   b. 14
   c. 21
   d. 28

5. The number of rotations per second that the rotor turns and produces voltage curves is known as _____.
   a. speed
   b. rpm
   c. cycle
   d. frequency

6. The typical stator has _____ phases.
   a. 4
   b. 1
   c. 2
   d. 3

7. The alternator requires _____ diodes in order to provide full-wave rectification.
   a. 6
   b. 5
   c. 4
   d. 3

8. A conducting diode can provide a voltage drop of as much as _____ volt(s).
   a. 1
   b. 2
   c. 3
   d. 4

9. A _____ _____ is necessary in an alternator charging system.
   a. cutout relay
   b. current regulator
   c. voltage regulator
   d. both *a* and *b*

10. The device in an alternator regulator that connects the battery to the rotor windings when the alternator produces electricity is the _____.
    a. voltage regulator
    b. field relay
    c. current regulator
    d. cutout relay

11. With an electromechanical regulator, the rotor windings _____

_____ at high alternator speed and output.

a. produce magnetism
b. short out
c. ground out
d. become effective

12. In a transistorized regulator, the device that is necessary to turn field voltage back on again is the _____ _____.

a. resistor *R1*
b. transistor *TR2*
c. transistor *TR1*
d. zener diode

13. The first item to check before testing the charging circuit is the _____.

a. battery
b. alternator
c. regulator
d. stator

14. When testing the charging system, it is satisfactory if the results are within _____ percent of the manufacturer's specifications.

a. 14
b. 12
c. 10
d. 8

15. The alternator must produce at least _____ amperes before you can perform the diode-stator test.

a. 7
b. 15
c. 23
d. 31

16. An alternator must produce at least _____ more amperes than the entire accessory load.

a. 11
b. 9
c. 7
d. 5

For the answers, turn to the Appendix.

In the early days of the automobile, it was necessary for the operator to start the engine with a hand crank. In other words, the driver had to insert a crank into the front of the engine and turn it by hand until the engine started operating. This task required both skill and physical strength and made the operation of the automobile very inconvenient for those who could not crank the engine. Moreover, without an electrical starting system, the early engines had design limitations in respect to displacement and compression ratio.

In 1910, Charles F. Kettering began to work on a practical electrical automotive starter. The resulting system first appeared on the 1912 Cadillac; other manufacturers quickly adopted it for their own passenger vehicles. This resulted in an increase in the popularity and widespread use of automobiles.

With the development of the starting motor, the complete electrical system came into existence. For example, a storage battery was then necessary to furnish the current to operate the starter motor. Also, a generator was needed to charge the battery in order to replace the electrical energy used by the starter.

The starting system provides the power to turn the internal combustion engine over until it can operate under its own power. To perform this task, the starting motor receives electrical power from the battery, and it converts this energy into mechanical energy, which transmits through the drive mechanism to the engine's flywheel.

Starting System Design

Battery

The typical starting system has five components: battery, starting switch,

Chapter 20

OPERATION AND TESTING OF THE STARTING SYSTEM

battery cables, starter solenoid or switch, and starting motor (Fig. 20-1). The battery supplies electrical energy in the form of current flow for the starting circuit. The starting motor can draw a large amount of current from the battery in order to turn the engine over. The starter for a large V-8 engine, for example, may require as much as 300 amperes of starting current.

Starting Switch

The starting switch activates the system. In the modern automobile this switch is part of the keyed ignition switch. The ignition switch usually has four positions: accessories, off, on (run), and start. In addition, the switch on late-model automobiles has a lock position that secures the steering wheel.

All the ignition switch positions except start have detents. That is, the switch remains in those positions until moved by the operator. However, when the driver turns the ignition switch to start and then releases it, the switch springs back to the on, or run, position. Consequently, the start position represents the actual starting switch portion of the ignition switch itself because it applies battery voltage to the solenoid.

Starting Safety Switch

Vehicles with automatic transmissions also have a starting safety switch, sometimes called a *neutral safety switch* (Fig. 20-2). This device prevents the starting system from operating when the transmission is in gear. If the vehicle had no safety switch, it would be possible to turn the engine over at any time. If the engine happened to start with the transmission in gear, the vehicle would lunge forward or backward, which is a dangerous situation.

Starting, or neutral safety, switches can connect in either of two places within the starting system control circuit. For instance, the switch can connect between the ignition switch and the solenoid so that the safety switch must close before current can flow to the solenoid. The manufacturer can also place the safety switch between the solenoid and ground so that the switch must close before current can flow from the solenoid to ground.

Cables

The starting circuit requires two or more heavy-gauge *cables* (Fig. 20-3). Two of these cables attach directly to the bat-

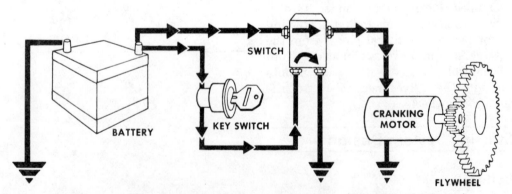

Fig. 20-1. A schematic of a simple starting system. (Courtesy of General Motors Corp.)

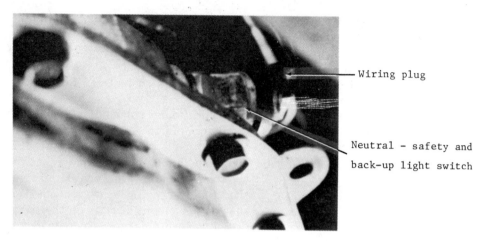

Wiring plug

Neutral - safety and
back-up light switch

Fig. 20-2. *A neutral safety switch mounted on the side of the transmission.*

tery. One heavy cable connects between
the battery negative terminal and a good
ground (on negatively grounded battery
systems). If this cable does not directly attach to the engine, the vehicle usually has
additional cables running from the engine
to the vehicle frame or body.

The second main heavy-gauge cable

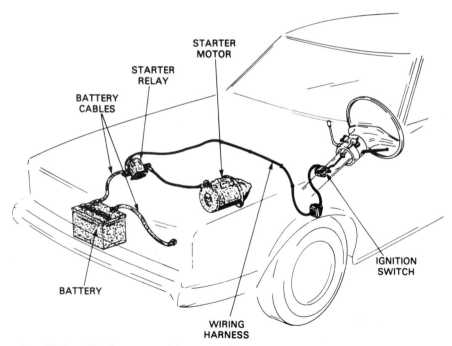

STARTER
MOTOR

STARTER
RELAY

BATTERY
CABLES

IGNITION
SWITCH

BATTERY

WIRING
HARNESS

Fig. 20-3. *The battery cables carry battery current flow to and from the
starter. (Courtesy of Ford Motor Co. of Canada Ltd.)*

clamps onto the battery positive terminal and connects to the starter solenoid. On vehicles where the solenoid does not directly mount on the starter, two cables are necessary—one from the battery terminal to the solenoid and the second from the solenoid to the starting motor terminal. In any case, these cables carry the heavy current flow from the battery to the starter and from the starter back to the battery.

Starter Solenoid

The *starter solenoid* is an electromagnetically operated heavy-duty switch that can have two distinct functions. First and most important of all, the solenoid switch opens and closes the circuit between the battery and cranking motor (Fig. 20-4). The battery must supply a great deal of current flow to the starter before it can crank the engine. If this high-current flow (up to about 300 amperes) passed through the ignition switch, it would rapidly burn out the switch. Consequently, the solenoid switch prevents this from occurring by supplying heavy-duty contacts through which the high current can flow without damage.

Second, many solenoids also shift the cranking pinion into mesh with the flywheel ring gear. Manufacturers accomplish this action by linkage between the solenoid plunger and the shift lever on the cranking motor. However, solenoids that do not mount directly on the starter do not perform this function; instead, they just act as a heavy-duty switch that carries the high current flow.

The solenoid shown in Fig. 20-4 consists of two windings, plunger, and heavy-duty switch. The two windings, designated as *pull-in* and *hold-in,* produce a combined magnetic field strong enough to pull in the plunger. The current producing this magnetic field in the windings comes from the battery via the ignition switch.

The two windings have different-size wires, but they have the same number of turns. The heavy pull-in winding is necessary to start and complete the plunger movement into the air core inside the windings. However, as the air gap between the plunger and windings decreases, the magnetic pull from the hold-in winding is sufficient to retain the plunger in the retracted position.

The plunger moves in and out within the air core, formed between the two windings. One end of the plunger attaches to the shift lever through linkage. The other end of the plunger has a pointed nose that contacts and closes the heavy-duty switch as the plunger retracts; this switch controls the circuit between the battery and starting motor.

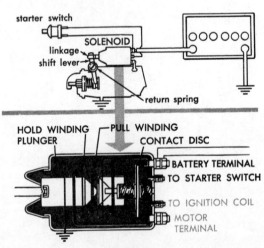

Fig. 20-4. *The location and design of a typical starter-mounted solenoid. (Courtesy of Delco Remy)*

Solenoid Operation

As the driver turns the ignition switch to the start position, it directs current flow to both the pull-in and hold-in windings within the solenoid (diagram 1 of Fig. 20-5). As a result of this current flow, both windings produce a magnetic field large enough to pull the plunger inward. This action closes the solenoid switch contacts, connecting the battery directly to the starter, and pulls the pinion into mesh with the flywheel.

The closing of the solenoid contacts also partially shorts out the pull-in winding because it connects across the main contacts (diagram 2 of Fig. 20-5). As a result, the increased current flow through the

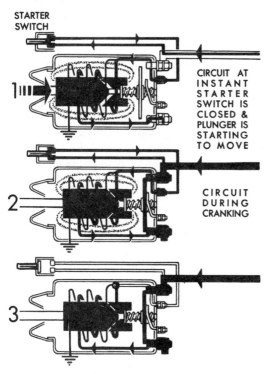

STARTER SWITCH

1

CIRCUIT AT INSTANT STARTER SWITCH IS CLOSED & PLUNGER IS STARTING TO MOVE

2

CIRCUIT DURING CRANKING

3

Fig. 20-5. The operation of a typical solenoid. (Courtesy of Delco Remy)

pull-in winding only occurs during the movement of the plunger from the extended to the retracted position.

When the driver releases the ignition switch to the run position, the ignition switch breaks the circuit between the battery and the solenoid (diagram 3 of Fig. 20-5). Therefore, current no longer reaches the hold-in winding from this source. However, there is a flow of current from the battery, through the solenoid contacts, then through the pull-in winding (in a reverse direction), and through the hold-in winding to ground. With the same number of turns in each winding and the same amount of current flowing through both, the magnetic field created in each winding is opposite and therefore counteracts each other. Consequently, tension of the plunger return spring causes the plunger to move outward to the at-rest position. This breaks the cranking motor circuit and moves the drive pinion out of mesh with the flywheel.

Starting Motor

Function

The *starting or cranking motor* itself is nothing but a device that converts electrical energy to mechanical energy in order to turn the engine over for starting. The starter is a special type of electric motor designed to operate under great overloads and to produce high horsepower for its size. However, the starter can only do this for a short period of time, since high current is necessary to operate the unit; this current flow creates considerable heat.

Therefore, if the starting motor opera-

Fig. 20-6. *Extended starter operation can cause serious internal damage due to high temperature. (Courtesy of Delco Remy)*

tion is continuous for any length of time, accumulated heat causes serious damage. For this reason, this motor must never operate for more than 30 seconds at a time (Fig. 20-6), with a rest in between of at least 2 minutes. This permits the heat within the motor to dissipate into the air.

Starter Motor Design—Housing

All starting motors are much the same in general design and operation, differing mainly in the type of drive mechanism used. Basically, the starter motor consists of a housing, fields, armature and brushes, end frames, and drive mechanism (Fig. 20-7). The starter *housing,* or *frame,* is a heavy cylindrical machined case that

serves several functions. For example, this assembly encloses and protects the internal starter components from damage due to the entrance of moisture or other foreign materials. In addition, the housing supports the field coils and forms a conducting path for the magnetism produced by current passing through the coils. As you recall, iron is a much better conductor of magnetic lines than air.

Starter Field Coils and Pole Shoes

Field coils, along with their pole shoes, fit inside the iron starter housing or frame (Fig. 20-8). These components securely attach to the inner surface of this assembly by means of screws. However, the field coils have a design that insulates them from the housing; but the coils connect to a terminal, protruding through the outer surface of the housing.

The design of the field coils and pole pieces is such that they produce strong electromagnetic fields within the starter itself, as current passes through the starter. The manufacturer forms the field coils by wrapping heavy insulated, flat copper strips around the pole shoes. These strips easily carry the heavy current flow needed for starting purposes.

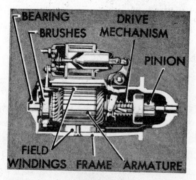

Fig. 20-7. *The design of a typical starter motor. (Courtesy of Delco Remy)*

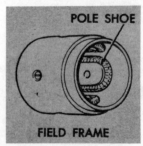

Fig. 20-8. *The location of a field coil and pole shoe inside the field frame. (Courtesy of Delco Remy)*

The magnetic field produced by the field coil concentrates itself at the pole shoe. This provides the field coil with either a magnetic N or S polarity, depending on which direction the current flows through the coil.

When current passes through a starter with two field coils, the current flow creates two strong electromagnets on either side of the housing. One of the fields produces an N polarity in its shoe, while the other an S polarity, due to the fact that the coils are wound around their respective pole shoes in opposite directions.

Between these two pole shoes exists a strong magnetic field that flows from the N pole shoe to the S pole shoe (Fig. 20-9). The field then completes its circuit back to the N pole by means of the iron field frame or housing.

The field coils connect in series with the armature winding through the starter brushes. This design permits all the current passing through the field coil circuit also to flow through the armature windings.

and operates between the drive and commutator end frames and the field windings (Fig. 20-10). When the starter is in operation, the current flowing through the armature produces a magnetic field in each of its conductors; the reaction between the armature's magnetic field and that produced by the field coils causes the armature to rotate.

The armature itself consists of two main components (the armature windings and commutator), which mount onto an armature shaft. The armature windings are heavy, flat copper strips instead of wire or cable, so that the windings can handle the heavy current flow. The windings are made up of a number of coils of a single loop each. The sides of these loops fit into slots within the armature core but are insulated from it. Each slot contains the side of two coils.

The coils connect to each other and to the commutator so that the current from the field coils flows through all the armature windings at the same time. This action creates a magnetic field around each armature winding, resulting in a

Armature

The *armature* is the only rotating component within the starter. This device fits

Fig. 20-9. *The magnetic circuit between the field coils in a two-pole starter.* (Courtesy of Delco Remy)

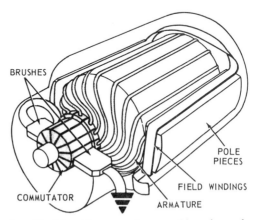

Fig. 20-10. *The armature and brushes of a starting motor.* (Courtesy of Deere & Co. Technical Services)

repulsion force all around the conductor. This force causes the armature to turn.

The commutator assembly presses onto the armature shaft. This device is made up of heavy copper segments, separated from each other and the armature shaft by insulation. The commutator segments connect to the ends of the armature windings.

Brushes

The starting motor has two to six *brushes*. These devices ride on the commutator segments; they carry the heavy current flow from the stationary field coils to the rotating armature windings via the commutator segments.

Manufacturers form the starter brushes under high pressure from a mixture of powered carbon and copper. The formed brush itself usually has one or more heavy pigtail leads of flexible copper wire securely fastened to the brush.

The brushes mount on and operate in some type of holder. In some cases, the holder may be in the form of a pivoting arm that operates inside the starter housing or frame. However, in many starters, the brush holders secure to the commutator end frame. In either case, the brush holder supports the brushes in position and have coil or flat springs to hold the brushes against the commutator with the correct pressure. Finally, alternate brush holders are insulated from the housing or end frame while those in between are grounded.

Commutator End Frame

The *commutator end frame* is a metal plate that bolts to the commutator end of the starter housing. Depending on starter design, this component has several functions. In all cases, for example, the end frame supports the commutator end of the armature in a bushing (a special type of bearing). Also, on many starter motors, the commutator end frame also contains the holders that support the brushes.

Drive Housing

The *drive housing*, sometimes known as the *drive end frame*, has several functions. First of all, this housing supports the driving end of the armature shaft by means of a bushing. Second, this heavy iron component contains the mounting flange by which the starter motor attaches to the engine.

Starter Operation

Before beginning the discussion of how a simple starter motor operates, let's first take a moment and review a few fundamentals concerning the action of a conductor within a magnetic field. Figure 20–11 illustrates the relationship between the magnetic field of a permanent magnet, the magnetic field around a current-carrying conductor, and the direction of the force exerted on the conductor. Note that the

MAGNETIC FIELD

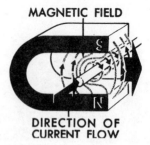

DIRECTION OF CURRENT FLOW

Fig. 20–11. The relationship between the magnetic field produced by a permanent magnet and the one produced by current passing through a conductor. (Courtesy of Delco Remy)

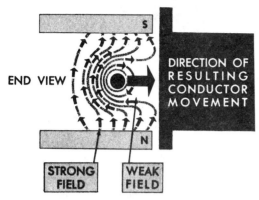

END VIEW

DIRECTION OF RESULTING CONDUCTOR MOVEMENT

STRONG FIELD

WEAK FIELD

Fig. 20–12. A current-carrying conductor within another magnetic field moves toward the weak field. (Courtesy of Delco Remy)

magnetic lines of force, from the permanent magnet, pass from the N to the S pole, as shown by the arrows. In addition, observe that the flow of current in the conductor is in the direction illustrated, which is away from you.

Using the right-hand rule for conventional current flow, you should be able to see that when the direction of current through the conductor is as shown, the magnetic lines of force around the conductor are in a clockwise direction (indicated by the circular arrows around the conductor). Observing the end of the conductor

(Fig. 20–12), note that to the right of the conductor, the magnetic field from the permanent magnet and the circular field around the conductor oppose each other. However, to the left of the conductor, the two magnetic fields are in the same direction, and the field is therefore stronger.

Consequently, when a current-carrying conductor is within another magnetic field, its normal field of force distorts, creating a strong field on one side of the conductor and a weak field on the opposite side. This action forces the conductor to move in the direction of the weak field. In Fig. 20–12, this movement is to the right. The more current flowing through the conductor, the stronger is the force exerted on it.

With these facts in mind, let's examine the operation of a simple starting motor with a one-turn armature (Fig. 20–13). When current flows through the field coils, which assemble around the two pole pieces, a magnetic field forms. Using the right-hand rule for coils, you can see that the direction of current flow tends to increase the magnetic field between the two poles.

Situated between these two poles is a U-shaped armature winding, connected to a two-segment commutator. In the ar-

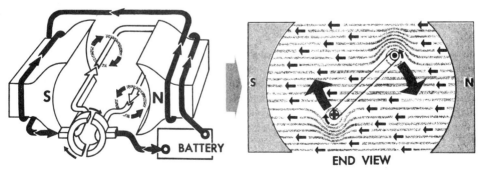

Fig. 20–13. The operation of a simple single-turn armature starting motor. (Courtesy of Delco Remy)

mature position shown, current flows first from the battery around the right-hand field coil. Then, the current crosses over to the left-hand field coil, through the field coil, and enters the left commutator segment. From this segment, the current flows through the armature winding, entering on the side nearest the S pole and leaving the armature on the side nearest the N pole, to the right-hand segment. From the right-hand segment, the current returns through the right-hand brush to the battery.

The magnetic field around the armature winding is in the direction shown by the circular arrows. The interaction between this magnetic field and the strong field produced between the two field coils causes the left-hand side of the winding to move upward while the right-hand side moves downward. This action creates a clockwise rotation in the armature winding.

Since the armature winding and commutator assemble together in one unit, they must rotate together. Therefore, the movement of the winding causes the commutator to turn also. Thus, by the time the left-hand side of the winding has swung around toward the N pole, the commutator segments will have reversed their positions relative to the brushes. Consequently, current flows in the opposite

Fig. 20-15. The location of the brushes in the static neutral zone. (Courtesy of Delco Remy)

direction in the winding with respect to the current flow in the previous armature position. But since the winding has turned 180 degrees, the force exerted on it tends to rotate the winding again in a clockwise direction.

There is a static neutral point, always halfway between the pole shoes (Fig. 20-14). This point is where the direction of current must be changed in the armature winding in order to maintain its rotation in the same direction. This is true whether the motor has two, four, or six field poles.

When the current flows through the armature winding, creating another magnetic field, the normal field between the pole pieces becomes distorted because lines of force supposedly do not cross each other. This action therefore shifts the neutral point. Consequently, manufacturers usually locate the brushes back of the static neutral point (against the direction of rotation) to prevent excessive arcing and to obtain more efficient operation (Fig. 20-15).

Cranking Motor Circuits

Two Coil, Four-Pole Starter

In the example used to explain starter operation, we used a simple motor with two poles and two brushes. However,

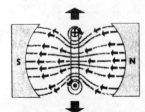

FORCES BALANCED AT NEUTRAL POINT

Fig. 20-14. The static neutral point of the winding between the pole shoes. (Courtesy of Delco Remy)

many starters in use have more than two field coils and brushes. For example, some cranking motors have four pole shoes, two field coils, and four brushes (Fig. 20–16). Although this unit has only two field coils, the additional pole shoes provide the starter with four-pole action, while keeping the resistance low in the circuit.

Notice in Fig. 20–16 the path of the current through the cranking motor. Using the right-hand rule for coils, observe that, in operation, the poles with the field windings have an N polarity at the face of their respective pole shoes. Their lines of force move through the armature, enter the pole shoes without windings, pass into the starter housing, or frame, and back to the original pole shoe with the winding to complete the magnetic circuit. With this design, there are as many lines of force entering the S pole as leaving the N pole, making the magnetic strength the same for both poles. Finally, in all cranking motors, the adjacent pole shoes have opposite polarity so that in any four-pole unit there are an N, S, N, and S pole in sequence around the housing.

Four-Coil, Four-Pole Starter Circuit

Another type of four-pole starter has four field coils and four brushes (Fig. 20–17). In this unit, the field windings pair off so that half the current flows through one set of field windings to one of the insulated brushes. The other half of the current flow passes through the other set of field windings to the other insulated brush. By the use of four field windings of low resistance, it is possible to create more ampere turns with a resulting stronger magnetic field. This design produces a starting motor with greater torque or cranking ability.

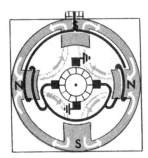

Fig. 20–16. A starter circuit with four pole shoes, two field coils, and four brushes. (Courtesy of Delco Remy)

Fig. 20–17. A starter circuit with four pole shoes, four field coils, and four brushes. (Courtesy of Delco Remy)

In the cranking motor shown in Fig. 20–18, the manufacturer insulates all brushes. Half the brushes in this unit connect to the starter terminal while the other half connect the ends of two field

Fig. 20–18. A four-pole cranking motor circuit with insulated brushes. (Courtesy of Delco Remy)

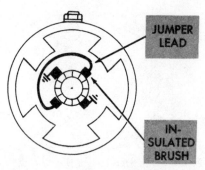

Fig. 20-19. Jumpers or equalizing bars connect insulated brushes together. (Courtesy of Delco Remy)

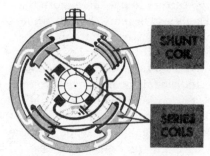

Fig. 20-20. A starter motor circuit with a shunt coil. (Courtesy of Delco Remy)

coils. In this situation, the opposite ends of all the field coils attach to ground.

As a rule, all insulated brushes connect together by means of jumper leads (Fig. 20-19). Consequently, the voltage equalizes at all brushes. Without these equalizer leads or bars, there may be conditions that cause arcing and burning of the commutator segments. This action would eventually insulate the brush contact from the commutator surface, thereby preventing cranking.

The four-pole, high-voltage motors just described, with a straight series circuit, can reach an extremely high top free speed. This high free speed can be a negative factor. Consequently, manufacturers sometimes install one or more shunt-connected coils for the purpose of limiting motor rpm (Fig. 20-20).

The magnetic strength of the shunt coil during starter operation remains constant and does not vary with speed. As a result, the speed of the armature revolving through this strong magnetic field creates a greater counter voltage in this coil, which limits the amount of current flow and the top speed of the motor.

However, during engine cranking, the shunt coil, with its many turns of rela-

tively small wire, forms a magnetic force similar to the force provided by each of the series coils. Therefore, the starter provides normal cranking performance with less current flow and at a safe top free speed.

Six-Coil, Six-Pole Starting Circuit

Figure 20-21 illustrates a six-coil, six-pole, six-brush starting motor circuit. The manufacturer uses this circuit in motors designed for heavy-duty service. In this case, the current splits three ways after entering the starter terminal, with one-third flowing through each pair of field windings to one of the three insulated brushes. Increasing the number of circuits

Fig. 20-21. A starter circuit with six pole shoes, six field coils, and six brushes. (Courtesy of Delco Remy)

through the cranking motor helps to keep the resistance low so that a high current can flow, developing a high horsepower within the unit.

Starter Drives

Bendix

As mentioned earlier in this chapter, one of the main design differences between starter motors is in the type of drive used. In this respect, cranking motors can use three types of drives: the Bendix, Dyer-shift, and overrunning-clutch. The *Bendix drive* depends on inertia to provide meshing of the drive pinion gear with engine flywheel. In other words, a motor with a Bendix drive does not have an integral solenoid to push the pinion into mesh.

A typical Bendix drive consists of a drive pinion gear, sleeve, spring, and drive head (Fig. 20–22). The drive pinion has a counter balance on one side that normally unbalances the pinion gear. In addition, the drive pinion has screw threads on its inner bore.

The Bendix sleeve, which is hollow, also has screw threads cut on its outer diameter. These threads match with the ones in the pinion. The pinion itself fits loosely upon the armature shaft and connects through the spring to the drive head, which keys to the armature shaft. Therefore, the sleeve is free to turn on the armature shaft within the limits permitted by the flexing of the spring that attaches to both the sleeve and head via the fastening screws.

Bendix-Drive Operation

As the driver turns the ignition switch to the start position, the starter armature begins to revolve. This rotation transmits through the drive head and spring to the sleeve so that all these parts pick up speed with the armature (diagram 1 of Fig. 20–23).

The pinion, however, being a loose fit on the sleeve's screw thread, does not pick up speed along with the sleeve. In other words, the increased inertia of the drive pinion, due to the effect of the counterbalance, prevents it from rotating. As a result, the threaded sleeve rotates within the pinion. This action forces the pinion

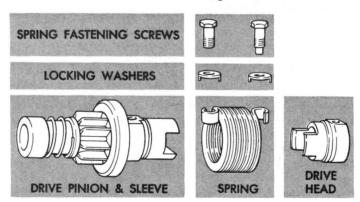

Fig. 20–22. A parts breakdown of a Bendix drive. (Courtesy of Delco Remy)

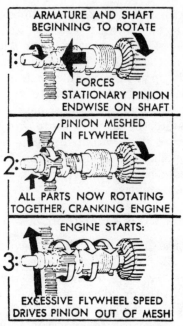

Fig. 20-23. Bendix drive operation. (Courtesy of Delco Remy)

gear endwise along the armature shaft until it meshes with the teeth on the flywheel ring gear (diagram 2 of Fig. 20-23).

As soon as the pinion reaches the pinion stop, the pinion gear begins to spin along with the sleeve and armature. This rotation transmits directly to the flywheel. The Bendix spring, in this situation, absorbs the shock of the pinion gear meshing with the flywheel.

When the engine starts, the pinion gear spins at a higher speed than that of the armature (diagram 3 of Fig. 20-23). This causes the pinion to rotate in its threads relative to the sleeve. Thus, the pinion backs out of mesh from the flywheel teeth. The Bendix drive, therefore, automatically meshes the pinion with the teeth of the flywheel ring gear to provide cranking and automatically demeshes the pinion as soon as the engine is running.

Dyer-Shift Drive

The *Dyer drive* is a special type of drive mechanism that shifts into mesh with the flywheel either through manually operated linkage or an electrical solenoid (Fig. 20-24). This type of drive provides a positive meshing of the drive pinion gear with the flywheel teeth before the cranking motor switch closes. In other words, the drive pinion meshes with the flywheel *before* the armature begins to rotate. This action eliminates the clashing of the pinion teeth with the flywheel as well as the possibility of broken or burred teeth on either unit.

The manufacturer uses the Dyer drive on heavy-duty installation, where it is very important that the pinion engage before armature rotation begins. In this situation, engagement of the pinion while in motion would be impossible, due to the high horsepower developed along with the acceleration of the armature, as the cranking motor begins to operate.

The Dyer drive mechanism itself consists of thrust washers, shift sleeve, pinion guide, pinion spring, pinion, pinion stop, and cotter pin (Fig. 20-25). The pinion guide is a snug fit on the spiral splines of the armature shaft. The pinion, which has integral splines matching those on the armature, fits loosely on the armature-shaft splines.

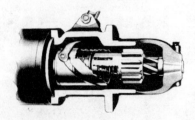

Fig. 20-24. A typical Dyer-drive installation. (Courtesy of Delco Remy)

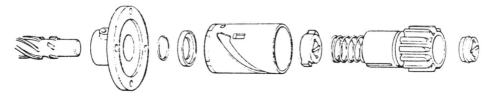

| ARMATURE SHAFT | CENTER BEARING | THRUST WASHERS | SHIFT SLEEVE | PINION GUIDE | PINION SPRING | PINION | PINION STOP |

Fig. 20-25. The parts breakdown of a Dyer drive. (Courtesy of Delco Remy)

Figure 20-26 illustrates the drive assembly at rest. In this position, the pinion guide, which drops into milled notches in the armature shaft splines, retains the drive pinion. The movement of the pinion guide through the operation of the shift lever can only release the pinion from this at-rest position.

Dyer-Drive Operation

When the operator moves the ignition switch to the start position or depresses the manual starter control, the action causes movement of the shift lever. The lever, in turn, moves the shift sleeve, pinion guide, pinion spring, and pinion endwise along the armature shaft. This action meshes the pinion gear with the flywheel teeth (diagram 1 of Fig. 20-27), provided that the teeth align properly. Further movement of the shift lever also closes the starter motor switch and cranking takes place.

If the teeth on both the pinion and flywheel do not align, meshing cannot

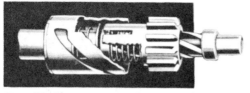

Fig. 20-26. A Dyer drive in the at-rest position. (Courtesy of Delco Remy)

take place at once. The pinion, in this case, just rotates against the flywheel teeth until alignment and meshing occur.

The pinion rotates because it is a snug fit on the armature shaft splines while the pinion guide is a tight fit. The continued forward movement of the pinion guide causes it to rotate as it follows the spiral splines on the shaft. This rotation transmits, by means of two lugs on the pinion guide, to the pinion itself. Consequently, the pinion rotates without any further forward movement, until alignment takes place. Then, it is thrust forward into mesh. The pinion stop limits the forward movement of the pinion.

As the shift lever completes its travel, the cranking motor switch closes. This action is due either to movement of mechanical linkage on the shift lever or travel of the solenoid plunger (diagram 2 of Fig. 20-27). As the motor armature begins to turn, the shift sleeve returns to its original position, rotating back out of the way.

The instant the engine begins to operate, it attempts to drive the pinion faster than the armature is rotating. As a result, the pinion gear and guide spin back out of mesh with the flywheel teeth (diagram 3 of Fig. 20-27). The pinion guide also drops into the milled section of the armature shaft splines, locking the pinion in the out-of-mesh or at-rest position.

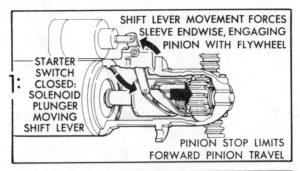

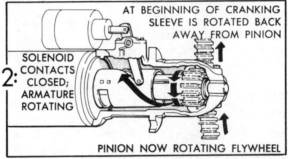

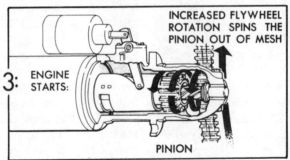

Fig. 20-27.   Operation of the Dyer drive. (Courtesy of Delco Remy)

Overrunning Clutch Drive

Another type of drive moved in and out of mesh by the shift lever (either manually or electrically) is the *overrunning clutch* (Fig. 20-28). The shift lever activates the drive pinion, and the pinion along with the overrunning clutch mechanism moves endwise along a splined armature shaft, moving the gear into or out of mesh with the flywheel teeth

The overrunning clutch portion of the drive unit consists of a shell, pinion, and

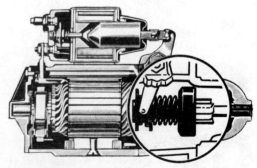

Fig. 20-28.   A starter with an overrunning clutch drive. (Courtesy of Delco Remy)

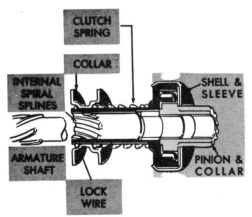

Fig. 20-29. The components of an overrunning clutch drive. (Courtesy of Delco Remy)

collar (Fig. 20-29). The shell and sleeve assembly have internal splines to match the splines on the armature shaft. Some units have straight splines while others have spiral splines.

The pinion and collar assembly fit within the shell. The manufacturer machines notches into the shell and assembles a hardened steel roller into each notch (Fig. 20-30). The notches have a

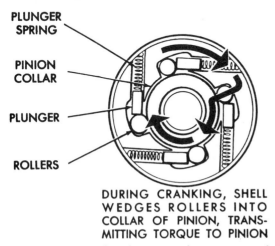

DURING CRANKING, SHELL WEDGES ROLLERS INTO COLLAR OF PINION, TRANSMITTING TORQUE TO PINION

Fig. 20-30. The design and operation of the overrunning clutch. (Courtesy of Delco Remy)

slight inward taper, allowing adequate room for the rollers in the position shown. Consequently, the pinion collar can turn freely in the direction that tends to move the rollers against the springs.

When the pinion meshes with the flywheel teeth, during starter operation, and the armature begins to spin, the shell rotates in the same direction as the armature (clockwise viewing the drive end in Fig. 20-30). As a result, the rollers tend to rotate between the shell and collar and to wedge tightly into the smaller area of the notches. In this position, the rollers force the pinion to rotate with the shell. Thus, cranking torque transmits from the shell to the pinion, causing the engine to turn over.

Overrunning Clutch Drive Operation

When the driver turns the ignition switch to the start position or depresses the manual starter control, the shift lever moves the drive assembly endwise along the armature shaft. This action meshes the pinion with the flywheel teeth. If the pinion and flywheel teeth do not align, the pinion spring compresses as the shift lever movement continues to push on the collar. However, after the cranking motor switch closes and the armature begins to turn, the pinion rotates only the width of half a tooth before alignment takes place; and the spring forces the pinion into mesh.

The overrunning clutch then transmits torque from the armature, through the shell, pinion, and to the flywheel. But the clutch permits the drive pinion to rotate freely (freewheel) in respect to the remainder of the clutch assembly and armature *after* the engine begins to operate. This action is due to the fact that when the engine begins to run, it tends to drive the pinion gear faster than the armature rotates. As a result, the rollers return to the position shown in Fig. 20–31. The pinion gear can rotate freely in respect to the shell. This feature prevents the engine from driving the armature at excessive speeds.

The shift lever moves the overrunning clutch pinion away from the flywheel as soon as the engine starts, and the driver releases the ignition switch to the run position or releases the starter control. If for some reason this is not done, the drive pinion would remain in mesh and continue to overrun the armature. The overrunning clutch can withstand this condition for a brief period. However, if the overrunning effect continues for a long period, the unit overheats and ultimately seizes. This, of course, would allow the armature to spin at high speeds.

Drive Pinion Gear Reduction

The pinion teeth not only transmit the cranking torque directly from the starter drive to the flywheel but also provide the necessary gear reduction between the cranking motor and engine (Fig. 20–32). This is necessary to permit an electric motor of only a few horsepower to turn over an engine that may have several hundred horsepower at cranking speed.

To accomplish this, there are approx-

Fig. 20–31.   The rollers move into the wide portion of the notches as the clutch begins to overrun. (Courtesy of Delco Remy)

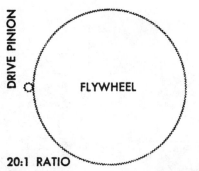

20:1 RATIO

Fig. 20–32.   The gear reduction provided by the pinion. (Courtesy of Delco Remy)

imately 15 to 20 teeth on the flywheel for every tooth on the drive pinion. This means that the cranking motor armature spins approximately 15 to 20 times for every engine revolution. Therefore, the cranking motor armature turns at 1,500 to 2,000 rpm to turn the engine over at 100 rpm.

Testing the Starting System

The easiest way to test the starting system is under actual operating conditions. You can perform such a test with a SUN VAT-40 following this procedure (Fig. 20–33).

1. Check each of the meter's mechanical zero, and adjust them as necessary.

2. Rotate the load increase fully counterclockwise to the off position.

3. Connect the tester load leads to the battery terminals—red to positive and black to negative.

4. Set the volt selector to INT. 18V.

5. Place the test selector in starting position 1.

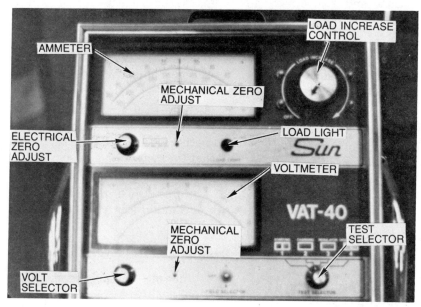

Fig. 20-33. A SUN VAT-40 starting and charging system tester.

6. Adjust the ammeter to read zero, using the electrical zero adjust control.

7. Connect the green clamp-on ampere pickup around the vehicle's ground battery cable, disregarding polarity (Fig. 20-34). If more than one cable connects to this battery post, place the clamp around all the cables.

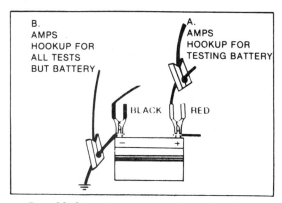

Fig. 20-34. Test connections for the ammeter. (Courtesy of Sun Electric Corp.)

8. Test the battery to make sure it is in serviceable condition, following the procedures outlined in Chapter 14.

9. Turn off all lights and accessories and close the vehicle's doors.

10. Prevent the engine from starting, using one of these methods.

a. On engines with externally mounted ignition coils, remove its high-tension cable from the distributor cap; then ground it, using a jumper lead.

b. On engines with integral-mounted ignition coils, disconnect the ignition switch lead from the ignition system assembly. Do not permit this lead to touch ground.

11. Crank the engine while observing the green voltmeter and the red ammeter reading. Note the results.

12. Restore the engine to its normal

starting condition, and disconnect all meter leads from the battery.

Results and Indications

Compare the readings against manufacturer's specifications. The starting system is satisfactory if:

1. The ammeter reading does not exceed the maximum amount specified. *Note:* If no ampere specifications are available, a rule of thumb is:

    a. Starter current draw for a large V-8 engine should be under 250 amperes.

    b. Starter current draw for a small V-8 and a six-cylinder engine should be under 200 amperes.

2. The voltmeter reading should be under the amount specified. *Note:* If the manufacturer does not provide a specification, the voltage should be 9.6 volts or higher.

3. The cranking speed should be normal.

4. If the starting circuit does not perform as stated, perform voltage drop tests on the cables and solenoid to determine whether the trouble is in the starter, solenoid, or cables.

Testing Internal Starter Components

Armature

If the testing sequence indicates that the starter itself is defective, remove and disassemble the starter, following the manufacturer's instructions. Then, test the armature and field winding, using the following procedures.

To test the armature for an open circuit, follow these steps.

1. Place the armature on a growler (Fig. 20-35). Then, using the two-pronged tester, span adjacent commutator bars as illustrated.

2. Rotate the armature back and forth to get the maximum reading on the meter. As necessary, adjust the voltage control so that the meter hand reaches about midpoint on the scale.

3. Rotate the armature and test each pair of commutator bars in turn. Note the results.

Results and Indications

1. All voltage readings should be approximately the same as you test each commutator bar with an adjacent bar.

2. A wide deviation in any reading indicates an open circuit. If you cannot repair the open circuit, replace the armature.

Fig. 20-35. Testing an armature for open circuits. (Courtesy of Deere & Co. Technical Services)

Testing for Grounds

To test the armature for grounds on a growler:

1. Place one test point on the iron core of the armature and the other point on a commutator bar (Fig. 20-36).

2. Observe the test lamp on the growler. The lamp should not light while performing this test. If it does, the armature has a grounded armature and requires replacement or rewinding.

Testing for Shorts

To test an armature for shorts on the growler (Fig. 20-37):

1. Place the armature on the growler, and turn the control switch on.

2. Place a thin strip of steel or hacksaw blade on the armature core. Then rotate the armature slowly. Note the results.

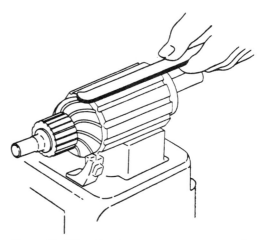

Fig. 20-37. Testing an armature for shorts. (Courtesy of Deere & Co. Technical Services)

Results and Indications

If the metal strip or blade vibrates over a winding, that particular winding has a short circuit. A short-circuited winding sometimes results from metal within the commutator that electrically bridges the gap from one bar to the next. In this case, removing the metal should clear up the short circuit. However, if it does not correct the problem, rewind or replace the armature.

Testing the Field Winding

To test the field winding for grounds with a test light from a growler (Fig. 20-38):

1. Disconnect the field winding ground connection.

2. Connect one test point to the field frame or housing and the other to the field connector terminal.

3. Observe the test lamp. If the test lamp lights, there is a ground in the field

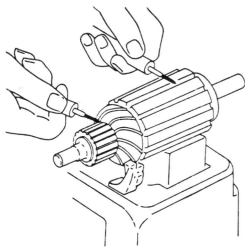

Fig. 20-36. Testing an armature for grounds. (Courtesy of Deere & Co. Technical Services)

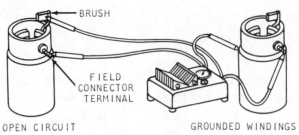

Fig. 20-38. *Testing the field coils for grounds and opens. (Courtesy of Deere & Co. Technical Services)*

winding. In this case, repair or replace the field windings.

To test the field winding for an open circuit with the test light (Fig. 20-38):

1. Connect the test points to each end of the field winding.

2. Observe the test light; it should *now* glow. If it does not, the field winding is open and requires repair or replacement.

Testing Brush Holders

To test the brush holders with a test lamp:

1. Connect one test point to an insulated brush holder and the other to the housing or end frame, depending on starter design.

2. Observe the test lamp. It should *not* glow. If it does, repair or replace the brush holder.

3. Repeat the process on any and all other insulated brush holders.

4. Connect one test point to a grounded brush holder and the other to the housing or end frame.

5. Observe the test lamp. It *should* glow. If not, repair or replace the brush holder.

6. Repeat the procedure on any and all other grounded brush holders.

Review

This section will assist you in determining how well you remember the material in this chapter. Read each item carefully. If you can't complete the statement, review the section in each chapter that covers the material.

1. Automobiles with an automatic transmission have a _____ _____ switch in the starting system.
   a. neutral safety
   b. keyed ignition
   c. all of these
   d. electrical solenoid

2. In some starters the device that actually pulls the pinion into mesh with the flywheel is the _____ _____.
   a. starter solenoid
   b. ignition switch
   c. starter switch
   d. field windings

3. The solenoid discussed in this chapter has _____ winding(s).
   a. 1
   b. 2
   c. 3
   d. 0

4. The rotating component of the starter is the _____.

a. brushes
b. shoes
c. fields
d. armature

5. The components that carry the current from the field coils to the armature are the _____.
   a. brushes
   b. holders
   c. shoes
   d. windings

6. The components within the starter that produce a strong stationary magnetic field are the _____
   _____.
   a. field housing
   b. field coils
   c. commutator segment
   d. starter brushes

7. A heavy-duty starter will have _____ field coils, pole pieces, and brushes.
   a. 3
   b. 4
   c. 5
   d. 6

8. The type of starter drive that operates on inertia is the _____
   ____.
   a. overrunning
   b. Dyer
   c. Bendix
   d. none of these

9. The type of drive where the pinion meshes with the flywheel teeth before the armature begins to rotate is the
   _____.

a. overrunning
b. Bendix
c. Dyer
d. none of these

10. The type of drive unit in which the pinion freewheels after the engine starts is the _____.
    a. Bendix
    b. overrunning
    c. Dyer
    d. none of these

11. There are about _____ teeth on the flywheel for each one on the pinion gear.
    a. 15 to 20
    b. 20 to 25
    c. 25 to 30
    d. 30 to 35

12. The current draw of a starter on a large V-8 engine should be to specifications or more than about _____ amperes.
    a. 175
    b. 200
    c. 225
    d. 250

13. If during the growler test the steel strip vibrates, the armature winding has a (an) _____.
    a. open
    b. ground
    c. short
    d. none of these

For the answers, turn to the Appendix.

Beginning in the early 1960s, some domestic automobiles were factory-equipped with the first emission control device. This device was the first attempt to curb or control the increasing problem of air pollution, which was gaining a great deal of public attention. Since then, many state and federal regulations have been put into effect, forcing vehicle manufacturers to install a greater number of additional control devices in order to meet a given air quality standard.

The development and introduction of these various devices to control different forms of air pollution have led to considerable changes in engine and vehicle design along with tune-up procedures. As a result, a simple tune-up is no longer simple. On newer vehicles, for example, the tune-up technician not only is responsible for making sure that the engine is mechanically sound and that the fuel and ignition systems are functioning properly but also must perform an emission-control tune-up. This latter tune-up is necessary to ensure that all emission control equipment is performing to specifications and that the vehicle is not emitting excessive amounts of harmful emissions into the atmosphere.

An emission-control tune-up also must be an integral part of any tune-up because the operation of the modern automobile engine centers around the control devices. Since the controls have caused some changes in engine design, the satisfactory operation of the engine itself depends to a great extent on how well the emission control devices are functioning. In other words, these devices must be operating normally in order for the engine to perform satisfactorily and meet all emission standards.

_____ Chapter 21

AUTOMOTIVE EMISSION CONTROLS, OPERATION AND SERVICING OF CRANKCASE DEVICES

Types of Air Pollution

Natural

In order to understand the need for the automobile to have all the various emission control devices, let us first examine the various types of air pollutants and their main sources. Air pollution basically results from the injection into the atmosphere of any foreign substance that not only is an eyesore but is detrimental to man as well as animal and plant life. These contaminants are divisible into two categories: natural pollutants and man-made pollutants.

There have always been *natural sources* of air pollution. For instance, when the volcano Mt. St. Helens erupted, it spewed millions of tons of ash and smoke into the air. Then prevailing winds carried these contaminants for hundreds of miles. Another type of common air pollution is dust that high winds are also responsible for stirring up into the atmosphere.

Trees and plants give off a gaseous form of air pollution. Conifer (evergreen) trees give off, for example, terpene hydrocarbons; rotting vegetable matter in forests emit methane hydrocarbons. *Hydrocarbons* basically are a compound of hydrogen and carbon atoms.

Man-Made Pollutants

There are many sources of *man-made air pollution*. For example, people who live in cities expose themselves to man-made pollution in the form of chemical fumes from factories, smokestacks, and chimneys, in addition to many types of harmful emissions from automobiles (Fig. 21-1). Man-made pollution of this type is sometimes referred to as *smog*—a combination of the two words *smoke* and *fog*.

Fig. 21-1. Air pollution (smog) can hang over heavily populated cities. (Courtesy of Ford Motor Co. of Canada Ltd.)

A typical example of a smog situation occurs in Los Angeles. Los Angeles itself is in a basin, or a valley, with the Pacific Ocean to the west and the mountains to the east. When the wind comes up from the mountains, it blows the smog out over the ocean, and the air in the city is reasonably clean. But when there is no wind, the air is still, and the smoke from industry along with automobile pollutants does not blow away. Thus, the mountains trap the smog over the city; the dirty, still air covers Los Angeles like a blanket, which gradually builds up to a thick, smelly layer of smog.

Also, under normal conditions, the warm air near the ground would rise to the cooler layers of the atmosphere. This would carry the smog up and away from the city. However, Los Angeles and similarly located cities are subject to a weather condition called an *inversion*. Under this condition, a relatively warmer layer of air hovers above the basin in which the city lies. The inversion layer shuts off the movement of ground-level air and keeps the smog near the ground.

As this condition worsens, it aggravates respiratory ailments such as emphysema, restricts oxygen to the circulatory system, causes eye irritation, and increases crop losses. In addition, smog damages paint on vehicles and rots rubber tires, hoses, and belts.

Conditions and Ingredients That Cause Smog

Smog is simply the result of a photochemical reaction in the atmosphere. This reaction takes place between hydrocarbons and nitrogen oxides when exposed to sunlight (Fig. 21-2). Some natural amounts of gaseous hydrocarbons enter the atmosphere; these are not the main concern. The hydrocarbons and nitrogen oxide emissions that are, come from the exhaust of a motor vehicle. The hydrocarbons (HC) are particles of fuel that the engine's combustion process did not burn.

Added to these hydrocarbons are the nitrogen oxides (NOx), which form by a chemical union of nitrogen atoms with one or more oxygen atoms. These oxides form more quickly under extreme heat conditions such as in the combustion chamber of an engine.

Also emitted from a vehicle's exhaust is carbon monoxide (CO). Carbon monoxide is an odorless, poisonous gas. If inhaled in sufficient quantity, it can cause nausea, headaches, and even death. Although CO is a dangerous gas, it is a separate problem from that of smog.

Under ideal combustion conditions, CO does not form. Instead, the process should form carbon dioxide (CO_2). Carbon dioxide results when a carbon atom unites with two oxygen atoms to form a harmless gas. Carbon monoxide, on the other hand, occurs when one carbon atom unites with only one oxygen atom. Since carbon monoxide is a harmful gas, federal automotive emission standards limit its emission from the automobile along with nitrogen oxide and unburned hydrocarbons.

Sources of Hydrocarbon Emissions from the Automobile

Hydrocarbons can emit from three different areas of the automobile (Fig. 21-3). For example, about 60 percent of the automobile's hydrocarbon emissions are expelled with the exhaust gases. Another 20 percent enter the atmosphere from the engine's crankcase while 20 percent discharge from the fuel tank and carburetor vents.

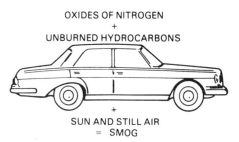

OXIDES OF NITROGEN
+
UNBURNED HYDROCARBONS

+
SUN AND STILL AIR
= SMOG

Fig. 21-2.   Conditions and ingredients that cause smog.

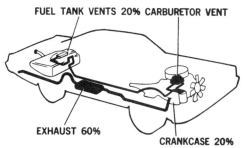

FUEL TANK VENTS 20% CARBURETOR VENT

EXHAUST 60%

CRANKCASE 20%

Fig. 21-3.   Sources of hydrocarbon emissions. (Courtesy of Chrysler Corp.)

However, effective emission control systems can eliminate or reduce these harmful emissions. For instance, manufacturers install devices that effectively control crankcase emissions and fuel vapor losses from the fuel tank and carburetor. These accounted for about 40 percent of the total hydrocarbon emissions from the automobile before control systems.

Manufacturers have also considerably reduced hydrocarbon, nitrogen oxide, and carbon monoxide emissions through various controls. These controls include such things as electrical-assist chokes, spark-advance controls, heated air cleaners, air pumps, catalytic converters, and exhaust gas recirculation systems. These particular systems along with the evaporation control device are explained in Chapters 22, 23, and 24.

Emission Control Standards

By 1968, the federal government and many states established emission control standards. These standards have become more stringent in regard to the allowable emissions by the automobile and light to intermediate-size trucks. Before 1968, for example, an average automobile could produce hydrocarbon emissions from the exhaust at a rate of 1,250 parts per million (ppm), with a carbon monoxide level of 6 percent of the total exhaust volume.

However, starting in 1968, a vehicle with a similar engine, operating in certain states, could not emit more than 650 parts per million hydrocarbons and a 5 percent volume of carbon monoxide. Of course, all new automobiles and light trucks must not discharge from their exhaust more

than 175 ppm of hydrocarbons and 0.5 percent by volume carbon monoxide gas in order to remain within the standards.

Obviously, the federal standards and state emission regulations have changed a great deal since 1968. In some cases, the standards were downgraded because certain vehicles at the time could not meet the requirements. But all new vehicles must meet a given standard in order to be sold in this country.

The main point is that these standards or regulations do exist. Consequently, when tuning a vehicle, you must make the necessary adjustments so that the total vehicle emissions are in compliance with the law. A federal or state agency is responsible for supplying the garages or service centers with the regulations and for enforcing them.

Crankcase Devices— Function

The first device factory-installed on automobiles in an attempt to reduce hydrocarbon emissions was the positive crankcase ventilation (PCV) system. The basic function of this system was, and still is, to prevent hydrocarbon emissions from escaping from the crankcase into the atmosphere. These emissions amounted to about 20 percent of the total hydrocarbon pollution from the automobile.

Need for a Ventilation System

Some unburned air/fuel mixture and other byproducts of combustion escape past the piston rings on the compression and power strokes. This unburned mixture (hydrocarbons) and the other contaminants form what are commonly known as *blowby gases,* which enter the crankcase and are detrimental to the engine. For example, the hydrocarbons that can condense mix with the oil to reduce its viscosity and lubricating properties. Also, moisture from the combustion process condenses, mixes with the oil, and forms sludge deposits. Finally, the pressure of the blowby gases and the movement of the crankshaft, rods, and pistons create a pressure buildup within the crankcase. This pressure eventually builds to a point where the engine seals do not contain it, and oil leakage past the seals soon results.

Consequently, every internal combustion engine must have a ventilation system so that it can breathe. Breathing within an engine crankcase is the direct result of permitting a charge of fresh air to enter the crankcase and mix with the blowby gases. Then, the ventilation system removes this mixture from the crankcase area.

Types of Ventilation Systems

Road-Draft Tube

Before the introduction of positive ventilation systems, a *road-draft tube system* took care of the breathing requirements of most engines (Fig. 21-4). This system consisted of a road-draft tube along with an open breather cap. The draft tube fitted into the lower crankcase or rocker-arm cover and projected down the side of the engine until it terminated near the base of the oil pan.

Installed over an opening in the crankcase or opposite rocker-arm cover was a

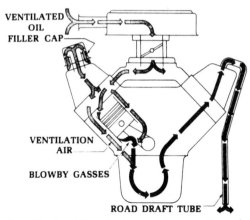

Fig. 21-4. The design and operation of a road-draft tube ventilation system.

breather cap. This cap was open, which simply means that the cap allowed atmospheric air to pass through and enter the crankcase itself. However, the cap had a filtering element to prevent dust in the air from entering the engine.

The operation of this system was relatively simple. With the vehicle in motion, air flowed past the opening in the base of the road-draft tube, creating a low-pressure area, or vacuum. This vacuum caused atmospheric pressure outside the engine to force a quantity of fresh air through the breather cap. The air passed through the crankcase, picking up the hydrocarbons, water vapor, and other contaminants. Then, the combined gases flowed out the end of the road-draft tube and into the air stream. Although this action ventilated the crankcase, it also contributed to the pollution problem.

Although the road-draft system was simple in its operation, it was not very efficient at low vehicle speeds. For instance, unless the vehicle was moving at 20 to 25 mph, the air velocity around the draft tube was insufficient to create enough of a vacuum to draw the vapors from the

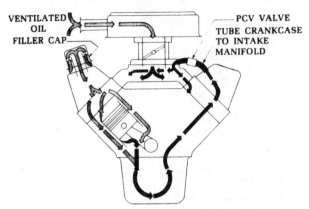

VENTILATED
OIL
FILLER CAP

PCV VALVE
TUBE CRANKCASE
TO INTAKE
MANIFOLD

Fig. 21-5. The design and operation of an open positive crankcase ventilation system.

crankcase. As a result, the formation of sludge increased in the crankcase. On the other hand, at high vehicle speeds, there was so much air flow that the resulting crankcase vacuum pulled some oil from the crankcase along with the vapors. This created excessive engine oil usage at high speeds.

Positive Ventilation Systems—Open Type

The first positive ventilation system that eliminated the road-draft tube completely, as well as that system's inherent problems, was the *open type* (Fig. 21-5). In this particular system, the manufacturer still installs an open-type oil breather cap into the upper portion of the crankcase. This cap along with its filtering element performs the same function as the cap in the road-draft tube system.

However, in place of the road-draft tube, the manufacturer installs a positive crankcase ventilation (PCV) valve into the crankcase. In the engine shown in Fig. 21-5, the valve fits into the opposite rocker-arm cover from the breather cap location. The valve, in turn, connects into the intake manifold via a PCV hose.

The PCV valve may be nothing more than a metered orifice or flow jet. However, the majority of systems use a valve similar to the one shown in Fig. 21-6. This particular valve consists of a housing, valve plunger, and calibrated spring. The valve housing has two openings. One opening connects into the crankcase while the other fits inside the PCV hose, leading to the intake manifold.

Operating in a special bore inside the housing is the plunger valve. The function of the plunger is to meter the flow through the system during different operating phases of the engine—idle, heavy acceleration, and cruise.

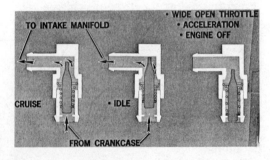

TO INTAKE MANIFOLD

• WIDE OPEN THROTTLE
• ACCELERATION
• ENGINE OFF

CRUISE   • IDLE

FROM CRANKCASE

Fig. 21-6. The design and operation of a typical PCV valve. (Courtesy of Chrysler Corp.)

The action of the plunger itself is under the control of intake manifold vacuum and the tension of the calibrated spring. During periods of high vacuum such as engine idle and deceleration, the vacuum overcomes the spring's tension, and the plunger bottoms in the manifold end of the valve housing (center diagram of Fig. 21-6). Because of valve face and seat design, this position restricts but does not completely stop the flow of crankcase vapors to the intake manifold.

When there is a zero vacuum condition in the intake manifold, such as when the engine is not running or is operating at wide-open throttle, the calibrated spring moves the plunger so that it bottoms on the crankcase end of the valve (right-hand diagram of Fig. 21-6). In this valve position, little or no fumes from the crankcase can enter the intake manifold.

At any engine rpm between idle and wide-open throttle, the valve plunger assumes a position determined by the resulting manifold vacuum (left-hand diagram of Fig. 21-6). In other words, when spring tension equals the pull of vacuum, the plunger assumes a give position in its bore in the housing. This position then determines the flow rate during that particular phase of engine operation. Consequently, the flow rate through the valve is lower at idle but higher during cruise conditions.

In the event of an engine backfire, the valve plunger assumes the same position during heavy acceleration. In other words, the valve seats against the crankcase side of the housing. This action is due to gas pressure from the intake manifold and the action of the spring. As a result, the closed valve stops any fire attempting to travel through the valve to the crankcase where it possibly would ignite the volatile blowby gases.

Open PCV System Operation

When an engine with the open PCV system (Fig. 21-5) is in operation at idle rpm, the PCV valve permits about 1 to 3 cubic feet (0.03 to 0.09 cubic meters) of air per minute to enter the open breather cap. This air flows through the crankcase, picking up hydrocarbon, moisture, and other gaseous forms of combustion by-products. Then, these vapors move through the PCV valve and through the PCV hose to the intake manifold, where they mix with the air/fuel charge. Finally, the entire charge enters the various combustion chambers where it burns.

During moderate acceleration and cruising, the PCV valve opens more than at idle. As a result, it allows a higher flow rate of approximately 3 to 6 cubic feet (0.09 to 0.17 cubic meters) of air per minute to pass through the open breather cap. This flow, along with the increasing amount of crankcase vapors, after passing through the PCV valve and hose, absorbs into the air/fuel mixture within the intake manifold. The additional air flow at this time does not affect engine performance as the entire charge moves into the combustion chambers.

Under heavy acceleration, intake manifold vacuum decreases considerably while crankcase vapor pressure builds up. As mentioned earlier under PCV valve operation, if a zero vacuum exists in the intake manifold, the valve closes; under moderate acceleration, it assumes a position based on spring tension and manifold vacuum. Consequently, under a heavy acceleration condition, the valve's closed or nearly closed position does not permit the increasing amounts of crankcase vapors to pass into the intake manifold. Therefore, the pressure in the crankcase forces some of these vapors out the open

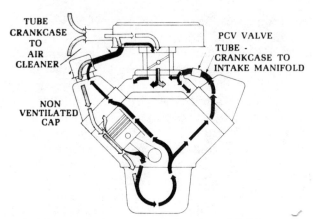

TUBE
CRANKCASE
TO
AIR
CLEANER

PCV VALVE
TUBE -
CRANKCASE TO
INTAKE MANIFOLD

NON
VENTILATED
CAP

Fig. 21-7.   The design and operation of a closed PCV system.

breather cap and into the atmosphere. For this reason, an open PCV system only partially controls crankcase vapors and therefore is only 75 percent efficient.

Closed PCV System—
Function and Design

In order to achieve 100 percent control of crankcase emissions, manufacturers added several modifications to the open system in order to seal it from the atmosphere during heavy acceleration. However, these components did not alter the other basic phases of the open PCV system operation.

Figure 21-7 illustrates a typical *closed PCV system*. This system not only includes the PCV valve and hose, as in the open system, but also a special cap and an additional PCV hose. The cap used with the closed system also serves, in many cases, as an oil-filler cap. However, in the closed PCV system, the cap has no air openings to the atmosphere.

The cap has one port opening, which accommodates the second PCV hose. This hose runs from the cap to the air cleaner. The hose connection on the air cleaner can be either on the clean or dirty side of the filter element.

When the hose connects to the dirty side of the air cleaner, a PCV air filter is necessary to trap foreign particles that would otherwise enter the crankcase. Some manufacturers install this filter inside the air cleaner housing where the PCV hose connects (Fig. 21-8). However, in other cases, the filter may also be inside the closed oil-filler cap.

Closed PCV System Operation

During all other phases of engine operation except during heavy acceleration, the

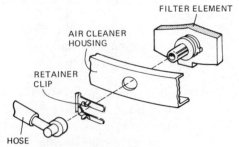

FILTER ELEMENT

AIR CLEANER
HOUSING

RETAINER
CLIP

HOSE

Fig. 21-8.   A PCV filter inside the air-cleaner housing.

closed PCV system (Fig. 21-7) operates in much the same way as the open type. The only real difference is that the air entering the crankcase comes through the inlet PCV hose connected to the air cleaner. Then, the air flows through the crankcase, PCV valve, and into the intake manifold.

Under heavy acceleration conditions, any excess vapors from the crankcase flow back up through the air inlet PCV hose and into the air cleaner. From there, these vapors mix with the incoming air and flow into the carburetor. Next, the entire mixture passes into the combustion chambers via the intake manifold. Due to this arrangement, any built-up crankcase vapors cannot escape into the atmosphere from the system. Therefore, the closed system provides 100 percent control of crankcase hydrocarbon emissions and completely ventilates the engine in order to prevent the buildup of sludge and other contaminants harmful to the engine.

Servicing the Closed PCV System—Purpose

A PCV system requires routine maintenance, or it does not function properly, causing rough idle, sludge, oil dilution, oil leakage through engine seals, and air pollution. The system requires periodic maintenance due to the nature of the materials flowing through it, mainly crankcase vapors. These vapors tend to form sludge and sediment, which can plug up the entire system.

In an event of a rough idle, never attempt to compensate for this condition by disconnecting the PCV system or by making carburetor adjustments without checking the ventilation system. The removal of the PCV components from the engine adversely affects fuel economy and engine

ventilation. Keep in mind that on non-PCV engines, the crankcase hydrocarbons are lost to the atmosphere while with the PCV system these fuel vapors burn in the combustion chambers. This improves the fuel economy of the vehicle.

If you disconnect the PCV system, the crankcase also does not have proper ventilation. This shortens engine life due to the formation of sludge and the loss of oil through engine seals.

On the average, most engine manufacturers recommend service on the PCV system at a given mileage or at least once a year. This service includes such things as inspecting the operation of the PCV valve, checking the hoses and carburetor passages for deposits, and cleaning or replacing the PCV air filter.

Checking the Operation of the PCV Valve

To check the operation of a typical PCV valve, follow this procedure.

1. Start the engine and permit it to idle at normal operating temperature.

2. Remove the PCV valve from the rocker arm. If the valve is not plugged, you can hear a hissing noise as air passes through the valve.

3. Place your finger over the inlet of the valve. You should feel a strong pulling effect of engine vacuum (Fig. 21-9).

4. Reinstall the PCV valve in the valve cover.

5. Then remove the crankcase inlet air cleaner or filler cap (Fig. 21-10).

6. Hold a piece of stiff paper over the opening in the rocker-arm cover. After allowing about a minute for the crankcase

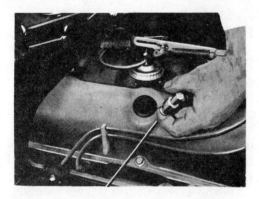

Fig. 21-9. Testing the operation of the PCV valve with your finger. (Courtesy of Chrysler Corp.)

Fig. 21-11. A typical PCV tester.

pressure to reduce, it should pull the paper against the opening in the rocker arm cover with considerable force. *Note:* Some technicians prefer to use a PCV tester similar to the one shown in Fig. 21-11 to perform the same check. The tester itself fits over the opening in the rocker-arm cover, and crankcase vacuum moves the test ball into the safe zone if the system is functioning properly.

7. Shut off the engine, and once again remove the PCV valve from the rocker-arm cover (Fig. 21-12). Then, shake the valve. You should hear a clicking noise, which indicates the valve plunger is free within its housing bore.

8. If the PCV system passed all the previous tests, its operation is satisfactory.

9. If the system failed either checks 2, 3, 6, or 7, replace the PCV valve and recheck the system. Do not attempt to clean the old PCV valve unless it is the type

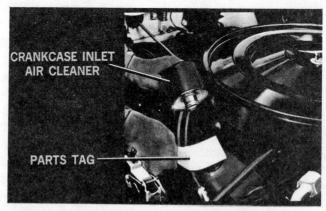

Fig. 21-10. Checking the operation of the PCV system with a piece of paper. (Courtesy of Chrysler Corp.)

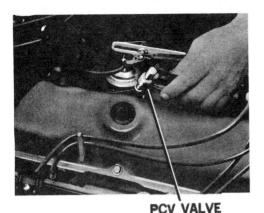

PCV VALVE

Fig. 21-12. Checking the PCV valve plunger for freedom of movement. (Courtesy of Chrysler Corp.)

that can be completely disassembled because there is no way to clean and inspect a sealed-type valve properly.

10. If the system with a new installed valve again fails to pass check 6, inspect the PCV hose and its carburetor passage in the lower part of the carburetor. Replace a plugged hose or clean out restricted passages using the following procedures.

Replacing a PCV Hose

All PCV hoses, both the inlet hose and the hose from the valve to the intake manifold, require replacement if cracked, plugged, or damaged. When replacing either or both of these hoses, only use the special hose made for PCV systems. Do not use ordinary heater hose because it cannot withstand the effects of the blowby gases.

To replace a typical PCV hose:

1. If so equipped, loosen and slide the hose clamps back out of the way.

2. Twist each fitting end of the hose

slightly, and remove it using a steady pulling action.

3. Using the old hose as a guide, cut a new piece of PCV stock to the proper length.

4. Slide the clamps over the new hose, and install it over the ends of both fittings. Then, tighten the clamps securely.

Cleaning the PCV Passages in the Carburetor

To clean the PCV passages in the carburetor properly, follow these steps.

1. Following the manufacturer's instructions, remove the carburetor from the intake manifold. However, it is not necessary to disassemble the carburetor in order to clean out the PCV passages.

2. Turn a drill by hand through the passages to dislodge the solid particles. As necessary, use a drill smaller than the diameter of the openings so that you remove no metal. Then, blow the passages clean with low-pressure compressed air.

3. Reinstall the carburetor, and then recheck PCV system operation.

Servicing PCV Air Filters

Air-Cleaner Type

A polyurethane-type foam filter like the one shown in Fig. 21-8 is not serviceable by cleaning. Consequently, when this filter is dirty or requires preventative maintenance, replace it following this procedure.

1. Remove the air cleaner cover.

2. Unsnap or remove the hose from the filter fittings on the air cleaner housing.

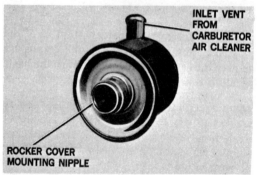

Fig. 21-13. Servicing the element within a PCV cap with oil. (Courtesy of Chrysler Corp.)

3. Slide the retainer clip from the filter nipple, and remove the filter element from the air cleaner housing.

4. Insert a new element, and then install the new filter retainer clip, supplied with the element kit. If a new clip did not come with the kit, clean and reinstall the old retainer clip.

5. Reinstall or snap the hose onto the filter fitting on the air cleaner housing.

6. Reinstall the air cleaner cover.

Cleaning and Servicing the Filter in the Filler Cap

To service a typical filter within the filler cap:

1. Remove the cap from the rocker-arm cover and disconnect its PCV hose.

2. Soak the cap completely in solvent.

3. Allow it to drain dry. Do not use compressed air to dry this type of filter because the air pressure will damage the element.

4. Inspect the cap and filter assembly. If the cap shows any signs of damage or is still fully to partially clogged, replace the entire cap.

5. If the cap is still serviceable after cleaning and drying, invert its inlet fitting from the air cleaner (Fig. 21-13). Then, fill the opening with SAE 30 oil, until oil drains from the mounting nipple.

6. Reinstall the cap onto the rocker-arm cover and connect its PCV hose.

Review

This section will assist you in determining how well you remember the material in this chapter. Read each item carefully. If you can't complete the statement, review the section in the chapter that covers the material.

1. The first factory-installed emission-control devices came out in the early _____.
    a. 1970s
    b. 1960s
    c. 1950s
    d. 1940s

2. The two gaseous ingredients of smog are nitrogen oxide and _____.
    a. carbon
    b. CO_2
    c. CO
    d. hydrocarbons

3. The first federal emission-control standards came into effect in _____.
    a. 1966
    b. 1967
    c. 1968
    d. 1969

4. The first factory-installed emission-control device was the _____ system.
    a. NOx
    b. PCV
    c. CO
    d. hydrocarbon

5. The first PCV system was the _____
   _____ type.
   a. closed
   b. open
   c. road-draft
   d. pressurized

6. The closed PCV system is _____ percent efficient.
   a. 100
   b. 75
   c. 50
   d. 25

7. The PCV system should receive service
   at least every _____ months.
   a. 6
   b. 9
   c. 12
   d. 15

8. If a PCV system does not pass the
   crankcase vacuum test, first replace
   the _____ and then retest the
   system.
   a. carburetor
   b. filter
   c. hose
   d. valve

9. You should use a _____ to clean
   out the PCV passages in the carburetor.
   a. chisel
   b. drill
   c. screwdriver
   d. brush

For the answers, turn to the Appendix.

System Function and Types

Due to California's stringent emission-control laws, all automobiles sold in that state, beginning in 1970, had to have an evaporation emission control (EEC) system. However, federal requirements for the installation of EEC devices began in 1971. Thus, all domestic vehicles, regardless of where sold, had to have this system, after that date.

The EEC system (Fig. 22-1) has a design that effectively reduces the escape of the gasoline vapors from both the vehicle's fuel tank and the carburetor vents into the atmosphere; these vapors amount to about 20 percent of the total hydrocarbon emission from the vehicle. Since the fuel vapors are essentially unburned hydrocarbons, their release into the atmosphere contributes to the formation of photochemical smog. Consequently, trapping the vapors in the EEC system and then burning them in the engine reduce their potential as air pollutants and provide a slight increase in a vehicle's fuel economy.

Since 1970, manufacturers have produced two basic types of EEC systems: one using crankcase storage and the other using canister storage. All 1970-1971 Chrysler and some Ford vehicles, for example, employed the *crankcase* as the vapor storage area. In this system, basically, fuel vapors from the tank and carburetor accumulated in the engine crankcase. Then on engine restart, the PCV system drew the vapors from the crankcase and into the engine.

All automobiles, starting with the 1972 model, had the popular *charcoal canister*. Because this particular type of system is

_____ Chapter 22

OPERATION AND SERVICING OF EVAPORATION EMISSION CONTROLS

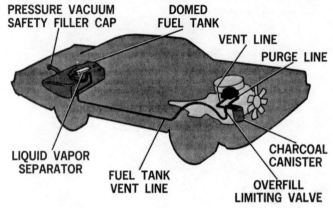

Fig. 22-1.   A typical EEC system. (Courtesy of Chrysler Corp.)

the most common, this chapter concentrates on its design, operation, and servicing. Just keep in mind, that each vehicle manufacturer can modify the system somewhat to fit a vehicle's configuration. Consequently, it may be necessary for you to follow the manufacturer's specifications and instructions when servicing a particular system.

System Design

Filler Cap

A typical EEC system consists of a pressure-vacuum filler cap or valve, an overfill-limiting device, liquid-vapor separator, rollover devices, a fuel-filter separator, carburetor vents, and charcoal canister (Fig. 22-2). The fuel tanks on EEC systems require a special cap that is different from those on non-EEC–equipped vehicles. These caps are the sealed type, which prevents any fuel spillage due to fuel surging within the tank and the escape of fuel vapors into the air.

The cap may also contain a combination pressure and vacuum valve (Fig. 22-3). This valve protects the tank from physical damage in the event of a system malfunction or damage to a vent line, which can cause either excessive pressure or vacuum. If the cap does not have this valve, the manufacturer installs a similar unit in the vent line to the canister.

The fuel cap on some late-model vehicles secures with a two-step latching device and has an extended skirt (Fig. 22-4). The cap has two pairs of tangs arranged like those on a radiator cap. These permit the attendant to break the tank-to-cap seal, in order to relieve tank pressure without separation of the cap from the filler tube. To remove the cap completely, another 90-degree turn of the cap is necessary. Both features prevent tank pressure from forcing fuel from the tank if the person removes the cap too quickly.

An exact replacement *must* be used for an EEC cap. Never install, for example, a cap without the pressure-vacuum valve onto a system that requires one. If you do, vacuum lock may develop in the fuel system, or the fuel tank may sustain damage by fuel expansion or contraction.

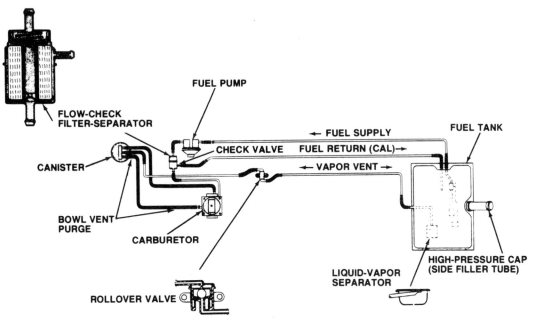

Fig. 22-2. A schematic showing the components of an EEC system. (Courtesy of Chrysler Corp.)

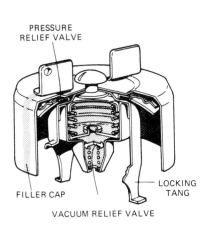

Fig. 22-3. The combination pressure and vacuum valve in an EEC filler cap.

Pressure-Vacuum Valve Operation

Figure 22-5 shows the action of the *pressure valve* when the fuel tank has excessive pressure. In this situation, the vacuum valve has closed, but the pressure valve is open. This action occurs when there is excessive pressure that, if not relieved, could damage the tank itself. With the pressure valve in this position, excessive air pressure can pass around the valve and out through the cap's vent opening. When the pressure drops, the valve again closes.

Figure 22-6 illustrates the operation of the *vacuum valve* when the tank requires venting to the atmosphere in order to prevent a vacuum lock. In this situation, the vacuum valve has moved up, and this valve position permits atmospheric air to

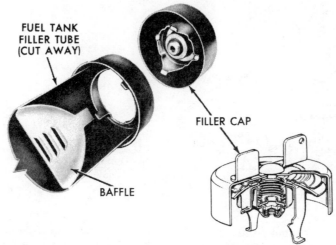

FUEL TANK
FILLER TUBE
(CUT AWAY)

FILLER CAP

BAFFLE

Fig. 22–4.   A fuel cap with a two-step latching mechanism. (Courtesy of Chrysler Corp.)

enter the cap's air vent, pass around the open vacuum valve, and enter the fuel tank. This action equalizes the air pressure in the tank to that of the atmosphere. As soon as this is done, the valve quickly closes.

Overfill-Limiting Devices

EEC systems usually have some form of *overfill-limiting device*. This device is sometimes in the form of an inverted dishpan inside the fuel tank or a small tank mounted on the inside, upper surface of the tank. This unit takes up about $\frac{1}{10}$ of the main tank's volume, or about the space of 2 gallons of fuel.

The smaller tank, sometimes known as an *expansion tank* (Fig. 22–7), has a series of small holes machined into it. The size of these openings is such that it requires 10 to 15 minutes to fill the expansion tank with fuel from the main tank during the refueling procedure. As a result, there is about a 2-gallon area above the level of the fuel in the main tank when its gauge reads full. This space takes care of any fuel expansion in the tank, in the event the refueled automobile sits in the sun for a prolonged period. The space also serves as a vapor collection area.

Other types of overfill devices serve the same purpose. These include the use of an overfill-limiting valve in the charcoal

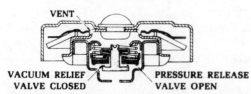

VENT

VACUUM RELIEF
VALVE CLOSED

PRESSURE RELEASE
VALVE OPEN

Fig .22–5.   The operation of the pressure valve in the EEC fuel cap.

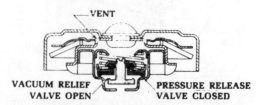

VENT

VACUUM RELIEF
VALVE OPEN

PRESSURE RELEASE
VALVE CLOSED

Fig. 22–6.   The operation of the vacuum valve within an EEC fuel cap.

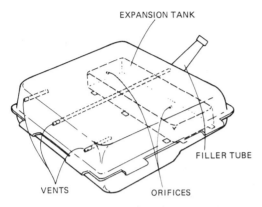

EXPANSION TANK

FILLER TUBE

VENTS   ORIFICES

Fig. 22–7. The location of a typical expansion tank.

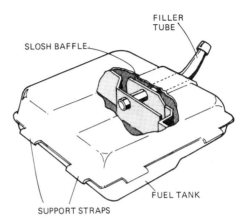

FILLER TUBE

SLOSH BAFFLE

SUPPORT STRAPS

FUEL TANK

Fig. 22–8. The location of the filler tube can prevent the complete filling of the fuel tank.

canister or canister vapor line (Fig. 22–1) or a special fuel tank filler pipe extending down into the tank (Fig. 22–8). In the latter, the fuel tank does not accept fuel after the end of the filler pipe, inside the tank, is covered with fuel. This action leaves a space for fuel and vapor expansion.

Liquid-Vapor Separators

Open-Cell Foam Type

All EEC systems also require some form of *liquid-vapor fuel separator*. This device prevents liquid fuel from reaching the charcoal canister. There are three common types of separator units: the open-cell foam, the standpipe, and float.

Figure 22–9 shows a *foam-type liquid-vapor separator* mounted on the fuel tank. With this type of device, fuel vapors alone can pass through the open-cell foam as they move from the tank, through the orifice, and into the vapor line to the canister. Any liquid droplets of fuel cannot pass through the foam material and, therefore, do not enter the vapor line. The

liquid, in this case, just returns to the fuel tank.

Standpipe Separator

Figure 22–10 is a schematic of a *standpipe-style separator*. This device fits above the fuel tank and has lines going to each corner of the tank. These multiple vapor lines serve two functions. First, they constantly act as vents for the fuel tank as the engine consumes gasoline. Second, the lines provide a liquid fuel

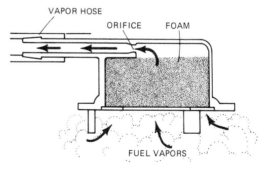

VAPOR HOSE

ORIFICE   FOAM

FUEL VAPORS

Fig. 22–9. An open-cell liquid-vapor separator.

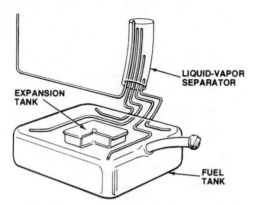

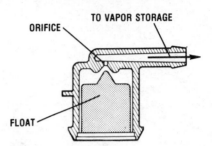

Fig. 22-11. The design of a float-type liquid-vapor separator.

Fig. 22-10. A schematic of a standpipe style of liquid-vapor separator.

drain, into the tank, of any fuel droplets contained in the separator.

As fuel vapors condense in the separator from the standpipes, the resulting liquid drains back through the shortest standpipe or a drain opening in one of the pipes to the fuel tank. Also, if the driver parks a vehicle with a standpipe separator on an incline, any collected fuel that does not drain back remains in the separator until the vehicle operates on a level road. This eliminates the flooding of the charcoal canister with liquid fuel. Consequently, the standpipe separator constantly acts as a baffle to prevent fuel from ever entering the canister regardless of the amount of fuel-vapor condensation or vehicle attitude.

Float Separator

Figure 22-11 illustrates the third common type of separator, the *float type*. This float-type separator also mounts directly on top of the fuel tank; it consists of a sealed float that rises in the housing with incoming liquid gasoline. On the end of the float is a needle valve, which contacts a seat over an orifice opening in the separator housing. This opening has a fit-

ting that connects to a vent hose and line leading to the canister.

When the float reaches its uppermost position, where the valve shuts off the orifice, neither fuel vapors nor liquid fuel can transfer to the charcoal canister. The valve remains closed until the fuel drains back to the tank. At this point, vapors can once again pass through the orifice and flow to the canister.

Rollover Leakage Protection Devices

Beginning in 1976, domestic automobile manufacturers began to install *rollover leakage protection devices*. In other words, each vehicle has more and more devices to prevent fires caused by liquid fuel leaks, in case the vehicle rolls over after an accident. Some of these devices are discussed in Chapter 6; this chapter covers only those incorporated into typical EEC components.

Figure 22-12 is a schematic of a Chrysler EEC system, showing several of these devices, which include a rollover valve, a flow-check filter separator, and a redesigned fuel cap. All the rollover devices operate on the check valve principle. That is, they usually permit vapor flow in one direction but prevent liquid

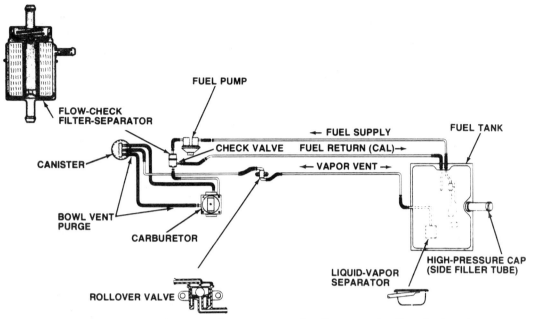

Fig. 22-12. A schematic showing typical rollover protection devices incorporated into EEC components. (Courtesy of Chrysler Corp.)

gasoline that accumulates in the same line from flowing in the opposite direction. The only exception to this rule is in the case of the fuel filler cap, which may have valving that controls tank pressure and vacuum.

The *rollover valve* fits either into the midpoint in the vapor vent line (Fig. 22-12) or into a rollover type vapor-separator valve on top of the fuel tank. In either case, this one-way valve allows a 360-degree vehicle rollover without liquid fuel leaking from the tank to the canister. This fuel would soon overfill the canister and cause an external leak.

The *flow check valve* in the filter separator permits vapors to flow from the separator to the fuel tank. But it prevents liquid gasoline, in case of an accident, to pass back through the separator and into the carburetor float bowl. A supply of fuel, from the tank to the carburetor via

the filter separator, would pass through the open needle valve in an inverted float bowl, causing a serious leakage problem.

The modification made to the filler cap in order to prevent leakage after a rollover accident, was to its pressure relief valve. Basically speaking, the modification just increased the opening pressure of the relief valve in order to prevent liquid gasoline from opening the valve if the tank should invert. All other functions of the cap remained the same.

Liquid-Vapor Filter Separator

The EEC system may have a *filter separator* with a check valve. The separator itself (Fig. 22-13) has been used on many vehicles for some time, even before the advent of the EEC system. The

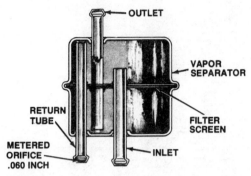

Fig. 22-13. A common liquid-vapor filter separator without the check valve. (Courtesy of Chrysler Corp.)

basic function of this device is to prevent engine flooding or vapor-locking due to high underhood temperatures. These temperatures can overheat the fuel in the line to the carburetor, causing it to expand to a point of vaporization. This results in excessive pressure in the fuel line, which can unseat the carburetor needle valve and permit too much fuel to enter the carburetor. Consequently, the engine floods. If the fuel in the line completely turns into a vapor, it can cause a vapor lock in the line, which affects pump operation to a point where there is no fuel delivery to the carburetor.

The separator in Fig. 22-13 has three fittings: an inlet, outlet, and vapor return. The inlet fitting attaches via a hose or line to the fuel pump outlet. The separator's outlet fitting attaches directly into the hose or fuel line to the carburetor. The remaining fitting has a metered orifice and connects by means of a vapor line back to the fuel tank.

When the engine is operating, fuel from the pump fills the vapor separator. Fuel from the bottom of the unit passes through the outlet fitting and into the fuel line to the carburetor. Any vapors that accumulate when the engine is running or is off, rise to the top of the separator, where they pass through the orifice and fitting into the return line to the fuel tank.

Carburetor Vents

All carburetors must have some form of external vent for the float bowl. This vent releases vapors from the bowl to prevent the buildup of pressure due to engine heat. Otherwise, the pressure would cause percolation of the fuel in the bowl and engine flooding.

Vehicles built before the addition of the EEC system had a vent that opened directly to the atmosphere. However, on a vehicle with the later-type EEC system, this external vent connects to the vapor storage canister by means of a hose (Fig. 22-14). While in many cases this vent is always open to the canister, some carburetors use mechanical linkage and a

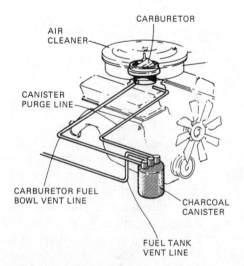

Fig. 22-14. On a vehicle with a newer EEC system, the carburetor's external vent connects into the charcoal canister.

valve to open the vent when the throttle valve closes.

Charcoal Canister

The late-type EEC system uses one or more *charcoal canisters,* instead of the engine crankcase, to store fuel tank and carburetor vapors. This canister (Fig. 22–15) fits underneath the hood and holds a given amount of activated charcoal granules. These granules hold up to one-third of their own weight in fuel vapors.

A typical canister holds 300 to 625 grams of charcoal. Each gram of activated charcoal has a surface area of 1,100 square meters, or more than a quarter of a mile. As a result, the total surface area of the charcoal within the canister is equivalent to 80 to 165 football fields.

The activated charcoal acts as a good vapor trap not only because of its greater surface area but also because the vapor molecules attract to the surface of the carbon by absorption. However, this attracting force is not very strong. Conse-

quently, fresh air entering the filter at the base of the canister and flowing through the charcoal can easily remove the vapor molecules from the carbon.

A typical canister has three fittings, located on its top (Fig. 22–15). A hose, connected to one fitting and line, carries the fuel vapors from the fuel tank to the canister. A second hose, attached to the canister, carries vapors from the carburetor vent to the canister. The third fitting accommodates the purge hose, which carries accumulated vapors within the canister into the carburetor base or air cleaner.

Canister System and Operation

Vapors collecting in the fuel tank and float chamber flow through vent lines, into the charcoal canister (Fig. 22–16). The carbon in the charcoal granules absorbs these vapors as soon as they enter the canister. Thus, the vapors remain in the canister until purged from the charcoal.

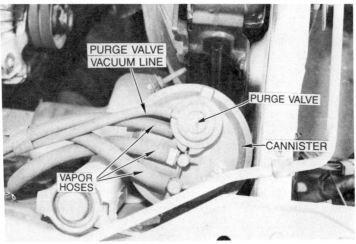

Fig. 22–15. A typical charcoal canister installation.

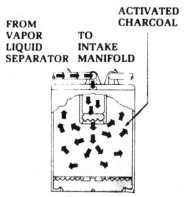

Fig. 22-16.   Collecting fuel vapors from the tank and carburetor float bowl enter the canister and absorb into the carbon granules.

In order to remove these vapors, the canister undergoes a process known as *purging*. This process involves moving an amount of fresh air through the filter located below the charcoal granules. The air, in turn, dislodges the vapor molecules from the carbon and carries them out of the canister (Fig. 22-17).

Types of Purging Methods

Constant Purge

Practically speaking, three types of purging methods are used on domestic EEC systems: the constant purge, variable purge, and two-stage purge. Two factors determine what method the manufacturer will use. The first factor is the actual amount of fresh air that must pass through the canister in order to remove the vapors and reactivate the charcoal (carbon) granules. The second factor, which relates closely to the first, is that this air flow can have little effect on either the engine's air/fuel ratio or the driveability of the vehicle.

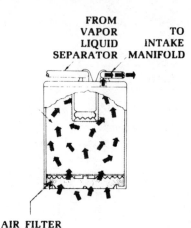

Fig. 22-17.   Purging the canister occurs as an amount of fresh air passes through the unit.

When the manufacturer uses the *constant-purge method*, the rate of purging air through the canister remains fixed, regardless of consumption of air by the engine. Manufacturers accomplish this by teeing into, for example, the PCV line at the carburetor, thereby using intake manifold vacuum to draw air through the carbon granules within the canister (Fig. 22-18). Even though, in this situation, intake manifold vacuum varies with engine loads, an orifice within the purge line provides a relatively constant air-flow rate through the canister.

Variable Purge

In a *variable purge system*, the manufacturer connects the canister purge line to the air cleaner (Fig. 22-19). In this case, the amount of purge air drawn through the canister is in proportion to the amount of fresh air pulled into the engine. Consequently, the more air that enters the engine, the more purge air passes through the canister.

Figure 22-19 shows two alternate locations for the purge line connection at the

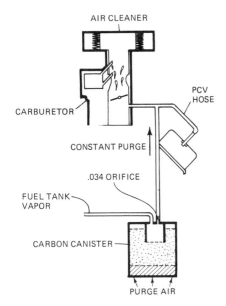

Fig. 22–18. A schematic of a constant-purge EEC system.

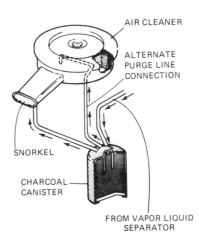

Fig. 22–19. A schematic of a variable-purge EEC system.

air cleaner. The purge line that enters the air-cleaner housing near the snorkel is acted upon by air velocity passing through the snorkel. In other words, velocity of the air flow past the purge line opening creates a low-pressure area. This vacuum, in turn, causes atmospheric pressure to force air through the canister filter. The amount of this air flow is in proportion to the vacuum created at the purge line opening.

The other location of the purge line can be on the clean side of the air-cleaner element. In this situation, the difference in pressure or the pressure drop across the air filter itself is sufficient to cause atmospheric pressure to push air through the canister. As in the snorkel-connected type, the amount of purge air depends on the amount of pressure drop or vacuum at the end of the purge line. In other words, more purge air flows when there is a high

vacuum at the end of the purge line than under a low vacuum condition.

Two-Stage Purge

In some instances, neither the constant nor variable purge system can provide the necessary air flow to purge the canister. To overcome this particular problem, some manufacturers use a *two-stage purging process*. This process involves the use of a purge valve located on top of the canister (Fig. 22–15 and 22–20). This valve operates by means of a ported-vacuum signal, which opens a second passage from the canister to the intake manifold. A *ported-vacuum signal* is one taken from a passage above the throttle valve. Consequently, there is no vacuum in this passage when the throttle valve closes; however, the signal increases in proportion to the amount the driver opens the throttle valve.

In another design of an EEC system utilizing a ported-vacuum signal, the canister does not have a purge valve. Instead, this system has an additional

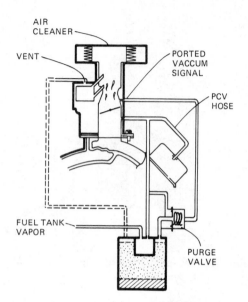

Fig. 22-20. A diagram of an EEC system using two-stage canister purging.

ported-vacuum connection on the carburetor, responsible for purging the canister. This port is above the upper portion of the throttle valve, so that there is no purge flow through the purge line at idle. However, the flow increases as the throttle opens. This system improves hot-engine idle quality by completely eliminating canister purging at idle.

EEC System Service

An EEC system should not require a great deal of maintenance in normal service, except for canister filter replacement or the replacement of cracked and damaged vapor hoses. Manufacturers recommend that the oiled foam or fiberglass filter in the bottom of most canisters be replaced at periodic intervals. These service intervals may range from 12,000 to as much as 30,000 miles or 1 to 2 years. This

form of preventive maintenance is necessary since outside air passes through the filter, and the air contains given amounts of dust, dirt, and other contaminants. Of course, if the vehicle is driven under severe conditions with a great deal of these contaminants in the air, the filter requires replacement more often.

Canister Filter Replacement

To replace a typical canister filter:

1. Mark all the canister hoses as to their proper locations on the canister. This action prevents installing a hose on the wrong fitting after servicing the canister.

2. Remove all vapor hoses from the canister fittings.

3. Loosen the hold-down clamps, and remove the canister from its mount.

4. If so equipped, remove the canister base, and pull the old filter from the bottom of the canister (Fig. 22-21). In some cases the filter is held in place by a ring or retaining bar.

5. Install the new filter pad under the

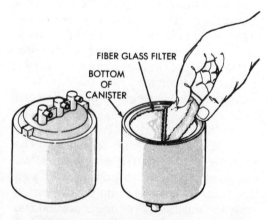

Fig. 22-21. Replacing the filter in a charcoal canister. (Courtesy of Chrysler Corp.)

retainer or bar, and reinstall the base cover.

6. Reinstall the canister into its mount, and tighten its hold-down clamps securely.

7. Reconnect all vent hoses to their proper canister fittings.

Vent Hose Replacement

Any EEC hose requires replacement if it is cracked or damaged. The hoses used in this system have a specific design suitable for carrying fuel vapors. Consequently, if hose replacement becomes necessary, use only fuel-resistant hose or hose designed for EEC systems.

To replace a typical hose:

1. If so equipped, loosen and slide back both hose clamps.

2. Twist the hose slightly around its fitting, and then remove the hose, using a straight, steady pulling action.

3. Using the old hose as a guide, cut a new hose of the proper diameter, to the correct length from a section of hose stock.

4. Reinstall the clamps over the hose.

5. Install each end of the hose over its fitting. Then, position and tighten each hose clamp down about $\frac{1}{4}$ inch from each end of the hose.

Review

This section will assist you in determining how well you remember the material in this chapter. Read each item carefully. If you can't complete the statement, review the section in each chapter that covers the material.

1. An EEC system was a requirement on all domestic automobiles beginning in _____.
   a. 1970
   b. 1971
   c. 1972
   d. 1973

2. All 1972 and later automobiles had _____ fuel vapor storage.
   a. filter
   b. crankcase
   c. canister
   d. carburetor

3. An overfill-limiting device provides about a _____ -gallon area above the level of the fuel in the tank when its gauge reads full.
   a. 2
   b. 3
   c. 4
   d. 5

4. The device that stops fuel from reaching the canister is the _____.
   a. pressure-vacuum valve
   b. filler cap
   c. overfill-limiting device
   d. liquid-vapor separator

5. Rollover devices began to appear on domestic vehicles in _____.
   a. 1975
   b. 1976
   c. 1977
   d. 1978

6. The device that prevents liquid fuel from the tank from reaching the canister in case of an accident is the _____ _____.
   a. filter separator
   b. flow valve
   c. rollover valve
   d. filler cap

7. Later-model EEC systems have the external carburetor vent connected in the _____.
   a. canister
   b. filter
   c. tank
   d. snorkel

8. A typical canister contains _____ grams of charcoal.
   a. 325
   b. 100 to 425
   c. 200 to 525
   d. 300 to 625

9. There are _____ methods commonly used by manufacturers to purge the canister.
   a. 1
   b. 2
   c. 3
   d. 4

10. In a variable purge system, the purge line connects to the _____ _____.
   a. engine crankcase
   b. air cleaner
   c. intake manifold
   d. PCV hose

For the answers, turn to the Appendix.

Exhaust Emission Legislation

As in the case of both crankcase and evaporation emission control devices, California was first in limiting exhaust emissions with legislation passed in 1966 and 1967. These particular laws applied only to new automobiles and some light trucks first sold in that state. However, the Federal Air Quality Act of 1967 set exhaust emission standards that applied nationwide to all 1968 new vehicles.

Purpose of Control Devices

As a result of not only California but also federal legislation, manufacturers had to begin installing a variety of exhaust emission control equipment to automobiles and light- to medium-size trucks in order to meet given emission levels. These controls have the purpose of reducing hydrocarbons (HC), carbon monoxide (CO), and nitrogen oxide (NOx) emissions from an engine's exhaust.

To make it easier for the reader to understand the function, design, and operation of the various controls, this text subdivides them into the following general groups: engine modification, air injection, exhaust gas circulation, and catalytic converters. *A given automobile or light truck can have all or only a few of these devices installed on it, depending on its model year, engine size, and type.*

Engine Modification— Function

With the advent of strict exhaust-emission–control standards, automotive en-

_____ Chapter 23

EXHAUST EMISSION CONTROL DEVICES

_____

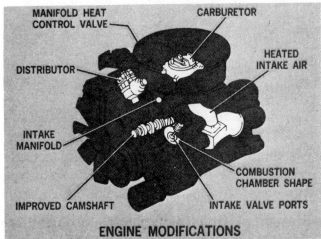

Fig. 23-1.   *Typical modification made to an engine in order to control exhaust emissions. (Courtesy of Chrysler Corp.)*

gineers and scientists reasoned that the best way to control emissions was to burn the fuel as completely as possible inside the engine. This philosophy led to many design changes within the engine—built-in modifications to reduce the level of HC, CO, and NOx. These engine design changes include alterations to the shape of the combustion chamber, design of the piston, reduced compression ratio, and changes in the intake manifold and the camshaft. Along with the changes in engine design, there are also modifications to the carburetor, air cleaner, and advance mechanisms of the distributor (Fig. 23-1).

Engine Design Changes

Combustion Chamber and Pistons

Certain portions of the combustion chambers, cylinder walls, and pistons remain relatively cool during the burning of the air/fuel charge. Consequently, the burning air/fuel charge within close prox-

imity to these areas does not reach ignition temperature. In other words, the normal flame front from combustion "snuffs" out as it approaches these areas. As a result, these unburned hydrocarbons eject from the cylinder with the rest of the exhaust gases on every exhaust stroke, polluting the atmosphere. Figure 23-2 illustrates the common "quench" areas within a single cylinder.

Within the modified emission-control engine, the manufacturer has eliminated

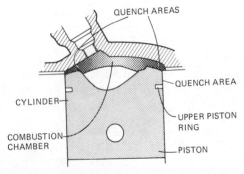

Fig. 23-2.   *The common quench areas within an unmodified cylinder.*

the quench pockets and close clearance spaces by redesigning the combustion chamber and piston (Fig. 23-3). In regard to the shape of the redesigned combustion chamber, manufacturers have opened the closed or nearly closed areas near the ends of the chamber. This action has fairly well eliminated the quenching of the burning air/fuel mixture in these areas.

The elimination of the quench area near the upper portion of the piston and cylinder wall, however, is a somewhat more difficult task. A typical approach to solving this problem is the repositioning of the top ring nearer to the head of the piston. This action reduces the size of the small pocket formed between the top of the ring and the top of the piston but did not eliminate it. Consequently, there is still a small quench area between the upper ring and the cylinder wall during the combustion process. However, the resulting hydrocarbon emissions from the reduced quench pockets are within tolerable limits.

Reduced Compression Ratios

Another design feature of the exhaust-emission–modified engine is a *lower compression ratio*. Engines with high-compression ratios must burn high-octane

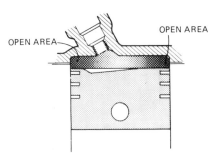

Fig. 23-3. A combustion chamber and piston modified to reduce quench areas.

leaded fuel and have high combustion-chamber temperatures. These high temperatures, in turn, create oxides of nitrogen (NOx), a primary air pollutant.

Since 1970, manufacturers have lowered compression ratios to an average of about 8:1 to permit the use of low-octane low-lead or unleaded fuel. This action resulted in reduced levels of NOx emissions and in some cases a lowering of hydrocarbon emissions.

Manufacturers have used several methods to reduce compression ratios within the emission-modified engine. These changes include the altering of combustion chamber design, modifications to the piston head, and altering the engine's stroke.

Intake Manifold Modifications

To reduce carbon monoxide levels, manufacturers have altered the design of the intake manifold to assure more rapid vaporation of the fuel during engine's warm-up. This design change mainly includes the reduction of the thickness of the manifold floor between the inlet and exhaust runners within the manifold. This modification reduces the time necessary for the heat from the exhaust gases to preheat the air/fuel mixture in the inlet runners. By increasing the heat transfer, the air/fuel mixture vaporized faster. As a result, the engine can operate satisfactorily with leaner mixtures during the warm-up period. This brings about a reduction in CO emissions.

Camshaft Modifications

Another modification made to some engines to lower NOx emissions is to the camshaft (Fig. 23-4). A modified cam-

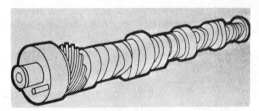

Fig. 23-4. In order to reduce NOx emissions, some camshafts are modified to alter valve overlap. (Courtesy of Chrysler Corp.)

shaft provides extended valve overlap, which causes some dilution of the air/fuel mixture. This action lowers the peak combustion chamber temperatures. In other words, by increasing valve overlap, the camshaft reduces the quality of the air/fuel mixture by preventing the complete purging of the exhaust gases from the cylinders. This in turn lowers the peak

combustion chamber temperatures and the formation of NOx.

Carburetor Modifications

Carburetors on emission-controlled engines are modified in various ways to reduce CO and HC during various phases of engine operation. The actual number of carburetor design changes depends on the design and size of the engine as well as the year model of the vehicle. In other words, these factors, for the most part, determine the allowable CO and HC emissions by a given vehicle. Consequently, some carburetors have more modifications than others.

Since all vehicle manufacturers have had to make design changes in their individual carburetor circuits, it would be im-

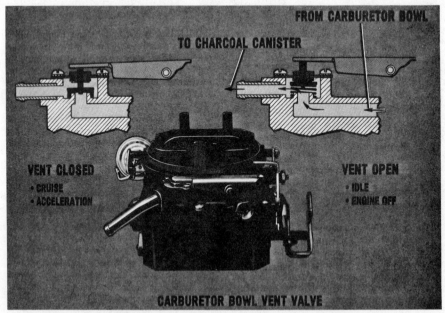

Fig. 23-5. A carburetor with a mechanically operated bowl vent valve. (Courtesy of Chrysler Corp.)

possible in the space provided to cover them all. Therefore, this chapter presents an overview of the main carburetor alterations in the following circuits: float, idle, high-speed light load, and choke.

Float Circuit Modifications

The design change made to the float circuit is for controlling fuel vapors generated in the float bowl. Vehicles with the EEC system have a carburetor that routes these fuel vapors either into the crankcase or, in the case of later-model vehicles, into the charcoal canister.

In some vehicles, this vent always remains open; however, Fig. 23–5 shows a carburetor that uses a mechanically operated vent valve. This vent valve, which activates through throttle-valve linkage, remains closed during cruise and acceleration, but the linkage opens the valve during idle or when the engine is off.

Figure 23–6 illustrates a solenoid-assisted, vacuum-operated bowl vent valve used on other carburetors. With this

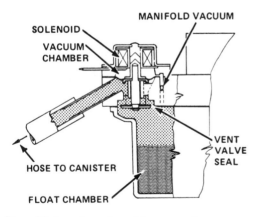

Fig. 23-6. A solenoid-assisted vacuum-operated bowl vent valve. (Courtesy of General Motors Corp.)

device, bowl vapors vent to the canister only when the engine is *not* running. Unlike its mechanically operated counterpart, the solenoid therefore prevents any canister venting of the bowl when the engine is idling or during any other phase of operation.

Idle-Circuit Design Changes

To maintain leaner air/fuel mixtures during idle engine operation, carburetors have such modifications as fixed idle-mixture adjusting screws and restrictions, hot-idle compensator, and idle enrichment system. Some early-model exhaust-emission–equipped vehicles had idle-mixture adjusting screws that the mechanic could only turn out a given amount. In other words, the manufacturer slotted the threaded shank of these screws and installed a lock pin into the carburetor casting that prevented the mechanic from turning these screws out, past a given amount.

However, there was a drawback to this method of limiting the idle mixture. That is, the mechanic could not remove the screws easily to clean the idle circuit during a carburetor overhaul.

Figure 23–7 shows a carburetor with idle limiter caps installed over the mixture-adjusting screws. These plastic caps perform about the same function as the stop pins on the earlier adjusting screws. That is, the caps allow only about $\frac{7}{8}$ of a complete turn of the mixture adjusting screws. With this arrangement, the vehicle's air/fuel mixture at idle is set to a precise amount at the factory. Then, these caps are installed over the adjustment

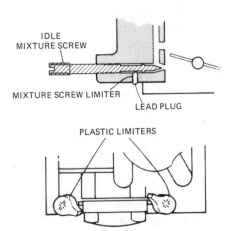

Fig. 23-7.   *Limiter devices prevent the excessive movement of the mixture-adjusting screw.*

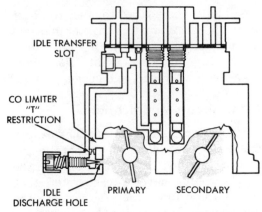

Fig. 23-8.   *An idle circuit restrictor regulates the maximum amount of fuel flow into the engine during idle operation. (Courtesy of Chrysler Corp.)*

screws in order to prevent the factory setting from being changed.

After their initial installation, the technician should only remove these caps for one of two reasons. First, it is necessary to take the caps off in order to remove the adjusting screws during a carburetor overhaul. Second, the caps can also be removed if it becomes necessary to readjust the idle mixture beyond what is allowable by the limiter cap, in order to meet a given emission standard. However, in either case, the mechanic must put the caps back on after making carburetor adjustments.

Idle-Circuit Restrictions

An alternate method of limiting idle-mixture enrichment is a restrictor placed into the idle circuit (Fig. 23-8). This restrictor may be used by itself or in conjunction with a limiter cap. In either case, the restriction helps to regulate the fuel flow more precisely into the engine during idle operation.

Hot-Idle Compensator Valve

Many carburetors now used on exhaust-emission-controlled engines have a hot-idle compensator valve (Fig. 23-9). This valve allows additional air to enter the engine from below the throttle valve to prevent hot-idle stalling. This condition can occur frequently on exhaust-emission-controlled engines due to its higher underhood operating temperature.

When the underhood temperature is high, the fuel in the float bowl can boil, and the resulting vapors flow into the air horn via the internal vents. This makes the idle mixture excessively rich, which raises both the CO and HC emission levels.

When the underhood temperatures are below a set amount, the bimetallic strip closes the attached valve. In this valve position, the normal air flow for the idle circuit is around the edges of the throttle valve or through an air passage designed for this purpose. However, when the tem-

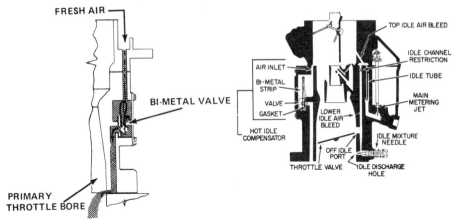

Fig. 23-9. A typical hot-idle compensator valve. (Courtesy of General Motors Corp.)

perature reaches a predetermined level the bimetallic strip lifts up and opens the attached valve. This action permits some additional air to pass through the additional air inlet and mix with the overly rich air/fuel mixture. This additional air flow leans the mixture out and reduces the exhaust emissions. In addition, the leaner air/fuel mixture causes the engine idle speed to increase somewhat, which increases the coolant flow that will help reduce engine temperature. The valve once again closes as underhood temperature goes back down.

Idle Enrichment System

Figure 23-10 illustrates a carburetor with an idle enrichment system. This system increases the enrichment of the normal idle circuit in order to reduce cold-engine stalling. The system itself consists of an idle-enrichment diaphragm valve and a thermo switch. The diaphragm receives its vacuum signal from the intake manifold through the thermostatic vacuum switch.

The thermo switch senses engine coolant temperatures. For example, when the engine is cold, the switch is open. Consequently, the switch passes vacuum to the diaphragm, which moves a valve to block the idle-enrichment air bleed. As a result, the idle vacuum signal to the idle well increases, which causes additional fuel flow to the idle circuit.

During engine warm-up, the thermo switch closes. Thus, it cuts off vacuum to the diaphragm and valve. This action opens the idle-enrichment air bleed, which in turn reduces the idle vacuum signal to the idle well. As a result, there is a decrease in fuel flow through the idle circuit.

Modifications to the Part-Throttle System

In some carburetors, manufacturers also provide a factory adjustment for the part-throttle (high-speed light-load) system. This adjustment is made at the fac-

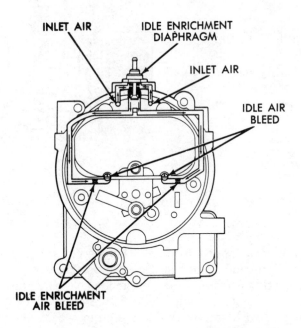

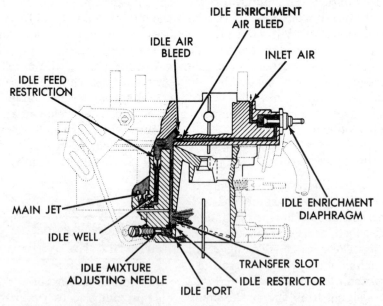

Fig. 23-10.   A carburetor that has an idle enrichment system. (Courtesy of Chrysler Corp.)

tory to provide leaner mixtures during part-throttle operation.

In the carburetor shown in Fig. 23–11, the part-throttle adjustment consists of a pin pressed into the side of the power piston and extends through a slot in the wall of the piston's bore. When the power piston is down in its bore (economy position), the pin stops on top of the flat surface of the adjustment screw located in the cavity next to the power piston. The adjustment screw itself is held from turning by the tension of a spring beneath the head of the screw.

The adjustment screw is preset at the factory. During a production flow test, a technician moves the adjustment screw up or down, which in turn places the tapered metering rods, operated by the power piston, at the exact point in their respective jet orifices. The resulting air/fuel mixture is sufficiently lean to meet exhaust emission standards. *Note:* This particular adjustment screw is preset at the factory and no attempt should be made to change the adjustment. If for some reason a float bowl replacement is necessary during carburetor service, the new bowl assembly has a preset adjustment screw.

Altitude Compensation

Many carburetors built since 1975 have an altitude-compensating device built into the main-metering (high-speed light-load) system. The purpose of this device is to maintain, as closely as possible, the same air/fuel mixture when a vehicle is operating at high altitudes as it normally has at sea level.

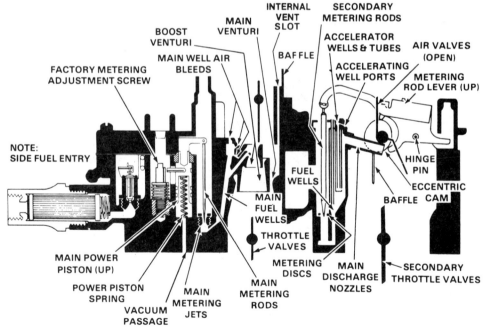

Fig. 23–11. A factory-adjusted power piston (Courtesy of General Motors Corp.)

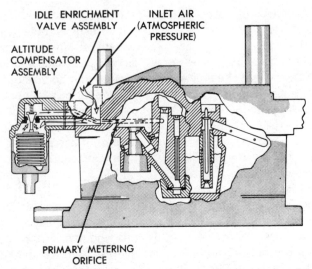

IDLE ENRICHMENT
VALVE ASSEMBLY

INLET AIR
(ATMOSPHERIC
PRESSURE)

ALTITUDE
COMPENSATOR
ASSEMBLY

PRIMARY METERING
ORIFICE

Fig. 23–12. A carburetor with a pressure-sensitive aneroid bellows.
(Courtesy of Chrysler Corp.)

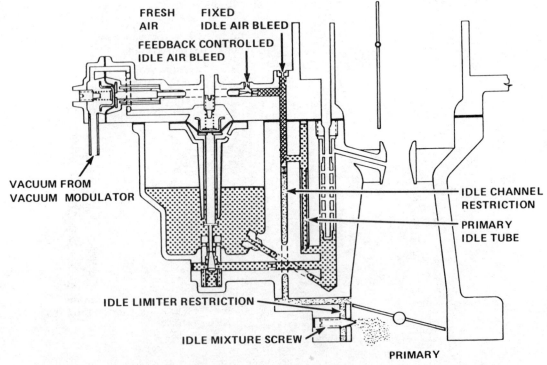

FRESH
AIR

FIXED
IDLE AIR BLEED

FEEDBACK CONTROLLED
IDLE AIR BLEED

VACUUM FROM
VACUUM MODULATOR

IDLE CHANNEL
RESTRICTION

PRIMARY
IDLE TUBE

IDLE LIMITER RESTRICTION

IDLE MIXTURE SCREW

PRIMARY

Fig. 23–13. A carburetor that incorporates an electronic control of the
air/fuel mixture from the idle and main-metering systems. (Courtesy of
General Motors Corp.)

Atmospheric pressure is greatest at sea level, but it reduces with increases in altitude. Consequently, less air enters the carburetor at higher altitudes. As a result, the engine operates richer as a vehicle climbs to areas above sea level, resulting in poor driveability and high CO emissions.

While some altitude-compensating devices are mechanical, the most widely used is an automatic device using an aneroid bellows. An *aneroid bellows* is an accordion-shaped device that responds to changes in atmospheric pressure by expanding or contracting. As a vehicle, for example, travels into a high-altitude area, pressure decreases, and the bellows expands. However, at sea level, the bellows contracts.

Figure 23-12 is a schematic of a Carter Thermo Quad carburetor with a pressure-sensitive aneroid bellows. The bellows in this carburetor operates an air valve that opens an auxiliary air tube into the main-metering system at high altitude. This action leans out the air/fuel mixture from the main-metering system in proportion to the altitude at which the vehicle is operating above sea level. In other words, the amount of valve opening and corresponding leaning out of the mixture vary with the changes in altitude.

Electronically Controlled Carburetors

The carburetor shown in Fig. 23-13 is an electronically controlled unit utilized on a V-8 with a specially designed catalytic converter. This particular carburetor has vacuum diaphragms in the idle and main-metering systems that provide precise control of the air/fuel mixture from these two particular circuits for good emission control.

Figure 23-14 illustrates the remaining components of the electronic fuel control system. These units include an oxygen sensor in the exhaust pipe or manifold, manifold vacuum switch, coolant temperature switch, vacuum modulator, and electronic control unit (ECU).

In operation, signals from the oxygen sensor, manifold vacuum switch, and coolant temperature switch are fed to the ECU. The ECU, in turn, directs a signal to the vacuum modulator indicating how much to feed to the vacuum diaphragms in the carburetor's idle and main-metering systems. The diaphragms react to the incoming vacuum signal and provide a precise control of the intake air/fuel ratio required by the catalytic converter for good emission control.

Choke System Modifications

To control CO and HC emissions during engine warm-up, manufacturers have modified the automatic choke system. These modifications basically are in the system in order to regulate how long the choke valve will remain on during engine warm-up. Although these modifications differ somewhat among automobile manufacturers, the design changes all do the same thing—supply heat faster or for longer periods to the choke valve's bimetallic spring. This opens the choke valve faster and permits it to stay open for longer periods even when the engine is shut down.

The most common types of modified choke spring heaters to control emissions are the electrical assist, coolant assist, and choke hot-air modulator. Figure 23-15 shows a carburetor-mounted *elec-*

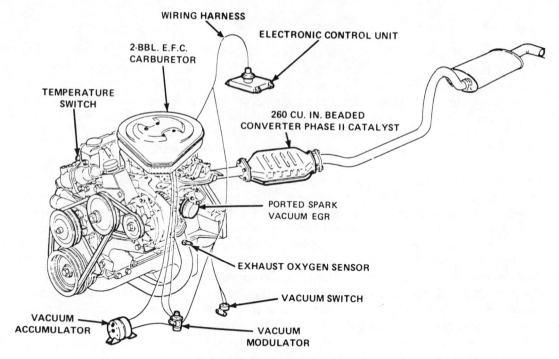

Fig. 23–14. *The components that support the electronic fuel control system. (Courtesy of General Motors Corp.)*

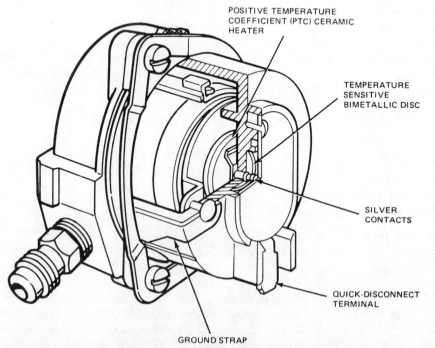

Fig. 23–15. *A typical carburetor-mounted electrical-assist choke system. (Courtesy of Ford Motor Co. of Canada Ltd.)*

trical-assist choke system. In this system, the bimetallic spring that closes the choke valve when the engine is cold receives its heat from two sources: the exhaust manifold and the ceramic heater. For example, when the engine is first started and cold, the bimetallic spring receives heat only from the exhaust manifold. However, when the engine temperature reaches a predetermined amount, the electric-assist choke mechanism turns on to supply additional heat, which opens the choke valve faster.

To accomplish this task, the heating element connects in series with a temperature-sensitive thermostatic switch. This switch has contacts that are open below about 60°F. (15°C.) in order to prevent the electric-heat assist mechanism from operating. At this time, the choke bimetallic spring receives its heat from the pipe connected to the manifold.

When the engine temperature rises about 60°F. (15°C.) either during engine operation or starting, the temperature-sensitive contacts close. As a result, the heating element becomes operational and provides additional heat to open the choke quickly.

The electric power for this type of choke system usually comes from the alternator. Therefore, the choke system only receives power when the engine is operating and the alternator is producing voltage and current flow. However, some carburetor-mounted, electrical-choke systems operate continuously. These units receive their power from the ignition switch whenever it is on.

Figure 23–16 shows an engine-mounted electric-assist choke heater. This assembly mounts on a recess in the intake manifold and receives heat from the manifold-heat crossover passage. But this unit also

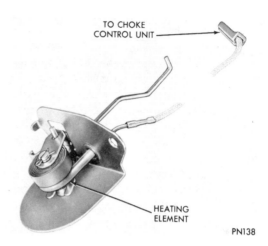

TO CHOKE
CONTROL UNIT

HEATING
ELEMENT

PN138

Fig. 23–16. An electrical-assist choke heater mounted on the intake manifold. (Courtesy of Chrysler Corp.)

has a heating element that activates at a given engine temperature to open the choke quickly.

In operation, with the engine below 80°F., the bimetallic choke coil reacts to exhaust heat from the crossover passage within the intake manifold. As the engine reaches approximately 80°F. (27°C.), a control switch, mounted on the engine, turns on the heating element to cause a fast and positive choke opening. The control unit then turns the heating element off after about 5 minutes.

Coolant-Assisted Chokes

For many years, some manufacturers have used engine coolant to heat the bimetallic spring of carburetor-mounted choke assemblies. In some earlier designs, manufacturers used coolant along with exhaust gas temperature to heat the bimetallic spring, thus opening the choke. In a few cases, coolant alone was the heat medium. However, now many coolant-assisted units work in conjunction with an electrical heater.

In any case, coolant passes through a special compartment in the choke housing (Fig. 23–17). The housing then heats as the engine reaches its normal operating temperature. The resulting hot compartment temperature unwinds the bimetallic spring and permits the choke valve to open.

The main benefit derived from using a coolant-operated choke is that this unit reduces overchoking after the engine has been shut down for a short period. The reason for this is that the coolant holds heat longer than air; consequently, the choke coil remains warm longer when exposed to heat from the hot coolant. Therefore, the engine receives a lesser amount of choking action on restart.

Choke Hot-Air Modifier

A few later-model General Motors engines have a modified version of an automatic choke system heated solely by exhaust gas temperature (Fig. 23–18). In this system, the heat for the automatic choke assembly comes from a heat stove mounted into the intake manifold, around which exhaust gases flow. The heat from

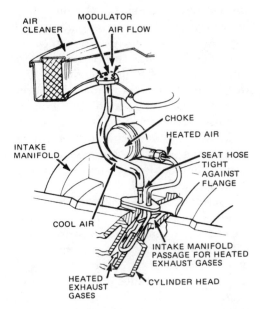

Fig. 23–18. A hot-air modifier choke system used on a carburetor-mounted automatic choke. (Courtesy of General Motors Corp.)

these exhaust gases radiates into the tubing that forms the stove.

A small amount of vacuum applied to the choke housing draws the heated air from the stove and into the choke housing. This heat, in turn, acts on the bimetallic spring, which causes the choke valve to open.

The main difference between this latter system and the earlier types is that the early systems permitted cool air from outside the air cleaner to pass through the heat stove tubing, where it received heat from the exhaust manifold gases. However, in the modified version, the manufacturer connects the open air tube to the air cleaner.

Connected to the end of the cool air hose that fastens to the air cleaner is a hot-air

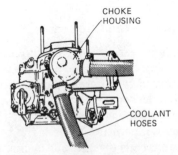

Fig. 23–17. A typical coolant-assisted, carburetor-mounted choke assembly.

modulator check valve (CHAM-CV). This valve controls how much air passes through the hose to the heat stove during given air-cleaner temperatures. For example, at air-cleaner temperatures below about 68°F., the check valve closes. Consequently, the air that enters the heater tubing must pass through a tiny hole in the modulator. This action restricts hot air flow over the bimetallic coil and results in a slower choke warm-up and opening. As the temperature rises above about 68°F., the modulator valve opens to permit more air flow for faster choke warm-up.

Carburetor Assist Devices

Along with the various circuit changes within the carburetor itself, manufacturers have also added one or more assist devices onto the carburetor. These devices primarily serve either the purpose of further reducing exhaust emissions or improving the driveability of the vehicle. These assist devices include such units as a choke vacuum brake, choke delay valve, deceleration valve, dashpot, and antidieseling or air-conditioning solenoid.

Choke Vacuum Brake

Most automatic chokes mounted directly on the carburetor itself have a metal vacuum piston to open the choke slightly against bimetallic spring tension after the engine starts. This action provides the additional air flow through the carburetor in order to prevent the engine from stalling due to an overrich mixture.

However, engines with a manifold-mounted bimetallic spring (Fig. 23-16) use a vacuum brake assembly for the same

purpose (Fig. 23-19). This unit is nothing more than a diaphragm and spring, mounted inside a plastic or metallic housing. The diaphragm has an attached rod that connects through linkage to the choke-valve shaft. Consequently, any movement of the diaphragm causes the rod and attached linkage to open the choke valve slightly against bimetallic spring tension, or it permits spring tension to close the valve.

The diaphragm chamber on one side connects, via a fitting and hose, to the intake manifold while the other side is open to the atmosphere. Therefore, when the engine is operating under moderately low-load conditions, its vacuum pulls the diaphragm to the left (Fig. 23-19). This action causes the diaphragm rod and its attached linkage to open the choke slightly against bimetallic spring tension. As a result, additional air flow enters the carburetor through the air horn to prevent stalling while the bimetallic spring is still cold.

When engine vacuum drops to zero as during acceleration, the spring on the vacuum side of the diaphragm pushes it

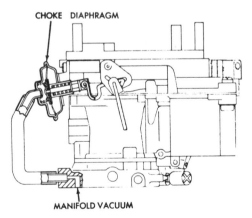

CHOKE DIAPHRAGM

MANIFOLD VACUUM

Fig. 23-19. A typical vacuum brake assembly. (Courtesy of Chrysler Corp.)

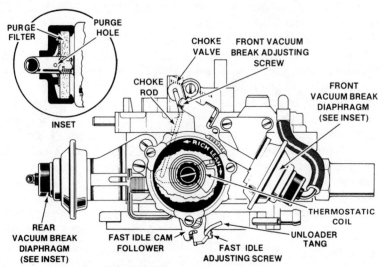

Fig. 23-20. A carburetor that uses two vacuum-brake assemblies to control choke operation. (Courtesy of General Motors Corp.)

more toward the right. This movement through the diaphragm rod and linkage reduces the pulling action on the choke shaft. Consequently, if the bimetallic spring is still cold, it once again slightly closes the choke valve. This action when the engine is cold increases the air/fuel mixture necessary for cold-engine acceleration. However, if the engine and bimetallic spring are hot and the choke valve is open, decreased vacuum on the diaphragm has no effect on choke-valve position.

On some late-model Rochester carburetors, there are two vacuum brake diaphragms to provide mixture control better during engine warm-up (Fig. 23-20). These two assemblies provide more choking of the engine when it is cold and less as it warms up, thus reducing emissions during this period.

Choke Delay Valves

Some late-model choke systems with either a vacuum piston within the carbure-

tor-mounted choke assembly or a vacuum brake like the one just described have a choke delay valve. Figure 23-21 illustrates one version of this type of valve. This valve delays the opening of the choke for a period of time in order to improve driveability and cold-engine warm-up.

The delay valve fits into the vacuum

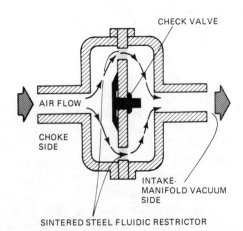

Fig. 23-21. A choke-delay valve slows the opening of the choke valve.

hose between the intake manifold and either the choke vacuum piston or vacuum brake. The valve has a sintered-steel fluidic restrictor, which filters intake manifold vacuum, making it take longer to act on the choke piston or diaphragm. As a result, vacuum must be in the hose for 15 to 30 seconds before it affects the piston or diaphragm.

The check valve within this unit permits immediate release of the vacuum in order to let the choke close quickly anytime the vacuum in the manifold drops to zero. This action is necessary to provide adequate choke closing if the engine should stall when cold, in order to facilitate restarting the engine.

Deceleration Valve

Many carburetors also have a deceleration (decel) valve (Fig. 23–22). This valve prevents the engine cylinders from misfiring during deceleration and sending an unburned charge of hydrocarbons through the exhaust. The valve accomplishes this task by providing additional air and fuel during deceleration.

The valve shown in Fig. 23–22 fits onto

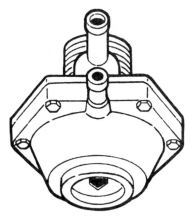

Fig. 23–22.   A common type of decel valve. (Courtesy of Ford Motor Co. of Canada Ltd.)

or near the intake manifold. One end of the valve connects to the manifold—either directly or by means of a hose. The other end connects to a deceleration section within the carburetor, which contains a fuel pickup tube and an airbleed.

A diaphragm within the decel valve reacts to intake manifold vacuum via a vacuum fitting. For example, when a given engine is decelerating and intake manifold vacuum is high, the spring-loaded diaphragm opens the decel valve within the assembly. This action permits additional air and fuel to pass through the valve, as long as vacuum remains above 20 inches of Hg, usually about 5 seconds during normal deceleration.

When engine vacuum drops, the diaphragm spring reseats the valve. This cuts off the additional air and fuel entering the engine, and the normal carburetor circuitry once again provides the necessary mixture for proper engine operation.

Dashpots, Antidiesel and Air-Conditioning Solenoids

As mentioned in Chapter 9, many carburetors have a dashpot, an antidiesel, or air-conditioning solenoid. These units are also assist devices used to improve the driveability of the vehicle and to reduce exhaust emissions. For a further discussion of these particular components, refer to Chapter 9.

Thermostatically Controlled Air Cleaners

Function

Another internal part of the exhaust emission control system is the thermostatically controlled air cleaner (Fig. 23–23). This device preheats the air com-

Fig. 23–23. A typical thermostatically controlled air-cleaner assembly.

ing into the carburetor continuously on severe winter days and during the engine warm-up period in warmer climates, causing improved fuel vaporization and distribution. This action results in a leaner fuel requirement, which permits the use of a weaker, fast-acting choke bimetallic spring and overall leaner carburetor calibration. Consequently, the thermostatic air cleaner, modified choke spring, and leaner carburetor bring about a reduction in CO and HC emissions during starting and warm-up. Finally, this type of air cleaner also reduces carburetor icing during warm-up, which can cause engine stalling.

Design

Figure 23–24 shows a typical heated air-inlet system. This system consists of a manifold shroud, heated air tube, vacuum motor, and temperature-sensing vacuum valve. The manifold shroud fits over one of the exhaust manifolds. On one end of this shroud is an opening that accommodates the heated air tube. The shroud

acts as a heat stove; that is, the shroud absorbs heat from the exhaust manifold and in turn preheats the air coming into the shroud chamber. This heated air passes through the heat tube to the air cleaner snorkel.

The vacuum motor fits on top of the snorkel. This motor is nothing more than a spring-loaded diaphragm acted upon by intake-manifold vacuum. The diaphragm connects through linkage to the heat-control door inside the snorkel and activates this door when the air coming into the air cleaner is below a predetermined temperature.

The door itself controls air flow into the air cleaner from two different sources. For example, when the door closes, heated air from the shroud is cut off, and the snorkel is wide open to outside air flow. However, when the door opens, only air passing through the shroud and heat tube enters the air cleaner.

The temperature-sensing vacuum valve mounts inside the air cleaner. A vacuum hose to the intake manifold carries engine vacuum through this valve to the vacuum

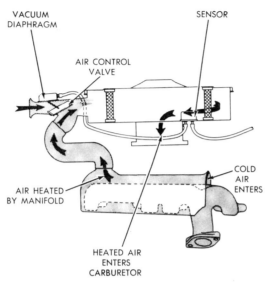

VACUUM
DIAPHRAGM

SENSOR

AIR CONTROL
VALVE

COLD
AIR
ENTERS

AIR HEATED
BY MANIFOLD

HEATED AIR
ENTERS
CARBURETOR

Fig. 23-24.   A schematic of a thermostatically controlled air-inlet system. (Courtesy of Chrysler Corp.)

motor. The temperature-sensitive valve itself controls the opening and closing of the door in the snorkel by regulating the strength of the vacuum signal to the vacuum motor, according to air temperature.

Operation

Figure 23-25 illustrates two positions of the heat-control door. When the temperature in the air cleaner is below about 85°F. (29°C.), the temperature-sensitive vacuum valve is in the closed position. Thus, it permits full manifold vacuum to the vacuum-motor diaphragm. The diaphragm, in turn, opens the heat-control door through linkage (right diagram of Fig. 23-25). This door position cuts off cool air flow through the open end of the snorkel and permits only heated air from the manifold shroud to pass into the air cleaner.

As the air temperature in the cleaner reaches about 128°F. (53°C.), the temperature-sensitive vacuum valve opens. This action permits the valve to bleed off the vacuum signal to the vacuum motor; then the diaphragm spring within the motor causes the heat-control door to close (left-hand diagram of Fig. 23-25). This door position permits outside cooler air to pass through the snorkel and to enter the air cleaner and cuts off heated air from the shroud.

Between 85°F. (29°C.) and 128°F. (53°C.), the heat-control door actually assumes a position based on the actual temperature within the air cleaner. In other words, at temperatures between these figures, the door moves slowly from the open to the closed position, with the amount of vacuum bleeding by the vacuum valve and the diaphragm spring controlling the actual door position.

Under a heavy acceleration condition with zero or very low vacuum in the intake manifold, the heat-control door closes.

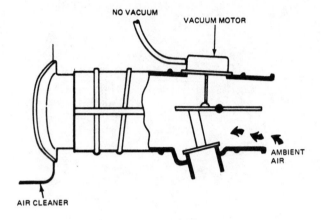

NO VACUUM

VACUUM MOTOR

AMBIENT AIR

AIR CLEANER

VALVE CLOSED

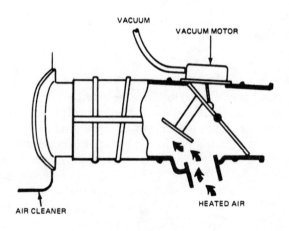

VACUUM

VACUUM MOTOR

AIR CLEANER

HEATED AIR

VALVE OPEN

Fig. 23–25. Operation of the thermostatically controlled air cleaner. (Courtesy of Ford Motor Co. of Canada Ltd.)

This door position permits maximum outside air flow through the snorkel to the engine. The door moves to this position due to the loss of vacuum to the diaphragm. Consequently, its spring moves the diaphragm, linkage, and heat-control door to the closed position.

Spark Advance Control Devices

Along with a thermostatically controlled air cleaner, emission-controlled vehicles have some form of spark-timing control system. Automotive engineers and scientists discovered early on, while attempting to lower vehicle exhaust emissions, that the proper timing of the ignition spark reduced harmful pollutants. Consequently, each automobile manufacturer has developed different types of spark-timing controls according to engine requirements and emission control standards for each model vehicle.

Although these spark control devices differ among manufacturers, their overall function is the same. That is, the controls keep the ignition timing retarded during idle and low-speed operation, when the air/fuel mixture is rich. The retarding ignition timing, during these periods, reduces the peak combustion temperature because the ignition occurs when cylinder pressure is lower. This action helps to reduce NOx formation. But at the same time, the greatest combustion temperature occurs at the end of the combustion process, which results in higher exhaust temperatures in order to reduce the amount of HC in the exhaust.

An efficient combustion process should begin with an advanced spark. However, when combustion occurs at an early point in the process, higher NOx emission levels result, due to higher combustion temperatures. In addition, later in the combustion process, the exhaust gases are cooler. Consequently, they do not heat up the exhaust manifolds as much, which results in a greater amount of HC emissions in the exhaust. Spark control devices reverse this process by firing the air/fuel mixture slightly later in the cycle. This action reduces the peak temperature at the beginning of the cycle and increases it toward the end of the combustion process.

Types of Spark-Control Devices

A separate discussion of all the systems used by the various automobile manufacturers is beyond the scope of this chapter. However, the text presents an overview of some of the main approaches used to control distributor spark advance. These include the dual-diaphragm vacuum advance, delay valves, transmission-controlled spark, and electronically controlled timing.

Dual-Diaphragm Vacuum Advance

Figure 23-26 shows a distributor with a dual-action vacuum advance. This retard-advance mechanism consists basically of two diaphragms: a vacuum retard and a vacuum advance. The purpose of the retard diaphragm is to retard the ignition timing from 4 to 10 degrees during engine idle. This diaphragm receives a vacuum signal directly from the intake manifold. Therefore, full manifold vacuum acts on the diaphragm, which is sufficient to overcome diaphragm spring tension and pull

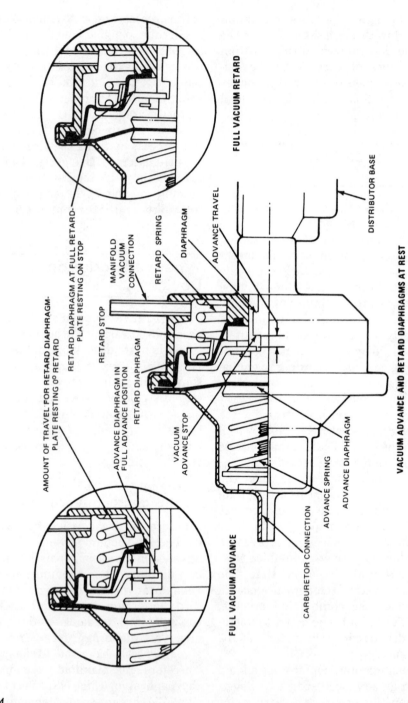

FULL VACUUM RETARD

DISTRIBUTOR BASE

MANIFOLD VACUUM CONNECTION

RETARD STOP

RETARD SPRING

DIAPHRAGM

ADVANCE TRAVEL

AMOUNT OF TRAVEL FOR RETARD DIAPHRAGM-PLATE RESTING 0° RETARD

RETARD DIAPHRAGM AT FULL RETARD-PLATE RESTING ON STOP

ADVANCE DIAPHRAGM IN FULL ADVANCE POSITION

RETARD DIAPHRAGM

VACUUM ADVANCE STOP

FULL VACUUM ADVANCE

CARBURETOR CONNECTION

ADVANCE SPRING

ADVANCE DIAPHRAGM

VACUUM ADVANCE AND RETARD DIAPHRAGMS AT REST

Fig. 23–26. A typical dual-diaphragm advance-retard mechanism. (Courtesy of Ford Motor Co. of Canada Ltd.)

554

the retard diaphragm to the right. This action retards ignition timing.

The advance diaphragm, on the other hand, receives its vacuum signal from a fitting above the carburetor throttle plates. In other words, the advance diaphragm receives a ported vacuum signal.

In operation, this ported vacuum signal applies itself to the advance diaphragm as the throttle valve opens. As a result, this signal along with the diaphragm spring moves both diaphragm assemblies to the left, overriding the retard side. This action provides the engine with normal vacuum advance. However, once the engine returns to idle, the dual-diaphragm advance unit once again returns to the retarded position.

Temperature-Sensitive Vacuum-Control Valves

If an engine idles for some time in hot weather with retarded ignition timing, it tends to overheat. Therefore, it is necessary to override a retarded advance system when the engine overheats. Manufacturers accomplish this through a temperature-sensitive vacuum-control valve (Fig. 23–27).

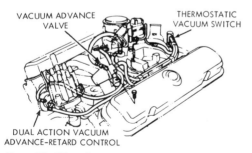

VACUUM ADVANCE VALVE

THERMOSTATIC VACUUM SWITCH

DUAL ACTION VACUUM ADVANCE-RETARD CONTROL

Fig. 23–27. A temperature-sensitive vacuum switch is necessary to override a retard advance system if the engine overheats. (Courtesy of United Delco)

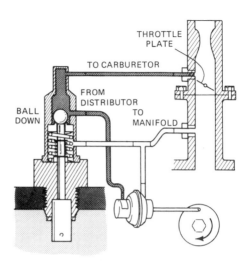

THROTTLE PLATE

TO CARBURETOR

FROM DISTRIBUTOR

BALL DOWN

TO MANIFOLD

Fig. 23–28. Design and operation of a typical temperature-sensitive vacuum switch at normal engine-operating temperatures.

This switch is nothing more than a thermostatically operated valve. The valve, in turn, controls three port openings. One of the openings connects via a hose or line to the carburetor's ported vacuum fitting (Fig. 23–28). The second port connects via a hose to the vacuum advance side of the dual advance mechanism. The final port on the valve connects into a hose or line, which has full manifold vacuum applied to it.

When the engine is operating at normal temperature, the valve assumes the position shown in Fig. 23–28. In this position, full manifold vacuum applied itself to the retarded side of the vacuum advance; carburetor-ported vacuum passes to the advance side of the dual-diaphragm unit. Consequently, the engine idles with retarded timing. But the vacuum advance begins to function as soon as the engine begins to accelerate.

Figure 23–29 illustrates what occurs within the switch when the engine over-

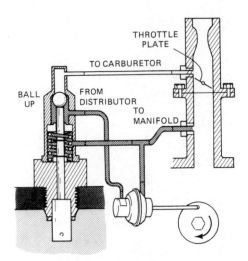

Fig. 23–29. Operation of a temperature-sensitive vacuum switch when an engine overheats.

heats. In this case, the ball valve moves upward, uncovering the vacuum passage from the distributor, and switches off the carburetor-ported vacuum. As a result, full manifold vacuum applies itself to both sides of the dual-vacuum advance unit. The advance diaphragm overrides the retarded side, and the timing advances 4 to 10 degrees. This action makes the engine race at idle and causes faster coolant circulation to reduce engine temperature. When the engine cools down, the switch reverts to the position shown in Fig. 23–28.

Spark Delay Valves

During periods of moderate acceleration with both a dual-diaphragm or standard vacuum advance mechanism on the distributor, engine combustion temperatures rise to cause excessive NOx emissions. To counteract these emissions, manufacturers retard the spark somewhat through the use of a spark delay valve. This valve delays full vacuum advance from the distributor by restricting the amount of vacuum acting on the advance diaphragm.

Figure 23–30 shows the installation and design of a typical spark delay valve. The valve itself fits into the vacuum line between the ported-spark carburetor fitting and the vacuum advance diaphragm. Consequently, the ported vacuum signal to the advance unit must pass through the valve.

The valve contains a sintered metal restrictor, which resists flow to delay spark advance. The amount of this delay depends on the porosity of openings within the sintered metal. In addition, the valve has an elastomer, which opens by vacuum on the diaphragm side. This action occurs when the ported-vacuum signal drops to zero as the throttle closes. Finally, in most cases, the valve has color coding that designates the delay time provided by the valve. Consequently, when replacing this valve, always use a new valve of the correct color coding.

OSAC Valves

The *orifice spark advance control* (OSAC) valve is a device used by Chrysler Corporation to control NOx and HC emissions (Fig. 23–31). This valve delays spark advance during vehicle acceleration by restricting the signal from the carburetor's ported-vacuum fitting to the vacuum-advance unit. This delay may be from 10 to 27 seconds, when the throttle moves from idle to the part-throttle position.

The restriction within this unit is in one direction only. Therefore, during closed throttle deceleration or wide-open throttle acceleration, there is no delay in retarding the spark. The retarding of the spark in these situations is brought about by a one-

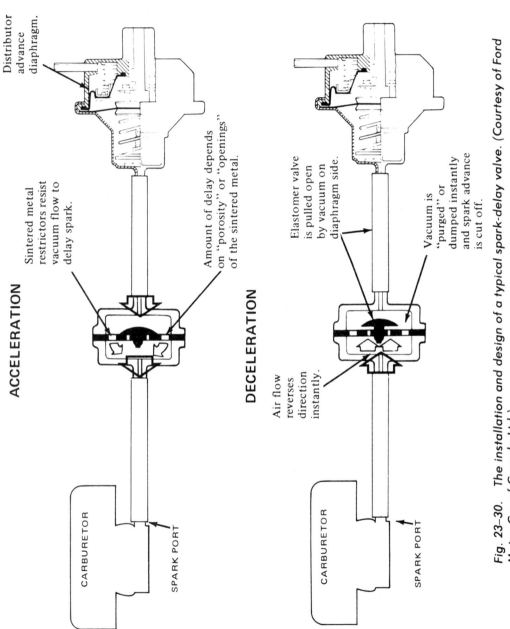

ACCELERATION

Distributor advance diaphragm.

Sintered metal restrictors resist vacuum flow to delay spark.

Amount of delay depends on "porosity" or "openings" of the sintered metal.

CARBURETOR

SPARK PORT

DECELERATION

Elastomer valve is pulled open by vacuum on diaphragm side.

Vacuum is "purged," or dumped instantly and spark advance is cut off.

Air flow reverses direction instantly.

CARBURETOR

SPARK PORT

Fig. 23-30. The installation and design of a typical spark-delay valve. (Courtesy of Ford Motor Co. of Canada Ltd.)

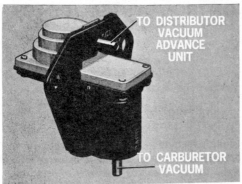

Fig. 23-31. An OSAC valve. (Courtesy of Chrysler Corp.)

way valve, which bypasses the timing delay orifice.

Some OSAC valves also contain a thermocontrol device to retain reliable driveability during engine warm-up. This portion of the device mounts into the air-cleaner assembly and senses carburetor inlet air temperature (Fig. 23-32). Consequently, the OSAC system has a design that makes it operational when ambient temperature is higher than about 58°F.

The thermocontrol device consists of a bimetallic disc. This disc opens the one-

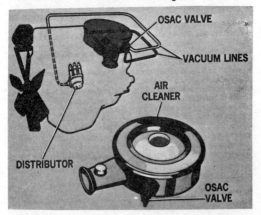

Fig. 23-32. The thermostatic control portion of an OSAC valve mounted into the air-cleaner assembly. (Courtesy of Chrysler Corp.)

way valve whenever it senses temperatures below 58°F. With the one-way valve open, the vacuum signal is unrestricted during all phases of engine operation. When the air temperature within the air cleaner reaches about 60°F., the bimetallic disc again closes the one-way valve, and the OSAC valve delays normal vacuum advance.

On some OSAC systems, a *thermo-ignition control* (TIC) *valve* senses engine temperature and switches full manifold vacuum directly to the vacuum advance. This action occurs if the engine should overheat. The valve has a similar design and operates in much the same manner as the temperature-sensitive vacuum control valve, mentioned earlier in this chapter.

Transmission-Controlled Spark

Beginning in 1970, some vehicles came from the factory with a *transmission-controlled spark system* (TCS). The purpose of this system was to prevent any distributor vacuum advance when the vehicle was in the lower gear ranges or traveling slowly. This action lowered cylinder peak operating temperatures during this time and thereby reduced NOx emissions.

Figure 23-33 illustrates a typical TCS system. This system consists of a solenoid-operated vacuum-advance switch, transmission switch, temperature switch, and time relay. The solenoid-operated switch, which energizes by the grounding of a normally open transmission switch, controls vacuum to the advance mechanism within the distributor. For instance, when the solenoid is in the nonenergized position, it cuts off vacuum to the vacuum advance, and vents it to the atmosphere through a filter at the opposite end of the solenoid. This venting action prevents the

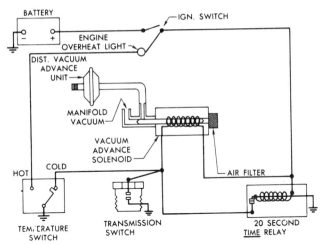

Fig. 23-33.   The components of a TCS system.

vacuum advance from becoming locked in an advanced position. As the solenoid energizes, the plunger uncovers the vacuum port and shuts off the air vent. This permits vacuum to act on the vacuum-advance diaphragm.

Two switches and a time-delay relay control the operation of the vacuum-advance solenoid. The transmission switch used with a manual transmission senses shift-lever position, while the switch used with an automatic transmission operates from hydraulic fluid pressure. In either case, the switch provides a ground circuit for the solenoid-operated switch when the vehicle is in high gear, but it breaks the circuit when the vehicle is in reverse, neutral, or the lower forward gear ratios.

The thermostatic coolant-temperature switch provides a cold override of the TCS system below about 90°F. In operation, the relay opens the vacuum solenoid switch during starting and for a few seconds after the engine is operating. This provides normal vacuum advance for starting and warm-up.

Some TCS systems have a dual temper-ature override switch. In addition to the cold override provision as mentioned, the dual switch also has a hot override terminal. With this design, the thermostatic switch provides a ground to energize the vacuum solenoid when coolant temperature exceeds about 232°F.

The time-delay relay is an electrically operated on-off type of switch. When its coil energizes, it begins to heat the bimetallic strip in order to open the normally closed relay points in about 20 seconds. This action occurs after the driver turns on the ignition switch. During this 20 seconds, the vacuum advance solenoid energizes through the closed relay points.

If for some reason the engine has not started within this 20 seconds and the time relay has completed its cycle, it cuts off, via the solenoid, vacuum advance operation until the relay cools off. In other words, once the relay has passed through a cycle with the ignition switch on, it must cool off before reactivating the solenoid. It should be obvious then that the time-delay relay opens the solenoid vacuum switch during starting and for the first few seconds after the engine starts, no matter if the engine is warm or cold. This provides normal vacuum advance to facilitate starting the engine.

TCS System Operation

Figure 23-33 shows the system components at their at-rest position with the engine off and cold. In this situation, the temperature switch cold-terminal contact points are in the closed position. Also, the time-delay relay points are closed, and the transmission switch points are open. As a result, the vacuum solenoid deenergizes, and its plunger shuts off the port to the vacuum advance unit.

When the driver turns on the ignition switch, a circuit is complete from the ignition switch, through the vacuum solenoid, and to ground through the temperature switch (Fig. 23-34). At the same time, another circuit is complete from the ignition switch through the time-delay coil and to ground. Also, as long as the relay points remain closed, they provide a path

to ground for the vacuum solenoid. With either the temperature switch or the time-delay contacts providing a ground circuit, the vacuum advance solenoid energizes, permitting vacuum to the distributor.

In low and intermediate forward gear operation with the engine temperature above about 93°F., the temperature cold-override and transmission switch points are open (Fig. 23-35). Also, if 20 seconds have elapsed, the time-delay points are also open. This switch action breaks all the normal grounds that had energized the solenoid. Therefore, the solenoid de-energizes, permitting its plunger to block vacuum to the advance mechanism and open the vacuum advance vent port to the atmosphere.

As the transmission shifts into high gear, the transmission switch points close (Fig. 23-36). This completes the circuit from the ignition switch, through the solenoid switch, and to ground. As a result, the vacuum-advance solenoid energizes, permitting vacuum to pass through the valve and to the advance unit.

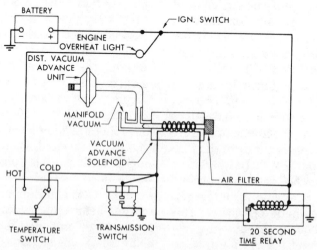

Fig. 23-34. TCS system operation with the cold-override energized.

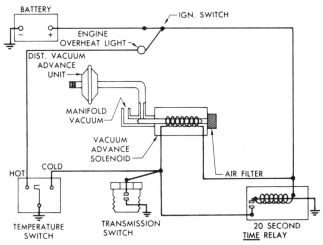

Fig. 23-35. *TCS operation in the lower forward gear ratios with the engine at normal operating temperature.*

If the coolant temperature of a system with a heat override feature reaches about 232°F., the hot override points close (Fig. 23-37). This action completes the electrical circuit of the vacuum solenoid to ground no matter what gear range the transmission is in. Consequently, the solenoid energizes and provides vacuum to the advance mechanism.

Electronically Controlled Timing—Function

Up to this point, this text has described several ways of controlling ignition timing by slightly altering the normal operation of the vacuum advance mechanism. However, in many cases, the vacuum advance as well as the centrifugal advance

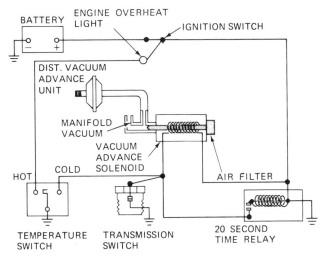

Fig. 23-36. *TCS operation in high gear with the engine warmed up.*

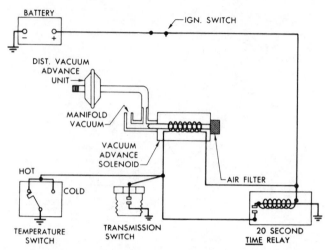

Fig. 23-37.   TCS operation with engine temperature at or above 232°F.

mechanisms often cannot react fast enough to changes in engine operating conditions to meet emission control standards and fuel mileage requirements. As a result, manufacturers have developed computer-controlled ignition-timing systems to provide more precise timing advance during the various phases of engine operation. These systems work in conjunction with electronic ignition systems.

Design of a Typical Electronic Spark-Control System

Figure 23-38 is a schematic of a Chrysler electronic lean-burn system, which uses an electronic ignition system and spark-control computer to regulate ignition timing. The computer adjusts ignition timing automatically, according to signals received from the various system sensors.

The spark control computer (Fig. 23-39) mounts onto the air cleaner. The early-model computer for this system had two printed circuit boards inside: the ignition schedule module and the ignition-timing control module. However, the computer used on recently built vehicles has only one circuit board, which performs both functions.

The ignition schedule module receives signals from various engine sensors; after computing them, it determines the exact spark-timing requirements of the engine. Then, the ignition schedule module directs the timing module to advance or retard the ignition timing accordingly.

Depending on system design, it may have six or seven sensors (Fig. 23-40), which feed information to the computer. These include a start pickup coil, run pickup coil, coolant-temperature sensor, air-temperature sensor, carburetor switch sensor, throttle-position transducer, and vacuum transducer. The start pickup coil fits inside the distributor. Its function is to provide a fixed amount of advance during engine cranking.

The run pickup coil is also inside the distributor. This coil supplies a basic timing signal and permits the computer to deter-

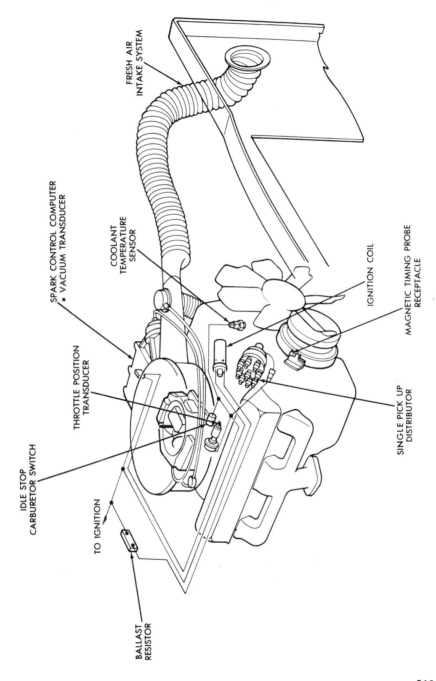

FRESH AIR
INTAKE SYSTEM

SPARK CONTROL COMPUTER
• VACUUM TRANSDUCER

COOLANT
TEMPERATURE
SENSOR

IGNITION COIL

MAGNETIC TIMING PROBE
RECEPTACLE

THROTTLE POSITION
TRANSDUCER

IDLE STOP
CARBURETOR SWITCH

TO IGNITION

SINGLE PICK UP
DISTRIBUTOR

BALLAST
RESISTOR

Fig. 23–38.   A schematic of Chrysler's lean-burn electronic ignition and spark-control systems. (Courtesy of Chrysler Corp.)

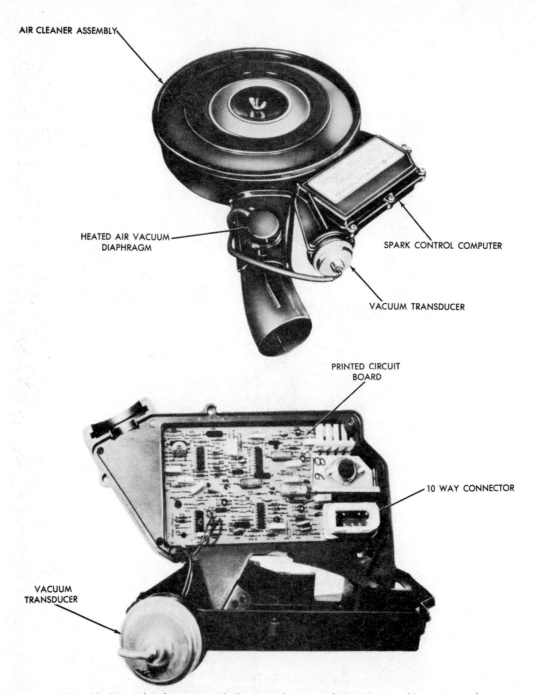

AIR CLEANER ASSEMBLY

HEATED AIR VACUUM
DIAPHRAGM

SPARK CONTROL COMPUTER

VACUUM TRANSDUCER

PRINTED CIRCUIT
BOARD

10 WAY CONNECTOR

VACUUM
TRANSDUCER

Fig. 23-39.   The location of the spark control computer. (Courtesy of Chrysler Corp.)

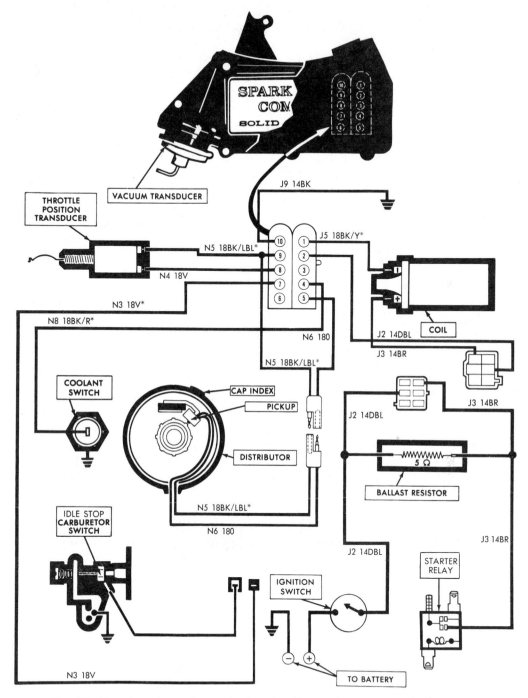

Fig. 23–40.   A wiring schematic showing the various sensors in the system. (Courtesy of Chrysler Corp.)

mine engine rpm. In later model systems, both the start and run pickup coils are combined into one coil to provide all timing signals to the computer. This coil is shown in Fig. 23–40, as the pickup coil.

The coolant temperature sensor mounts into the water-pump housing. This sensor signals the computer when the coolant temperature is low, so that it can regulate the timing accordingly, in order to improve the driveability of the vehicle during the warm-up period.

The air temperature sensor fits inside the computer. This device is a *thermister,* which provides a varying amount of resistance with changing air temperature. For example, as air temperature increases, resistance decreases; as temperature decreases, resistance increases. This action varies the degree of timing in accordance with air temperature.

The carburetor switch senses two operating phases of the engine. That is, the sensor informs the computer if the engine is at idle or at off-idle. This signal, of course, is necessary so that the computer can regulate the ignition timing during these periods of engine operation.

The throttle position transducer connects to the throttle lever. A *transducer* is a device that changes mechanical movement into an electrical signal. The transducer itself has a coil and a movable metal core. The small amount of voltage applied to the coil varies in strength as the core moves within the coil. This varying voltage signal is interpreted by the computer. In the case of the throttle position transducer, this core movement informs the computer of the position and the rate of change in the position of the throttle plates.

The vacuum transducer also mounts onto the air cleaner and spark control com-puter. This device contains a diaphragm, activated by engine vacuum. Movement of the diaphragm with changes in engine vacuum moves the core within the transducer coil to signal the computer of the various changes in engine vacuum. As a result, the computer alters ignition timing according to engine load.

In this system, the computer depends on distributor shaft rotation to direct a crankshaft position signal to the control module. In other types of systems on the market, the computer receives crankshaft position information from a sensor mounted on the front of the engine and from a disc attached to the crankshaft (Fig. 23–41).

In this situation, the signals taken from the crankshaft are more accurate than those from the distributor shaft. This is mainly because the gears or chain driving the camshaft along with the gears rotating the distributor shaft have operating tolerances or a given amount of looseness. While these tolerances are small, they can combine to cause a significant difference between crankshaft position and ignition timing.

Figure 23–42 shows the location of the magnetic timing-probe receptacle at the front of a typical engine. This receptacle accommodates a magnetic probe used in conjunction with special testing equipment to check ignition timing on some electronic timing systems. This special equipment is discussed in Chapter 25.

Air-Injection System

The *air injection system* has been used extensively since the passage of the first exhaust-emission-control standards. Manufacturers have used this system on

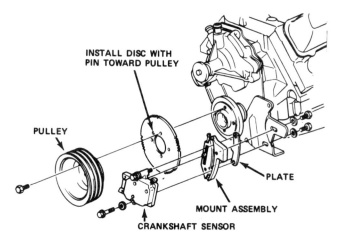

INSTALL DISC WITH
PIN TOWARD PULLEY

PULLEY

PLATE

MOUNT ASSEMBLY

CRANKSHAFT SENSOR

Fig. 23–41. A crankshaft position sensor and rotating disc. (Courtesy of General Motors Corp.)

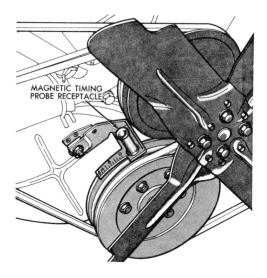

MAGNETIC TIMING
PROBE RECEPTACLE

Fig. 23–42. The location of a typical timing probe receptacle. (Courtesy of Chrysler Corp.)

vehicles with and without engine modification to reduce the levels of HC and CO content within the exhaust gases. In other words, the air injection system (Fig. 23–43) is an add-on system that can function well on most gasoline engine designs.

The design of the air injection system is such that it introduces fresh air, with its oxygen content, into the exhaust of an operating engine. This process causes further oxidation (burning) of the hydrocarbons (HC) and carbon monoxide (CO) left in the hot exhaust. In other words, the oxygen in the air combines with the HC and CO to reduce their concentration further, permitting them to oxidize and produce harmless water vapor (H_2O) and carbon dioxide (CO_2).

On some vehicles, the air injection system injects this air into the base of the exhaust manifold to assist the oxidation process in this area. However, other systems inject the air through the cylinder head, at the exhaust port, causing the oxidation process to begin within the area of the exhaust port.

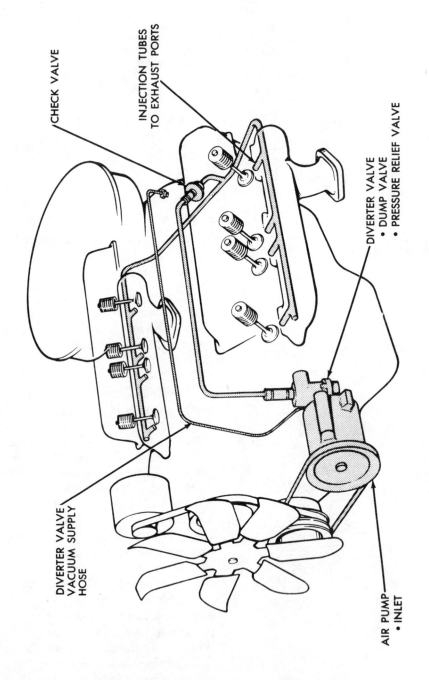

CHECK VALVE

INJECTION TUBES
TO EXHAUST PORTS

DIVERTER VALVE
• DUMP VALVE
• PRESSURE RELIEF VALVE

DIVERTER VALVE
VACUUM SUPPLY
HOSE

AIR PUMP
• INLET

Fig. 23-43. The design of an air injection system. (Courtesy of Chrysler Corp.)

Design of the Air Injection System

Air Pump

The typical air-injection system consists of a belt-driven air pump, combination diverter and pressure-relief valve, check valve, and air injection manifold (Fig. 23–43). The belt-driven air pump mounts onto the front of the engine. The engine crankshaft pulley drives this vane-type pump, which in turn supplies a high volume of air at low pressure to the injection system (Fig. 23–44).

The *air pump* consists of a centrifugal filter and a set of vanes that rotate inside the pump housing. The centrifugal filter mounts on one end of the pump's rotor shaft and therefore turns at pump rpm. This filter cleans the air as it enters the inlet port of the pump, which eliminates the need of a separate pump air cleaner and hose connections.

The *centrifugal filter* consists of a vaned wheel that, when rotating, actually opposes normal air entry into the pump; this

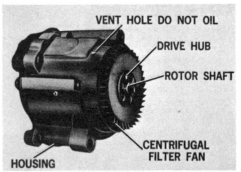

Fig. 23–44. A typical air-injection pump. (Courtesy of Chrysler Corp.)

opposition is not sufficient to hamper the flow substantially. However, the opposing force causes the discharge of any foreign particles in the air from entering the pump.

In operation, the air enters the pump inlet by passing between the vanes of the centrifugal filter (Fig. 23–45). The vanes of the filter assembly are rotating at a relatively high rpm. Consequently, the rotating vanes strike any heavier-than-air foreign particles attempting to enter the pump with the incoming air and rebound them out and away from the pump. In

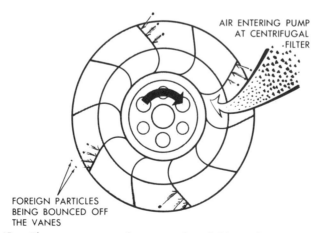

Fig. 23–45. The operation of a centrifugal filter. (Courtesy of United Delco)

other words, the vanes force the foreign particles to move out of the filter in a direction opposite to the flow of the air coming into the pump.

The pump also has a set of two vanes mounted on a rotor inside the pump housing (Fig. 23–46). The pump pulley, through a shaft, drives the rotor that rotates on an axis different than the center line of the pump bore. The vanes, on the other hand, turn about the center line of the housing bore.

The vanes fit into slits in the rotor and are 180 degrees apart. A set of seals (two per vane) provide a seal between the vanes and the rotor.

The vanes are in constant contact (or rather near contact) with the pump housing bore as the rotor turns. Consequently, the vanes constantly slide back and forth in the sealed rotor slits during pump operation. This action is necessary because the vanes and rotor operate on different centers.

Air-Pump Operation

As the pump begins to operate, a vane moves past the inlet port. This action increases the volume in the pump chamber near the inlet port, which has the effect of producing a vacuum. This vacuum draws the air through the centrifugal filter and

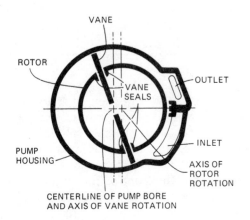

Fig. 23–46. A schematic of air pump construction.

into the pump chamber (*A* of Fig. 23–47).

As the first vane continues to rotate within the housing bore, the second vane passes the inlet port (*B* of Fig. 23–47). At this point, the air previously pulled into the pump is now trapped between the two vanes. As the vanes continue to turn, they trap and carry the air into a smaller area of the chamber. This compresses the air.

Continued rotation of the first vane takes it past the outlet port (*C* of Fig. 23–47). Once the valve passes the outlet port, the compressed air exhausts out the port and into the remainder of the injection system. Although this discussion has concentrated on only one cycle, note that

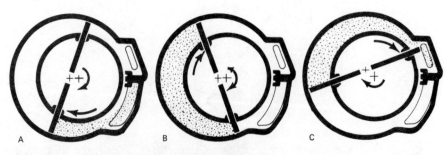

Fig. 23–47. Air-injection pump operation.

two cycles are made during each complete revolution of the rotor.

Diverter Valve

The *diverter valve* can be a separate unit connected to the pump by a hose or bolted to the pump. The purpose of this valve is to prevent a backfire in the exhaust system during engine deceleration. When an engine decelerates, there is a strong vacuum in the intake manifold, which applies itself just beneath the carburetor throttle plate. This draws a rich mixture of fuel into the cylinders.

This rich mixture is not completely burnable during the engine power stroke, so that much of the mixture exits the cylinders through the exhaust valves. If at this time the injection pump continued to supply air to the manifolds or exhaust ports, this air would combine with this mixture, and a backfire would occur. The diverter valve prevents the backfire by momentarily exhausting the air pump's output, so that it does not reach the exhaust valve area during the initial stages of engine deceleration.

The diverter valve shown in Fig. 23–48

consists of a diaphragm and spring that control the operation of a double-acting metering valve. For example, the sudden rise in intake manifold during deceleration creates a strong vacuum condition over the diaphragm on its spring side. This vacuum causes the diaphragm and its attached metering valve to move upward against the return-spring tension.

This upward movement of the valve (closed position) causes two reactions within the system. First, the upward portion of the valve seats to cut off injection air to the exhaust manifold. Second, the lower portion of the valve unseats to bypass momentarily or divert the pump output through the silencer material to the atmosphere.

However, this diversion of pump air flow only lasts momentarily. This is due to the orifice hole in the diaphragm assembly, which soon equalizes the vacuum on both sides of the diaphragm. Consequently, the return spring quickly brings the diaphragm and metering valve back down into the normal operating (open) position in a matter of seconds. In other words, the diverter valve, in effect, turns off the air supply suddenly in order to pre-

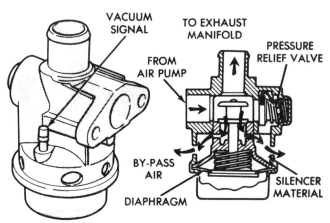

Fig. 23–48. The design of the diverter valve. (Courtesy of Chrysler Corp.)

vent a backfire and then turns it back on gradually for the purpose of starting the oxidation process in the exhaust manifold or ports.

Relief Valve

The diverter shown in Fig. 23-48 also has a *pressure relief valve*. This valve controls pressure in the system by exhausting excessive pump pressure at higher engine rpm to the atmosphere through the silencer.

The assembly consists of a valve body, which encloses a preload spring, movable valve, and valve seat. When the air pressure of the pump builds up to a predetermined value, it forces the valve off its seat, compressing the spring. As a result, excess pump pressure exhausts through the silencer to the atmosphere.

As the air pressure drops below the preload tension of the spring, it closes the valve, which prevents further exhausting of pump pressure. In other words, the preload tension of the spring determines at what air pressure the valve opens and consequently system pressure during all phases of pump operation.

Check Valve

A *check valve* (Fig. 23-49) fits into the air-injection manifold. This valve has a one-way diaphragm, which allows pump air pressure to enter the manifold but prevents hot exhaust gases from backing up into the hose and pump. In other words, the valve protects the system from damage from corrosive gases in the event of drive belt failure, abnormally high exhaust system pressure, or air hose rupture.

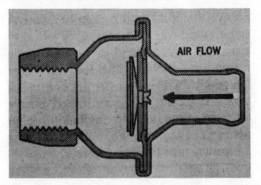

Fig. 23-49. A typical injection system check valve. (Courtesy of Chrysler Corp.)

Injection Manifolds and Tubes

The system shown in Fig. 23-43 has two injection manifolds, which incorporate a number of stainless-steel tubes—one for each engine cylinder. The manifolds distribute the air to the tubes while they direct the injected air into the exhaust ports close to the exhaust valves, near the manifold side of the port, or into the exhaust manifold itself.

Injection System Operation

When the engine is operating, the air pump displaces a large volume of low-pressure air. This air passes through a hose to the diverter valve, which is normally open. From the diverter valve, the air moves through the check valve and into the air manifolds. The manifold then distributes the air to each one of the tubes in the exhaust ports or manifolds. If at any time the air pressure within the manifold exceeds the preload on the relief-valve spring, the valve opens and lowers manifold air pressure.

During engine deceleration, the diverter valve closes. This action momentarily exhausts pump air into the atmosphere, which prevents a backfire within the exhaust system. However, within a few seconds, the valve once again opens to permit normal operation of the injection system.

Aspirator-Type Air-Injection Systems

Function and Design

Since 1975, General Motors, Chrysler, and Ford have used a much simpler type of air injection system on some of their vehicles. This system is known as either the *aspirator-air* or *pulse-air injection system.*

The aspirator- or pulse-air system does not use an air pump to force air into the air manifolds. Instead, this system uses exhaust pressure pulsations to draw fresh air into the exhaust system. Each time an exhaust valve closes, there is a period when the pressure within the manifold drops below atmospheric pressure. During these low-pressure (vacuum) pulses, air from the clean side of the air cleaner (Fig. 23–50) moves into the exhaust manifolds. This air in turn provides the oxygen necessary to oxidize the HC and CO in the exhaust manifolds as well as supply needed oxygen to the catalytic converter.

The aspirator system shown in Fig. 23–50 consists of a steel tube, one-way aspirator valve, and length of hose from the valve to the air cleaner. The steel tube flanges into the exhaust manifold. This tube carries the air from the aspirator valve itself to the exhaust manifold.

Threaded into the open end of the steel tube is the aspirator valve. This valve

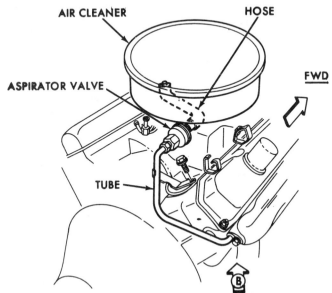

AIR CLEANER   HOSE

ASPIRATOR VALVE

FWD

TUBE

Fig. 23–50. The design of an aspirator-type air-injection system. Courtesy of Chrysler Corp.)

(Fig. 23–51) is a one-way check valve, which permits air to flow from the clean side of the air cleaner, through the steel tube, and to the exhaust manifold. However, the same valve prevents exhaust gases from backing up the steel tube, hose, and into the air cleaner.

The one-way aspirator valve may contain a spring-loaded diaphragm (Fig. 23–51) or have a metal reed valve. However, both valve designs operate in much the same manner and connect via a hose to the clean side of the air cleaner.

System Operation

When an engine with this system is idling or operating at low speeds, the

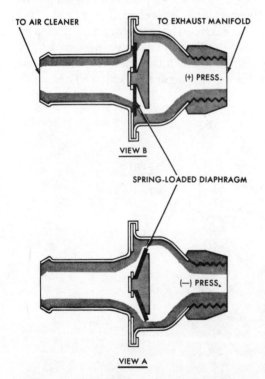

VIEW B

SPRING-LOADED DIAPHRAGM

VIEW A

Fig. 23–51. The design and operation of an aspirator valve. (Courtesy of Chrysler Corp.)

aspirator-air valve opens due to the pulsing negative pressure within the exhaust manifold. In other words, the valve opens each time there are low-pressure (vacuum) pulses, which occur each time an exhaust valve closes. When the diaphragm or reed valve opens (view *A* of Fig. 23–51), atmospheric pressure forces fresh air from the clean side of the air cleaner, through the aspirator valve, steel tube, and into the exhaust manifold.

When the exhaust gas pressure rises above that of the atmosphere, the spring closes the diaphragm or reed valve (view *B* of Fig. 23–51). Now, the assembly acts as a one-way check valve to prevent exhaust gases from backing up into the air cleaner. This usually occurs more at high engine rpm, where the vacuum pulses follow each other too quickly for the valve to respond by opening. Consequently, the internal spring simply keeps the diaphragm or reed valve closed. Consequently, no fresh air enters the exhaust manifolds during these periods, and the exhaust gases cannot flow back to the air cleaner.

Exhaust Gas Recirculation System

An *exhaust gas recirculation (EGR) emission-control system* reduces the amount of nitrogen oxide (NOx) produced during combustion. Under normal circumstances, nitrogen and oxygen do not combine unless temperatures exceed 2,500°F. However, this and even higher temperatures along with maximum pressure occur within the engine's combustion chambers when ignition timing is correct. Therefore, when temperatures are higher than 2,500°F., nitrogen and oxygen rapidly combine to form large amounts of NOx.

There are basically two ways in which peak combustion chamber temperatures are held down to prevent the formation of NOx. One way is through the use of a spark control system. The other, and very efficient, method is to dilute the incoming air/fuel mixture with a small amount of an inert gas. An *inert gas* is one that will not undergo a chemical reaction.

Due to the fact that exhaust gas is relatively inert, manufacturers use it to dilute the air/fuel mixture. This action is done by routing small amounts of exhaust gas (about 6 to 10 percent) from the engine's exhaust system to the intake manifold. This concentration of the inert exhaust gas mixes with the air/fuel mixture, entering the various cylinders, to lower the mixture's ability to produce heat during combustion.

Exhaust gas performs this function basically because it contains no oxygen. Consequently, the resulting air-fuel-exhaust gas mixture is not as powerful when ignited; it therefore creates less heat than an undiluted air/fuel mixture would otherwise produce.

Not all engine-operating phases produce excessive NOx emissions. For example, because the engine produces very small amounts of NOx at idle, exhaust gas recirculation is not necessary or desirable at that time. In addition, the EGR system is inoperative during wide-open throttle operation for more efficient engine operation and vehicle driveability. Therefore, the main engine operating period at which the EGR system should function is at vehicle speeds of 30 to about 70 mph, when NOx formation is highest.

Even during these periods, at certain engine temperatures exhaust gas circulation may not be necessary. For instance, when engine temperature is low, the for-mation of NOx is less. Consequently, operation of the EGR system is not necessary and the system is therefore made inoperative in most cases. This improves engine warm-up and improves vehicle driveability.

Design of the EGR System

Intake Manifold

Figure 23-52 illustrates a typical exhaust gas recirculation system, which consists of a modified intake manifold, EGR valve, vacuum amplifier, CCEGR (coolant-controlled exhaust gas recirculation) valve, EGR delay timer, and solenoid. In order to tap the continuous supply of the inert exhaust gases without external pipes or connections to the exhaust system, manufacturers cast an additional exhaust gas passage into the complex runner system within the intake manifold (Fig. 23-53). In other words, instead of having only one exhaust passage to preheat the intake runner floor, an EGR manifold has two—one that serves as the exhaust crossover, while the second passage routes the inert gas to the intake runners.

EGR Valve

Separating the two passages within the manifold is a vacuum-controlled shut-off and metering valve, referred to as the *EGR valve*. This valve is a spring-loaded, vacuum-operated, poppet-type valve (Fig. 23-54). The assembly contains a spring-loaded diaphragm that attaches to a tapered EGR valve. The spring side of the diaphragm housing has a port opening that connects into a vacuum source, while

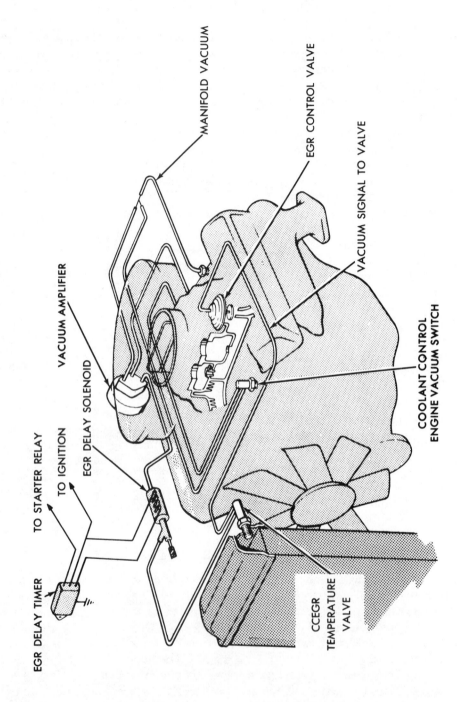

MANIFOLD VACUUM

EGR CONTROL VALVE

VACUUM SIGNAL TO VALVE

VACUUM AMPLIFIER

EGR DELAY SOLENOID

TO STARTER RELAY

TO IGNITION

EGR DELAY TIMER

COOLANT CONTROL
ENGINE VACUUM SWITCH

CCEGR
TEMPERATURE
VALVE

Fig. 23–52. The components of a typical EGR system. (Courtesy of Chrysler Corp.)

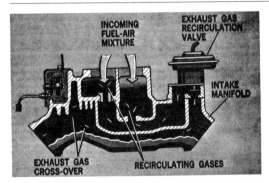

Fig. 23-53. An intake manifold with an EGR passage and ports cast into it. (Courtesy of Chrysler Corp.)

the other side has a vent opening to the atmosphere.

In operation, the valve is in the closed position by the action of the spring and opens when a given amount of vacuum acts on the diaphragm. For example, in the left-hand diagram of Fig. 23-54, the spring is holding the diaphragm and its attached tapered valve in the closed position. As a result, exhaust gases, from the crossover passage, cannot enter the EGR passage leading to the intake manifold.

When the vacuum acting on the diaphragm reaches about 3 inches of Hg, the diaphragm begins to open the valve. The valve reaches its full open position somewhere between 5 to about 8.5 inches of Hg, depending upon system design (right-hand diaphragm of Fig. 23-54). As a result, the actual position of the tapered valve meters the flow of exhaust gases into the intake manifold in proportion to the amount of applied vacuum on the diaphragm. Even with the tapered valve in the wide-open position, the flow still has limitations due to the size of the orifice formed between the valve stem and the wall of its seat. This area, as shown in Fig. 23-54, is relatively small.

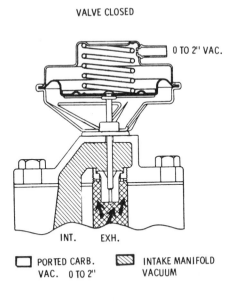

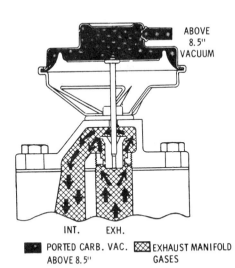

Fig. 23-54. The design and operation of an EGR valve. (Courtesy of General Motors Corp.)

Vacuum Sources Used to Operate an EGR Valve

Ported Vacuum

Manufacturers can use one of two vacuum sources to operate an EGR valve: either *ported vacuum* or *venturi vacuum*. When ported vacuum is the source (Fig. 23–55) the carburetor has a slot-type port machined into the throttle body. As the throttle valve opens during engine acceleration, it exposes the slot to a progressively increasing percentage of intake manifold vacuum. As a result, there is no vacuum signal to the EGR valve with a closed throttle valve. But as the valve opens, the signal increases, which in turn opens the EGR valve in proportion to the intensity of the vacuum signal applied to its diaphragm. In other words, the amount of valve opening and exhaust-gas recirculation depends on throttle position and intake manifold vacuum.

Due to the important fact that the ported-vacuum signal cannot be more than intake manifold vacuum, the EGR valve does not function under wide-open throttle acceleration. In other words, as intake manifold vacuum drops extensively during heavy acceleration, so does the ported-vacuum signal. This action prevents any exhaust gas recirculation during extended wide-open throttle operation. Therefore, an EGR valve operated by a ported signal opens progressively during periods of moderate vehicle acceleration between speeds of 30 to 70 mph, but the valve closes when there is weak manifold vacuum, produced during prolonged wide-open throttle conditions.

Venturi-Vacuum-Controlled EGR Valve

An alternative method of providing a vacuum signal to an EGR valve is through the use of a venturi-vacuum control system. This system consists of a vacuum tap, amplifier, and dump valve (Fig. 23–56). The tap, like the main fuel nozzle, is nothing more than a projected opening into the throat of the venturi. As such, the tap also has a low pressure

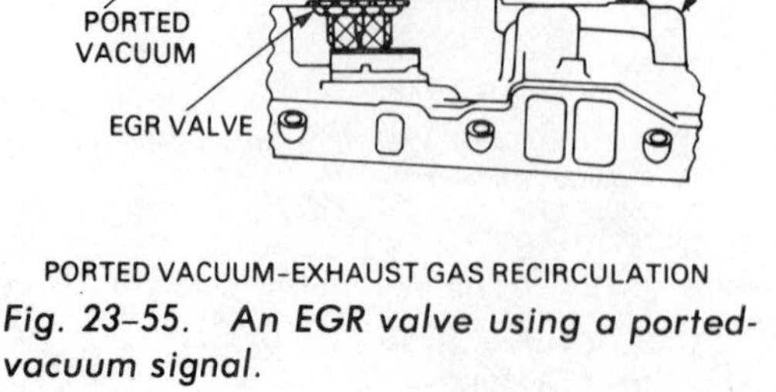

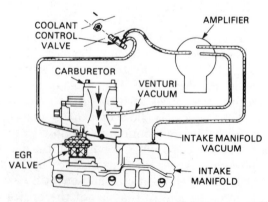

PORTED VACUUM-EXHAUST GAS RECIRCULATION

Fig. 23–55. An EGR valve using a ported-vacuum signal.

VENTURI VACUUM EXHAUST GAS RECIRCULATION

Fig. 23–56. An EGR valve operated by a venturi-vacuum signal.

(vacuum) applied to its opening when a considerable amount of air flows through the carburetor.

In operation, the amount of the venturi-vacuum signal depends mainly on the amount of air flow through the venturi itself. For instance, during engine idle (closed throttle), the air flow through the venturi is very slow. This results in a zero or very low vacuum signal from the tap. However, as the throttle valve opens and air flow increases, the tap signal increases in proportion to the rise in air flow.

Even when there is a great deal of air passing through the venturi, such as during high engine rpm, the tap signal is too weak to activate the EGR valve diaphragm. To overcome this problem, the system requires an amplifier to boost the tap signal sufficiently to open the EGR valve. The amplifier performs this function by storing intake manifold vacuum in a reservoir inside the unit itself or externally mounted on the firewall. The reservoir also guarantees an adequate vacuum source to activate the EGR valve, regardless of the variations in manifold vacuum.

Since the reservoir maintains a relatively steady vacuum source to the EGR valve, a dump diaphragm is necessary to prevent the EGR valve operating at wide-open throttle (WOT). In operation, the diaphragm senses when the throttle valve is wide open, and it responds by venting the stored reservoir vacuum to the atmosphere. In other words, the diaphragm compares venturi tap and manifold vacuum. When tap vacuum is equal to or greater than manifold vacuum, the diaphragm "dumps" reservoir vacuum. This action limits the signal to the EGR valve to manifold vacuum, which during WOT is very low or zero. Thus, the EGR dia-

phragm spring closes the valve until reservoir vacuum increases.

Coolant-Controlled Exhaust Gas Recirculation (CCEGR) Valve

The EGR valve system, using either a ported- or venturi-vacuum signal, utilizes an engine coolant temperature control valve. This CCEGR valve (Fig. 23-57) threads into the radiator's top tank and tees into vacuum line between the amplifier and the EGR valve.

The function of this valve is to prevent exhaust gas recirculation at low engine temperature. For example, until coolant temperature reaches about 65°F., the valve remains closed. This prevents the amplifier signal from reaching the EGR valve. Thus, the EGR valve cannot react to any amplifier signals until coolant temperature reaches about 65°F.

In some models, a similar valve fits into the thermostat housing (Fig. 23-52). This CCEGR valve operates in a similar manner to the one mentioned earlier, but it does not activate until coolant temperature within the engine reaches 90°F.

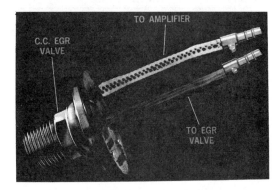

Fig. 23-57. The design of a CCEGR valve. (Courtesy of Chrysler Corp.)

EGR-Delay System

The venturi-controlled EGR system (shown in Fig. 23–52) also has a time-delay system. The purpose of this system is to prevent exhaust gas recirculation for about 35 seconds after the driver turns on the ignition switch. This action improves engine starting and initial vehicle driveability.

The basic system consists of a delay timer and solenoid. The delay timer mounts onto the firewall inside the engine compartment, and it electrically activates the solenoid for about 35 seconds once the ignition switch is on.

The solenoid has a plunger that controls two vacuum ports, which tee between the vacuum amplifier and the CCEGR valve. Therefore, when the relay energizes the solenoid, it cuts off the vacuum signal to the CCEGR and EGR valve. However, after 35 seconds, the relay de-energizes the solenoid, and its plunger permits the amplifier signal to reach the CCEGR valve. If this valve is also open, normal exhaust gas recirculation occurs.

Catalytic Converters

In order to meet stricter exhaust-emission-control standards, manufacturers began to install catalytic converters on domestic automobiles, beginning in 1975. This device fits into the exhaust system between the engine's exhaust manifold and the muffler (Fig. 23–58). Although from the outside the converter looks similar to a muffler, it does not serve that function. Instead, the catalytic converter changes harmful exhaust emissions (HC and CO) into byproducts of combustion, namely, carbon dioxide (CO_2) and water

vapor (H_2O); and in some cases, it reduces the concentration of NOx in the exhaust.

Types of Catalytic Converters

Oxidation

Two basic types of converters are used today: oxidation and reduction. The *oxidation converter* turns HC and CO compounds into water vapor and carbon dioxide by directing these pollutants and the exhaust gas through a catalyst in the presence of oxygen. A catalyst is a substance that causes a chemical reaction without being changed by the reaction. Since the catalyst only encourages rather than takes part in this reaction, the process does not use the catalyst up.

Since this converter oxidizes the HC and CO pollutants, the process generates considerable heat. The heat of the catalyst ranges from about 900 to 1,600°F., with the exhaust gas at the outlet of the converter being 50 to 200°F. higher than at the inlet end. However, in spite of this intense heat, the oxidation process does not generate the flame and radiant heat associated with an actual burning-type reaction.

Reduction Converter

An oxidation type converter has little effect on NOx because the control of this pollutant requires a separate reaction called reduction. *Reduction* is a chemical process in which oxygen is taken away from a compound. Therefore, this process is the opposite of an oxidation reaction. In other words, in the reduction converter, the reaction changes NOx to harmless

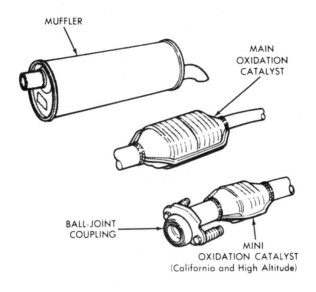

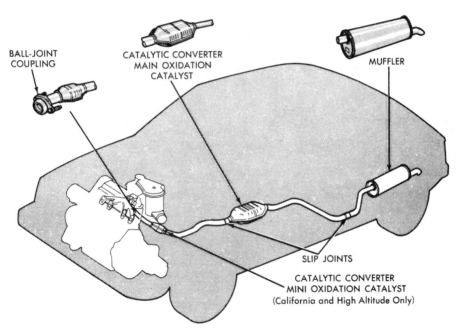

Fig. 23-58. A typical catalytic converter installation. (Courtesy of Chrysler Corp.)

nitrogen (N_2) and CO_2 by chemically promoting the shift of oxygen from the NOx to the CO compounds.

Oxidation Converter Design

Figure 23-59 illustrates the construction of a typical oxidation converter, which consists of a shell, substrate, flow diffuser, and stainless-steel mesh. Manufacturers make the converter housing or

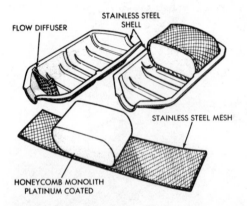

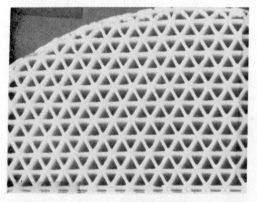

Fig. 23-59. The construction of an oxidation converter. (Courtesy of Chrysler Corp.)

shell of two stamped metal pieces welded together to form a round or oval assembly. The outer housing or shell is made of aluminumized or stainless steel because of the high temperatures associated with the oxidation process, which the metal must withstand.

Each side of the shell supports the catalytic element. This element consists of a substrate upon which the manufacturer deposits the catalyst and through which the exhaust gases must flow. The substrate may be in the form of tiny ceramic or aluminum oxide pellets or a ceramic or aluminum-oxide, honeycomb, monolithic element as shown in Fig. 23-59.

The manufacturer deposits the catalyst onto the pellet or monolithic substrate. The two common catalyst elements generally used are platinum or a mixture of platinum and palladium. Either or both of these metals provide the chemical activity, operating temperature, and durability required by an effective catalyst in the oxidation converter.

Between the converter inlet and the catalytic element is a flow diffuser (Fig. 23-59). This device is necessary with monolithic-type substrate to allow a uniform flow of exhaust gas over the entire area of the element. If the unit did not have a diffuser, the gases would tend to flow only through the center portion of the substrate.

The stainless-steel mesh has three functions. First, it protects the monolithic substrate material from damage due to shock or severe jolts by acting as a cushion. Second, the mesh also protects the catalytic element from thermo shock caused by temperature extremes. Finally, the mesh keeps the monolithic element in proper position during the final assembly of the converter shell.

Reduction Converters— Location and Design

The *reduction converter* fits into an exhaust system in front of the oxidation converter. The main difference in design between the two units is in the substrate and catalyst. In the reduction converter, there are two substrates of different sizes, one coated with platinum and the other rhodium. *Rhodium* is the catalyst used to remove the oxygen from the NOx emissions.

Three-Way Converters

Beginning in 1978, two domestic automobile manufacturers, Ford and General Motors, began using a two-stage, three-way converter that controlled HC, CO, and NOx emissions (Fig. 23-60). The front half (first stage) of this converter type has a reduction-oxidation catalyst that controls NOx, HC, and CO. This portion of the converter has a monolithic substrate with a rhodium and platinum catalyst. The rear portion of the converter (second stage) has only a platinum catalyst to oxidize HC and CO emissions further.

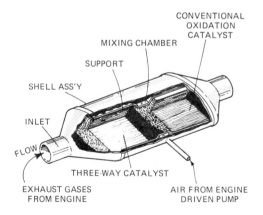

CONVENTIONAL
OXIDATION
CATALYST

MIXING CHAMBER

SUPPORT

SHELL ASS'Y

INLET

FLOW

THREE-WAY CATALYST

EXHAUST GASES
FROM ENGINE

AIR FROM ENGINE
DRIVEN PUMP

Fig. 23-60. A three-way converter controls HC, CO, and NOx emissions.

Figure 23-61 shows the installation of a two-stage converter. As mentioned earlier in this chapter, this special reduction-oxidation converter system also incorporates an electronically controlled carburetor and an exhaust-gas oxygen sensor. This sensor continuously monitors the unburned air/fuel ratio in the exhaust, and it directs a signal to the electronic control module, which also receives signals from the throttle-angle switch, two vacuum switches, and the ignition control side of the ignition coil. The module then directs a signal to the solenoid regulator that controls the vacuum supply to the carburetor's power valve. This action provides precise control of the air/fuel ratio needed by the two-stage converter.

Secondary Air Supply

In some cases, the manufacturer may also supply the catalytic converter with a secondary air supply (Fig. 23-61). This supply comes from an air injection system, which uses an air pump or an aspirator valve. The purpose of this secondary air supply is to provide oxygen to aid the catalytic action of the platinum and palladium. The resulting oxidation produces a high temperature, which is one of the main requirements for breaking down HC and CO into water vapor and CO_2.

In the case of some two-stage converter systems, the air injection system supplies air to the exhaust port or manifold so that it passes through the whole converter during engine warm-up. However, when the engine reaches its normal operating temperature, a vacuum signal from a temperature vacuum switch redirects the injected air to the middle of the converter. The additional air then enters only the rear half

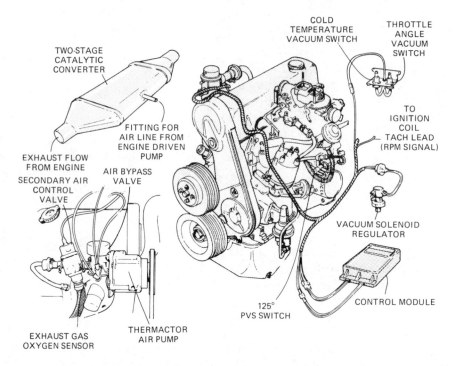

Fig. 23-61. The components necessary to operate a typical two-stage, three-way converter.

of the converter, where it finishes the oxidation process of any remaining HC and CO compounds (Fig. 23-62).

Use of Unleaded Fuel

Vehicles with catalytic converter systems require unleaded fuel. The lead and phosphorus additives used in leaded gasoline greatly reduce the catalyst's efficiency because the lead plates the catalyst and forms a coating. This in time prevents the exhaust gases from reaching and reacting with the catalyst material. As a result, continuous use of leaded fuel eventually causes the catalyst to lose its ability to promote oxidation of HC and CO emissions.

As mentioned earlier, manufacturers prevent the use of leaded fuels on vehicles with catalytic converters by reducing the size of the fuel filler neck. This type of filler neck accommodates the smaller unleaded gasoline pump nozzles found in service stations. In addition, automobiles that require unleaded fuel have labels reading "unleaded gasoline only," usually next to the fuel filler neck and sometimes on the instrument panel.

Review

This section will assist you in determining how well you remember the material in this chapter. Read each item carefully. If you can't complete the statement, review the section in the chapter that covers the material.

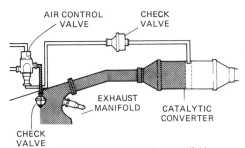

Air is injected into the exhaust manifold during engine warm-up.

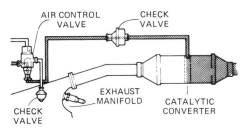

Air is injected into the mid-section of the catalytic converter during normal hot engine operation.

Fig. 23-62. The operating phases of a two-stage, three-way converter.

1. In an engine modified to reduce emissions, manufacturers redesigned the combustion chamber and pistons to reduce _____ areas.
   a. quench
   b. hot
   c. cool
   d. static

2. The average compression ratio of an exhaust-emission–modified engine is about _____.
   a. 11:1
   b. 10:1
   c. 9:1
   d. 8:1

3. To prevent engine stalling and to reduce emissions, many carburetors have a _____ _____ valve.
   a. hot decel
   b. emission reduction

   c. hot-idle compensator
   d. antistall vent

4. Altitude-compensating devices are built into the _____ system.
   a. choke
   b. idle
   c. main-metering
   d. low-speed

5. Electronically controlled carburetors are found on vehicles with a specially designed _____ _____.
   a. exhaust system
   b. catalytic converter
   c. intake manifold
   d. ignition system

6. Choke hot-air modifiers are found on some _____ _____ engines.
   a. General Motors
   b. American Motors
   c. Ford-built
   d. Chrysler-built

7. The valve that retards the opening of some automatic chokes is the _____ _____ _____ valve.
   a. choke retard
   b. choke delay
   c. vacuum brake
   d. hot-air modifier

8. The thermostatic air cleaner preheats the air primarily on winter days and during engine _____.
   a. starting
   b. acceleration
   c. idle
   d. warm-up

9. During heavy acceleration the thermostatic air-cleaner door is _____ _____.
   a. partially closed
   b. fully closed
   c. fully open
   d. partially open

10. At idle, the retard diaphragm of the dual-action, vacuum-advance units retards ignition timing _____ degrees.
    a. 2 to 8
    b. 4 to 10
    c. 6 to 12
    d. 8 to 14

11. The unit that actually blocks vacuum from the vacuum advance in the TCS system, described in this chapter, is the _____ _____.
    a. vacuum advance solenoid
    b. transmission switch
    c. delay relay
    d. temperature switch

12. In a system with electronically controlled ignition timing, the _____ _____ actually adjusts the timing, according to signals received from various sensors.
    a. ignition module
    b. spark control computer
    c. vacuum transducer
    d. pickup coil

13. The system that forces air into the exhaust to oxidize HC and CO compounds further is the _____ _____.
    a. thermostatic air
    b. air injection
    c. catalytic converter
    d. lean burn

14. The device that prevents dust from entering the air pump is the _____ _____.
    a. diverter valve
    b. rotor vanes
    c. air cleaner
    d. centrifugal filter

15. The component within the air injection system that prevents a backfire is the _____ _____.
    a. diverter valve
    b. air pump
    c. relief valve
    d. check valve

16. The aspirator-type air-injection system has no _____ _____.
    a. air hose
    b. steel tubing
    c. air pump
    d. air cleaner

17. The EGR system reduces NOx by introducing a (an) _____ _____ into the intake manifold.
    a. volatile gas
    b. inert gas
    c. atmospheric air
    d. gas compound

18. When an EGR valve operates by venturi vacuum, a(an) _____ is necessary.
    a. amplifier
    b. booster
    c. rectifier
    d. slot

19. The oxidation converter changes HC and CO compounds to _____ _____ and _____.
    a. water vapor HC
    b. water vapor CO
    c. water vapor N_2
    d. water vapor CO_2

20. The catalyst used in a reduction converter is _____.
    a. platinum
    b. rhodium
    c. palladium
    d. aluminum

For the answers, turn to the Appendix.

The testing and servicing of the various types of exhaust emission control systems found on the modern automobile are a vital portion of every tune-up. In other words, changing the spark plugs, points, and condenser or checking the operation of the electronic ignition system are only some of the aspects of a complete tune-up. The emission control devices also require testing and servicing as necessary because these units in most cases not only interact with other engine systems to reduce harmful emissions but do so while still maintaining vehicle driveability and reasonable fuel economy.

Since exhaust emission control devices interact with the engine, fuel, ignition, crankcase, and evaporation emission control systems, these units or systems must be in good operating condition before attempting to test the exhaust controls. Otherwise, these controls cannot perform their function of reducing harmful emissions from the vehicle. This text covers the various engine condition tests in Chapter 5 and carburetor servicing and testing in Chapters 10, 24, and 26. The ignition testing and servicing procedures are found in Chapters 16, 18, 25, and 26; while crankcase and EEC systems are discussed in Chapters 21 and 22.

_____ Chapter 24

TESTING AND SERVICING OF EXHAUST EMISSION-CONTROL DEVICES

Equipment to Test Exhaust Emission-Control Devices

Before discussing the testing and servicing of the many types of exhaust controls, it is important for the reader to be familiar with the various pieces of equipment used by the industry for this purpose. These include such items as the vacuum gauge, timing light, tachometer, infrared exhaust analyzer, propane-enrichment equipment, and vacuum pump. In previous chapters, you have already learned the purposes for and how to use the vacuum gauge, timing light, and tachometer. Consequently, this chapter discusses the infrared analyzer, propane-enrichment equipment, and portable vacuum pump.

Infrared Analyzer

An *infrared analyzer* (Fig. 24-1) is a device that measures the amount of hydrocarbons (HC) and carbon monoxide (CO) in a vehicle's exhaust. Both of these compounds are harmful air pollutants. Hydrocarbons in a vehicle's exhaust represent unburned gasoline. If the engine does not burn up all the fuel during the combustion process, raw gasoline goes out the tailpipe and registers as HC on the meter. A fouled spark plug, a defective spark plug wire, or burned valves causes an abnormally high reading on the HC meter simply because the combustion process in the affected cylinders did not burn up all the fuel. In addition, an excessively rich air/fuel mixture from the carburetor increases the HC level. However, this condition shows up more apparently on the CO meter than the HC meter.

The meter on the analyzer measures HC emissions in parts per million (ppm) or grams per mile (g/mi). The industry uses ppm or g/mi as the HC measurement basically because there are much smaller amounts of it in a sample of a vehicle's exhaust. One part-per-million is equal to 0.0001 percent of the total exhaust sample. Finally, typical specifications for the allowable HC emissions range from as high as 900 ppm for early-model automobiles to a low of 175 ppm from a current-model vehicle.

Fig. 24-1. An infrared analyzer accurately measures the amount of HC and CO in a vehicle's exhaust.

Carbon monoxide (CO) is a colorless, odorless, tasteless, poisonous gas that results from incomplete fuel combustion. In other words, CO is a byproduct of gasoline after it burns within the combustion chambers. An abnormally high CO level can only be due to an excessively rich air/fuel mixture, while a low CO reading indicates a lean mixture.

On the analyzer's CO meter, the richness or leanness of a mixture is shown by the position of the needle. The richer the mixture, for example, the higher the needle deflects, indicating a greater percentage of CO in the exhaust sample. If the vehicle has a choke valve stuck closed, a restricted air cleaner, or an extremely high carburetor float level, the CO needle shows this by swinging into the high numbers on the scale.

A lean fuel mixture produces the lowest CO emission. However, if the mixture is too lean, the engine misfires intermittently or totally. This misfire may not be heard. But it is definitely there whenever the analyzer shows a low CO reading and a high HC reading or one that fluctuates between the low and high ends of the scale.

The analyzer measures the amount of CO in the exhaust, using a percentage figure. A specification table may show a percentage range for CO emission from 0.05 for current-model vehicles to as high as 6 percent for early-model automobiles.

The infrared analyzer measures the amount of HC and CO in a vehicle's exhaust by comparing a sample of its content with the surrounding air. An analyzer does this by pulling two "samples," one from shop air and the other one from the vehicle's exhaust via a probe inserted into the tailpipe, into two separate glass tubes. Then, an infrared beam shines through both tubes. The beam passing through the exhaust sample refracts or bends due to the impurities within the sample. The machine then gauges the amount of refraction and converts it to electrical signals to drive the HC and CO meter needles.

The two meters, located on the analyzer in Fig. 24-1, indicate the amount of HC and CO concentration. Both meters have dual scales. The HC meter indicates reading in ppm from 0 to 500 and from 0 to 2,000. The CO meter, on the other hand, has readings that range from 0 to 2.5 or from 0 to 10 percent, depending on which range button is pushed.

Other than the task of measuring emission levels to determine if a vehicle's exhaust emissions comply with legal standards, the infrared analyzer has three other common usages. First, you can perform emission tests with this machine at various engine speeds and conditions to uncover quickly a variety of engine, ignition, and fuel-system malfunctions. Second, the analyzer provides the accuracy and range for checking and adjusting most carburetors, except those found on many vehicles with catalytic converters. Finally, the analyzer serves as a valuable quality-control tool after a tune-up to make sure that all the repair work and adjustments corrected a noted problem and restored the vehicle to manufacturer's specifications.

Warm-up and Calibration of the Infrared Analyzer

To prepare the analyzer for testing a vehicle's emissions (Fig. 24-1):

1. Depress the zero button on the mode control and permit the analyzer to operate

5 to 15 minutes, depending on machine design.

2. Depress the ppm, HC lo-scale and the percent, CO lo-scale buttons.

3. Using the zero control knobs, set the HC and CO meter needles to zero.

4. Depress and hold the span button on the mode control. Then, adjust the span knobs of both the HC and CO meters until both their needles read on the respective set lines.

5. Release the span button and recheck the zero adjustment on both meters.

General Testing Procedures

Vehicles without Catalytic Converters

To test a vehicle's exhaust for HC and CO content:

1. Depress the Hi-HC and CO meter scale buttons.

2. Insert the sampling probe about 12 inches into the vehicle's tailpipe. *Note:* Be sure that the vehicle's exhaust system is airtight; do not connect a high-velocity exhaust-removal system to the tailpipe while performing the test. Any air leaking into the exhaust system can dilute the exhaust gas and affect the reading. Also, when performing the test on a vehicle with dual exhaust, test each side separately to ensure that you have an exhaust sample from each bank of cylinders.

3. Depress the test selector button on the mode control.

4. With the air cleaner installed, operate the engine at idle or the rpm specified by the manufacturer. *Note:* The engine must be at normal operating temperature.

5. Note and record the reading on both the HC and CO meters. If the HC meter reads less than 500 ppm or the CO meter reads less than 2.5 percent, depress both meter LO buttons for more convenient scale readings.

6. Increase engine speed to 2,500 rpm and hold. Note and record the HC and CO readings. Both should be as low as or lower than the reading taken at idle. *Note:* When testing some electronic fuel injected vehicles without a load, only the idle readings will be accurate. Testing of these engine types at 2,500 rpm requires the use of a dynamometer to load the engine.

7. Return the engine to idle. After a momentary increase on deceleration, both readings should return to the levels recorded in step 5.

8. After completing these tests, depress the zero button on the mode control. Depressing the zero button during intervals between testing procedures, maintains the analyzer for use without the need for further warmup and increases filter life.

9. To turn the analyzer completely off, depress the off button on the mode control.

10. Remove the sample probe from the tailpipe.

Testing Vehicles with Catalytic Converters

With a few exceptions, the procedure just outlined for testing exhaust emissions with an infrared analyzer applies to vehicles with catalytic converters. One of the notable differences is in the test results. The HC and CO readings should be much lower, because the converter reduces these emissions so that the analyzer barely reads the remaining concentrations. This is especially true with the CO level. For this reason, many manufacturers no longer provide CO percentages with their tune-up specifications. However, if the vehicle is a gross pollutor, the analyzer of course indicates the levels of the increased emissions.

Another difference in the procedure is the area into which you insert the test probe. In many cases, the probe still fits into the tailpipe. However, in a few instances, manufacturers provide a plug in the front of the converter (Fig. 24-2) for access to the probe. This permits the analyzer to sample the exhaust gases before they enter the catalytic converter. This is necessary if the technician is to use the infrared tester to make carburetor air/fuel ratio adjustments.

Without the test plug, the technician can use the machine to check a vehicle's emissions against federal and state standards, and the analyzer indicates if the levels are within limits. But in many cases, the CO emissions, due to converter action, are so low at idle that the analyzer

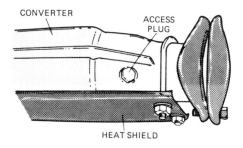

Fig. 24-2. Some converters have a plug access for the infrared probe, so that the analyzer can sample the exhaust gases before they enter the converter.

is no longer an accurate tool for carburetor adjustments. In these situations, the manufacturer recommends the use of propane adjustment, which this chapter explains later.

The key as to when you should use an infrared analyzer in adjusting a carburetor, is in the manufacturer's specifications for the particular vehicle on which you are working. These specifications are either on a decal located under the hood, or in the appropriate service manual. In either case, these specifications will inform you as to the exact procedure to follow in order to set idle mixture and speed properly along with the CO levels. By following these instructions, you should have no difficulty in obtaining the proper idle mixture that provides a smooth idle and low emissions.

Results and Indications— Idle Speed

1. If at idle the HC and CO readings are within specifications, the engine and the ignition, fuel, and emission control systems are functioning normally.

2. If the analyzer indicates a high HC reading and a low CO level, the carburetor may be set too lean, causing a misfire, or the misfire is due to an open spark plug cable or fouled plug.

3. If the tester shows high HC but normal CO levels, this indicates either low engine compression, vacuum leak, arcing ignition points, improper ignition timing, or missing or incorrect thermostat.

4. If both HC and CO readings are high, the problem can be that the air/fuel ratio is extremely rich, the PCV system is inoperative, the heat-riser valve is stuck open, the air-injection system is inopera-

tive or disconnected, the thermostatic air-cleaner preheat door is sticking, or the catalytic converter is defective.

5. If the analyzer indicates a normal HC reading but a high CO level, either the air cleaner is restricted, the choke valve is stuck partially closed, carburetor is out of adjustment, the idle speed is not to specifications, or the PCV valve has a restriction.

Results and Indications—2,500 RPM

1. If at 2,500 rpm, the HC and CO levels are at or slightly below those noted at engine idle, the engine and the fuel, ignition, and emission control systems are functioning correctly.

2. If the analyzer shows a high HC but a low CO reading, there is a fouled plug or defective spark plug cable, extremely lean air/fuel mixture, or a floating exhaust valve.

3. If the HC reading is high while the CO level is normal, there is most likely a vacuum leak, sticky valve, or arcing, bouncing, or misaligned contact points.

4. If the test reading indicates normal HC but high CO levels, the choke valve is partially closed, the air filter is restricted, or the carburetor has a defective high-speed or power circuit.

PCV System Test

You can perform many other special tests with an infrared analyzer. These include testing of the PCV system, carburetor accelerator pump, and the carburetor power valve.

To check to see if the PCV system is functioning properly:

1. With the engine idling at normal temperature, note the CO reading.

2. Remove the PCV valve from the engine but leave it connected into the hose to the carburetor or intake manifold.

3. Observe the CO reading on the analyzer; it should drop to a lesser value than the one noted in step 1.

4. Plug the open end of the PCV valve and again note the CO reading. It should be greater (richer) than the one in step 3.

Results and Indications

No changes in the CO readings indicate the PCV system is not functioning. Clean and replace the PCV valve and hoses as necessary and retest the system.

Accelerator Pump Test

To test the accelerator pump within the carburetor:

1. Start the engine and permit it to operate at its normal hot-idle rpm.

2. While observing the CO meter, quickly open and release the throttle.

3. The engine should increase its speed without hesitation, and the CO meter should indicate an increase in the percentage of CO.

Results and Indications

If the CO reading decreases more than 0.5 percent before increasing or it does not increase at all, the carburetor requires an accelerator pump, linkage adjustment, or repair of the pump mechanism.

Power-Valve Test

To test the operation of the carburetor power valve or power system:

1. Start the engine and permit it to reach normal operating temperature.

2. While operating the engine at 2,500 rpm, quickly snap the throttle wide open and then release it.

3. Note the reading on the CO meter. The meter should show a slight but quick increase. This indicates that the power valve or system is functioning.

Results and Indications

If the reading on the CO meter does not increase, the power valve or system is inoperative and requires service. *Note:* Accelerator pump operation also causes an increase in the CO reading, but that increase is much higher than one caused by the operation of the power valve and occurs at a lesser throttle opening point. Remember that the power valve test is made by opening the throttle valve with the engine operating above 2,500 rpm. The accelerator pump usually does not function at this higher engine speed. If there is any doubt that the accelerator pump may still be functioning during the power valve test, repeat the test, beginning at a slightly higher engine speed.

Carburetor Adjustments

When adjusting a carburetor with an infrared analyzer, you must remember two things. First, each turn of the mixture adjustment screw should affect the air/fuel mixture. For example, when you turn an adjustment screw out (counterclockwise), the mixture should enrich, and the CO level increases. On the other hand, a clockwise movement of the adjustment screw leans the air/fuel mixture, which decreases the CO reading. However, should you make the mixture so lean as to

cause one or more cylinders to misfire, the HC level increases.

Second, always perform all carburetor idle and mixture adjustments as per the manufacturer's recommended procedure. When, for instance the manufacturer provides a CO setting, use it and the analyzer to make the adjustment. On early-model vehicles where CO specifications are not available, use a setting that is below state and federal standards and normal for the year and make of the vehicle being tested. If you are not able to obtain the desired HC and CO levels by following the manufacturer's instructions, there may be other problems such as faulty ignition, engine compression, air injection system, or catalytic converter. You should test all these areas before condemning the carburetor.

Although the adjustment procedures vary somewhat between manufacturers, the following one is one commonly employed by the industry and is especially useful when adjusting an overhauled or repaired carburetor. *Note:* Chapter 10 also explains how to adjust a carburetor's mixture for the lean-best-idle and how to perform a lean-drop procedure through the use of a tachometer.

1. As necessary, remove the limiter caps from the mixture adjustment screws.

2. As designated by the manufacturer, disconnect the air injection hose to the manifolds, remove and plug the vacuum hoses to the EGR valve and vapor-storage canister, and turn on the headlights and air conditioner.

3. Lightly seat each mixture adjustment screw. Then, back out each screw the number of turns specified by the manufacturer. If no specifications are available,

turn each screw out about 2 1/2 turns or to its internal stops, if so equipped.

4. Start the engine and permit it to reach normal operating temperature.

5. Calibrate the infrared analyzer as described earlier, and insert its probe into the tailpipe or access hole in the catalytic converter. Then, depress the analyzer's test button.

6. Using a tachometer, adjust engine idle speed to the manufacturer's specifications.

7. Turn the mixture adjusting screw in, until there is a definite drop in rpm on the tachometer. Then, slowly rotate the adjustment screw out (counterclockwise) until the tachometer needle stabilizes on the highest rpm. Repeat the process on the other adjusting screw (two- and four-barrel carburetors). If the stabilized rpm is over the specified curb-idle speed specification, reduce engine rpm by adjusting the idle-speed screw or solenoid. Repeat the process on two- or four-barrel units to make sure that both primary idle circuits are in balance. At this point, the engine is operating at lean best idle.

8. Install the air cleaner.

9. Check the HC and CO readings. If the readings are too high, gradually lean the mixture by turning the adjustment screws in clockwise 1/16 of a turn, one at a time. Continue to adjust the mixture screws equally to obtain the lowest HC reading and the smoothest possible idle. *Note:* It will be necessary for you to wait for the HC and CO reading to stabilize after each adjustment. This can require 7 to 10 seconds from the time you change the mixture until the results appear on both meters. Also, readjust the idle speed

after each mixture adjustment to maintain the specified engine rpm.

10. Continue gradually to adjust the mixture screw in order to obtain the lowest CO reading without increasing the HC reading. Stop the procedure when the HC and CO readings are within the manufacturer's specifications and legal limits, with the engine operating smoothly. *Note:* If the adjustment process takes longer than two minutes, clean out the engine by running it at about 2,000 rpm for a few seconds.

11. Install new limiter caps as necessary over the idle-mixture adjusting screws with their tangs against the full-rich stops.

12. As necessary, turn the headlights and air conditioner off, and reconnect all hoses or lines removed and plugged under step 2.

13. Remove the analyzer test probe from the tailpipe and disconnect the tachometer.

Propane Enrichment—Idle Adjustment

Many manufacturers recommend that the technician use propane enrichment when setting the idle mixture adjustment and curb idle speed on their vehicles. With the advent of the catalytic converter, there is normally an almost unmeasurable percentage of CO emitting from the tailpipe. As a result, the infrared analyzer is not always accurate enough for mixture adjustment. Consequently, the idle mixture can be set too rich, and the analyzer may not indicate the problem.

In addition to the pollution problems,

operating a catalytic-converter–equipped vehicle with an over-rich idle mixture can create several problems. For example, a rich mixture over a period of time reduces the effective life of the converter. Also, this same mixture causes the converter to produce a strong rotten-egg smell at the tailpipe. Finally, an excessively rich mixture can produce a rough idle or even engine stalling.

Artificial enrichment through the use of propane involves injecting a controlled amount of this gas into the carburetor at idle and noting the effect on engine idle speed. Manufacturers recommend propane for this purpose because it is readily available in small pressurized containers and mixes well with the air/fuel mixture. Figure 24-3 shows a propane enrichment tool that consists of the propane cylinder, main metering valve, propane metering valve, length of hose, and adapters to connect this hose to the carburetor or air cleaner.

When this tool is injecting propane into the engine, there is a direct three-way correlation between the carburetor's air/fuel ratio, the amount of propane emitted, and the gain or loss in engine rpm. For instance, with a constant supply of propane to a carburetor, adjusted to a given air/fuel mixture at idle, there should be a specified increase (gain) in engine speed. However, if the rpm gain is less than that specified by the manufacturer, the air/fuel mixture is too rich. On the other hand, an rpm gain more than specifications indicates a ratio that is too lean.

Many manufacturers require that the mechanic adjust the carburetors on their vehicle through the use of propane enrichment. As with many other service techniques, each company has slight differences in its recommended procedure for this adjustment. Therefore, when using propane enrichment to adjust the air/fuel mixture on a given vehicle, always refer to the tune-up decal or service manual for the exact procedure.

There is insufficient space available in

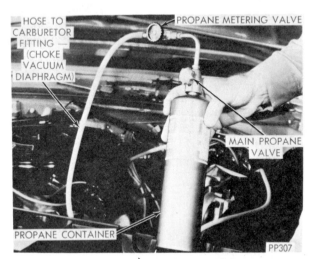

Fig. 24–3. Many vehicles require the use of this propane-enrichment tool to adjust idle mixture and speed. (Courtesy of Chrysler Corp.)

this chapter to explain all the propane-assisted mixture-adjustment procedures used by the various manufacturers. Consequently, this section will present one method used by the Ford Motor Company to familiarize you with the process.

To check and adjust the air/fuel mixture on a typical Ford vehicle, using propane enrichment, follow this procedure.

1. Disconnect the PCV inlet hose to the air cleaner. Then, cap or plug the air-cleaner fitting.

2. Disconnect the EEC purge hose from the air cleaner.

3. If specified on the decal tag, disconnect the air-injection supply hose from the check valve or from the diverter-valve outlet.

4. Connect a tachometer to the engine.

5. If the vehicle has a vacuum brake release, disconnect and plug its vacuum hose.

6. Set the parking brake and block the wheels.

7. Start and run the engine at fast idle until it reaches normal-operating temperature.

8. As indicated on the engine decal or in the service manual, adjust the idle speed to the normal slow idle or to a specified idle-mixture adjusting rpm.

9. As specified, place the transmission in neutral or drive.

10. Insert the adapter of the propane hose into the air-cleaner connection from which you removed the EEC hose. Then, close the propane metering valve and fully open the main propane valve.

11. While holding the propane bottle *upright*, slowly open the propane-metering valve until the engine reaches its highest idle rpm (the maximum rpm gain). Opening this valve any further causes engine speed to drop as the mixture becomes excessively rich.

Results and Indications

Compare the idle rpm gain to that listed on the tune-up decal or in the service manual. If the rpm increase is within specifications, remove the propane tool adapter from the air cleaner, and disconnect the tachometer from the engine. Then, remove the caps or plugs and reconnect all hoses removed under steps 1, 2, 3, and 5.

If the rpm gain is too high, adjust the mixture as follows:

1. Remove the air cleaner and plug any disconnected vacuum hoses.

2. As necessary, remove the idle-mixture screw limiter cap by prying it off carefully. Be careful not to damage the adjustment screw.

3. Start the engine and turn the mixture screw counterclockwise slowly and carefully to enrich the mixture. Continue this process until the rpm increases by the exact same amount that the test reading exceeded the specifications. For instance, if the rpm gain is supposed to be 40 rpm and the actual gain is 70, adjust the screw until the engine speed increases 30 rpm.

4. Reinstall the air cleaner and readjust the idle speed to specifications.

5. Using the propane tool, recheck the idle mixture.

6. If you removed the limiter caps, install new ones with their tangs resting against the full-rich stops (Fig. 24–4).

If the rpm gain is too low, adjust the mixture as follows.

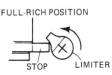

FULL-RICH POSITION
STOP   LIMITER

Fig. 24-4. The installation of a new limiter cap against its full-rich stop.

1. Remove the air cleaner, and plug any disconnected vacuum hoses.

2. As necessary, remove the idle-mixture screw limiter caps by prying them off carefully. Be careful not to damage the adjustment screws.

3. Start the engine and turn the mixture screws clockwise slowly and carefully to lean the mixture. Continue the process until the rpm drops by the same amount as the original rpm gain *was below the specified amount.* For example, if the rpm gain is 20 and should have been 50, adjust the mixture screws until the engine speed drops by 30 rpm.

4. Reinstall the air cleaner, and reset engine idle speed to specifications.

5. Recheck the idle mixture with the propane tool.

6. If you removed the limiter caps, install new caps with their tangs resting on the full lean stops (Fig. 24-5).

7. Remove the propane tool adapter from the air cleaner, and disconnect the tachometer from the engine. Then, remove the caps or plugs and reconnect any lines or hoses disconnected under steps 1,

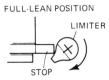

FULL-LEAN POSITION
LIMITER
STOP

Fig. 24-5. The installation of a new limiter cap against its full-lean stop.

2, 3, and 5 listed under the original propane test procedure.

Vacuum Pumps

Hand-Operated

Two common types of vacuum pumps are used for diagnostic purposes: the hand- and electrically operated assemblies.

The hand-operated vacuum pump and gauge assembly (Fig. 24-6) is a very useful tool for the tune-up technician. This device can test most types of vacuum-operated device such as a delay valve, vacuum motor, or vacuum-advance diaphragm with the unit on or off the vehicle. In addition, since the tool is hand-operated and therefore requires no electrical power, it provides the mechanic an easy and accurate method of checking vacuum devices not only in the shop but on a road call.

The portable pump shown in Fig. 24-6 consists of a vacuum gauge, vacuum pump, inlet and outlet ports, release trigger, along with a hand grip and pump handle. The vacuum gauge connects externally via a hose to the component being tested and internally to the vacuum pump. The dial scale of the gauge has readings ranging from 0 to 30 inches of Hg and 0 to 76 millimeters of Hg.

The vacuum pump is inside the main housing. The pump handle mechanically activates this pumping mechanism. It in turn evacuates the air from any component being tested, thus creating a vacuum.

This pump requires two valve-controlled ports: an inlet and outlet. The inlet

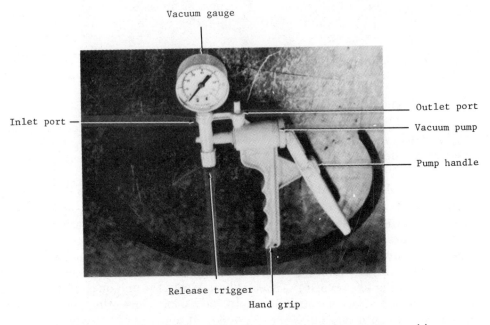

Fig. 24-6.   A hand-operated vacuum pump and gauge assembly.

port connects via a hose to the unit that you are testing. The outlet port, on the other hand, provides an opening for the pump directly into the atmosphere.

The release trigger has one important function. It vents all or part of any vacuum built up by the pump assembly into the atmosphere. In other words, by coordinating the movements of the pump handle and trigger, the operator can easily pump up a *specific* amount of vacuum within a unit, with this piece of equipment.

The hand grip and handle merely provides a means by which the mechanic can hold and activate the pump assembly. The palm of the mechanic's hand fits over the pump handle, with the fingers encircling the hand grip. This construction permits ease of control with one hand, leaving the other free to perform other tasks.

Electrically Operated Vacuum Pumps

Most distributor machines and some engine analyzers also have a vacuum test device on its console. In other words, these machines have a built-in vacuum pump, vacuum gauge, and necessary controls to operate the pump for testing vacuum components. This form of vacuum pump assembly performs the same function as the hand-operated unit but requires electrical power to operate.

Testing Exhaust Emission Control Devices

As mentioned in the last chapter, a large number of exhaust emission control devices are used on automobiles. The number, type, and design of these devices depend largely on the particular manufacturer, the vehicle's engine size, type, plus the year model of the vehicle. Consequently, when testing a particular emission device, it is necessary to use factory instructions and specifications.

For this reason, this chapter presents only samples of typical procedures in order to familiarize you with them. The procedures included in this section are testing of a choke-delay valve, thermostatically controlled air cleaner, dual-diaphragm distributor, spark-delay valve, OSAC valve, TSC system, air injection sytem, EGR system, and catalytic converters.

Testing a Choke Delay Valve

To test a typical choke delay valve, as found on some late-model Ford engines:

1. Remove the valve from the vacuum line between the intake manifold and the choke vacuum diaphragm or piston.

2. Connect a hand-operated vacuum pump to the manifold side of the valve and a vacuum gauge to the other (Fig. 24–7).

3. With the vacuum pump, apply 10 inches of vacuum to the valve. Then, note the number of seconds necessary for the second vacuum gauge to indicate the 10-inch reading.

4. Compare this time delay in seconds to factory specifications. Replace the valve if the delay period is not within factory tolerances.

Testing a Typical Thermostatically Controlled Air Cleaner

To test a thermostatically controlled air cleaner, follow these instructions.

1. Make sure that all vacuum hoses and the heat stove-to-air cleaner flexible connections are attached and in good condition.

2. Remove the air cleaner cover. Then, tape a thermometer next to the air-cleaner sensor (Fig. 24–8). The tape holds the thermometer alongside the sensor and prevents engine vacuum from pulling it into the air horn.

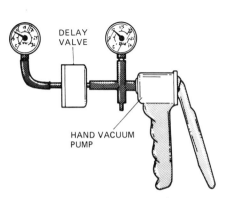

Fig. 24–7. Testing a typical external choke-delay valve.

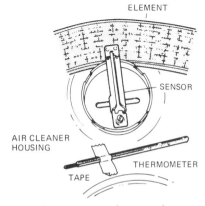

Fig. 24–8. Testing the air-cleaner sensor operation with a thermometer.

3. Replace the air-cleaner cover, but do not install its wing nut.

4. With the engine shut off, observe the heat-control door (damper) position through the snorkel opening. The snorkel passage should be open to the air cleaner element (Fig. 24–9). If not, check for binds in the linkage.

5. Start and idle the engine. With the air temperature below about 85°F., the heat-control door within the snorkel should be up or in the heat-on position (Fig. 24–10).

6. When the damper door begins to move down to open the snorkel passage, remove the air-cleaner cover and observe the thermometer reading. It should be between 85°F. and 115°F.

Testing the Vacuum Motor Diaphragm

If the damper door does not close completely or does not open at the correct temperature, check the vacuum motor as follows.

1. Turn off the engine. Next, disconnect the vacuum line from the diaphragm.

2. Connect the hose of a portable vacuum pump to the diaphragm fitting (Fig. 24–11). Then, apply 20 inches of vacuum to the diaphragm. The diaphragm should not lose more than 10 inches of vacuum in 5 minutes.

3. Bleed off the vacuum from the hand pump. Next, apply 5 inches of vacuum to

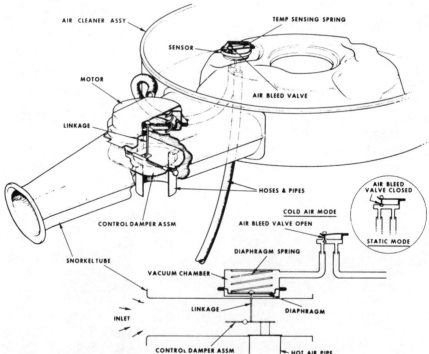

Fig. 24-9. Position of the control damper door with the engine shut off.
(Courtesy of United Delco)

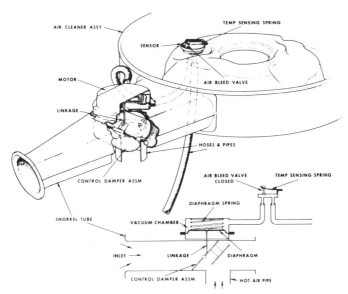

Fig. 24-10. Position of the damper door with the engine operating with an underhood temperature of less than 85°F. (Courtesy of United Delco)

the diaphragm while observing the damper door. It should begin to lift from the bottom of the snorkel.

4. Increase the vacuum on the diaphragm between 9 to 10 inches. The damper door should move to the full-up position.

5. If the vacuum diaphragm does not perform adequately, replace it following the steps outlined later in this chapter, and recheck air-cleaner operation.

6. Should the vacuum diaphragm operate satisfactorily, replace the sensor, as explained later in this chapter, in order

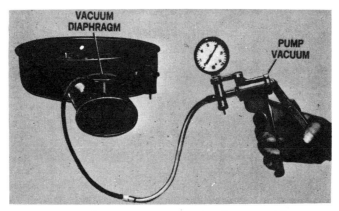

Fig. 24-11. Testing the vacuum motor diaphragm with a vacuum pump. (Courtesy of Chrysler Corp.)

to correct the damper-door malfunction. Then, recheck the operation of the unit as outlined earlier in this section.

Removing and Replacing the Vacuum Motor Diaphragm

To replace a typical vacuum motor diaphragm:

1. Remove the air-cleaner assembly from the engine and disassemble it.

2. Disconnect the vacuum hose from the vacuum motor diaphragm fitting. Then, tip the diaphragm slightly forward to disengage its lock and rotate counter-clockwise.

3. When the diaphragm is free from the snorkel, slide the entire assembly to one side in order to disengage its operating rod from the heat-control damper door (Fig. 24–12).

4. With the vacuum diaphragm assembly removed, check the damper door for freedom of operation. When the door is in the up position, it should fall freely when released. If it does not, check the door-to-snorkel side walls for interference by foreign material. Also, check the hinge pin

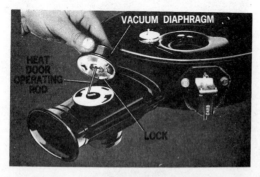

Fig. 24–12. Removing the vacuum-motor diaphragm assembly from the air-cleaner snorkel. (Courtesy of Chrysler Corp.)

for foreign matter. If interference exists, use compressed air to blow the material out of the affected areas.

5. Insert the operating rod of a new diaphragm assembly into the damper door.

6. Position the tangs of the diaphragm assembly into their respective openings in the snorkel. Next, turn the diaphragm assembly clockwise until its lock engages.

7. With a vacuum pump, apply 9 to 10 inches of vacuum to the diaphragm assembly fitting (Fig. 24–11). The damper door should move freely to the full-up (heat-on) position. *Note:* Do not operate the damper door manually because this can cock the rod and diaphragm, which restricts the normal movement of the door.

8. Assemble the air cleaner, and install it on the engine. Then, retest the operation of the damper door to make sure that it opens at the correct temperature.

Removing and Replacing the Air-Cleaner Temperature Sensor

Follow these instructions for replacing a typical temperature sensor.

1. Remove the air cleaner from the engine and disassemble it.

2. Disconnect the vacuum hoses from the sensor fitting. Then, remove the sensor's retaining clips (Fig. 24–13).

3. Remove the sensor and gasket.

4. Position a new gasket onto the air-cleaner housing and install the new sensor (Fig. 24–14).

5. While supporting the sensor on its outer diameter, install two new retaining

Fig. 24-13.   Removing the sensor retaining clips. (Courtesy of Chrysler Corp.)

Fig. 24-14.   Installing a new sensor in the air cleaner. (Courtesy of Chrysler Corp.)

clips securely, making sure that the gasket compresses to form an airtight seal. *Note:* Do not support the sensor by its guard during this process. This can damage the bimetallic strip.

6. Install the vacuum hoses onto the sensor fitting. Then, reassemble the air cleaner.

7. Install the air cleaner onto the engine and test damper door operation.

Testing a Dual-Diaphragm Vacuum-Advance Distributor

To test both the advance and retard diaphragms of a distributor with a dual-purpose vacuum advance:

1. Following the manufacturer's recommendations, connect both a timing light and tachometer to the engine.

2. Remove and plug both vacuum hoses to the distributor.

3. Clean off the timing marks on both the crankshaft pulley and timing flange. Then, go over the specified timing marks to brighten them with white chalk.

4. Operate the engine at the recommended timing rpm and observe the initial (basic) timing (Fig. 24-15). As necessary, readjust the timing to the manufacturer's specifications.

5. Unplug and connect the intake manifold vacuum hose to the inner (rear) vacuum chamber fitting, and then observe the timing setting with the timing light. The timing should immediately retard usually 5 to 10 degrees from the basic timing specifications (Fig. 24-16). If

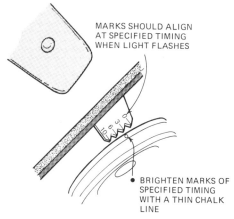

MARKS SHOULD ALIGN AT SPECIFIED TIMING WHEN LIGHT FLASHES

BRIGHTEN MARKS OF SPECIFIED TIMING WITH A THIN CHALK LINE

Fig. 24-15.   Checking initial timing with a timing light.

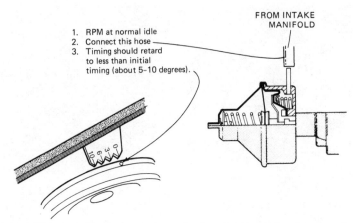

1. RPM at normal idle
2. Connect this hose
3. Timing should retard
   to less than initial
   timing (about 5-10 degrees).

FROM INTAKE
MANIFOLD

Fig. 24-16.   Testing the vacuum retard side of a dual-diaphragm distributor.

the rear diaphragm fails to retard the timing the number of degrees specified by the manufacturer, the distributor vacuum unit is defective and requires replacement. *Note:* You can test the diaphragm at this point to verify a leaky diaphragm with a vacuum pump.

6. Adjust engine rpm to 2,000.

7. While checking the timing with the light, unplug and connect the carburetor vacuum hose to the outer (advance) diaphragm. The timing should immediately advance (Fig. 24-17). If not, a problem exists either in the advance diaphragm or in the distributor. In this situation, check the diaphragm for leakage with a vacuum

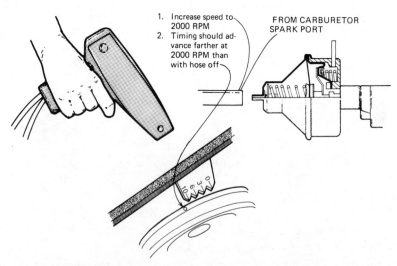

1. Increase speed to
   2000 RPM
2. Timing should advance farther at
   2000 RPM than
   with hose off

FROM CARBURETOR
SPARK PORT

Fig. 24-17.   Checking the advance portion of a dual-diaphragm distributor.

pump, and the distributor for a stuck breaker plate.

8. Return the engine to the normal hot-idle setting, and recheck the timing with the light. The timing should retard in the same manner as during step 5.

Servicing and Testing Vacuum-Advance (Spark) Delay Valves

Some manufacturers recommend that the spark-delay valve be replaced at regular intervals, such as every 12,000 vehicle miles or 12 months. In addition, since the spark delay must vary with different engine applications, the valve has color-coding for identification. Therefore, when replacing a valve, it is important that the new valve be the same color as the original.

If you suspect a delay valve is malfunctioning, you can test it following this procedure.

1. Remove the carburetor vacuum hose from the valve. Then, connect a hand-operated vacuum pump to this valve fitting.

2. Remove the hose from the opposite end of the valve, and connect the hose from a vacuum gauge to this fitting (Fig. 24–18).

3. Apply 15 inches of vacuum to the valve with the hand pump.

4. Note the vacuum reading on the gauge connected into the opposite end of the valve. Depending on specifications, the needle should rise a given amount in the specified number of seconds. If it does not, the valve is defective and requires replacement.

5. Reverse the pump and gauge connections on the valve in order to check the valve's release operation. After applying 15 inches of vacuum, the second gauge reading should rise immediately. If not, the valve is defective and requires replacement.

Testing an OSAC Valve

The OSAC valve on a Chrysler automobile may be on the firewall or air cleaner. To test this valve on the vehicle (Fig. 24–19):

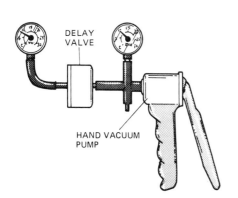

Fig. 24–18. Testing a spark-delay valve.

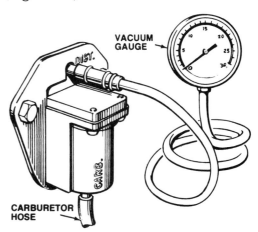

Fig. 24–19. Testing an OSAC valve.

1. Remove the distributor vacuum hose from the OSAC valve. Then, connect the hose from a vacuum gauge over the DIST. fitting on the valve.

2. Start the engine and permit it to reach normal operating temperature.

3. Set the parking brake, and operate the engine at 2,000 rpm in neutral.

4. Observe the needle on the vacuum gauge. The valve is operating properly if you observe a very gradual rise in vacuum. It perhaps requires 20 seconds for vacuum to obtain a stabilized level, depending on the engine and vehicle.

Results and Indications

1. If the vacuum reading immediately increases to the same level as manifold vacuum, the OSAC valve is defective and requires replacement. *Note:* If the valve has a temperature-override feature, it should permit an immediate vacuum increase below 60°F. Therefore, heat and cool the temperature-sensing portion of the valve in order to check its operation

above and below 60°F. before condemning the valve.

2. If no increase in vacuum occurs on the gauge at any time, the valve is defective and requires replacement.

Testing a Typical TCS System

You can check the operation of a transmission-controlled spark system following this procedure (Fig. 24-20).

1. Check all vacuum hoses and electrical wiring for proper routing, connection to their respective units, and damage. Repair or replace any damaged components.

2. Tee a vacuum gauge into the vacuum hose at the distributor vacuum advance.

3. Raise and block the rear wheels of the vehicle off the ground, or place the vehicle on a dynamometer.

4. Start the engine and permit it to run

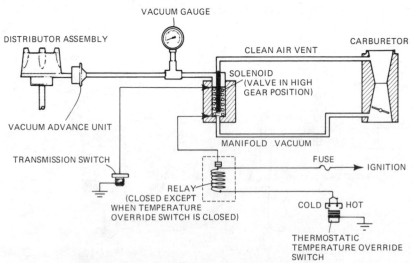

Fig. 24-20.   Testing a typical TCS system.

at slightly above idle speed at the normal operating temperature, and with the transmission in neutral or park.

5. Observe the vacuum gauge. A zero reading indicates the TCS system is functioning properly at this point.

6. Place the transmission in gear; while observing the vacuum gauge, speed up the engine until the transmission is in high gear.

Results and Indications

1. The vacuum reading at the distributor should be zero with the transmission in first and second gear, but it should immediately rise to indicate manifold vacuum as the transmission reaches third or its highest gear ratio. If not, check the transmission switch for continuity, between its electrical terminal and ground, with an ohmmeter.

2. If the transmission switch checks out, connect a jumper lead to the positive battery terminal. Then, apply power directly to the vacuum solenoid positive or ignition switch terminal. With the engine running at curb idle, there should be a full manifold vacuum reading on the gauge. If no vacuum appears on the gauge, check to see if there is vacuum in the hose leading into the vacuum solenoid valve before diagnosing the valve as failed.

Testing a Typical Air-Injection System with an Infrared Analyzer

You can test the overall effectiveness of an air injection system with an infrared analyzer. To peform this check:

1. Start the engine and bring it to normal operating temperature.

2. As outlined earlier in this chapter, calibrate the infrared analyzer. Then, insert its sampling probe into the tailpipe.

3. Set the idle-speed screw on a step of the fast-idle cam that operates the engine at about 1,000 rpm.

4. Depress the test mode selector button on the analyzer, and then note the HC and CO readings.

5. While maintaining the same engine speed, disconnect the air supply hose leading from the air pump to the exhaust manifold.

6. Again note the HC and CO reading on the analyzer. An increase in HC and CO level indications should occur with the hose disconnected if the system is functioning properly. If the analyzer shows little or no increase in HC and CO readings, examine all the components of the air injection system as follows.

Checking Air Injection System Components

Drive Belt

1. Inspect the pump drive belt for wear, cracks, or deterioration. Replace it as necessary.

2. Check the tension of the belt (Fig. 24-21), using a strain tension gauge. Then, adjust belt tension as necessary. *Note:* Belt settings vary slightly between different system manufacturers. However, a typical setting for a used belt is 55 pounds and for a new belt, 75 pounds.

Air Injection Pump

To check the injection pump:

1. Start the engine and permit it to reach the normal operating temperature.

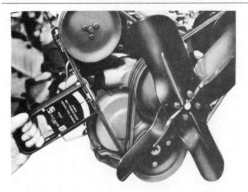

Fig. 24–21. Testing belt tension with a strain gauge. (Courtesy of General Motors Corp.)

2. Set the parking brake and place the transmission in park or neutral.

3. Shut off the engine and remove the outlet hose from the air pump.

4. Start the engine and slowly accelerate it to approximately 1,500 rpm while feeling the air flow from the pump's outlet port.

Results and Indications

If the air flow increases as the engine accelerates, the pump is operating satisfactorily. However, if the air flow does not increase or is not present or the pump is noisy, proceed as follows.

1. Check the belt for proper tension.

2. Check for a leaky pressure relief valve (on pumps so equipped). Air may be heard leaking out of the valve with the pump operating.

3. If belt tension is satisfactory and the relief valve is not leaking, remove the pump for overhaul or replacement.

4. To determine if excessive noise is the fault of the air pump, operate the engine with the pump drive belt removed. *Note:* The air pump is not a completely noiseless

unit. Under normal conditions, its noise level increases slightly in pitch as the engine accelerates. Consequently, before replacing a pump for excessive noise, make sure that it has operated in excess of the 100 mile break-in period. In addition, make certain that pump alignment and mounting are correct. *Caution:* Do not introduce oil into the air pump. This may quiet the pump for a little while, but it does not fix the problem permanently and eventually leads to premature pump failure.

5. If pump alignment and mounting are correct and the pump produces excessive noise, remove it for repair or replacement.

Diverter Valve

1. Inspect the condition and routing of all lines to the valve, especially the vacuum signal line. All lines must be secure, without crimps, and not leaking.

2. Disconnect the vacuum signal line at the diverter valve. Then, start the engine.

3. Check for a vacuum signal at the end of the disconnected line (Fig. 24–22).

4. Reconnect the vacuum hose to the diverter valve. Next, check for air escaping through the diverter valve muffler, with the engine rpm stabilized at idle.

5. Manually open and quickly close the carburetor throttle valve. At this point, a momentary blast of air should discharge through the diverter muffler for at least 1 second (Fig. 24–23).

6. If no air discharges from the muffler, replace the valve because it is not internally serviceable. *Note:* Although diverter valves sometimes are similar in appearance, their design is such that a particular valve fits the requirements of a given engine. Therefore, always use the

Fig. 24-22. *Checking for a vacuum signal at the end of the diverter valve vacuum line. (Courtesy of United Delco)*

correct valve when a replacement is necessary.

Air Manifolds and Hoses

1. Check all the hoses for holes or deterioration.

2. Inspect all injection manifolds for holes or cracks.

3. Check all the hose and manifold connections.

Fig. 24-23. *Testing diverter valve operation. (Courtesy of United Delco)*

4. Check all the routing of the hoses. Any interference between the hoses and any object may cause wear.

5. If you suspect a leak on the pressure side of the system, check the involved component or connection with a soapy water connection (Fig. 24-24). With the air pump operating, bubbles form if a leak exists. However, be careful to keep the soapy water solution away from the centrifugal filter of the pump.

6. If any hose is found defective, replace it. *Note:* Manufacturers form air hoses of special high-temperature material. Therefore, if a hose requires replacement, use only the proper type hose.

Check Valve

You should inspect a valve whenever it is necessary to disconnect the hose from the valve or when you suspect that the valve has failed. A check valve failure is obvious when an inoperative air pump shows signs of exhaust gases passing through it.

Fig. 24-24. *Testing a hose connection for leaks. (Courtesy of United Delco)*

Fig. 24-25. The normal direction of air flow through a check valve. (Courtesy of General Motors Corp.)

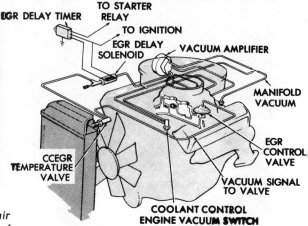

Fig. 24-26. Inspecting and testing a typical EGR system. (Courtesy of Chrysler Corp.)

To check a valve, orally blow through it toward the air manifold; then, attempt to suck back through the valve. Normal air flow should be in one direction only—toward the air manifold (Fig. 24-25).

Air Injection Tubes

There is no periodic inspection or service for the air injection tubes. However, when necessary to remove the cylinder heads or exhaust manifolds from the engine, inspect all the tubes for carbon build-up and for warpage or burned holes.

To service the exposed tubes, remove any carbon buildup with a wire brush. If any of the tubes is warped or burned out, replace it or, as necessary, the entire air-injection manifold assembly.

Inspecting a Typical EGR System

A typical EGR system requires a complete inspection and testing, on an average of every 12,000 miles or 12 months, in order to assure proper function of the system. When inspecting the system (Fig. 24-26):

1. Check all hoses and connections between the carburetor intake manifold, EGR control valve, vacuum amplifier, EGR delay solenoid, and temperature valve. Replace any hoses that appear hardened or cracked or have faulty connections. *Note:* When replacing several hoses to a single unit, it is a good idea to disconnect one hose at a time and immediately replace it with the new one. This action prevents you from connecting the new hoses to the wrong fittings.

2. Check that all valves and gaskets are in their proper position and not damaged. Repair and replace damaged components as necessary.

Testing an EGR Control System and Valve

To operationally check the EGR control system and valve, follow this procedure.

1. Start the engine and permit it to reach normal operating temperature.

2. With the engine idling in neutral, rapidly accelerate it to approximately 2,000 rpm but not over 3,000 rpm.

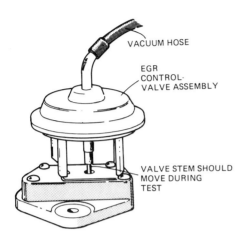

Fig. 24-27. *Checking the operation of the EGR control system and valve.*

VACUUM HOSE

EGR CONTROL-VALVE ASSEMBLY

VALVE STEM SHOULD MOVE DURING TEST

3. Observe the EGR valve stem (Fig. 24-27). Visible movement of the EGR valve stem should occur during this procedure, which you can determine by the change in the relative position of the groove on the EGR valve stem.

4. Repeat the procedure several times to confirm stem movement.

Results and Indications

1. Movement of the stem indicates the control system is functioning correctly.

2. If the preceding check or a driver complaint points to faulty operation of the system, use the service diagnosis chart (Table 24-1) to determine the problem area.

Testing the EGR Valve and Passages

If the control system functions properly, you should test the EGR valve and passages for exhaust gas flow. To perform this check:

1. Connect a tachometer to the engine.

2. Start the engine and permit it to reach normal operating temperature.

3. Disconnect the vacuum hose to the EGR valve, and insert over its fitting the hose from a hand-operated vacuum pump.

4. With the engine idling in neutral, apply a vacuum signal of 10 inches to the EGR valve.

5. Note the rpm on the tachometer.

Results and Indications

1. Idle speed should drop 150 rpm or more with the vacuum signal applied. This rpm drop confirms that exhaust gas recirculation is taking place.

2. If the speed change does not occur or is less than the specified minimum, there are exhaust deposits in the EGR valve or intake manifold passages. In this situation, it is necessary to remove the EGR valve, inspect and clean its passages along with those within the intake manifold.

EGR Valve Service

If the previously mentioned tests or diagnosis indicate that the EGR valve may have excessive deposit buildup, remove the valve from the engine. Then, inspect the condition of the poppet valve and seat area. If the deposits exceed a thin film, clean the EGR valve using this process.

1. Apply a liberal amount of manifold heat control valve solvent to the poppet valve and seat area. *Note:* Exercise extreme care when applying the solvent so as not to spill any of it on the diaphragm, as this may cause diaphragm failure.

Table 24-1
EGR SERVICE DIAGNOSIS CHART

Condition	Possible Cause	Correction
EGR valve stem does not move on system test.	a. Cracked, leaking, disconnected or plugged hoses.	a. Verify correct hose connections and the leak check to confirm that all the hoses are open. If defective hoses are found, replace them.
	b. Defective EGR valve, ruptured diaphragm, or valve stem frozen.	b. Disconnect the hose from the EGR valve. Connect external vacuum source, and 10 inches of Hg or greater, to the valve diaphragm. If no valve movement occurs, replace the valve. If the valve opens, approximately 1/8-inch travel, pinch off the supply hose to check for diaphragm leakage. Valve should remain open 30 seconds or longer. If leakage occurs, replace the valve.
EGR valve stem does not move on system test, operates normally on external vacuum source.	a. Defective CCEGR valve.	a. Bypass valve so that the amplifier is connected directly to the EGR valve. If normal operation of the EGR valve stem is restored, replace the CCEGR valve.
	b. Defective controls system—plugged passages.	b. **Ported-vacuum control system:** Remove the carburetor and inspect the port (slot type) in the throttle bore and associated vacuum passages in the carburetor throttle body, including limiting orifice at the hose end of passages. Use suitable solvent to remove the deposits and check for flow with light air pressure. Normal operation should be restored to the ported-vacuum control EGR system.
	c. Defective vacuum control unit (amplifier).	c. **Venturi-vacuum control system:** Remove the venturi signal hose from the nipple on carburetor. With the engine operating at

Condition	Possible Cause	Correction
		idle, apply a vacuum of 1 to 2 inches of Hg to the venturi signal hose. (On models having the EGR delay system, remove the hose from delay solenoid and apply 1 to 2 inches of vacuum to the hose.) Engine speed should drop a minimum of 150 rpm and the EGR valve stem should visibly move 1/8 inch or more. If this does not occur, replace the vacuum control unit.
	d. Plugged carburetor venturi signal passage.	d. If the vacuum control unit (amplifier), operates normally in previous test, a plugged vacuum tap to carburetor venturi is indicated. Use suitable carburetor solvent to remove the deposits from the passage and use light air pressure to verify that the passage is clear.
	e. Defective EGR delay system.	e. Disconnect the electrical connection to the solenoid and repeat system test. If the valve stem moves, reconnect the solenoid and disconnect timer. Repeat system test and observe the valve stem. If there is no movement, replace the solenoid. If there is movement, replace the timer.
Engine will not idle, dies out on return to idle, or idle is very rough or slow.	a. Control system defective—EGR valve open.	a. Disconnect the hose from the EGR valve and plug hose—recheck idle. If satisfactory, replace the vacuum control unit (amplifier).
	b. High EGR valve leakage in the closed position.	b. If vacuum hose removal does not correct, remove the EGR valve and inspect to ensure the poppet is seated. Clean out the deposits if necessary, or replace the valve if found defective.

(cont.)

Table 24–1
EGR SERVICE DIAGNOSIS CHART (Cont.)

Condition	Possible Cause	Correction
Weak wide-open throttle performance.	a. Defective vacuum control unit (amplifier).	a. Disconnect the hose from the EGR valve and plug the hose. Road test the vehicle; if performance is restored, replace the vacuum control unit.
At ambients below 55°F. vehicle exhibits poor driveability and choke loading characteristics.	a. Leaking CCEGR valve.	a. Leak test and if necessary replace the CCEGR valve.
At ambients below 55° before thermostat opens, vehicle idles roughly or stalls on return to idle after steady speed driving.	a. Leaking CCEGR valve.	a. Leak test and if necessary replace the CCEGR valve.
On starting, engine runs up, then stalls on return to idle.	a. Vacuum hose connections to the EGR delay solenoid made improperly.	a. Connect the hoses properly as shown in the appropriate hose routing figure.
Vehicle surges, hesitates or stalls on attempt to drive away after 1–3 hour cool-down.	a. Defective EGR delay system.	a. Test the delay system and if malfunction replace the appropriate component.

2. Allow the solvent about 30 minutes to soften up the deposits.

3. Connect a hand vacuum pump hose to the diaphragm fitting, and apply sufficient vacuum to open the poppet valve fully. *Note:* Do not push on the diaphragm to open the valve; use a vacuum source only.

4. Use a sharp edge tool to scrape carefully the loosened deposits from the poppet valve and seat. *Note:* If after cleaning the valve you notice excessive wear on the stem, valve, or seat, replace the assembly.

5. Using a new gasket, replace the EGR valve on the engine. Then, torque its mounting screws to 10 foot-pounds.

6. Connect the vacuum line to the valve, and test the system as outlined earlier.

Catalytic Converters— Factors Reducing Service Life

Federal laws require that a catalytic converter provide at least 50,000 miles of use before service is necessary. However, certain factors reduce the life of the converter and require its replacement or servicing. Other than physical damage, these factors include the use of the wrong fuel, poor engine condition, or improper service procedures.

Unleaded Fuel

Vehicles with catalytic converters must utilize an unleaded fuel. The lead additives in leaded fuel greatly reduce the efficiency of the catalyst. The lead itself plates the catalyst to form a coating that prevents the exhaust gas pollutants from reaching and therefore reacting with the catalyst. Consequently, the continuous use of a leaded fuel eventually causes the converter catalyst to lose its ability to promote the oxidation of HC and CO compounds.

Even in a situation of the emergency use of leaded fuel in a vehicle, the converter sustains some damage. The return to the use of unleaded fuel permits the converter to regain some, but not all, of its efficiency. In reality, how much efficiency the converter does regain depends on how long the leaded fuel was used. The problem in dealing with this particular situation is that there is no known procedure for testing the remaining converter efficiency.

Engine Condition

Proper engine condition and maintenance are necessary to prevent overheating the catalyst. Excessively high catalyst temperature reduces the converter's service life. On the average, converters operate well at internal temperature up to 1,500°F. However, at temperatures above this, the catalyst begins to melt or break up.

When any engine is in poor mechanical condition or requires a tune-up, the exhaust gas passing into the converter will contain excessive amounts of hydrocarbons. These excessive amounts of HC change the converter into a catalytic furnace, where the temperatures are high enough to destroy the catalyst.

Even when an engine is in good condition and tuned properly, its improper use can create excessive converter temperature. For instance, operating the engine at idle for long periods is one of the worst operating conditions for converter life. At prolonged idle, the engine develops more heat than at normal highway speeds. Therefore, never operate an engine with a converter more than about 10 minutes, at idle, at a time.

Service Precautions

To prevent fuel vapors from reaching the converter and causing high temperatures during vehicle maintenance, follow these general rules.

1. Use an oscilloscope, if available, for isolating misfiring cylinders, instead of shorting or removing spark plug wires from an operating engine.

2. If an oscilloscope is not available, never operate an engine more than 30 seconds with one spark plug wire removed or shorted.

3. Do not crank an engine over for more than 60 seconds when flooded or firing intermittently. In the case of a flooded engine, repair the cause of the flooding condition first. Then, dry out the engine as necessary before starting, by removing the spark plugs.

4. Never operate the engine more than 10 minutes at idle.

5. Do not attempt to start a vehicle with a standard transmission by pushing

it. Instead, use a spare battery and jumper cables.

6. With a vehicle in motion, never turn off the ignition switch.

7. Always repair substandard operating conditions such as dieseling, heavy surging, backfiring, or repeated stalling. These conditions can lead to premature converter failure.

Converter Inspections

To check converter condition physically:

1. Inspect it for physical damage such as a ripped skin or a crushed shell.

2. Inspect for holes or damage to the exhaust pipe leading to the converter.

3. Examine the tailpipe. Pellets coming out of the tailpipe are an indication that the internal stainless-steel basket assembly containing the pellets is breaking up.

4. If the outside of the converter shows damage or pellets are emitting from the tailpipe, replace the converter.

Testing the Converter

There is no accurate method to test the efficiency of a catalytic converter. However, you can check a converter for restrictions and to see if it is reducing HC and CO emissions by following these recommended procedures.

1. Attach a vacuum gauge to the engine. Then, test the converter for restrictions in the same manner as you would for a plugged exhaust system. Chapter 5 explains this test in detail. If the converter has a restriction, replace it.

2. Calibrate an infrared analyzer and insert its probe into the vehicle's tailpipe.

3. Thoroughly tune the engine, making

all the operational adjustments necessary to meet manufacturer's as well as the appropriate emission control specifications.

4. After making all the required adjustments, check the HC and CO levels on the infrared analyzer. If the engine along with the ignition, fuel, and emission control systems are functioning properly but the analyzer still indicates HC and CO levels that are still too high, the catalytic converter is most likely defective and requires replacement or servicing.

Catalytic Converter Service

If a pellet-type converter, such as made by AC-Delco and used by GM and AMC, is no longer reducing HC and CO emissions, you can refill it with a new charge of catalyst. However, the monolithic converters used by Ford and Chrysler are not serviceable and require replacement. To service a typical pellet-type converter:

1. Raise the vehicle on a hoist.

2. Attach an aspirator (Fig. 24-28) to the vehicle's tailpipe. If the vehicle has

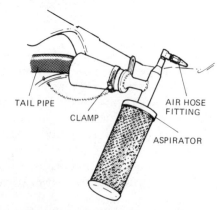

TAIL PIPE   AIR HOSE
                     FITTING
     CLAMP
                 ASPIRATOR

Fig. 24-28. Attaching an aspirator to the tailpipe.

a dual-exhaust system, plug the other tailpipe.

3. Connect a compressed air-line coupling to the fitting on the aspirator. This action creates a vacuum within the converter that holds the pellets in position.

4. Remove the catalytic converter's drain-and-fill plug:

   a. For a pressed-in plug, drive a small chisel between the plug and the converter shell to deform it. Next, remove the plug with a pair of pliers.

   b. For a threaded plug, use a 3/4-inch hex wrench to remove it.

5. Clamp the vibrator and catalyst container into position over the converter fill opening (Fig. 24–29). *Note:* A special adapter is necessary if the converter had a pressed-in plug.

6. Disconnect the compressed air-line coupling from the aspirator and snap it in place on the fitting of the vibrator. This

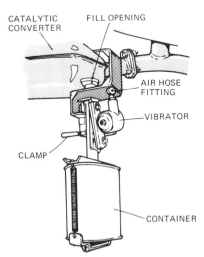

CATALYTIC CONVERTER

FILL OPENING

AIR HOSE FITTING

VIBRATOR

CLAMP

CONTAINER

Fig. 24–29. Attaching the vibrator and catalyst container in place over the converter fill opening.

action drains the catalyst pellets from the converter housing.

7. After the process removes all the pellets from the converter, disconnect the air-line coupling. Then, remove the container from the vibrator unit.

8. Dispose of the used catalyst pellets.

9. Fill the container with the new replacement catalyst pellets.

10. Intall the fill-tube extension to the vibrator unit. *Note:* An adapter is necessary on those converter types, using a press-in plug.

11. Connect a compressed air-line coupling to both the vibrator unit and the aspirator.

12. Connect the catalyst container to the vibrator unit.

13. Turn on the air supply. The pellets will move and pack themselves into the converter housing.

14. When the vibrator container is empty, disconnect the air line at the vibrator.

15. Remove the vibrator unit. Then, make sure that all the catalyst from the container has entered the converter, and it is full.

16. Wipe the threaded fill plug with an antisieze compound. Next, thread it into the converter housing, and torque it to specifications. *Note:* A special service plug with a bridge is necessary, with the converters originally equipped with a pressed-in plug. Torque this plug also to specifications.

17. Disconnect the air-line coupling from the aspirator, and remove it from the tailpipe.

18. Lower the vehicle sufficiently to start the engine. Then, check the converter drain plug for leaks.

19. Remove the vehicle from the hoist.

20. Using an infrared analyzer, check the vehicle for the specified HC and CO emissions.

Review

This section will assist you in determining how well you remember the material in this chapter. Read each item carefully. If you can't complete the statement, review the section in the chapter that covers the material.

1. The instrument that measures the amount of HC and CO in a vehicle's exhaust is the _____
_____.
   a. vacuum gauge
   b. vacuum pump
   c. infrared analyzer
   d. compression tester

2. In order to measure a vehicle's HC and CO emissions, the analyzer takes in samples of the exhaust and ____
_____ _____.
   a. bottled oxygen
   b. shop air
   c. bottled nitrogen
   d. bottled propane

3. After completing a test with an infrared analyzer, you should always depress the off or the _____ button.
   a. zero
   b. span
   c. hi
   d. lo

4. A high CO level reading at idle indicates
   a. a rich air/fuel mixture
   b. low compression
   c. a misfiring spark plug
   d. a defective plug wire

5. When performing an accelerator pump test with an infrared analyzer, the _____ level should increase.
   a. CO_2
   b. NOx
   c. HC
   d. CO

6. Propane enrichment is necessary when making idle-mixture adjustments on vehicles with a(an) _____
_____ _____.
   a. PCV system
   b. EEC system
   c. catalytic converter
   d. air pump

7. Artificial-enrichment idle-mixture adjustment requires injecting _____ _____ into the carburetor.
   a. oxygen
   b. propane
   c. nitrogen
   d. diesel

8. If, during the artificial enrichment, idle-mixture adjustment procedure, the engine rpm gain is below specifications, _____ the air/fuel mixture.
   a. lean
   b. enrich
   c. decrease
   d. increase

9. To test a choke- or spark-delay valve, a vacuum gauge and a _____ _____ are necessary.
   a. infrared analyzer
   b. vacuum pump
   c. compression tester
   d. engine analyzer

10. When testing the vacuum motor of a thermostatic air cleaner, it should begin to open as you apply _____ inches of vacuum to the diaphragm.

a. 2
b. 5
c. 8
d. 11

11. To check the operation of a dual-diaphragm vacuum advance requires the use of a tachometer and a(an) _____ _____.
    a. compression tester
    b. engine analyzer
    c. timing light
    d. vacuum gauge

12. With the engine at normal operating temperature, an OSAC valve should delay spark advance for about _____ seconds.
    a. 14
    b. 16
    c. 18
    d. 20

13. You can use a(an) _____ _____ to test the operation of an air injection system.
    a. infrared analyzer
    b. vacuum gauge
    c. compression tester
    d. engine analyzer

14. When installing a new air-pump drive belt, adjust its tension to _____ pounds.
    a. 65
    b. 75

c. 85
d. 95

15. A typical EGR system requires inspecting and testing on an average of every 12 months or _____ miles.
    a. 4,000
    b. 8,000
    c. 12,000
    d. 16,000

16. Federal laws require that a catalytic converter provide at least _____ miles of service.
    a. 50,000
    b. 40,000
    c. 30,000
    d. 20,000

17. Catalytic converters operate well with internal temperatures up to _____ °F.
    a. 700
    b. 1,000
    c. 13,000
    d. 15,000

18. Test a catalytic converter for restrictions with a _____ _____.
    a. compression tester
    b. engine analyzer
    c. vacuum gauge
    d. infrared analyzer

For the answers, turn to the Appendix.

Function

The tune-up technician must be very familiar with and competent in the use of various forms of test equipment. With the aid of this equipment, the technician can perform two very important tasks. For instance, the test instruments when properly used quickly pinpoint malfunctions within the engine and the ignition, fuel, electrical, and emission control systems. In other words, these machines rapidly decrease the period of time necessary to locate a problem area and reduce completely guesswork as to the cause of a malfunction. In addition, this same equipment is an excellent quality control tool. That is, the machines inform the technician (1) if the completed work corrected a given problem and (2) if the engine along with its various systems is performing to specifications, after the completion of a tune-up.

Types of Test Equipment

The two basic types of test equipment used by tune-up technicians, other than those previously described in this text, are the engine analyzer and the dynamometer. The *engine analyzer* (Fig. 25–1) is the actual piece of equipment used to test the condition of the engine as well as the ignition, fuel, electrical, and emission control systems. Since this analyzer performs so many functions, it must as a consequence have many types of instruments mounted in its console. These instruments include such items as the oscilloscope, voltmeter, ohmmeter, ammeter, dwell meter, tachometer, vacuum gauge, along with an HC and CO meter.

Chapter 25

TUNE-UP
TEST
EQUIPMENT

Fig. 25-1.   A typical engine analyzer.

The *dynamometer* (Fig. 25-2) is also a piece of test equipment that performs many functions. For example, the dynamometer can load a vehicle in such a way that the operator can measure the engine's horsepower output. Furthermore, through the use of the dynamometer, the technician can test the accuracy of the test vehicle's speedometer.

The dynamometer and the engine analyzer form an excellent diagnostic team. By placing a malfunctioning vehicle on a dynamometer and connecting its engine to an analyzer, the technician can actually duplicate the road speed and load conditions under which a problem occurs. By doing so, the operator can then easily locate the source or cause of the problem

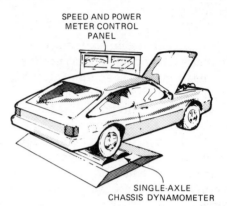

SPEED AND POWER
METER CONTROL
PANEL

SINGLE-AXLE
CHASSIS DYNAMOMETER

Fig. 25-2.   The dynamometer tests engine horsepower and torque output.

with the engine analyzer. In conclusion, some manufacturers specify that the only accurate way of checking the operation of their fuel-injected engines for excessive HC and CO levels is with the vehicle placed under a load at certain engine speeds.

Engine Analyzer

The typical engine analyzer has a number of individual test instruments. This text has already discussed many of the test instruments such as the tachometer, ammeter, dwell meter, ohmmeter, voltmeter, vacuum gauge, HC and CO meters, in addition to the timing light. Consequently, this particular chapter presents only a brief review of these units and concentrates on the oscilloscope, cylinder balance tester, timing advance unit, and electronic timing unit.

Tachometer

The SUN 1115 analyzer, shown in Fig. 25-1, has a RPM / 100 tachometer. This instrument measures crankshaft revolu-

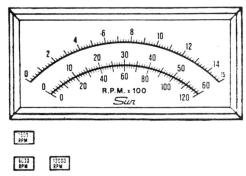

Fig. 25-3. The rpm/100 tachometer of the SUN 1115 analyzer. (Courtesy of Sun Electric Corp.)

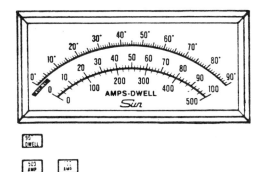

Fig. 25-4. The amps-dwell meter of the SUN 1115 analyzer. (Courtesy of Sun Electric Corp.)

tions-per-minute (rpm) from 0 to 12,000. If, for example, the operator moves the amps-dwell-rpm knob into the auto-tach/dwell position, the red 0 to 1,500 and the blue 0 to 6,000 scales activate (Fig. 25-3). In this case, engine speed determines which scale applies and which indicator lamp is lit. When engine rpm is in the 0 to 1,500 range, the 1,500 rpm indicator light is on. However, if engine rpm is in the 0 to 6,000 range, the 6,000 rpm indicator lamp lights. On the other hand, with the amps-dwell-rpm knob in the 12,000 rpm/dwell position, only the blue 0 to 12,000 scale along with the 0 to 12,000 rpm indicator lamp activates.

Amps—Dwell Meter

As in the case of many other engine analyzers, the SUN 1115 incorporates several individual instruments into one meter; this is the case of the amps-dwell meter. The lower portion of this meter (Fig. 25-4) registers the amount of current flow (amperes) in a given electrical circuit. This particular ammeter has scale readings that register 0 to 100 amperes on the upper scale and 0 to 500 on the lower scale. Which scale the technician reads, depends

on whether the amps-dwell-rpm knob is in the 100 A position or the 500 A position.

As in the case of any dwell meter, the dwell portion of this unit measures and registers the average dwell for all cylinders in terms of degrees of distributor cam rotation. The red dwell scale activates when you place the amps-dwell-rpm knob in the *automatic tach dwell* or the 12,000 rpm/dwell position (Fig. 25-5).

This particular dwell meter has another function. It can measure distributor resistance. This particular test determines the amount of primary-circuit resistance from the negative terminal of the coil through the distributor to the engine ground. The technician activates the meter for this particular test by placing the amps-dwell-rpm knob in the dist. res. position. If the resistance is normal, the pointer of the meter stays in the black dist. res. portion of the scale (Fig. 25-4).

Volt-Ohmmeter

This engine analyzer also has a combination volt-ohmmeter (Fig. 25-6). The volt meter section of this unit measures voltage—the difference in electrical pressure in volts between any two points

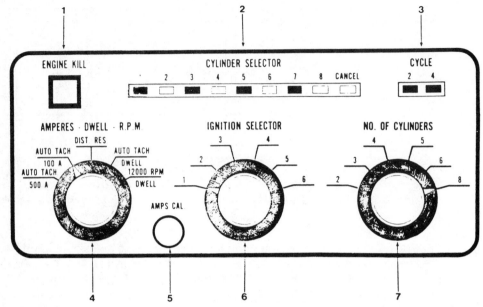

Fig. 25–5.   The center panel of a Sun 1115. (Courtesy of Sun Electric Corp.)

in a circuit. Note in Fig. 25–6 that the volt meter has two scales, one reading 0 to 20 volts while the other can read either 0 to 4 volts or 0 to 40 volts. The 0- to 20-volt scale is necessary for checking 6- and 12-volt electrical systems, while the 40-volt position is for 24-volt systems. The 0- to 4-scale is used primarily for voltage drop tests. The volt-ohm knob

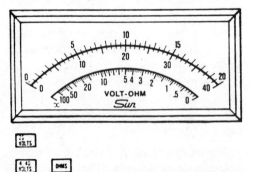

Fig. 25–6. The combination volt-ohm-meter of a SUN 1115 analyzer. (Courtesy of Sun Electric Corp.)

position (Fig. 25–7) determines which scale of the volt meter you will read.

The ohmmeter portion of the unit indicates the resistance in ohms between any two points in a circuit. Note that in Fig. 25–6 the bottom scale on the volt-ohm meter is for measuring ohms. If you would place the volt-ohm knob in the ohm position, the resistance in the circuit is shown as marked on this scale (0 to 100 ohms). If on the other hand you set the knob to the ohms × 100 position, the ohms reading on the scale requires multiplication by 100 in order to obtain the correct value. Finally, with the knob set to the ohms × 1,000 position, the scale is read on the meter and then multiplied by 1,000.

Note also on the control panel in Fig. 25–7 the ohms cal knob. This particular knob is necessary to zero the ohms scale whenever the volt-ohm control knob is in the ohm position. In this situation, the technician must clamp together the two

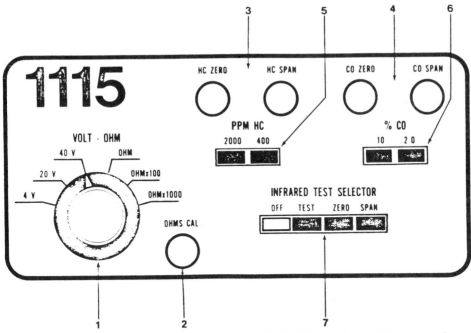

Fig. 25-7. The right panel controls of a SUN 1115 analyzer. (Courtesy of Sun Electric Corp.)

ohm leads and adjust the ohms cal. knob until the pointer is zero on the ohms scale. However, when the volt-ohm knob is set to either the ohm × 100 or the ohm × 1,000 position, the tester automatically sets the pointer to zero; that is, these two positions are self-calibrating.

Vacuum Gauge

The vacuum gauge (Fig. 25-8) measures the amount of vacuum produced by the engine. *Vacuum* is the difference in pressure. Vacuum, in this case, is a measurement of the difference in pressure between what is found inside the intake manifold of an operating engine and the atmosphere. The common measurement for a vacuum is either in inches or millimeters of mercury (Hg).

The vacuum gauge shown in Fig. 25-8 has two scales. The upper scale reads from 0 to 30 inches of Hg. The lower scale, on the other hand, ranges from 0 to 700 millimeters, for comparison with international vehicle specifications.

Fig. 25-8. The vacuum gauge of a SUN 1115 engine analyzer.

Ppm HC Meter and Percent CO Meter

The SUN 1115 also incorporates an infrared analyzer. The infrared analyzer measures the amount of hydrocarbons and carbon monoxide in a vehicle's exhaust. The level of hydrocarbon emission is a direct result of mechanical engine condition, temperature, and ignition. Carbon monoxide, on the other hand, is a byproduct of fuel after the combustion process burns it within the cylinders. An overly rich fuel mixture, for example, causes a high reading on the CO meter.

Figure 25-9 illustrates the ppm HC meter. This meter has two scales—one reading 0 to 2,000 ppm, while the other reads 0 to 400. The hydrocarbon buttons on the panel (Fig. 25-7) allow the operator to select either the 2,000 or 400 scale of the ppm HC meter.

Also note in Fig. 25-9 the three indicator lights on the ppm HC meter. The 2,000-ppm and the 400-ppm lights, one at a time, come on whenever the operator depresses either the 2,000- or the 400-hydrocarbon buttons. The low flow indicator light illuminates in yellow whenever the exhaust-gas–sampling system becomes

restricted due to clogged filters, kinked pickup hose, etc. This indicator light is a warning that the infrared system requires maintenance.

Figure 25-10 shows the percent CO meter and its indicator lights. Note that the scale readings on this instrument measure from 0 to 10 percent and from 0 to 2 percent. The carbon monoxide 10 and 2 buttons on the console permit the selection of either the high or low percent CO meter range by the operator. The 10 percent CO or the 2 percent CO indicator light automatically come on, corresponding to the button the operator presses.

Also note on the console (Fig. 25-7) the other infrared controls, including the infrared test selector buttons as well as the HC and CO zero and span knobs. The infrared test selector buttons are the master control for the hydrocarbon and carbon monoxide exhaust emission meters. These buttons include test, zero, and span. When the zero button is in, both the ppm HC and the percent CO meter pointers can be zeroed. When pushing in the span button, the mechanic can adjust both pointers for full-scale deflection, using the span control knobs. With the test selector button in, both the HC and CO meters are

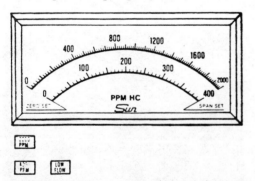

Fig. 25-9. The ppm HC meter of the SUN 1115 analyzer. (Courtesy of Sun Electric Corp.)

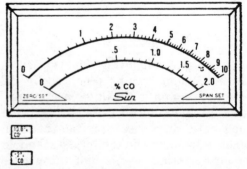

Fig. 25-10. The percent CO meter of a SUN 1115 analyzer. (Courtesy of Sun Electric Corp.)

ready for use. The HC, CO, zero, and span control knobs provide the adjustments for the zero and full-scale deflections of both the ppm HC and percent CO meters. These adjustments are necessary to ensure the accuracy of both meters for the vehicle that the operator is testing.

Oscilloscope

The *oscilloscope* is a tool designed to aid in diagnosing ignition system malfunctions. Through its proper use, the technician can readily locate abnormal conditions in the ignition system by comparing the patterns observed on the scope screen with those of a standard trace from a normally operating system. In addition, the oscilloscope can often indicate abnormal combustion chamber temperature, pressure, and air/fuel ratio.

The oscilloscope itself converts the complex electrical voltage developed during the ignition cycle into a graphlike picture. This graphlike picture (waveform) represents all phases of the ignition cycle at the same instance they occur in the operating engine. This permits accurate observation of the factors affecting ignition system operation that were once assumed in theory only. Also, since a properly operating ignition system presents a characteristic pattern (waveform), any deviation from this pattern indicates some type of malfunction.

To understand and use an oscilloscope properly, the operator must be quite familiar with two factors. First, the technician must have a good understanding of the principles of the operation of the ignition system, because this knowledge simplifies interpretation of the oscilloscope patterns during ignition system testing. Second, the technician must understand the significance of the basic trace or waveform that appears on the scope screen. Otherwise, the indications are meaningless. When this waveform is understood thoroughly, the operator can very quickly obtain more information about the ignition system of any engine and what is happening in that system faster than with any other conventional testing instrument.

Controls and Hookup

The large number of controls on a typical oscilloscope makes the unit appear formidable, but the use of these controls can be mastered very easily. The first thing to understand about the controls on the oscilloscope is that they have no effect on the ignition pattern waveform other than its overall size, brightness, focus, and so on. The ignition system itself determines the shape of the pattern waveform because the pattern itself represents actual ignition system operation. The controls simply permit the operator to regulate the way the waveform is viewed. Figure 25–11 illustrates the scope panel of controls for a SUN 1115 oscilloscope. This panel consists of a function selector, panel height control, pattern position control, cylinder select mode control, five pattern adjustment controls, and pattern position control.

The function selector control (Fig. 25–11, item 1) is a four-position rotary switch used to select the waveform that the scope will display. The first position (secondary) causes the oscilloscope to display secondary waveforms. The second and third positions (primary plus and primary minus) are control positions used for positive and negative primary wave-

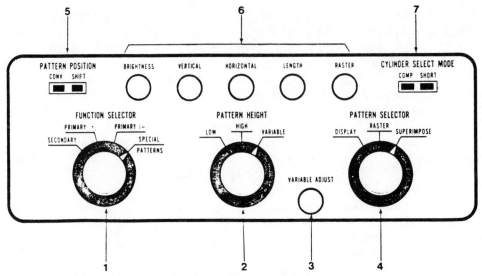

Fig. 25–11. *The scope panel of controls for the SUN 1115 engine ana-*
lyzer. (Courtesy of Sun Electric Corp.)

forms. The fourth position (special patterns) is necessary to permit the scope to
display special waveforms picked up at
the alternator output terminal or the positive battery terminal. In addition, this
special pattern position can also be used
for viewing other waveforms such as fuel
injection.

The pattern height control (Fig. 25–11,
item 2) is a three-position switch utilized
to select the vertical height of the waveform displayed on the scope screen. Whenever the operator desires to display either
primary or secondary ignition waveforms,
this control is set in the low position, and
the left-hand (0 to 25) scale on the screen
will be the measuring device. On the other
hand, when the control is in the high position, the operator would measure the same
waveforms using the right-hand (0 to 50)
scale as the measuring device. The third,
or variable adjust, position provides a
means of adjusting the vertical display of
any waveform used on the scope screen.

Note also in Fig. 25–11 the variable ad-

just knob to the right of the pattern
height control. This variable adjust knob
provides the means of manually adjusting
the vertical height of the pattern on the
scope screen. This control is only opera-
tive when the pattern height knob is set in
the variable position.

The pattern selector control (Fig. 25–11,
item 4) is a three-position rotary switch
that provides a means of selecting just
how an ignition waveform is to appear on
the scope screen. For example, in the display position, all the ignition waveforms
appear in a horizontal chain across the
screen. In this situation, the cylinder 1
pattern is at the left (except for its firing
line), while all the other patterns follow to
the right *in the engine's firing order.*

In the raster position the operator views
all cylinder patterns at full-screen length.
The pattern of cylinder 1 is at the bottom,
and the other cylinder patterns are evenly
spaced above, again in the engine's firing
order.

In the superimposed position, the operator views all the individual waveforms simultaneously. In other words, all cylinder pattern waveforms are in place one behind the other on the zero line of the scope screen.

The cylinder selector mode (Fig. 25-11, item 7) consists of two buttons: a short button and a compare button. With the short button in, the eight buttons on the cylinder selector on the center panel of the analyzer are operational to short out the engine cylinders as necessary to perform a cylinder power balance test. By depressing this short button and then selecting an individual or a group of buttons on the cylinder selector, the analyzer electronically shorts out the ignition of the corresponding engine cylinders. This shorting of individual or groups of cylinders provides an accurate and convenient means of determining the comparative overall operating efficiency of each engine cylinder.

With the compare selector depressed, the operator can use the eight buttons on the cylinder selector to display certain patterns on the scope screen. The depressing of the compare button switches the function of the cylinder selector to permit it to alter the waveform pattern displayed on the scope. For example, with the ignition system waveform being viewed in the display manner, pushing any one of the cylinder selector buttons causes the corresponding cylinder waveform to be removed from the normal display and to appear enlarged and centered above the others on the scope screen. This particular feature allows the operator to enlarge any cylinder's pattern as necessary for more detailed examination. In addition, this compare button function also allows two or more cylinders to be superimposed for close examination. Finally, the releasing of the cylinder selector button permits the enlarged waveform to return once again to its usual position in the display pattern on the scope screen.

The pattern position control (Fig. 25-11, item 5) consists of two buttons (conventional—conv—and shift). When the pattern selector is in either the raster or superimpose position and the conv button in, the ignition pattern displayed on the screen begins with a spark line on the left end of the pattern and the firing line at the right end of the pattern. However, depressing the shift button results in a pattern shift to the right, causing the waveforms displayed to begin with the firing line at the left. Consequently, in display with the shift button in, the firing line of cylinder 1, which normally appears at the far right, is moved or shifted to the far left.

Hookups

Figure 25-12 illustrates typical oscilloscope lead connections to the engine. Basically speaking, only two test lead connections are made to the ignition system: the pattern pickup device that transmits the signal from the ignition system to the scope and a timing pickup that synchronizes the scope operation with engine speed. In Fig. 25-12 the chrome pattern pickup clamp fits around the secondary coil wire. Two wire leads emit from the base of the chrome pattern pickup. The red primary pickup connects to the negative terminal on the ignition coil (negative ground ignition systems) or to the positive terminal on positive ground ignition systems. The black ground primary pickup connects to any good engine ground. Finally, the red trigger pickup clamps around the number 1 spark plug wire, close to the distributor cap.

Screen

The oscilloscope converts the complex electrical voltages developed during the

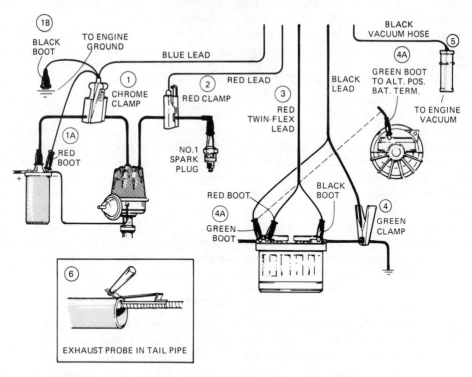

Fig. 25-12.   Typical oscilloscope lead connections to an engine.

ignition cycle into a visual display that appears on the scope screen. The SUN oscilloscope shown in Fig. 25-1 has a 20-inch screen with vertical and horizontal divisions. The vertical line on the left edge of the tube provides a range of 0 to 25, which the operator reads as 0 to 250 volts or 0 to 25 kv (killovolt), depending on whether the screen is displaying a primary or secondary waveform. A *kilovolt* is a unit of electrical measure equaling 1,000 volts. The vertical scale on the right edge of the tube provides a range of measurement from 0 to 50. The operator reads this as 0 to 500 volts for a primary waveform display, or 0 to 50 kv for a secondary waveform display.

Notice also on the oscilloscope screen shown in Fig. 25-13 the number of horizontal lines beginning at zero and equally spaced up to the top of the screen. These horizontal lines have several functions. The lines equally divide the total screen into increments, which make it easy for the operator to measure the height of various portions of the waveform. If the operator is using the left-hand scale, each line division is worth 1 volt or 1,000, depending on whether viewing primary or secondary waveforms. On the other hand, if the right-hand vertical line is the measuring unit, each horizontal line represents 2 volts, 20 volts, or 2,000 volts, again depending on whether the operator is viewing a primary or a secondary waveform.

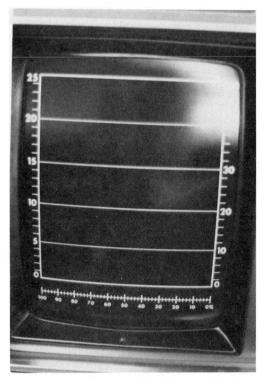

Fig. 25-13. The oscilloscope screen of a SUN 1115 engine analyzer.

The zero line on the oscilloscope screen also has another very important function. It acts as a scale to measure the amount of dwell. When adjusting a single cylinder trace to just the length of the zero line, the operator can then read the dwell in a percentage form.

To accomplish this, the screen shown in Fig. 25-13 has a single scale below the horizontal line. This scale reads from 0 to 100 percent, in increments of 2 and 10 percent. With this arrangement, the single scale can represent up to 45 degrees dwell for an eight-cylinder engine; 60 degrees dwell for a six-cylinder engine; and 90 degrees for a four-cylinder engine. Therefore, the actual measurement on the scale, of a 30-degree dwell period, of any single

eight-cylinder trace would be about 66 percent.

Ignition Waveform Patterns— Secondary

The second most important factor in learning to use the oscilloscope is the interpretation of the waveform patterns. The pattern, or waveform, basically speaking, is a picture of voltage in relationship to time. If, for example, the operator centers a single secondary waveform between the left and right vertical lines and on the zero horizontal line on the scope, all vertical traces from the zero line upward represent induced negative voltage on a negatively grounded engine. From the zero line downward, the images represent positive voltage. Consequently, the negative voltage is measurable by comparing the trace to the graduations on the scope screen. In addition, the horizontal movement of the trace represents time measured in degrees of distributor rotation, termed *dwell time*.

The pattern illustrated in Fig. 25-14 is a standard ignition secondary waveform. This waveform is the most informative because it shows overall ignition system operation. Notice in Fig. 25-14 that the secondary waveform is divided into three sections: firing, intermediate, and dwell section.

The *firing section* of the waveform represents the period in which the actual firing of the spark plug takes place. This section has only two lines: the firing and the spark. The *firing line* is the vertical line *AB* indicating the voltage required to overcome the plug and distributor rotor gaps and any other resistance in the secondary circuit. Point *A*, in the pattern il-

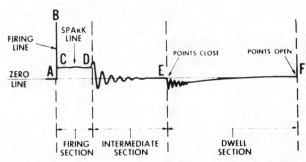

Fig. 25-14.   The secondary waveform of a standard ignition system.
(Courtesy of Sun Electric Corp.)

lustrated, represents the instant at which the breaker points have separated, causing the magnetic field to collapse through the coil windings. This results in the induction of high voltage in the secondary windings indicated by the vertical rise from *A* to *B* in the pattern. The actual height of point *B* indicates the exact voltage required to fire the plug after overcoming the plug gap, rotor gap, and ignition wire resistance. This voltage is sometimes known as the *firing* or *ionization voltage*. Firing or ionization voltage, then, is the actual amount of voltage necessary to overcome the resistance in the plug wires, the rotor gap, and the spark plug gap. Also, this voltage must convert a compressed air/fuel charge into ions that will conduct the current flow across the plug gap.

The *spark line* is a horizontal line indicating the voltage required to maintain the arc across the spark plug air gap. This spark line appears in this illustration as line *CD*. Notice in the illustration that there is a noticeable drop in secondary voltage to point *C* once the arc of current is flowing between the spark plug electrodes. Once the compressed air/fuel mixture ionizes, there is a noticeable drop in secondary voltage requirement to keep the arc of current flowing across the gap. The required voltage, in this case, is

shown by the relative distance from the zero line to the spark line.

Also notice in the illustration that the spark line *CD* is rather flat and lasts for an appreciable period of time as shown by the horizontal length of the line. In this situation, the measurement of spark line duration is in thousandths of a second, with the full length of a typical trace of a single sparking cycle taking only about 0.01 second at an engine speed of 2,000 rpm. Of course, the actual time requirement at other engine speeds would be in proportion to the rpm.

The arc of the spark in the air gap acts as a voltage regulator. This is the reason the secondary spark line remains relatively flat, indicating direct current voltage in the secondary circuit for the duration of the spark.

At point *D*, the plug stops firing. Voltage is no longer available to overcome the resistance of the plug wire along with the rotor and plug air gaps. Consequently, the arc at the plug dies out or extinguishes. At this time, the intermediate section of the oscilloscope trace begins.

The intermediate section, sometimes referred to as the *coil-condenser zone*, is seen as a series of gradually diminishing oscillations that disappear or nearly disappear by the time the dwell section begins. Beginning at point *D*, the remaining coil energy dissipates itself as an oscillating current that gradually dies out as it approaches point E.

The oscillations result from the combined effects of the coil and condenser in dissipating this energy. Note at point D the voltage increases in the negative direction. This is because the spark plug is open-circuited, thereby permitting voltage in the coil to increase. This is followed by a series of four or more oscillations, moving first in one direction and then the other until they diminish or nearly diminish as the points close.

These oscillations in the secondary are due to primary coil and condenser action. As soon as the points open and the plug begins to fire, the condenser begins to discharge back through the primary coil toward its other plate. Then, the current changes direction and passes through the coil in the opposite direction. This zigzagging continues until all the voltage induced in the primary coil diminishes.

However, as the voltage zigzags through the primary coil from one plate of the condenser to the other, it is also inducing voltage in the secondary coil, first in one direction and then the other; this gradually diminishes with the induced voltages in the primary coil. It should be apparent then that what you see in the *intermediate section* in the secondary reflects the action of the condenser discharging its stored energy through the primary windings until this energy dissipates as heat. The main difference as to what you see in the intermediate section in the secondary circuit is that here you see induced a.c. voltages in the secondary coil that are higher than those seen in the primary waveform. This chapter presents an interpretation of the primary waveform later.

The *dwell section* represents the period of time during the ignition cycle in which the breaker points are in the closed position. The dwell section begins at point E (Fig. 25-14). As the points close, they short out the condenser so that there is a rapid charge across the condenser from battery voltage to zero. Before the points closed and after the oscillations died out in the intermediate section, battery voltage appears across the condenser.

The point-closed signal is shown in the secondary pattern as a short downward line followed by a series of small, rapidly diminishing oscillations. These oscillations represent induced voltages in the secondary, which results from the rapid charge across the condenser as the points close and the buildup of the magnetic field around the primary coil. After these series of oscillations, the dwell section continues until the points open, which signals the beginning of the next waveform, shown at point F of Fig. 25-14.

The oscilloscope can actually measure the duration of the dwell section. If the straight section of the dwell line is centered on the zero line with points A and F of the basic pattern also centered on the left and right vertical line of the scope screen, the operator can read the percent of dwell on the scale below the zero line.

Interpreting Primary Waveforms

The primary waveform has a similar appearance to the secondary. However, the primary pattern is not quite as sensitive or informative as the secondary. Consequently, technicians only use this particular waveform to verify a suspected problem in the low voltage or primary side of the ignition system.

As in the case of the secondary waveform, the primary pattern represents voltage in relationship to time. However, in the case of the primary trace, the voltage is quite a bit lower. Therefore, when using an oscilloscope such as the SUN 1115, the operator would read the primary voltage, using the left-hand vertical scale, which reads from 0 to 25. This in turn is read as 0 to 250 volts when interpreting a primary waveform.

As in the case of the secondary pattern, a primary waveform is divisible into three sections: firing, intermediate, and dwell (Fig. 25–15). In the *firing section,* the screen displays a series of rapid oscillations that take place in the primary circuit during the point in which the spark plug actually fires. These oscillations continue for the actual duration of the spark and can be seen from point *A* to point *C* of Fig. 25–15.

Also note in Fig. 25–15 the vertical rise of the waveform from point *A* to point *B,* followed by the diminishing oscillations.

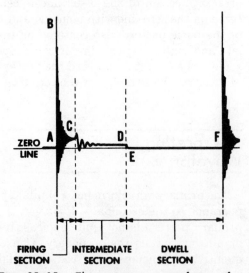

Fig. 25–15. The primary waveform of a standard ignition system. (Courtesy of Sun Electric Corp.)

These oscillations represent the initial and repeated charging and discharging of the condenser with the resulting self-induced voltage surges in the primary circuit while the spark plug is firing. As the spark bridges the gap and energy drains from the coil, the amplitude of these oscillations diminishes until the spark extinguishes, as indicated at point *C.*

The *intermediate section* of the primary pattern is shown from *C* to *D* on Fig. 25–15. As in the secondary pattern, this intermediate section is a series of gradually diminishing oscillations that disappear or nearly disappear by the time the dwell section begins. In this section also, these oscillations represent the continuing discharge of the condenser back and forth through the primary circuit. Since during this time the condenser has a charge that is still higher than the battery or any other portion of the circuit, it causes current to flow in the reverse direction back through the primary circuit. The current has no place to go but around the circuit to the other plate of the condenser, charging it in an opposite direction. This process continues during the intermediate section, giving an alternating current and voltage in the primary, which the scope screen indicates as the oscillating lines. Due to the dissipation of energy in the spark and the resistance of the primary circuit, these oscillations die out rather rapidly, as shown by their decreasing amplitude on the trace.

As with the secondary intermediate section, there should be four or more of these large oscillations, followed by what appears to be a fairly straight line as the waveform approaches point *D.* This rather short and flat line appears above the zero line and represents battery ignition voltage across the condenser.

The intermediate section ends at point

D, and the *dwell section* begins simultaneously. The section begins at point *E* as the points close, which appears on the waveform as a faint downward line from point *D* to point *E*. The screen displays the remaining portion of the primary dwell section by a horizontal line that extends from point *E* to point *F*. At point *F*, the points again open and the beginning of the next waveform commences.

Types of Ignition Waveforms

The pattern selector knob on the scope panel controls the type of waveform viewed by the operator. These controls do not affect the actual shape of the pattern but only control the type of waveform to be viewed. The selector has three control positions: superimposed, raster, and display.

Superimposed Pattern

A *superimposed pattern* (Fig. 25-16) is a display obtained by simultaneously placing the patterns of all cylinders one behind the other. This type of pattern provides a convenient method of testing the ignition system for overall uniformity. By expanding the waveform horizontally to fill the space completely between the two vertical reference points on the screen, the operator can quickly detect any variation in the basic pattern.

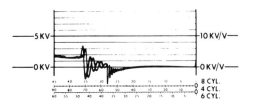

Fig. 25-16. A secondary superimposed pattern. (Courtesy of Sun Electric Corp.)

Raster

The *raster pattern* is one of the most outstanding advancements in ignition scope testing. Raster permits individual cylinder identification while viewing all the cylinders simultaneously (Fig. 25-17). The pattern itself makes use of the vertical size of the scope screen by stacking the patterns of each cylinder's ignition cycle one above the other, so that all the individual patterns are vertically distributed on the screen. This permits the scope to display, at full screen width, the patterns of the individual ignition cycles, permitting the operator detailed close-up inspection of all engine ignition cycles simultaneously. In addition, the raster pattern is especially helpful for individual cylinder identification of any variation in pattern waveform observed while using a superimposed pattern.

With the timing pickup connected into the circuit of spark plug 1, the screen displays the pattern waveform representing the ignition cyle of cylinder 1 at the bottom of the screen. The remainder of the pattern waveforms appear in the normal firing order sequence, starting with cylinder 1 at the bottom and working upward. This places the pattern waveform of the

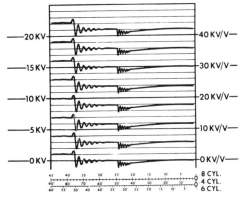

Fig. 25-17. A secondary raster pattern. (Courtesy of Sun Electric Corp.)

last cylinder in the firing order at the top of the scope screen.

Also note in Fig. 25-17 that with the raster pattern, as with the superimposed pattern, the firing lines of the basic pattern waveform are not seen. However, by pushing in the shift button of the pattern position control, the firing line moves from the right of the screen to the left, where the operator can see it.

Figure 25-18 illustrates a raster pattern showing primary waveforms. In this situation, the operator views the primary waveform for all individual cylinders. In the case of the secondary raster pattern, cylinder 1 appears at the bottom of the screen, and the last cylinder in the firing order appears at the top.

Display

With the pattern selector control in the *display* position, the scope will trigger, beginning a new sweep of the trace, only once for every complete ignition cycle for all cylinders. Consequently, with the timing pickup connected to the spark plug cable 1, the waveform viewed on the scope screen begins on the left with the pattern

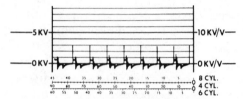

Fig. 25-19. A secondary display pattern. (Courtesy of Sun Electric Corp.)

for cylinder 1 (Fig. 25-19). Then the trace moves from left to right, displaying all the ignition cycles in the engine's firing order.

Note in Fig. 25-19 that the firing line of cylinder 1 appears at the extreme right or the end of the trace. This is necessary because when it fires, spark plug 1 triggers the scope to begin a new trace. However, by depressing the shift button of the pattern position control, the firing line of cylinder 1 is moved to the left side of the screen.

The importance of the display pattern is that the operator can measure the firing voltage of all the cylinders individually or simultaneously. To accomplish an accurate measurement, the operator first adjusts the base of the pattern's firing line to the zero line on the scope's screen. Then, all that is necessary to make a measurement is to compare the height of one or all firing lines against the vertical scales on the right or the left side of the screen. Of course, which scale the operator uses depends on whether the pattern height control is in the low or high position.

Abnormal Scope Patterns—Secondary

Variations in the secondary pattern waveforms indicate components that are faulty or improperly adjusted. The following sections describe some of the most

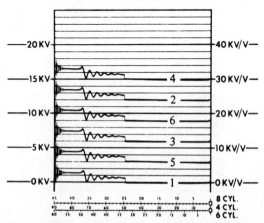

Fig. 25-18. A primary raster pattern. (Courtesy of Sun Electric Corp.)

common problems in the secondary circuit, which you can detect by examining an oscilloscope waveform. Unless specified, the following conditions will be most noticeable with the scope controls set for superimposed or raster or by the removal of a cylinder's waveform from the normal display pattern, by pushing in the cylinder compare button of the cylinder select mode.

Reverse Polarity

Figure 25-20 illustrates a secondary waveform pattern of an ignition system with *reverse polarity*. In this situation, the pattern is upside down. That is, the spark line is below the zero line, and the point-close signal is above the zero line. The main cause of this condition is the incorrect connection of either the vehicle's battery or the ignition coil.

Unusual Point-Close Signals

Figure 25-21 shows an *unusual point-close signal*. Note in this illustration the rise in voltage observable above the zero line, after the point-close signal. This type of condition can only result if the secondary coil is receiving an induction of higher voltage.

In the normal ignition circuit, the secondary coil only receives this induction of high voltage when the rubbing block

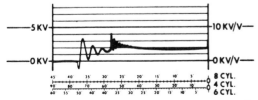

Fig. 25-20. A secondary waveform with reversed polarity. (Courtesy of Sun Electric Corp.)

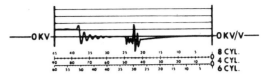

Fig. 25-21. An unusual point-close signal, caused by weak contact point spring tension. (Courtesy of Sun Electric Corp.)

pushes the points open. However, before doing this, the current flow in the primary coil must cease. This is accomplished normally by the opening of the contact points and the action of the condenser.

Since the coil has some induced high voltage during the point-close signal, there is most likely some problem in the contact points. In most cases, this condition is the result of points that do not close tightly enough because of a weak point spring tension.

Figure 25-22 points out another abnormal point close signal. Note that in this illustration when the points close, the first oscillation is the shortest, and the second oscillation is the longest of all. This indicates that when the points first close, something keeps them from completely seating. However, by the time of the second oscillation, the points fully seat. The most common cause for this type of situation is dirty, burned, or misaligned points.

Abnormal Point-Open Signals

Figure 25-23 points out an *abnormal point-open signal*. Note in the illustration,

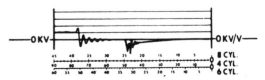

Fig. 25-22. An unusual point-close signal, caused by dirty, burned, or misaligned points. (Courtesy of Sun Electric Corp.)

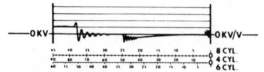

Fig. 25-23. An unusual point-open signal, caused by either dirty or pitted points, defective condenser, high-charging voltage, or a shorted ballast resistor. (Courtesy of Sun Electric Corp.)

at the far right end of the dwell line close to the vertical scale, the *hash marks*. This blip or spot of light indicates the point arcing that can be caused by dirty or pitted points, defective condenser, high charging voltage, or a shorted ballast resister.

Figure 25-24 illustrates another unusual point-open signal. Note in this illustration that the spark line is not a straight horizontal line but appears as a series of small oscillations. In addition, the actual firing line begins approximately at the center of the spark line and not in its normal position, at the end of the dwell line. This is another example of excessive point arcing caused by a faulty condenser action, usually brought about by a loose condenser pigtail, an open condenser, or a condenser with high series resistance.

Shorted Coil Windings or Leaky Condenser

Figure 25-25 illustrates a raster display that plainly shows a problem in the intermediate section. Note in this figure the

Fig. 25-24. A poor point-open signal due to faulty condenser action. (Courtesy of Sun Electric Corp.)

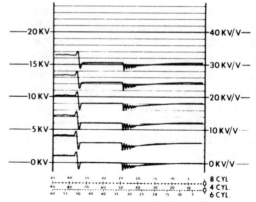

Fig. 25-25. A raster display showing a problem in the intermediate section. (Courtesy of Sun Electric Corp.)

lack of oscillations in the intermediate section. This indicates either a short in the coil or a leaky condenser. To determine which component is malfunctioning, first observe the point-open signal in order to determine condenser action. If the point-open signal is normal, the coil has shorted windings and requires replacement.

Worn Cam Lobe

The operator can spot the next two abnormal conditions on a superimposed pattern; however, they are more easily seen on a raster waveform. Note that in Fig. 25-26 the point-closed signal for the same cylinder is consistently out of alignment, while the signal for the remaining cylinders are all in line. This is an indication that one cam lobe on a distributor shaft is worn.

The distributor cam of the six-cylinder engine viewed in this waveform is hexagonal in shape. Therefore, it has six flat sides, and there are 60 degrees of distributor shaft rotation from the high point of any lobe to the high point of the next lobe. If one lobe becomes worn, it contacts

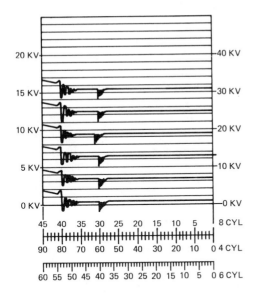

Fig. 25-26. A raster pattern showing one worn cam lobe.

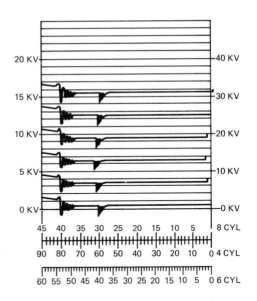

Fig. 25-27. A raster pattern showing variations in dwell.

the rubbing block of the contact point later than normal. This causes the dwell to be longer on the affected ignition cycle than on any of the others. Furthermore, since the lobe is worn down, it permits the points to close sooner than normal on the next cycle.

Dwell Variation

Figure 25-27 points out clearly another problem occurring within the dwell zone. Note in this illustration the curve effect at the point-close and -open signals, which indicates variations in dwell. The possible causes of this condition are uneven distributor cam lobes, bent distributor shaft, worn distributor shaft, or bushings, or in some cases worn timing chain or gears.

Open Plug Circuit

Figure 25-28 represents an abnormal pattern, showing an open secondary circuit in one of the ignition cycles. Notice

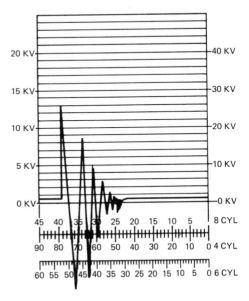

Fig. 25-28. A secondary pattern indicating an open plug circuit.

the large oscillation for the affected cylinder, and the waveform has little or no spark line. The most probable cause of this particular problem is a disconnected or open spark plug cable. Although this problem is apparent with the scope showing a superimposed pattern, the easiest way for the operator to locate the affected cylinder is to adjust the scope to either the display or the raster mode.

Excessive Resistance

Figure 25–29 is a superimposed pattern showing a problem in the firing section. Note in this particular situation the high and short spark line. This indicates high resistance in the circuit between the distributor's cap and spark plug. The cause of this particular problem can be a damaged or loose cable or in some cases a wide spark plug gap. As with the open circuit, the operator can easily locate the malfunctioning circuit by adjusting the pattern selector to either raster or display.

Fouled Plug

A *fouled spark plug* is one in which a conducting material such as carbon be-

comes lodged between the center electrode and the ground electrode or between the center electrode and any portion of the metal shell. In any case, this foreign material forms an electrical current path that grounds out the high voltage surge. Consequently, an arc does not cross the plug's air gap to fire the air/fuel mixture.

Figure 25–30 shows a display pattern of an eight-cylinder engine with the plug of the second cylinder in the firing order fouled out due to carbon. Note in this illustration the low firing line, which indicates that high voltage was not necessary to ionize the air/fuel mixture between the plug's air gap. Also note how the spark line slopes downward slightly from the firing line to the first coil oscillation. Of course, this abnormal condition would be very obvious to the operator with the pattern selector on raster.

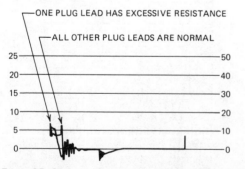

Fig. 25–29. A superimposed secondary pattern showing high resistance somewhere between the distributor cap and spark plug.

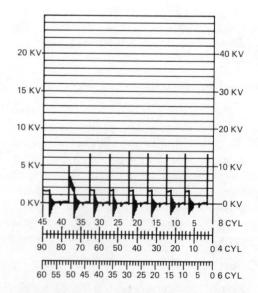

Fig. 25–30. A secondary display pattern indicating a fouled spark plug.

Fig. 25-31. A secondary superimposed pattern with an erratic firing line.

Erratic Firing Line

The *erratic jumping* of the firing line in any cylinder (Fig. 25-31) indicates inconsistencies in the air/fuel mixture of the affected cylinder. This condition may result from a sticking or worn valve, air leaks, or carburetor problems. In any case, the inconsistent mixture offers various amounts of resistance to the spark that the scope shows as an erratic, jumping firing line.

The unusual firing line shown in Fig. 25-32 also is a good indication of variations in the air/fuel mixture. In this situation, the spark line of one cylinder slopes up toward the end of its firing zone. If this condition occurs at high engine speed, a valve may be sticking open. This, of course, results in a leaner mixture near the end of combustion and greater resistance to the continuation of the spark. This trace can also result from air leaks or carburetor problems.

Fig. 25-32. A spark line that slopes up toward the end of the firing zone is a good indication of a leaner mixture near the end of the combustion.

Wide Spark Plug Gap

A single trace of the ignition cycle of a cylinder with a large spark plug gap is shown in Fig. 25-33. Note in this waveform the high firing line. The high firing line results from the fact that the ignition coil must produce a greater voltage in order to force current across the wide gap. Following the high firing line is a short and high spark line, which indicates a shorter firing period of the spark plug. In other words, since the coil must produce a greater voltage, not only to initiate the arc but to maintain it, the coil itself loses its stored energy quickly. Consequently, the actual arcing period at the spark plug gap ends prematurely.

Narrow Plug Gap

The pattern of an ignition cycle of a cylinder with a narrow gap plug is just opposite of the one shown in Fig. 25-33. In this

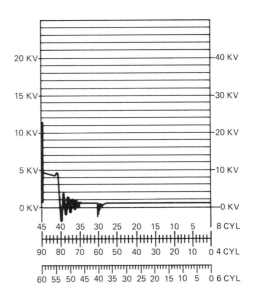

Fig. 25-33. A secondary waveform showing a plug with a wide gap.

situation, the waveform shows a short firing line (Fig. 25-34) followed by a long and low spark line. The short firing line indicates that the coil does not have to produce a high voltage in order to initiate the arc at the spark plug gap. The long spark line shows an increase in the length of time the arc appears across the spark plug gap, while the height of the firing line represents the reduction in voltage necessary to sustain the arc.

Uneven Firing Lines

The operator utilizes the display pattern for measuring the actual height of the firing lines. While doing so, the operator may encounter three abnormal conditions: uneven firing lines, one excessively high firing line, or all firing lines too high.

A display pattern with *uneven firing lines* (Fig. 25-35) may result from one or more factors. For example, the higher

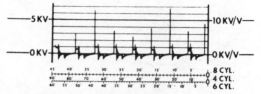

Fig. 25-35.   A display pattern with uneven firing lines. (Courtesy of Sun Electric Corp.)

than normal firing lines can result from excessive plug wire resistance, wide spark plug gap, or a lean mixture. In this regard, an unbalanced carburetor, one which is improperly adjusted, causes every other firing line in the display pattern to be either high or low. Shorter than normal firing lines result from either a fouled plug, a short in a plug wire, low compression, or excessively rich fuel mixture. However, in this latter case, every other firing line would have to be low.

One Firing Line too High

Figure 25-36 illustrates a display pattern with the fourth ignition cycle in the firing order showing an *excessively high firing line*. The problem in this case cannot be in the rotor, coil wire, or coil, since a malfunction in these components would affect all cycles. Consequently, the fault must be in the cap tower, plug wire, spark plug, or the cylinder itself because only one of the firing lines is too high.

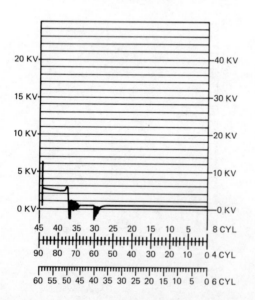

Fig. 25-34.   A secondary pattern indicating a spark plug with a narrow gap.

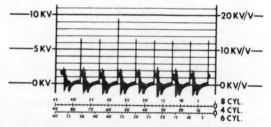

Fig. 25-36.   A secondary display waveform showing one high firing line. (Courtesy of Sun Electric Corp.)

To isolate the exact problem, remove the spark plug wire from the plug and ground it securely. You must ground the wire totally so that there will be no spark. If the firing line falls below about 5 kv, the trouble is in the plug or the cylinder (with the plug wire grounded, the spark plug and the cylinder are out of the circuit). Consequently, if the firing line is low, the cause of the problem must be the spark plug or the cylinder.

To check these components, remove the spark plug and inspect it for an enlarged or worn gap. If the plug is satisfactory, check the cylinder for carbon buildup by performing a compression test. Carbon buildup normally increases the compression ratio, which offers increased resistance to the voltage in the circuit and causes the high firing line.

If, on the other hand, the firing line did not fall below 5 kv when you grounded the plug wire, the problem is in the plug wire or the distributor cap. In this situation, substitute a reliable plug wire for the suspected wire, and ground the new one. If the firing line goes down to about 5 kv, the original plug wire is defective. However, if the firing line is still too high with the substitute wire grounded, the problem lies in the cap tower.

All Firing Lines too High

A display pattern on which all the firing lines are too high indicates a problem common to all the cylinders or ignition cycles (Fig. 25-37). This problem may be either or a combination of late ignition timing, carbon buildup in the cylinders, high operating temperature, worn or widely gapped plugs, overall lean fuel mixture, excessive rotor air gap, defective coil wire,

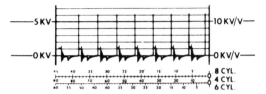

Fig. 25-37. A secondary display pattern in which all the firing lines are too high. (Courtesy of Sun Electric Corp.)

defective coil, worn distributor cap, high engine speed, or heavy engine load.

To isolate the cause of the high firing lines, ground the plug wires on two or three cylinders, one at a time. If during these tests the high firing line disappears, either the plug, carbon buildup within the cylinder, lean mixture, timing, or engine temperature is the cause of the problem. Check the plugs, compression, fuel mixture, and timing to isolate which is causing the malfunction.

If the high firing lines remain after grounding the plug wires, the problem is in either the coil, coil high tension wire, distributor cap, rotor, or, infrequently, the entire set of secondary wires. To isolate which one is at fault, first check the coil high-tension wire for excessive resistance with an ohmmeter. Then, check the distributor cap segment and rotor electrode for deterioration due to arcing. If these components are satisfactory, check the entire secondary wire set for excessive resistance with an ohmmeter, and check coil operation on a reliable coil tester.

Transistorized Ignition System Patterns

Up to this point, this chapter has discussed normal and abnormal patterns of the standard ignition system. Let us turn our attention to both the primary and secondary patterns of transistorized ignition systems. The systems that this chapter discusses are Delco-Remy, Prestolite, Motorcraft, and Chrysler.

Before examining any of these systems, which do have some noticeable differences, it is an appropriate time to explain the similarities and the basic differences between a transistorized pattern and the waveform of the standard ignition system. For example, you can interpret the firing section of a transistorized secondary trace in the same way as for a standard system; the same things are happening in both types of systems. Consequently, the most noticeable difference between the two waveforms are in the intermediate and dwell sections.

In the intermediate section, there is no condenser oscillation. This, of course, is due to the fact that transistorized ignition systems have no condenser. Therefore, the oscillations in this section result from the action of the coil and are representative of the coil condition.

In the waveform of the standard ignition system, the dwell section begins with the points close signal. However, within a transistorized system, the dwell section of the waveform begins with the transistor on signal. In some systems, this signal appears much like the point-close signal of the standard waveform—a downward line indicating a sharp drop to zero voltage.

Unlike the standard ignition waveform, the length and shape of the transistorized waveform dwell section vary somewhat among systems. For example, some systems have a design that lengthens the dwell section at higher engine speeds. Also, during the dwell section, some systems have slight voltage ripples or voltage humps. These are normal, when viewing specific waveforms.

At the very end of the dwell zone in a standard ignition system pattern, the firing line appears as a sharp upward line as the contact points open. However, within a transistorized pattern, there may be a jagged, upward-sloping line leading to the firing line. Again, this is a normal situation in many transistorized systems.

HEI, Prestolite, and Dura-Spark I Systems

The primary and secondary waveform patterns of the Delco-Remy HEI, the Prestolite, and the Motorcraft Dura-Spark I systems are very similar in appearance. Consequently, this chapter discusses these systems together. However, at the appropriate time, the text points out any major differences among them.

Figure 25-38 illustrates a typical primary superimposed pattern for these systems. Notice in this waveform the absence of the condenser oscillations at the beginning of the trace and the small current hump toward the end of the dwell period. Except for these differences and the transistor on and off signal in the dwell zone, this pattern is quite similar to the one for the standard ignition system.

Figure 25-39 shows a typical secondary superimposed pattern for these systems. The oscillations noticeable at the beginning of the dwell period, indicated by the transistor on signal, are *coil* oscillations, not condenser oscillations. Notice again the current hump appearing in the dwell section of the pattern. This hump that may also appear as a voltage ripple is normal. This hump or ripple is due to the action of the control module circuitry and may occur in the middle or toward the end of the dwell period.

The dwell period for HEI and the

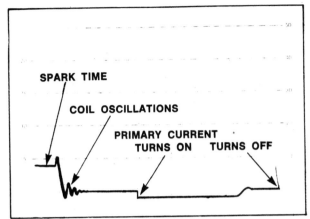

Fig. 25-38.   A primary waveform of the HEI, Prestolite, and Dura-Spark I systems.

Motorcraft Dura-Spark I systems changes with engine speed (Figure 25-40). At idle and low speed, for example, dwell period may only be 40 percent of the total waveform. However, as engine speed increases, the dwell period lengthens to as much as 60 percent of the total pattern.

The oscilloscope patterns of the HEI system, as used on uneven-firing V-6 engines, is somewhat different from those of other engines. Figure 25-41 shows the primary and the secondary raster patterns of a typical V-6. Notice in this illustration that the intermediate section of three of these cycles is much longer than the other three. Also note how the dwell zone of cylinders 1, 3, and 5, in the

engine's firing order, the cylinders 2, 4, and 6 are in alignment on the scope screen.

Motorcraft Dura-Spark II System

The primary and secondary waveforms for the Dura-Spark II systems are slightly different from those of the Dura-Spark I system. Note, for example, the oscillations within the firing section of the primary pattern of a Dura-Spark system shown in Fig. 25-42. These coil oscillations may not be as high as those found in a standard system, but there should be

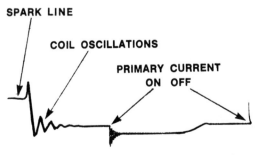

Fig. 25-39.   A secondary pattern of a HEI, Prestolite, or Dura-Spark I system.

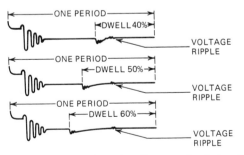

Fig. 25-40.   The dwell period of the HEI and Dura-Spark I system changes with engine speed.

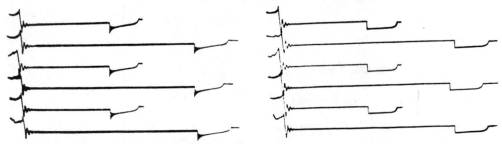

Fig. 25–41. A secondary raster pattern of an unevenly firing V-6 engine. (Courtesy of Sun Electric Corp.)

more of them. Furthermore, the dwell section of the Dura-Spark II system should be longer.

Figure 25–43 illustrates a secondary superimposed pattern of the Dura-Spark II system. Notice that in this secondary pattern a current hump or voltage ripple appears in the dwell section. Note, however, that this is a gentle curve, which decreases toward the end of the dwell.

Chrysler Ignition Patterns

Figure 25–44 shows the primary pattern of Chrysler's electronic ignition system. Notice that there is no intermediate section as in the electronic systems mentioned earlier. In the Chrysler system, the transistor turns on at the end of the firing section. After the transistor turns on, the dwell period is seen as a long, straight line with no humps or voltage ripples.

Figure 25–45 illustrates the secondary pattern of the Chrysler electronic system. Notice also that this pattern does not have an intermediate section, and the transistor turns on at the end of the firing line. However, in the secondary pattern, there is a series of coil oscillations after the transistor turns on. These oscillations represent the buildup of primary current flow in the coil, which causes a slight voltage induction in the secondary winding.

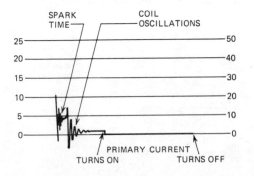

Fig. 25–42. A primary pattern of a Dura-Spark II system.

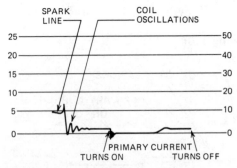

Fig. 25–43. The secondary waveform of a Dura-Spark II system.

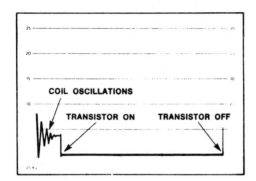

Fig. 25-44. A primary pattern of a Chrysler electronic ignition system.

Oscilloscope Alternator Patterns

The operator can view a waveform picked up at the output alternator terminal by placing the function selector switch in *special patterns* and connecting the green special patterns pickup lead to the alternator output (positive) terminal (Figs. 25-11 and 25-12).

With these conditions met and the engine operating at the specified speed, the oscilloscope will show a trace similar to the one shown in Fig. 25-46. The trace illustrated consists of a smooth rippled

line, which is an indication of normal alternator output. The pattern height, in this case, may vary somewhat with alternator output. Finally, if any of the diodes or the stator windings are defective, the trace is different from the one shown.

Figure 25-47 shows typical faulty alternator traces, which are usually only repairable by removing the unit from the vehicle and rebuilding or replacing it. In view *A*, the pattern is of an alternator with two diodes of the same polarity that are open. In this case, alternator output is greatly reduced.

In view *B*, the trace is also due to two diodes that are open. However, in this situation, there is an open positive and an open negative diode.

View *C* illustrates a pattern caused by a single open diode. Note in the waveform that one ripple is missing and the ripples next to it are somewhat compressed.

The pattern in view *D* shows what happens to alternator output when two diodes connected to different windings are open. Note in the illustration that two full ripples are missing.

Views *E* and *F* both show conditions caused by a short in diodes. View *E* for example shows the great effect on the waveform caused by just one shorted diode. View *F*, on the other hand, shows almost no alternator output due to two

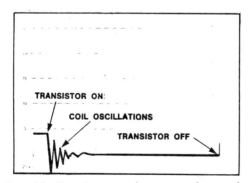

Fig. 25-45. A secondary waveform of a Chrysler electronic ignition system.

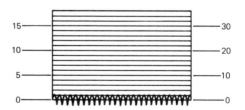

Fig. 25-46. The oscilloscope waveform of a normally functioning alternator.

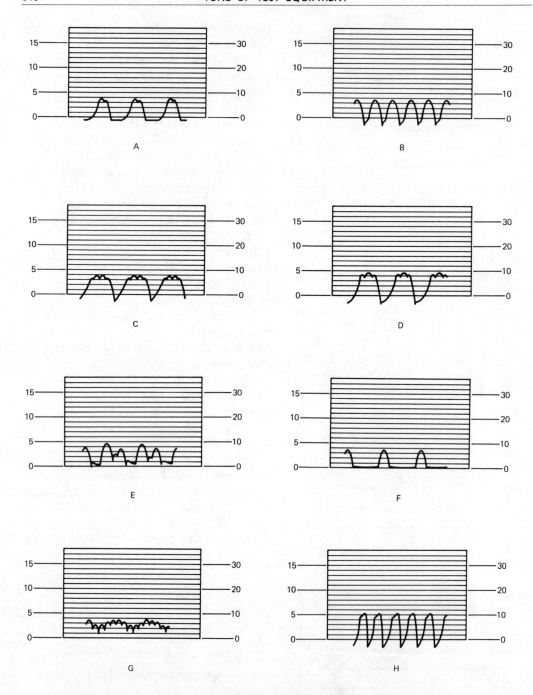

Fig. 25–47.   Waveforms showing abnormal alternator output due to defective diodes or stator windings.

diodes of the same polarity, which are shorted.

View *G* is a trace of an alternator in which none of the diodes has completely failed. However, one diode offers high resistance to current flow.

View *H* is an alternator pattern very similar to one caused by shorted diodes. However, in this situation, the abnormal pattern is the result of shorted stator windings.

Cylinder Balance Tester

The cylinder balance tester provides a means of shorting out cylinders individually or in combinations. This determines just how well the engine runs on the remaining cylinders.

The balance test compares the change in engine operation with one cylinder at a time or with similar groups of cylinders shorted-out. The test results show whether any particular cylinder or combination of cylinders is developing its share of power. For example, the less power produced by a given cylinder, the less rpm will be lost as the operator shorts out the cylinder.

Two control panels on the SUN 1115 console provide the means to perform the balance test. For example, on the scope panel of controls (Fig. 25–48) is the cylinder select mode control, which consists of two buttons. When performing the balance test, the operator depresses the short button. This action activates the eight buttons on the cylinder selector.

The cylinder selector is found on the center panel of controls (Fig. 25–49). The cylinder selector itself consists of a series of buttons identified by numbers 1 to 8. These buttons are the push-to-set, push-to-release type, which the operator can set and release individually or in any combination. By depressing any individual or group of buttons, the ignition of the corresponding cylinders electronically shorts out. Then, the operator can read the amount of rpm drop on the tachometer.

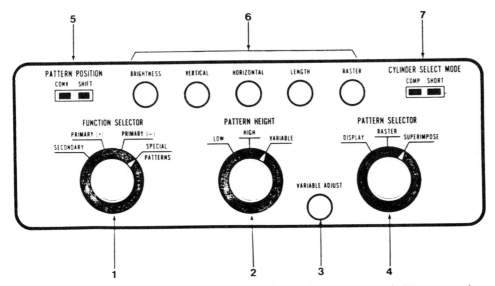

Fig. 25–48.   The cylinder mode control is on the scope panel. (Courtesy of Sun Electric Corp.)

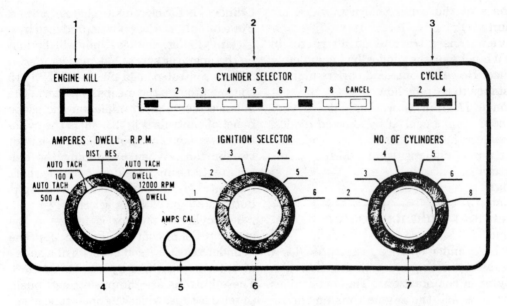

Fig. 25–49.   *The center panel has a cylinder selector, consisting of nine buttons. (Courtesy of Sun Electric Corp.)*

Finally, the ninth button, identified as *cancel,* when depressed simultaneously releases all the buttons.

Timing Advance Unit

The SUN 1115 engine analyzer also has a timing light with a timing advance unit. This unit is sometimes referred to as a *powered timing light.* The operator uses this unit to test and set the initial timing and to test quickly the action of the advance devices. In other words, the power advance unit of the light measures the amount of advance of the spark due to the action of the mechanical and vacuum advance mechanisms or the electronic control devices.

The timing advance unit itself has two controls: the timing light switch and the rotating indicator control (Fig. 25–50). The timing light switch is nothing more than an on-off switch for the timing light.

Fig. 25–50.   *The controls of a SUN 1115 timing light.*

The rotating indicator control has a number of degree markings used to measure the amount of spark advance.

When the timing advance unit is in operation, it electronically moves the engine-timing marks in relationship to the rotation of the indicator control. For example, when switching on the timing light and aiming it at the timing marks, the operator can move the timing mark on the rotating crankshaft pulley so that it aligns with the zero mark on the engine's timing scale. Then, the technician can measure the amount of advance by noting which degree, marked on the rotating control, lines up with the stationary marking on the control unit. This process, of course, is accomplished at given engine speeds, and the results compared to specifications supplied by the manufacturer.

Magnetic Timing Unit

The SUN 1115 engine analyzer shown in Fig. 25–51 also has a MAG-81 magnetic timing unit. This unit also works in con-

junction with the analyzer to measure the amount of ignition timing on vehicles equipped with a magnetic timing pickup receptacle. However, in place of the conventional timing light, a MAG-81 magnetic timing unit displays initial timing and the timing advance information *digitally* in the readout window of the unit (Fig. 25–51).

The MAG-81 basically consists of a magnetic probe and a front panel, which consists of a readout window, control switch, and offset angle knob. The magnetic probe, which connects via an electrical harness to the left side of the front panel, fits into a receptacle on the engine near the engine timing mark bracket (Fig. 25–52). The probe itself picks up a signal from the engine crankshaft, which indicates engine top dead center. The magnetic timing unit then uses this information to provide a digital readout of the exact engine timing at any moment and at any speed.

The readout window displays timing information in digital form. In other words, the readout window displays a series of

Fig. 25-51. A SUN MAG-81 magnetic timing unit.

Fig. 25–52. A typical magnetic timing receptacle. (Courtesy of Chrysler Corp.)

numbers representing basic ignition timing, or any advancement in timing due to the action of the mechanical or vacuum advance mechanisms. Finally, numbers in

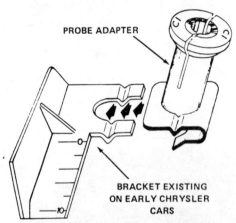

Fig. 25–53. The timing receptacle is usually offset a number of degrees from the zero or TDC mark on the timing bracket. (Courtesy of Sun Electric Corp.)

the printout window also verify correct adjustment for the offset angle of the magnetic probe receptacle.

Between the timing window and the offset angle knob is a two-position function switch. The technician uses the manual position of the switch for testing magnetic timing of current model vehicles. The manufacturer of this unit has set aside the other position for future application of this device; therefore, it is not used at this time.

The offset angle knob is necessary to compensate for the offset angle of the timing receptacle. In other words, the probe receptacle, in most cases, is offset a number of degrees from the zero degree mark on the timing bracket (Fig. 25–53). The offset angle may range from a minus 9.5 degrees on AMC and General Motors vehicles to as much as minus 135 degrees on Ford-built automobiles. Before actually performing the magnetic timing check, the technician adjusts this knob one way or the other until the correct number of degrees of offset angle appear on the readout window.

Chassis Dynamometer

The chassis dynamometer is another very important diagnostic tool, found in many tune-up specialty shops. The chassis dynamometer measures the mechanical power of the vehicle at the drivewheels and provides the operator with a readout in units of road speed and power. In addition, the chassis dynamometer along with an engine analyzer permits the operator to examine engine systems in detail with the vehicle operating under a loaded condition.

Value of the Dynamometer

The experienced tune-up technician knows that an engine operates differently under load than when running without one. There are, of course, many reasons for this phenomenon. For example, ignition timing is different between the loaded and unloaded vehicle, due to the action of the vacuum advance mechanisms. Similarly the air/fuel ratio also varies greatly as the load on the engine increases. Furthermore, since compression pressure is definitely higher with the throttle plate partially to fully open, the coil must produce a higher voltage to cause an ignition spark to occur in a loaded engine.

Manifold vacuum also varies greatly between the unloaded and loaded engine. For instance, vacuum is generally 16 to 21 inches of Hg at idle, whereas under a light load, it is 14 to 16 inches of Hg. However, under a heavy load condition such as rapid acceleration, driving at very high speeds, or climbing a long, steep hill, the manifold vacuum is 0 to 10 inches of Hg.

Obviously, it is very important to test the engine and its accessories while each unit is functioning under conditions simulating those on the road. At the same time, the technician can measure the output of the engine both before and after servicing and compare the results. The power output in this case is the power delivered to the rear wheels to drive the vehicle on the highway.

However, operating the engine under a load in the shop is far more important than measuring the horsepower delivered to the rear wheels because the average vehicle owner has little understanding of the significance of horsepower. What is important to him is that the service work put the vehicle back in top running condition.

Rated Horsepower

When discussing the dynamometer, the term *rated horsepower* comes up very often. The vehicle manufacturer usually provides a measurement of the rated horsepower of the engine. However, this is the horsepower delivered by a stripped engine, without a fan, alternator, transmission, driveline, rear axle, and the effect of dragging brakes. In other words, the manufacturer rates the engine under ideal laboratory conditions and provides a measurement taken at the peak of the engine's horsepower curve.

On the other hand, when the engine operates in a vehicle, it drives a number of accessories. As a result, the engine power delivered to the rear wheels is less than the rated value due to the power losses through the preceding units. In addition, the engine in a motor vehicle must operate under widely varying conditions of temperature, speed, humidity, and atmospheric pressure. Therefore, a given engine rated at 300 horsepower may show only 125 horsepower at the rear wheels on the dynamometer. It should be obvious then that the horsepower measured and indicated on the dynamometer actually has little value to the vehicle owner other than for comparison purposes.

Road versus Dynamometer Testing

For a great many years, tune-up technicians have recognized road testing as an acceptable procedure for checking out engines that they have serviced or determining what engine repairs or adjustments are necessary. However, road congestion in the well-populated areas along with the high hourly rate paid to mechanics makes road testing somewhat hazardous and expensive. Therefore, the use of the *chassis dynamometer* to test and check out the vehicle safely and quickly, right in the shop, has become very desirable.

Dynamometer Design

The typical chassis dynamometer consists of two rollers, a remote control pendant, and readout instruments. The two trunnion-mounted rollers (Fig. 25–54) cradle the vehicle's drive wheels. One of the rollers couples directly to a power absorption unit. The power absorption unit applies a varying load on this roller upon command from the operator. The power absorption unit then acts as a very effective brake, which applies, through the roller, resistance to drivewheel rotation. The greater the load applied by the ab-

Fig. 25–54. The roller assembly of a Clayton dynamometer.

sorption unit to the roller, the more horsepower is necessary to turn it at any given speed. Thus, at constant drivewheel speed, the horsepower output can be made to vary by changing the load, applied by the absorption unit. Also, the operator can vary the horsepower output with a constant load applied to the drivewheels by changing the engine speed.

The other roller drives a tachometer generator. This unit supplies electrical current for operation of the dynamometer's readout instruments.

The remote pendant (Fig. 25–55) is a hand-held control used to activate the power absorption unit. The control itself has two buttons: on and off. When the technician pushes the on button in, the power absorption unit begins to load the roller. The off button, on the other hand, de-energizes the power absorption unit, thus releasing the load from the roller.

The speed and power instrument panel of a Clayton dynamometer is shown in Fig. 25–56. This panel contains two large, illuminated meters: speed and power. The speed meter has a range of 0 to 120 miles per hour (0 to 200 kilometers per hour). The power meter reads 0 to 100 or 0 to 200 horsepower (0 to 80 or 0 to 160 kilowatts). Which scale the operator uses depends upon the position of the switch on the face of the instrument box, which provides for full or half-scale readings.

Fig. 25–55. The hand-operated remote pendant controls the operation of the power absorption unit.

Fig. 25-56. The speed and power instrument panel of a Clayton dynamometer.

Review

This section will assist you in determining how well you remember the material in this chapter. Read each item carefully. If you can't complete the statement, review the section in the chapter that covers the material.

1. The testing device that can measure engine power is the _____.
   a. dynamometer
   b. voltmeter
   c. tachometer
   d. speedometer

2. The instrument for measuring electrical pressure is the _____.
   a. tachometer
   b. ammeter
   c. ohmmeter
   d. voltmeter

3. The instrument that measures the amount of hydrocarbons within a vehicle's exhaust is the _____ meter.

   a. CO
   b. HC
   c. CO_2
   d. NOx

4. The best instrument for diagnosing ignition system malfunctions is the _____.
   a. tachometer
   b. ammeter
   c. oscilloscope
   d. both *a* and *b*

5. In the _____ position, all the ignition waveforms appear in a horizontal chain across the screen.
   a. raster
   b. superimposed
   c. display
   d. both *b* and *c*

6. The SUN 1115 has _____ oscilloscope leads.
   a. one
   b. two
   c. three
   d. four

7. The _____ section of a waveform represents the period in which
the plug actually fires.
a. intermediate
b. firing
c. arcing
d. dwell

8. In a secondary pattern, coil and condenser oscillations appear in the _____
_____ section.
a. dwell
b. arcing
c. firing
d. intermediate

9. In an oscilloscope pattern of an ignition cycle, the section representing
the period when the points are closed
is the _____.
a. intermediate
b. firing
c. dwell
d. arcing

10. The _____ waveform is not
as informative as the secondary.
a. raster
b. superimposed
c. primary
d. display

11. The waveform in which all the cylinder patterns are stacked vertically,
one above the other, is the _____.
a. raster
b. display
c. superimposed
d. parade

12. The waveform commonly used to
measure the height of the firing voltage is the _____.
a. firing
b. display
c. superimposed
d. raster

13. The operator sees the effects of dwell
variation more easily in the _____
_____ pattern(s).
a. display
b. superimposed
c. raster
d. both b and c

14. If the firing line is missing from a secondary pattern, the _____
circuit is open.
a. point
b. coil
c. plug
d. condenser

15. A secondary ignition pattern with a
high firing line and short spark line is
due to _____ _____
_____.
a. an enlarged plug gap.
b. a narrow plug gap.
c. shorted coil.
d. high engine compression.

16. The secondary _____ section
is about the same in both standard
and transistorized ignition system
patterns.
a. intermediate
b. firing
c. dwell
d. raster

17. The dwell section of a transistorized
ignition-system waveform begins
with _____ _____
_____.
a. a point-close signal.
b. a point-open signal.
c. a transistor-on signal.
d. a transistor-off signal.

18. The pattern of a Chrysler transistorized ignition system has no _____
section.

a. display
b. firing
c. dwell
d. intermediate

19. The device that measures the amount of spark advance is _____ _____ _____.

a. the timing advance unit.
b. the oscilloscope.
c. the cylinder balance tester.
d. the dwell meter.

20. The device that measures ignition timing on vehicles with a magnetic timing pickup receptacle is the _____ _____ _____.

a. timing advance unit.
b. oscilloscope.
c. MAG-81.
d. dwell meter.

21. The device that measures power at the drive wheels is the _____ _____.

a. vacuum gauge.
b. chassis dynamometer.
c. oscilloscope screen.
d. SUN MAG-81.

22. The component of the dynamometer that actually loads the vehicle is _____ _____ _____.

a. the speed instrument.
b. the tachometer drive.
c. the power instrument.
d. the power absorption unit.

For the answers, turn to the Appendix.

Every vehicle manufacturer publishes tune-up procedures and specifications for its particular automobiles. This data may be found either in the service manual for the particular vehicle or on a decal underneath the hood. The information in the service manual applies only to one or more automobiles produced by a given manufacturer. The tune-up decal, on the other hand, provides the technician with information only about the vehicle he is working on.

Tune-up mechanics who work within independent garages or tune-up specialty shops do not have available to them all the service manuals for all automobiles. Therefore, if no other data are available, the tune-up technician must depend entirely on the specifications and procedures outlined on the tune-up decal. This could be a real probelm because older vehicles did not have the decal, and the decals on the newer vehicles become illegible after a period of time.

However, several independent companies along with manufacturers of test equipment publish their own tune-up specifications and procedures. This information is also available in bound volumes or on specification cards for each automobile. The use of the bound volumes or specification cards reduces the size of the technical library that the service center needs, but at the same time provides the necessary information for the mechanic to perform a thorough tune-up.

Factory Procedures

The factory service manual on a particular vehicle provides the mechanic with all the necessary information on how to test the condition of the engine and its

Chapter 26

TUNE-UP TEST PROCEDURES

related systems. Along with this information, the manual also specifies certain types of equipment that the mechanic can use to perform a given test or procedure. In the automobile dealership environment, the mechanic follows these procedures and uses the recommended test instruments.

Equipment Manufacturers' Procedures

It is apparent that the mechanic working in an independent garage or tune-up specialty shop is again placed at a disadvantage. It would appear that the mechanic must know many different procedures and possibly must be proficient with many types of testing equipment in order to make a living. However, automotive-testing equipment manufacturers have solved this problem by providing the technician with not only excellent test equipment but standardized test procedures applicable to most automobiles.

Although these test procedures vary somewhat between equipment manufacturers, they all perform the same function. The procedure provides the technician with a step-by-step testing sequence, designed to locate malfunctions within the engine or its related systems.

Equipment manufacturers recommend that the technician follows the test procedure before and after the tune-up. Performance testing a vehicle before the actual work on the engine and its subsystems begins provides the technician with vital information as to their condition, thereby eliminating guesswork and the replacement of nondefective parts. Lastly, manufacturers also recommend

the use of their test procedures as a quality control tool after the completion of the tune-up. This assures that the engine and its related systems are functioning satisfactorily and to specifications.

Sun Procedures

Sun Electric Corporation, as do any other test equipment manufacturers, provides with its equipment given tune-up or performance test procedures. The procedure consists of testing the engine and the ignition, fuel, electrical, and emission control systems at given rpms with the engine analyzer. During the procedure, the mechanic notes the conditions of the various systems and components on a performance test report.

Figure 26-1 shows an engine performance test report that the technician uses with either a SUN 1115 or a TUT-1015 SUN Engine analyzer. The upper portion of this form is set aside for information about the customer and the vehicle brought in for a tune-up. The most important question in this section is the reason for the test.

In any form of diagnostic work, the most important thing to do before starting the test is to get the customer's story. What particular problems has the owner been having with the automobile, and why is the vehicle in for a tune-up? What are the specific complaints?

By knowing exactly what the complaint is and noting it on the form, the technician can begin to look for probable causes during the test sequence. The result of this, of course, is locating and correcting the customer's complaint and eliminating costly comebacks.

The manufacturer divides the remain-

SUN 1115/TUT-1015
ENGINE PERFORMANCE TEST REPORT

Customer Name _____ Phone _____ Date _____

Address _____ City/State _____ License _____

Make/Year/Model _____ Mileage _____ Mileage Since Tune-Up _____

Engine _____ Transmission—Auto ☐ Std ☐   Air Conditioning—Yes ☐ No ☐

Carburetor _____ Ignition Type _____ Air Pump—Yes ☐ No ☐ Converter—Yes ☐ No ☐

Reason For Tests _____ Tested By _____

TEST MODE	TESTS	READ	ENTER SPECIFICATIONS	TEST RESULT	GO	NO GO
#1 **CRANKING**	COIL OUTPUT	SCOPE (DISPLAY)	KV (MIN)			
	STARTER CURRENT	AMMETER	AMPS (MAX)			
	BATTERY VOLTAGE	VOLTMETER	VOLTS (MIN)			
	ENGINE VACUUM	VACUUM GAUGE	STEADY			
#2 **CHARGING**	CHARGING SYSTEM	AMMETER	SHOWS CHARGE			
	DIODE STATOR	SCOPE (ALT)	EVEN RIPPLE			
#3 **IDLE**	RPM	TACHOMETER	RPM			
	DWELL	DWELL METER	DEGREES			
	INITIAL TIMING	TIMING LIGHT	DEGREES			
	CARBON MONOXIDE	CO METER	%			
	HYDROCARBONS	HC METER	PPM			
	ENGINE VACUUM	VACUUM GAUGE	INCHES			
	PCV	TACH. VACUUM GAUGE	RPM · VAC			
#4 **1200 RPM** **LOW** **CRUISE**	COIL POLARITY	SCOPE (DISPLAY)	VISUAL			
	SPARK PLUGS	SCOPE (DISPLAY)	KV			
	MAX COIL OUTPUT	SCOPE (DISPLAY)	KV (MIN)			
	SECONDARY INSUL.	SCOPE (DISPLAY)	VISUAL			
	SECONDARY RESISTANCE	SCOPE (RASTER SHIFT)	VISUAL			
	COIL, CONDENSER	SCOPE (RASTER SHIFT)	VISUAL			
	BREAKER POINTS	SCOPE (RASTER SHIFT)	VISUAL			
	CYLINDER TIMING	SCOPE (SUPER-CONV)	VISUAL			
	CARBON MONOXIDE	CO METER	%			
	HYDROCARBONS	HC METER	PPM			

TEST MODE	TESTS		1	2	3	4	5	6	7	8			
#5 **CYLINDER** **POWER** **BALANCE**	ENGINE	TACHOMETER						BASE RPM					
	SHORTED RPM												

TEST MODE	TESTS	READ	ENTER SPECIFICATIONS	TEST RESULT	GO	NO GO
#6 **SNAP** **ACCELERATION**	SPARK PLUGS UNDER LOAD	SCOPE (DISPLAY)	KV (MAX)			
	ACCELERATOR PUMP ACTION	CO METER	% (MAX)			
#7 **2500 RPM** **HIGH** **CRUISE**	TIMING ADVANCE	TIMING LIGHT	DEGREES			
	DWELL	DWELL METER	DEGREES			
	CHARGING VOLTS	VOLTMETER	VOLTS			
	CARBON MONOXIDE	CO METER	%			
	HYDROCARBONS	HC METER	PPM			
	ENGINE VACUUM	VACUUM GAUGE	INCHES			

Sun DIAGNOSIS AND TRAINING GUIDE

0692-0951 (8710)   Printed in USA

Fig. 26-1. A typical engine performance test report. (Courtesy of Sun Electric Corp.)

ing portion of the test form under sub-titles: test mode, test, read, specifications, test result, go, no-go. Under the test mode column are seven sections. These refer to the phase of engine operation at which the technician will perform tests.

The test column refers to the actual components that a given procedure evaluates. For example, under cranking test mode 1, the procedure evaluates coil output, starter current draw, battery voltage, and engine vacuum.

The read column specifies which instruments the technician uses during a given procedure. For example, during charging test mode 2, the technician gathers information from both the ammeter and the scope.

Under "enter specifications" are spaces in each test mode for specific specifications. The technician uses either the SUN specification cards, underhood sticker, or manufacturers' manuals and bulletins to obtain the specifications needed. Where no factory specifications are available, the mechanic will base the decision (go, or no-go) on testing experience on good engines of the same make and model as the vehicle being tested.

Under the heading "test results" spaces are available, in each test mode, for data received from the various instruments. In other words, after the test is complete, the technician writes in these blanks the data received from the instruments. For example, after the cranking test, if the coil output is 24 Kv, the technician would write this information in the "test result" block.

The *go* and the *no-go* are nothing more than *Pass* and *Fail* blocks of the test form. In other words, if a component or number of components failed a given test, the technician would check the no-go block across from the defective components.

Tune-up Procedures with a Sun 1115

To prepare the Sun 1115 engine analyzer for this procedure:

1. Plug the analyzer's power cord into a proper a.c. outlet.

2. Turn the a.c. power switch (left end of panel) to the on position. With the switch on, the sign, meters, and scale indicators light, and a waveform appears on the scope screen.

3. Position the gas calibrate switch at the rear of the tester in the operate position.

4. Depress the zero mode control button of the infrared test selector to allow the exhaust analyzer to warm up while you finish preparing the tester.

Positioning the Scope Controls

To prepare the scope for the tune-up test procedure (Fig. 26–2):

1. Push in the pattern position conv. (conventional) button.

2. Adjust the brightness control as necessary.

3. Adjust the vertical control so that the scope pattern line rests on the screen's zero line.

4. Adjust the horizontal control knob to align the left end of the scope waveform with the left edge (0 to 25 KV line) of the scope screen.

5. Adjust the length control knob to align the right edge of the scope pattern with the right edge (0 to 50 KV line) of the scope screen. *Note:* To adjust the length control properly, the no. of cylinders knob

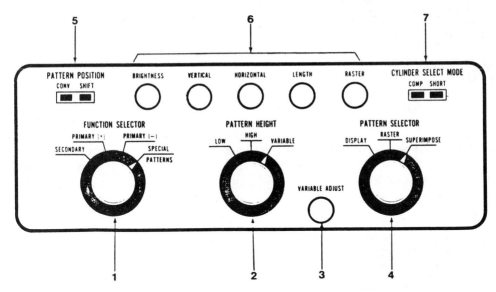

Fig. 26-2. The scope control panel of a Sun 1115 engine analyzer. (Courtesy of Sun Electric Corp.)

must be set at 8 or the engine must be operating.

6. Set the function selector knob to the secondary position.

7. Adjust the pattern height knob to high. Set the pattern selector knob to the display position. *Note:* The raster control knob does not require adjustment at this time. Only adjust the raster knob as required during the test procedure.

Positioning the Analyzer's Test Controls

To adjust the analyzer's controls correctly for the upcoming test, follow this procedure (Fig. 26-2).

1. Push the cylinder select mode short button.

2. Depress the engine kill button to the green position. (*Green* is the run position, while *red* indicates that the ignition system is disabled and the engine will not function.)

3. Push the cylinder selector red cancel button.

4. Push the appropriate cycle button. Depress the fourth button for most automotive engines, with the exception of the rotary or others with two-cycle ignition.

5. Adjust the amperes-dwell-rpm knob to the auto-tach/100 A position.

6. Zero the ammeter with the amps cal. knob. Then set the amperes-dwell-rpm knob to the auto-tach/500 A position.

7. Set the ignition selector knob to position 1, except as follows.

a. Adjust the knob to position 2 for Delco HEI and Prestolite Bid systems.

b. Set the control to position 4 for any capacitive discharge (CD) system.

8. Adjust the no. of cylinders knob to correspond to the number of cylinders of the engine being tested.

9. Set the volt-ohm knob to the 20v position (Fig. 26–3).

Calibrating the HC and CO Meters

To calibrate the HC and CO meters (Fig. 26–3) in preparation for the test:

1. Permit the depressed zero mode control button to remain in at least 5 minutes in order to warm up the tester.

2. Push in the ppm HC 400 and the percent CO 2.0 buttons.

3. Adjust the HC and CO zero knobs until both meter pointers read on the respective zero set line.

4. Depress and hold in the span mode control button while adjusting both the HC and CO span knobs until both meter pointers read on the span set line.

5. Release the span button and recheck the zero adjustment.

6. Push in the test button. *Note:* During the first 15 minutes of operation, the HC and CO meters may require slight additional calibration adjustments. You can check calibration at any time by repeating the above steps. However, it is not necessary to remove the sample probe from the tailpipe or to stop the engine in order to recheck the calibration of the unit.

Analyzer Lead Connections to the Vehicle

To connect the analyzer's lead connections properly to a vehicle with a negative ground system, follow these instructions (Fig. 26–4).

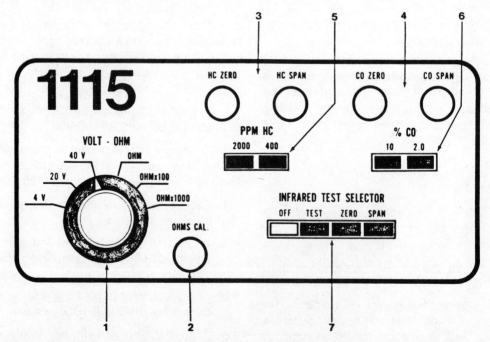

Fig. 26–3. *The right panel of controls of a Sun 1115 engine analyzer. (Courtesy of Sun Electric Corp.)*

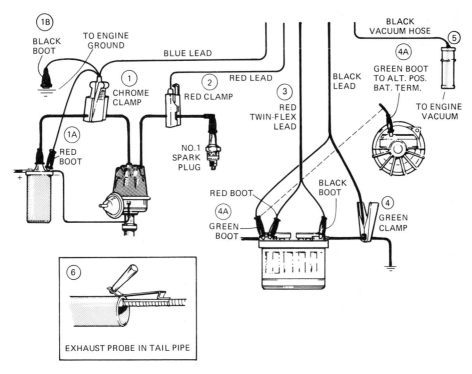

Fig. 26-4.   The engine analyzer's lead connections to the vehicle.

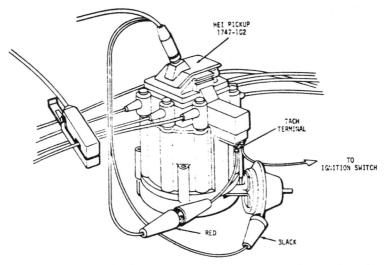

Fig. 26-5.   The special adapter necessary to connect the analyzer's pattern pickup lead to a GM HEI ignition system with the coil in the distributor cap. (Courtesy of Sun Electric Corp.)

1. Clamp the chrome pattern pickup around the secondary coil wire. *Note:* On GM HEI systems, with the ignition coil within the distributor cap, use the special adapter as shown in Fig. 26-5.

2. Connect the red primary pickup connector to the negative terminal of the ignition coil (on electronic ignition systems, connect it to the specified terminal).

3. Connect the black (ground) primary pickup lead to any good engine ground.

4. Clamp the red trigger pickup around spark plug wire 1, close to the distributor cap.

5. Connect the volt-ohm leads to the battery post: red to positive and black to negative.

6. Clamp the green ammeter pickup lead around the negative battery terminal with its arrow pointing away from the battery. *Note:* If there is more than one negative battery cable, clamp the pickup around all the cables.

7. Connect the green special pattern pickup lead to the positive (+) battery post. *Note:* If accessible, clamp this lead around the alternator output (+) terminal.

8. Connect the vacuum hose to a source of full engine vacuum.

9. Insert the infrared sampling hose into the vehicle's tailpipe about 12 inches (Fig. 26-4).

Testing Procedures— Cranking Test 1

To perform this particular test:

1. Disable the engine's ignition system by disconnecting the secondary coil lead from the distributor cap. Position this lead clear of any ground. (To disable all HEI ignition systems, push the engine kill button so that it shows red.) Then, turn off all lights and accessories. Crank the engine and:

a. Note the cranking coil output in kilovolts on the 50 KV scale on the scope screen. *Note:* This particular test is void when using the engine kill button on the HEI ignition systems.

b. Read and note the cranking starter current on the blue 500-amp scale of the ammeter.

c. Read and note the cranking battery voltage on the red 20-volt scale on the voltmeter.

d. Read and note the cranking vacuum on the analyzer's vacuum gauge.

Results and Indications— Coil Output

If the coil output is below specifications, check the *no-go* block on the test report and look for the following problems.

1. Battery voltage is too low. Check the cranking battery voltage test results on the report. If it also is below specifications, perform both battery and starter tests.

2. Dwell is too low. Check the dwell during idle mode test 3.

3. The bypass ignition circuit is defective. In this situation, test the bypass circuit with a voltmeter.

4. Primary ignition current is low. In this case, check for excessive resistance in the primary circuit and contact points. Also, check for the possibility of the incorrect coil for the vehicle.

5. The ignition coil or condenser is bad. Check each unit on an appropriate tester.

6. The coil wire to the distributor cap is defective. Test the unit with an ohmmeter. *Note:* On electronic ignition systems, follow the appropriate test procedure to locate the cause of low coil output.

Starter Current

If starter current was too high during the cranking mode, mark *no-go* on the test report and check for the following problems.

1. The battery is either discharged, defective, or too small for this application. Perform a complete battery test and check the battery's rating against specifications.

2. Either a battery cable, starter solenoid, or starter motor is defective. Perform a complete starting system test.

3. The engine is too tight or excessively hot. In this case, cool the engine off and retest.

Battery Voltage

If battery voltage is below the specified minimum, check the *no-go* space on the report form. Then, perform the same tests as for excessive current draw.

Engine Vacuum

If the engine vacuum reading is uneven or much lower than normal, mark the no-go block on the report form and check for the following problems:

1. Vacuum leaks. In this situation, examine all vacuum hoses, including those leading to emission controls and accessories. Replace any defective hose.

Also, tighten all engine manifold bolts including those holding the carburetor in place.

2. Engine in poor mechanical condition. Test the engine with a compression and leakage tester.

Test 2—Charging

To perform this particular test:

1. Turn the amperes-dwell-rpm knob to the auto-tach/100 A scale.

2. Set the function selector knob to special patterns.

3. Set the pattern height knob to variable. Then, adjust the variable adjust knob to the full clockwise position.

4. Set the pattern selector knob to raster.

5. Prepare the engine to operate by inserting the coil's high tension wire into the distributor or by releasing the engine kill button to its green position. Start the engine and accelerate to 2,000 rpm. Then note the following:

   a. The alternator's output on the blue 100-amp scale of the ammeter.

   b. The condition of the diode's stator as indicated by the scope pattern. As necessary, use the raster control knob to space the scope pattern for best viewing.

6. Return the engine to idle speed.

Results and Indications

If the ammeter shows low output or the alternator waveform on the scope is abnormal, mark the no-go space on the test report and check the following.

1. Loose or worn out fan belt. Check fan belt tension; replace the belt as necessary.

2. Very high accessory load. In this case, check the current draw with the ignition key on and the engine stopped. Add this reading to the output obtained, and compare it to specifications.

3. Defective alternator. Recheck the alternator output with the amps pickup at the alternator output terminal with all the accessories on and the engine operating at 2,000 rpm. If alternator output is still low, proceed to item 4.

4. Defective voltage regulator. Use the appropriate starting and charging system tester to bypass regulator and check alternator output. If the voltage regulator is satisfactory, remove the alternator for repair or replacement.

5. Defective diodes or stator windings. If the scope pattern indicated an uneven ripple, either the output diodes or stator windings are defective. In this case, remove the alternator for repair or replacement.

Test 3—Idle

To perform this test:

1. Turn the amperes-dwell-rpm knob to the auto-tach/dwell position.

2. Adjust the function selector knob to the secondary position.

3. Set the pattern height knob to high.

4. Set the pattern selector knob for a display pattern.

5. Start and warm up the engine until the choke is open and the engine is at normal curb idle speed. Then, read and note the results of the following:

a. The rpm on the red 0 to 1,500 rpm scale of the tachometer.

b. The dwell on the red dwell meter scale.

c. The initial ignition timing with the timing light.

d. The percentage of carbon monoxide on the CO meter.

e. The amount of hydrocarbon emissions in ppm on the HC meter.

f. The amount of intake manifold vacuum on the vacuum gauge.

g. The operation of the PCV valve, following manufacturer's recommended procedures.

Results and Indications—Idle RPM

If the idle speed is not to specifications, mark the no-go space on the test results. Then check the following:

1. Carburetor idle speed and/or mixture screws out of adjustment. To correct this problem, readjust the screws following the manufacturer's recommended procedure.

2. The choke plate sticking or not fully open. Perform any repairs or adjustments as necessary to correct the problem.

3. Idle solenoid, if so equipped, out of adjustment. Readjust solenoid, following factory instructions.

4. The test was not performed under specified conditions. Check the specifications in the motor's manual or on the underhood sticker; perform the test as specified.

5. Poor engine mechanical condition. In this case, perform an engine compression and leakage test.

6. Improperly operating emission control devices, especially the EGR valve. Test and service the systems following the manufacturer's recommendations.

Dwell

If the dwell is either too high or too low, mark the no-go block on the report form. Then check for the following:

1. Ignition points out of adjustment. Reset the points to specifications.

2. Defective distributor. In this case, make a complete distributor test on an appropriate distributor machine. Then, repair or replace the distributor as necessary. *Note:* On electronic ignition systems, always follow the manufacturer's recommendations when testing the distributor.

Ignition Timing

If the ignition timing is either too early or too late, mark the no-go block on the report form. Next, check for the following:

1. Timing adjusted improperly. Reset the timing to specifications.

2. Defective distributor advance mechanism. Remove and test the distributor on an appropriate distributor tester. Then, repair or replace the defective mechanisms.

3. Engine not operating at the proper speed or the vacuum retard unit not disconnected during the test, if so specified. Reset the engine to the correct speed or disconnect the hose to the vacuum retard unit on the distributor. *Note:* Before adjusting the ignition timing to specifications, always make sure that the dwell is correct and the engine is operating at the specified rpm.

Carbon Monoxide Level

If the CO reading is not to specifications, mark the no-go space on the report form and check the following:

1. Incorrect carburetor settings. Perform mixture adjustments following the factory recommended procedure.

2. Incorrect float adjustment. Readjust the float to specifications.

3. Dirty air cleaner. In this situation, clean or replace the element.

4. Improper idle speed. Adjust the idle speed, following the manufacturer's recommended procedure.

5. Oil in the crankcase diluted with gasoline or the engine has excessive blowby. Make all repairs necessary to correct the faulty condition.

Hydrocarbon Level

If the HC reading is not to specifications, mark the no-go space on the test report. Then, check for the following:

1. Mechanical problem in the engine. Perform a compression or leakage test.

2. Ignition system malfunction. Test and service the ignition system.

Engine Vacuum

If the vacuum reading is unsteady or below the specified minimum, mark the no-go space on the test report. Then, check for the same possible causes as for cranking engine vacuum.

Positive Crankcase Ventilation Valve Operation

If the rpm, CO, or vacuum does not change after testing the valve as outlined in Chapters 5, 21, and 24, mark the no-go space on the report form and then check for the following:

a. Defective or plugged PCV valve. Clean or replace the valve and retest the system.

b. Restriction in the PCV hose or its vacuum source, or the hose is cracked and leaking. Perform repairs as necessary.

c. Incorrect PCV valve for the engine. Replace the valve with the correct one.

Test 4—1,200 RPM, Low-Cruise

To perform this particular check:

1. Start the engine and operate it at approximately 1,200 rpm.

2. Then, perform the following checks:

a. The polarity of the coil of a display pattern.

b. The spark plug firing voltages of all cylinders, using a display pattern.

c. The maximum coil output (available voltage) of the display pattern. *Note:* To perform this test, it is necessary to remove one of the spark plug wires with insulated pliers, and hold it away from the spark plug.

d. The display pattern for secondary insulation. In this situation, it also is necessary to remove a spark plug wire from the plug.

e. A raster waveform for excessive secondary resistance.

f. A raster waveform for coil and condenser condition.

g. A raster pattern for the condition of the breaker points.

h. A superimposed pattern for cam lobe accuracy.

i. The percentage of carbon monoxide on the CO meter.

j. The amount of hydrocarbon emissions on the HC meter. After taking this reading, push the zero button on the infrared test selector.

Results and Indications— Coil Polarity

If the display pattern shows an inverted waveform (firing lines extend downward), mark the no-go space on the report form. Then check the following:

1. Incorrect coil installed on the engine or the ignition coil primary wires improperly connected. The wire connections should match battery ground polarity. Replace the coil and correctly connect the primary wires to the coil.

2. Battery either installed or charged backwards. Reconnect the battary properly or check its polarity at the terminals with a volt meter.

Spark Plug Firing Voltage

If there is more than 3 kv difference in any of the firing voltages or all the firing lines are excessively high or low, mark the no-go space on the test report form. Then, check the following:

1. Defective resistor spark plugs; incorrect spark plug or rotor gaps; defective distributor cap or rotor; or secondary wires that have high resistance or are open. In this situation, visually inspect all components and check secondary wires

with an ohmmeter. Replace defective components as necessary.

2. Improper air/fuel mixture. In this case, check the automatic choke and carburetor adjustments. Also check for vacuum leaks. After finding the cause of the problem, make adjustments and repairs as necessary.

3. Initial timing or advance not to specifications. In this situation, check the ignition timing test results in the idle mode and the timing advance test in the high cruise mode. Then, correct initial timing as necessary or remove the distributor and check the advance mechanisms on an appropriate distributor tester.

4. Electronic distributor trigger coil connected incorrectly. In this case, reverse the connections to the coil and retest.

Maximum Coil Output

If the coil output is less than the minimum specified, mark the no-go space in the report form and check for the following:

1. A too low dwell reading. In this case also see the dwell test results in the idle mode and later from the high cruise mode. Then, reset the contact points or remove the distributor for further testing on an appropriate distributor tester.

2. Excessive resistance in either the ignition switch, primary circuit, or points. Check these components with a voltmeter or ohmmeter.

3. Low-charging system voltage. In this case, also check the amount of charging volts in the high cruise mode test. As necessary, make a complete charging system test with an appropriate analyzer.

4. Poor insulation in the secondary circuit. If the coil output is under 25 kv and the lower extent of the waveform is intermittent or missing, test for insulation breakdown in either the wires, cap, or rotor.

5. Defective coil or condenser. Check each component on appropriate tester. Then, replace the defective component.

Secondary Insulation

If the coil output is less than 25 kv and the lower extent of the waveform (downspike) is not steady and equal to about one-half the height of the upward extent, mark the no-go block on the test report. Then, check the system for defective wires, distributor cap, rotor, or coil. *Note:* The loss of the lower extent to high output systems such as in a HEI that produces over 30 kv is not uncommon. The spark jumps inside the distributor cap, even on a good system, when the operator removes the spark plug wire from the plug terminal.

Secondary Resistance

If one or more of the spark lines slant excessively or are too short, mark the no-go block on the test report form. Next, check for excessive resistance in either the spark plugs, wires, rotor, distributor cap, or the coil tower. Isolate the problem using a grounding probe, and replace defective parts.

Coil and Condenser Oscillations

If the intermediate section of the waveforms shows a reduction in the number and size of coil-condenser oscillations, check the no-go block on the test report. Then, check for the following:

1. Defective coil or condenser. Check each unit on appropriate tester and replace the defective part.

2. Points, condenser, or pigtail loose in the distributor. In this situation, check distributor operation on an appropriate distributor tester.

3. In some electronic ignition systems, such as Chrysler electronic ignition, there will not be any oscillations in the intermediate section. Consequently, the coil may be satisfactory.

Breaker Points

If the point-close and-open signal is irregular or shows signs of arcing, mark the no-go space on the test report. Then, check for the following defects:

1. Dirty, burned, or misaligned contact points. If the points are defective, replace them. Then, test the condenser.

2. Weak contact point spring tension. Adjust spring tension or replace the contact points.

3. Dwell or primary current is too high. In this situation, check and adjust dwell. Then, measure the primary current flow, and make any adjustments or repairs necessary to bring primary current flow to specifications.

4. Incorrect coil or ballast resistor for vehicle. Check both units and replace incorrect parts as necessary.

5. Charging voltage too high. Check the test results in the high cruise mode. Then, perform a complete charging system test.

Dwell Variation

If the point-open signals vary more than specified, usually plus or minus 2 degrees, there is excessive dwell variation. In this case, mark the no-go block on the test report and check for the following defects:

1. Defective distributor cam. Remove and test the distributor on an accurate distributor tester.

2. Worn or defective breaker plate or shaft bushings, or incorrect contact spring tension. In this situation, also remove and test the distributor.

3. A problem in the engine such as a defective distributor bushing within the block or loose timing chain or gears. Inspect these items for wear; make needed repairs.

Carbon Monoxide Level

If the carbon monoxide level during this test mode is not to specifications, mark the no-go block on the test report. Then, check the same items as for an incorrect CO reading during the idle test mode.

Hydrocarbon Level

If the HC reading is out of specifications, mark the no-go space on the test report. Then, check for the same defects as for an excessive HC level during the idle test mode.

Test 5—Cylinder Power Balance

To perform this particular test:

1. Set the pattern selector knob for a display pattern.

2. Start and operate the engine at the desired test speed. Then, record the base rpm on the test report.

3. One at a time, press the cylinder selector buttons until all cylinders have been shorted out and then released.

4. Note and record rpm produced with each cylinder shorted-out. The amount of drop and allowable variation depends upon the type of engine, number of cylinders, and speed at which you performed the test.

Results and Indications

If rpm during this test does not change or changes very little on one or more cylinders, mark the no-go block on the test report. Then, check for the following defects:

1. Problems within the ignition system. In this case, check the results of the scope test in the low cruise mode. Then, repair or replace any defective components.

2. Problems within the engine. Perform compression and leakage tests to ascertain the mechanical condition of the engine.

3. Problems in fuel mixture or distribution. In this situation, always check for vacuum leaks and carburetor adjustment and balance.

Test 6—Snap Acceleration

To perform this test:

1. Push the test button on the infrared test selector.

2. With the engine warmed up and at curb idle, quickly snap-accelerate the engine and release the throttle while observing the spark plug firing lines on the scope screen.

3. Note the cylinders with excessively high or low firing lines.

4. Again, snap-accelerate the engine and permit it to return to idle speed. Then, wait a few moments for the CO reading to peak on the meter. Record the maximum CO reading on the test report.

Results and Indications— Spark Plugs under Load

If the firing lines do not increase moderately or evenly or the firing voltages exceeded the maximum specified, mark the no-go block on the test report. Then, inspect the spark plugs for wear, incorrect gap, or fouling. Clean, regap, or replace the spark plugs as required.

CO Level under Load

If the CO reading decreases more than 0.5 percent before increasing or does not increase, mark the no-go space on the test report. Then, check for lean air/fuel mixtures, caused by faulty accelerator pump or high-speed circuit operation. Make repairs or adjustments to the carburetor in order to correct the defect.

Test 7—2,500 RPM High-Cruise

To perform this test:

1. With the engine operating at normal temperature, set its speed to approximately 2,500 rpm.

2. Turn the timing light switch on, and aim the timing light at the engine timing marks. Then, adjust the rotating control on the back of the timing light assembly until the timing mark on the rotating pulley aligns with the zero mark on the engine timing scale. Next, note on the test report the number of degrees of actual advancement.

3. Read and note the number of dwell in degrees on the dwell meter.

4. Read and note the number of charging volts on the 20v scale of the voltmeter.

5. Read and note the carbon monoxide percentage on the CO meter.

6. Read and note the amount of hydrocarbon emission on the HC meter.

7. Read and note the amount of intake manifold vacuum on the vacuum gauge.

8. Stop the engine.

9. Push in the zero button on the infrared test selector.

Results and Indications— Timing Advance

If the timing advance is either too little or too much, mark the no-go space on the test report. Then, check the distributor for the following defects:

1. Leaking or inoperative vacuum advance chamber. If the vehicle has a transmission control spark system, recheck the vacuum advance operation as specified for the type of system. Also check the vacuum chamber with an external vacuum source for leaks and the vacuum supply line or hose to the distributor for obstruction.

2. Sticking or inoperative mechanical advance. In this situation, disconnect the hose from the vacuum advance and repeat the test. This action checks the action of the mechanical advance only. If there is still too little or too much advance, remove and repair the distributor as necessary.

3. Incorrect distributor for engine. Remove and replace the distributor with the correct one for the engine.

Dwell

Some electronic ignition systems incorporate a dwell change as an integral part of its design. Consequently, before condemning the system, check the specifications and recommendations for the particular system being tested. However, if the dwell changes more than allowable for the system being tested, mark the no-go block on the test form. Then, remove and test the mechanical condition of the distributor in an appropriate tester. Repair or replace the distributor as needed.

Charging Voltage

If the charging voltage is higher or lower than specified, mark the no-go block on the test report. Then, make a complete charging system test and make necessary repairs or replacements in order to correct the defect.

Carbon Monoxide Level

If the CO reading is not within specifications, mark the no-go space on the test report. Then, check for the following defects:

1. Plugged air bleeds or restricted air cleaner. Clean out the air bleeds or the entire carburetor. Replace a restricted air cleaner.

2. Metering rods out of adjustment or the installation of incorrect main metering jets. Adjust the metering rods as necessary or replace the jets.

3. A leaky power valve, accelerator pump, or accelerator pump check valve. In this case, check each component and make any repairs or replacements as necessary.

4. High float level. Adjust the float as required.

Hydrocarbon Level

If the HC reading is not within specifications, mark the no-go block on the test report. Then, check for the following problems:

1. Plugged high-speed passages or jets. Clean the passages, jets, or carburetor as necessary.

2. Incorrect metering jets or metering rods out of adjustment. In this case, replace the jets with the correct size or adjust the metering rods to specifications.

3. Intake manifold or carburetor air leaks. Tighten all attaching hardware or replace gaskets as necessary to stop the air leaks.

4. Incorrect float level. Adjust the float to specifications.

5. Ignition system malfunction. Test and service the entire system as necessary.

Engine Vacuum

If the vacuum reading is unsteady and lower than during the idle mode test, mark the no-go block on the test form. Then, check for the following defects:

1. Mechanical engine problems. Check the cylinder balance test results. Then, perform as necessary a compression and leakage test.

2. Exhaust system restricted. Make any repairs or replacements as necessary.

3. Ignition timing not advancing properly. Check the results of the timing advance test. Make necessary repairs or replacements to the distributor or system.

Testing Ignition Timing Advance with Magnetic Timing Unit

On certain vehicles, you can check initial ignition timing during the idle mode and the total timing advance during the 2,500 rpm high-cruise mode with a magnetic timing unit. To perform these tests using a MAG-81 Sun magnetic timing unit, follow these instructions.

1. As necessary, insert the proper probe adapter into its slot in the timing bracket (Fig. 26-6).

2. Insert the magnetic pickup probe into the opening in the adapter or receptacle so that the probe tip is in contact with the engine vibration dampener. *Note:* In some installations, the lock ring on the probe contacts the adapter before the probe tip contacts the vibration dampener. This design permits the probe, in this situation, to enter the adapter to the proper depth for test purposes.

3. Make certain that the probe and lead assembly are clear of fan, pulleys, etc.

4. Turn the oscilloscope a.c. power on. This lights the MAG-81.

5. Prepare the scope tester and make all test connections as shown in Fig. 26-4, except for the red trigger pickup that fits around spark plug lead 1.

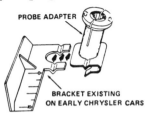

PROBE ADAPTER

BRACKET EXISTING ON EARLY CHRYSLER CARS

Fig. 26-6. The installation of a probe adapter into its slot in the timing bracket. (Courtesy of Sun Electric Corp.)

6. Connect the probe harness to the receptacle on the left side of the MAG-81 control panel (Fig. 26-7).

7. Start the engine and adjust the offset angle knob until the proper setting appears in the readout window.

8. Connect the red trigger pickup around the number one spark plug cable. With the engine at curb idle, the initial timing setting of the engine should appear in the digital readout window.

9. Increase engine speed to 2,500 rpm. Then, note the amount of total advancement appearing in the readout window.

Results and Indications

If initial timing and the total advance curve of the distributor at 2,500 rpm are incorrect, perform the same checks and adjustments that you would normally make if you noted the problem through the use of a timing light and a timing advance unit.

Testing a Vehicle on a Dynamometer

Preparation

To prepare a vehicle for testing on a Clayton chassis dynamometer:

1. Raise lift and engage roll brakes. To do this, move the lift brake lever located at the left front of the dynamometer, away from the power absorption unit.

2. Drive the vehicle squarely onto the dynamometer rollers (Fig. 26-8), attempting to center it so that the drive wheels are clear of the roller end frames.

3. Lower the lift and release the roll brakes by moving the lift/brake lever toward the power absorption unit.

4. Start the engine and place the transmission in a forward gear to permit the drive wheels to rotate slowly. This permits the vehicle to center itself in the

Fig. 26-7.   The control panel of a Sun MAG-81.

Fig. 26-8. Attempt to center the drive wheels so that they are clear of the roller end frames.

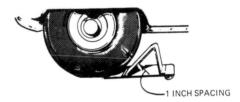

1 INCH SPACING

Fig. 26-9. The proper installation of wheel chocks.

c. If applicable, level of automatic transmission fluid.

d. Tire pressure. Inflate all tires to normal road pressure.

7. Connect an engine analyzer to the vehicle, following the manufacturer's recommended procedures or the one presented earlier in this chapter.

Testing the Vehicle

A technician can use the dynamometer for several purposes. For example, when in operation, the unit can load the vehicle in such a way that the operator can check the vehicle's power output at the drive wheels. Also, during this same test, the technician can check the vehicle's speedometer for accuracy against the dynamometer speed meter.

The other main function of the dynamometer is to simulate an actual road condition in which a particular malfunction occurs. In this way, the mechanic checks the operation of the engine and its subsystems on an engine analyzer as the malfunction occurs. This type of testing would be impossible without the dynamometer.

Level Road Load Check

To test a vehicle simulating level road load operation, follow this procedure.

rollers. *Note:* Check to see that the drive wheels are clear of the roller frame. If the tires are rubbing on the frame, reposition the vehicle as instructed in step 2. *Caution:* On front-wheel drive vehicles, the drive wheels tend to drift across the rollers as they rotate. In this situation, steer the vehicle to keep it from drifting. Then, position the front-wheel guide devices as instructed in the manual provided by the dynamometer manufacturer.

5. Place two wheel chocks ahead of the stationary wheels. For vehicles with rear-wheel drive, place the chocks ahead of the front wheels. For front-wheel-drive vehicles, install the chocks ahead of the rear wheels (Fig. 26-9).

6. Prior to performing the test on the vehicle, check each of the following:

a. Oil level in the crankcase.

b. Cooling system heat indicator.

1. Start the engine and permit it to reach normal operating temperature.

2. Accelerate the vehicle to 55 mph.

3. Observe the power meter (Fig. 26-10). If the power is less than 10 horsepower, press the load button. Then, observe the power meter as it approaches the desired reading and the speed meter as it drops to 50 mph.

4. Release the load button. *Note:* Pressing the on or load button increases the load on the vehicle, while pressing the off or unload button decreases the load. The actual load remains constant with both buttons released.

5. If the power meter indicates more than 10 horsepower, ease up on the accelerator until the speed reading is 45 mph.

6. Press the unload button and watch the power meter drop to the desired reading as the speed meter approaches 50 mph. Then, release the unload button.

7. When 10 horsepower shows on the power meter at 50 mph, the dynamometer has placed a level road load on the vehicle.

At this point, set aside the remote control pendant as this load will remain on the vehicle until changed.

8. Check the operation of the engine and its subsystems on the engine analyzer. Check such items as spark plug firing voltages on a display pattern; excessive secondary resistance or plug fouling on a raster pattern; the condition of the coil, condenser, and breaker points on a raster pattern; and the carbon monoxide and hydrocarbon levels.

Wide-Open, Full-Throttle Load Test

To perform this test:

1. Accelerate the vehicle to 3,000 rpm.

2. Press the load button while gradually depressing the throttle to maintain engine speed over 2,500 rpm.

3. Release the load button when the throttle is wide open and the engine speed is 2,500 rpm.

4. Observe and note the reading on the power meter. *Note:* If you are unable to

Fig. 26-10. The power and speed meters of a Clayton dynamometer.

reach 2,500 rpm the dynamometer is overloaded. In this case, press the unload button until the engine reaches this speed. *Note:* On a vehicle with automatic transmission, avoid depressing the accelerator to the floor and into a downshift condition.

5. On the engine analyzer, check the operation of the engine and its subsystems. Check for such items as excessive firing voltages; breakdown in secondary insulation; excessive secondary resistance and plug fouling; faulty coil; condenser; or breaker point operation; insufficient or excessive timing advance; engine vacuum; and carbon monoxide and hydrocarbon levels.

6. Decelerate the engine and apply the vehicle brake slightly to stop the rollers. *Note:* If you have operated the vehicle at full throttle for several minutes, it is a good idea to run the engine at approximately 2,000 rpm for a short time in order to circulate engine coolant. This prevents "hot spots" from resulting inside the engine and causing boil-over.

7. Remove the wheel chocks.

8. Move the lift control lever away from the power absorption unit. This raises the lift plate and engages the roller brakes.

9. Drive or back the vehicle off the dynamometer slowly.

Dynamometer and Engine Analyzer Testing for a Specific Problem

In most cases, if a vehicle malfunctions, it will do so under the wide-open, full-throttle load test. In other words, with a vehicle under a full load by the dynamometer, any defect within the engine and its subsystems should become apparent on the scope screen or other analyzer instruments.

However, if the malfunction does not occur during this test, the operator can simulate the road and load condition with the dynamometer. The operator must simply operate the vehicle at the road speed under which the problem occurs, while manipulating the load on and off buttons. When the vehicle achieves the road speed and load under which the problem occurs, the technician can then locate the actual cause of the malfunction on the oscilloscope screen or its related instruments.

Review

This section will assist you in determining how well you remember the material in this chapter. Read each item carefully. If you can't complete the statement, review the section in the chapter that covers the material.

1. Standardized test procedures are provided by _____ _____ .
   a. vehicle manufacturers
   b. test equipment manufacturers
   c. engine manufacturers
   d. both *a* and *b*

2. The Sun test report form mentioned in this chapter has _____ columns.
   a. 5
   b. 6
   c. 7
   d. 8

3. When preparing a Sun 1115 analyzer for the test procedure, set the pattern selector to the _____ position.

a. display
b. raster
c. superimposed
d. primary

4. When preparing a Sun 1115 analyzer for the test procedure, clamp the red trigger pickup around spark plug wire _____ close to the distributor cap.
   a. 6
   b. 4
   c. 2
   d. 1

5. If the engine kill button shows red, the ignition system _____ _____.
   a. is inoperative
   b. is operational
   c. operation is delayed for 20 seconds
   d. operation is delayed for 5 minutes

6. During the charging test, the function selector knob should be in the _____ _____ position.
   a. primary (+)
   b. primary (–)
   c. special patterns
   d. secondary display

7. If during the idle test the dwell is either too high or low, check for _____.
   a. a defective ignition switch
   b. a defective coil
   c. points out-of-adjustment
   d. a defective condenser

8. If the CO level is too high during the idle test, check for _____ _____ _____.
   a. a lean air/fuel mixture
   b. a rich air/fuel mixture
   c. an ignition system malfunction
   d. low compression

9. If coil polarity is incorrect, check the connection to the battery and the _____ _____.
   a. contact points
   b. ballast resistor
   c. ignition switch
   d. ignition coil

10. When checking the condition of secondary resistance on the scope screen, the lower extent of the waveform should be _____ the height of the upper extent.
    a. 1/2
    b. 1/3
    c. 2/3
    d. 3/4

11. If the dwell variation is too great, check for _____ _____ _____.
    a. a worn distributor cam
    b. points out of adjustment
    c. a faulty condenser
    d. a faulty coil

12. If the spark plug firing voltages are too high during the snap-acceleration test, check the condition of the _____ _____.
    a. ballast resistor
    b. contact points
    c. spark plugs
    d. ignition coil

13. If the dwell varies excessively at 2,500 rpm, check the condition of the _____.
    a. contact points
    b. distributor
    c. condenser
    d. ignition coil

14. If engine vacuum drops excessively at 2,500 rpm, the _____ _____ may have a restriction.
    a. exhaust system
    b. injection system

c. induction system

d. emission-control system

15. After centering a vehicle's drive wheels on the dynamometer's rollers, install the _____ _____ ____.

a. antiskid device

b. retaining devices

c. wheel chocks

d. tie-down cables

16. If you can't achieve 2,500 engine rpm during the dynamometer full-load test, the _____ _____ _____.

a. transmission is overloaded

b. dynamometer is overloaded

c. dynamometer is malfunctioning

d. engine has too much power

For the answers, turn to the Appendix.

ANSWERS TO CHAPTER REVIEW SECTIONS

Chapter 1

1. c	5. a	9. d	13. b
2. a	6. c	10. b	
3. d	7. b	11. c	
4. d	8. d	12. a	

Chapter 2

1. d	6. b	11. d	16. a
2. b	7. d	12. d	17. d
3. a	8. c	13. d	18. c
4. a	9. a	14. a	19. a
5. c	10. b	15. b	20. c

Chapter 3

1. c	4. a	7. a	10. c
2. a	5. b	8. d	11. d
3. d	6. c	9. b	12. b

Chapter 4

1. c	4. b	7. c	10. a
2. a	5. d	8. b	11. b
3. d	6. a	9. d	12. c

Chapter 5

1. c	6. a	11. d	16. b
2. a	7. d	12. a	17. a
3. d	8. c	13. b	18. c
4. b	9. b	14. a	19. b
5. b	10. a	15. d	20. d

Chapter 6

1. a	5. d	9. c	13. c
2. d	6. c	10. b	
3. b	7. a	11. a	
4. c	8. b	12. d	

Chapter 7

1. b	4. d	7. a	10. a
2. c	5. c	8. c	11. d
3. a	6. b	9. b	12. a

Chapter 8

1. d	8. b	14. c	20. c
2. c	9. b	15. c	21. b
3. a	10. c	16. a	22. a
4. b	11. d	17. b	23. a
5. c	12. a	18. d	24. b
6. d	13. b	19. d	25. c
7. a			

Chapter 9

1. a	5. b	9. c	13. c
2. a	6. b	10. d	14. c
3. d	7. a	11. b	15. d
4. c	8. b	12. b	16. a

Chapter 10

1. a	5. b	9. d	13. c
2. b	6. a	10. d	14. b
3. c	7. c	11. a	
4. b	8. c	12. a	

Chapter 11

1. a	6. a	11. d	16. c
2. d	7. c	12. c	17. a
3. c	8. c	13. b	
4. c	9. b	14. a	
5. b	10. a	15. d	

Chapter 12

1. d	6. c	11. c	16. b
2. d	7. a	12. c	17. c
3. a	8. a	13. b	18. d
4. b	9. b	14. a	19. a
5. c	10. d	15. b	20. b

Chapter 13

1. b	5. a	8. b	11. a
2. b	6. d	9. a	12. b
3. c	7. c	10. c	13. d
4. a			

Chapter 14

1. c	5. d	9. a	13. d
2. b	6. c	10. b	14. c
3. d	7. b	11. c	
4. a	8. b	12. a	

Chapter 15

1. b	6. c	11. b	16. a
2. c	7. b	12. a	17. a
3. a	8. a	13. c	18. c
4. a	9. c	14. c	19. c
5. d	10. d	15. b	20. b

Chapter 16

1. b	6. b	11. b	16. c
2. a	7. a	12. b	17. b
3. d	8. d	13. d	18. a
4. c	9. d	14. a	19. b
5. c	10. a	15. b	20. c

Chapter 17

1. d	4. c	7. d	10. a
2. b	5. b	8. c	
3. a	6. a	9. b	

Chapter 18

1. b	4. b	7. a	10. a
2. a	5. d	8. d	11. c
3. c	6. c	9. b	

Chapter 19

1. b	5. d	9. c	13. a
2. a	6. d	10. b	14. c
3. c	7. a	11. c	15. b
4. b	8. a	12. d	16. d

Chapter 20

1. c	5. a	9. c	13. c
2. a	6. b	10. b	
3. b	7. d	11. a	
4. d	8. c	12. d	

Chapter 21

1. b	4. b	6. a	8. d
2. d	5. b	7. c	9. b
3. c			

Chapter 22

1. b	4. d	7. a	10. b
2. c	5. b	8. d	
3. a	6. c	9. c	

Chapter 23

1. a	6. a	11. a	16. c
2. d	7. b	12. b	17. b
3. c	8. d	13. b	18. a
4. c	9. b	14. d	19. d
5. b	10. b	15. a	20. b

Chapter 24

1. c	6. c	11. c	16. a
2. b	7. b	12. d	17. d
3. a	8. a	13. a	18. c
4. a	9. b	14. b	
5. d	10. b	15. c	

Chapter 25

1. a	7. b	13. d	19. a
2. d	8. d	14. c	20. c
3. b	9. c	15. a	21. b
4. c	10. c	16. b	22. d
5. c	11. a	17. c	
6. b	12. b	18. d	

Chapter 26

1. b	5. a	9. d	13. b
2. c	6. c	10. a	14. a
3. a	7. c	11. a	15. c
4. d	8. b	12. c	16. b

INDEX